D0392070

INTERNATIONAL HANDBOOK OF MANAGEMENT

McGRAW-HILL SERIES IN INTERNATIONAL DEVELOPMENT

ALDERFER · *Local Government in Developing Countries*
BENJAMIN · *Higher Education in the American Republics*
BRANNEN AND HODGSON · *Overseas Management*
BRYCE · *Industrial Development: A Guide for Accelerating Economic Growth*
BRYCE · *Policies and Methods for Industrial Development*
DAVID · *International Resources in Clinical Psychology*
DUNN · *International Handbook of Advertising*
EICHER AND WITT · *Agriculture in Economic Development*
ETTINGER · *International Handbook of Management*
HARBISON AND MYERS · *Education, Manpower, and Economic Growth: Strategies of Human Resource Development*
HARBISON AND MYERS · *Manpower and Education: Country Studies in Economic Development*
MEIER · *Developmental Planning*
MONTGOMERY AND SIFFIN · *Politics, Administration, and Change: Approaches to National Development*
POWELSON · *Latin America: Today's Economic and Social Revolution*
REIMANN · *International Finance Library*
SINGER · *International Development: Growth and Change*
STALEY AND MORSE · *Modern Small Industry for Developing Countries*
WALINSKY · *The Planning and Execution of Economic Development: A Non-technical Guide for Policy Makers and Administrators*

PREFACE

The history of the economic development of various nations indicates that the velocity of their growth stood in direct proportion to the extent that their people brought into play and availed themselves of their *own* human and material resources and the then available technology in industry, agriculture, commerce, and public administration. The men who played then, and are playing now, the role of leaders in the economic growth of a country are the managers, the directors of economic enterprises of whatever size or description. They are the managers who must employ technology to convert old and newly discovered material resources into products or services acceptable and salable in the marketplace.

These directors must so "manage" enterprises that the economic aspirations of expectant peoples are fulfilled by the employment of means in harmony with their own spiritual longing and needs. And it is they who must find the key to the release of the human potentials in their countrymen for their economic betterment.

When economic development is pursued for its own sake, it is apt to be without compassion and empty of the joy of achievement, because it is contradictory to the total hopes of the people it meant to serve. "Forced draft" economic growth can gain social validity only when economic development aims and the means for reaching them are deeply rooted in and have grown out of the natural evolvement of the very people it is intended to benefit. Economic development is more than merely building factories, dams, and highways, employing skilled and unskilled laborers, training supervisors, and using the results of technology to the utmost human extent. Economic development, particularly in underindustrialized or predominately agricultural countries, becomes a blueprint of an untrodden road to a new structure of a society. And the more rapid the pace by which such economic development proceeds, the more fierce will be the strains on the existing fabric of society and culture in those countries.

The realization that an accelerated or even a slow pursuit of economic development in underdeveloped countries will have a profound and lasting effect on the social structure and culture of their peoples should compel the directors of economic enterprises to think in terms not only of wages paid or goods produced and sold, but of social and cultural values to be enhanced. Without such awareness by the directors of enterprises and without their weaving that cognizance into their economic action, the road to further economic development can be strewn with violent strife and strident discord. Fortunately, a reservoir of skill, experience, and insight can be tapped by peoples on the way to accelerated growth. That this reservoir is to be drawn on more often and more wisely is, I believe, one of the purposes of this book.

It is for that reason—economic growth through human and humane progress—that the Comité International de l'Organisation Scientifique (CIOS), founded in 1924, has, through its Board of Governors, sponsored this book. The opinions of the editors and contributors of articles expressed in this book are their own. They do not necessarily reflect the viewpoint of CIOS, its officers, governors, or members.

CIOS is glad to be associated with an additional effort—which the articles in this book demonstrate—to spread knowledge, experience, and understanding of the arts and science of managing among the present and future directors of the world's daily work.

A. M. Lederer
PRESIDENT OF CIOS, 1960–1963

FOREWORD

In the industrialized nations a wealth of information is available to the manager of business operations about how business problems have been analyzed and solved by others. The similarity of traditions and conditions makes many of these examples applicable to situations in identical cultural and economic environments. For the international activities of national and multinational business organizations, and especially for managers responsible for economic development in lesser-developed countries, only a small amount of such information has been accumulated. The literature of management covering their problems is as yet meager.

Where great differences in culture and conditions exist the applicability of the experience of one country to another is sharply limited. In most instances the manager of international operations and economic development projects is confronted by unprecedented problems. For him there are no routine solutions to be drawn from experience. In fact, he is rarely in a position to recognize the similarity of his problems with those existing elsewhere. Hence the principal task of management in such novel environment consists in developing analytical techniques in order to pose the right questions and work out the right answers to concrete problems of policy making and operations.

This Handbook was conceived for the purpose of helping managers in international and development activities to ask the right questions. The separate articles are not meant to suggest patterns of management, but rather to acquaint the reader with the great variety of problems encountered in worldwide operations. It is hoped that they will contribute to a needed systemization of thought in the planning and performance of business activities.

In the United States two organizations have contributed substantially to the formation of a body of information on international management, the Council on International Progress in Management and the American Management Association. The former, representing the leading professional associations of managers, is the American constituent body of the international management organization, Comité International de l'Organisation Scientifique

(CIOS), a nongovernmental agency with consultant status in the Economic and Social Council of the United Nations. The American Management Association is the largest membership association of managers in America and conducts an extensive program of education, research, and publication. The concepts of international management as reflected in the activities of these leading organizations constitute a substantial part of an emerging body of information about international business and problems of the lesser-developed economies.

Transfer of the practices and principles of management based on the experience of one country to the needs of other nations calls for cautious application of experience from abroad. Differences in cultural traditions, in the role of consumer, labor, and management in the economy, in the functions of government and of private enterprise make the uncritical adoption of management practices that have succeeded elsewhere risky. Even among highly developed industrial countries we find great differences in the motivations of men, in concepts of authority and of acceptable conduct in human relations, in national and religious and in political and class traditions. These social differences are obstacles to the introduction of foreign practices in managerial operations. Such differences must be taken into consideration when designing plans and procedures for international business activities. As conditions determining the success or failure of a program, they force managers to adjust borrowed practices to the prevailing social and ethical environment. In international business development, even more than differences in language, differences of traditional values must be understood as conditioning factors in adapting foreign management methods to local needs.

Fundamental to the study of international management is the necessity of establishing sound methods of fact finding to avoid blind imitation and mechanical acceptance of outside experience and to facilitate an appraisal of local economic requirements and concepts of value. Certainly, the student of international business and the entrepreneur seeking to benefit from foreign productivity methods can learn from the experience of others. Case histories of mangement even from different cultures can often provide useful examples.

Because management depends on the cooperation of people, familiarity with local conditions and with concepts of value is a necessary ingredient of business direction. This explains the prevailing practice of American corporations operating in foreign countries of reducing the number of American nationals abroad to a minimum and preferring, wherever possible, to set up managerial staffs of local origin. They know that persons rooted in their societies can best understand the conditions for success or failure of business in their homeland. It is obviously more desirable to recruit effective managers locally, teaching them the technical requirements and proven management practices, than attempt to convey to a nonnational employee all the complexities of cultural and social values and traditions of the foreign environment.

In the management theory of the industrialized countries several sets of principles have been formulated by pioneer thinkers of management. Among these are the principles of scientific management of Frederick W. Taylor, the principles of industrial management of Henry L. Gantt, the principles of industrial administration of Henri Fayol, the principles of policy determination of Paul E. Holden, the principles of manufacturing management of Leon Pratt Alford, the principles of organization of Lyndall F. Urwick, along with the principles listed in Lawrence A. Appley's "Management in Action." These are rules of managerial conduct which can supply valuable guidance for the direction of affairs, wherever they may be conducted. But behind all these principles stands the assumption of a social order that rewards productivity and offers incentives for risk taking and personal effort.

The great success of the industrialized nations in increasing productivity and output must be attributed to the existence of a social climate favorable to production. In addition to education and technical skills, the greatest contributing factor in the production of national and personal wealth is the ability to organize human cooperation. The prosperity, as well as the poverty, of nations is the result of human behavior. Human beings and their attitudes determine the fate of a nation. This can be demonstrated by the example of nations that became rich in spite of the absence of major natural resources.

Neither the Swiss nor the Danes nor the Japanese have been favored by nature, but they are prosperous because of their ability to manage business within realizable economic goals. They have created a climate stimulating to innovation and production. Perceptible in the industrialized nations of the world is a dominating urge for self-improvement in labor and management that promotes prosperity. This all-pervading urge is not an unworthy expression of greed, but a persistent search for excellence that motivates the people, whatever their place on the social ladder may be.

Between 1947 and 1963 the world's seven most advanced nations (the United States, Canada, Britain, France, West Germany, Japan, and Italy) doubled their industrial production and raised their agricultural output by nearly 50 percent. The economic system responsible for this astounding increase in production and productivity is characterized by the adoption of advanced methods in management. The grammar of motives common to these countries rests on the contributions of businessmen and farmers and of all other persons participating in production and on their self-assumed responsibility for improving the efficiency of their activities. The prevailing system of penalties and rewards for decision making is predicated on motivation for innovation and heightened productivity. Unless such motivation is stimulated in lesser-developed nations, there will be limits to the impact on the economic development of proved management methods borrowed from successful enterprises abroad.

In the postwar years, the advanced countries added more to their total product in twenty years than they had added in the preceding fifty. This impressive increase in output of industry and agriculture could not have come about without the contributions of labor and its motivation for greater productivity. The introduction of new management methods in these industrialized countries has increased the rewards of labor without reducing the returns of risk-taking enterprise. It has brought about an unprecedented output per man-hour and at the same time the highest standard of living for the common man and his family, comparable to and even higher than the standard enjoyed by princes of earlier ages.

The population explosion and the reluctance to adopt new attitudes and methods of doing business account for existing low living standards and economic and technical backwardness. In contrast, in only four generations, the United States, by adopting new methods of management and by orienting its education and social order toward goals of productivity, has demonstrated that determined dedication to change can bring prosperity.

Management is not an exact science. But in pursuing its goals it avails itself of the scientific method. It starts with an examination of conditions as they are. It seeks to reduce risks by evaluating all the knowable factors that may affect attainment of its goals. In true scientific manner it applies measurement to work processes; it uses scientific research methods and quantitative data in appraising business problems. It seeks to verify assumptions by experiment. It bases its values on the sum total of all observable factors that may influence its results. Modern management converts business from a "game" of chance into one of skills.

In the use of scientific methods management applies the findings of many sciences. It benefits from the work of psychologists and sociologists, of economists and anthropologists. It applies statistics and mathematical computation, engineering, and natural sciences to the solution of business problems. The practice of management in the industrialized nations is not based on a codified set of generally accepted rules; it uses whatever elements of the whole body of science may promise results, in a given situation. In the end there is noticeable progress in the art of directing business paralleling the successive adoption of new ideas and methods in operating business organizations.

Systematic study of management problems in the now industrialized countries began at about the same time, when the idea of individual human freedom changed the course of history. Freedom of decision making and risk taking, paired with personal responsibility for superiority of products in a competitive market, became the force that brought about the industrial revolution.

Toward the end of the eighteenth century, economists and managers of enterprise began to be concerned with the rationalization of human labor. Innovation in manufacture soon proved to be the key to the supply of more goods to more people at lower cost. Methods of problem solving that had increased industrial productivity were found applicable to agriculture. An initial concern with the division of labor resulted in specialization of labor and better planning of the cooperation of participants in the work process. The result was an increase in output paralleled by a reduction of cost. Manufacturers adopting improved production methods in the form of better work organization soon brought to the competitive market lower-priced goods. Out of competition for the favor of the consumer there came a general tendency to plan production and distribution so that business volume could expand with the ever-growing number of customers. Modern management is consumer-oriented. It seeks to maximize output and minimize cost, so as to increase sales by bringing its products within the reach of purchasing power of ever-larger consumer markets.

The attention of producers in search of improved management methods at various stages of the development of better practices was focused on different problems. Near the end of the last century the work process stood in the center of the methodical study. Taylor and his associates and contemporaries developed time and motion study as measurement tools. They rearranged factory layout, introduced mechanical tools to fit the ability of workers to perform, and separated work preparation from simplified machine operations. Introduction of the conveyor belt, the assembly line, and piecework wage incentives were characteristic of this period. The next concern of management was the improvement of cooperation within the organization by establishing better human relations. This concern with the actions of men resulted in intensified search for better forms of organization. It was found that the structure of a business organization often determined the effectiveness of all its constituent parts. Consequently, business-organization building by efficient design of the corporate hierarchy became a major concern of management. Better planning of work loads and control of work schedules resulted from the contributions of Gantt to the practice of business direction. Concurrent with the concern for better use of time, labor, and materials came a growing practice of scheduling and budgeting the requirements of money, machines, materials, and manpower.

Efforts to understand the motivations of labor led to a concern with problems of wages and nonmonetary incentives. It was found that in addition to economic motivation there existed a wide range of noneconomic factors affecting the productivity of labor. Study of work environment, human relations, and group psychology led to improvements in labor relations that contribute greatly to manufacturing efficiency. The postwar years have added many management techniques in the fields of operations research, computer use for planning, value engineering, use of market studies, and of sophisticated mathematical methods on all levels of business operations.

The concern with international business and problems of economic development of the lesser-developed nations have added a new dimension to management theory. This encounter with a great variety of conditions all over the globe has led to an intensified study of cultural and economic conditions of management success. Local differences in the social traditions and conditions are so much a determining factor in international management that their interpretation and the adjustment to them have become a new focus of management science. This explains the great diversity in the themes of the articles contained in this Handbook.

The opinions expressed by the authors of articles in this volume are their own. Their papers will suggest many questions to be asked in tackling management problems and also some solutions.

This book owes much to its support by management organizations. It came about with the help of the CIOS and the Council for International Progress in Management. To these and the many altruistic contributors of articles, the editor expresses sincerest thanks.

K. E. Ettinger

CONTENTS

INTERNATIONAL CORPORATE ACTIVITIES

PROBLEMS IN FINANCING

SPECIAL DEVELOPMENT PROBLEMS

RURAL MANAGEMENT PROBLEMS

TRAINING OF MANAGERS

SCIENTIFIC MANAGEMENT AND ECONOMIC DEVELOPMENT

John F. Mee, Ph.D.

Impact of Scientific Management on Economic Development

Virtually all nations in the world are faced with the task of increasing their rates of economic growth. Levels of economic welfare that exist among the various communities of the world are relative in degrees of poverty, illiteracy, ill health, and human satisfactions. Countries which have experienced the greatest degrees of economic development are challenged to maintain and increase their standards of productivity, health, education, employment, and income. The relatively less fortunate peoples of countries with low rates of economic growth have rising expectations for an improvement in their economic environments. What reasons can be given for the differences of economic growth among nations? Why did some nations generate industrial societies while others remained in predominantly agricultural economies? How can a nation initiate a management movement that will stimulate and facilitate its economic growth and contribute to greater human satisfactions?

Explanation for the differences in the levels and rates of economic growth among nations can be given in economic, psychological, and sociological terms. However, the greatest single factor or key for unlocking the forces of economic growth in any nation is *management,* both public and private. Any historical analysis of the economic development of a nation discloses the interrelationships between the economic, social, political, and technological environment and the prevalent management concepts and value system of the times.

Scientific Management: Concept and Definition. The principal purpose of scientific management is the realization of maximum prosperity for both employers and employees with proper consideration for the services created for the consumers. It seeks an increased output per unit of human effort by means

Dr. Mee is Professor of Management at Indiana University, Bloomington, Indiana.

of "knowing exactly what you want men to do and then seeing that they do it in the best and cheapest way." It provides an approach for increasing the world's wealth by eliminating the waste of human energy, time, materials, and inefficient methods of organization and operations.

Scientific management is characterized by the form of organization and procedures in purposeful human endeavors which rest on factual information from systematic scientific investigation and analysis—instead of on tradition or on policies determined through trial and error. It entails all the resources of science. The most efficient methods of work are established to accomplish a task; the workman is instructed how best to perform the work; and he is offered an incentive to do it in the prescribed manner. Desired results are determined and then achieved by the best attainable methods, practices, tools, and equipment. Scientific management provides the means for economic growth through maximizing productivity for the mutual benefit of all concerned, instead of tolerating conditions of scarcity, poverty, and inefficiency.

Economic Factors. Economic theorists have tried to explain the economic growth of nations in various ways. In general, their major criteria may be summarized under the following classifications:

1. Entrepreneurship or management
2. Capital accumulation and technological advancements
3. Division of labor and specialization
4. Population changes to increase demand

Economists have argued that the entrepreneurs or managers are the prime movers in any economy. It is believed that an economy does not grow either naturally or steadily; instead, it is stimulated by leaps through the efforts of industrial leaders who wish to exploit new products, new methods of work, new sources of materials, or new markets. Capital accumulation permits increasing productivity by means of mechanization and technological assistance for human labors in the manufacturing and marketing of goods. Division of labor and specialization among workers lead to a reduction of time required to produce commodities. Each worker can use his personal talents and improve his dexterity to increase his wages. Population growth through a net reproduction rate is assumed to provide a continually increasing demand for an increasing supply of consumer goods. Obviously, purchasing power must increase with the population increase.

Economists have provided rational explanations with logical reasons for the economic growth of a community. However, there appear to be some additional factors for economic growth that lie outside an economic system proper. Psychologists and sociologists are expected to explain the more irrational reasons for the economic development of certain countries at particular times. The motivations for people to save and invest for capital accumulation seem to entail psychological rather than economic variables. Causes of change in an economic order and the acceptance of technological improvements in some economies and not in others can be explained better by the behavioral scientists than the economists.

Professor Paul Lazarsfeld, in an attempt to illustrate the results of irrational actions on economic results, asked the question, "What rational capitalist would have invested in Gutenberg?" Few people at the time of Gutenberg's invention of the movable-type printing press could read. Those who could read had little time for reading. New type-printed books lacked the distinctive custom-made qualities of the conventional ones. Political upheavals could occur. Some skilled workers would suffer unemployment. In retrospect, an economist would have difficulty explaining the justification for financing the Gutenberg project.

Psychological and Social Factors. The Gutenberg illustration describes the problems of a country in the process of creating the climate for economic growth. The labor force is not educated or trained for mechanical production. There is little demand for new products. Little demand causes the entrepreneur to consider the risks too great for the use of his capital. The existing environment is not ready for a revolutionary technology. Somehow change is essential for economic progress. How can such change be effected? What psychological or sociological factors can effect change by initiating the forces that lead to economic development and growth? The major psychological and sociological explanations for economic growth in a society are:

1. The willingness of the people to accept change and innovations of all kinds
2. The opportunity and the desire of the people for education, and their abilities to apply science and technology for economic purposes
3. The desire of the people to seek and work for material advantages that will improve their standards of living, health, and education
4. The desire of the people to consume goods and commodities as a means for increasing their state of happiness
5. The motives of people to attain economic goals through organized efforts and feel self-satisfaction from the achievement of their goals
6. The strong need for achievement or accomplishment in some of the people (the managers or entrepreneurs) and their willingness to take great risks in economic endeavors with the expectations of great economic gains that will enhance their personal statures and feelings of superiority

The economic growth of a country is related to both economic factors and human factors. Even though economic resources may be available, the social and political environment must be suitable for the work of entrepreneurs or managers to seek economic objectives through the utilization of both human efforts and the facilitating resources of capital and technology.

Any study of the nations that have achieved a high level of economic development will show the presence of *scientific management* at the initial stage of economic growth. Furthermore, no nation has experienced much economic development without the presence of scientific management as the means for assembling and utilizing the resources available to the economy.

Scientific Management Factor. Stefan H. Robock, a past Deputy Director of Area Development of the Committee for Economic Development, has stated, "If any single factor is the key for unlocking the forces for economic growth in the underdeveloped areas of the world, that factor is management." Capital alone will not meet the needs of those countries that are attempting to improve their economic conditions. Although many nations are in need of both private and public capital, their greatest needs are the management skills to employ existing capital efficiently through scientific management methods and business managers. They find little success in trying to adapt foreign technologies and methods without the essential management skills that have employed capital, human efforts, and technological aids in the economically advanced nations.

The economic status of any country can be evaluated historically in terms of the management concepts and the value system of the government and the industrial managers. Too often, the governmental and industrial leaders of an underdeveloped area are prone to overemphasize capital and investment as a means for stimulating economic growth. Primary emphasis should be given to the development of managerial and human resources. Economic growth in a community stems from a governmental environment that permits the managers or entrepreneurs to have freedom of choice in the utilization of scientific management practices and economic resources for the pursuit of economic and social goals. The value system must provide opportunity for all members of the society to advance economically and socially.

Emergence of Scientific Management. The rapid rate of economic growth in the countries of Europe and North America began early in the twentieth century. During the same period of time, the concepts and techniques of scientific management were conceived and employed. The ideas and mechanisms of scientific management were not compatible with the environment of an agricultural economy, or a manorial system of land ownership, or colonialism, or authoritarian leadership. Economic growth was stimulated by the practices of scientific management when the political and social environment accommodated the technological improvements of the scientists and the inventors. When the people of some nations chose to build an industrial society, scientific management provided the process for increasing the production and consumption of goods and services.

Scientific management was not an invention. It was a discovery of a new way of thinking about the ways and means for increasing the productivity of people. The essence of scientific management is *the achievement of planned objectives.* Waste and inefficiency must be eliminated in human work, and the savings must be divided among all concerned. Waste can benefit nobody. The desired result is a softening of the struggle for existence, the development of human talents, and the increasing of the happiness of workers.

Conventional and Systematic Management. Prior to the discovery of scientific management philosophies and mechanisms, the managers of industrial enterprises were confined to conventional or systematic management practices. The distinguishing features of conventional management are the acceptance of practices already in existence and the choosing, by guess, from among those methods which have been developed by others. Traditional methods prevail as obstacles to innovation and progress. Systematic management is distinguished by the collection and classification of the records of past practices in order to determine the relative value of methods of work for choosing the most suitable alternative. Under conventional or systematic management practices, a manager confronted with the problem of moving work in progress would be limited to choices in the size of tote boxes or wheelbarrows. By the use of scientific management, he would design a conveyor belt or a monorail. The philosophy of scientific management leads to better methods for greater productivity and higher wages. Economic growth is facilitated.

Time Perspective, Management Concepts, and Value System. Scientific management introduces a new value system into an economy. At such time as a country strives to change to an industrial society, the concepts of scientific management can provide the bridge to economic progress. Furthermore, those concepts will develop a value system that will influence the attitudes, decisions, and behavior of the managers and workers. One of the key characteristics of the value system generated by scientific management is the pursuit of *progress toward a better way of life.* A practical approach to life supersedes a theoretical approach. A steadily rising standard of living is desired and expected. Education is valued highly. Personal health and economic well-being are cherished. A happier existence is expected by using technology to increase human production and consumption of material commodities. Greater satisfactions evolve from productive work than from voluntary leisure. Economic growth is a consequence.

Scientific Management Philosophy and Mechanisms

The basic principles of scientific management may be used by the political and industrial leaders of those nations in the process of stimulating their rates of economic growth as they work to build industrial economies. For purposes of illustrating the fundamental principles which generated the management movements in some of the industrial societies of the world, the philosophies and mechanisms of the most influential authorities will be presented. Their concepts of scientific management were advanced in their countries at a time when work occupied a key place in the value system of their economies.

Scientific management could not benefit national economies while prevalent systems of value were based upon a desire for leisure and minimum work for bare personal needs instead of productive work for a market, or upon the prestige of an aristocracy with power over people instead of a democracy with power through people to develop an industrial society for economic growth and greater human satisfactions.

The achievements of scientific management resulted from an environment where cultural, social, and religious traditions were firmly oriented around work. Both political and industrial leaders sought ways and means to elevate human workers to a higher level of efficiency, earning power, and dignity.

Early English Management Concepts. Prior to the discoveries of scientific management, the great industrial benefits from the Industrial Revolution involved the substitution of machinery for unaided human efforts. Some authorities in England anticipated the later management movement. Their advanced management philosophies appeared early in the nineteenth century and illustrate how new ideas about management emerge as a nation begins to build an industrial economy.

Charles Babbage explained the benefits that are realized from the division of work and the intelligent organization of workers when he proclaimed:[1]

> . . . that the master manufacturer, by dividing the work to be executed into different processes, each requiring different degrees of skill or of force, can

[1] Charles Babbage, *On the Economy of Machinery and Manufacturers,* Charles Knight, London, 1835, pp. 175–176 (reprint of this edition by Augustus M. Kelley, New York, 1963, available).

purchase exactly that precise quantity of both which is necessary for each process; whereas if the whole work were executed by one workman, that person must possess sufficient skill to perform the most difficult, and sufficient strength to execute the most laborious, of the operations into which the art is divided.

He further stated that competition resulting from machinery and the division of labor required each employer to make a constant effort to reduce costs by:

1. The discovery of improved methods
2. The knowledge of the precise expense of every process
3. The knowledge of which processes offer the greatest possibility of cost reduction through study

Babbage anticipated the mechanisms of time and motion study for scientific management practices. He also predicted the importance of the service objective to all concerned when he wrote:[2]

> The first object of every person who attempts to make any article for consumption is, or ought to be, to produce it in perfect form; but in order to secure to himself the greatest and most permanent profit, he must endeavour, by whatever means in his power, to render the new luxury or want which he has created, cheap to those who consume it. The larger number of purchasers thus obtained will, in some measure, secure him from the caprices of fashion, whilst it furnishes a far greater amount of profit, although the contribution of each individual is diminished.

In the cultural conditions of an industrial society, the system provides for higher worker wages from greater productivity, lower prices to the consumers, and profits to the employer through reduced costs and greater sales volume.

Alexander Ure explained the English factory system in terms of *mechanical, moral,* and *commercial* principles. These principles were considered subservient to and in harmony with the interests of the workers, the employer, and the government. All three used, for their mutual interests, the powers of science, labor, and capital. He stated that "when the whole are in harmony, they form a body qualified to discharge its manifold functions by an intrinsic self-governing agency, like those of organic life." This concept preceded F. W. Taylor's belief in harmony rather than discord as a principle of scientific management. Ure wrote that "The grand object of the manufacturer is, through the union of capital and science, to reduce the task of his work people to the exercise of vigilance and dexterity."

Scientific Management in America. America followed the processes of England and France in the development of an industrial economy. The kind of economy that a country develops depends mostly on the kind it wants. The attitudes, values, and cultural traditions of the people of a nation determine its economic levels of accomplishment. Its economic destiny is shaped more by psychological and sociological factors than by material resources.

In the early stages of the American industrial economy, some pioneers in what has been classified as scientific management observed the opportunities to reduce waste in manufacturing and to increase productivity and prosperity for all segments of society.

[2] *Ibid.*, pp. 119–120.

Frederick W. Taylor described the fundamental philosophy and values of scientific management when he stated:[3]

> The art of management has been defined as "*knowing exactly what you want men to do and then seeing that they do it in the best and cheapest way.*" Furthermore, "The principal object of management should be to secure the maximum prosperity for the employer coupled with the maximum prosperity for each employee."
>
> Scientific management has for its very foundation the firm conviction that the true interests of the two are one and the same; that prosperity for the employer cannot exist through a long term of years unless it is accompanied by prosperity for the employee, and vice versa; and that it is possible to give the worker what he most wants—high wages—and the employer what he wants—a low labor cost—for his manufactures.

In *Shop Management* (1903), Taylor expanded on his earlier paper, "A Piece Rate System" (1895). He stated that the best management rests on a foundation of high wages and low costs. The aims of each business establishment should be as follows:

1. Each workman should be given, in so far as possible, the highest grade of work for which he is qualified by ability and strength.
2. Each workman should be called upon to turn out the maximum amount of work which a first-rate man of his class can do.
3. Each workman, when he works at the best pace of a first-class man, should be paid 30 to 100 percent (according to the nature of the work which he does) beyond the average of his class.

In order to practice management as an art, Taylor advocated the application of the following principles:

> *A Large Daily Task.* Each man in the establishment, high or low, should daily have a clearly defined task laid out before him. This task should not in the least degree be vague or indefinite, but should be circumscribed carefully and completely, and should not be easy to accomplish.
>
> *Standard Conditions.* Each man's task should call for a full day's work, and at the same time the workman should be given such standardized conditions and appliances as will enable him to accomplish his task with certainty.
>
> *High Pay for Success.* He should be sure of large pay when he accomplishes his task.
>
> *Loss in Case of Failure.* When he fails, he should be sure that sooner or later he will be the loser by it.

When an establishment has reached an advanced state of organization, in many cases a fifth element should be added, namely: The task should be made so difficult that it can only be accomplished by a first-class man.

In *The Principles of Scientific Management* (1911), Taylor develops his earlier principles in a different manner. He emphasizes the importance of the substitution of scientific knowledge and incentive on the part of manage-

[3] Frederick W. Taylor, *The Principles of Scientific Management,* Harper & Row, Publishers, Incorporated, New York, 1919, p. 13. (Italics mine.—J. F. M.)

ment for the previous reliance on the initiative of the workman by incentive. The principles or "new duties" for management, as listed by Taylor, are given as follows:

1. They develop a science for each element of a man's work which replaces the old rule-of-thumb method.

2. They scientifically select and then train, teach, and develop the workman, whereas in the past he chose his own work and trained himself as best he could.

3. They heartily cooperate with the men so as to ensure that all work is done in accordance with the principles of the science which have been developed.

4. There is an almost equal division of work and responsibility between the management and the workmen. Those forming the management take over all work for which they are better fitted than the workmen, while in the past almost all the work and the greater part of the responsibility were thrown upon the men.

According to Taylor, his fundamental principles of scientific management were applicable to all kinds of human activities, from the simplest individual acts to the work of great corporations, which calls for the most elaborate cooperation.

Taylor gave warning that mechanisms and techniques can produce the desired benefits only when they are made to serve the underlying philosophical principles of scientific management, which are known as:

1. Science, not rule-of-thumb management methods
2. Harmony, not discord between managers and workers
3. Cooperation, not individualism among the members of an organization
4. Maximum output, in place of restricted output of work
5. The development of each man to his greatest efficiency and prosperity

The mechanisms and techniques of scientific management are applied primarily to the activities of operative work performance. Emphasis is placed upon the scientific setting of work standards and predetermined results from workers. Before the start of any work activities, there is a determination of what shall be done, how it shall be done, when it shall be done, and the cost of doing it. The major techniques for setting and maintaining work standards involve time study, motion study, tasks, and wage systems. To Taylor, enabling workers to enjoy their greatest prosperity and highest state of efficiency depended on turning out their largest daily output of work, and he demonstrated the effectiveness of his managerial approach by many experiments.

Taylor advocated the differential piece rate as the best method of incentive pay for high productivity. Production standards are set by time and motion study, and two rates of pay are determined for each job. The higher piece rate can be earned by those first-class workmen who produce at a rate equal to or greater than the standard rate of production—30 to 100 percent beyond the average of their class. A first-class workman is one who is scientifically selected and trained for his class of work and jobs. The amount of incentive under the *higher differential piece rate* varies with the class of work. For ordinary light machine-shop work, a workman can earn at least 30 percent more than day wages, with higher earnings possible for heavier and more highly skilled work, up to 100 percent. A workman who fails to produce at the standard rate is paid at the *lower differential piece rate,* which is slightly more than day wages. Unless a workman can qualify as a first-class man and produce at the standard rate of production, he is penalized severely even though he earns the ordinary day rate of pay for his class of work.

Time and Motion Study. The foundation of scientific management started with time study. Before the development of its techniques, there was no proper manner for predetermining the amount of work that a man could do before he actually began to do it. Motion study attempted to find and perpetuate the scheme of least waste methods in productive work.

Frank B. Gilbreth summarized the purposes and methods of time and motion study as follows:[4]

1. To obtain all the existing information about the art or trade being investigated that is possessed by the present masters, journeymen, and experts.
2. To get the most exact information regarding the time required to perform each smallest element of the operation, so that in building up the standard method synthetically the quickest elements and motions may be selected, in order that the workman can use a method consisting of elements requiring the least time to perform.
3. To determine which motions and elements are the least fatiguing, so that the worker may be caused no unnecessary fatigue in his work.
4. To determine the amount of actual rest that each kind of work requires, so that neither the manager nor the man himself injure the worker by trying to make him do too much in order to secure higher wages.
5. To determine the personal characteristics of each worker for certain kinds of work, so that he may be assisted in entering that job for which he is best fitted.

It is the science of eliminating wastefulness resulting from the use of unnecessary, ill-directed, and inefficient motions of workers so that the one best method of each type of work can be established.

The Task. Gilbreth defined the task as the quantity of work of prescribed quality to be done in a given time, or the time required to do a certain quantity of output in a certain way as established by scientific time study. It is based on the one best method of performing the operative procedures of work to be done by a worker who has been scientifically selected for the task because of his qualifications for it.

According to *Henry L. Gantt,* a basic requirement for the practice of scientific management is the ability to distinguish between fact and opinion. He stated that "the most important asset which either a man or a nation can have is the ability to do things." Getting the facts consisted of:[5]

1. Finding out the proper day's task for a man suited to the work
2. Finding out the compensation needed to induce such men to do a full day's work
3. Planning so that the men may work continuously and efficiently

[4] Frank B. Gilbreth, *Primer of Scientific Management,* D. Van Nostrand Company, Inc., Princeton, N.J., 1912, p. 13.

[5] H. L. Gantt, "Work, Wages, and Profits," *Engineering Magazine,* 1911, p. 22.

The benefits to be derived from investigations of the facts are an increase in output, a decrease in cost of product, better workmen attracted by higher wages, and improvement of the quality of the product.

Dr. Alex Rathe, in his study *Gantt on Management*,[6] identified some of the most lasting and useful of Gantt's concepts and principles, which are listed as follows:

1. *Man is a goal-oriented creature.* The most effective method of getting workmen interested in their work is to set a task, an objective. This principle provided the foundation for his "task and bonus" plan.

2. *Planning and control provide for proper methods.* Proper results will be achieved from proper methods. This concept was the key to the Gantt Charts which showed by equal divisions of space on a single horizontal line at the same time the following:

Equal divisions of time
Varying amounts of work scheduled
Varying amounts of work done

The Gantt Charts illustrated the vital relationships between work and time that established the basic principle for all planning and control activities.

3. *Task setting is superior to driving or urging men to more strenuous toil without any well-measured standard of how much work is reasonable under the prevailing conditions.* This principle preceded the present concept of management by objectives. Results took priority over activities.

4. *The "task and bonus" principles* provided for the payment of a bonus to workmen who completed all the work assigned to them for the day. Gantt reported that it was possible to get "from two to three times as much work done as is usually done, pay 20 to 50 percent increase in wages, and still save about 40 percent in wage cost." A reduction in overhead will also follow.

5. *The authority to issue an order entails the responsibility to see that it is carried out.*

6. *Training is the responsibility of management, because it can increase productivity.*

7. *Proper work habits lead to greater productivity.* Gantt believed that men are influenced by certain incentives in addition to financial ones. Workmen who are trained in proper work habits find enjoyment in work as well as livelihood.

8. *Management is a leadership function: its mission is progress.* It is the administration of human affairs with emphasis on the importance of the individual.

Gantt believed that the problems of leadership are most easily solved when approached through scientific research. He highlighted the importance of making producers out of the vast numbers of busy people whose energies are being wasted by inefficient methods of work. According to Gantt, scientific management is a way of achieving national wealth. He warned that "the business system must accept its social responsibility and devote itself primarily

[6] American Management Association, New York, 1961.

to service, or the community will ultimately make the attempt to take it over in order to operate it in its own interest."

Rewards for Increased Productivity

The application of the philosophy and mechanisms of scientific management to human work has rewarded some nations with increasing levels of prosperity and human welfare. People are limited in their consumption of goods and services to the amount they can produce. Prosperity flows from a value system in which workers and managers cooperate to eliminate waste and inefficiency from the use of human resources.

Modern concepts of value for measuring the success of management set criteria for the rewards of at least three groups:

1. The ideal of service to customers. As stated by Howard Coonley in 1924, "The justification for any undertaking whether great or small, individual or collective, is accomplishing service to the community."
2. The prosperity of the workers. Taylor taught that, "The principal object of scientific management should be to secure the maximum prosperity for the employer coupled with the maximum prosperity for each employee."
3. The profit motive for investors and managers.

Unless the political leaders and industrial managers of a nation accept this value system as a guide to managerial thinking and actions, conflict, resistance, and strife will prevent improvement of work performance standards through waste elimination or cost reduction techniques.

In a Latin American country, a group of industrial managers were receiving information about the opportunities for cost reduction in their manufacturing operations. When it was shown how the savings from cost reduction could generate economic growth by lowering prices, raising wages, and developing new products, they objected. Their spokesman said that they did not need to raise wages because their workers could not get more pay anywhere else and that prices could not be lowered because of their protective agreements. They considered only their personal profits from cost reduction because of increased worker efficiencies. They rejected the national benefits from the opportunity to increase the purchasing power of employees and increase the volume of sales because of lower prices. Their unenlightened value system retarded economic growth for customer satisfactions and worker benefits.

Cultural Conditions and Productivity. Problems preventing the development of an industrial society can stem from the influences of cultural traditions and beliefs reflected in the value system for work performance and management practices.

1. The setting of tasks and work performance standards from the use of time and motion studies to establish wage incentive systems may suffer resistance in countries where manpower exists in abundance, such as India. Workers prefer payment in relation to family needs based on the number of children instead of personal efficiency in their jobs.
2. In countries such as Taiwan, the eldest son is presumed to be the head of any undertaking whether or not he is qualified. Such a cultural tradition is contrary to the scientific management requirement for selecting and training the personnel most suitable for the work assignments.

3. In some South American and Asian countries, the concept of time in relation to work accomplished is poorly understood. Consequently, the use of production planning and control devices such as simple Gantt Charts can have limited application without prior training and worker education programs. Wage incentive systems such as the differential rate piece payment and the task and bonus plan require careful installation and explanation to the workers. They presuppose an understanding of the importance of time.

Scientific management is most successful in aiding the economic development of countries that have a cultural environment with a scale of values that permits people to be ranked or rewarded for what they can do instead of who they happen to be. Individuals must be able to achieve status through achievements of work instead of being limited to family inheritance. Workers should be able to compete for any kind of work by virtue of qualifications instead of being permitted to perform only certain jobs because of caste or birth. An essential requirement is that of a specific labor contract relationship with an employer instead of one which involves kinship, political, religious, and other dependencies.

Scientific management can stimulate economic growth in a nation when its cultural environment and value system provide for the release of individual talents in the pursuit of personal productivity for personal satisfactions and rewards.

Changing Concepts for Industrial Development

A modern value system for industrial development may involve a change of concepts and practices among managers and workers. Experimentation is essential. Progress will be laborious and accompanied by mistakes and frustrations.

New concepts of value different from old cultural conditions with conventional management can be achieved by experimentation and demonstration. Psychological factors may be more important than economic factors in effecting a change of employee attitudes toward productivity. Great emphasis is placed upon the selection and training of workers when the techniques of scientific management are introduced. From actual demonstration of the rewards for productivity to a few selected individuals, many others will accept the new methods in the hope of personal gains.

Classic Examples. In the process of determining and demonstrating the value system of scientific management, the following examples may be cited for increasing the efficiency and wages of operative workers:

1. When applied to the simple operation of loading by hand a railroad car with pig-iron castings, the performance of the individual worker increased from 12½ to 47 tons a day. Originally a work gang of about 75 men were loading 92-pound pig-iron castings on a railroad car and averaging about 12½ tons per man per day. Through time and motion study analysis, it was determined that 47 tons per day should be the proper task. The next step was the scientific selection of the workmen who had qualifications for the task. One man was selected for experimentation with the new standard task. By following the instructions for the best method of performing the job, he averaged a little more than $1.85 per day, which was a 60 percent increase over his previous

earnings of $1.15 per day. Furthermore, he was under load only 43 percent of the work day and free from the weight load 57 percent of the time worked. By resting at proper intervals, he was able to maintain an even gait without suffering exhaustion. After the first man selected proved that the best method of work could increase wages and productivity, one man after another was picked and trained to perform the task and receive an increase of 60 percent in wages.

2. When applied to bricklaying, the day's accomplishment rose from 1,000 to 2,700 bricks.

3. When applied to the manufacture of cotton goods, it increased the output 100 percent.

Change Requires Education. When change is introduced to an economy with the intent of applying better management practices, there can be no substitute for a concurrent educational program to properly prepare both managers and workers. Failures may occur unless the conditions of the work environment are investigated and the managers plan carefully the effects of the change. A few examples follow.

In China an airstrip was being constructed with stones broken to proper size by hand labor. The decision was made to provide technological aid to the human efforts and increase productivity by means of a small stone-crusher. When the crusher was put into use, all other work stopped while the employees watched it. The use of the stone-crusher was discarded so that regular work could continue. When technological aids are introduced, the employees must be prepared and educated for the change in the work environment.

In French Morocco, leather goods have always been made by craftsmen who produce a complete product such as a purse. If the craftsmen would cooperate in an organized effort, their productivity and earnings would increase. By means of specialization and division of work, the craftsmen could each concentrate on a cutting, sewing, or tooling operation. In the same amount of time, they could produce more and better products. However, they would have to change their concept about work. They would have to replace the individual's satisfaction value of creating a total product with another value based upon higher earnings through increased productivity and group effort.

In Indonesia, the manager of a shipping company decided to increase productivity by using two large boats for island deliveries instead of many small ones. He had freedom of choice to succeed or fail with his plan. However, he used his opinion instead of investigating the facts concerning the depth of the water in the island harbors. The big boats could not enter the shallow waters. He was willing to effect change, but he failed to investigate the situation and suffered frustration.

Organization for Productivity Increases

Organization provides the vehicle for people to release their energies toward the accomplishment of work assignments that can be more productive by concerted efforts than by individual struggles. In countries where the cultural traditions have provided organizational experience in only family or tribe organizations, the workers will need orientation and introduction to the forms and purposes of industrial organization. New concepts of authority, responsibility, and human relationships must be accepted.

Henri Fayol first related the functions of business to the functions of management in France in 1916. He stated that all activities in industrial undertakings can be divided into six groups:

1. Technical (production, manufacture, adaptation)
2. Commercial (buying, selling, exchange)
3. Financial (search for and optimum use of capital)
4. Security (protection of property and persons)
5. Accounting (stocktaking, balance sheet, costs)
6. Managerial (planning, organizing, command, coordination, control)

Henri Fayol (*Administration Industrielle et Générale,* 1916) formulated some general principles of management. They are listed and explained as follows:

Division of work. This led to specialization and delegation of authority.

Authority. This was the right to command and to make oneself obeyed.

Discipline. This developed obedience, diligence, energy, and respect.

Unity of command. This provided for orders from only one superior.

Unity of management. This consisted of one manager and one plan for all operations with the same objective.

Subordination of individual interests to the general interest. This provided for the reconciling of conflicting interests.

Remuneration. The reward for work done should be fair and satisfactory.

Centralization. This involved finding the proper degree of centralization for each concern.

Scalar chain. This referred to the line of authority by all communications to and from the highest authority.

Order. This required a place for everything and everything in its place.

Equity. This dealt with uniform treatment and fairness for all.

Stability of tenure for personnel. This provided for success by tenure of managerial personnel.

Initiative. This meant the freedom and power to conceive and execute activities.

Esprit de corps. This led to organization strength through harmony and unity.

Fayol, in his attempt to provide a discipline for the teaching of management, developed a logical management philosophy. He was the first authority to relate the functions of a business to the functions of management, and then to provide principles for the guidance of the management function in the conduct of business activities. His concepts of the elements of management (planning, organizing, command, coordination, and control) have had great influence on the development of management thought. He made his contributions to management thought independently in France at about the same time that scientific management was developing in the United States.

Productivity from proper organization comes from establishing the most effective relationships among the work tasks, the people assigned to the work tasks, and an efficient work environment. Organization provides for the best division and specialization of work according to the essential functions of the business and the assignment of managerial, supervisory, and worker personnel to the work functions and tasks. In scientific management, an organizational form is based upon achieving the established goals through the work functions and not upon the status or favored positions of people.

Criteria for Obtaining Industrial Cooperation

In all modern management philosophies and practices, the basis for industrial cooperation is the concept which gives prime importance to the value and dignity of human beings. The economic future of any nation will be shaped by the achievement needs of its people and their value system of organized work with technological aids. The following criteria can determine the degree of industrial cooperation for economic growth:

1. The consideration of human beings and their personal dignities as the primary value.
2. The integration of personal, industrial, and national goals through the development of an identity of interests among all segments of society.
3. The proper use of management talents to effectively employ the fruits of human effort and technology to increase the prosperity of both managers and workers.
4. The development of the need for achievement among the people in an economy by means of work opportunities with incentive rewards for personal efficiency and productivity.
5. The intelligent use of capital equipment and technological aids essential for permitting humans to do human work and enjoy relief from animal work.
6. The establishment of a value system that can generate economic development and progress from competitive forces rather than industrial strife and conflict.

Within the present century, no nation in the world has enjoyed any appreciable economic growth without the presence and practice of the fundamental concepts and principles of scientific management. Furthermore, scientific management has not found its way into any nation which lacks the interest and desire to build an industrial economy. A close relationship exists between the acceptance and practice of scientific management and the degree of industrial development and economic growth of a society.

The political and business leaders of developing countries may choose between industrialization as a feasible approach to satisfactory standards of living and health for their people, or the continuation of a national economy based on subsistence agriculture. *The building of an industrial economy will depend upon the success of small industrial pilot enterprises.* In any country, the individual enterprises must operate within an "external environment" of political, economic, social, and technological forces; however, each enterprise also has an "internal environment" of management leadership, human skills and talents, financial and physical resources, and an element of "know-how" for the achievement of desired results. The basic philosophy and techniques of scientific management applied to pilot or pioneering enterprises in an economy can provide the leadership and successful example for others to follow in the struggle to generate economic growth for human satisfactions.

The practices of scientific management have pioneered the way toward industrialization in several countries where the need for achievement has existed among a few political and business leaders.

The concept and the principles of scientific management may not be applied successfully in all cultures and economic climates. Unless the public administrators, the business administrators, and the people of a nation are willing to accept dignified and productive human work as a means for generating economic growth, scientific management practices can have minimum influence on the economy. To any nation aspiring to improve conditions of economic development, the principles of scientific management have proved their value and effectiveness in maximizing the productivity of human efforts in organized economic endeavors. The economic factors and the behavioral-personality factors are interdependent in a national environment.

APPLICABILITY OF MANAGEMENT PRINCIPLES IN UNDERDEVELOPED ECONOMIES

Leon C. Megginson, Ph.D.

Eugene C. McCann, Ph.D.

As Carl A. Roos so aptly phrased it, "Everyone must live better." But to live better, the people of a given country must do one of three things: they must work more intensely through the expenditure of greater effort; they must work more efficiently and effectively by utilizing more advanced machines and methods; or they must employ a combination of both methods. This study is concerned with the second alternative, that is, raising productivity by improving management techniques and practices.

Need for Management Development

If a country is to raise its income, it must utilize effectively all available resources, internal and external and material and nonmaterial. Effective resource utilization includes, among other things, the channeling of human resources into those activities which would be the most productive and which, therefore, would do most to raise the standard of living of its people. In the past, the "resources" of the underdeveloped nations have included only material goods; too frequently, the resource with the greatest potential, people, has been ignored. More specifically, managerial talent has not always been recognized as an economic resource. But recognizing management talent as a source of wealth is not enough; developing nations must take action to generate and

---

Dr. Megginson is Professor of Management at Louisiana State University, Baton Rouge, Louisiana.

Dr. McCann is Assistant Professor of Management and Assistant Dean of the College of Business Administration at Louisiana State University, Baton Rouge, Louisiana.

accumulate this important economic resource, just as positive steps are taken to generate and accumulate capital.[1]

The development of managerial talent must become a part of the national policy of a developing country if it is to achieve its goal. The expansion of this resource can no longer be considered a field of private endeavor, or the responsibility of the industrial organizations alone. For a nation even to enter the race to industrialize, it must encourage and facilitate the training and development of managerial personnel to direct efficiently the affairs of its business and governmental organizations.[2] Only through effective management of these organizations will the supply of goods and services increase rapidly enough to raise the standards of living of its people.

Apparently, reticence exists among the aristocratic classes of certain underdeveloped countries to the encouragement of the expansion, training, and elevation of the position of managerial classes. The aristocrats reason that the managerial classes may gain political influence at the expense of the aristocracies. Although such a phenomenon could conceivably occur, the fact remains that if a nation is to expand industrially, a managerial class must be developed. A high positive correlation exists between the extent of managerial development in a country and the economic well-being of that country. The question of which comes first, management development or industrial development, is academic; neither element can exist without the other. Also, there is little reason to believe that the mass of working people have been, or will be, exploited by the emerging professional managerial class.[3]

Recognizing management development as being essential to economic development leads one to determine ways and means of achieving that development. Two general propositions hold true concerning management development in industrial societies. First, the general direction of management development is the same in all industrial societies. Second, progress toward industrialization can be quickened or hindered by certain factors affecting management development. Underlying both these propositions is the constant effort by management scholars to develop more fully a theory of management and the propagation of the laws and principles derived from it. But, without a theory of management, there can be no teaching of management. Even though no comprehensive theory of management has yet been developed which is universally accepted, a core of principles does exist. These principles are true, regardless of time, place, organization, or level within an organization.[4]

[1] F. Harbison and C. A. Myers, *Management in the Industrial World: An International Analysis*, McGraw-Hill Book Company, New York, 1959.

[2] This thought has been excellently stated by Mariano Sanchez Rodrigo in "Formación de directores de empresa mediante un programa nacional," *Productividad*, Revista de la Comisión Nacional de Productividad Industrial, April–June, 1960, pp. 24–29: "Las consecuencias de una política formativa equivocada, pueden ser le lamentables consecuencias para el país, con el agravante de que sólo se pondrían de manifiesto a largo plazo y por ello no sería fácil corregirlas hasta pasados algunos años."

[3] Harbison and Myers, *op. cit.*, pp. 121–122.

[4] For a further discussion of this proposition, see L. C. Megginson, "The Pressure for Principles: A Challenge to Management Professors," Paul M. Dauten (ed.),

Universality of Management Principles

The universal applicability of management principles is accepted by management theorists because the organic functions of management are deemed to be the same at all levels of management and in all organizations. This concept of a body of knowledge with universal applicability was the central theme of Taylor's scientific management.[5] Among various organizations and at various levels within organizations, certain management functions receive greater emphasis than others. For instance, top management may devote more time and effort to the planning function than do first-line supervisors; but planning takes place at both levels—planning, and the other organic functions of management, exist at all management levels of an organization.

The universality of management concept is not restricted to certain nations or societies of the world. Execution of the organic functions of management varies from culture to culture, but the functions themselves and the principles they involve are constant. The functions and principles involved in managing a small organization are the same as those involved in running a large organization; the functions and principles involved in managing a statewide organization are the same as those involved in managing a foreign-based organization.[6]

Examples of Universal Management Principles

An example of a universally true principle of management is the division-of-labor principle or the principle of specialization. This principle is rooted in nature. As Fayol acknowledged, " . . . it is observable in the animal world, where the more highly developed the creature, the more highly differentiated its organs; it is observable in human society, where the more important the body corporate, the closer is the relationship between structure and function. As society grows, so new organs develop destined to replace the single one performing all functions in the primitive state."[7]

Even in the most primitive societies, one can observe that as the economy grows, there is a tendency toward specialization or division of work. In underdeveloped countries the specialization of work is one of the first observable consequences of the emerging industrial development. This principle is universally true because it is based upon a cause-and-effect relationship that is true in every situation where it is *permitted* to operate.

Another universally true management principle concerns centralization. The principle of centralization states that there is a tendency for decisions to be

---

Current Issues and Emerging Concepts in Management, Houghton Mifflin Company, Boston, 1962, pp. 46–49; and L. C. Megginson, "L'Arte dell'Amministrazione," *Rivista Internazionale di Scienzé Economiche e Commerciali,* vol. 9, no. 8, pp. 755–768, August, 1962.

[5] Frederick W. Taylor, "The Principles of Scientific Management," as reprinted in H. F. Merrill, *Classics in Management,* American Management Association, New York, 1960, p. 92.

[6] Jerome Barnum, "Management Movement Here and Abroad," *Advanced Management-Office Executive,* International Edition, January, 1962, pp. 22–27.

[7] Henri Fayol, *General and Industrial Management,* Pitman Publishing Corporation, London, 1949, p. 20.

referred upward through the various levels of the organization in opposition to the exception principle, for authority to remain undelegated at the top echelon of the organization, and even for physical facilities to be concentrated in one location. These observable phenomena stem from the fact that " . . . in every organism, animal or social, sensations converge towards the brain or directive part, and from the brain or directive part orders are sent out which set all parts of the organism in movement."[8]

Still another principle that is universally true is the principle of standardization. This principle states, in effect, that the " . . . best practice should be determined, expressed in terms of definite units or standards and adapted as a pattern for use in operation, in performance, and in planning and control."[9]

This principle evolved from Taylor's statement that " . . . *there is a best way in doing everything*, and [that] that best way can always be formulated into certain rules; [that] you can get your knowledge away from the old chaotic rule-of-thumb knowledge into organized knowledge."[10]

The principal of standardization was at the heart of Taylor's *Scientific Management* and later was an integral part of the concepts of Frank and Lillian Gilbreth.[11]

Underlying the Industrial Revolution and the present emphasis upon automation is the principle of transfer of skill. This principle states that[12]

> . . . the attention and skill required of a worker to use a tool or operate a machine is inversely related to the thought and skill transferred into its mechanism.
>
> Corollary 1: Thru the application of the principle of the transfer of skill, the worker becomes an adjunct to the tool or machine.
>
> Corollary 2: The transfer of skill from the expert workman to the machine makes the quality and quantity of work produced dependent upon the machine, not upon the machine operator.

This principle has been utilized repeatedly throughout history—from the time of the development of the ax, wheel, and knife, until today's blind rush toward automation. Essentially, this principle says that man is capable of performing all tasks himself but is manifestly more efficient if his skills can be transferred to machines.

Effects of Culture, Philosophies, and Attitudes on Applicability of Principles

Although this listing of management principles is by no means all-inclusive, it does help prove the thesis of the transferability, or universality, of the principles of management. However, it must be realized that in addition to

[8] *Ibid.*, p. 33.

[9] W. B. Cornell, *Organization and Management in Industry and Business*, 3d ed., The Ronald Press Company, New York, 1947, p. 56.

[10] Taylor, *op. cit.*, p. 95. Italics in Merrill.

[11] Frank D. Gilbreth, "Science in Management for the One Best Way to Do Work," reprinted in Merrill, *op. cit.*, pp. 245–291.

[12] L. P. Alford and H. R. Beatty, *Principles of Industrial Management*, The Ronald Press Company, New York, 1951, rev. ed., pp. 11–12.

the body of knowledge that encompasses the principles of management, there are at least two other factors that help a manager achieve his success. One of these factors is his own unique managerial philosophy which encompasses his sense of values, customs, beliefs, and assumptions concerning his environment. The other factor is the manager's knowledge of the environment. Knowledge of the environment is vital because one's management philosophy must be compatible with his environment. Dr. Robert D. Calkins made the observation that administration is informed, rational, and deliberate action that draws upon the knowledge of the physical and social sciences and uses many of the unspoken techniques of these two fields of study. However, it is " . . . overwhelmingly concerned with the choice of ends, ways, and means for the attainment of desired results. It is curbed by moral codes and ethical principles; and it is driven by springs of ambition and devotion that largely escape analysis."[13]

Therefore, a given manager in a given company in a given country will be successful if he knows and is able to apply the principles of management, and if his personal philosophy is compatible with the environment in which he is operating.

It must be borne in mind that although management occurs within an economic context, it also exists within a cultural, political, psychological, and social context. Although there is a science of management, that science is modified by the art of management. Coping with environment has always been and always will be a challenge to management. But the notion is accepted that one important factor of environment, culture, can serve as an impediment to the effectiveness of a manager. As a matter of fact, one of the biggest failures of American management abroad is its general disregard for, and unfamiliarity with, the customs, laws, and conditions of the foreign country in which it is called upon to operate.[14]

In certain areas of the world, the culture, the stage of economic and technological development, and the personal philosophies of managers may impede or even preclude the successful application of management principles. Moreover, in some regions of the world, businessmen fail to recognize the fact that management contains a science. These businessmen consider management to be strictly an art and conclude, therefore, that management does not contain principles and cannot be set down, codified, or communicated. To their way of thinking, experience is the only teacher. As one can readily see, if management is considered strictly an art, there is no need or urge to seek out and understand management principles; for, by definition, management principles do not exist.

However, knowledge of management principles does not automatically transform itself into management efficiency.[15] At least two vital ingredients need to be added—experience and proper attitude. One develops into an

[13] *Faculty Requirements and Standards in Collegiate Schools of Business,* American Association of Collegiate Schools of Business, New York, 1955, p. 151.

[14] J. W. Houser, "The Delicate Job of American Management Abroad," *Advanced Management-Office Executive*, January, 1962, pp. 20–21.

[15] R. F. Gonzalez and Claude McMillan, Jr., "The Universality of American Management Philosophy," *Journal of the Academy of Management,* April, 1961, p. 33.

effective manager through the thoughtful application of management knowledge and principles. The second ingredient, proper attitude, implies a willingness on the part of a would-be effective manager to make a sincere effort to apply the management principles of which he is aware and continually to broaden his management knowledge. One cannot develop to his full management potential and ignore, or pay only lip service to, management principles; he must put forth a sincere effort to apply them effectively. Knowledge alone is not enough, for, as Henri Fayol stated: "It must be admitted that proclamation [of management principles] is not enough. The fact is that the light of principles, like that of lighthouses, guides only those who already know the way to port, and a principle bereft of the means of putting it into practice is of no avail."[16]

As mentioned above, one of the most frequently employed tools of management is the scientific method. This method is simply the application of logic or orderly thinking to the solution of a problem. Strange as it may seem to the U.S. manager, businessmen in some cultures rarely, if ever, utilize the scientific method in decision making. The effective utilization of the scientific method requires patient, careful, orderly thinking and the ability to see reality objectively. In some cultures, however, the people tend to be quite impatient, impulsive, and emotional, and to disregard objectivity. In such cultures, basing decisions on emotion and impulse is expected because spontaneous expression of one's feelings is expected and not necessarily undesirable.

In the place of cold, relentless logic, individuals in these cultures rely heavily upon intuition to point out solutions to problems. Thought proceeds in a series of direct revelations or perceptions of "truths" concerning the problem from its inception to its ultimate solution. The perceptions are independent of any reasoning process and, therefore, are neither verifiable nor repeatable. The individual tends toward action which is improvised and poorly thought out. His culture teaches him to rely on intuition for solutions to problems. In short, the characteristics the culture spawns and the environment emphasizes clash with the characteristics necessary for the effective utilization of the scientific method.

The stage of economic development and the level of technology frequently play an important role in determining the applicability of management principles. Generally, the lower the level of economic development, the lower the level of understanding of the management process. This relationship may reflect inadequacy in general education, but more frequently, it reflects a lack of education for business. In addition, this relationship reflects the scarcity of opportunities in underdeveloped areas for many people to gain worthwhile management experience. In underdeveloped areas there are few opportunities for formal education for business and relatively few persons are capable of gaining worthwhile management experience.

Throughout the less developed areas of the world, wide gaps exist between technological possibilities and the level of technology practicable. Frequently, these gaps are a reflection of economic size or the diseconomies of relatively small scale. In turn, diseconomies of small scale must be borne because the

[16] Fayol, *op. cit.*, p. 15.

available markets are small—perhaps relatively few people can afford to buy certain manufactured products. When such circumstances prevail, specialized machinery is not likely to be economical, and a high level of worker specialization is not easily achieved.

Examples of Inapplicability of Principles

Perhaps some brief examples will illustrate how the culture, the level of economic and technological development, and the philosophy of managers can hinder the application of management principles.

One of the principles that Fayol discusses concerns the subordination of individual interest to general interest.[17] He explains that in any group the interest of the group should supersede the interest of the individual. This principle implies the presence of team-mindedness and a feeling of equality among men. Such characteristics are not found in all cultures, however. Whereas Americans tend almost instinctively toward cooperative effort, people in some other cultures tend almost instinctively away from cooperative effort. In these other cultures, extremely individualistic behavior, which is common, renders the team or cooperative approach to goal achievement almost useless. Teamwork requires subordination of the individual's will to the group's will—a phenomenon which has little appeal to the individualistic person.

Teamwork, as noted earlier, also implies the presence of a concept of equality among men. This concept is relatively useless in cultures where strong master-servant, authoritarian relationships prevail between superiors and their subordinates and where they are mindful of their respective positions. These cultures disallow American-style cooperative effort. A caste system is an obstacle to the application of management principles.

A principle of management exists which states: "The minimum overall time required to perform a group of successive tasks on one product is obtained by performing the tasks arranged with a maximum overlapping."[18] This principle simply indicates that before step one of the process is completed, step two is begun; before step two is finished, step three is begun, and so on. In this manner, the overall time required for performing all the steps or tasks of the process is less than it would be if step two were not begun until step one was completed.

An American firm producing abroad may not employ the same type of machinery that is used in the present plant. The parent plant may utilize expensive single-purpose machines. In the overseas plant, however, perhaps no single-purpose machinery is used. Rather, the machinery is a multipurpose type which, if altered slightly, can be used for many different operations. Economical utilization of special-purpose machinery requires long, high-volume production runs. Large production capacity requires, in turn, mass markets. But mass markets do not exist overseas for many types of goods. The size of the market for a particular good in a particular region may require, therefore, the use of only multipurpose machinery. The use of multipurpose

[17] *Ibid.*, p. 26.

[18] George R. Terry, *Principles of Management*, Richard D. Irwin, Inc., Homewood, Ill., 1960, p. 202.

machinery may preclude the overlapping of the successive tasks or steps of production. Therefore, although the principle is still true, it is not applicable in that specific situation because of mitigating circumstances caused by the environment.

Summary

This article has tried to develop two related but contrasting thoughts. First, an effort was made to prove that there exists a systematic body of knowledge that encompasses a core of management principles that are true in all managerial situations regardless of size, kind of operation, or geographic location. If this core of knowledge is developed, promulgated, and utilized in underdeveloped countries, it will lead to increased effectiveness among managers in those countries and, therefore, to higher standards of living for their people. However, the effective utilization of the principles of management may be modified by the individual managerial philosophies of the managers attempting to apply them. This philosophy, in turn, is modified by the cultural environment in which the managers are operating. In any given area, therefore, the culture, the level of economic and technological development, and the attitudes of the manager may seriously impede the successful application of management principles to underdeveloped countries. However, because culture is a man-made phenomenon, man can change it. Certainly, education will play a large role in initiating and influencing cultural changes.

THE VALUE AND DIGNITY OF HUMAN BEINGS AS A BASIS OF INDUSTRIAL COOPERATION

Carl Heyel

Ever since the late 1920s, and intensified by the social problems of the Great Depression, there has been increasing preoccupation on the part of management in all industrialized countries with the human side of operations. Prior to that time, industrial engineers had been seeking most of the answers to efficient operation in improved production processes and more refined budgeting for cost controls and the like. Even in the stress and strain of World War II production, the question of employee morale and motivation was always of high-priority concern in the factories, not excluding Russia, where in some instances cosmetics for women workers were considered essential items.

Human relations has been much belabored in supervisory and management development courses in American industry. "How to Get Along with People," "How to Motivate," "How to Handle Grievances" have become stock titles in all such training programs—to say nothing of the shelves of books and numerous magazine articles on the same subjects. What more should be said about the value and dignity of human beings as a basis of industrial cooperation?

The fact is that there have been some wide pendulum swings in management attitudes on the subject ever since the famous Chicago "Hawthorne experiments" of the Western Electric Company in 1923–1926 and 1927–1932 triggered the so-called "human relations movement." In recent years the effects of automation and the more centralized control through new decision-making techniques have appeared to work against many of the tenets of the "human relationists," and the differences between extreme positions may well be a source of confusion. Our purpose here is to attain a balanced view.

Mr. Heyel is a management consultant, editor of a management encyclopedia, and author of management textbooks.

Effect of the Hawthorne Experiments

The Hawthorne experiments had such a profound effect in ushering in the new preoccupation with worker motivation, participation, satisfaction, and the like that it may be well to tell the story again briefly. These experiments represent the most ambitious single investigation ever attempted to determine what factors significantly influence the efficiency and productivity of working groups.

The investigators began what they at first thought would be a more or less routine study of the effect of illumination on production. A test group of employees was chosen, and a suitable assembly operation was set up. Conditions were standardized, and it was found that production did indeed increase as illumination increased. But when the analysts *decreased* the illumination within very broad limits, they found to their surprise that production still continued to go up! Obviously, some variable or variables were at work that were more important than illumination.

As a result of the unexpected findings a second, more ambitious research study was undertaken. This experiment consisted of an exhaustive investigation of the production of five girls who were continuously engaged in the repetitive assembly of small electrical relays. The girls were subjected to all sorts of changes in their working conditions. They took six rest pauses a day, worked without rest pauses, worked short hours and long hours. They were switched around in their chairs, and given different kinds of relays to assemble. Detailed records were kept on such factors as the weather outside and whether the girls came to work tired after parties or fresh after a good night's sleep. There were changes in the form of incentive payments and in the quality of supervision.

The results of all these observations were again unexpected. No matter what the changes, the girls' total output continued to rise throughout the period of the experiments, reaching a total increase of 30 percent. The conclusion reached was that the increases in output were due, not to any of the changes in tangible working conditions, but rather to the *social relationships* of the girls and *their attitude toward supervision*.[1]

The girls were interviewed in depth and were asked to reply to detailed questionnaires. The investigators, in their final explanation of the results, placed great emphasis on the apparent influence of the *sense of participation and belonging*. The girls knew that they were taking part in an interesting experiment, and they were consulted on details that affected them. They realized that they were part of something that management considered important, and this affected the pride they took in their work. The investigators

[1] In the Hawthorne experiment, the experimental room was devised and maintained by the Western Electric Company. Much of the analysis was done by Prof. T. N. Whitehead and his associates at the Harvard Graduate School of Business Administration, under the direction of Prof. Elton Mayo. The story is told in F. J. Roethlisberger and W. J. Dickson, *Management and the Worker*, Harvard University Press, Cambridge, Mass., 1939.

also concluded that the informal organization and social relationships which the girls developed by working together were as important as the formal organization, and were even of more significance than physical factors and changes in pay.

A later study of fourteen male operators in a wiring room, designed to obtain more exact information about social groups within the company, reinforced the findings from the relay test room.

Following the Hawthorne experiments there was a tremendous swing by management to a deep preoccupation with the human and social aspects of work. In industrial relations literature and from the platforms of management gatherings both in the United States and abroad, the Hawthorne findings were quoted extensively. The findings provided an apparent scientific basis for the arguments that were increasingly being advanced by socially conscious spokesmen for government, business, and academic circles, to the effect that human relations had been a neglected factor in productivity.

In the United States this new trend in management thinking had a marked influence on the type and content of management training programs for all levels—supervisors, "middle management," and top executives. In many cases the preoccupation with the human reactions on the job led to rather extreme emphasis on psychological and even near-psychiatric approaches. While there later was a reaction against giving analysis and advice to subordinates on alleged personality defects, and a swing back to stressing performance on the job, the net result was a salutary concern to have all supervisors and higher executives, both in the plant and in the office, think about what constitutes constructive leadership on the job, about effective techniques of communication and teaching, overcoming resistance to change, instilling pride in work, and achieving identification with company objectives.

Another direct result of the Hawthorne experiments was the impetus they gave to "undirected" employee counseling. This was carried to great lengths by the Hawthorne management, which made a skilled interviewer available to each shop department. Complete confidence was absolutely guaranteed, and the interviewer never argued or gave advice.

Under this philosophy, whatever corrective action takes place comes about through increased understanding, through thinking and self-help stimulated by the questions. Not many companies, of course, could afford the luxury of such an elaborate setup, but the techniques of this form of counseling—that is, largely listening—are now widely applied as part of formal employee and executive appraisal plans. (That this was no short-lived enthusiasm at Hawthorne is indicated by the fact that the counseling procedure was in force for twenty years, from 1936 to 1956. Since then the program has been curtailed, and the counseling techniques have been incorporated into Western Electric's general supervisory development programs.)

Insights into Motivation

In the years since World War II, a great deal of attention has been given to the question of human motivation. Social scientists have sought to develop theories about the motivation of people at work on the basis of firsthand observations in industrial situations, studies reported upon by clinical psychologists, the reactions under controlled experiments of nonindustry groups such as school children and military units, and the "living examples" furnished by employee-sharing and incentive programs.

We shall come back to these later. At this point, however, we should mention some ideas about motivation advanced by A. H. Maslow.[2] These ideas have since won general acceptance by psychologists and provide valuable insights to anyone concerned with getting the best out of people in our industrial society today.

Dr. Maslow postulates five basic needs which, he says, are organized into successive levels. For example, *hunger* is a basic physiological need. But when there is plenty of food, higher needs emerge. When the higher needs are satisfied, newer and still higher needs come to the fore, and so on. Thus gratification becomes as important a concept in motivation as deprivation. A want that is satisfied is no longer a want.

Below we give, necessarily simplified, these levels of basic needs, starting with the lowest. (It should not be assumed that a need must be entirely satisfied before the next one emerges. Most normal people are partially satisfied in all their basic needs at the same time.) Perhaps the greatest significance of this insight is the new light it throws on motivations of workers in advanced stages of a society's industrial development, hence standard of living. Where a lower level of needs is guaranteed as a matter of course, the other levels will assume greater importance.

The Physiological Needs. These are hunger for food, sexual gratification, and shelter.

The Safety Needs. If the physiological needs are relatively satisfied, a set of needs emerges for protection against danger and threats. In an ordered society a person usually feels safe from extremes of climate, tyranny, violence, and so on. Expressions of safety needs are thus seen in preferences for job security, insurance, and the like. Other manifestations are preferences for the familiar rather than the unfamiliar, the known rather than the unknown. These are normal reactions. Arbitrary management actions giving rise to uncertainty can have an adverse effect at any level in the organization. The tendency toward resistance to change is human and universal.

The Love Needs. (Some writers term these "social" needs.) If the physiological and safety needs are fairly well taken care of, the needs for love and affection and "belongingness" will emerge, and the cycle will repeat itself with this new center. The person now seeks affectionate relations with people in general, a place in his group. If he is deprived of these goals, he will want to attain them more than anything else in the world, and, in Dr. Maslow's words, "he may even forget that once, when he was hungry, he sneered at love." In our society, the thwarting of these needs is the most common cause of severe psychological maladjustment.

The Esteem Needs. Practically everyone has a need for self-respect and for the esteem of others. This results in the desire for strength, adequacy,

[2] A. H. Maslow, "A Theory of Human Motivation," *Psychological Review*, vol. 50, 1943.

confidence, independence, reputation or prestige, recognition, attention, and appreciation. These needs are rarely completely satisfied. They are of special importance in our discussion because today the typical industrial and commercial organization does not offer much opportunity for their satisfaction to employees at the lower levels. It is the recognition of these needs that has focused so much attention upon ways to provide employees with a sense of participation. Extreme advocates call for very broad participation indeed, covering even allocation of work and setting of the work pace, and criticize Taylor's scientific management as deliberately thwarting these esteem needs.

The Need for "Self-actualization," for Self-fulfillment. Even if all the needs thus far mentioned are satisfied, we can still expect that a new discontent and restlessness will develop unless the individual is doing what he is fitted for. Dr. Maslow writes: "A musician must make music, an artist must paint, a poet must write, if he is to be ultimately happy. What a man can be he must be. This need we may call self-actualization." The clear emergence of these needs rests upon prior satisfaction of the physiological, safety, love, and esteem needs. People who are satisfied in these needs are basically satisfied people, and it is from these that we can expect the fullest and healthiest creativeness.

An important point about these basic needs is that in the average person they are more often unconscious than conscious. An executive made aware of them will often obtain a clarifying insight into seemingly contradictory behavior. ("We agree to their wage demands—now why can't we get productivity?")

"Democratic" versus "Authoritarian" Management

The foregoing ties in with the continuing emphasis that has in recent years been given by many industrial psychologists and others interested in the industrial application of the social sciences to the advantages of so-called "democratic" versus "authoritarian" management and to more "participative" management in general. An executive who is "democratically oriented" is one who thinks of himself as a coordinator of his group rather than "boss." He believes subordinates should have more voice in running the department or division and listens to ideas and suggestions from them. He passes adequate explanations on to his subordinates when changes are made and is prepared on occasion to give in to a subordinate if there is disagreement on how something should be done.

The advocates of democratic management contend that with all that is now known about the reactions of people in groups, about individual motivations, and about worker satisfaction, an entirely new theory of management is called for, one that permits more self-fulfillment or self-actualization by the worker.

Under this concept, an executive or supervisor is seen not so much as the directive head of his group but rather as its representative in the next higher group in the organization. The department head and the members of his work group are interdependent, whereas under the authoritarian system the superior's authority and the subordinate's dependency are emphasized. The latter view is considered unrealistic by the proponents of democratic management, since, they point out, in many situations the superior must depend on his subordinate. The principle is illustrated by what Rensis Likert has called the "linking pin" concept of supervision,[3] illustrated in Figure 1. In (*a*), loops are drawn around each individual and his superior, indicating that the pairs represent the primary working and communication relationships. In (*b*), illustrating the "linking pins," loops are drawn around each superior and all of his subordinates. (This concept has proved to be of special pertinence

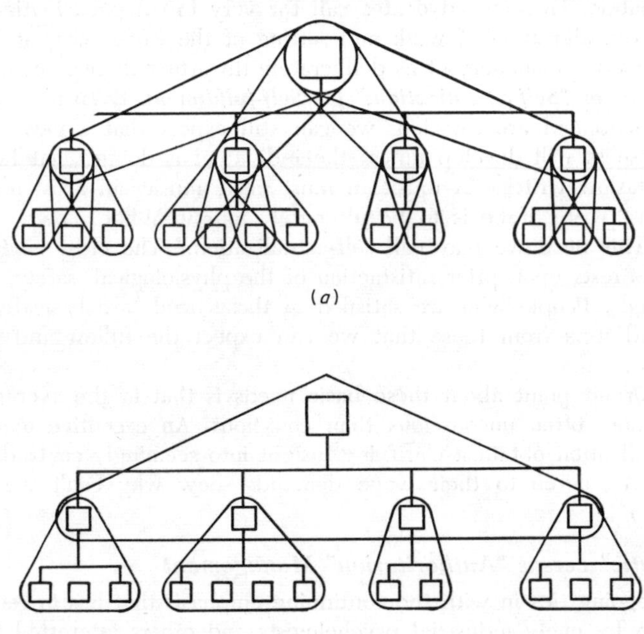

Fig. 1. (*a*) "Man to man" and (*b*) "Linking pin" concepts of supeior-subordinate relationships. (*After Likert.*)

where the group consists of creative professional workers, such as those engaged in research and development.)

Incentive Plans and the Newer Concepts of Motivation

It is understandable that developments such as those discussed thus far would cause many people to question individual incentives or piecework plans. By the beginning of the "human relations movement" such plans had been brought to a point of wide application in industry, and they are still very widely used.

These plans, of course, rely practically altogether on a single motivation—additional monetary reward for additional effort—and if recognized industrial engineering procedures are followed, the production standards against which individual performance is measured are set by a professional methods de-

[3] Rensis Likert, "Developing Patterns in Management," in *Strengthening Management for the New Technology,* General Management Series, no. 178, 1955, and Part II in *Changing Patterns and Concepts in Management,* General Management Series, no. 182, 1956, American Management Association, Inc.

partment. In recent management literature there has been increasing advocacy of replacing such plans with group bonus plans and company-wide profit-sharing plans, relating the bonus either to company profits or company savings as a whole or to departmental saving effected by voluntary group effort. These, it is claimed, are much more conducive to harmonious relationships, continuing productivity, and dedication to the objectives of the enterprise as a whole.

In an attempt to support this view, industrial psychologists and others have cited numerous case study examples of worker opinions polled in specific plants, showing shortcomings of engineered performance standards and incentive systems or citing beneficial results when the newer philosophies of participation, group cohesiveness, and the like were applied. The literature cannot be reviewed extensively here; but to give the flavor of the general nature of these reports, two examples are cited as typical. Presently we shall comment on the validity of such criticisms if an incentive plan is soundly engineered and installed in such a way as to achieve employee cooperation.

The first example, related by William Foote Whyte,[4] concerns a paint room, where women spray-painted wooden toys and hung them on hooks which carried them into a drying oven. The girls were expected to reach engineered performance standards in six months, but there was a serious problem of absenteeism and turnover. The girls claimed that the standards were impossible, and many hooks went into the oven empty. They complained of the oven heat, fumes, and general messiness. The foreman decided to meet with the girls and discuss their problems. They claimed that the room was poorly ventilated and too hot and asked for some large fans. The foreman got management approval to install three fans.

The girls' attitude was so improved that the foreman arranged for another meeting. The girls then complained that the time study men had set the conveyor too fast. They asked to be allowed to control the conveyor speed themselves—to be able to vary it during the day.

After meetings between the foreman and the standards men, it was decided to try the girls' idea, and a control was installed, containing a dial for "low," "medium," and "fast." Medium speed was just a little above standard. The girls experimented with this and established the following pattern: For the first half-hour each day the control was set at slightly above medium. The next 2½ hours were at high speed. For a half-hour before and after lunch the speed was set at low. Thereafter the control was again changed to high and left there until the last forty-five minutes, when it was changed to medium.

The girls now reported that the pace was comfortable. Scarcely a hook went by empty, and rejects leveled off. Two months before the end of the six-month learning period, production was 30 to 50 percent above standard, and the girls were collecting base pay, learner's bonus, and regular bonus.

This story typifies case studies purporting to show the possibilities, even in fairly mechanized operations, of applying the new concepts of participation—although in this instance there was an anticlimactic ending. The girls were earning more money than many skilled workers, and the latter knew it. Whyte

[4] William Foote Whyte, *Money and Motivation*, Harper & Row, Publishers, Incorporated, New York, 1955.

reports that without consultation the superintendent revoked the learning bonus and returned the painting operation to its original status. The hooks again moved at a constant speed, production dropped, and within a month all but two of the girls had quit. The foreman stayed for several months but then left for another job.

The second example is from Douglas McGregor:[5]

> The practical logic of incentives is that people want money, and they will work harder to get more of it. . . . Incentive plans do not, however, take account of several other well demonstrated characteristics of behavior in the organizational setting: (1) that most people also want the approval of their fellow workers and that, if necessary, they will forego increased pay to obtain this approval; (2) that no managerial assurances can persuade workers that incentive rates will remain inviolate regardless of how much they produce; (3) that the ingenuity of the average worker is sufficient to outwit *any* system of controls devised by management.
>
> A "good" individual incentive plan may bring about a moderate increase in productivity (perhaps 15 per cent), but it also may bring a considerable variety of protective behaviors—deliberate restriction of output, hidden jigs and fixtures, hidden production, fudged records, grievances over rates and standards, etc. It generally creates attitudes which are the opposite of those desired.

The Reaction

The cumulative effect, in some companies, of all the emphasis on human relations was to swing the pendulum pretty far—to a "do-gooder's" philosophy of personnel administration, Inevitably, there were second thoughts. Was all this talk about the human factor in industry taking on the aspects of a fad? Was "democratic" supervision simply "soft" supervision? Were all the interesting case studies nothing more than anecdotes—isolated case-book material without any general significance?

Participative management, the questioners pointed out, is all well and good, but should girls really be allowed to set conveyor speeds? Are we becoming overly concerned with patting workers on the head, giving them expressions of approval to bolster their self-esteem? Do engineered performance standards really rob a worker of human dignity? Where should management draw the line in giving up its prerogatives?

These growing doubts were accentuated in the United States by the sharp business recession of the late 1950s. Cost-conscious managers felt that there were many "frills" that could be cut from industrial relations practices, and many felt that they were in a position to adopt somewhat more of a "get tough" policy with organized labor. Typical of the questioning attitude are the following observations by Malcolm P. McNair in the *Harvard Business Review:*[6]

> Too much emphasis on human relations encourages people to feel sorry for themselves, makes it easier for them to slough off responsibility, to find excuses for failure, to act like children. . . .

[5] *The Human Side of Enterprise,* McGraw-Hill Book Company, New York, 1960.

[6] Malcolm McNair, "Thinking Ahead: What Price Human Relations?" *Harvard Business Review,* March–April, 1957.

> It has become the fashion to decry friction, but friction has its uses; without friction there are no sparks, without friction it is possible to go too far in the direction of sweetness and light, harmony, and the avoidance of all irritation. . . .
>
> The overemphasis on human relations, with all its apparatus of courses, special vocabulary, and so on, tends to create the very problems that human relations deals with. It is a vicious circle. You encourage people to pick at the scabs of their psychic wounds.

The Search for Proof

To seek answers to questions such as those raised above, there have been numerous attempts by social scientists to put a somewhat firmer scientific base under all the admonitions to encourage participation, to provide scope for individual goal setting, to consider social relationships, and the like. To see whether such human relations practices could actually be tied in to increased production, a number of controlled experiments were undertaken, incorporating as much as possible of the rigor employed in experiments in the physical sciences.

In this search for hard-core evidence, the sacrosanct Hawthorne experiments themselves came under some critical review. In 1953, twenty years after the original Hawthorne reports, a British social scientist, Michael Argyle, published a paper entitled "The Relay Assembly Test Room in Retrospect."[7] He carefully reexamined all the reported results, subjecting them to tests for statistical significance, evaluated the types of controls that had been set up, and reconsidered all the possible influences on the final measurements. He flatly stated:

> It is clear that the three groups of physical factors considered [rest periods, shorter hours, changes in pay] could easily have been responsible for the whole of the observed increase of output, although there is insufficient evidence to show whether they were or not. . . . It was concluded that only about half of the 30 per cent increase was due to the method of payment. This figure was arrived at by comparison with two control groups, but no conclusions can be based on comparisons of single case studies where there is no control of other important conditions. . . . It is thus not possible to say how much increase was due to the wage change. . . . There is no quantitative evidence for which this experiment is famous—that the increase in output was due to a changed relationship to supervision.

It is interesting to note that this British paper apparently made no impression upon American management literature. Since 1953 the Hawthorne experiments have continued to be cited with the traditional approbations and interpretations.

The Harwood Manufacturing Corporation Study

One of the most widely quoted of the carefully controlled statistical studies is that of the Harwood Manufacturing Corporation.[8] The company

[7] Michael Argyle, *Occupational Psychology*, vol. 27, 1953.

[8] L. Coch and J. P. French, Jr., "Overcoming Resistance to Change," *Human Relations*, August, 1948.

manufactures clothing, chiefly pajamas, and at the time of the study, 1948, employed 500 women and 100 men.

When girls were transferred to new work because of, say, a change of style, their output dropped below the 60 units per hour standard for fully trained workers and tended to stay down, even after a reasonable readjustment period and even when the changes were quite small. Those who succeeded in regaining standard did so slowly, taking longer than a "green" worker. There was also a good deal of conflict with supervisors, time study men, and management generally.

To test the effects of allowing the girls to participate more in a needed change, the company developed a series of experiments when four groups of girls had to be transferred to new work. The work was all about equally difficult, and the changes were of about the same magnitude. One of the groups was used as a control, and for it the customary transfer procedure was used.

For the other groups, meetings were set up at which a manager discussed the need to cut costs. He showed two seemingly identical pairs of pajamas. One had been made the year before, and the other was made by the new method at half the cost. Animated discussion ensued. The workers agreed that cost reductions were possible and necessary and came forward with suggestions. Management then presented its plan for making a job study and training operators for the new job, and explained how the new rate would apply.

The control group showed all the typical symptoms found in previous transfers. Its output after transfer averaged only about 50, with close standardization of output around the average. In the first forty days of the experiment about 17 percent of the group left the company. The rest caused trouble with supervisors and time study men and brought in the union to dispute the new rate.

Results with the participating groups showed a remarkable contrast. Output not merely recovered, but climbed quickly to about 70. Interest and cooperation shown in the initial discussions carried over to the jobs. Workers referred to "our job" and "our rate." There were no difficulties with supervisors and no major grievances, and none of the workers left the firm. The investigators reported that intergroup competition quickly developed and sped the process of achieving higher output.

The Norwegian Shoe Factory

A group of Norwegian investigators[9] was impressed with the Harwood findings but felt they should be confirmed by a more detailed study which would be more closely controlled and would employ more refined methods of statistical analysis, in order to be sure that the results could be attributed to the variables under study and not to random or unknown causes. They chose for their study a shoe factory in southern Norway, with 1,600 employees. The department studied employed 400 men and women organized in almost identical work groups. Nine 4-employee groups took part in the experiment, because they were going to be assigned to work on a new product.

[9] John P. French, Jr., Joachim Israel, and Dagfinn Ås, "An Experiment in Participation in a Norwegian Factory," *Human Relations*, 1960, no. 1.

Four areas of decision making were used: (1) allocation of articles to be produced, (2) length of training, (3) division of labor, and (4) assignment of jobs. Two of the experimental groups were allowed "moderate participation," and the other three were allowed only "weak" participation—that is, they participated only in allocating the articles. The control groups were permitted *no* participation. Detailed production records for all groups were supplied by management.

Ten weeks after the training, extensive postexperimental questionnaires were answered by the group members. The variations in the production of the groups, and in the answers to the questionnaire, were subjected to extensive statistical-significance analysis to determine the statistical probability that the results could have been due to other factors than the ones under review.

As far as tangible results—actual production—were concerned, the experimental groups did *not* differ significantly from the control groups. All kept fairly close to standard. However, the two groups that had been permitted the greater amount of participation took a relatively shorter time to reach the standard level of production. One of these groups increased beyond the level but took fifteen weeks to do so. This experiment must therefore be disappointing to anyone seeking to make an open-and-shut case for participation in terms of increased productivity. With respect to attitudes toward management and job satisfaction in general, the authors concluded from the questionnaire analysis that they had adduced statistical support for their hypothesis (which might appear obvious) that the effects of participation hold only for subjects who experience only as much participation "as they consider right and proper" and that the effects of participation increase with decreasing resistance to the methods adopted by management to assure participation.

We have, of course, given only the bare bones of these Norwegian results, limiting ourselves to the tangible effects on production. The authors speculate on participation in general and on employee attitudes revealed by the questionnaires. They find moderate support for relating participation to feelings of satisfaction, and to labor-management relations. Despite the apparent inconclusiveness of this much more statistically refined version of the Harwood experiment, the authors surprisingly conclude that it seemed to yield consistent results, but that "the American experimental manipulation was more relevant to production and hence produced stronger forces affecting production."

University of Michigan Studies

Another widely quoted source of quantitative analytical data on human relations in industry is the University of Michigan Research Center. In recent years this group has conducted extensive research into the effect on productivity of several organizational variables, with emphasis on the type of supervision. Included are studies of 72 foremen in charge of maintenance gangs for the Baltimore and Ohio Railroad; 224 Prudential Insurance Company office supervisors; over 300 supervisors in the Caterpillar Tractor Company; and employees of The Detroit Edison Company. The general conclusion of the investigators is that "democratic" supervision, as against close or "autocratic" supervision, is related to higher output. Job satisfaction on the part of employees is also reported as generally greater under democratic leadership. In the Prudential study, an average difference of 10 percent in production was found between matched departments under different supervisors. The studies seemed to indicate that pressure for production on the part of the supervisors was completely unrelated to productivity, even to be inversely related to it. Surprisingly, when other data of the studies were analyzed, the evidence indicated that the foremen who spent more time on supervision had more productive sections, even though the same studies showed that close supervision was related to low output. It was concluded that to obtain high output a foreman had to tread a narrow path, spending a lot of time on supervision and yet not supervising too closely!

The Industrial Controls Corporation

Industrial Controls is the disguised name of a medium-sized company (1,000 employees) in which a group of investigators from the Harvard Business School made an exhaustive six-month study, in 1955, of a department with 45 industrial workers. The stages of this research, including selection of the company, collection of preliminary data, and processing and reporting upon the data, extended over more than two years.[10] The study was designed to test eighteen basic hypotheses about factors which were thought to determine the behavior of any work group and the individuals in it, viz., the effects on productivity and worker satisfaction of such factors as acceptance by the group, differences in social and educational background, degree of interaction required by the job, rewards by management, and differences in social and educational background of an individual as compared with the norms of the group. They also covered observations about informal leadership, factors determining acceptance by the group, tensions arising from confusion as to "status" within the group, and the like.

Statistically speaking, the results of this detailed study were decidedly mixed. In the words of the authors:

> A document of some 200 pages was prepared which recorded our hits, our near-misses, our gross errors, etc. . . . In some few cases we were right "on the nose"; in some more cases we were not "on the nose" but in "the right direction"; and then there were a substantial number of cases in which we were "way off." In some cases the actual behavior in terms of productivity and satisfaction was at a variance of 180 degrees from the behavior we had expected and predicted.

But the published study is valuable, nevertheless, in terms of the insights into motivation and behavior which are provided by the speculations and extended discussions of the authors in which they glean illuminating perspective out of varying and sometimes contradictory results.

[10] A. Zaleznik, C. R. Christensen, and F. J. Roethlisberger, *The Motivation, Productivity, and Satisfaction of Workers: A Prediction Study,* Harvard University, Graduate School of Business Administration, Division of Research, Boston, 1958.

Significance—On Balance

Looking back upon all that we have said in this article, what should the balanced appraisal be? The following remarks are offered as a guide to those in management who are confronted with practical problems of output and quality but who also have an awareness of the importance of the individual human being in every production group.

1. There is as yet no exact science of human relations. It is not possible to predict the specific results in terms of *worker output* to be obtained by extending the degree of participation by employees, improving their "job satisfaction," clarifying their attitudes toward management, and so on.

2. A manager will be well advised to take advantage of the swing toward greater stress on cost and immediate output as measures of executive effectiveness, and insist upon results from people without too many qualms about friction and harmony and the workers' liking for him as a person. But this does not mean that he should dismiss as of no consequence all the preoccupation with human relations that has become increasingly prevalent over the past few decades. Instead of looking for a "standard package" of formalized techniques, an executive should take the commonsense view that "treating people like people" results in a more responsive working force.

3. Putting real thought into overcoming resistance to change, into effective communication, into putting workers at their ease when instructing them or checking on them, into getting them to work as a team for the objectives of the company—all these are definitely part of good executive technique. At the same time, it will be well to beware of going overboard on some of the notions advanced about seeking employee views on every change, about allowing employees to allocate work or set their own pace, and the like.

4. The concept of "democratic" management is sound—within limits. Yes, if it means careful indoctrination of the worker by management and the supervisor on what is expected of him, careful teaching of methods, solicitation of suggestions, voice for the employee *to the extent feasible* in work allocation, and then a minimum of "breathing down the employee's neck." Yes, *if by his experience in his own department or division* the executive knows that his people are ready for it. No, if he has "green" help, if methods have undergone a significant change, if the quality record is poor, or if there has been a past record of poor management-employee relationships.

5. Contrary to much of the human relations literature, individual-incentive systems, *properly engineered* and installed in a way to achieve full employee understanding and cooperation, are still a powerful motivator. As recently as 1960, Arthur A. Rath, a pioneer in the field, had this to say:[11]

> Based on observation in hundreds of plants, large and small, in every type of industry, it is my conviction that nothing will stimulate an employee to perform at his top capacity as will individual incentives—a system of compensation which links his reward as directly as possible with his *own efforts.*

[11] Arthur A. Rath, "The Case for Individual Incentives: Management's Most Potent Motivational Tool," *Personnel Journal,* October, 1960.

> This position is based not only on 40 years of personal contact with problems of worker productivity, but also on parallel professional experience of others, the testimony of operating executives, and by confirming evidence of published surveys.

It goes without saying that the plan must be one that adheres to modern industrial engineering principles.

6. Employee participation should be encouraged *in matters which are within the employees' province.* They should be given ample explanation about changes, and their opinions and suggestions should be welcomed. Key employees will often have good ideas on how work can be done better, and, as is advocated by the practitioners of "work simplification," the supervisor can use these ideas in supplementing the work of the professional methods and systems people in the plant or office. Management should have a policy of paying well for any usable ideas. However, *management should not step away from its right and duty to manage.* With engineered performance standards in use, the opportunities for democratic direction are, if anything, enhanced. Since methods and expected output are established, the department head can leave conscientious employees to be their own taskmasters and concentrate on planning for and servicing the department.

7. There is no conflict between the concept of *participation,* as exemplified in successful group-incentive plans, and the drive of *individual competition,* as shown in the success of individual-incentive plans—as long as there is ingrained acceptance of the idea of individual responsibility for performance. To be successful, group plans require that employees be ready for them. Engineered group incentives can, with proper management philosophy, develop a feeling of solidarity, individuals helping one another.

8. Finally, even though there is no solid statistical evidence correlating job satisfaction with tangible output, management should not forget about satisfaction and concentrate solely on output. The conclusion to be drawn from research is that we should revise a fundamental notion about job satisfaction: It is not the *cause* of something (for example, increased production) but rather the *result* of something (the conditions under which the work is done). Hence, job satisfaction is an *output,* not an *input.* But it should always be a desired output, and for long-run operating efficiency it is intelligent to take the position that a balance may well be struck which sacrifices some productivity for job satisfaction.

WORK STUDY—THE COMPREHENSIVE MANAGEMENT SERVICE

Russell M. Currie, C.B.E.

Introduction

The techniques of work study as applied in Europe are used by the International Labor Office in newly developing countries as an aid to the more efficient use of the public service, the more rapid expansion of agricultural production, and the swifter developing of the manufacturing sectors of the economy. No novelty is claimed for many of the elements in these techniques; but it is asserted that the contribution of Europe, in which Great Britain has been the leader, has been in the direction of welding these techniques into a coordinated approach and incorporating within them a due regard for human factors. Hence, while it might be possible to say that work study is nothing new, it can be said that what *is* new is the intensity of the approach, which has produced abundant evidence of success in application.

A Top Management Job

Top management's use of work study has been a feature of the industrial practices of the past twenty-five years. Top management has frequently called for the development of efficiency techniques that could be applied to the personal situation of the top manager and especially to the large-scale problems with which he has to deal. Work study provides this coordinated approach; and long experience has shown that not only is the successful introduction of work study a top management responsibility, but that the techniques in their broadest sense have such a wide application that they are no longer something that can be conveniently forgotten from day to day once the

---

Mr. Currie is President of the European Work Study Federation. He was formerly Head of the Central Work Study Department, Imperial Chemical Industries, Ltd., London.

initial gesture of support has been made. This is why it is regrettable to see work study men fighting, as it were, with their backs to the wall, defending their right to conduct time studies, when what they should be doing is teaching higher management to apply formal critical examination to its own activities.

Of course a great deal depends upon the view we ourselves take of what work study means. If it means only "stopwatch thumping," therbligs,[1] and bonus schemes for repetitive work, then we cannot complain if management takes only a very limited view of our capabilities. Modern work study indeed consists of a whole galaxy of techniques capable of analyzing, critically examining, evaluating, and communicating improvements in any field, industrial or otherwise. It is in fact a top management tool and hence a top management responsibility.

The Object of Work Study

First of all let us define the object of industry as "to supply the goods and services needed by the community with the minimum consumption of real resources."

The goods and services constitute our standard of living, which we can improve only if we minimize the use of our real resources and reduce wastage of them. Embodied in this definition we see therefore the real meaning of the word "productivity." It is a ratio between what you take out in the way of goods and services and what you put in in the way of real resources. Higher productivity is getting the same or more goods and services from less resources. That is the problem which faces us—and when faced with a problem it is wise to apply a logical sequence of thought:

1. Define the basic problem.
2. Analyze, to determine relevant factors.
3. Collect information on relevant factors.
4. If necessary, supplement information collected by assumptions.
5. Find or reach toward a solution to the problem.
6. Check the dependence of the solution upon the assumptions to see whether the assumptions are of critical importance.

We have already defined the broad basic problem of productivity which affects us so vitally. Let us collect factual information on this problem, avoiding opinions or ideas sanctified only by antiquity. Let us make assumptions, if we have to. Let us reach toward this problem of productivity, and let us check by our results the dependence of the solution upon the assumptions we have made. To all intents and purposes the year of the birth of British work study was 1947. The war was over, and we decided to get the measure of our position. How did Britain's productivity stand in relation to that of other countries? What was the rate of change? What were the trends?

We started from the humbling realization that productivity in Britain was

[1] Therbligs—a name given by Frank B. Gilbreth to each of the specific divisions of movement, according to the purpose for which it is made. These therbligs cover movements or reasons for the absence of movement. To each therblig there is assigned a specific color, symbol, and letter for recording purposes.

increasing at only 1½% per annum. We decided that this was not going to be good enough, and that we should have to do more to earn our keep. We resolved at that point in time to go into a high gear to increase our productivity, and so we began to develop work study.

This same feeling of urgency is growing in newly developing countries at the present time. They too have a balance-of-payment problem. To remedy that position, commodity industries must increase sales at home as well as abroad. This can only be done by reductions in the cost of production. If the wheel can be turned in this direction and govern its own impetus, national wealth will increase and still further developments can then be financed.

Work study has the advantage of transcending all political divisions, whether local or national. It bridges the traditional tragic division between management and labor and unites the team. It is true that you may read from time to time in the press stories of labor unrest and strikes in Britain—it is unfortunate that the newspapers do not regard people working happily together as news. The truth is that in Britain today many of the suspicions of the past are dying. And here let me take the opportunity of stressing that the British trade union movement, to which many of my friends belong, is in the vast majority of cases cooperating with management on the matter of work study. But they do this only when they are satisfied that management is using modern work study and not the old-fashioned, outdated, and distorted concept of time and motion study. Progressive trade unionists, and there are more of them each year, rightly maintain that they have a vested interest in increasing national productivity, for it is their members who will share in the fruits of it.

European countries are not slow in taking up and developing the techniques which will enable them to continue their dramatic improvement. As President of the European Work Study Federation, I have presided at the three congresses so far held. They are a demonstration of the upsurge of the use of work study, and speaker after speaker gave evidence of the rapidly increasing contribution it is making to their productive efficiency in the major European countries.

Six Lines of Attack

What are the means of increasing productive efficiency? Here, revised in the light of experience, is the six-pronged attack that we made on the problem.

1. Improve basic processes by research and development.
2. Provide more and improved physical means of producing.
3. Simplify and improve the product, and reduce the variety.
4. Improve methods of operation.
5. Improve organization planning and control.
6. Improve manpower effectiveness at all levels.

Let us look at these one by one. We all know the vital necessity of research and development of all kinds to give industry a constant "blood transfusion" of new ideas. It is no use having the ideas in our heads or even in the heads of those who work in the laboratories and research departments; we have got to have them working for us, as the second and third lines of attack above suggest. Now let us look at the fourth line of attack—the simplest of all to write and the hardest to achieve. It was an American, I think, who said,

"If we use yesterday's methods in business today, we will be out of it tomorrow."

The fifth line of attack reminds us that we may be afflicted with inflation. Some of our economist friends believe that we must have 3 to 4% per annum inflation for a healthy economy. If we are not constantly trying to improve our organization, planning, and control, we shall get all of 4 to 5%—in increased cost, since the cost of manpower is going up at approximately double that rate, and this is an increase calling for increasing productive efficiency.

The sixth line of attack, of course, is aimed at the manager, and not just the man at the bench; when one considers how much good—and how much damage—an executive can do by his decisions, compared with what a payroll worker can do, it becomes obvious that the campaign for greater effectiveness must permeate all levels in an organization. In any case, all through our lives we need food for the mind as well as the body, and there is no doubt that keeping one's own methods of work under constant scrutiny is a shortcut to the full life!

There are people who will find these six lines of attack a blinding flash of the obvious; but only the conscious archangel will believe that he has always applied all these lines of attack as effectively as he could have done. But it is not a question of whether one has or has not applied these methods of increasing productive efficiency: it is a question of how intensely one has applied them.

Let us study the lines of attack again.

Lines of attack	Term	Results
1. Research and development 2. Physical means of producing	Long term—require capital	No limit to results
3. Standardization and simplification	Medium term—may require capital	Results subject to limits
4. Methods of operation 5. Planning and control 6. Manpower effectiveness	Short term—require little capital	

The six points are grouped into those which are long-term and those which are medium- or short-term. The long-term attacks are not limited in their possible results. The short-term attacks consist really of getting the best out of what we have. Whether one looks at it from an individual point of view, or from the point of view of a company, a single organization, or a whole nation, it is only by getting the best out of all our existing resources that we will generate the national wealth, or the individual wealth, and so have the capital to exploit to the full the long haul of the first and second lines of attack.

We ought to consider a little more closely what we mean by resources.

Our definition of the purpose of industry depended upon economy in manpower (both brain and brawn), materials, and capital equipment. After long and careful study of these resources back in 1947, we realized something that had not been fully understood before: *All these resources are essentially the result of manpower.* No matter how abundant a country's raw materials may be, they are of no use under the ground or out in the fields. They do not contribute to the comfort of man until the hand of man has worked them and brought them to a place where they can be used. We realized also that capital equipment in any form is merely the energy and wisdom of men in the past stored up for present and future use. Whichever of the basic resources we considered, we came back at length to manpower; and now came the real understanding of the dignity and depth of meaning of the word "work."

To return to the six lines of attack, who is to deploy these resources along these fronts? The responsibility falls of course on management in the broad sense of the word. Let me offer a definition of management, with the object of stimulating thought: "The organization and control of human activity directed to specific ends." If I may expand this simple definition—organization is the planning function, and control is the implementation of that plan; the words "human activity" are used as a further reminder that in the last analysis the only thing that matters is human work and the people who do it; the reference to "specific ends" implies that management must know where it is going in order to be able to do its job. And by management I mean not only the management of a factory—I am talking of the management of government, the management of trade unions, and the management of the fighting services and of the public services, as well as the management of industry. What I say about management is intended to refer to all those who are privileged to determine policies and to guide others in the implementation of them.

What Work Study Means

If management is going to "organize and control," management must have facts on which to judge: so now you see what is meant by "work study." One tires of hearing the polysyllabic names which experts often give to themselves and the things they hold sacred. But I never tire of using the following definition, which describes the concept and function of work study as we see it:

> Work study is the systematic, objective, and critical examination of all factors governing the operational efficiency of any specified activity in order to effect improvement.

Again this definition is worth examining word by word. The examination must be "systematic" in order to appeal to the intelligent brain; it must be unprejudiced and objective if we are reaching toward rough justice; it must be constructively critical; and it must cover *all* factors—we have made a number of fine failures in the earlier days through not realizing that the human factors were as important as the other ones. We must be quite clear what our specified activity is, and we must be genuinely seeking improvement, no matter how much the existing way of doing things may be challenged.

It should be difficult to reconcile this definition with the long-outdated concepts of time and motion study as something designed to make people work harder. Wherever work is done, work study as defined above can also be done.

However, the words "work study" are only a label. What matters is what is in the package. What is in the package concerns one man and his job. He may be a very important man, or we may be considering large numbers of men and their jobs together. Matters of scale must be taken for what they are, and it is nonsense to say that work study is something that only the big firm can afford. Some of the finest work study is being done by small firms of a few dozen people, with first-class management in the lead.

The following diagram defines simply the two main tools required and defines their purposes.

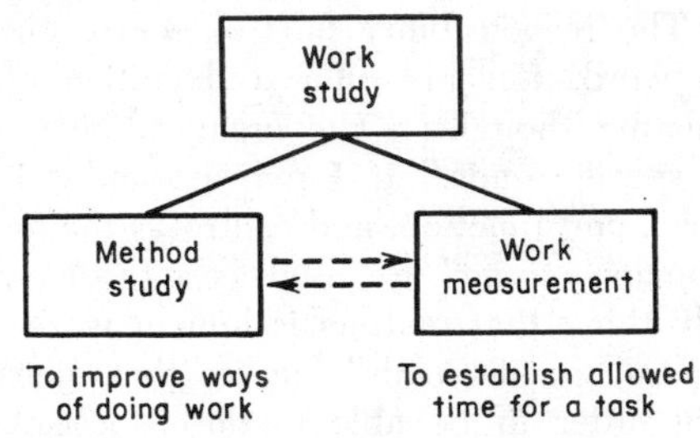

Each of these also represents a major group of tools for tackling widely different sizes and types of jobs—the broad surveying techniques for tackling major problems and using statistical and mathematical evaluation. It is also true that work study includes techniques for solving problems in very fine detail—if it is economically important to do so, or, for example, in aircraft design, where the safety of human life is concerned. But in general let us remember that it is a pity to waste time on small details when a broad approach is really needed. In one instance, a study was made involving five workmen; we studied everything, we got the seats the right height and painted the wall behind the right color, and everything was motion-studied so that all the tools and materials were within easy arm reach. Alas, in a very short time proper method study eliminated the job altogether!

Method Study

Let us examine method study more closely.

> Method study is a systematic and analytical approach to problems which will enable all the relevant factors to be evaluated so that decisions may be made.

Many people wonder when work study originated. I suggest that the honors really go to the first man—even if he wore the skins of wild animals and lived in a cave—who consciously thought about his work. We hear much of the great pioneers, and great tribute is due to Taylor, for example, for his contribution to time study. But there is ample evidence that time study was being carried on in the Old Derby China Works, in England, as long ago as 1792, by one Thomas Duesbry. This was sixty-four years before

Taylor was born. These arguments can be carried on indefinitely, and there is always fresh evidence on the antiquity of applied common sense, which is what work study really is. Last year, for example, a member of the Indian Government presented the author with a book on work study, entitled *The Art of Government,* done in India in 212 B.C.[2] The book includes records of a careful study on an elephant stable and on a harem . . . !

Here are the objectives of method study as we see them:

1. Improved buildings and workplace layout
2. Improved design of plant and equipment
3. Improved use of material, plant and equipment, and manpower
4. More efficient handling of material
5. Improved flow of production
6. Standardization of methods
7. Improved safety standards
8. Better working environment

We cast the net widely indeed, and try to apply method study at the very earliest stage of design. Hard experience has taught us that we must learn to erase our mistakes on the drawing board rather than with a concrete-breaker after they are built. That of course is why my company has such an apparently large work study staff—just over 2,000 men full-time. Even this number is not large enough to deal with the vast range of complex problems that exists. Up to now we have found no limit to the problems and certainly no limit to the capacity of method study to tackle them, within the confines of what is economic, of course. This versatility of method study is disciplined within the basic procedure:

Select	the work to be studied
Record	all the relevant facts
Examine	the facts critically in ordered sequence
Develop	the best method under prevailing circumstances
Install	that method as standard practice
Maintain	that standard practice by regular checks

This procedure provides us with a pattern of disciplined thinking and makes sure that we set out with clear terms of reference; that we set down the facts as they are—what is true, and not what is merely believed to be true; that we apply critical thinking to these facts and seek the best method, and so on. Consider in closer detail the "examine" stage of the procedure:

What is achieved?
How is it achieved?
When is it achieved? } *Why?*
Where is it achieved?
Who achieves it?

This questioning sequence is the means by which the facts that have been objectively and faithfully recorded are subjected to ruthless scrutiny. The procedure is based on Kipling's poem "Six Honest Serving Men," but unfortunately Kipling did not develop the best way of putting these serving men

[2] *Kautilya's Arthasastra,* English translation, Mysore Printing and Publishing House, Mysore, India.

to work. Here is the critical examination sheet which makes sure that no question is omitted and that all answers are properly recorded.

Description of Element	METHOD STUDY CRITICAL EXAMINATION SHEET	Reference .... Page Date ....

The present facts		Alternatives	Selection for development
What is achieved?	*Why?*	What *else* could be achieved?	What *should* be achieved?
How is it achieved?	*Why that way?*	How *else* could it be achieved?	How *should* it be achieved?
When is it achieved?	*Why then?*	When *else* could it be achieved?	When *should* it be achieved?
Where is it achieved?	*Why there?*	Where *else* could it be achieved?	Where *should* it be achieved?
Who achieves it?	*Why that person?*	Who *else* could achieve it?	Who *should* achieve it?

Unless this has been done, almost all the value of the ordered thinking will be lost. In essence this is the simple form which is saving many millions of pounds where method study is applied to questions at the highest level. There is nothing particularly new in method study itself: what is new is the intensity of the ordered thinking that can now be applied to the restless search for improvement that characterizes the use of all work study techniques.

The other main group of evaluation techniques is under the general heading of work measurement. I do not think people realize its power—especially now that it is linked with other great evaluation techniques, financial, mathematical, and technical. Remember also that since computers have "come down to earth," the range and speed of work measurement have been enhanced in the same way as has happened in other fields of activity.

> Work measurement is the application of techniques designed to establish the time for a qualified person to carry out a specified job at a defined level of performance.

In other words the fundamental task of work measurement is the evaluation of the work content of a job, remembering what we have said above about the importance and universality of human work. In their expanded form the objectives of work measurement are seen to be quite broad:

1. Basis of comparison of alternative methods
2. Correct initial staffing with manpower
3. Continuous economy of manpower
4. Effective planning of production and maintenance
5. Realistic labor costing
6. Basis for sound incentive schemes

In the definition we mentioned a specified job. Clearly the job must be done by a specified method, since if one changes the method, the time established and agreed will be unrealistic.

Work Measurement

During a method study one tries to arrive at the best method from the alternatives that we have examined and evaluated; and a very important technique in this evaluation is work measurement, which will give us the answer to how long the various methods will take. Correct staffing has been mentioned—and the significance of this is that if one gets the right staffing at the start, one avoids any subsequent difficulties with redundancy when it is discovered that there are too many men on the job. I have not yet met an engineer or a maintenance man who failed to insist that he was conducting planned maintenance. Those words can mean almost anything, of course; but there is a vast difference between modern preventive maintenance and a little black book containing a few antiquated pencil notes! Similarly, the words "incentive scheme" can mean almost anything; but if one is seeking a basis for sound schemes, and not bribery and corruption, one has in work measurement the foundation upon which management and labor can reach toward rough justice with reasonable confidence to all concerned.

To put the many and various techniques of work measurement into true perspective, the following diagram may be useful:

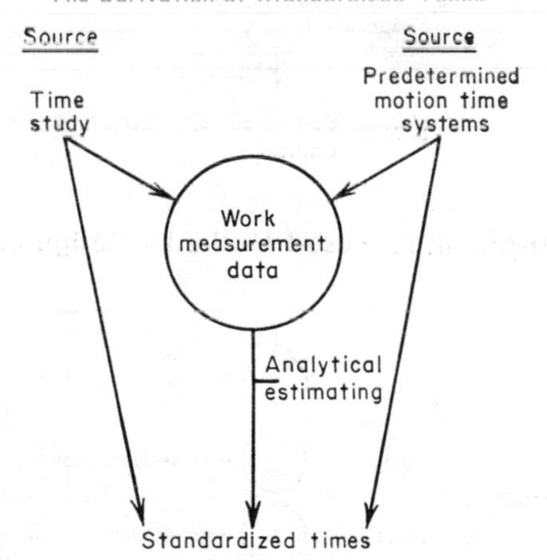

Time study appears in the diagram as a "source" technique; and in modern work measurement we no longer direct a time study of a job toward arriving at the work content of that particular job. All time study should be directed toward the production of carefully codified work measurement data, and providing the specifications are adequate, a library of values is compiled which can be used anywhere that it is applicable. It appears certain that this compilation of data will one day become an international proposition. This is especially true with the considerable development of what we in Britain call by the generic title of "predetermined motion time systems" (such as

MTM,[3] Work Factor, Basic Motion Times, etc.), and they have a vital contribution to the aim of compiling an exhaustive library of work measurement data. My own company is probably the biggest user of these systems anywhere, and we now know their limitations and their possibilities. We use data whenever we can, and when it is not yet available, or the conditions are not suitable for measurement, we make controlled use of the less accurate but still useful technique of analytical estimating, carried out, of course, by work study staff who have a thorough knowledge of the job they are concerned with.

Some Results

Having all too briefly explained the versatile and penetrating power of the techniques of modern work study, I shall now illustrate some of the ways in which the proper application of these techniques can economize money,

Critical Examination of Existing and Proposed Methods

Case Example I: Existing Method—Operation of Existing Plant

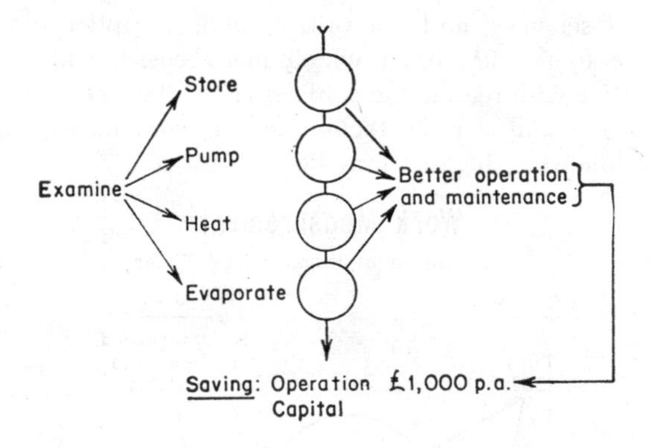

Case Example II: Proposed Method—Design of New Plant

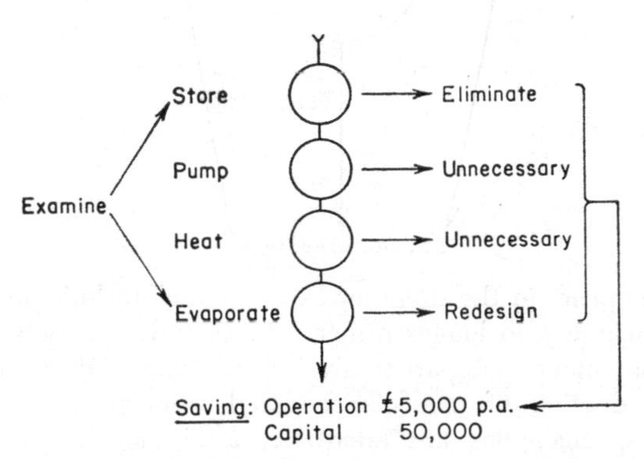

[3] MTM is Methods Time Measurement, an American system of predetermined motion times based on the work done by various firms and by the Society for the Advancement of Management in America. This is a proprietary system, as are also "Work Factor" and "Basic Motion Times."

time, effort, and materials. Here, for example, is a very small part of a major study of a modern chemical process plant. We have two such plants, and found that by better operation and better maintenance of this small part we saved costs of about $3,000 a year. Then we had to build a third plant. By then we had learned to apply work study in design. We looked first at the necessity for storage, which had always been accepted as necessary to effective operation. Through work study, we found we had no need to store; and if one does not need to store, one does not need to pump. Furthermore, one does not have to reheat—so all these processes were eliminated. After the evaporator had been redesigned to meet the new conditions, we found that we were saving $150,000 worth of capital costs, and in addition to that $15,000 a year in operation costs.

This approach does not apply only to process plants—it can be used with effect for any kind of construction. Here, for example, is a work study in design, for a sales warehouse in Jamaica (5,000 widely different items) which was redesigned in my department:

	Floor area, sq. ft.	Estimated capital cost, £
After detailed consideration based on past experience	46,000	92,000
After applying work study	36,000	72,000
Saving	10,000	20,000

Note: Time taken for study, 2½ man weeks. Final design also allowed for future expansion without layout alteration.

Here are some comparative details covering the use of work study in designing three different canteens and the reductions in capital costs that were effected:

Original design, cost in £	After work study	Percentage saving
23,000	13,000	43
9,400	6,000	28
158,000	120,000	24

Finally, in the category of building construction, here are some typical savings using work study on construction sites:

Operation		*Saving*
Erecting 17-ton columns	32%	erection costs
Fixing hardwood skirting	37%	labor costs
Handling masonry	47%	increased output
Laying floor slabs	50%	reduced laying time
Placing cement/sand screed	89%	increased output
Laying precast concrete	100%	increased productivity

To turn to a slightly different field, questions are often asked about engineering maintenance. "You can't apply work study to nonrepetitive engineering activities," I am often told, which of course is complete nonsense. In point of fact, maintenance is one of the most rewarding of all fields for work study. This is illustrated by the story of a medium-sized works with 300 employees. There was no capital expenditure during the six years covered by the study recorded in the following diagram. The recorded total output increase is entirely due to first-class works management, integrating properly applied work study into the management team. It can be seen that the total number of maintenance hours drops over the six-year period, but there was no redundancy. The intake of new staff was stopped, and so no hardship was caused by unemployment. Output per maintenance hour rose sharply to almost twice what it had been, and the saving on direct labor was about $80,000 a year, excluding the profitability from increased output.

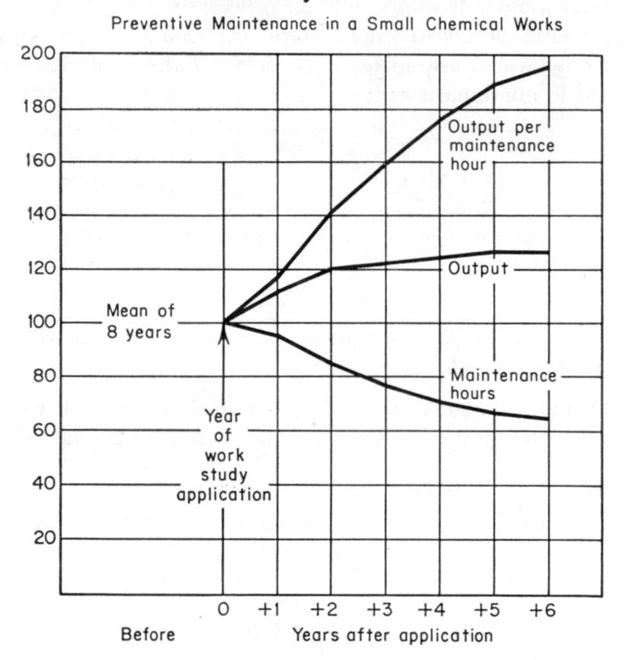

What about the effect of all this on supervision? Many of our foremen have told me that in the old days they had to contend with complaints from the management—now they have to contend with their men if the maintenance planning is not effective. The supervisor's job is changing. Work study, and the individual-incentive scheme based on work measurement, tend to make every man his own supervisor.

When considering where to start work study, obviously the best place tactically is in one's own office—there is no force so strong as the force of example. The next case history concerns our own mail room—such rooms being "sitting ducks" for work study every time. Here in tabulated form is the record:

Costs

Total cost of alterations:	£1,000
Investigators' salaries:	900

Savings
  Salaries (staff reduced from 7 to 4): £2,400 p.a.
  Faster collection and distribution of mail
Other Significant Savings
  30% of original floor space
  Airmail and inland postage cost
  Stationary
Savings Outside Mail Room
  Mail pouches replaced by envelopes throughout the company

While on the subject of typical gains and savings due to work study, I should like to pay tribute to a great organization which is at present engaged on a very aggressive work study program—British Railways. They now have six work study schools, and are increasing their work study as rapidly as they can. Already 1,400 men are fully employed, applying work study over practically the whole range of railway activity. Here is only one of thousands of examples of their achievements, news of which is coming in daily:

Locomotive Servicing Depot

Locos previously serviced	36
Locos now serviced by same men	52
Extra loco availability due to reduced time in servicing	5
Savings per year:	
Labor	£ 90,000
Capital	25,000
Total	£115,000
Cost of investigation	£ 2,000

A Coordinated Approach

Let me draw together the many threads that have run through this discourse and give you a broad picture of what the basic discipline called work study has come to mean today.

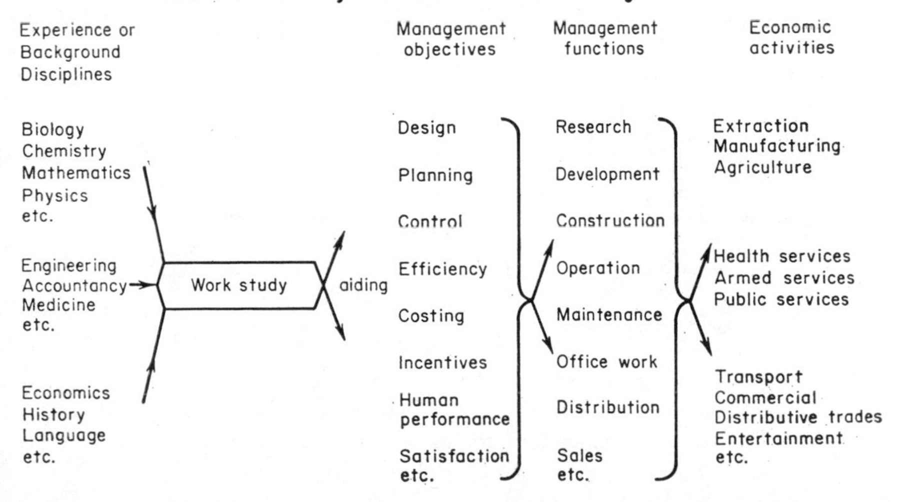

This diagram shows how work study helps in putting together the specific contributions of various sciences, technologies, and arts that can be brought to bear and coordinated through the techniques. Following through from the left-hand side one sees how those who have undergone their theoretical training and those who, denied graduate training, have learned from their experience at least the need to think logically, are ready for training in work study. This basic discipline of intensive analysis and evaluation helps them to arrive at a proper approach to the problems that occur wherever work is done. It is not suggested, by the way, that they work as lone troubleshooters. Sometimes they will work on their own, and sometimes in teams, say, of two or three people; and always of course they work as fully collaborating members of the larger management team. The remainder of the diagram demonstrates that in whatever field of economic activity management shares common objectives and discharges common functions, work study is now being applied. I hope to have demonstrated, by the small selection of case examples I have quoted, that work study can contribute to management in all these fields, whether the organization concerned is large or small.

This last point is rather important. There is fundamentally no difference in the approach whether the study covers a whole industry or what might be termed "the waggle of a finger."

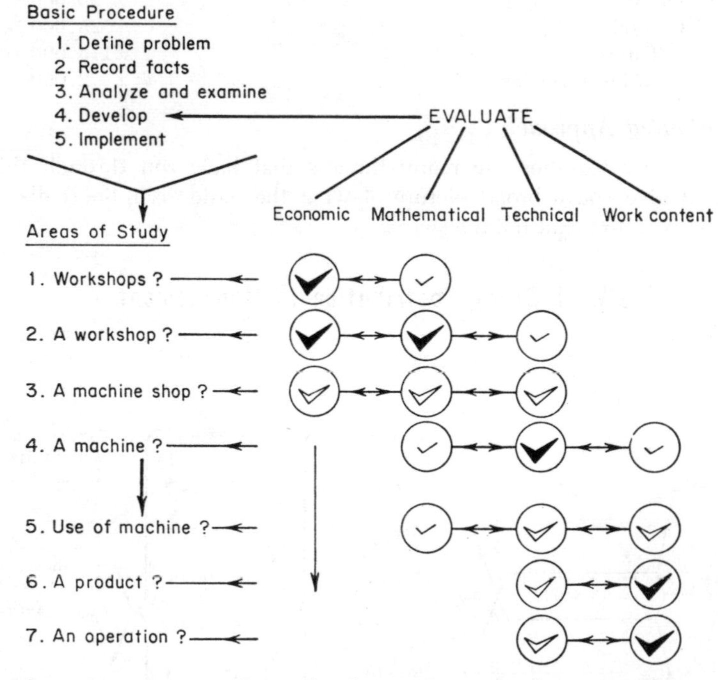

The first step is to analyze the facts, the second is critical examination of the facts, the third step is the development of improvements, and finally there are the endless human and technical problems of implementation. All through these successive stages alternatives will be thrown up; some of them look possible, some of them impossible, but we must not be deceived by their looks—all must be evaluated fully. Here is an example, to be followed through on the diagram above. Let us take as an instance a railway repair function, something that might be called "workshops." The basic question that might be asked here is: "Why not let the repairs out to contract?" In the instance I am quoting the economic light showed green so they moved on to the second-order study: the critical examination of a single workshop. Here the question might be: "Where shall we put it?" If the green light shines at the end of the second study, we move on to the third stage—a machine shop. There are many questions here: What capacity, what layout, what type of machine tools, covering what type of work? So we descend to the fourth-order study of a machine tool itself: What capacity of tool, what degree of flexibility, a general-purpose tool or a specially designed tool, and so on. Thence we move to the fifth-order study—the job itself; and of course we can go on from there to an individual operation within the job or to an element within that operation. All through these studies we require constant evaluation. The most important kind of evaluation is, of course, financial. We want to know what it is going to cost, and what the profitability will be over the life of the whole project on the particular job. Then we have the increasing use of mathematical evaluation, particularly with the dramatically rapid development of computer science.

The next type of evaluation might be called technical, and there is no need to stress its importance. But due emphasis should be placed upon the importance of the new kind of evaluation by work measurement of the work content of jobs, be they large or small. Measurement techniques are available that can be used to the economic limit justified in the particular job on hand.

A first-order study might be done only once. In fact, one might try to deduce a general rule that, as the scale of the study diminishes, so the number of studies is likely to be larger. To produce the line to its furthest point, one might say that in studying single jobs the studies would almost be continuous. It ought to be clear that all the evaluation techniques apply at all stages of study and that at no stage can work measurement—the evaluation of human effort—be left out.

Nonfinancial Dividends

Furthermore, material gains are not the only benefits to be derived from work study. According to one medium-sized firm, the by-products of work study are that it:

1. Acts as a catalyst to straight thinking
2. Creates and maintains a restless urge to improve
3. Improves trade union relationships
4. Reveals organizational flaws
5. Attracts better workers
6. Tends to reduce labor turnover
7. Provides a valuable training ground for higher responsibility.

How can work study possibly improve relationships with trade unions? The same firm comes up with the answer. It is because individuals matter more;

frustrations caused by waiting for jobs or materials are diminished; work measurement eliminates injustices caused by guesswork; and the level of earnings is at least maintained, with less overtime, and consequently more leisure. Here is a practical demonstration of the fact that industry is of men, not machines.

But there is a sting in the tail of this medium-sized company's experience. In introducing work study, lip service is not enough: management itself must manage better. Success in work study, according to this experience, demands the following:

1. Support and drive from top management by word and deed
2. First rate work study staff with thorough training
3. Sound appreciation of all levels of work study aims and activities
4. Close integration with other functions of management
5. Willingness to accept change
6. Realization that "it doesn't pay to do work study on the cheap"

How to Start

As previously mentioned, it will be wise to discuss top management's role in starting work study in a concern. It is most important that attention should be given to every facet of this activity. The decision to install work study is an admission by top management that there is room for improvement at all levels. It is top management's gesture that resistance to change is a thing of the past at their level and primarily, therefore, a sign of management's good intentions. But by himself the work study officer can do little. His main task is to show clearly to the manager what are the problems that deserve his attention; only the manager can find time to integrate problem solutions into the human team. When this is not understood, the manager merely finds one more cause for depression. To all his existing troubles he adds another: a work study program that gets him nowhere.

Work study, then, is a management exercise demanding wholehearted effort. It is no good thinking that it can be tried out as a casual experiment without proper preparation and organization. If someone untrained and inexperienced tries to use the techniques "to see what happens," then inevitably the result will be disappointment and failure. Work study techniques, though they appear simple in themselves, have far-reaching effects and can eventually achieve dramatic savings; but in the hands of the wrong person they can cause a great deal of harm, particularly in labor relations.

First it must be accepted that work study cannot be done "on the cheap" and that its adoption must have the full drive of senior management behind it. Lip service is not enough. Management should be quite sure that they understand the need for work study, and have a clear idea of the service it can provide within the management framework. They should not expect sudden miracles but be prepared to back the work study team in its efforts.

As an example let us assume that work study is to be introduced into a medium-sized, well-established manufacturing concern. (The procedure would be broadly the same in any organization.)

The first step is to appoint someone in full-time charge. Where possible, the position should be filled by promoting a suitable person from the existing staff and having him properly trained. If no suitable candidate can be found within the organization, the position should be filled by recruiting with the utmost care a trained person from outside. It cannot be too strongly emphasized that the successful introduction and application of work study depends in the last analysis upon the caliber of the man appointed.

The task requires enthusiasm, persistence, and those qualities of leadership which command respect and trust both from management and men. A person of character and ability is essential; an inquiring mind is needed, allied with plenty of common sense. If technical problems will be involved, then adequate technical training is a definite advantage.

While training and knowledge are essential, experience has shown that the problems involved in applying work study are mostly psychological, and therefore the nontechnical qualities which should be looked for in an ideal work study officer are of fundamental importance. These could be summarized as:

1. Power of logical thought
2. Imagination
3. Determination
4. Tact
5. Integrity
6. Personal acceptability
7. Power to inspire confidence

One cannot expect any man to possess such a list of qualities in equal measure, but nevertheless thought should be given to them and the candidate assessed against the ideal with a view to making sure that he has at least some degree of each attribute. Although a man might fulfill the requirements in every other respect, if he is tactless, for instance, he will not succeed as a work study officer.

As status is important, the work study officer should be made directly responsible to the factory manager or to a higher executive. At the same time, it should be made quite clear from the outset that his job is advisory (a staff function), and that he is there to provide a service to line management in the discharge of its functions and must on no account usurp that authority.

The number of personnel who should be employed on work study in any organization will depend on many factors. Besides the size of the organization, there will be the type of work involved. For instance, where a large number of people are doing exactly the same job, then the proportion of work study staff will be small. At the other extreme, when work study is being applied to nonrepetitive work, such as engineering maintenance, the proportionate number will be much greater. In all cases, however, the economic return will far outweigh the cost of such staff.

Another factor in determining the size of the work study staff will be the extent to which it is economically justifiable to apply work study. In some small concerns one individual will be quite able to carry out all necessary investigations and make whatever studies are required. In such cases it frequently happens that he accepts responsibility for routine planning as well as carrying out the investigations and implementing them, working closely with line management.

The following is a suggested organization chart for a medium-sized firm, showing where the work study officers (W.S.O.) of various categories should fit in.

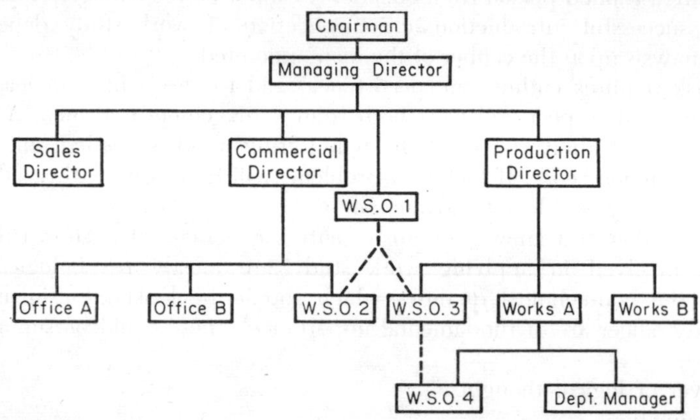

In all countries it is the more progressive industries and managements that are adopting work study. It is also true that, the more progressive the company, the more insistence there is on the work study staff being properly trained. This can be done only by attending a first-class, well-established training course, which should last for a minimum of three months full time. Even after this the work study officer will need practical experience under guidance.

It has been proved that simply putting a raw recruit into a work study department without formal training is a most misguided policy and, indeed, is economically unsound. After the work study officer is trained, he must be provided with opportunities to keep himself up to date by attending refresher courses where available, taking part in conferences, and maintaining contacts with other companies on work study techniques.

Management must also keep up to date, with sufficient knowledge for executive control, and give constant encouragement to the work study staff. No work study officer should be regarded as infallible or treated as if he were. The application of work study is a team responsibility.

As mentioned previously, the number of work study staff required by an organization will vary widely, and it is wise, particularly in the initial stages, to concentrate on the quality of the staff rather than the quantity.

The quantity can always be expanded as savings start to accumulate. It should, however, be remembered that some part of the work study staff must always be engaged on the maintenance of existing work study applications. The remainder will, of course, be available to break fresh ground, but this in turn will need maintenance. Managements have to be prepared, therefore, to adapt work study organizations to meet this continuing progress.

Many firms have found it beneficial to employ a consultant to help introduce work study in the early stages. This policy can have tremendous value in giving confidence to a new work study staff and in building up for all employees a knowledge of the true purpose of the activity. A reputable consultant can advise on the selection of the permanent staff and indeed sometimes arrange for their training.

The choice of the consulting firm is of very great importance, for only the most reputable are good enough. It is far better to pay 10% more and get 100% better results. In all countries today there are far too many small concerns promising splendid results which, all too late, they prove unable to produce. There should be no danger of disappointment from a well-established firm, who will have a reservoir of experience to draw upon.

To gain a complete understanding of work study one must start from the top and work downward. It is a discipline of very great power, instilling in everyone's mind at all levels a restless urge to improve. The managing director must be prepared, in spite of all his multifarious duties, to spend whatever time is necessary to ensure that his senior staff appreciate the importance of work study. He will thus ensure their support in its application throughout the company. He should also make it clear that, whatever the results, there will be no recriminations for anyone. This is particularly true in the initial stages. Success or failure can depend almost entirely upon the care and thoroughness with which this is done.

If possible all management should attend some form of appreciation course—say, three days for the most senior and up to two or three weeks for middle management. Supervisors should be included, so that they too have a clear understanding of the subject. Interest can be stimulated by visits to other companies who have already made use of work study and applied it properly, extensively, and successfully. Free and open discussion must be encouraged at all levels. There is nothing to hide in the application of the techniques.

It is a wise policy to time the appreciation courses to coincide with the completion of the work study officer's training course. He will then be equipped to run the courses if they are done internally with, perhaps, some outside assistance. All who attend the courses must clearly understand the answers to the first questions about work study:

What is it?
How does it work?
What benefits does it bring?
Whom does it affect?

For the purposes of work study appreciation courses, managements can be conveniently divided into three groups: (1) directors and other senior executives, (2) executives at the middle level, and (3) junior executives. Administration, sales, and research should all be included, as they must be made aware of the role of work study in increasing productivity and thus be prepared to cooperate in its application.

The most highly organized industries tend to have the highest degree of trade unionism among their employees, and since trade unions exist to concern themselves with the hours and conditions, including financial conditions, governing the work of their members, it is natural that they should pay particular attention to any changes in those hours and conditions that are proposed by managements. That is why many firms go to great trouble to make sure that, at the outset of the application of work study, the trade unions are brought into the picture at the earliest possible moment. By "earliest possible moment" is meant at the first intention to apply work study.

In such consultations there must be no hesitation in discussing honestly all the problems involved, and the ways of overcoming them. Since the basic principle of work study is to find and state the facts, the same attitude must inspire discussion with the trade unions, otherwise there can be no real understanding or the building of permanent confidence. This is a stage which cannot be left out, or even shortened, and hence adequate time must be found for it.

Just as management has its problems in gaining understanding and confidence in the true purpose of its intentions in applying work study, so the progressive trade unions have similar problems. Many organizations now find it most rewarding to include the senior trade union officials in their training programs. In the United Kingdom the trade unions are now running their own work study courses. They realize that work study can provide opportunities for higher earnings by strengthening the economy of the company concerned.

Conclusion

This book is being produced primarily, I believe, for those in newly developing countries who wish to see their lands prosper and contribute to the wealth and well-being of the world. With this in mind, I should like to conclude with a simple quotation from *Gulliver's Travels.* When Gulliver visits the King of Brobdingnag, the King expresses his astonishment at the destruction which his fellow kings wreak upon one another's countries. "And he gave it for his opinion that whoever could make two ears of corn or two blades of grass to grow upon a spot of ground where only one grew before, would deserve better of mankind, and do more essential service to his country than the whole race of politicians put together." This, of course, is the purpose of good government; it is the purpose of good management as a supporter of good government; and it is the purpose of work study, as the comprehensive service to good management.

DIVISION OF LABOR

Joseph W. Towle, Ph.D.

The "division of labor" is both a characteristic of organization and a basic function of management. Nevertheless, it is frequently taken for granted and neglected in modern theories of organization. While the economic fact of the division of labor was enunciated almost two centuries ago by Adam Smith in his *Inquiry into the Nature and Causes of the Wealth of Nations,* the significance of this fundamental concept seldom receives adequate attention in current discussions of management, administration, and organization.

Smith's analysis emphasized the opportunities in organized work for the specialization of personnel through the logical division of labor. He reported three basic reasons for the increase in efficiency and productivity of workers when this principle is applied: "First, to the increase of dexterity in every particular workman; secondly, to the saving of the time which is commonly lost in passing from one species of work to another; and lastly, to the invention of a great number of machines which facilitate and abridge labour, and enable one man to do the work of many" (Adam Smith, *An Inquiry into the Nature and Causes of the Wealth of Nations,* Thomas Dodson, Philadelphia, 1796, p. 18). Observers of our mass-production and mass-marketing economy recognize the efficacy of Smith's conclusions. In the modern industrial organization, workers concentrate on specialized tasks, improve their skills in performing these tasks, and use the best available tools and machinery.

In traditional organization theory the division of labor has been described as an economic or management principle. In some circles, however, the concept and the use of principles have fallen into disrepute. For example, the

---

Dr. Towle is Professor of Management at Washington University, Graduate School of Business Administration, St. Louis, Missouri.

authors of one textbook on administration and organization make this statement:[1]

> We consider a principle synonymous with a law; and both should embody a high degree of regularity. This consistency should provide reasonable predictability, as with the law of gravity or the principles of thermodynamics. We have generally refrained from talking about principles in this book because we have not been able to identify such regularities in organization practice.

It is suggested here that the division of labor can be identified with regularity in organization planning and practice and might well be considered to be a basic principle. Such a principle is not a dogmatic or legalistic control over managerial action. Rather, it is a guiding truth which can be useful in the planning of work when certain specific conditions exist. The regularity of the principle of the division of labor is a fact because it operates whenever two or more people join together to perform related tasks and to achieve specifically determined goals.

Fundamental to Organizational Planning

Empirical studies of organizations reveal that the division of labor as a management process is carried on continuously as enterprises are established, developed, and expanded. In viewing either an embryonic or a mature organization, some logical basis or criterion is employed for the division of the work and the assignment of tasks to individuals. Either by careful planning or by casual delegation of activities, the manager of an enterprise multiplies his own abilities by dividing his responsibilities and assigning duties to others. One definition of organization implies this process when it says, "Organization is the form of every human association for the attainment of a common purpose."[2] In this concept of organization, "the form of human associations" describes the structural relationships which exist between the functions or jobs in an enterprise. This structure is based on an assumption that the total amount of work to be accomplished has been divided and is assumed by various members of the work group. The entire organizing process is a threefold task, namely, the division of work, the combination of duties and units of activities, and the coordination of individual tasks or groups of workers performing tasks. Both from a practical and from a theoretical point of view, it is important to understand *how the work is divided* and *who is responsible* for this phase of the organizing function.

The organizational structure of an enterprise, which is frequently depicted by an organization chart, is a part of the formal plan of operations developed by the management of the enterprise. Although some managers fail to crystallize this part of their plans and avoid the development of an organization chart, the relationships existing between the individuals performing the functions or activities in the organization actually constitute this structural plan. In fact, many managers have such a plan of organization and simply do not recognize it.

[1] John M. Pfiffner and Frank P. Sherwood, *Administrative Organization*, Prentice-Hall, Inc., Englewood Cliffs, N.J., 1960, p. 59.

[2] James D. Mooney, *Principles of Organization*, Harper & Row, Publishers, Incorporated, New York, 1947, p. 1.

Formal and intentional organizational planning may be done by an individual or by a group of individuals. It is usually recognized that the formal plan established by the management of an enterprise may be altered greatly by the behavior, the personalities, and the sentiments of the incumbents in the positions in the organization. Nevertheless, the formal planning of activities usually results in a more efficient achievement of the objectives, even though the informal and personal relationships deviate somewhat from the planned organizational structure.

Two classes of organizational planning may be recognized. The *primary planning* for an organization in which the overall structure of functional or job relationships is established is most likely to be performed by a high-level executive council or a management committee. On the other hand, *secondary planning*, the more frequent, day-to-day division of work and the planning of assignments for individuals, is more often done by a single executive or supervisor of work groups. Especially in "job shops" or "intermittent production activities" is the supervisor required to analyze each new job, divide it equitably, and distribute it to available workmen. In business activities where production or operations are continuous, the supervisor is expected to divide and assign work to individuals less frequently. Obviously, the primary organizational planning for an enterprise in which the major functions, departments, and divisions are established is a responsibility of top management and requires frequent reappraisal and action.

Limited Participation in Decisions

Some of the newer theories of organization and management urge the extension of "participative management" to all areas of the enterprise. One authority states:[3] "All component parts of any system of management must be consistent with each of the other parts and reflect the system's basic philosophy. In an authoritative form of organization, decisions are made at the top; in a participative form, they are made widely throughout the organization." Certainly, the use of consultative supervision is advisable in the solution of most management problems, but the division of work and the delegation of assignments are management functions which are shared with difficulty.

In most instances it would be time-consuming and inefficient for the manager to apply the "participative principle" in all stages of the planning activity. Conflicts between members of groups and dissatisfactions develop when managers attempt to be completely democratic in the distribution of work loads. There are times when strong, fair leadership is more effective than participation. Thus, it is suggested that the division of labor and the assignment of work loads may be done successfully in an authoritarian manner by the manager. His ability to be fair and his use of democratic leadership techniques in other supervisory situations make it possible for him to make authoritarian decisions regarding work assignments which are acceptable to his subordinates.

This division of labor and assignment of work in an industrial concern are done with ease by the experienced manager. The establishment of new jobs

[3] Rensis Likert, *New Patterns of Management*, McGraw-Hill Book Company, New York, 1961, p. 222.

in the organization may be done hastily as a matter of expediency as work is acquired, or it may be a carefully planned and directed activity. In building a new organization or in assigning new work in the operating concern, advance planning of job requirements contributes to efficiency. This concern for the proper allocation of duties leads the manager to the development of a logical process in the division of work.

The Division-of-Labor Process

In original organizational planning, as well as in the day-to-day direction of operations, work must be divided and delegated. A principle frequently called *functionalization* is operating when work is divided and duties and activities are clearly identified prior to their assignment to workers. As activities are grouped together because of their similarity or their relationship in the flow of operations, organizational functions are established. This grouping of activities into functions and the relating of the various functions to each other lead to the establishment of the overall structure of the enterprise. The preliminary division of work usually requires the following steps:

1. *The clarification and analysis of organizational objectives.* An awareness of the goals to be achieved is essential to efficient organizational planning.

2. *The determination of the total work load necessary to achieve objectives.* An overall view is taken of all tasks required to achieve the purposes of the enterprise.

3. *The division of the work load and the identification of duties, activities, and functions in the enterprise.* The separation of duties and activities in the enterprise is accomplished on the basis of (*a*) the skills required of workers performing the tasks, (*b*) the types of work performed, (*c*) the machinery or equipment used to perform the work, (*d*) the nature of the materials used in the work processes, (*e*) the locations or place at which the work is performed, (*f*) the time at which the work is performed, such as on the day shift or night shift, and (*g*) the sequence of required activities in the operations. The same criteria used for this division of work may be used for the combination of tasks or the grouping of activities into departments or divisions within the organization.

4. *Job analysis and job description.* Completion and reappraisal of the division of labor occurs with the analysis, description, and clarification of tasks. The job description is fundamental to job evaluation (wage and salary administration), personnel training, and other organization work.

5. *The assignment of tasks to individual workers.* This delegation of work to subordinates is the ultimate goal of the division of labor. In most enterprises, reappraisals and changes in original divisions of labor are necessary to maintain balanced work loads and efficient operations.

Too frequently managers assume that original divisions of labor are permanent and changes in work loads are unnecessary. This false assumption and the inability of managers to perceive the changes taking place in their organizations result in inequities and inequalities in work assignments. For the avoidance of uneven work loads and for the maintenance of balance in operations there is a constant need for managers to reappraise the divisions of labor in their areas of responsibility and to take corrective action when necessary.

Patterns of Organization in the Barytes Mining Industry

Management principles may be employed as specific tools in problem solving or as general guides to management action. A concept like the division of labor is used almost instinctively by the experienced manager as he plans and organizes work. For some, this separation of duties and functions is easy and natural; for others, it is more difficult and requires concentrated attention.

In the application of this principle, there are three patterns of the division of labor which should be noted. First, there is the natural tendency in an industry for workers and groups of workers to compete and share in the work opportunities which are available (no single individual plans this distribution of jobs). Second, there is the planning of work at the lowest level of labor and skill, with either the workmen themselves or their immediate supervisors planning the division of work. And third, there is the planning of work by the management of an organization, in which the functionalization of activities starts at the top, the highest level of work, and major divisions of the organization are established before work-level tasks are analyzed, divided, and assigned to workers. It is possible, of course, that the second and third patterns are operating simultaneously within an enterprise, with organization planning being carried on at both top management and operating work levels at the same time.

All three of these patterns for the division of labor may be found in the history of the barytes mining industry in Washington County, Missouri. This ore is barium sulfate, known locally as "tiff," and found in pockets or veins near the surface of the ground. It is a white, stonelike substance, sometimes containing iron or other impurities, and when ground into a white powder it is used in a variety of products. The largest market in the period following World War II has been the demand for its conversion into a drilling mud used in the drilling of oil wells.

As late as the 1930s, the mining of this ore in Missouri was carried on by hand miners, using ordinary picks and shovels. Although the early miners found large quantities of the ore near the surface of the ground, it later became a common practice for miners to sink shafts from ten to forty feet deep. In these mining fields a "tiff-digger" was an individual entrepreneur, working on his own time and using his own methods. Any laborer with a few basic tools needed only to obtain permission of a landowner (who received a royalty for the ore produced) to become a miner or tiff-digger.

In the hand mining process, the tiff-digger usually found it necessary to sink a circular hole four or five feet wide into the ground to locate a deposit or vein of ore. After this hole was several feet deep, he frequently dug a "tunnel" following the vein of ore, which he extracted and brought to the surface. The division of work for the miner usually became a necessity when the mining shaft was more than six feet deep. He needed and obtained a partner or an assistant—sometimes his son, or even his wife, who assisted him with his tiff-digging. As the mining shafts became deeper, it was more efficient for the work to be divided by having the assistant or one worker stationed on the surface of the ground hauling the excess dirt, as well as the ore, to the top of the shaft with the use of a windlass. This division of labor introduced mechanical equipment, the windlass, which permitted the lowering of a large bucket on the end of the windlass rope. The miner in the shaft would deposit the ore or the excess dirt into the bucket, then it would be pulled to the surface with the windlass and deposited on the ground nearby.

Another application of the division of labor occurred in this mining operation when the tiff-digger and the windlass operator found it more efficient to have another assistant, or a third partner, who would clean and stockpile the ore after it was brought to the surface. Further mechanization of this simple mining operation took place when the individual responsible for the cleaning and preparation of the ore for sale developed the "rattle-box." This ingenious piece of equipment was a large wooden box on rockers, or "half-wheels," with holes in the bottom. After thorough drying, large chunks or pieces of the ore were placed in the box, which was pushed back and forth on its rockers until the dirt and impurities were rubbed off and fell through the holes onto the ground. Although there was some waste in this process because the ore is rather soft, it did give the tiff a clean appearance.

A division of work in the entire industry developed naturally. The transportation of the ore from the mining field to a railroad shipping point, as well as the purchasing of the ore from the miner and its subsequent shipment to the ultimate market, developed in the industry as independent occupations for individual entrepreneurs. Throughout this mining area the function of "tiff-hauling" developed early as a separate occupation. For this activity a worker needed a team of horses and a wagon or truck, when they were available. Usually a load of between one and five tons of ore was hauled to market at one time. This division of labor in the industry permitted an enterprising worker to own his own equipment, to negotiate individually with miners in the field, and to haul the ore to the local market near railroad transportation facilities. For this service he received a payment by the ton. In most cases this tiff-hauler did his own work in loading and unloading his wagon, or truck, and stacking the ore after its sale to the local purchasing agent. In rare instances these tiff-haulers divided their activities and had assistants who helped them with the loading and unloading of the ore.

A third, and more influential, independent businessman in this industry was the barytes merchant or buyer, who purchased the ore from the miner and stored it until the proper time to ship it in carload lots to ultimate consumers. These barytes merchants frequently owned the land on which the ore was mined and received a royalty payment for each ton of ore mined on their holdings. The functions of the barytes merchant included all buying, warehousing, and shipping activities. In Figure 1, the division of labor in the early barytes mining industry in Missouri is depicted. While the activities of the miners, haulers, and merchants were specifically planned and divided into jobs by the individuals themselves, the natural division of work in the industry permitted independent operators to enter these occupations and work under their own supervision.

The mining of barytes ore by hand was eventually replaced with more completely mechanized procedures. The entrepreneur who desired to establish a modern tiff mining operation needed capital to invest in a tiff mill with a gasoline- or diesel-powered shovel, heavy trucks for hauling equipment, a water supply for a sluice, a jig-type operation for the separation of dirt and stone from the ore, and miscellaneous other equipment. The planning of work activities, including the division of labor in this enterprise, was made with little reference to the techniques and activities of the old-fashioned tiff digger.

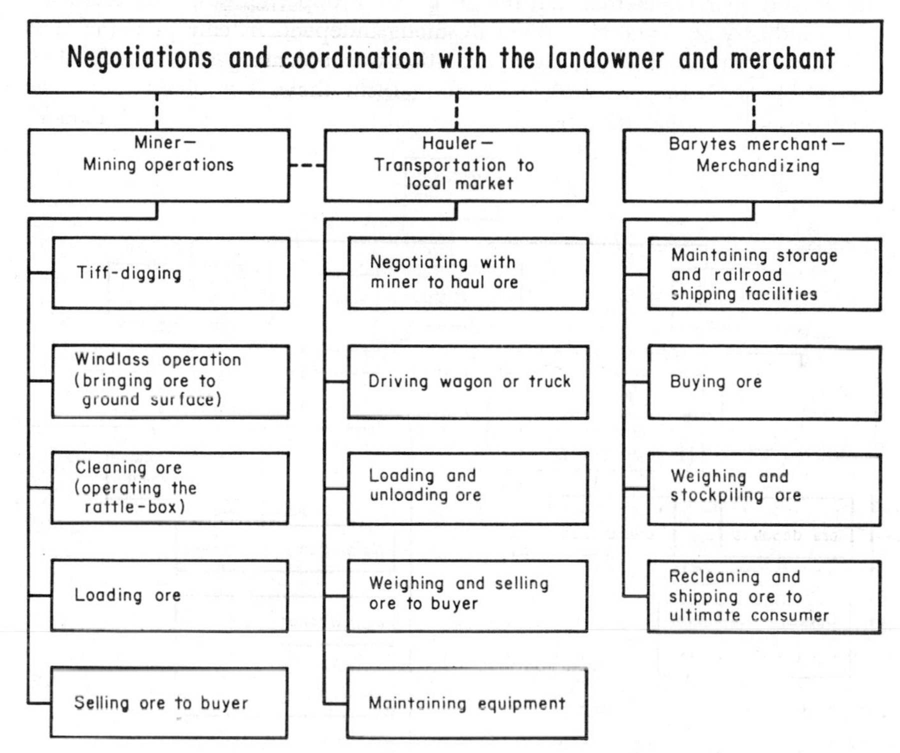

FIG. 1. Division of labor in the barytes mining industry in the late nineteenth and early twentieth centuries.

Figure 2 shows the functional organization of the modern barytes mining operation, which is now locally known as a tiff-washer. In the efficient operation of such a mill a diesel-powered shovel digs the earth in large quantities and loads it onto heavy-duty, off-road, diesel-powered hauling equipment which trucks the earth to the mill. The length of this haul varies, but is seldom more than a mile or two.

At the tiff mill the hauling equipment dumps the earth into a large washer in which a log-washer (perhaps a steel tube) with large blades rotates over a moving platform or conveyor. Water pours over the deposit and puts the clay in solution, which overflows as the tiff and rock pass over the platform. The material passes through a screen where it is sized at $3/4$ or $7/8$ inch into a large jig, where a gravity separation occurs. This mill operation permits, through this washing and grinding process, the separation of the barytes ore from the rock or gravel. These materials are stored in tanks or in piles for sale or disposal. The ore coming from the tiff-washer is ground into rather fine particles. This product is therefore different and more easily purified than the ore procured in large chunks.

This brief analysis of mining operations in the barytes industry illustrates the application of the division-of-labor principle in the development of an industry and in organization of the enterprise. The three patterns of organization are recognized here. In the early practice in the barytes mining fields, miners and merchants took advantage of their opportunities, and the work in the industry was naturally divided among independent entrepreneurs. The second pattern for dividing work activities was operating as the individual miner obtained assistants and assigned to them the duties of operating the windlass and cleaning the ore. The third pattern is recognized in the modern

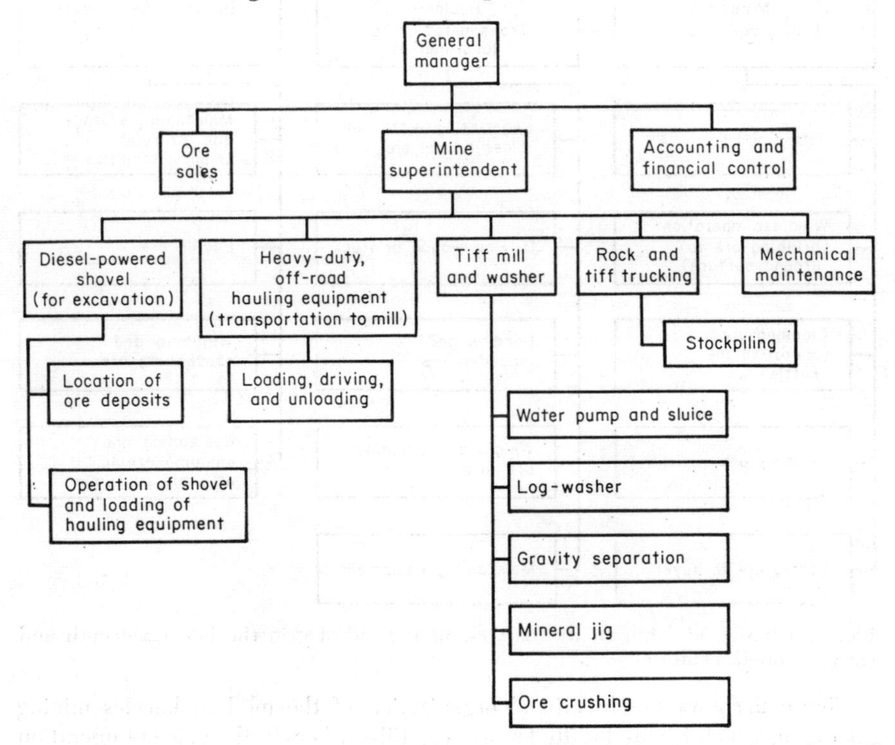

Fig. 2. Functional organization of a modern barytes mining operation. A modern tiff mill employing 15 or 20 workmen could produce between 50 and 100 tons of ore per day; under the former hand mining system a single miner could seldom produce more than 2 tons per week.

tiff mill, where the general manager is required to functionalize his enterprise, divide the tasks, and make work assignments to his employees. All these patterns are variations in the application of the division-of-labor principle.

Line and Staff Organization—An Application

The introduction of specialists into an organization and the establishment of staff departments represent a unique application of the division of labor. These additions to an operating group are made for purposes of efficiency, improved planning, better communications, greater productivity, and the like. The duties and specialized tasks performed by staff workers provide particular forms of assistance to operating managers, because qualified and trained people concentrate their efforts in narrow fields of activity. Although staff work frequently represents new or additional services for an organization, a good portion of the staff work in industry results from a division of labor, the separation of specific functions from line or operating activity, and the assignment of these duties to the specialists who devote their full time and complete attention to them.

Figure 3 presents the organization chart for a small manufacturing plant and illustrates the division of work in the enterprise into line and staff activities. In most operating firms the *line activities* are recognized as those basic functions which are essential and directly concerned with the achieve-

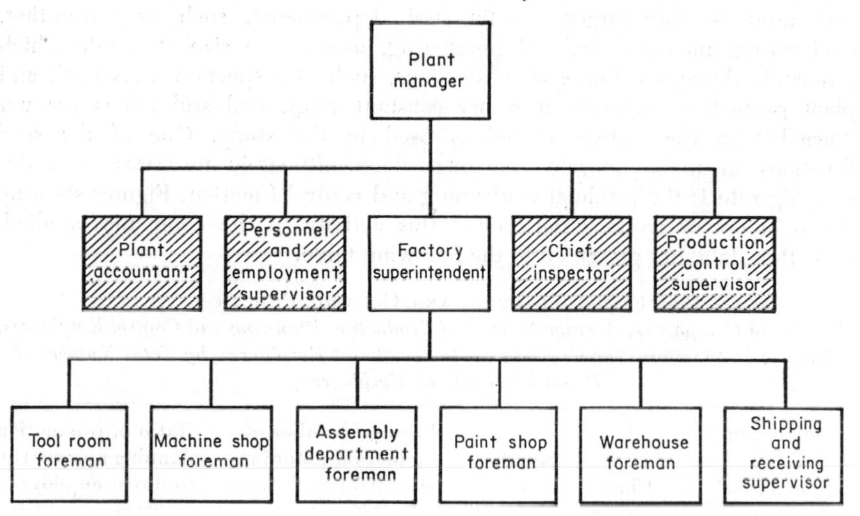

FIG. 3. Organization chart for a manufacturing plant. Staff departments in this organization consist of functions handled by the chief inspector, production control supervisor, personnel and employment supervisor, and plant accountant. All other departments are line departments. The principle of the division of labor was applied as these activities were separated from line functions and established as specialized services for the entire organization.

ment of the objectives of the organization. In this manufacturing firm, the line functions would include machine shop work, assembly, painting, storage, shipping, and similar activities. The *staff activities* in the organization would consist of the informative, advisory, and service activities, as well as the specialized managerial controls established to make the line organization more efficient and more productive. In this simple illustration of a manufacturing plant the application of the division of labor is easily recognized. As the plant organization expanded and became more productive, specialized activities were separated, taken from line managers, and delegated to qualified staff workers. The common acceptance of this form of organization attests to the effectiveness of dividing managerial responsibilities in such a manner.

Illustrations of the use of the division-of-labor principle in the establishment of staff departments in manufacturing organizations may be found in a research study reported by DeSpelder.[4] In this study of 152 manufacturing

[4] Bruce Erwin DeSpelder, *Ratios of Staff to Line Personnel,* Research Monograph 106, The Ohio State University, Bureau of Business Research, Columbus, Ohio, 1962.

companies in the automotive parts industry, the numbers of employees in specialized activities, such as accounting, engineering, maintenance, purchasing, and production planning and control, were compared to the total numbers of employees in direct production activities. These comparisons clearly indicated that in very small organizations some of these staff functions are performed by the production personnel themselves, but in the larger concerns, through a division of labor, specialized staff workers are given these activities.

One of the important findings of this research is the conclusion that as companies become larger, certain staff departments, such as accounting, engineering, maintenance, and purchasing, increase in size at a rate which ultimately decreases. Other staff functions, such as inspection, personnel, and plant protection, increase at rather constant rates, and still others are not amenable to the statistical analysis used in the study. One of the staff functions in manufacturing concerns which ultimately increases at a decreasing rate is the production planning and control function. Figures showing the numbers of workers performing this activity in the companies studied, and other data, are presented in the following table.

PRODUCTION PLANNING AND CONTROL FUNCTION

[*Number of Companies, Average Number of Production Planning and Control Employees, Ratio of Production Planning and Control to Direct Employees, by Total Number of Direct (Production) Employees*]

Number of direct (production) employees	Class midpoint	Number of companies	Average number of production planning and control employees		Ratio of production planning and control to direct employees	
(X)	(Xm)	(N)	(Y)	(Yc)	(Y/Xm)	(Yc/Xm)
5–25	15	14	0.00	0.00	.000	.000
26–50	38	19	1.16	0.00	.031	.000
51–75	63	22	1.74	0.35	.028	.006
76–100	88	15	2.07	1.57	.024	.018
101–149	125	13	2.77	3.35	.022	.026
150–250	200	21	4.24	6.81	.021	.034
251–399	325	14	8.86	12.17	.027	.037
400–700	550	14	15.86	20.57	.029	.037
701–1,299	1,000	12	39.00	32.47	.039	.032
1,300–2,400	1,850	6	35.83	37.19	.019	.019

Note: The estimating equation is $Yc = -2.82 + 0.051X - 0.0000161X^2$ (Yc = estimated number of indirect employees required by a company employing X number of direct employees).

SOURCE: Bruce Erwin DeSpelder, *Ratios of Staff to Line Personnel*, Research Monograph 106, The Ohio State University, Bureau of Business Research, Columbus, Ohio, 1962. Data supplied in 1956 by 150 manufacturers of new, functional, metallic automotive parts. Two divisions were excluded since they were receiving partial functional assistance from their headquarters' production planning and control department.

The Ohio State study of the ratios of staff to line workers defines production planning and control functions as "All work concerned with the planning, routing, expediting and scheduling of production, as well as the control of inventories of materials and product. . . . "[5] Reference to the figures in the table shows that none of the 14 companies studied with less than 25 employees has specialists or staff departments performing the production planning and control activity. For these companies this work has not been divided and separated from the other parts of the production function. However, the 19 companies having between 25 and 50 employees in production work have an average of 1.16 employees performing the production control function, the 15 companies with more than 75 and less than 101 employees in direct production work have an average of 2.07 people in production planning and control activities, and so on. Conclusions from this analysis regarding the separation of staff functions from direct production activities are applicable only to the automotive parts industry, but the relevancy of the division of labor to all line and staff organizations is apparent.

Conclusion

In summary, it should be reiterated that the division of labor appears to be an important management tool which is neglected in current discussions of organization and administration. On the other hand, it is frequently recognized as a universally applicable concept in the planning and organizing of tasks. Every supervisor and every manager employs the principle in evaluating the capacities and interests of workers and in assigning duties and responsibilities. Even the functionalization of management and staff activities requires adherence to this principle.

Many fundamental management techniques, such as job analysis and evaluation, work simplification, and production scheduling, employ the principle of the division of work, and more sophisticated management controls and decision-making procedures are based on successful applications of the theory. Certainly, the clarification of responsibilities and the development of capable personnel in an enterprise are facilitated with management's awareness and consistent application of this concept of the division of labor. Present-day administrators are indebted to Adam Smith for his recognition of this principle and its presentation many years ago.

[5] Ibid., p. 30.

THE TRANSFERENCE OF MANAGEMENT TECHNIQUES

David L. Chewning, A.B.

From time to time proposals have been made for the creation of a "Business Peace Corps" whose purpose would be to introduce American management methods into newly developing countries around the world. Usually it is also suggested that such a program should begin in countries where there is a widespread knowledge of English and a strong private business sector. The program would be staffed by retired businessmen on pension and receiving minimum government compensation.

It is true that know-how in business management is one of the highly developed characteristics with which the American culture has become identified. Accurate accounting, systematic inventory and quality controls, planned purchasing, and delegations of executive authority are all illustrative of established and accepted ways of doing business in our environment. The contributions made to our productivity and standard of living by these management and decision-making tools are so generally recognized and acknowledged that those who specialize in economic assistance to developing countries have naturally had the impulse to include them uncritically in development programs abroad. My own experience in two thoroughly dissimilar developing countries, Burma and Puerto Rico, suggests a need for raising several important questions about the validity of this practice and about the usefulness of a Business Peace Corps.

1. Are these modern and sophisticated techniques in fact transferable to an economic situation where tradition governs the decision-making process and the state of economic and social development is in some cases literally centuries removed from our own?

2. If so, can an effective transfer be accomplished without preconditioning the economic leadership and environment?

Mr. Chewning is a Senior Associate of Robert R. Nathan Associates, Inc.

3. If such an acceptance and environment are achieved, how can modern management tools be introduced with good effect at the level of business operations? Where should the process begin? How can managers at the operating level be persuaded to give the new ideas a fair try?

4. Are language and cultural differences barriers to effective application of new management techniques?

5. Are retired American businessmen the best means for introducing modern management techniques to newly developing nations?

An Environment Must Be Created to Accommodate Modern Management Ideas

When talking about the possibility of transference, consideration must be given to the varying types of business organizations to which the new management ideas are to be addressed. Burma during the U Nu era provides an excellent example of a country emerging from colonial rule as a socialist or semisocialist state. Here, the business community was made up of large government commercial and industrial organizations, large private foreign business operations, and a multitude of small indigenous firms, privately owned and family controlled. The needs and, more important, the motivation of these organizations differed, as did the opportunities for management progress.

In countries such as Burma, government business operations are frequently tradition-bound, cautious, and lacking in a profit motivation. Large foreign firms are usually farther advanced in management methods but are restricted somewhat by host country controls and practices. Small indigenous firms may be so small as working units that they are uneconomic to tackle, and the owners may resist anything that makes tax evasion more difficult. These small businesses are also inhibited in too many instances by unwillingness to share control of business management beyond close family bounds and by an abhorrence of minority participation.

For all these reasons, the initiator of new management ideas will very likely run head on into ideas about management that have long been abandoned in our own system. Many of these have been perpetuated uncritically even in terms of whether improvements could or should be made. The very first task, then, is to establish the will to progress and to progress beyond the point just of public policy pronouncement. The communication of such policy and its enforcement at operating levels of business are steps that cannot be overlooked. This requires education and initiative at the top echelon of government, along with the creation of understandable, workable methods of communicating to operating business levels, both private and governmental, the policy decisions and the means for their implementation.

In Burma this was rarely achieved, and management improvement programs were spotty, ill-defined, poorly supported, and rarely worth the effort. In fairness to the local leaders, foreign advisers sometimes contributed to this chaos because too many of them, representing many disciplines and many countries, failed to grasp the importance of implementing programs in the development process. A good plan or an adequate policy does not of itself cause action to follow.

A curious related phenomenon, in Burma at least and probably typical of other newly developing countries, is the acceptance of technological advance and the rejection of management improvements in the same project. This took place to a ridiculous degree in the case of the Burma Pharmaceutical Institute, a modern multimillion-dollar government-owned manufacturing facility created in Burma in the mid-1950s to produce alcohol, certain biological products, and a diet supplement in the form of vitamin-fortified yeast tablets.

The principal and supporting volume of the entire operation was to come from the yeast operation. Consequently, the plant was opened in July, 1957, to produce 1 million yeast tablets per day. The idea was to make available a vitamin supplement, free and on a national basis, to a vulnerable health group comprised of pregnant women, nursing mothers, infants, and schoolchildren.

By September, 1958, the factory had produced 330 million tablets, 205 million of which had been turned over to various government agencies for distribution. There was, however, no evidence that the vulnerable health groups had received any appreciable number of tablets. Moreover, there was considerable evidence that recipient government departments had haphazardly issued small quantities of tablets to their own employees and put the balance in dead storage where they deteriorated rapidly under tropical weather conditions. Another 125 million tablets had piled up in the factory's warehouse, but production was continuing at the million-per-day rate.

Obviously, no plans had been made by the appropriate government agencies for purchasing and distributing the tablets to the target groups. The crisis that brought the stupendous mess to cabinet-level attention was not so much the failure to meet the objectives of the program but the depletion of the working capital of the factory. Only a tiny portion of the distributed tablets had been paid for, and almost no funds had been budgeted to take care of distribution needs. It was only with the greatest difficulty that government officials could be persuaded to stop production until these management omissions could be taken care of. Further remedial action was then delayed ad infinitum.

In this case the fault clearly lay with the top echelon, and the story illustrates a fundamental weakness in the political management aspect of government. The failure to follow up a policy decision with a program to provide funds, coordination, and control of all agencies involved leads inevitably to total collapse of a much-needed national health program.

That an Environment Can Be Created Is Proved by Development in Puerto Rico

Puerto Rico, like Burma, is an underdeveloped country. It has a serious lack of natural resources to form the base of an industrial economy. It has an infinitely greater problem of overpopulation, as its population density exceeds that of China, India, and the Indonesian Islands. It suffers from the limitations imposed by outmoded traditions of business management. Yet Puerto Rico has become a showplace of what can be accomplished through systematic planning and implementation of development programs. This success cannot be explained on the basis of its economic and political ties to the United States. The really critical factor has been the creation of a will to develop within an atmosphere carefully created by an enlightened and properly trained leadership.

With this sort of leadership, *fomento,* the Spanish word for development, has become a vital and pervasive symbol in Puerto Rican life. *Fomento* means more than just the Economic Development Administration, which has spearheaded industrial promotion efforts of the Commonwealth. It means the whole national effort, private and public, to improve the economic life of the island. The results flowing from the environment do not need to be elaborated here. They do dramatize some actions and motivations that were tragically missing in the Burmese environment and suggest some ingredients that must go into any newly developing country's efforts to move into the modern world.

Perhaps the most significant step in Puerto Rico's development within a conducive environment of public policy was that it found a way to import good managers through the device of U.S. capital investment. Thus it did not have to train its own people as managers overnight, though they are absorbing solid management "know-how" by working with U.S. managers. Puerto Rico's program also placed much emphasis on basic education and vocational and mid-management training.

Transference Is Neither Simple Nor Easy

In most developing countries, newly independent and seeking better ways of life, government and economic structures of the past were not oriented to development as a major national objective. Institutions and management practices of the past which may have been quite adequate to meet the needs of colonial or semicolonial situations are no longer relevant. The new objectives may be reasonably clear, but what will be entailed in achieving them is probably quite vague. Thus there is a tendency to continue the old institutions and management methods.

A case in point is the Civil Supplies Management Board in Burma, an agency created by the British at the end of World War II to ration and distribute critical commodities during a period of social and political chaos in a country recently ravaged by war. Today the institution still exists with much the same organization and procedural structure, but with a wholly different purpose. Its present mission is that of importing and distributing, at low rates, a range of essential commodities such as, for example, sugar, textiles, canned milk products, and building materials. This is a routine but very large merchandising operation and virtually a government monopoly in its field. As such, it seemed a logical point for the effective introduction of modern management techniques. A management development program was instituted, and foreign management development advisers were assigned, one from Robert R. Nathan Associates, Inc., and one, an accounting specialist, from the Public Administration Service. Several serious problems became evident from the outset.

The Policy Level of Government Did Not Support Moves to Establish an Effective Merchandising Operation. It takes more than lip service from this level of government to stimulate lower-level management progress in operating government agencies or in private business. In Burma much ado was made at the top about "efficiency," but little was done about making it possible to achieve the management goals called for.

For example, in spite of the fact that a foreign exchange budget and allocation controls necessarily existed at cabinet level, the operating agency responsible for buying textile imports never succeeded in getting from higher government levels a flexible system for the release of foreign exchange funds on which a planned, properly timed, and economic buying program could be built. Funds were doled out as inventories appeared to reach replenishment levels; requests for funds lay unanswered for intolerably long periods of time. No doubt other agencies of the government suffered from poor budget administration, but in the case of the CSMB good price opportunities were missed, good merchandising practices became well-nigh impossible, and worse, perhaps, the commodity buyers lost all motivation to efficiency and economy.

Operating Managers Were Not Ready for Significant Change in Methods. Here the cultural and language barriers rose up to haunt the path of management advance. Somehow those in charge did not really quite know what the objectives of their operation were or just how far they would be allowed to go in bringing about new methods without danger of serious censure. More important, they lacked the training and cultural background needed to recognize what changes might be worthwhile and what innovations would merely be disruptive. No real guides existed in Burmese language publications, and the English learned in liberal arts institutions at home and abroad did not include much from the realms of business and industry. Many managers were too old, too entrenched, too enmeshed in the old colonial ways to give any encouragement or even toleration to new ideas. All these things combined to build up a pattern of resistance or indifference.

Existing Methods Were Too Primitive to Provide a Solid Basis for Growth. Normal organization, and procedures for planning, controlling, and assessing the operations of this big merchandising enterprise simply did not exist. In a multimillion-dollar business whose principal task was to buy and sell goods, there were no inventory controls, no buying plans, no sales projections, no means for disposing of slow-moving items, none of the standard operating procedures that are necessary for even minimal success. In an enterprise employing about 4,000 people there were almost no personnel procedure, no wage standards, no training efforts.

Management Advisers Had Difficulty in Finding Working Counterparts. For reasons already described there were few indigenous officials prepared to work with the assigned management advisers in preparing the way for introduction of new ideas and methods. For example, a young Burman with considerable Western-type training had been designated as statistical officer of the business. But since he now *was* the statistical officer, he felt no further interest in developing useful data. His immediate status goal had been achieved. This situation was quite acceptable to the chief executive officer who, in any event, had no concept of how to use statistical data in the decision-making processes of the merchandising operation he headed.

Even the Few Officials Who Wanted to Help Were Utterly Lacking in a Sense of Timing. In a merchandising operation, perhaps more than in any other kind of commercial enterprise, there is a compelling urgency to act at just the proper moment of opportunity. This concept was wholly out of step with the prevailing Burmese cultural pattern, as were habits of long hours and hard work. In 1959, for example, the purchase of cotton yarn from India under the US 104D agreement was delayed seriously in minor banking technicalities involving opening letters of credit. As a result, the timing of the CSMB purchase was badly disturbed, and unnecessary shortages of yarn took place in many districts of Burma.

Establishing a Program to Deal with Characteristic Problems

Forget about Sophistication. It became immediately apparent that the transference of the objectives, not the specific methods, of modern American management was the real target of the management development program. The sophisticated techniques of U.S. business simply were not applicable. For example, the introduction of simple, hand-posted accounting methods was something the CSMB chief accounts officer could understand. Elaborate punched-card systems were beyond his comprehension, although some months into the program a small demonstration project using a simple mechanical system was undertaken successfully.

Establish a Few Top-priority Projects and Concentrate on Them. Priorities had to be on the basis of what could be done, not what the need might be in terms of achieving American management standards. Getting a tightly controlled procurement program under way would have been a major accomplishment in establishing an effective merchandising operation. However, this was not possible, and it was therefore necessary to begin the management development program wherever there was any awareness of what was trying to be accomplished. In the CSMB case, such opportunities occurred in the accounting department and in the office of the official who would have been designated, in American parlance, the administrative vice president. The heads of these departments became working counterparts for the foreign advisers, and almost all approaches to CSMB management were made through them.

A Simple Program Was Devised. The program was designed to strengthen, to develop, and to add to existing services. It was rationalized with top CSMB officials on the basis that a comparatively modest investment of time and money could substantially improve services and reduce costs. Thousands of successful management improvement programs in organizations around the world were cited as precedent for such expenditures. It was also pointed out that operating capital was available for such a purpose and that the program need not depend upon government appropriations. The principle that a reasonable portion of profits should be used to sustain and improve the enterprise was emphasized as the essence of good business economics. The following three-step program[1] was proposed, and it is quoted directly here to illustrate how simple and unsophisticated the approach had to be:

[1] Quotation from management development proposal made to Chairman of CSMB, Rangoon, Burma, in May, 1958.

Step No. 1 *Establish Firm Long Range Objectives for Management Improvement.*

These should be presented as lucidly as possible to the Commissioner and subsequently to the controlling Board for understanding, approval and support. It is vital to show that time and money, in reasonable amounts, must be budgeted and that a disciplined, imaginative effort must include the participation, support, and ideas of the top executive leaders of Civil Supplies Management Board. The people who have the most influence on events are those who are willing to propose plans for improvement. It should be kept in mind, however, that an improvement plan is something like a navigator's compass. It is a valuable instrument to show you where you want to go, *PROVIDED* you also have the creative ingenuity to get there. Some of the objectives might include improvements in:

1. The development of more skilled and productive employees both at supervisory and work levels.
2. Providing means for relieving top management executives of burdensome routine work.
3. Providing more systematic means for accumulating accurate and timely information (Dynamics Statistics) for decision making purposes.
4. The development of means for planning and reviewing systematically the work of all operating departments.
5. Establishing means for gathering foreign markets intelligence and consumer research data.
6. Reducing the costs of Civil Supplies Management Board in order to contribute large revenue to the Union Government.
7. Establishing a more clearly defined chain of command.
8. Introduction of more modern office methods and equipment.

An effective way for the Board to take part in this program might be to devote one meeting each month to the planning and review of the management improvement effort.

Step No. 2 *Reorganize the Major Functions of the Enterprise.*

In order systematically to pursue the objectives just outlined, it will be necessary to provide an organizational framework capable of meeting expanded responsibilities. (A simple organization chart was provided to illustrate an organizational arrangement that could prove effective.)

Step No. 3 *Establish a Series of Improvement Projects.*

To set the administrative improvement program in motion it will be wise to organize a series of special projects. These can be set up within the framework of the newly proposed organization. Each project should be placed in the charge of a project leader whose programs will be systematically reviewed (according to a time schedule) by a senior executive of the Civil Supplies Management Board. The projects presented here have been selected because:

1. They appear to meet immedate needs of CSMB and could be undertaken at minimum cost and disruption of regular work.

2. When viewed together they comprise the nucleus of a small experimental program to which other projects may be added in the future as a means for broadening into an overall program of improvement.

The secret of successfully carrying out such a program of improvement lies in starting promptly, even if in rough fashion; in adjusting to circumstances as the program progresses; and in injecting ideas and criticisms of the top executives during the course of the program. Projects in the proposed program should include these types of action:

1. *Those that strengthen existing services* such as introduction of modern office machines, establishment of clearcut lines of authority and delegations of power, and improvement in statistical data for decision making.
2. *Those that train and develop employees* such as definite training plan, an incentives and awards plan, and the use of foreign study grants to provide badly missing technical and professional skills.
3. *Those that add essential new services* such as data concerning the foreign markets in which commodities were purchased, establishment of an internal audit system to evaluate and guide all operating departments, and the publication of operating manuals to provide standards of work for the entire enterprise.

Obviously these steps were not the only things that needed to be done. They were the actions that under existing circumstances seemed most likely to succeed and to demonstrate the value of simple, practically applied management methods.

A complete working outline was prepared for each of nine management improvement projects, and detailed manuals were drawn up for the more complex ones, such as the use of statistics in management decisions and the introduction of punched-card accounting in a few promising demonstration areas.

Just as this program got under way, the Burmese Army took over the functions of civil government. One of its first acts was to cancel the arrangements under which the foreign advisers had been made available to the CSMB and other government agencies. Word that has trickled out of the country since that time is that much of the program was attempted and with some success.

There Is No Unique Prescription for Transference of Management "Know-how"

Although the management development project with the CSMB in Burma was terminated before the changes suggested could show their full effect, a measure of progress could be assessed. One of the top executives had developed a real interest, certain accounting reforms had been inaugurated, and some development plans had been put together and groundwork laid for further advancement.

More rapid advancements were made in similar projects in Puerto Rico, where a better development climate existed and effective managers came along with U.S. investment. In neither case, however, would it have been possible to superimpose an "off-the-shelf" structure of American managerial techniques upon the existing commercial-industrial system.

To revert to the proposal for a "Business Peace Corps" drawn from the ranks of retired U.S. businessmen of proved capacity, serious questions arise as to whether such men can constructively advance management practices in newly developing countries.

The introduction of new ideas requires considerable cultural empathy and a reflective analytical approach. While some American businessmen who might consider service in a senior business corps would have the sort of flexibility required, many years of top-level executive experience in a situation over which he has full control do not necessarily provide a businessman with these qualities.

In addition, living conditions would be a new and, perhaps, distasteful experience; language barriers would almost inevitably be present, even in countries where English is widely spoken; in many countries a socialist economy with which a business executive might feel less than sympathetic would have to be dealt with; and, finally, the very basic tools needed even to begin a program of improvement would be missing.

Recruitment for development work abroad is not easy, and to the extent that the ranks of retired businessmen can furnish qualified personnel they should, of course, be utilized. But in the final selection, patience, sympathy with unfamiliar points of view, flexibility, and adaptability should be weighed in the balance with knowledge of managerial techniques. These qualities may perhaps be found more often in younger men and even in men whose experience has not been confined entirely to business management.

One other fundamental conclusion that can be drawn from these experiences in Burma and Puerto Rico, and from the experience of others working with similar problems in a wider range of newly developing countries, is that there is no single and unique prescription for introducing good management. Just as in the U.S. economy no accounting or personnel program can be taken from one company or one business environment and applied without change, neither can U.S. methods of management and direction be simply and uncritically transferred from this country to a newly developing country.

The fact remains, however, that, no matter how difficult the task, rationalized management techniques are sorely needed in the growth process of newly developing countries and must receive equal emphasis with planning as a key aspect of development programs.

MANAGERIAL PERFORMANCE STANDARDS

Virgil K. Rowland

There is probably no top manager anywhere in the world who does not have some type of performance standards for his subordinate managers, and no department head who does not have some standards of performance for the supervisors under him.

Subordinate managers know this, of course; they know they must meet certain standards or they will soon be demoted or fired. And they want to exceed the standards if they can, because they hope eventually to get salary increases and promotions as their skill improves. But too often they do not have a clear idea of what the standards are, and they devote a great deal of time and attention trying to find out, time and attention that could well be devoted to productive work.

The reason they do not know is that their superiors have not told them, or have not told them in a way they can understand. In other words, superiors have not written down the standards and given them to their subordinates to serve as a day-by-day guide. Instead, they have merely indicated obliquely from time to time how well they expect the subordinate managers to perform.

Lacking written standards, the subordinate managers, who are constantly trying to find out what the boss really wants, often read unintended meanings into his most casual remarks. Even a raised eyebrow can convince a subordinate that he has transgressed some sort of standard, and he makes up his mind that he will never fall under the boss's displeasure in the same way again.

The unfortunate part of this is that the standards which the subordinates

---

Mr. Rowland is Assistant to the Chairman of the Detroit Edison Company and an author of studies and books in the field of management. Thanks are due to the American Management Association for permission to use copyrighted material from his book of the same title.

deduce in this way are generally not the standards that their superior really wants emphasized. Many top managers and department heads might be astonished—and very unpleasantly so—if they knew the standards their subordinate managers are trying to observe. In a great many companies, the list might run something like this:

- Don't get into any disagreements.
- Always tell the boss what he wants to hear.
- Never look idle. If you haven't anything to do, have three or four folders on your desk and appear to be studying one of them.
- Always be available when the boss wants you, even if you have to neglect your work to be there.
- Dress well, but not conspicuously.

In fact, wherever the standards are not in written form, it is likely that the ideas the subordinates have of them are irrelevant or that the standards they are trying to observe are much lower than they should be. This is true in highly industrialized countries and also in developing countries, where it is perhaps even more important that every manager pull his weight, since there is less likely to be a margin for error. And it is true of all subordinates from the rank-and-file workman to the executive near the top.

It was not until the Industrial Revolution was more than a century old that companies in the United States were brought to realize this, even in the case of the workmen. Then Frederick W. Taylor, "the father of scientific management," showed how the lack of rational standards was keeping production down to one-half or one-third of what it might have been. It has taken more than another half-century for U.S. companies to realize that what is true of production workers is also true of managers. Even today, comparatively few U.S. companies, and probably fewer in Europe, have written standards for their managers. Those that do have them are finding that the standards make it possible for them to raise performance more than they had thought possible.

The reason for the delay is, of course, that the manager's job is much more complex than that of the rank-and-file worker. It is easy to specify a standard of so many pieces per hour for a production worker, so many words per minute for a typist, or so many orders for a salesman. A manager, on the other hand, must be judged on many facets of performance that seem difficult or impossible to reduce to figures. He is expected to train those under him and improve their skills, to keep their morale high, to plan their work efficiently, to make suggestions for improvement, and to keep in mind the interests of the business as a whole as well as the set tasks before him.

Yet a technique for setting managerial standards, including standards for the intangibles, does exist, and developing countries can adapt it to their needs just as they can adapt the techniques of time and motion study that Taylor and others in the scientific management movement developed.

The technique is actually a very simple one, and it has the dual advantage of producing written standards and fostering understanding of them at the same time. It also makes it possible for a company to have higher standards for its managers than it has had in the past.

All that is necessary is that the boss get together with his subordinates in a quiet room, either individually or in a group, and determine with them (*a*) what they are supposed to be doing, and (*b*) how well they are supposed to be doing it. The only "props" the boss will need are a number of large sheets of paper, a roll of sticking tape, and a crayon.

The group approach is used where there are a number of subordinate managers on the same level who are doing approximately the same type of work—a group of first-line production foremen, for example, or a group of office supervisors or district sales managers.

For higher managers whose work is unique within the company, such as, for example, a marketing director or a head of manufacturing, the individual approach is used.

Using the Group Approach

Group sessions, with the immediate superior as the presiding officer, are called, first, to determine the segments of the subordinate managers' job, i.e., *what* they are supposed to be doing, and second, *how well* they are supposed to be doing it. Sometimes more than one meeting may be needed for each of these phases; sometimes there need be only two sessions.

Determining the "What." In opening the discussion on the "what" of the managerial job, the boss at first confines himself to stimulating the discussion. He begins by explaining the purpose of the meeting, then asks his subordinates to suggest the things that they, as managers, do in the course of performing their jobs.

As suggestions are made from the floor, he writes each one down and attaches it to the wall with the tape in a spot where everyone can see it. During this phase of the meeting, he himself makes no comments. Many of the suggestions will be poorly phrased, and some will merely duplicate in different words suggestions that have already been made. Nevertheless he posts them all as given. At this time he is not trying to produce a finished list, merely a preliminary list that will serve as a basis for further discussion.

When the group has exhausted its ideas, or when it is evident to the boss that no really new ones are being offered, he calls a halt to this part of the meeting and initiates discussion of each suggestion in turn. Here the group itself will begin to eliminate some of the repetition. For example, one list contained both "Get subordinates to realize how important it is not to make a mistake" and "Training employees." With both items posted in plain sight, others in the group were quick to point out that the first of these "segments" is merely a facet of the second.

There will, of course, be some disagreements among members of the group about the various segments of the job, and the boss can guide the discussion by asking pertinent questions, both of individuals and of the group as a whole, and express his own views if he wishes. But he need not dominate the meeting to get good results; in fact, results will not be good if he merely lays down the law. Often he will find the Socratic method of asking questions and analyzing answers adequate to ensure that the list as finally agreed upon by the group will be one that he himself can agree to without reservations. If he feels that some important segment of the job has not been mentioned at all, he can ask: "What about . . . ? Isn't that something you all do?"

A final list developed in a meeting for first-line supervisors in office or factory will probably include such major job segments as the following:

1. Work assignment
2. Work scheduling
3. Enforce punctuality
4. Train employees
5. Have contacts with employees

Probably the boss could write the segments of the job down in a better way from the viewpoint of literary style. But if the subordinate managers have suggested the language, they understand it better than they would the most elegant job description. In the course of the discussion, many of them will be learning that there are some segments of their jobs they have not been paying enough attention to, or have been neglecting entirely. The boss, too, will be learning; he will come to see that there are certain of his subordinates whom he must work with on some phases of their job because they are unsure of the extent of their responsibilities.

The steps in determining the *what* of the management job in a group session, then, may be summarized as follows:

1. Write down every item suggested until a good list is compiled.
2. Let the group discuss each item and either discard it or accept it, either as it stands or after some rewriting.
3. Make a list of the tasks everyone agrees are the responsibilities of the job.

Setting the Standards. The list so produced, however, is not necessarily the really final one. It will be used, rather, as a means of getting discussion on standards started, and it may be modified or enlarged as that discussion proceeds.

When the standard-setting session is called, the boss posts the list and begins by pointing to the first item and asking: "How will we know when this is well done?"

Some standards can be set in figures—the number of days or weeks a supervisor should take to bring a new employee up to full production, the amount of scrap permissible, the attendance rate, and so on.

Others will embody no figures, but will be very definite nevertheless. Take, for example, this standard set by a group of plant managers for their own performance in the selection of foremen, which was one of the responsibilities on their list of job segments: "Selection of foremen is up to standard when the new supervisor gives evidence of good work as shown by (1) lower costs, (2) lower scrap, (3) higher productivity, (4) better attendance on the part of his employees, and (5) fewer complaints from his employees."

In the company in question there are regular reports on all these factors, and it will be easy to see whether the plant manager has made a wise selection. The standard also included the proviso that the plant manager should be able to show that his selection had not been haphazard but according to plan; that is, he should have interviewed a sufficient number of candidates, checked references, and so on.

Again, a group of regional sales managers had included in their list of job segments (1) "Reporting any significant competitive products" and

(2) "Teaching field representatives how to make proper use of reference manuals."

For the first, the standard set was: "Performance in this respect is satisfactory when the sales manager has reported any significant competitive products he has had an opportunity to observe, and when subsequent events prove the soundness of his judgment."

For the second, the sales managers worded the standard: "The regional sales manager's performance is satisfactory when a field representative seldom makes recommendations or commitments that show unfamiliarity with the manuals and seldom requests information that is to be found in the manuals."

Even on the more intangible aspects of the manager's job, standards can be, and have been, worked out. For example, one group of sales managers worked out the following standards for the segment of their job that they had called "motivating employees":

A manager's performance in motivating is good when:

1. His employees work at their maximum potential toward predetermined goals.
2. Morale of employees is at a high level.
3. The manager analyzes the basic drives of each employee and provides the opportunity for the employee to progress in the direction of his needs.
4. The manager recognizes good performance.
5. He sets up good incentive plans.
6. He conducts contests.
7. He lets people know what is expected of them.
8. He is fair and ethical in his treatment of employees.
9. He gives thoughtful consideration to employees' suggestions.
10. He gives employees an opportunity to exercise initiative within prescribed limits.
11. He maintains good personal habits.
12. He counsels with employees, correcting them diplomatically and letting them know where they stand.

The Individual Approach

Where the individual approach is used, there are only two participants—the superior, who is probably the chief executive of the organization, and the man for whom standards are to be set. While it would be quite possible to use an ordinary sheet of paper and have the two men work at one desk or table, experience has shown that here too the technique of posting suggestions on the wall is useful. Neither man has to crane his neck to see what is written, which makes it much easier to combine items, condense the list, or add to it.

Below is a partial transcript of an individual standard-setting discussion between a company president and his sales vice president. Here they are discussing market coverage, which they have already agreed is a part of the vice president's job:

PRES.: "Scope of the product"—we agreed that was part of market coverage. How can we use that as a unit of measurement? [He writes at the top of a new page, "Your performance in market coverage is good when (1) . . . ."]

V.P.: Well, what I had in mind there was the completeness of our line. When one of our salesmen goes into a customer's office, he needs to be able to handle all his painting needs, and supply not only the paints but the related needs. I think we could amplify our related lines somewhat.

PRES.: Yes, I think so too. But where does *your* performance come into it?

V.P.: Our salesmen know what the customers need. It would merely be a case of my getting the information back from them through divisional and regional managers. Then I could assemble the data and discuss it with you.

PRES.: How often should this happen?

V.P.: Offhand, I'd say annually. After all, we can't move too fast on new products, and many of those suggested won't be feasible.

PRES: That's right, but some of them may help us increase our sales revenue. One thing I want to mention right now, however, is that our discussion isn't designed to make you do a lot more work. The purpose is to help you do your job better by using your specialized talents more effectively.

V.P.: I understand that. But I think it's something I should be doing.

PRES.: I agree. But you've got to remember that most of the segments of your job had to do with getting performance from your regional managers, and getting them, in turn, to do a better job of supervising the district managers.

V.P.: That's right. But it seems to me that this is a matter of getting the regional managers to do something they really should have been doing all along. I should have been asking for the information, and they, in turn, should have been asking their district managers for it.

PRES.: OK. Now, how will we word this portion of the standard?

V.P.: Well, we could say that my performance is satisfactory when I supply you with annual data for recommended additions to the line and there is evidence that the information has come from the salesmen through the district and regional managers.

PRES.: Suppose I word it [writes] "Data for recommended additions to the line are presented at least annually, and there is evidence that the data have been supplied by the sales force through its own line organization."

V.P.: I think we should add that the data should come from the whole country. Let's say a recommendation should be received from at least 75 percent of the salesmen before I should recommend an addition to the line.

PRES.: 75 percent may be enough for you and me, but I think the Board of Directors would want an even higher percentage before approving capital expenditures to broaden the line.

V.P.: Maybe we should split it then and say 75 percent for items that require less than $5,000 in capital expenditure and 90 percent for anything over that.

PRES: That's more like it. If I know our salesmen, these things will have a tendency to build up as they chat with each other at their meetings.

V.P.: Yes, and if they get the new lines they ask for, it stands to reason they'll work hard to sell them.

PRES: Now let's see how we'll make this standard read. We said [he writes again] that "performance is satisfactory when you supply annual data from the field for recommended additions to the line drawn from recommendations from 75 percent of the salesmen in cases where the new items will require less than $5,000 in new capital . . . "

V.P.: Better make it $3,000.

PRES.: OK, that's better. [Writes again] . . . $3,000 in new capital, and recommendations from 90 percent of the salesmen when the capital cost is greater than that." That's it. Now for the second item on the list—share of the market.

V.P.: Let's say my performance on that segment is satisfactory when we have 30 percent of the market. Last year we had 28.2, and that gives me something to shoot at.

PRES.: Do you think that's realistic? Can we really expect to gain that much?
V.P.: Yes, I do. We had only 25.9 the year before last, and I think we're still gaining. Our advertising budget is larger this year, too.

How High Should Standards Be?

It will generally be possible, in either group or individual standard-setting sessions, to raise standards somewhat. In a group meeting, some of the managers who are falling below the standards met by others can be brought to see that they should be setting their sights higher, and eventually the average for the group should rise perceptibly. In an individual session, the boss will often have an opportunity to learn ways in which he can help his subordinate meet higher standards. For example, broadening the line, as suggested by the vice president of sales in the example above, may help him to raise the company's share of the market because customers may prefer to buy the regular products from a concern that can also supply them with all the accessories.

Standards should not, however, be set too far above current levels at first. If a standard seems to be unattainable, people are discouraged from trying to attain it. Any standard set for a group of managers, for example, should be attainable at least by the majority of them, not merely by the very best. In the case of an individual standard-setting session, the standard should not be so high that the individual himself does not feel reasonably confident he can reach it. Standards can always be raised later if it appears that higher levels are feasible.

The real purpose of the standard-setting is not to determine who should be fired although the standards may occasionally be used for that purpose. Rather it is to improve the performance of the managers and to lead them to place emphasis on the phases of their job that the boss considers most important.

Take a group of first-line plant foremen. Some of them will do an excellent job, the majority a passable job, and a very few will be doing rather poorly. If they can be brought to recognize the importance of meeting definite standards, the best may not improve at all—they will probably be meeting the standards already. But the average foreman will raise his performance somewhat, and the poorest will undoubtedly do so as well—the poorest may even raise their performance to the point where they are doing as well as the average man formerly was. These changes will mean a substantial gain for the company.

Importance of the Discussion

It is sometimes asked why the boss himself cannot write down the standards, or have a staff man do it, or perhaps borrow standards from another company. All these techniques have been tried, and none of them works as well as the discussion method in which every person has an opportunity to participate in setting the standards by which he will be judged.

If standards are borrowed from another company, they may be completely inapplicable—methods, equipment, and personnel may be entirely different. If a staff man does the job, or if the boss himself does it, the standards are quite likely to be too low—for, as Taylor found when he first went into industry, the boss's idea of what the average person can do is likely to be the average of the past, and often this is far lower than the standard those on the job *could* meet. Conversely, many of those affected by the standards may think they are too high if they are imposed from without, but they cannot long maintain this viewpoint when they learn, in a group meeting, that others on the same level consider them entirely reasonable. Nor can a manager, in an individual standard-setting session with his boss, maintain that *no* improvement is possible, and if he is allowed to set the degree of improvement himself, he will be sure it is attainable.

Above all, the discussion and the arguments back and forth that may take place in a group or individual meeting give the participants an understanding both of what they should be doing and of how well they should be doing it that can be obtained in no other way. They know what the job segments and the standards mean because they have themselves selected the phrasing.

GOAL SETTING, RISK TAKING, AND QUANTITATIVE METHODS

Dr. T. Paulsson Frenckner

Introduction

Management in one form or another is probably just as old as human activity. In technical fields where man is using more and more refined instruments, exactly formulated goals and quantitative measurement are self-evident. We could mention as examples the construction of houses, machines, bridges, etc., while in that which concerns management functions —e.g., product pricing, financial planning, and personnel policy—action has more numbed hands. The main instruments are routines, rules of thumb, and intuition.

Plants and sales markets are growing. Administration costs increase. Nonnecessary commodities gain greater importance. All these changes increase the significance of the management decision process. Could it not become more precise and improved? Of course individual managerial instruments have been improved, such as bookkeeping, costing, pricing, and budgeting. Every scientist who studies managerial decisions is, however, struck by the lack of specifically formulated action goals in management. There are often no definite criteria when management must take risks and uncertainty into regard. To the extent that quantitative methods are used they are usually not integrated into a combined managerial decision system.

The Study of Business Behavior

When a business firm buys, manufactures, or sells products or services, when it administers personnel, etc., we talk about the behavior of the com-

---

Dr. Frenckner is Professor of Business Administration at the Stockholm School of Economics.

pany. Behind the behavior in each situation we find a set of decisions which are made individually or cooperatively by different decision makers inside the company. What from the exterior takes the shape of business behavior could from the interior be considered the effect of a steering process inside the company.

The business firm and its behavior are studied mainly inside economics and business administration. In these sciences attempts are made to draw general conclusions about business behavior. The conclusions are built upon the assumption that actions could be predicted. The actions are supposed to be an expression either of economic rational behavior or of certain psychological regularities.

Rational behavior assumes goal-conscious actions.

From a study of business behavior and goal setting we may attain better decision-making practices in the future.

Costing Methods and Goal Setting

Classical economic theory postulates profit maximization as the objectives of the business firm. This is the reason for the use of marginal revenues and marginal costs. According to this theory it is profitable if the firm changes its price, increases its volume, etc., until the limit is reached where marginal revenues no longer cover marginal costs.

In practice we never speak of marginal revenues and marginal costs. They are difficult to determine by business records. However, theory has influenced practice, for example, in the justification of direct costing. A product or a business measure is judged as profitable only to the extent that it brings about a positive contribution above separable (or direct) costs. This contribution should express the difference between incremental revenues and incremental costs.

Also the competitive costing method, absorption costing or full costing, could be theoretically motivated. The different overhead burdens could be looked upon as planned contributions which management considers necessary to cover overhead costs in different parts of the company. In that way absorption costing could be looked upon as an instrument for the delegation of managerial power. Another theoretical motive for absorption costing could be cited in bidding. The full costs could then provide guidance for management in estimating the average costs in the long run for both its own and the competing companies. In duopoly and oligopoly situations, absorption costing could contribute toward stability. Companies are not drawn into temporary price wars but are still influenced so that they react similarly to changes that are affecting all of them, e.g., a price rise in raw materials.

Traditional Goal Setting: Profit Maximization

The debate concerning the choice of costing method illustrates the lack of exact goal setting in business. Direct costing is mostly motivated by short-run profitability. Absorption costing is an effect of long-run aims and of an effort to attain stability. The lack of exact goal setting also influences the way in which replacement, capital costs, and other engineering economy problems are judged.

In every business firm it seems necessary and desirable to formulate exactly what will be meant by profit and profitability. The following questions have to be answered:

1. How does the management wish to define mathematically the profit to be maximized, e.g., as a net profit according to absorption costing, or as a contribution to cover common costs according to direct costing?

2. How does the management wish to take into regard depreciation and other capital costs that could be defined historically on the basis of book-keeping data or *ex ante* as predicted demand of capital for the continuation of the business activity?

3. How does the management wish to choose between actions that are especially profitable in the short run and actions that are supposed to yield more in the long run?

4. If a decision has to be made upon data from a certain department, how should the subjective estimates of sales potentials, prices, costs, etc., be evaluated?

5. If the profit of different courses of action is dependent upon external conditions, such as trade conditions, how does the management wish to appraise the utility of a small but certain profit chance against one which is larger but more uncertain?

6. If the profit of different actions depends upon competitors' actions, how willing is the management to risk different countermeasures from their side?

7. How does the management wish to define profit with regard to variations in the price level, i.e., in the choice between investment in activities with constant real value but low rate of return, compared with (nominal) monetary investments with higher return?

Goals Other than Strict Profit Maximization

It is difficult to inquire into the real goals of management; often business people are not fully aware of the goals.

The desire to survive is sometimes mentioned among the goals for business activities. More exactly the goal could be formulated as a desire expressing maximum probability for survival or minimum probability for not surviving, but it could also be considered as a long-run profitability goal.

Among many businessmen the profit goal is taken as self-evident for every business firm. In cooperative activities, Federal and state companies, non-private hospitals, and many other organizations, the profit goal, however, takes a special form. It could, for example, be used to bring about a certain activity to minimize cost. In such cases it is important to formulate exactly the object of maximum gap between revenues and costs where one of these factors is constant.

As a complement more than an alternative for profit or survival goals, management people sometimes speak also of other goals. If these should be systematically examined regarding their influence on business behavior, they have to be formulated exactly and integrated with each other.

Among such goals—mostly subgoals—we find, for example:

1. Financial goals, such as consolidation of the financial position and high financial liquidity

2. Expansion goals, such as big market share and large turnover
3. Stability goals, such as satisfying profit or maintained physical capacity, purchasing power, or market potential
4. More personal or noneconomic goals, such as personal goodwill, high manager's compensation, percentage, personal prestige, and technical perfection

Sometimes behavior is observed that could be taken only as a sign of general conservatism or traditional routines in the lack of more precisely formulated managerial goals.

Further Specification of Goals

Company goals are often too generally formulated to be used for each single management decision. The fixing of different action goals in relation to each other suggests the possibility of various courses of action. For some goals, management aims at the highest possible goal satisfaction (goals to obtain); for others, it demands only a certain minimum goal satisfaction (goals to retain).

A precise statement of the goal structure is necessary on the following points:

1. Business actions could in many respects be limited. These constraints may originate from external or internal conditions. Some constraints mean that certain actions are excluded as such, e.g., illegal actions. In other cases a certain action is expected with certainty or with a lower or higher probability to have consequences which are definitely not desired by the management. The consequences could occur in certain trade conditions or depend upon counteractions from clients, suppliers, banks, etc.

2. Sometimes the constraint of the action space is an effect of goals other than profit maximization. These goals could be formulated as, for example, a minimum level with regard to cash liquidity, market share, etc. Every action that does not certainly or with probability reach above this threshold level has to be excluded.

3. Sometimes it is carelessly said that a company attempts to provide products of the highest quality at the cheapest price. As higher quality does not ordinarily mean cheaper price, this goal is imprecise. The decision maker has to aim either at the highest possible quality for a given price level or at the cheapest possible price for a given quality level, or has to express exactly what a decline in quality is worth in price or vice versa. Such functions for weighing different goals are extremely difficult to formulate for practical use.

4. Conflicts between different goals, for example, between profit maximization in the short run and maximization of survival probability, are extremely common when different interests are behind a company. In a family company, some owners could be interested in immediate dividends, others in expansion and better future profit potentials. For a consequent business management it seems absolutely necessary to overcome such goal conflicts by formulating an exact business policy, otherwise decision making could be unprofitably delayed.

5. Similar conflicts could occur between functional managers with different subgoals for their activities, if these subgoals were not consistent with each

other. The production manager could be interested in low manufacturing costs and the sales manager in a large turnover. This could lead to conflicts with regard to lot size and product line.

6. According to trade conditions, competition, etc., certain goals could dominate temporarily. Under pressure, financial goals could dominate profitability goals. In such cases it is extremely important that all decision makers consistently subordinate themselves to these dominating goals.

7. Sometimes it is purposeful to formulate temporary stage-goals. Maximum profitability in the long run is often too unrealistic as a guidance for individual decisions. Stage-goals could be formulated as a certain sales turnover, a certain cost reduction, a reduced personnel turnover, etc., for a given period. Such stage-goals necessarily have to be coordinated with the long-run goals of the company.

Certainty, Risk, and Uncertainty

A businessman has to base many decisions upon predictions. Actions are chosen with regard to their expected consequences. If the predictions are assumed to be certain, the choice is relatively simple. For every course of action its consequences are studied with regard to the satisfaction of different goals. From the known courses of action are excluded those whose consequences do not satisfy given constraints or minimum thresholds. Then the choice is made with relation to the goal or the goal combination for which maximum goal satisfaction is wanted.

Predictions are, however, seldom certain. Sometimes they can be formulated in terms of different probabilities for different events, and consequently for different outcomes of the courses of action at hand. We talk about a risk situation. For every event or state of nature the probability is assumed to be known. The sum of the probabilities for all events equals one.

In other cases it is not possible to determine probabilities for the different events. We talk about uncertainty. The decision has to be taken blindly. At best different events and consequences could be surveyed.

With risk or uncertainty it is not enough to have a precise statement of goals. It must also be defined how management will treat the risk and uncertainty. Decision criteria have to be formulated. Maximum mathematical expectation of goal satisfaction is one possible criterion in a risk situation. Sometimes, however, the decision maker will give more importance in goal value to some outcomes than to others. In uncertainty situations one possibility is to choose the action with the best goal value among the worst possible outcomes for each action. Additional criteria are discussed in the literature of the theory of games.

A Scheme for Decision

For many managerial decision problems it is rational to use a schematic step procedure. This could be described in the following way:

1. The decision maker specifies the set of alternative courses of action that are available to him.

2. He also specifies the different events (states of nature) which could arise.

3. For every combination of action and event the predicted outcome is evaluated with regard to the degree of goal satisfaction. If there are many goals, each outcome has to be evaluated with regard to each goal.

4. If possible, the probability of different events is determined.

5. If the management in such a risk situation uses the mathematical expectation of goal satisfaction as decision criterion, the expected outcome for each action is calculated on behalf of its outcomes and the probabilities for different events.

6. That action is chosen which has the best average outcome.

7. In other cases—especially in uncertainty situations where it is supposed to be impossible to determine probabilities for different events—another decision criterion has to be chosen.

8. The decision problem could be reduced if certain courses of action have to be excluded while their outcomes violate a restriction. A common restriction is that no action should be taken that could ruin the company.

9. It is also possible to exclude dominated actions, i.e., actions which show a goal satisfaction less than or equal to some other action for every possible event.

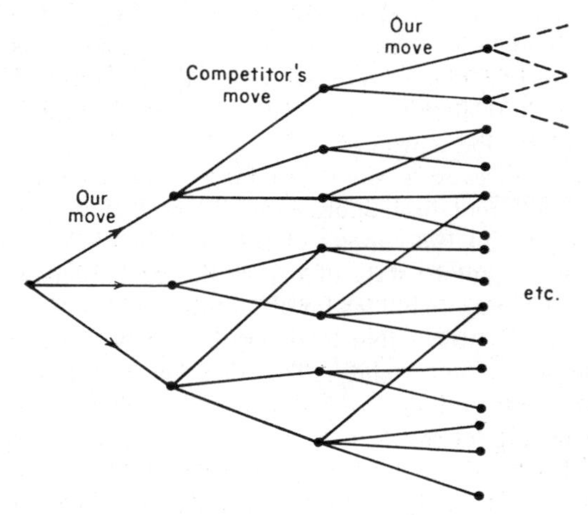

Sometimes the action choice refers to a decision variable that could take any value on a continuous scale. In the same way the probability for different events could be given in the form of a frequency function for different values of a variable. The probability of different events could be more or less subjectively determined.

Sometimes the outcomes of different actions are mainly dependent upon actions by one or more competitors. If one supposes a perfect knowledge of possible actions and outcomes for both one's own business firm and the competitors, and if one also supposes a knowledge of the competitors' goals, a rational decision according to a given decision criterion is still possible.

In many practical situations it is not possible exactly to define different actions, events, outcomes, goal satisfactions, and so on. Still, it could be useful to formulate the problem in those terms and evaluate outcomes with, for example, + +, +, − and − − for different degrees of goal satisfaction.

By using such a crude method, management could be helped to get a better survey of possibly good decisions compared with worse decisions.

If a decision process includes decisions at different times, the analysis could be made somewhat differently. By choosing one alternative, the decision maker is now limiting his choices in later decisions. Between the different moves by the decision maker there could be countermoves from nature or competitors. This is a typical situation in chess, bridge, etc. Sometimes such a decision process could be illustrated schematically as a "game tree." At each node are shown the possible courses of action. Our decision maker's choices at one time could be shown in one column, nature's or the competitor's choice in the next column, our decision maker's choice in the next column, and so on. If our decision maker could determine any probability for the different choices by nature or the competitor, this could be shown in the scheme. At each node the goal satisfaction of the outcome in question could also be noted. From looking at the right-hand side of such a game tree it is possible to say something about the long-run outcomes from choices between different courses of action at earlier stages to the left in the diagram on the opposite page.

Optimality, Satisfaction, or Flexibility

Whether or not business people in their day-to-day decisions really try to reach optimal behavior has been frequently discussed. Necessary information for formulating the decision problem exactly in accordance with the above-mentioned scheme is difficult to obtain. The costs of collecting data and their evaluation should also be taken into consideration. In statistical decision theory this has been done. In business it seems more common to formulate a set of minimum requirements with regard to profitability, market share, financial relations, etc. The search for courses of action is continued only until the point where the first action is found that meets all requirements. As the search process is improved, the requirements are strengthened, i.e., the aspiration level is raised. Thus, this so-called "satisficing"[1] procedure comes close to an optimizing procedure.

Another alternative to optimization could be mentioned. In business it is probably more important to avoid bad decisions than to find the very best ones. The states of nature and the countermeasures from competitors could change rapidly. A common decision criterion that is motivated in many situations is a kind of maximum flexibility. By this we mean that management attempts to keep open as many future courses of action as possible. With this decision criterion, the "game tree" formulation seems especially useful.

Quantitative Methods

A business activity could be described simply as a process with an input of material, labor, and other resources and an output of products or services. The process in its turn could be divided into subprocesses with inputs and outputs of different services. Many decisions result from a choice among acquisition of resources, allocation of available resources, or output

[1] The term "satisficing" has been coined by Professor Simon of the Carnegie Institute of Technology.

of products or services. The economic evaluation and analysis refer to the sacrifices to buy or use the resources and the utility or revenue value of manufactured and sold output. With specified goal-setting and decision criteria and newer methods of collecting and handling data, the use of quantitative methods as a basis of decision making is of more practical importance than before. Consequently, mathematical and statistical education has become more valuable to business people.

The acquisition of resources implies a dimension problem. Some problems of this kind have been treated quantitatively for a long time, for example, in the formulas for purchasing order size or lot size in production. The same formulas—based upon ordinary calculus—can also be used for determining appropriate cash reserves. When demand or production speed varies, the inventory problem can be looked upon as a queuing problem. A solution technique has been developed for telephone traffic problems. This same technique may also be used for determining optimal machinery use, the number of repair personnel, etc.

The allocation of available resources has to be made within the framework of capacity in manufacturing and sales possibilities. Financial limitations are also given. Considering these limiting factors, a product line problem can be formulated with the help of so-called mathematical programming. The goal can be formulated as maximum contribution to common costs within capacity and other limitations.

The output of products or services in competition with other companies mostly requires decisions about pricing, advertising and other sales activities, choice of originality and quality level of products, etc. In oligopoly situations there is a "game" problem; the outcome of our behavior is dependent also upon the competitors' behavior. Even if the game theory in such cases might be difficult to use for finding a unique optimal solution, its way of structuring the decision problem along the lines of the above-presented decision method could be useful for avoiding inappropriate decisions.

What Is to Be Gained?

Precise goal setting and formulation of decision criteria are necessary for using quantitative methods. The latter, however, are very much criticized because they give no more exactness than the data, and business data are usually inexact.

Even if the management does not believe in better decisions through quantitative methods, three other distinct advantages of the discussed approach to decision making should be stressed. First of all the formulation of decision problems in an exact way often shows up inconsistency or internal contradictions in the management process. Secondly, with exact methods it is much easier to take into consideration what changes or inexactness in data could mean for the optimum choice. Quantitative methods make sensibility analysis possible. It is also easier to understand the importance of so-called imponderables, i.e., variables that are not measurable. Thirdly, after a decision is made, it is much easier in the appraisal of its effect to locate responsibility and to gain experience which will facilitate future decision making.

Summary

The management function in business to a great extent means decision making. It is considered most desirable to make decisions rationally, in order to save time and irritation in the decision process and to check the outcome of earlier decisions as guidance for future decisions. Then it seems desirable

1. To formulate as precisely as possible goals and subgoals for different decision makers in the company so that they all cooperate as efficiently as possible toward maximum satisfaction of the company's main goal in the long run.
2. To formulate how risk taking and uncertainty should be regarded in current decision making.
3. To use simple analytical schemes or routines for all kinds of decisions, especially repeated ones.
4. To use quantitative methods for determining optimal or "satisficing" decisions and for studying, among other things, the sensitivity to inexactness in data and to changes in external and internal conditions.

PRINCIPLES OF LONG-RANGE PLANNING

Everett R. Walker

Successful enterprises have always done some long-range planning. A few years ago most such long-range planning was done only in fragments. It was extremely rare to find a plan carefully written down, documented, and controlled.

Today, in a highly competitive economy, no longer insular but already world-wide, a long-range plan is almost essential to success. There are certain fundamentals which need to be known in order to construct a long-range plan which will serve a business adequately. A knowledge of these basic principles makes possible the construction of a proper operating plan which, while not ensuring against failure, certainly makes success far more possible than trying to operate without such a plan or trying to make a plan built upon false fundamentals.

Advantages of Long-range Planning

It is proper to elaborate a little on why a long-range plan is needed and why it will contribute more to successful operation than will a short plan, a plan for only the next year, for example.

The whole world is changing. Now the incessant growth and dynamic change taking place in nearly every economy create an atmosphere in which individual companies must keep moving forward in order to keep on even terms with competition.

Markets for the sale of goods and services are constantly changing and enlarging. More and more people everywhere are finding ways to improve their living standards. People everywhere are changing their wants as the times change. It is possible to anticipate the wants of tomorrow, and a

---

Mr. Walker is Vice President of the State Mutual Life Assurance Company of America.

long-range plan makes the act of anticipating these wants a worthwhile thing to do, since it allows the thinking and planning company to progress faster than those companies which do not do it.

A long-range plan requires each member of a company to understand where his company wants to be in the future. This makes each person a real part of the company, sharing common goals and common success in their accomplishment.

A long-range plan makes people stretch their thinking, and then their actions, in order to attain the goals they thought about in the first place. Thinking and planning into the future tends to make people raise their ambitions and their wants, and such raising of ambitions makes each work harder to accomplish the increased goals thus set.

A long-range plan makes it easier for the top management of a company to see potential bad performance in the future and makes it possible to correct the bad performance before it causes serious trouble. Vigorous corrective action can only be taken when the need for the correction is known. Long-range planning, through the controls built into the plan, tells early when things are not going according to schedule and, since the plan has already been carefully worked out to attain goals known to be desirable, tells what to do to put the plans back into force again.

Fundamentals of Long-range Planning

It is the purpose of this article to describe the fundamentals for building a proper long-range operating plan for any enterprise—manufacturing-, sales-, or service-oriented.

First, a few definitions:

Long range: five years or more.

Objective: the end to which an activity is directed.

Operating plan: a specification of the objectives, policies, practices, and procedures for operating an enterprise, and the controls for holding each of these factors in proper relationship.

Quantitative: that which can be measured or estimated by numbers.

Qualitative: that which is related to or concerned with quality.

Forecast: a prediction of a future happening or condition determined from assumptions or known facts.

Controls: the examination of actual performance as it relates to predicted performance, the analysis of variances which appear, the notification to one in authority that the variances exist, and the course of action to be followed because the variances do exist.

As will be seen later on, a long-range plan cannot be put together by any one person in the enterprise. Every person with responsibility will ultimately contribute something, greater or smaller, to the construction of the plan. One person will ultimately put all the pieces together into a formal documented plan, but he will only be a collector and arranger of information supplied by others. The true facts will always be presented by everyone responsible.

Because a long-range operating plan is a complex thing to make, it is wise and necessary for the head man to be sure he has the willing cooperation of all his subordinates before asking for their help in constructing it. This means he must be enthusiastic himself and must somehow communicate his enthusiams to his helpers. This means he must be certain that all subordinates understand the need for the plan and will work to make it a success. This means many things, but above all it means that the head man must *want* a long-range operating plan himself—want it very badly—want it so the enterprise can move ever forward toward greater and greater success.

The principle is that until and unless the head man is certain that he wants a long-range operating plan, is sincere in his desire, and is enthusiastic about its possibilities for the enterprise, no long-range plan should ever be started. It will surely fail.

Quantitative Objectives

An important principle in long-range planning is for someone to know or to decide exactly where an enterprise wants to be each year for five years in the future. This is most often determined by the head man, be he called owner, president, chairman, director, or other name or title. It is impossible to plan for the future without goals being established, and proper goals cannot be determined by underlings. There are many places a business may want to be five years in the future. For instance, the business may want to be twice as big in five years as it is today. This can be measured in many ways. It may want to sell twice as many goods or services; it may want twice as much profit for every item sold; it may want to employ twice as many people, have a building twice as big, or earn twice as much money on each share of stock.

The important principle is that the head man must define exactly what he means by *twice as big*.

Since an entire long-range plan will be constructed on the goals set by the top man, it is imperative that the real goal be understood by all in the enterprise. Any time spent in being definite and precise at this point is time well spent, for failure to do so will inevitably cause much time to be wasted later.

The goals mentioned are quantitative goals—they can be expressed by numbers or amounts of currency. Later on there will be a discussion of qualitative goals, which are not expressed in numbers but are equally necessary for a successful long-range plan.

Most companies have traditional measuring sticks by which one company compares its present position within the industry with others in the industry. These traditional measures are the ones most frequently used first in declaring quantitative objectives. For example, in the shoe manufacturing industry the number of pairs of shoes manufactured or sold is usually one criterion for measuring progress; in the paper industry the number of tons of paper produced is used; railroads measure freight by the number of ton-miles. There is some purpose in using the traditional measures in establishing goals, for it is usually easy to determine where the individual enterprise is today in relation to its competition and thus to be more exact as to where the individual enterprise wants to be in five years.

The quantitative objectives set by top management must always be established *tentatively* at first. It is simple to see why. The top man may be very ambitious for the growth of his company and will thus set objectives for each of the next five years which are simply not attainable. His goal may be so unrealistic that any further effort is almost ridiculous. The goal must be tentative until all subsidiary goals are established and the results of the whole plan evaluated and priced out. For example, the paper manufacturer might want to double his sales of paper in five years. But subsidiary planning to accomplish the objective might indicate that to do so would require an addition to his plant and the purchase of much machinery for the new addition in order to produce the product which he hoped to sell. These additions would require capital in so large an amount that the cost of new capital, added to an already heavy financial investment, would make profits disappear entirely. But the planning might indicate that profits were entirely possible when sales were increased, not 100%, but only 75% in five years. With these facts before him, the president would be realistic and decide that his goal for the next five years would not be to double his sales of paper but only to increase them by 75%. The principle is that tentative goals be set at the start and modified later when planning has progressed to a point where the resulting whole picture can be seen and considered.

Planning Problems in an Unstable Economy

Tentative quantitative goals always have their roots in the economy of the country. As long as the economy is relatively stable, the tentative goals will probably need to be changed only when performance within the company fails to meet the goals. If the economy of the country or of the natural marketing district is not stable, long-range planning becomes somewhat more difficult, but by no means impossible.

An unstable economy simply means that the objectives will have to be reexamined more frequently than in a stable economy. Before any realistic quantitative goals can be established, there must be an appraisal of the economy and an appraisal of what that economy will be like three or five years hence.

If sufficient statistical background information is available, it can be useful in projecting a probable trend into the future. If no statistical information is available, or if available statistical information is not considered trustworthy, then other means must be employed by the planners to give some indication of what will probably occur in the future. Such means will probably be considered judgment based on the planners' experience.

A potentially unstable political situation also makes long-range planning difficult, but by no means impossible. The planner's job is simply to appraise the possibility of political upheaval and to make assumptions for the long-range plan which reflect the assumed situation and also the results which might be expected. A careful planner would surely make at least two assumptions, and perhaps more than two, depending upon his appraisal of the possibilities. He should establish two or more goals for his plan, each to be effective when certain anticipated events might take place.

This makes long-range planning more difficult than under a stable economy or in areas where political upheavals are not expected, but the added effort is worth putting forth in order to have a long-range plan.

One of the most important parts of a long-range plan is the establishment of controls to let management know of the progress being made toward the declared objectives. The subject of controls will be explored later.

Communication of Objectives

Having established tentative quantitative goals in terms of sales, profits, or whatever else was appropriate to the particular company, the president then notifies all his subordinates, in writing, of these tentative goals. Each subordinate then uses these tentative figures to plan his own operation. The sales manager, knowing how many units he is supposed to sell in each of the following five years, can plan on how many new salesmen he will have to hire and train, where these new salesmen should be placed geographically in relation to the existing sales force, when they must be hired, how much money it will cost for total salesman salaries, what he will need by way of increased advertising, what the general sales expense will be, how many new people will be needed in the head office to handle and service the additional sales volume, and, in fact, every item expressible in money or numbers which will be required of him in order to sell the required number of units.

The works manager, knowing the number of units he will be expected to produce in each of the next five years, can plan on how many new workers he will have to hire in each year, how many new machines he will need and when he will need them, how much additional raw material he will need and exactly when he will need it, how much additional power he must produce or purchase, and every other item which will be required for him to produce the units called for in the sales goal.

The treasurer, chief financial man, or chief accountant will not be able to go to work on the new sales goals at once. He must wait until the sales manager, the production manager, the purchasing agent, and everyone else in the organization have determined what they will each need in order to accomplish the sales goals established tentatively by the president. So he waits until all the secondary quantitative figures are made available to him. Then he can price out the whole plan. He will require each responsible person in the organization to submit a tentative budget for each of the five years. These budgets will reflect each and every item contemplated by each responsible officer and will put tentative prices on each. In this way, a total expense budget for the entire enterprise can be put together based on the tentative sales goals originally stated by the president.

At this point in the construction of the long-range plan, the accounting people have sufficient information in their possession to draw up a possible profit and loss statement for each year being considered in the plan. They have learned, for example, that the sales manager believes that for him to sell the increased units he will have to reduce his selling price per unit at the end of two years. This becomes of the utmost importance to the corporation because, if the production boss cannot reduce his costs at that same time, the profit picture may change radically and for the worse.

The accountants learn also that to finance the required equipment, additional debt borrowing will have to be consummated. This will add to the fixed charges for the period three years away, perhaps, and the fact must be known to general management before it can make a safe and useful decision to proceed with the plans.

This article will not detail all the procedures which must be carried on to construct a useful long-range plan. The purpose of some of the foregoing is to illustrate generally the interrelationship of all parts of an organization in the construction process and to illustrate the need for the establishment of *tentative* quantitative goals as a starting point. When the whole plan is "priced out" and management is satisfied with the results, then the objectives are declared in final form.

Assumptions need to be made. How large is the market for the product probably going to be in a few years, how much greater income per person is expected in five years if, indeed, per capita income is expected to increase at all, what technological improvements are expected to occur, and many other such questions have to be answered by making intelligent assumptions based on presently known facts. Intelligent assumptions *can* be made by thoughtful planners; they are an essential requirement for any successful long-range operating plan.

Qualitative Objectives: Fundamental Policies

It is relatively simple to explain and to understand the practical use of quantitative goals in long-range planning. It is not so simple to understand the use of qualitative objectives in planning. Yet the use of qualitative goals is important to a company in its long-range work. A qualitative goal is simply a statement about what the company stands for in its business life, one of the ways in which the company intends to operate or one of the things the company is trying to accomplish. It has no relation to money or to numbers. Perhaps it is easier to think of the whole lot of qualitative goals as making up the bedrock background—the credo—under which the enterprise will work.

A warning is necessary here: qualitative goals are usually such basic goals that planners and top management people are prone to consider them unnecessary to write down or to declare, and yet they are so fundamental to the success of the business that just the opposite point of view should be held.

They form the very highest and most fundamental policy of the company and will be the starting point for all the other operating policies which need to be established before the business can be efficiently operated.

Examples of Policy Declarations

An example or two will indicate the type of declaration which becomes a single qualitative objective. Almost any company would do well to declare that it was its purpose "to strive continually to keep operating expenses at the minimum level consistent with sound operating practice." Any board of trustees or directors would be fulfilling its duty to shareholders in saying this and in insisting that it be a basic policy of the company under which all other policy be written and observed. With this declaration the board would then be able to judge proposals presented to it for approval by management, and if any proposal could not be fitted under the declared policy, it would be entirely free to refuse its approval.

It can be agreed, of course, that there is no need for such a declaration; that any board and any top management would always operate to keep expense down, and that they would do so simply because any right-thinking businessman would do so instinctively. This may be true. The point is made, however, that the act of declaring the policy is in itself a good thing, and furthermore, the act of declaring the policy builds a foundation on which many more policies can be built.

Another example. All companies have employees, and it will be a good thing for a company to declare its position concerning them. This sort of declaration lets employees know exactly where they stand and can be so written as to make future employees want to join the organization. Better still, it will serve to guide and direct everyone in the organization in actions affecting employees under their control. Suppose, for instance, that the board of directors declared, "It is the objective of this company to develop a loyal, efficient, and enthusiastic organization by providing to all employees good working conditions, equitable treatment, just compensation for services, opportunity for advancement, recognition of their own personal dignity, and an understanding of the company's objectives and policies." Almost anyone would want to work under conditions like those stated.

Illustration of Secondary Policy

To illustrate how secondary policy could be written to implement this basic objective concerning employees, it may be helpful to write a few more policy statements which would ensure the carrying out of the basic objective at all levels of employees and in all parts of the enterprise. Once they were declared, everyone having personnel under his control would necessarily abide by them.

One policy might be, "It is company policy to fill vacancies by promotion or transfer from within the company." Thus the small piece of the basic objective—"opportunity for advancement"—is implemented. In answer to an applicant's question, "How do I get ahead if I come to work for your company?" the person doing the hiring would reply, "Let me read you our policy in this company." This is a perfect answer and would immediately make the company a desirable one to work for in the mind of the applicant. However, he still might not be satisfied. He might say, "How do I know you will ever remember me if I come to work for you? Do you have any written practices I can look at to be sure you can find me if the opportunity ever arises?" If all the forward planning had been properly done, the person doing the interviewing could reply, "Yes, we have practices already set up so you would be found and considered for promotion if you were qualified. Here's how it works. We keep a very complete record of every person employed by us. That record includes your skills, length of service, the work you have been doing, and a dozen other facts which would help us locate you and help us judge whether or not you were qualified for the better job. See, here it is written. It says, 'It is company practice to maintain complete records of relevant personnel information on all employees.'"

This imaginary conversation shows just one of the good things which come from having a policy and the practice to carry out that policy. It allows each boss in the organization to know what the company wants everyone to do under most circumstances which will arise. This allows managers to make decisions on a daily basis without having to go back to the boss to find out what to do. This makes for efficient operation of the enterprise.

Importance of Qualitative Objectives

The long-range operating plan insists that these qualitative objectives be considered, because without them there is not enough assurance that the organization can be kept in proper order to accommodate itself to the very ambitious *quantitative* goals which are established. To be certain that the organization can produce the required number of units called for under the plan and that it can sell these units, it is imperative that proper personnel policies, for instance, be made and that practices be established to ensure the carrying out of these policies.

Basic long-range qualitative objectives have to be declared concerning all the major parts of the business. Most companies which have already done this work have found that they can cover all pertinent areas by declaring somewhere around ten to fifteen major objectives.

The very first objective usually covers the basic purpose of the company. A shoe manufacturing company, for example, might declare its purpose (objective) to "make and sell the finest men's shoes in the world." Such an objective would tell us that the company was not interested in making very many shoes, because it says nothing about the price of the shoes to be produced. It simply says "the finest shoes." Obviously, "the finest" means just what it says, and to qualify under any such declaration the shoes would have to sell only to people who could afford to pay the highest prices in order to get the best available.

All objectives must be compatible with the basic one. The objective concerning sales would have to be something like "to sell our shoes only through the most exclusive shoe stores." This company could not hope to sell its shoes by putting them in cheap shoe stores or by offering them for sale in areas where there were very few rich men.

Some qualitative objectives can be expressed in one short sentence like the shoe manufacturer's, while others must be longer and more complete. The rule is to write each one in as concise a manner as possible but to encompass all the ideas the company wants to express. A more complex statement could be like the one published by a large American life insurance company. It reads, "Our objective is to fulfill the insurance needs of the greatest possible number of people; to keep open the way by which all who so desire can, in freedom, in confidence and in privacy, arrange secure financial benefits for themselves and those close to heart and mind." The principle is that each objective should be complete and very carefully thought out, because basic qualitative objectives are very rarely changed, and since they serve as the foundation stones for all the policy and practice which will later be developed in an enterprise, they must be absolutely correct expressions of the intent of the top company officers and of the board of directors.

Objectives should be prepared to cover all parts of the company. In addition to the basic purpose of the company (to manufacture and sell shoes, to provide and sell life insurance protection) they should cover the objectives for the people who work for the company, clerk, office boy, salesman, production workers, officers alike. An attempt should be made to express the intention of dealing ethically and within the law, to define the type of service the company wants to give to its customers, to indicate a desire to perform as efficiently as possible, to define the quality of the goods manufactured, to refer somehow to the financial strength to carry on under adverse economic conditions, and to define the company's goals toward improving the product or the service by research and development. There are other areas which could be covered, but all can usually be included in from ten to fifteen statements.

Approval of Policy Declarations

Once the basic objectives are declared, the long-range plan calls for policy and practice to be prepared and approved. Obviously no policy or practice can be tolerated which does not carry out or carry forward the basic qualitative objectives. To be sure that no policy is prepared which violates an objective, one person or group of persons is usually given the chore of examining each policy prepared and of judging its value and its content. In this way the company can be sure that every policy does indeed help to move the company toward its avowed objectives.

This work with qualitative objectives, policy, and practice is not easy. It must be done with careful thought by dedicated and well-informed people. It is not easy, but it is worth it.

Organization

A third important element in long-range planning has to do with the organization of the enterprise. Organization is the framework upon which any company is built. All planning for future activity must be predicated on having a system of organization which is tailored to the company objectives and then filling the organization with people who are competent and willing to do their assigned jobs well.

When one person is the entire business, no organizational problems exist, because the one man does as he wants to do, and success or failure comes solely from his efforts. But the minute the operation becomes too complex or too large for one man to do all the work, then organization must come into existence. One man must be the "boss" and another man must work for the boss. When more than two people are needed to carry on the affairs of the enterprise, real organization comes into being. As the number required to operate the business increases, more and more care must be exercised in defining each person's area of responsibility to avoid having two people responsible for a function or having needed functions not performed because no one knows the responsibility is his. Recognition of this fact is the beginning of organization.

Organization which allows overlapping of responsibility or allows areas where no one is responsible is poor, and will always work against successful operation of business.

It is not the purpose of this article to explore all the ramifications of organization or to do more than mention the principles of organization which have been built up over the centuries. But it must be mentioned that a thorough knowledge of these principles will give any planner a more complete knowledge of what makes business work and what makes for success in an enterprise. There are many books available for study.[1]

The purpose of this article is to show how organization fits in with successful long-range planning.

An organization structure designed for a company producing 1,000 units a week may be entirely inadequate or even entirely wrong for the same organization when it is ready to produce 10,000 units per week. For example, for a company to produce 1,000 units, it may require only 10 people on 10 machines. This requires only one supervisor, who could report directly to the president. When production is stepped up tenfold, it may require nearly 100 people to man the machines, but at about this point it requires five or six supervisors to keep the machines running at the same level of efficiency. It is probably wrong to expect the president to have all six supervisors reporting directly to him, because as the number of units produced increases, so do all the other jobs needed to run the company. Thus, instead of the president being concerned with only the additional five machine supervisors reporting to him directly, he also has many other people reporting to him from other areas. The president simply does not have enough time in a day to manage all the supervisors now reporting to him.

At this time organization requires another layer of supervision so that the president can find time to fulfill his normal function of managing. Good organization prescribes a new job, that of the machine shop superintendent, to whom the six machine supervisors now report. The new superintendent coordinates the work of the six machine supervisors and reports directly to the president. Thus coordination in the machine area, which is vital to smooth operation, is taken care of adequately. The president is not burdened with day-to-day coordination in this area and can do his own top managerial work successfully.

Long-range planning demands that situations such as the one just described be anticipated far enough in advance so that when proper progress has been made toward the quantitative goals already established, a definite action takes place. If it is not done this way, if the need for the extra job is not anticipated, it will be detrimental to the further objectives, and the whole plan may be thrown into trouble.

Planning Organizational Patterns

Many situations which arise in growing and expanding companies require forward planning along organizational lines. For example, when will the small, tightly knit group which started the business need extra help to keep the ex-

[1] Paul E. Holden, Lounsbury S. Fish, and Hubert L. Smith, *Top Management Organization and Control,* McGraw-Hill Book Company, New York, 1951; Alvin Brown, *Organization: A Formulation of Principle,* Hibbert Printing Company, New York, 1945; *Planning and Developing the Company Organization Structure,* American Management Association, New York, 1952.

pansion moving? When will the business require someone to be responsible for research and development? When will a full-time financial man be required? In how many years will the business be large enough to afford its own legal staff? Similar questions need to be answered and tentative plans made at once, so that the organization will be ready to receive these new jobs at the proper time.

It is suggested that the present organization be charted as a first step in forward planning. Once this is done, it will become easier to look into the future and make whatever plans appear to be proper. It is suggested that a new chart be drawn which will show exactly what is needed in, for example, five years. The quantitative objectives will have already been established. Those objectives will indicate what is needed as an organization in the future. Only these questions need to be asked by the planner: "In order to accomplish these objectives, what must we provide for in terms of men and machines, and how shall we align those men (jobs) to get the best results? Should the added workmen have one supervisor, or two, or three? To whom shall each be responsible, and to whom should their boss report?" Once the answers to these questions have been determined, a new organization chart can be prepared. This new chart will be tentative only, but it will have approximate dates on it showing when new jobs must be created and also showing the organizational placement of each.

The tentative organization chart should not be made public. It belongs only to the planner and to the chief executive officer. But it should be used frequently by each. In any growing business there are frequent pressures to alter the existing organization. Strong bosses are always trying to enlarge their areas of responsibility. Strong bosses frequently try to persuade the president to change the organization in order to make them even stronger by putting more people under their control. This is normal in business, and it is not wrong—that is, unless the change of organization requested at today's point in time will seriously damage the tentative future organization already decided upon by the president. If a change of organization now will not contribute toward the long-range organization, it should not be allowed.

The principle is that all organizational changes requested or contemplated should be reviewed and considered in the light of what the organization must be in the future in order to accomplish the previously agreed-upon objectives. If the contemplated change will be a step toward the future organization, then it can be allowed; if it will not advance the future organization or will hinder it, it should not be allowed. Organization changes made only to overcome a temporary situation are not usually helpful to the business in the long run. An ideal organization for five years in the future, well understood and agreed upon by the president, is an integral part of a long-range operating plan.

Controlling the Long-range Plan

It is wrong to expect any long-range plan to be perfect in all areas, particularly in its first few years. Indeed, it is probably not possible for any long-range plan to be entirely accurate with regard to actual happenings in any year. To learn where and when actual performance is *not* on the long-range target is the function of the controls.

Going back to definitions, "controls" means the examination of performance, the analysis of any variances which appear, the notification to one in authority that the variances exist, and the course of action to be followed because the variances do exist.

It may be helpful to consider the several parts of the definition and determine how such controls may be established. A hypothetical plan and situation will be helpful.

A shoe manufacturing company has determined through its long-range plan that it wants (and expects) to produce and sell 12,000 pairs of shoes in the year. Since it manufactures shoes of all kinds for all seasons of the year, the planners expect sales to be very stable at 1,000 pairs each month. The planners know from experience that they must have from 1,500 to 2,000 pairs of shoes in stock at all times in order to be certain to make deliveries on time, even though they might experience temporary work stoppages for any number of reasons.

Controls are established covering all the areas which contribute to these goals. For example, a control is established on sales, one on production, and one on inventory. In every month, therefore, a report is made to the proper authority. Such a report for the fifth month might be as follows (figures representing pairs of shoes):

Sales expected this month	1,000
Sales (actual) this month	960
Sales expected first 5 months	5,000
Sales made first 5 months	5,100
Production expected this month	1,000
Production (actual) this month	1,200
Production expected first 5 months	5,000
Production (actual) first 5 months	3,500
Inventory expected at end of 5 months	1,500–2,000
Actual inventory at end of 5 months	400

There are variances indicated in this report. These variances require analysis. Some corrective action needs to be taken at once, or, at least, some corrective action needs to be considered lest the trends shown continue. A study of this simple report tells management that something is wrong with the five months' production and something is wrong with the inventory. Further examination of the facts shows that production for the past month has been greater by 200 pairs of shoes than was expected. Sales results are substantially on target and present no problem. Analysis of these facts indicates that production in previous months has caused all the variances. It has been consistently lower than forecast in each month except the last one, when 200 extra pairs of shoes were produced. Further examination shows that six machines were producing poorly in the previous months but were now back in full production again, and an appraisal of the situation gives every promise that the machines will continue to produce at slightly above normal production. Since sales are expected to continue as planned, and since production is expected to be slightly over that expected, the planner might be entirely safe in recommending that nothing needs to be done at this point in time inasmuch as the overproduction expected will build up the inventory to a satisfactory level in the next few months.

If, on the other hand, examination shows that the 200 extra pairs of shoes produced in the last month were a result of some luck, and if expectations are that the overproduction will not continue, then an entirely different recommendation has to be made. The inventory is desperately low, and it appears that it will not increase in normal operation. So a recommendation is made that overtime work is necessary to build up the inventory to a safe level again, or that something else must be done to guarantee better production in order to build up the inventory. Since previous planning also has predicted a profit picture satisfactory to top management, and since overtime will change the predicted profit results, further study will have to be carried on and further recommendations made.

This simple hypothetical case points out the need for planning—present planning. Its relationship to long-range planning is clear, however. If the goals for this year are not made, the predicted increase in sales and production probably will not be made in the years to come unless some drastic (and probably very expensive) action is taken in the future to attain the progress wanted by top management.

Controls must be established for every critical factor in the plan—controls which will point out failures *early* and thus allow proper corrective action to be taken as soon as possible, and early enough so that the general progress will not be halted or impaired. Persistent failure to make sales goals might point at the need for replacing the sales manager; regular failure of production might result in further exploration of the work force and the machinery involved. Perhaps a change in organization may be indicated.

One of the most vital control points is the profit picture. In constructing the long-range plan, many assumptions have been made. For example, a profit on each pair of shoes sold has been assumed. It is imperative that strict controls be established which will tell management of anything which occurs which changes the profit assumptions. It is as important to learn of any increase in profit as it is to learn of any decrease in profit. An increase in profit, generally a rare circumstance, will probably change a lot of plans for the future years.

Keeping the Plan Up to Date

No one can look into the future—even as little as five years in the future—with any certainty of being correct in all areas. Most assumptions are based on the probable economic situation existing in the future. Since so many assumptions stem from basic economic assumptions, it becomes imperative for planners to be sure the basic economy is actually performing as assumed. In areas of relatively stable economy, planners are able to predict the future with some certainty of being correct, but even in stable areas there is always a possibility of gross error. In areas where the economy is less stable, the task of predicting the future is more difficult. Because of the importance of economic assumptions to the whole enterprise, control points must be very carefully established and watched over with regularity. The value of currency as expressed in its purchasing power is a basic unit which requires watching under some controls. Any strong inflationary trend will be observed quickly by planners, who will be able to change plans fast in order to protect their company against loss, or perhaps to capitalize on the trend and make the company move ahead faster.

Political upheavals may occur in some areas in the future. A carefully made long-range plan anticipates possible political upheaval in the future and *makes plans now* to be put into effect when and if the political change occurs. The competitive advantage to a company which has plans already formulated for use when a suspected contingency arises is obvious and most important. The way to make forward plans like this is exactly the same as for the original long-range plan: to try to anticipate what will probably happen to the economy and to make alternate plans which will be workable under those conditions.

A long-range plan sets out objectives for the next five years and allows management to decide exactly what it wants to accomplish in each of those five years. But once decided, there is still time to change goals and objectives in light of happenings as they occur. Once each year the long-range plan must be carefully reviewed by management. At this review period, the results of the past year are evaluated, particularly as they affect the plan for the four years yet remaining. It is at this review period that the quantitative objectives are considered for the next four years. Are they still feasible? Are they still possible? Are they still desirable from a management viewpoint? If they are all these things (and until a company gains experience in long-range planning, they probably are not), the original plan can be continued, with management setting new objectives to be added to the plan for the fifth year in the future.

If the objectives for the four years remaining on the plan at the review period are not satisfactory to management in light of happenings during the past year, they are changed and new objectives declared for the fifth year in the future.

A five-year plan is constructed each and every year either using the old four-year quantitative objectives, if they are still useful, or changing any or all of the quantitative objectives previously declared and adding an entirely new set of objectives for the fifth year in the future. Thus, there is always a plan for a full five-year period.

The once-a-year review of the long-range plan need not be its only review. If conditions change radically (unusual economic change, political upheaval), it would be in order to review the plan at once. Changes should be made whenever indicated by events.

One thought needs to be repeated. A long-range plan is difficult to produce, but its value is so great that no enterprise which wishes to grow and prosper should ever allow the difficulty to stop it from making the effort. A carefully worked-out long-range plan with adequate controls goes a long way toward making the success of an enterprise almost certain.

SUPERVISION

Amory A. Pakenham-Walsh, M.A., F.A.C.C.A., F.C.W.A.

The Task of Supervision

Employing Supervisors. A business undertaking may be run by one man, by a few individuals, or by a large number of individuals. In a one-man business there is no one to be supervised. When the man who operates his own business wants more work done than he can do himself, he employs others to help. Whether he owns the business or is responsible for it, he will wish to see that the employees do their assigned work in the right way. Watching over others at work is supervising.

In large undertakings with many employees, the owner-manager or the manager responsible to the owner has to arrange that the employees are supervised by some of their number, who are called supervisors. These supervisors are selected for their skill in the arts of supervision and for their knowledge of the work to be done. Skill in the art of supervising is the more important. In part it comes from innate abilities. In part it comes from education and training, for no matter how gifted a man may be as a leader, his ability to lead a team is significantly increased by appropriate training.

A supervisor must know, or be provided with means of knowing, what is required; that is, he has to be able to recognize proper performance. Where he has been promoted to supervisory status from the ranks of workers, he knows how to do the work himself and can therefore guide his subordinates. If, however, the subordinates have been properly trained in their tasks, they will not need to seek guidance from the supervisor on the work itself; rather, they will look to the supervisor when exceptional conditions arise, and they will also expect his help with personal difficulties. Although these resorts

---

Mr. Pakenham-Walsh is Lecturer in Management at Trinity College, University of Dublin.

to the supervisor might make only marginal demands on his time, they are effective pointers to the characteristics of supervisory work.

The Nature of Supervisory Work

To see that the right work is done in the right way calls for:

1. Targets in terms of quantity and quality
2. Standards of performance by which the work to be done by men and machines can be planned and controlled
3. Planning the work, which involves:
   a. Measuring the quantity and quality of the output from men and machines
   b. Measuring the input of materials, services, stores, such as fuel, lubricants, cotton waste, expendable tools, etc., and hours of labor against the standards of performance set

Targets and Standards of Performance. The targets and the standards of performance may be set for the supervisor by his manager, or they may be partly supplied and partly set by the supervisor himself. To the extent that the supervisor sets them, he is himself acting as a manager.

In general it may be said that, to secure cooperative working by all members of the group or team being supervised, group targets are superior to individual targets.

Planning and Control. The functions of planning and control extend to motivating subordinates to proper performance and to securing and maintaining the conditions in which this proper performance is reasonable and possible.

Successful motivation of subordinates depends upon the supervisor's skill in communicating to them in a way which they understand and which takes account of their attitudes, background, expectations, and training.

The conditions necessary to proper performance of the tasks set include:

1. Sufficient and regular supply of the means of production (materials, fuel, power, services, etc.)
2. Proper working order of the machines
3. Observance of measures and rules for the safety of the workers and protection of facilities
4. Attention to physical conditions of the workplace, i.e., to humidity, temperature, shelter, ventilation, light, etc.
5. Attention to the psychological needs of the workers

Communicating. The supervisor is a link between the members of his team and higher managers. In fulfilling his link role the supervisor might seem to be faced with a conflict between loyalty to his subordinates and loyalty to his superiors. This need not and will not be the case if organizational procedures are correctly drawn and if there is, at all levels, a real understanding of objectives.

In this connection, a main role of the supervisor will be to translate instructions from those above him into terms those below him can understand. For example, he may be adept at translating instructions received verbally into visual form. This is a great advantage, for nothing travels faster than a visual signal.

Communication Upward. The supervisor will also receive complaints and suggestions from those below. Some may be dealt with by the supervisor himself. For the others, be becomes the spokesman for his team, unless there is an officially appointed representative (other than the supervisor) for handling complaints and grievances. The representative method is the better arrangement. Where it exists, the supervisor should, of course, be approached by the workers' representative before the representative presents complaints to a higher level of management.

Employees' ideas for improving methods of work, safety, and other working conditions are a valuable source of innovation and production economies. Unless there is an explicit mechanism (for example, an official suggestions scheme), the supervisor should welcome, and pass up where appropriate, all suggestions, including those referring to his own supervisory practices.

Communication Downward. Three kinds of instruction will reach the supervisor:

1. General instructions, e.g., to keep the factory tidy, to look after the health of workers, to spread production loads as evenly as possible
2. Specific instructions, e.g., to produce 200 units on Tuesday, to open the factory door at 8 o'clock every working day
3. Instructions having general and specific elements, e.g., not to put female workers on heavy jobs

To the extent that instructions are general, the supervisor himself must decide the specific ways in which they should be implemented, for example, whether to have the floor cleaned once, twice, or three times each day. These things are left to his discretion, and the decisions he makes and specific instruction he gives constitute the supervisor's discretionary work. Discretionary work is management work.

To deal in terms of our examples, the work of carrying out the instruction not to employ women on heavy work has a discretionary element, in deciding what is heavy work. The class of worker excluded, however, is completely specific, namely, female.

The whole of an instruction to open the factory door at 8 o'clock every working day is specific. To carry out this kind of instruction involves the supervisor in prescribed work; though, it should be noted, whether the supervisor physically opens the door himself or instructs another to do it is left to his discretion.

To the extent that he may exercise discretion, the supervisor is given management powers. In doing prescribed work, however, he is simply acting as an agent for his superior.

Management. To carry out the tasks described as supervisory work calls for an ability to organize and a knowledge of, and sensitivity to, human nature. These essentials of managing are less easily acquired than technical knowledge and skill in the job being supervised. This is why supervisors require education and training in the management aspects of work and why it is not sufficient to select supervisory personnel on standards of technical proficiency alone.

For the supervisor, attention must be focused, not on the goods and services being produced, but on the human beings producing them. When the planning and control aspects of supervisory work are being properly performed, a supervisor should only exceptionally have to watch the technical operations of his subordinates. The time he has free from planning and control is better spent on their personal problems. The workers will, in turn, respond with good work. They will not respond as effectively if they sense the supervisor watching the work itself.

This approach assumes, and indeed requires, that the workers are properly trained in the technical aspects of the tasks they are expected to perform. To the extent that a supervisor must himself train his subordinates, he is not doing management work, but teaching work. Such teaching is better done away from the job. This problem will be further discussed in the final section.

Discipline. The maintenance of discipline by the supervisor has been left for discussion last. Given group targets, planning, and proper attention to the workers' physical and psychological needs, the maintenance of discipline should make only marginal demands on a supervisor's time and energy. Nonetheless, lapses will occur: workers will arrive late; they will fail to observe regulations about hygiene and safety; and they will become involved in disputes with one another. The lapses will be minimized if the supervisor deals with them promptly, firmly, and justly. He will be assisted in this by having available a published and well-understood code of suitable disciplinary measures, for example, fines, layoff from work, etc. And his stature in the eyes of his subordinates will depend on his own proper handling of reprimands; for example, he will always conduct a disciplinary interview with the offender in private.

Supervisory Behavior

High production levels can be obtained by technically competent, job-centered, and insensitive managers and supervisors. It has been found, however, in industrially developed countries like Great Britain and the United States, that the work groups or teams supervised in this way are among the most hostile to management and likely to indulge in showdowns and strikes on minor grievances.[1]

The reverse may also obtain. It is not sufficient for managers and supervisors to rely entirely upon building up good attitudes and providing job satisfaction. Many business undertakings in developed countries which can be credited with these qualities nevertheless are not highly productive because they lack the cohesion and determination which come from a scientific approach to performance.

Supervisory Training and Education. To obtain good performance from his unit or work group, a supervisor undoubtedly needs training and guidance in the application of the managing techniques of planning and control and performance goals. But he will not be successful in applying these techniques unless he has also been educated in the even more basic conception and appreciation of human nature. The response from his subordinates will depend on the confidence and interest he displays in them as men and women quite as much as on his competence to organize and control the jobs they are doing.

It is imperative, therefore, in a training scheme for supervisors, to make

[1] See Rensis Likert, *New Patterns of Management*, McGraw-Hill Book Company, New York, 1961, passim, but especially pp. 44–60.

sure that there is a responsive change in the behavior of the supervisor and that the effect of training is not manifested merely by a change in his verbal response.[2]

Supervisory behavior which has the most favorable impact is that which is seen to be consistent and which is governed by sincerity and principle.

The Making of a Supervisor

Selection. It has been emphasized that, to secure good performance from the group or team, the man or woman appointed as supervisor must have the right personal qualities and appropriate training.

The personal qualities required are intelligence, integrity, moral courage, vitality, and an interest in people.

Training. Required training includes instruction in:

1. Instructing others
2. Job methods
3. Job safety
4. Planning and control
5. Relations with other people, e.g., subordinates and superiors
6. Relations with institutions within the undertaking, e.g., committees, shop stewards
7. Relations with people and institutions outside the undertaking, e.g., customers, trade unions

To be really effective, training should take place away from the job so that the supervisor can learn the best methods. On-the-job training, by "sitting beside Harry," possibly inheriting out-of-date methods and unproductive practices, should be rejected. The same applies to the training of workers. As far as possible, the instruction of subordinates should not fall on the supervisor. This is work for a trainer, not for a supervisor.

Education. To maintain his or her performance, the supervisor must have the opportunity to grow. The opportunity to grow is best provided by facilities for education—education beyond the horizons of his supervisory job. As well as providing facilities (for example, time off, financial support), management should encourage the supervisor to make use of them by holding out to him prospects of promotion.

Promotion from Within. Just as the prospect of promotion is a condition of good supervisory performance, so it is a condition of good performance from the supervisors' subordinates. For the subordinates the prospect should be to become supervisors.

As far as possible, therefore, supervisors should be selected from among the employees of the undertaking. To this end, those likely to become good supervisors should be sought and encouraged to develop. Their development can be promoted by educational facilities and by the opportunity to work as deputy or assistant to the supervisor.

[2] Evidence of a change in verbal response without significant change in behavioral response can be obtained by comparing the supervisor's answers to a set of questions concerning his supervisory work with the anwers from his subordinates to the same set of questions concerning the felt impact of his supervisory work on them. See Likert, *op. cit.*, p. 91.

INVENTORY CONTROL

Albert Battersby

Reasons for Holding Inventory

Purpose of Stock. The purpose of any stock is to save money. A shopkeeper who did not keep stocks on his shelves would lose customers through poor service; a factory with no stock of an essential component would lose money through idleness. Stocks can therefore increase efficiency—but if not properly controlled they can also reduce it.

An individual stock center always occurs between two processes—an input process and an output process.

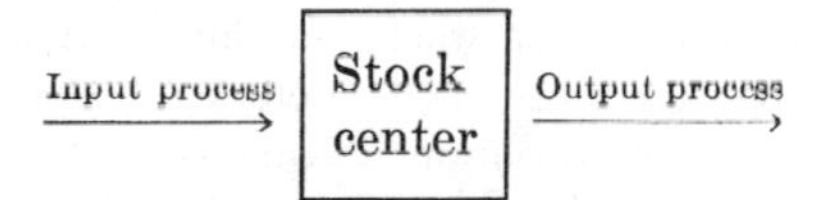

The input, for instance, might be the supplies a shopkeeper receives from the wholesaler, and the output would be his sales. In a factory, the input might be the production of a bolt and the output its use in assembling a gearbox.

The stock has a definite purpose: it enables the two processes to work independently of each other.

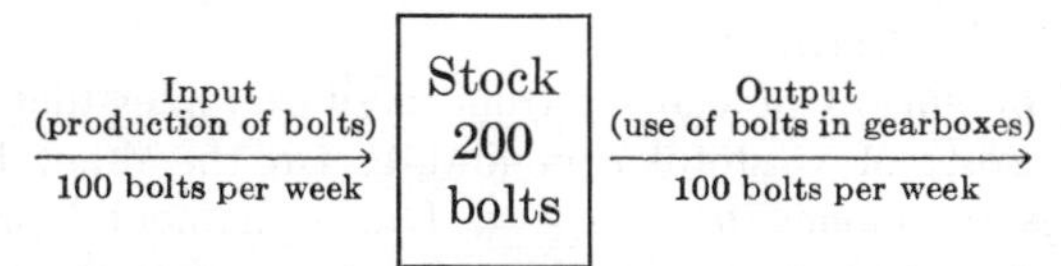

A stock of 200 bolts will allow the process of assembly to go on for two weeks after the production of bolts has stopped. This function is called *uncoupling* the two processes, and the extent to which a stock uncouples two processes

---

Mr. Battersby is Senior Lecturer at The Cranfield Work Study School, Cranfield, Bedford, England.

depends on its size. In practice, the uncoupling function is usually more complicated than in the simple example given here.

Furthermore, individual stock centers are connected together, the output process of one becoming the input of another, forming in all the total *inventory* of stocks in a company.

One reason for poor inventory control is a lack of awareness of this uncoupling effect of a stock. Systems installed arbitrarily without an understanding of their mechanism can lead either to excessive stocks or to violent fluctuations in stock levels.

Types of Stock. The concept of a stock as something which uncouples two processes leads to the classification shown in the following table.

Type of stock	Processes		Effect of shortage
	Input	Output	
Finished goods	Final inspection	Sale to customer	Loss of profit and goodwill
Work in progress	Manufacturing operation	Manufacturing operation	Interruption in smooth flow of material; some machines idle
Raw materials	Receipt from suppliers	Unpacking, inspection	Inability to produce; whole plant idle
Spare parts	Receipt from suppliers	Replacement of failed part	Delay in repairing machines which have broken down
Cash in hand	Receipt from bank	Cash payments	Loss of goodwill and discounts; possible interruption of labor and supplies

There are many other types of stock, not included in this list, which can be given only passing mention here. They include:

1. Stocks which smooth out variations in quality
2. "Speculative" stocks, which absorb fluctuations in price
3. "Strategic" stocks, which aim to uncouple a country from the shortages of war, e.g., the U.S government's stockpiles of tin, molybdenum, and other metals
4. "Negative" stocks, i.e., available storage space
5. Stocks of energy, as in a heat-storage cooker, an electric battery, or the reservoir of a hydroelectric station

Problem of Balance. One can see from these examples that lack of stock can lead to many sorts of wasteful expenditure. On the other hand, to provide stock also calls for money to be spent. The fundamental problem of control is to balance these two conflicting sets of costs so that the total cost is made as small as possible. Good stock control is concerned, then, with *quantities, times,* and *costs.*

Information Required for Inventory Control

Quantities. The pattern of demand is first settled by analyzing past sales to customers. This is the *output* process, and the amounts sold are almost certain to vary in a random manner from one sales period to another, possibly showing seasonal and long-term trends as well. The records of sales must be studied over several periods so that *expected* and *maximum* rates of demand may be deduced, either by exercising judgment or by using more formal statistical analysis.

The *input* process is "replenishment by the supplier"; it may also vary randomly, but in a different way from the output. The amount of the replenishment will have been determined by the order placed on the supplier and is therefore a fixed quantity. The time between placing the order and receiving the goods, called the *lead time,* may vary; here again, estimates of the expected and maximum lead times must be obtained by examining past records.

Example. The weekly sales of heating oil from an oil storage depot were 107, 54, 99, 77, 89, 74, 66, 81, 92, 86, 82, 61, and 72 tons. The average or expected sales are 80 tons; the maximum sales are estimated statistically as 125 tons. The depot is replenished by a 120-ton barge; the last seven deliveries took 12, 9, 10, 6, 11, 14, and 8 days. The average or expected lead time is 10 days, the maximum is 18 days; this is again deduced statistically as the highest figure which might occur if the series were continued for a very long time.

Past records of the stock level itself are less important than those of the input and output processes, but they may be useful in assessing the frequency with which the stock held has proved to be inadequate in the past.

Times. As the simple example on page 115 has shown, the uncoupling effect can be taken as meaning that a stock "buys" time. One most important figure for the stock controller is the *lead time* already mentioned; it is defined as the interval between deciding to place an order and the receipt of the goods. The lead time may include several elements, e.g., the delivery time itself as well as administrative time.

The *delivery time* is the interval between the receipt of the order by the supplier and delivery of the goods to the customer. It may be a variable quantity, in which case one will need enough figures to analyze the nature of the variation.

Administrative time comprises the time to select the supplier, decide the size of the replenishment, and prepare and send the order. It also includes any time which may be needed to unpack the goods on receipt, inspect them, and transfer them to the storage point, and deal with any accompanying paper work.

It is advisable before putting in a stock control system to examine these times carefully to see whether they can be reduced. Shorter lead times mean smaller capital investment in stocks; in one case, a lead time of eight weeks was halved by removing delays in administration. Consequently, the capital tied up in stock was also reduced by about half. The remaining time which needs to be considered is the *review time,* which is the interval between successive reviews of the stock level. In many cases it will be the same as the sales period—for example, if sales records are accumulated over weekly intervals, the stock level will also, in general, be checked once a week.

Costs. Costs come under two main headings: those associated with holding the inventory (stockholding costs) and those which its possession enables us to avoid.

Stockholding costs themselves divide into two classes. First come those associated with the physical processes of storage—rent, rates, taxes, and depreciation on the storage space; the cost of racks, bins, pallets, tanks, and handling machinery; the wages of storekeepers, clerks, and laborers; insurance; the cost of deterioration and obsolescence; heating, lighting, and maintaining the storage area. Then comes the cost of the capital invested in inventory, which may be interpreted as a cost of borrowing, an "opportunity" cost from alternative investment, or a control figure set as a matter of policy. It may lie anywhere between 5 and 30%, being usually higher in smaller companies. Under the second heading—costs *avoided* by having stocks—are shortage costs and some administrative costs. Shortage costs depend on the consequences of not having stock available when it is needed; for finished products they may arise from loss of customer goodwill or the need to supply from an expensive alternative source. Shortage of raw materials or work in progress may cause all or part of a factory to stop production. It is obvious that shortage costs are often hard to measure, and it is sometimes possible to use an arbitrary risk level instead.

Administrative costs which vary with the inventory level are ordering costs and review costs. Larger inventories can mean a lower frequency of ordering (or for work in progress, less frequent production changes). They also mean that stock levels may be reviewed at longer intervals with consequent saving.

Policy Figures. When accurate costs cannot be obtained (such as shortage costs), or when their exact definition is controversial (as for the rate of return on capital), managerial estimates will be needed. These estimates can then be widely applied—for example, a single decision to accept at 0.1% risk of running out of stock may be spread over 10,000 items in the knowledge that at any one time there would be a shortage of 10 items. When single estimates are widely applied in this way, they may fairly be called "policy" figures.

The Two-bin or S,s System

Any system of inventory control must answer at least two questions:

When do we re-order?
How much do we order at a time?

Each of these questions is answered by finding the best compromise between two conflicting goals: on the one hand, to avoid shortages or heavy administrative costs, and on the other, to keep stockholding costs as low as possible.

Two main systems of stock control have been devised to answer these questions. The first is called the Two-bin or S,*s* System: it uses a Re-ordering ***S,s*** Level, *s*, and a Re-ordering Quantity, S. The second, called the Constant-cycle or S,*t* System, is described later.

Re-ordering Level **(*ROL*)**. If the lead time for replenishment is, say, two weeks, then a new order must be placed when the total available stock is equal to two weeks' supply. It is obviously prudent to take two weeks' consumption at the *maximum* rate of sales which can be calculated statistically. In the heating oil example quoted previously, we had "expected" and "maximum" sales of 80 and 125 tons respectively in one week. The expected sales for two weeks are obviously $2 \times 80 = 160$ tons, but maximum weekly sales are not likely to occur in two successive weeks, so we cannot use $2 \times 125 = 250$ tons as our estimate. Instead, we take the excess of maximum over expected sales for one week, i.e., 45 tons, and multiply it by the square root of the number of weeks ($\sqrt{2} = 1.4$; $45 \times 1.4 = 63$ tons). Adding the answer (which is the "safety" or "buffer" stock for two weeks) to the expected sales gives the maximum sales for two weeks, $160 + 63 = 223$ tons, and this is the Re-ordering Level. The same can be done for any number of weeks.

Re-ordering Quantity (ROQ). Orders for large quantities of a material need only be placed infrequently, whereas for smaller quantities the orders have to be placed at shorter intervals. In the latter case the costs associated with ordering will be high, but the smaller average stocks which ensue incur lower inventory costs.

The economic Re-ordering Quantity is calculated so that the sum of the ordering and stockholding costs is minimized. The method of calculation is to multiply the administrative cost of placing an order by twice the rate of sales and then divide the result by the cost of holding stock. (The latter cost is often conveniently expressed as the product of the percentage stockholding cost and the unit value of the stock item, divided by 100.) The square root of the number obtained in this way is the ROQ. It is important that all the numbers used should be expressed in consistent units of measurement. If the stockholding cost is, say, 10% per *year*, then *annual* sales must be used; if the ordering cost is in pounds sterling, the unit value of stock must be in pounds also.

Example. The heating oil already discussed costs £10 a ton. At 20% per year, the stockholding cost is £2 per ton per year. The total fixed cost associated with a single replenishment order, regardless of its size, is £4. The annual rate of sales is forecast as 3,600 tons. Twice this rate multiplied by £4 is 28,800, which, when divided by the stockholding cost, gives 14,400. The square root is 120, so the ROQ is 120 tons.

Returning to the two questions at the beginning of this section, we now have the answers:

When do we re-order?—When the stock level falls to 233 tons.
How much do we order at a time?—120 tons.

More elaborate versions of these rules have been developed to suit special cases, but the basic principles remain the same.

The Constant-cycle or S,t System

One drawback of the two-bin system is that it requires stock levels to be continuously reviewed. It is more convenient to inspect the stock at fixed intervals or cycles, and this has given rise to the Constant-cycle System.

The answer to the question "When do we re-order?" is given simply as "Once a month" or "Every day" or "On Monday mornings," that is, in some way which describes a *constant cycle* of re-ordering.

There are various rules for determining the size of the replenishment, a common one being to restore the stock level to some predetermined value. This must be high enough to cover the uncertainties of demand during the lead time, as in the two-bin system, but with one important difference: the lead time must now include the review time—that is, the length of the re-ordering cycle.

Example. Suppose that in the heating oil case already discussed, we decide to review the stock and re-order every four weeks: the lead time goes up from two weeks to six weeks. Using the rule given on page 119, we find the safety stock to be $\sqrt{6} \times 45 = 110$ tons. The expected demand during the review interval is $4 \times 80 = 320$ tons, so the "target" stock is $110 + 320 = 430$ tons.

The amount to be ordered is then simply "Enough to restore the present stock level (including replenishments in transit) to 430 tons."

A constant-cycle system will always require a higher average stock, and therefore more working capital, than the corresponding two-bin system. The increase can be calculated and offset against any saving in administrative (review) costs.

BIBLIOGRAPHY

In a short survey, it is possible to deal with only the most elementary problems of inventory control. Of the references cited below, Battersby, Brown, and Magee present more comprehensive reviews. Fetter and Dalleck deal admirably with variable lead times and problems of controlling whole inventories as distinct from individual stocks. Colcutt and coworkers described an interesting case study which released £100,000 of capital.

Battersby, Albert: 1962. *A Guide to Stock Control,* British Institute of Management and Pitman Publishing Corporation, London.

Brown, Robert G.: 1959. *Statistical Forecasting for Inventory Control,* McGraw-Hill Book Company, New York.

Colcutt, R. H., Bansbury, Massy, and Ward: 1959. "A Method of Fixing Desirable Stock Levels and of Stock Control," *Operational Research Quarterly,* June issue, p. 81.

Fetter, Robert B., and Winston C. Dalleck: 1961. *Decision Models for Inventory Management,* Richard D. Irwin, Inc., Homewood, Ill.

Magee, John F.: 1958. *Production Planning and Inventory Control,* McGraw-Hill Book Company, New York.

START-UP PROBLEMS OF NEW INDUSTRIAL PRODUCTION

B. W. Berenschot

Investment in new production facilities and purchases of new plants and equipment is of considerable importance. Capital outlays have risen steadily over the last five years. It is estimated that the American industry invests close to $14 billion a year in modernization and expansion of manufacturing facilities.

In this study, the discussion will be focused on the start-up of new plants. The problems and situations in major expansions and in the start of the production of new products are similar. In this respect, it is interesting that 12% of the sales volume in industrial products in the United States is for items that were not in production four years ago.

Why Is a Start-up Different?

The problems in starting up new operations are different from the normal activities in an industrial organization. The start-ups happen infrequently and are of a project nature for the expanding company. In all phases of the start-up we see unusual activities:

- The labor market is investigated.
- The goods to be produced in the facility are selected.
- The company has to buy land in a new community.
- New (and better) machinery has to be selected and ordered.
- New distribution facilities and procedures have to be established.

For many of these activities, experts are engaged. These men are special-

---

The late Professor Berenschot (he died in January, 1964) was a Fellow of the International Academy of Management and President of the Fédération Européenne des Associations des Conseils en Organisation.

ists in a particular activity and sometimes in the particular geographical area that the company is interested in.

It is typical of a start-up project that a substantial number of people are involved. These people have to work together. Initially, they do not (or hardly) know each other, and as they are not familiar with the approaches and methods of operation of the others, adjustments have to be made.

Even more disturbing is the fact that the team changes in accordance with program stages during the project. In the very beginning the feasibility will be studied with emphasis on product selection, sales forecasts, and legal considerations. In the later stages of production, the completion of construction and the organization and training of personnel are more likely to get attention, the project team being completely different.

Difficulties in Planning

The constantly changing nature of the project makes it difficult to keep the partners in the changing team organized. It is not surprising that, in specific situations, inefficiencies can be identified easily. Many of these are related to activities that were identified too late during the preparatory stages:

- Inadequate survey of the labor market, resulting in difficulties in hiring desirable personnel
- Insufficient preparation of maintenance procedures—a problem which is sometimes not resolved in the first years of operation
- Improper selection of personnel, resulting in low efficiencies, high turnover, etc.
- Inadequate stipulations with the contractor on the dates for intermediate stages of the construction and equipment installation

This indicates a need for definition of all activities in the preparation of the start-up, a clear statement of the responsibilities of the team members, and a means of controlling the interrelations between the activities of the members.

Techniques used for the above-mentioned identification are similar to the planning and scheduling methods known as PERT (Program Evaluation and Review Techniques) and CPM (Critical Path Method). These have been extensively used in recent years to control activities in large projects.

Such methods of planning will show the relations between the numerous required activities. The advantage of being able to see these relations and to schedule and adjust the activities accordingly is even more important than a highly sophisticated program for each of the activities.

The Four Phases

The start-up project can be divided into four distinctively different phases.

1. *Orientation*. The original idea to start a new operation is investigated. In this phase, the scope of the project is determined.

2. *Concept*. In this phase, the financial feasibility of starting an operation in an area (state or country) is studied in detail. This includes a prediction about expected sales volume, product mix, size of the plant, etc.

3. *Design*. In the previous phases, the design of the plant (building,

equipment, personnel) was specified in general terms. Now, the preparation for construction starts with a design in detail, and the organization is specified. In this phase, expenditures for the investment start climbing.

4. *Construction and Preparation.* The plant is under construction, equipment will be installed, and personnel will be selected, trained, and organized. This phase ends with a pilot production stage.

The relations between the activities in these four phases are shown in Figures 1 to 4. Such charts cannot be complete; they present only a general and simplified picture of the interactions involved. A detailed network of the preparation activities would be different for each specific case, as would the importance of the elements that are mentioned.

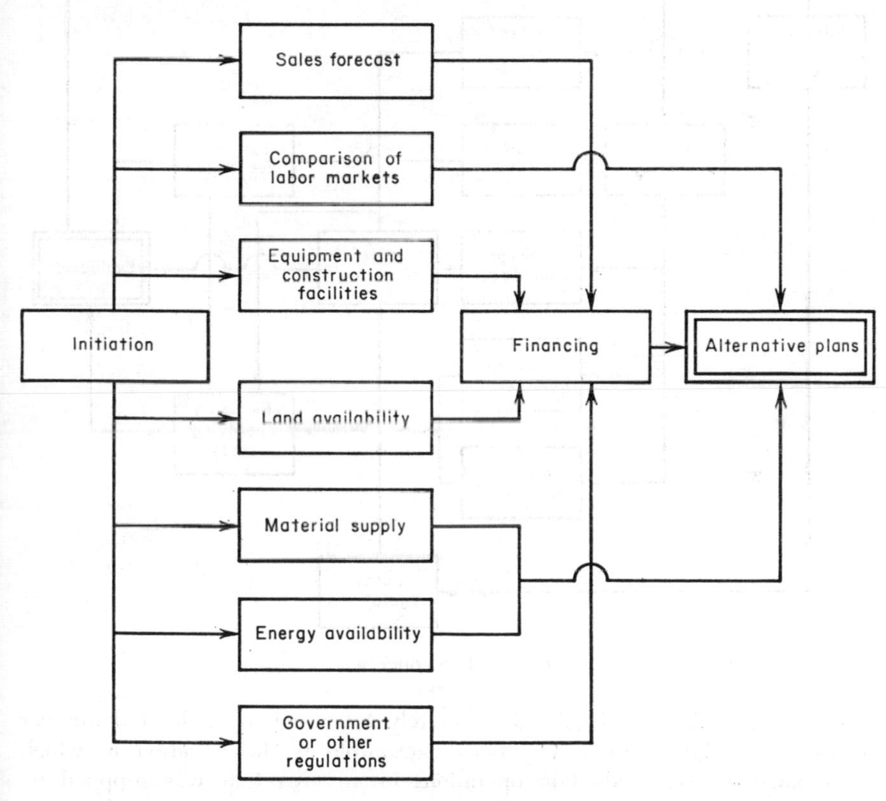

FIG. 1. Orientation.

Orientation. The project might start with any of the activities in the diagram:

- Increases in regional sales
- Material availability (e.g., mining industry)
- Government regulations (tariff changes, EEC)

The decision to start orientation is made at a top level in the organization. It will be followed by assignments at various other high levels to collect information of a general nature.

Almost always, these first informative steps are kept secret, and the objectives of the orientation will be indicated to a small number of people. If only for the sake of competition, the company will not publish its intentions in this stage.

Some of the more general aspects of the information needed can be obtained only from public agencies, especially if the orientation concerns a geographical area in which the company has no experience.

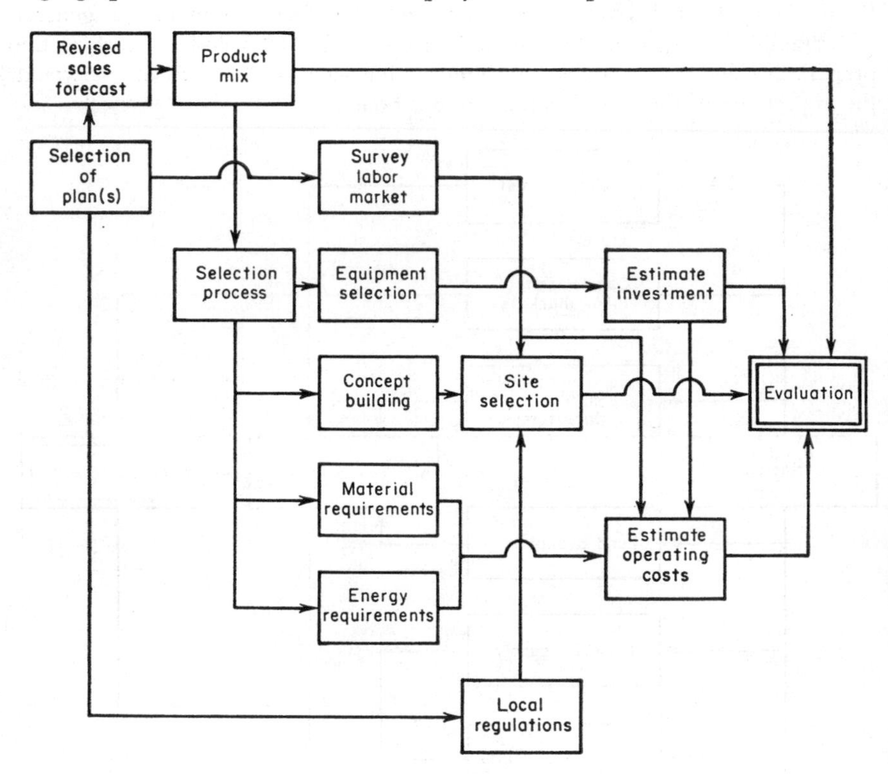

Fig. 2. The concept.

It can be a distinct disadvantage to rely too much on a limited number of sources of information. The perfect example is the situation in which a company started production operations in an area that was supplied by plants in other locations. The information provided by the local sales force was not at all dependable on subjects such as labor relations.

It is typical that the information is collected by independent departments. Except for the timing of completion, very little coordination is necessary between these groups.

The Concept. Figure 2 shows that in this stage the relations between the activities of the various groups involved become more complex. It will be impossible to make a selection of the processes and an estimate of the investment if the projected product mix is not known.

In this stage, contacts with outside experts start to develop. It will be necessary to contact the electricity or gas company. The selection of plant sites might even reach the stage of taking options on land. Contractors will be contacted in this phase. The preliminary design of the building might be subcontracted.

Another indication of the growing complexity of the project is that future participants become involved in the preparations of estimates.

The project now starts to develop, and there are indications of a need for a team—a team with a leader or coordinator. In some cases, a duplication or even a triplication of this phase might be desirable; it is not necessary to start this phase with only *one* plan. Because of the relatively low expenses, a few plans can be detailed in concept simultaneously, and calendar time will thereby be gained.

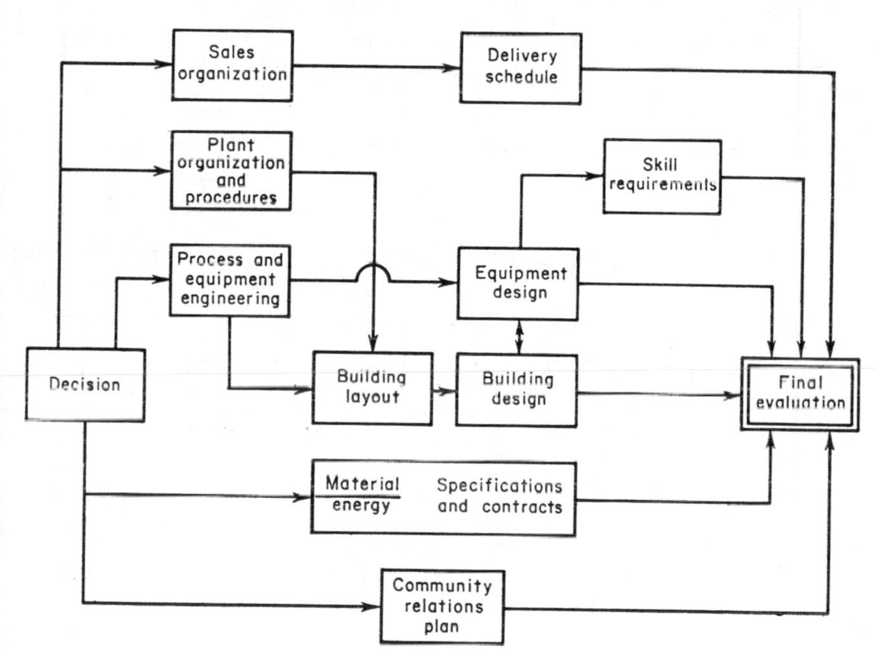

FIG. 3. The design.

The concept phase ends with a selection of the scope of the plant and a determination of the plant location. This decision is not final; it can and should be reviewed before construction starts. Nevertheless, it is an important decision because it initiates the detailed design and a rapid climb of the investment.

Design. The design phase is characterized by a preparation in considerable detail but without the investment in facilities. The building will be designed, but the construction is not started yet. The functional organization of the plant in this stage is developed while the payroll of the new plant is still minimal. It is possible to minimize the investment in capital goods at this stage. It makes feasible a final evaluation at the latest possible date.

In an actual situation, the design phase will not finish and change to the preparation phase for all activities simultaneously. Quite frequently, the clearing of the site starts during the design of the building. Material might be ordered or options taken during this phase.

At this critical stage, the specifications and standards are set for the various elements involved. Quantity, Quality, and delivery requirements are now determined. For no other reasons than these, the coordination of the design activities is essential for the success of the whole process.

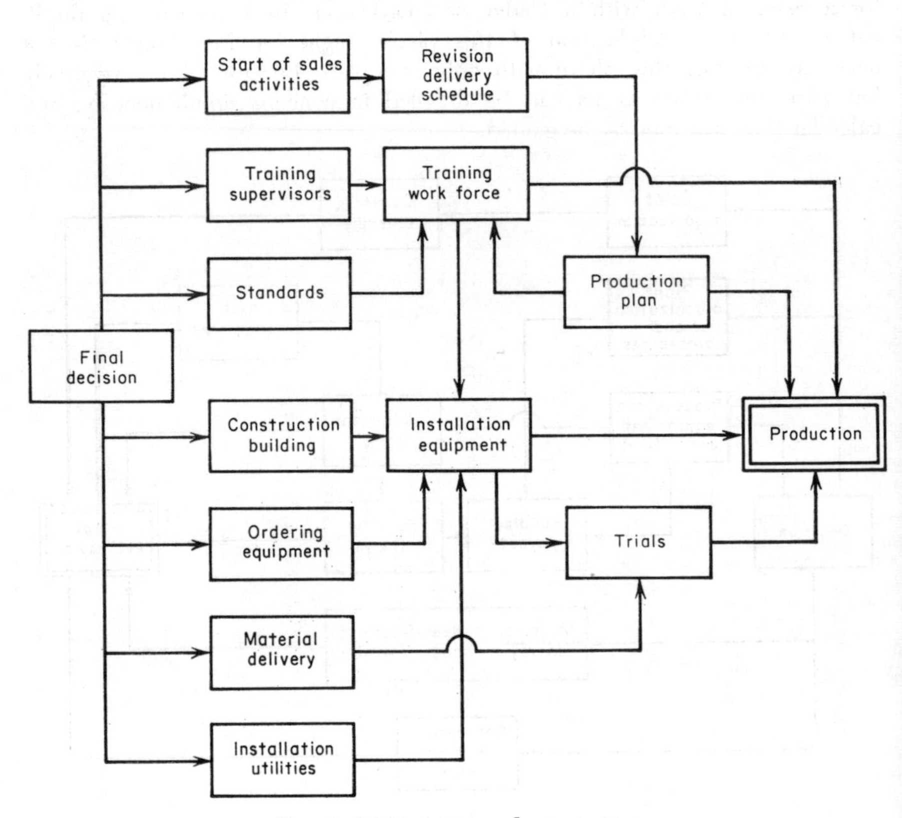

FIG. 4. Construction and preparation.

Construction and Preparation. Two major problem areas are typical here. A considerable pressure toward completion is normal for both construction and personnel preparation. In the latter group of activities, an unusual amount of training has to take place.

The Pressure

The date for the start-up of the new plant has been determined at the end of the design phase. During the final (construction) phase, all activities will be planned in relation to this important date. Sometimes meeting the start-up date looks like the only objective. Regardless of costs, this date has to be met. There are some good reasons for this.

As soon as construction begins, the company starts investing money on a large scale. The decision to build has been made, and a revision of plans is costly at this stage. As long as the plant does not produce, there is no return on the investment.

As soon as the decision is made to start the new plant, other sections of the company are influenced. The decision will change activities in the sales department; it might change production schedules in other plants, and the sales department might be authorized to make sales commitments.

Last, but not least, the previous phases are usually extended over a long period of time. The decision might have been delayed by delays in those phases. Once the decision is made, top management is inclined to an acceleration of the final stage in which the plans will be realized.

Transfer of Knowledge

At the beginning of the final phase, a considerable amount of preparation is completed in the design. There is very little doubt in the minds of the design engineers about the way the equipment should be operated. It has been our experience that the availability of this type of knowledge is generally overestimated by management.

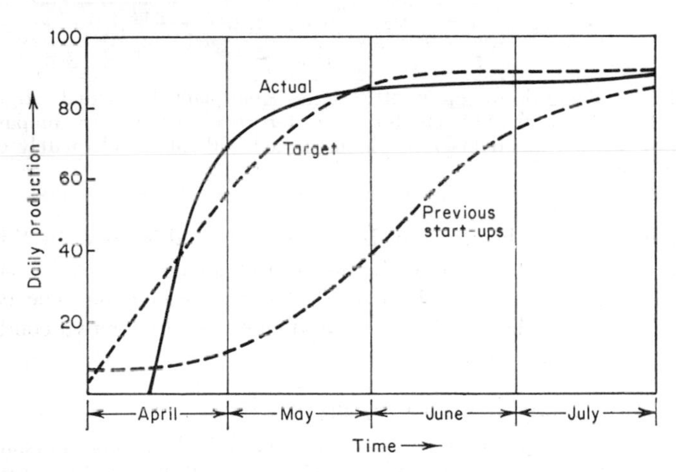

FIG. 5A. One measure of training benefits. Organized training of the production and maintenance force achieved this dramatic rise (solid line) in units produced by one plant (superceding target production), compared with the experience (dotted line) of the same corporation in previous start-ups. Training of foremen and the maintenance force began two months prior to start-up; the foremen trained their operators during the two weeks before the plant opened.

Firstly, this know-how is not complete. The new plant is never a carbon copy of other operations; every new facility will be blessed with improvements and other modifications. Secondly, from an operational viewpoint, the knowledge is in the wrong place. The planners and designers know each detail of the preparations, but they will not be operating the facilities. Production and staff people have to be selected and trained.

It is unreasonable to assume that this transfer of knowledge will take place automatically. Contacts between the design group and the operating group are usually insufficient, and the process of learning while doing is expensive and time-consuming. The problem of training a large number of people for their jobs in the new plant is unique. It will happen only once during the start-up. Therefore, it requires special attention from the plant

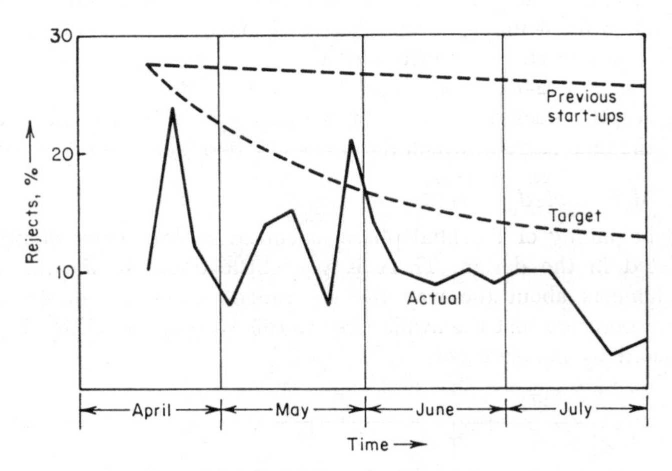

FIG. 5B. How training drops reject rate. At the same plant, the actual rate of rejects (solid line) declined sharply (better than target expectations), compared with previous experience (dotted line) in plants started without an adequately organized training program.

manager, who should be assisted by specialists in this area. In this phase, the company invests in the new facilities, and an insufficient investment in people will result in a slow and costly start of the production. The two parts of Figure 5 illustrate the difference in production results for two conditions in two similar (almost identical) plants.

Particular Conditions in Two Projects

The project of a plant start-up is not controlled by one person or one group alone. The required activities are the responsibility of different persons. The differences in background of these persons, in types of activity and ways of acting, are very great. In the various phases of starting the project, contributions are made by the sales manager, the architect, the design engineer, the contractor, the legal counselor, the plant manager, etc.

This separation of activities results in difficulties which can be compared with those in extreme forms of specialization. It calls for very special and unusual attention to the coordination between the specialized functions.

Where a new plant is to be added to the established activities of an organization, the preparation is not always present. The project has to be carried out by officers and departments in the company who are not normally concerned with these one-shot operations. This is especially true in the preparation of personnel for the new plant.

Those participating in the preparatory effort involved do not normally belong to one organizational unit and rarely have an opportunity to develop into a team.

As can be seen in Figures 1 to 4, the preparatory activities follow each other in a logical sequence. At different phases, these separate functions are interrelated. The consequence is that the total preparation time can be shortened if these activities are coordinated and the different functions are not carried on in isolation.

The Project Team

Cooperation between different functions and interests must be created through an organization geared to the company's objective. It can be focused upon a reduction of the lead time of the project or aimed at a reduction of the total costs. The company takes the initiative in forming this project team, and it should exercise great care in assessing capabilities and capacities when selecting the members. Some of the team members may be from the group of company employees; almost always, some of them will be outside experts. The leader of the team should be well qualified. He should have the ability to judge the capabilities and motivations of the members and arrange for the proper communication between them.

Some of our experiences with these project teams will be summarized briefly:

1. Each member of the team retains full responsibility for his activities in the project. For instance:
   a. The architect is responsible for the design.
   b. The contractor has full responsibility for the quality of construction and for meeting the scheduled dates.
2. All team members have to work according to schedules. The leader will use the schedules for progress control, and he can exercise his authority in coordinating activities according to these schedules. Some of the critical items in this coordination are:
   a. Completion of detailed specifications for the contractor.
   b. Completion of the installation of the equipment on a schedule geared to the production requirements.
3. The quality of the plans must be high. This can be accomplished only if two conditions are fulfilled:
   a. The necessary activities and their interrelations should be thoroughly analyzed in advance, and the time estimates should be based on realistic standards.
   b. The parties involved should participate in this analysis and have authority and responsibility for preparatory steps and performance on schedule.
4. The team members must meet regularly. Some members will be present at each meeting, while others will take part only when needed.
5. When the team is well selected, an element of sportsmanship will enter into the cooperation. The members will automatically feel responsible for making good their promises. They will seek to avoid becoming the cause

of delays. The team approach will make each member realize that progress on the total project will depend upon his ability to perform according to schedule.

Start-up Manager

It will be practical to assign someone as the start-up manager in an early stage (phase 1) of the preparations. He will be assigned to this project for its duration and should be reassigned only after the new plant is in production. It is clear from the variety of activities involved and from the authority handed to a project manager that the requirements for this function are extremely high. The problem is sometimes made greater by characteristic difficulties in the start-up phase of a project:

• The political aspects of the start-up will influence all activities to a great extent.

• The availability of suitable labor might create a dominant problem to the extent that it could determine the design of the equipment.

It has been our experience that a suitable man for the function or start-up manager is available only in exceptional cases. In most cases, another type of organization will be more practical.

Project Leaders

Under this other form of project organization, leadership of the team is assigned to one of the participating specialists, who is in charge of the activity of greatest importance to the current phase of start-up preparations.

In one particular situation, for example, the following organization was designed:

Phase	*Chosen project leader*
1. Orientation	Corporate personnel director (labor relations)
2. Concept	Division manager (process selection and design)
3. Design	Project engineer
4. Construction, preparation	Project engineer Plant manager

In this type of organization, continuity in the project becomes a problem. The chosen project leaders must cooperate. In practice, this means that in the transition stages between two successive phases two men will be coordinating the activities. This is not as serious a deficiency as it might appear, provided that a functional division of the activities is possible. In the transition from project engineer to plant manager in the above-mentioned case, the project engineer coordinated the construction and installation activities; the plant manager was responsible for the progress in all other areas.

Case History

The *Empresa Nacional Elcano de la Marina Mercante* is a Spanish shipping line which started operating about 1940 with a fleet of roughly forty somewhat old-fashioned ships The management decided to build a shipyard for the purpose of renewing its own fleet and of producing ships for other companies, thus increasing the country's shipbuilding capacity and helping to industrialize a nonindustrialized area.

The entire installation of this yard was very modern and can be compared with the best in Scandinavia and Holland. Its layout was well developed, with production following one straight line.

Starting up a shipyard in a nonindustrialized area where shipbuilding is unknown can be considered a problem, as this yard could not draw skilled manpower from the local labor market and had to meet quite an ambitious production schedule. Personnel had to be hired locally, and only key men could be hired from other shipyards in the country. Supervisory personnel could be hired to a very small extent, and often they were unfamiliar with modern section-building methods in ship production.

Unorganized training in this yard during the first phase of the start-up was impossible, because there were not enough skilled operators to show the new and unskilled ones their way in the job. Hiring skilled help from other yards was possible in some cases only with higher wages and promises of upgrading. Using existing training programs was not possible. Formal training had never been set up for jobs related to shipbuilding.

The problem therefore amounted to organizing the training of great numbers of operators, while little operating experience in modern methods of shipbuilding was available.

A double-purpose management program was adopted:

1. With the accent on training
2. With the accent on improving efficiency and control

The problems attended to were:

1. Training of skilled and semiskilled workers for numerous jobs; training of first-line supervisory personnel
2. Recruiting and selecting suitable candidates for training
3. Integrating the new personnel into their jobs and into the organization, thus forming the basis for a rapid start-up of production

These goals were attained by means of the following activities:

1. The formation of a capable training staff. For this purpose a group of men were selected and trained, consisting of (*a*) a naval architect acting as chief training engineer, and (*b*) two bachelors of science, acting as training engineers. This task force worked during the first phase. During the second phase the training department included (*a*) a bachelor of science, acting as chief training engineer, (*b*) two bachelors of science and two technicians, acting as training engineers, and (*c*) one selection officer. Along with the administrative clerks and secretary, this formed a staff department under the production manager. The first group was trained individually, and the four new men of the second group were trained in our training engineers course.

2. On the basis of the job analyses, test batteries were composed by an industrial psychologist for an effective selection of candidates for the courses for the various jobs. The selection officer was trained by the psychologist and given know-how, experience, and material in the field of personnel selection; he was also charged with the selection of practice and theory instructors.

3. On the basis of careful analysis of the job, each course was specially made to fit the requirements of production. Organization of the course was always adapted to the specific situation involved. Practice and theory instructors were chosen and trained. "Acting as instructor" was one of the phases in the training of a new first-line supervisor.

These three steps were followed by:

4. The training of a group of work study specialists and the organization of a work study department.

5. The transfer of our experience and knowledge in the field of standardization of times and methods.

6. The buildup of documentation and files for method and time data.

7. The training of work preparators for various production departments and the integration of work preparation into the organizational structure of the shipyard.

8. The improvement of means for the control of performance and efficiency.

The results of the assignment were as follows:

1. A total of 2,260 people were recruited and tested.

2. During the assignment more than 80 courses were given and more than 870 men trained.

3. The financial benefits of the faster start-up of production, in which 126 trainees were involved, exceeded by far the costs of preparation. During the first year alone, the benefits were roughly 8 million pesetas (at that time approximately $200,000).

4. Essential conditions of the skilled operator training were complete engaging of all future foremen concerned, their training them as instructors, and their assignment to the training of their own group of new personnel. The majority of the forty practice instructors were later involved in training courses for first-line supervisory personnel.

5. Invaluable by-products of the whole training setup were (*a*) a thoroughly prepared group of training analysts, who could be used for special work in various departments when the bulk of the training was done; (*b*) a well-informed group of shop engineers (naval architects) whose cooperation throughout the development of this plan was stimulated because of their contributions; and (*c*) a group of about thirty employees from the technical and drawing departments, who participated as theory instructors and now have a better understanding of the worker's attitude, his way of thinking, and his daily problems.

6. The turnover among trained operators proved to be only 5½%, which is a favorable minimum as compared with other factories in this area (roughly 20%).

7. A productivity increase was realized through (*a*) method improvement, (*b*) a rate-setting incentive scheme, (*c*) improvement of organization and working conditions, and (*d*) improvement of control.

The yard continues with accelerated training and has gradually reached full use of the work study techniques. Work study and training function hand in hand.

MANAGEMENT TECHNIQUES AND THEIR APPLICATION IN LESS DEVELOPED AREAS, WITH SPECIAL REFERENCE TO THE EXPERIENCE IN THE UNITED ARAB REPUBLIC

Ahmed Fouad Sherif, Ph.D.

Development and Spread of Modern Management Techniques

Although the development of modern industry in advanced countries can be traced back over the last two hundred years, the techniques used by modern industrial management can be traced back only to the early twenties. Work study techniques and wage incentive systems were put into widespread practice in the early decades of this century. Production-line techniques and continuous production systems were also a twentieth-century development. Marketing promotion and research were largely adopted in the thirties. Morale measurement and human relations made their appearance in the inter-war period, while personnel testing and selection, job evaluation, and accelerated supervisory training were widely installed during World War II. The most significant developments in industrial relations, production planning, and controllership techniques followed in the postwar years. Managerial planning, decision making, quantitative techniques, and management development came into practice in the early fifties. Indeed, the progressive adoption of modern management techniques in advanced economies coincided with the period of increasing drive for industrialization in less developed countries.

Management development has lagged behind the development of modern production techniques in industrialized countries, particularly where the application of the scientific method in management problem solving is concerned. Apparently, there are no strong reasons; this time lag could be avoided (and the same sequence of application does not have to be followed) in the case of newly industrializing countries. Deliberate measures for accel-

Dr. Sherif is Director of the National Institute of Management Development, Cairo.

erating the application of these techniques might conceivably narrow the gap and even promise a comparative advantage for the late starters. The absence of the rigidities of the established organizations, strong union pressures, and the possibility of developing a more integrated approach might facilitate this acceleration.

By contrast, the association of modern production technologies with the most rudimentary management techniques in newly established enterprises in less developed countries readily suggests that successful modernization in this connection involves a priori more than the direct transfer of universal methods. Most of these "universal" techniques are being transferred under the turn-key contract: shifting the burden of work in the plant construction stage, and in testing and initial operations, in well-established international companies. While the skills required for operating the plants can be readily imported or acquired, the installation of the corresponding management techniques involves something more. The chief difficulties in the way of effective use of modern management techniques are to be found in the wide and complex field of managerial attitudes, motives, behavior, aptitudes, and educational and cultural backgrounds.

Modern management techniques, like production equipment, have been conceived, developed, or put into practice by leading managers or progressive entrepreneurs in advanced countries, who acted as sponsors of some technique in response to specific problems pertaining to a specific environment and conditioned by certain limitations. The first series of modern management techniques introduced by Taylor, Gilbreth, Gantt, Emerson, and other scientific management leaders or efficiency experts were oriented toward faster production rates, method standardization for higher and more even quality, and labor-skill savings akin to the mechanical improvements introduced by James Kay, Hargreaves, Arkwright, Crompton, Cartwright, and other earlier mechanical inventors.

Viewed against the environment of management in less developed countries, the successful application of most modern management techniques calls for considerable adaptation. Work study and productivity techniques seem to have been the first to spread internationally through the promotional efforts of international organizations. Useful as they are, the partial adoption of these techniques might only increase the prevailing functions, resulting in inventory accumulation, excess capacities, and ineffective market planning. Also, their orientation to labor saving might run counter to the pressures for expanding employment. The successful introduction of these as well as other management techniques requires a great deal of dovetailing and an integrated approach based upon thorough understanding of the interrelations between various management functions and techniques.

The successful adaptation of these techniques is related to a multiplicity of factors operating on the capacity of management for assimilating new and more complex methods, also to the very methods of "transferring" them. Many variables are involved, including the prevailing forms of organization, the institutional framework, the education and sophistication of potential management personnel, etc. In a real sense, the whole problem of modernization of management techniques is fundamentally one of management development broadly conceived. It is according to this conception that some of these pertinent factors will be discussed in their bearing upon the possibilities of different functional techniques and against the background of the U.A.R. experience.

New forms of organization are emerging and gaining relative importance in the modern enterprise sector of many developing countries, while other conventional forms are declining in importance. In many developing countries, the expansion of the public sector through nationalization or establishment of new public enterprises has invariably been associated with a proliferation of public corporations, development organizations, and mixed-ownership or government-controlled corporations.

Conceptually, the emergence of these newer forms can be characterized as an induced separation between ownership and management. The owner-manager form of organization has been associated with a specific pattern of management behavior usually identified by low-volume, high-profit margins; strong propensity for quick returns and high-dividend distribution; and a lesser inclination to maintain a stable work force or to invest in training and developing professional high-level managers. In a real sense, these newer forms of organization favor a greater professionalization of management associated with a different pattern of managerial behavior. Emerging professional managers are more inclined to adopt the latest production technologies, the most modern plant and equipment; they are less desirous of short-term profit maximization and are more inclined to reinvest particularly in longer-term projects.

The newer organizational forms represent a step forward in so far as they attempt to provide a successful balance between government control and management autonomy, which has so far been successful in very few cases. The proliferation of these new forms is a manifestation of the diffusion of management function and departure from unilateral authority in decisions affecting product line, scale of operations, factory locations, manpower requirements, systems of industrial relations, and pricing and investment decisions.

In most developing countries, the private sector has generated little or no surplus of high-quality management potential for staffing other enterprises. In some countries, like the U.A.R. and India, well-established enterprises have virtually acted as training grounds for a sizable number of potential top managers for newly established public sector enterprises. Whenever prosperous large-scale private enterprises exist, government salaries are significantly lower than top management salaries in successful private companies. Senior executives are rarely willing to work for the public sector. The inevitable outcome of this supply situation is that the old bureaucracy constitutes an important source of top management recruitment, with the inevitable risk of transferring old methods.

In less industrialized countries that are importing modern management techniques, some of these techniques have seeped into local enterprises from progressive subsidiaries of foreign enterprises. Accelerated industrialization targets are to be attained mainly through developing national managers. However, the importation of management techniques has lagged behind the importation of modern technology. Engineering studies and blueprints are prepared with the help of foreign consultants or the very technical assistance of equipment manufacturers. But the transfer of related modern management techniques is rarely conceived as an integral part of the project. For a few projects, usually those being presented for loans, some formal appraisal of management is made. Whenever the assurance as to management quality or adequacy is lacking, the development lender often proposes the hiring of an experienced general manager or a good part of the management team. For more complex management techniques, a management contract, or a joint venture plus management contract with leading foreign firms, is often proposed.

Management in a less developed country has its own particular problems, which might still differ from those of advanced management responding to its experience in developing these problem-oriented techniques. Also, management in most developing countries functions in an essentially unfavorable environment, which requires managers to adjust, improvise, provide solutions, and, in particular, compensate for nonexistent facilities and services which, in a developed country, are available and often taken for granted by their counterparts there. As many management techniques are applicable only after some degree of adaptation, managers are typically called upon to resolve conflicts and maladjustments between received techniques and the prevailing environmental conditions and limitations.

Another feature of the process of assimilating modern management techniques is the tendency in many developing countries to accelerate the sharing of productivity gains. Manifold pressures, including the revolution of expectations, the demonstration effect of high mass consumption in advanced countries, and the growing power of unions, influence new national governments to act as a third force in a system of industrial relations conducive to the more immediate and directed sharing of productivity gains.

Applicability of Production Management Techniques

Production management problems in the process of industrialization are those involving a forced-pace changeover from primitive factory or artisan workshop to mass production systems involving highly mechanized and expensive plant. The transition specifically involves a shift from various types of intermittent production to continuous systems including an integrated assembly line, continuous flow processes, and a high degree of automation. The transition almost amounts to forced introduction of production systems, involving serious conflicts, maladjustments, and inadequacies inherent in the economic environment. Conflicts between environmental conditions and the requirements of newer systems give rise to production management problems which can be rationally formulated by asking "Which production system would be optimal in terms of its requirements and of a set of environmental conditions?" Pragmatically, the problem is "how" to cope with the conflicts involved.

Although the installation of these advanced systems gives rise to problems of a managerial rather than a technical nature, this aspect of production management has been susceptible to some pattern of vertical disintegration, shifting this part of the function to foreign consulting firms and equipment manufacturers. Thus the problems of installation and initial operations are taken over by foreign firms. Under different types of such management contracts, as well as under the joint venture arrangement, some diffusion in the performance of production management function is obtained. It amounts to some type of division of labor in the performance of the complex functions associated with the introduction and operation of a new production system.

Local enterprise managers are not completely relieved of their responsibilities for making basic decisions, such as those relating to plant capacity, selection of processes, etc., no matter what type of work-sharing arrangement seems most feasible. Considering the longer lead time involved prior to the start of economical, smooth operations, the decisions mean long-term commitments on the part of enterprise managers.

Active joint participation of the enterprise managers along with government and planning personnel has proved conducive to more realism in project selection and appraisal. Often those directly involved in implementing the projects develop a greater measure of consciousness of the soundness of a new project, stress its feasibility, discount the less tangible social profitability criteria, and inject more concern for the probabilities of success. The recruitment of a top management team at an early stage of project origination to participate in the project making has proved, whenever possible, a more successful practice than that of handing over a final project for implementation at a later stage.

Most modern industrial enterprise managers coming from the ranks of engineers and technologists display a greater propensity for adopting refined scientific techniques in the area of production management. As the economics of continuous production systems come to be appreciated by top management, new needs are discovered and a whole battery of new management techniques comes to be viewed as an integral part of the system. For example, the high fixed cost of stoppage induces the adoption of preventive maintenance, systematic procurement planning, and inventory control. The techniques of quality control and of product standardization and development will be adopted. Production-minded managers come to appreciate the importance of other managerial functions, as well as their interrelationship. General management training allowing for a modicum of exposure to the logic and uses, rather than the mechanics, of these techniques is designed to advance their use.

Applicability of Marketing Management

In most industrial enterprises the production function is typically regarded as the major activity. To cope with the marketing requirements of new production systems, top management approaches need drastic revisions. Three approaches to marketing can be identified as representing widespread concepts and attitudes, namely:

The Traditional Trader's or "Transaction" Approach. Top management's concept of marketing is frequently an extension of the traditional trader's approach. This identifies effective marketing with maximizing profit per transaction, taking advantage of price fluctuations and shortages regardless of the regularity of production schedules, the building up of long-term market relations, a system of market communications, or a stable sales organization.

The Agent's Approach. The sales function is delegated to wholesalers, transferring the goods physically from the producer to the retailer. Most wholesalers prefer to buy on a hand-to-mouth basis, allowing little regularity in production scheduling. Very limited feedback of information from the market to the enterprise manager is done by the wholesaler, resulting in management being literally isolated from the market.

The Physical Distribution Approach. In a growing number of new enterprises, management is "forced" to undertake the marketing function, in view of deficiencies in the wholesaler's system.

Management thinking in these cases has been centered upon physical aspects of distribution. The presence of excess capacity is not usually enough to pressure management into any form of sales promotion. The typical enterprise takes the demand for its products as given and does little to alter this demand. Further, where competition is present, few managers have any drive to increase their market share. Inevitably, management operates on the basis that production governs sales.

With these attitudes and approaches, enterprise managers are primarily concerned with plant operations, and they come to recognize marketing problems only under duress (e.g., inventory accumulation, shortage of working capital, intense foreign competition). In addition to lack of appreciation for modern marketing techniques and basic marketing education, there are some significant environmental factors conditioning these attitudes. New enterprises established under tariff protection in such stable industries as textiles and food processing, or those operating virtually in a seller's market, create situations that cause enterprise managers to feel that marketing is relatively unimportant.

The extent of the adoption of modern management techniques in marketing, the organization of the marketing management function, and the makeup of the management team ascertain the state of marketing management in industrializing countries. For example, very few enterprises use sales forecasting as the basis for production scheduling. Under pressure of planning, supervision, and authorities control, a larger number of public sector enterprises are undertaking sales projections and estimates. More refined techniques of market evaluation and sales forecasting are being appreciated in connection with investments in new facilities or the development of new products. In newer industries where minimum economic size exceeds domestic market needs, "surplus" has to be exported. The difficulties encountered in disposing of a growing surplus brought home the notion that marketing is decisive for the success of new enterprises. It is increasingly realized that the starting management team ought to include a sales manager with professional marketing skills to avoid any marketing problems relegated to "postoperative phase."

In some enterprises, the purchasing, selling, and storekeeping activities are combined in one department, usually called the "commercial department." Typically, the sales manager or the commercial manager is below the production manager; thus, the marketing function is made subservient to the production function. Very few top executives in these enterprises started their careers in marketing or have had any experience in this field. In the recurring conflict between production and sales as to lot size, variety, product design, and length of production run, the conflict is rarely resolved in favor of the sales department. Under these conditions, the emerging professionally trained sales manager has a basic job to do in converting top management to the modern concept of marketing.

As the professional marketing man gets integrated into the top management team, product development is increasingly accepted as a top management responsibility. Delegating product research to government research organizations, looking abroad to new product standards, designing products by imitation and thus divorcing product design from local market needs, all testify to the problems involved in incorporating product development as a function of top management. This would also require systematic feedback information, exposing the local producer to some imported quality competition, enforcement of minimum specifications standards for export sales, quality control agencies, and industrial research organizations. In many instances, government-forced price reductions and more liberal attitudes toward product research and advertising expenditures have forced the adoption of sales promotion and aggressive selling techniques.

Applicability of Personnel and Industrial Relations Techniques

In developing, adapting, or modernizing the prevailing industrial relations systems in less developed countries, the government in most cases plays the dominant role. The requirements of continuous production systems in terms of a stable, fully committed, highly motivated work force are increasingly recognized. More forceful are social pressures upon governments to introduce, through legislation and administrative discretion, measures for employment stabilization. In some cases, these measures have reduced the incentive for improving productivity and introducing mechanization in ancillary processes. The presence of excess labor and high labor costs seem to have generated a greater drive for expansion of production with the same work force. At times, lower prices for the consumer coupled with higher labor costs resulting from these institutional arrangements have created a profit squeeze, depleting the funds required for new investments in expansion and modernization of equipment.

Top managers are described as authoritarian in their relationships with subordinates. This is particularly true of owner-managers on the one hand and of the bulk of unskilled labor on the other. Protective labor legislation has largely emanated with a view to attaining a greater measure of stability through restricting management rights to fire, discipline, discharge, and use other "employment-reducing" prerogatives. The increasing awareness of human relations as practiced by modern management does not seem to suffice alone, or coupled with legislative and administrative pressure, in bringing about the modernization of management practices in this area. This suggests that it involves more than mere exposure to modern human relations practices.

Work study and related work rationalization techniques, like other labor-saving and possibly employment-reducing devices, tend to generate labor opposition, especially where there is a strong union. The government's role in cases of outright labor opposition can be considerably greater than the traditional role in advanced countries. In many situations where established industries are going through a process of modernization, the government concerned have not been equipped to handle the change effectively. Whenever an explosive management-labor situation developed, the authorities stepped in only to police the situation, control the mob, and limit the damage or violence. At times, many managers facing a deteriorating labor-management situation have positively invited government intervention, repeatedly relinquishing their autonomy in handling industrial relations problems. In less violent situations of labor sabotage, professional managers of public enterprises tend to disguise and suppress the symptoms until they are forced out into the open. In many developing countries strikes are banned, in specific sectors or in the economy at large, the rationale being the nation's inability to tolerate industrial strife. In any event, this, coupled with compensatory measures like restriction of management right to lockouts and stoppages, firing and discharging, etc., has not prevented work stoppage in newer forms and even the invention of new names for strikes.

With increasing governmental controls, growing power of unions, and the expansion of the public sector, pressures arise for the adoption of a more objective approach to the problem of justifying pay differentials. As enterprise managers learn about job evaluation techniques, they readily accept them as a highly valuable addition to their kit of tools. In the United Arab Republic, for example, some type of formal job evaluation in mixed and public enterprises is now almost universal. The general level of pay, including minimum wages and ceilings for executive salaries, is set by the government, and incorporated in the legislation, leaving the relative position of individual jobs, largely, to enterprise managers' autonomy. The extension of the job evaluation technique to include professional job groups, a development introduced in newly industrializing countries, happened only recently even in the United States. This is perhaps one area where management in developing countries ought to start from the point only recently reached by advanced management. The large-scale adoption of this technique has been hampered by many factors, including the need for more basic education for top managers, the inadequacy of outside consultants, and the lagging recognition of the need to win a larger understanding of job evaluation on the part of supervisors, employees, and union leaders. Higher and middle management, while usually possessing a better grasp of the job evaluation concept, often fail to see it in true perspective with regard to overall management objectives. An adequate background in the fundamental concepts of job evaluation is a major management training need.

By the same token, the introduction of modern personnel management techniques is closely related to development of the personnel function in management. The professional personnel director, representing a new viewpoint and new skills, would have to gain his place as an effective member of the management team. The staff concept applied to the personnel director and the concept of human relations skills as an integral part of the training of managers and supervisors at different levels would have to be incorporated in management thinking.

Applicability of Modern Controllership Techniques

Modern controllership techniques used in planning and control present a recent departure for enterprise managers in less developed countries. Historical or financial accounting techniques tend to be assimilated first, with the initial push coming from profit taxation and company laws, and with the larger corporate enterprises in the lead. The modernization of legal codes and institutional practices generates a growing demand for the professional services of chartered accountants. Public enterprises run along departmental lines, or, as public corporations, usually lag behind private corporations in developing a modern accounting system. Lacking the required measures of financial autonomy, the changeover to modern techniques is often dependent upon official realization of the inadequacy of traditional government accounting for the purposes of modern management. An aversion to providing accounting and financial data beyond the requirements of the law is often displayed by top managers coming from the ranks of engineers and technologists. Inevitably, this can be redressed only through the development of well-rounded generalists educated, among other things, in the uses of accounting data for control purposes. Lack of familiarity with basic management accounting naturally inhibits the engineer-manager in attempting to develop accounting as a management tool.

The symptoms of an undeveloped controllership function are manifold. There is a widespread tendency for average managers to conceive of accounting in terms of historical recording of financial transactions. At a subsequent stage, and under environmental pressures for greater cost consciousness, cost accounting and stock control are introduced. In only a few modernized enterprises is the system of accounting designed and installed with a view to providing the basic control information. When the initial management motive for developing an accounting system is mainly to comply with the requirements of credit institutions, tax legislation, or company regulations, the adequate accounting basis for control is usually lacking. Under the circumstances, typical owner-managers in small enterprises would quite rationally tend to develop a minimal accounting system. The concept is maintained that accounting records need only be rudimentary and oriented to external uses in the erroneous belief that this is more in line with secrecy safeguards and false economy notions. Professional managers in public enterprises and progressive private enterprises would be less reluctant to install more elaborate systems. The end product, as observed in a number of cases, might be the installation of a highly elaborate accounting system designed with little or no regard for managerial control purposes.

Without educating top managers in the potentialities of using accounting data for making day-to-day decisions, the proper design and the effective use of a management accounting system are not assured even when professional accounting organizations are adequate. In some developing countries like the U.A.R., India, or Chile, for example, professional accounting skills ranging from bookkeeping to full-fledged accounting can hardly be described as in short supply. The modern controller, however, as an effective member of the management team, requires a broader background than that of the specialist accountant as currently produced by existing commerce colleges, schools, and practicing institutions. In addition to prior accounting, this would have to cover related fields of finance, statistics, organization, and decision making. To develop into a controller, a professional accountant should grasp the function of controllership as related to these areas and acquire the ability to perform as a member of the management team.

In some countries, formal budgeting techniques are in use only in government departments and departmentally managed enterprises, while others confine themselves to end-of-the-year balance sheets. With the growth of the public sector and the growing acceptance of national accounting and comprehensive planning, a large number of public and mixed-ownership enterprises are adopting budgeting techniques. Through decrees, directives, requests from planning authorities, and follow-up forms, coupled at times with training and consulting, modern enterprises are both installing budgeting systems and adapting their information systems for public control purposes. Procurement budgeting in terms of foreign exchange requirements is one of the first areas of systematic budgeting appreciated by government agencies. In the absence of objective and acceptable budgeting techniques in situations of shortage and control, the enterprise manager is always tempted to build up reserves, inflate his requirements, and operate in terms of safety factors, contrary to the rational principles of inventory control. Another area of significance is that of credit budgeting. Systematic credit budgeting might actually economize cash needs and reduce the credit requirements, or improve the terms on which credit is made available. Central credit budgeting, based upon credit budgeting at the enterprise level, might help reconcile the necessity of creating credit to meet growing financial needs on the one hand, and of achieving a reasonable price stability on the other. It can also enhance the effectiveness of banking services and assure an adequate response from financial institutions to the requirements of enterprise.

Contribution of Management Training to the Modernization of Management Techniques

The application of modern management techniques in less developed countries is largely, we have seen, a problem of training and developing professional managers. Unfortunately few managers are eager to learn and adopt new or more complex techniques. This might be traced to the increasing subordination of enterprise managers to central direction and control, which inevitably leads to a habit or an attitude of expecting major decisions to be taken by central authorities and to a corresponding lack of responsibility and initiative except in the strongest-minded. Individuals who might be willing to pioneer new methods are often thwarted by resistance to change and reluctance to join in a departure from beaten paths. The schools and universities of most developing countries stress the purely academic aspect of education rather than skills. Occupational preferences do not favor the choice of management as a career.

MARKETING AS THE PRIMARY FACTOR IN PRODUCTION PROGRAMMING

Dr. Albrecht Kruse

During the last two decades millions of new products have been developed. One of the most spectacular innovations was television, introduced into the market after World War II. Its success was accompanied by expanding production of home appliances such as deep freezers, built-in electric ranges, tape recorders, room air conditioners, electric shavers, and combination washer-dryers. In the food field and among home cleansers, thousands of new products have been put on the market. Every household is familiar with aerosols and different plastics. Trade journals continue to be filled with descriptions of new products.

But nevertheless, a great many new products turned out to be complete failures. Statistical evidence proves that unsuccessful products outnumber items which have been introduced successfully into the market. A growing "degeneration" of products has been observed. Various surveys of new-product activities indicate that almost 90 percent of new products fail to survive their first two years. The mere fact that failure rates have not been reduced until now illustrates the complex nature of the question: Why do so many new products fail?

It is obvious to experienced management that little about new products can be tied to fact. A great deal of decisions are based therefore on a "hunch" method, which leads to unsound management judgments. Technical innovations are not closely connected with marketing considerations. There is an obvious interrelationship between products and markets in the sense that the product-line decisions of a firm will affect the choice of channel, and, conversely, channel decisions have to take into consideration the company's products and product line. Furthermore, advanced planning in effective in-

---

Dr. Kruse is Secretary General of the Institute of Marketing, Berlin.

ventory control is most important. It should be in accordance with the possible changes in the demand of the market and the productive capacity of the firm as well.

Marketing Considerations and Production Programming

An important conclusion is that marketing considerations should be a primary factor in production programming. Any effort to sell must begin with researching the customer's desire to buy. The high failure rates of new products reflect the failure to assemble these important facts and interpret them objectively. Many companies do not adhere to policies established in connection with long-range goals. They reduce the effort on a new product too soon. Persistence and continued promotional effort at this point can keep orders from dropping off abruptly. The marketing concept means that all steps, from developing a product until it will be introduced successfully into the market and give satisfaction to the final user, are not independent of one another but are links of a continuous chain. Sales promotion activities cost money and affect the price of the products to be sold. In a great deal of Continental textbooks it is held that they must result in higher selling costs and, hence, higher prices to consumers. Since markets are not perfect as far as most consumer goods are concerned, textbook arguments which fundamentally rest on terms of pure competition do not apply. Markets are not wholly "transparent" to buyers and sellers; they do not fit the perfect abstract patterns of firms with optimum efficiency and consumers whose decisions are exclusively rooted in price evaluation. The major task of sales promotion is to expand production and consumption, which induce on their part price reductions by internal economies of scale. On the other hand, advertising expenditures as an important part of promotional activities keep potential competition from "squeezing the market." Thus it is by no means certain that the company which first started all kinds of successful promotional activities will pass on their savings to the customers in the form of cover prices. Sales promotion, in general, may lead to higher or lower prices depending on the market position of the advertiser and his price policy.

Need for Refinement in Market Research

In spite of the progress that fact finding has made, one major obstacle to the greater use of marketing research is the confusing terminology of researchers. Those managers and firms who are supposed to approve the expenditure of large sums are very often confronted with experts who restrict their activities to refining the tools and say little about findings applicable to everyday decisions of management. Even when research is concerned with practical problems of production programming, serious uncertainties exist. Testing methods have inherent weaknesses, inaccuracy is tolerated, insufficient testing is done, and many products simply cannot be market-tested. The Edsel automobile failure is an outstanding example. The gap which often exists between the market as shown by research work and the real up-to-date market can be bridged by salesmen who are acquainted with the major results of fact finding and the pattern of consumer markets. Unfortunately, there are a number of companies whose salesmen are not as market-minded as they should be and do not fully understand the company's marketing plans and strategy or how they themselves fit into them.

What Is Adequate Advertising?

As promotional activities expand, advertising becomes more and more important. The principal media used are newspapers, magazines, radio, television, direct mail, motion pictures, handbills, classified columns in telephone directories and newspapers, and window and counter display materials. The alternatives in production programming depend to a great extent on the benefits and limitations of different advertising strategies. Unfortunately, the growing costs of advertising include an increasing rate of failure. Advertising costs in consumer goods industry range from a very low level—some firms record less than 0.02 percent—to 20 percent of sales and more (for some individual firms advertising costs were 50 percent of sales and up). A detailed compilation and analysis of statistical data shows that there are significant differences in advertising expenditures not only between different companies but also between different countries. The results of these investigations can be summed up as follows:

Country	*Advertising expenditures, percentage of Gross National Product* (1961)
United States	2.9
Great Britain	1.6
West Germany	1.04

Some other countries (e.g., France and Italy) show a lower rate of 0.8 percent.

A great number of devices and mathematical models have been developed in order to measure advertising effectiveness. They range from the analyzing of readership to more sophisticated mathematical approaches which attempt to correlate advertising expenditures to sales in some way or other. All these attempts have not been very successful. There is a direct relationship between sales and advertising which makes any kind of analysis and projection extremely difficult. The traditional percent-of-sales method of setting up the advertising budget and the high correlation between trends of advertising expenditures and business cycles are by no means a result of the effectiveness of the advertising.

More important than the problem of the effectiveness of advertising is the review of what were the goals of promotional activities in the past few years and of what has been accomplished. Such a critical review will disclose most interesting facts for the future production programming. There is evidence that production programming cannot be confined to marketing considerations of what should be done, but should also examine the significance of what has been done and consider the conclusions to be drawn. The mere fact that most companies are without a formal scheme of production programming, despite the pressure imposed upon them by the need to find new products in this age of rapid obsolescence, shows that projections of future trends in many instances today are not connected with a detailed reconsideration of former policies incorporating simple trial-and-error methods. On the close interrelation of the two tasks, market and production planning, depends the success of new products.

BUSINESS POTENTIAL OF DESIGN IN CONSUMER INDUSTRIES

Philip Rosenthal, M.A.

Manufacturers in many sectors of the consumer industry are faced with a unique problem of competition. As individual companies, of course, we are competing against other individual companies in our respective product lines. But we are also locked in a sector-by-sector battle to win a share of the consumers' discretionary or free income. Manufacturers of household goods, for example, must persuade the consumer to spend his money on their products instead of on more automobiles or more expensive vacation trips.

One way to create demand for a product is to convince the consumer that it offers him satisfactions beyond its practical use. In the long run, simply resorting to the "hard sell" is not enough. The manufacturer must offer products that create genuine pleasure because they have real aesthetic value and are in harmony with the taste of our times.

To produce and sell such a product, manufacturers must invest interest, time, and money in locating and developing suitable designers. They must establish a harmonious, dynamic relationship between designer, factory, salesmen, and retailer. Presenting and selling a product properly can be just as important as designing it properly. Companies with established markets may find it impossible to upgrade their product line and revamp their sales structure all at once. But it is possible to create an "island" of good taste within the overall program and gradually extend it.

Throughout this article I will use as a case history the experience of my own company in the area of china and glass.

If one looks at the long-term record of personal consumption, at least one trend is clear. With prosperity increasing, people have more and more free

Mr. Rosenthal is President of Rosenthal Porzellan, A. G.

money to spend, and they are spending it. But not all sectors of the consumer industry are benefiting equally from this increased spending.

What has happened in West Germany I believe to be indicative of a world-wide trend, at least within the more highly industrialized nations of the Free World and among the growing middle classes of the developing nations. In 1955, the average West German family spent 7.7% of its budget on purchases for the household, including 3.2% for furniture. By 1961, the share of spending for the household had grown to only 8.7%, and for furniture to only 4.1%. But while West German families spent only 0.9% of their budgets on cars and motor cycles in 1955, by 1961 they had pushed purchases of these products to 3.2% of their budgets. And they boosted their outlays for soap and cosmetics from a mere 2.7% share of their budget in 1955 to a 5% share in 1961—which represents more money than they spend on heat and light.

My own industry, the china industry, was one of the losers (again, relatively speaking) in this shifting of consumer preferences. In 1954, the china industry accounted for 0.892% of total consumer industry sales in West Germany. By 1961, its share had slipped to 0.720%.

Why are people increasing their outlay so much faster for things like automobiles and cosmetics than for things like furniture and china? The answer, I think, is that people's selection of "the good things in life" on which to spend their spare cash is based on an externalization of personal values. Observers of the market note what they call "a general upgrading of taste." By this they mean that people are spending more on "quality," whether it be in higher-grade soap or higher-fidelity phonographs. But underlying this urge for "quality" is not simply greater discrimination. Rather, it is in many cases the quest for prestige, the continuation of the old game of "keeping up with the Joneses." Quality is measured more by the status it bestows than by the genuine satisfaction which the object itself gives to the buyer.

Since even the prosperous middle classes of Western Europe and the United States have limits to their free income, it is obvious that if their interests lead them to spend more money on bigger cars, or second cars, or cosmetics, or trips to fashionable resorts, they will spend less for products they are less interested in. They will, for example, go on using their old dinnerware year after year, even though they may find it a "must" to replace their still good automobile every two years. They will buy these things in which they are not really interested only to the extent that they have to.

Manufacturers of products not favored by the dictates of current fashion, or in the scramble for prestige, can face their situation with two different attitudes. They can simply shrug their shoulders and settle for a modest increase of sales as the population increases, or they can take up the challenge of the marketplace and fight for a bigger share of the consumer's free income.

For those companies willing to take up the challenge, the key question is, "How do we increase the consumer's interest in our products?" If we are not content with having the sales of our products limited to fulfilling the consumer's bare needs, then we must give him other reasons for buying them. We must create demand.

It is possible to create interest in a product, and sometimes to increase sales dramatically, simply by bombarding the public with clever advertising and promotion programs. That may be especially true when manufacturers are competing against each other with rather similar "everyday" products such as chewing gum or cigarettes.

But when you are dealing with products which are not quickly consumed, and whose price involves a substantial investment rather than a casual conditioned expenditure, and when you are not simply competing against manufacturers who make similar products, but are trying to counter a massive preference for different *kinds* of products, then smart selling is not enough. To create interest and demand for these products, you must offer the consumer something more than simple utility. You must offer a product that will give its owner real satisfaction and pleasure that are inherent in the product itself and deep enough to convince him that he should spend his money on this product and not on something else.

The source of such satisfaction must be aesthetic, and the means of creating it is good design.

I mean "good design" in a very specific sense. Manufacturers of quality china, for example, have always been interested in "good design." For hundreds of years they have been producing china whose forms and patterns were created by true artists and were handed down from generation to generation, cloaked with tradition and respectability or perhaps they have been selling china designed by contemporary artisans who try to imitate these safe, respectable designs.

But for the manufacturer who wants to win a bigger share of the consumer's spending, it is obvious that safety and respectability are not the answer. These may win the loyalty of a limited buying public, but they do not create the excitement that will capture new buyers.

The great old designs first gained prestige because they somehow expressed the tastes and values and mood of the societies out of which they were created. They were genuine expressions of the aesthetic wellsprings of their time, and for this reason one may still get satisfaction from owning a really good and genuine antique. But relatively few genuine antiques are available, and no one can really be excited by dead imitations of the past passed off on the market as "traditional."

I am not suggesting that producers of household products should turn their backs on traditional designs only to pick up the banner of novelty for its own sake. Novelty might create a fad, but it is not the basis of solid, long-term sales growth.

Instead, manufacturers should seek designs which are genuine expressions of the living feelings of contemporary society. By creating something genuine for our time, we can strike deep chords in the public and stimulate real excitement and demand for our products.

I am suggesting what may seem like an awesome task. I am saying that we must venture out into this materialistic, externally oriented world, and say to the consumer, "Buy my product because it will give you a deep, personal satisfaction, instead of buying that fancy soap because it has a glamorous name, or that unnecessary new car because it will give you prestige." This may indeed be struggling against a massive tide, but I believe that the manufacturer who tries it will find there are growing undercurrents that will help him. I see plenty of signs all over the world—the "culture beam" is one of them—that people are realizing that simply spending to impress the other fellow yields very shallow satisfactions. I believe more and more people are looking for something more satisfying and are ready to listen to the man who offers it. My conviction that this is so stems from the experience of our own company. In the decade since we first started producing china and tableware with contemporary designs which we feel are attuned to our time, they have become by far the most important and fastest-growing part of our business.

The "modern look" in design is already well established. In fact, there is always the danger that it will become too well established, that manufacturers will fix on a popular style and make it into a cliché which can become as dead as the imitations of the styles of two hundred years ago.

The modern look has its roots partly in the "form follows function" philosophy of Germany's Bauhaus school before World War II, partly in the Scandinavian designs which drew both on the Bauhaus idea and on local folk art traditions. It is notable for its simple, clean, graceful lines, and its world-wide popularity seems to reflect the contemporary attraction toward a clean, open, uncluttered, direct way of life.

There is no fixed formula for identifying or producing the most successful modern design. In the earlier days of this movement, pure functionalism seemed to be the answer. More recently, the trend seems to be toward "functionalism plus"—a less rigid, less ascetic style that retains the clean functional look but adds to it a generally restrained embellishment, a rather more warm and personal note. This shift shows why manufacturers have to be alert to trends in popular taste, to adopt a dynamic approach, and not fix on one style, which can become outmoded. The manufacturer who wants to capture new markets must be a leader, not an imitator.

It is perhaps too early to know where these contemporary trends will lead. One should not assume from the influence of Scandinavia that the world will be engulfed by a single "modern" style that will wipe out regional and national cultural distinctions. That would be a pity. It is true that modern communications have produced great similarities in widely scattered and traditionally very different cultures. But what will probably happen is that these seeds from Scandinavia will take root in different countries and will blossom with distinctive national colorings, and that a rich cross fertilization will take place from one country to another.

I have been speaking about good design as the means of winning customers away from other kinds of products. It is obviously also an important competitive tool among manufacturers in the same field. Industrialization and standardization have tended to diminish the differences in quality between competing products. Design can thus be the critical factor in the competition between producers of similar items, other factors (such as sales techniques) being equal; good design can be applied to low-priced, mass-produced articles, although if a manufacturer is working on a very low unit cost basis, he will naturally have less cash to invest in developing designs.

Of course, the key to turning out well-designed products is to have good designers. This is a real problem, because if you are trying to turn out products that will be genuine and exciting enough to create demand, then you must have really creative artists designing them and not run-of-the-mill copiers. No company can afford to retain a large staff of fine artists. Our solution has been to supplement our small group of staff artists and artisans with a large number of outside designers who work on a commission basis. This enables us to get real variety from the best available talents. This outside group now creates or participates in the design of about 80% of our top-grade contemporary line.

One way to get fresh, exciting designs is by seeking designers from a wide variety of sources. This means using designers from different countries, and also finding designers who have distinguished themselves in fields which may be quite different from your own, but whose talents are transferable. Our company, for example, numbers among its outside designers a textile designer and a fashion designer who had never before worked with china.

The process of finding new designers, and of helping them work up new designs, demands from the manufacturer an investment of interest, patience, and money. Good designs are not born overnight, especially when they are created by people new to the particular materials. Only about one-third of the designs of designers considered by us finally enter production. When we find a promising designer, our company sometimes advances him money to give him time to develop his ideas. Ultimately, however, this is deducted from his royalties. The royalty system works very well, because it forces the artist to think about the economic and market factors, not just the purely artistic ones.

The final product must be the result of teamwork between the artist, the technicians, and the businessmen. There must be an interplay of ideas among them and compromises from all sides. Sometimes, for example, the technicians may reject an artist's idea because of technical considerations and suggest something else, which often leads to improving the artistic quality; very often an artist's idea opens up technical possibilities the technicians have not thought of. In our company, the outside designers work at the plant studio while they are doing a design for us, in order to help ensure this teamwork. Although staff designers have created their own designs, their main function is to work with the outside designers, serving as a link between them and the technicians.

The teamwork must not stop with the manufacture of the product. It must extend right through to the salesman in the retail store, or else the entire effort may be wasted. First of all, it is necessary to have sales personnel on all levels who understand and sympathize with what the designer and manufacturer are trying to achieve and who are capable of transferring their enthusiasm to the customer. In companies which have been stuck in the rut of tired, "safe," old-fashioned design, it may be necessary to go so far as to replace key personnel, if they are not flexible enough to adapt to the new program.

It is very important to have the right sales personnel in the retail shops. Because they are introducing something new to the public, a good part of their job is really educational. They must have a thorough knowledge and appreciation of the products, in order to be able to kindle appreciation and enthusiasm in the customer. Sales people of this type are rare. We have solved the problem by hiring well-educated, intelligent girls directly at the factory and training them for four weeks in production techniques, to give them a sound understanding of the product. They are then made available to the special retail outlets handling our top-grade contemporary line. The latter are more than glad to hire them. In the stores, the salesgirls receive further training. They learn about the individual designers and what they are trying to do, about proper presentation, some sales psychology, and of course, prices. Training in the store takes about three months.

Proper physical presentation of the product is also critical. If distinguished designs are thrown in with run-of-the-mill products in what I call the "hat rack" presentation, they will too often be swamped in a mass of mediocrity. Therefore, we decided it was necessary to exert strong influence on the retail outlets handling our top contemporary line.

We do this in two ways. We have set up in important European cities stores which carry our name and which our own architects design. Under the terms of our agreement with the store owners, these stores carry only our best contemporary designs, as well as products made by other companies—including our competitors—which have been selected by a panel of outside experts as meeting a high standard of taste and good design. The stores may select from the panel's recommendations, but they may not sell products which have not been approved.

The panel of seven experts was chosen by the company on the basis of their critical abilities in various aspects of design. They receive a fairly modest retaining fee from the company and decide on the designs to be included in our own top contemporary line (which is labeled with the trade name "Studio Line") as well as on the products of other companies which may be sold by the special retail outlets.

To help create public awareness and interest in what we are trying to accomplish, we help these outlets stage special events throughout the year. Typically, this would be a special showing devoted to the work of one of our top designers in all his different fields, with the designer on hand for a press reception to explain his work. These events have attracted great interest among the press, and their publicity value is obvious. For instance, we showed Emilio Pasion china designs along with his own fashion show.

When we first set out to establish special retail outlets a few years ago, the idea was new, and it was hard to find retailers willing to invest money in them. Therefore, we took an equity position in the first that were established. On the basis of these stores' success, we are now able to attract retailers who take full ownership. When necessary, we do help with the initial financing on a loan basis.

We have found that in the cities where these shops are established sales of our products are also dramatically boosted in other local retail outlets, much to the surprise of their owners, who often feared competition from the new shops. This would seem to support our basic contention that good design and proper selling can increase a product's total market.

In addition to these special shops, we have also made arrangements with many retail outlets—to date about 130—to set up special departments in their stores which are exclusively devoted to our "Studio Line." Our agreements with these outlets include certain standards of presentation which our own designers plan. For example, table settings are shown, not just china stacked on shelves. Many of the agreements also include commitments for a certain amount of window display space.

At first many retailers resisted the idea of setting aside a special department designed by us. They felt that this limited their freedom. However, this resistance has tended to disappear with the discovery that the special department draws customers and increases the store's entire business and prestige.

Until this year, all of our "Studio Line" could be sold through any retail shop, besides the special shops and departments. However, we are gradually setting aside important forms and designs within this line for sale only in the special outlets. By this means we succeed in improving the presentation of our top lines and help those shops and stores that went along with our ideas of presenting the merchandise with an idea behind it.

Unless a company has just been formed, it would find it impractical to launch such a program all at once, revamping its entire design, distribution, and sales approach. But this can be done gradually; a company can establish within its overall operation an "island" devoted to the concept of good contemporary design, and this is not too costly a venture. A separate corps of outside designers can be recruited for it, and a separate, undiluted distribution system established, composed of people who really believe in the new goals.

Within this system, the manufacturer can afford to maintain a rigid high standard, even if this means limiting sales for the time being.

This is the approach our company has taken. First we departed from our traditional line by adding contemporary designs created by the best designers we could find. These gradually became successful even through our conventional distribution channels. When we had a large enough group of such designs, we began setting them off with the "Studio Line" label. Now we are setting up a separate distribution system for them.

We believe that the philosophy and methods of approach I have just described have been responsible for much of our success, both in strengthening our position against our direct competitors and in increasing the total market for our product. At the beginning of this study I showed how the German china industry's share of total consumer purchases has been growing smaller. As evidence of the success of our policy of producing and properly selling products of contemporary design, I should mention that our own company's sales increased nearly fivefold between 1949 and 1962 and that our share of total consumer purchases has increased, in contrast to the trend for the china industry as a whole.

This seems to show that in certain types of consumer industries an apparently idealistic approach may be the most realistic policy. It also gives more fun, satisfaction, and pride to everybody concerned in it—and that cannot be measured in dollars and cents.

POLICY AND PROCEDURES IN DEVELOPING BUSINESS VENTURES

John D. Cassidy

Policy Considerations

The Problem. With the advent of jet aircraft the world has become a small place. Today few areas, however remote, are more than twenty-four hours away from any spot on earth. Together with the advances in global transportation and communications have come drastic changes in the outlook of people everywhere. All over the world, people have suddenly become conscious of what others are doing and of the way they are living. The appetite of those in the "have not" nations has become whetted by the desire to create a better way of life for themselves. They are desperately seeking to emulate the living standards of the more highly developed areas. This determination for the better life comes at a time when there is an intense global struggle between two economic philosophies, the free enterprise system and communism. The outcome of this struggle will affect the future course of history, economic and otherwise.

The world today is roughly divided into three areas, and each area contains about 900 million persons. First there are the already highly developed and industrialized components of the Free World, then the rapidly developing Sino-Soviet communistic area, and finally the less developed areas of the Free World, with which this chapter is mainly concerned.

In any discussion of the less developed nations, it is important to recognize that the people of these areas are in no way inferior, however "backward" their economies may appear to an outsider. We must recognize that, as education increases, so too will the scientific and industrial capabilities of the peoples of less developed nations. In many ways, the present state of the developing

Mr. Cassidy is Vice President of EBS Management Consultants Incorporated, New York.

nations has close parallels in the early days of American history. It is only a question of time before they, too, will take their places among the developed nations, and this time may be sooner than we realize, for these nations now have available to them advanced techniques which took other nations generations to develop. This has important implications which cannot be overlooked.

In a world where all peoples have equal scientific and industrial potential, the strongest side—from a military standpoint—is determined by numbers. It is therefore essential to the survival of the Free World, and of the way of life to which it subscribes, that at least a majority of the peoples of developing nations be able to find out for themselves the merits of the free enterprise system, else there is the risk that they will be overrun with communism.

But how can nations best be helped which have illiteracy rates approaching 85 percent, with inadequate schooling, little knowledge of local resources, erosion of readily available resources, inadequate land transportation, and a shortage of power? What should they develop first—basic industries, capital goods, or consumer goods?

Basic Industries, Capital Goods, or Consumer Goods. Experience suggests that all three of these areas must develop simultaneously and on an evolutionary basis. Basic industries require huge investments and sophisticated know-how. In many of the developing areas there is an abundance of local funds, but unfortunately, in most instances, these funds cannot be used to purchase equipment from abroad because little foreign exchange is available for this purpose. Local technical know-how is almost nonexistent, although there is a growing nucleus of well-educated individuals who can be taught the technical know-how.

Capital goods must for the most part be imported, because the facilities and the raw materials needed to produce them are not yet generally available. This means that these items must come from outside, and foreign exchange must be generated and conserved to purchase them, at least in the early stages of development.

The demand for consumer goods is rising at an unprecedented rate. "Cottage" industries have been springing up to supply some of these needs, but the items produced are generally of inferior quality, and even the local uneducated people know that some of this homemade merchandise does not measure up to imported products. The cottage industry relies on readily available local materials and on such other materials as are crudely generated from scrap.

Capital and Know-how, the Vital Missing Ingredients. It is most important for industrialists to recognize that there is not enough foreign exchange or money available for these nations to purchase the things they need from abroad. Therefore, the two vital missing ingredients are capital goods and technical know-how. Given these ingredients in adequate quantities, the developing nations of the world can and will progress at a satisfactory rate—basically under a free enterprise system. This is why the growth of these nations has particular appeal to businessmen of other lands who subscribe to the free enterprise system.

Many enterprising industrialists of the Free World are translating this common interest into action. They have found that it is mutually profitable to establish a joint venture and/or a license arrangement with local entrepreneurs. In such ventures, Free World industrialists are investing capital goods and technical know-how. Both parties stand to gain, not only from the standpoint of mutual security, but also from that of mutual profit.

Local Habits and Traditions. In considering a joint venture, however, the question arises as to whether we adjust production procedure to local habits and traditions or attempt to adjust local personnel to foreign production procedure, and it appears that we must do a little of both. We must accept existing situations and "roll with the punches" for now, while working toward the day when local personnel will more and more adopt sophisticated production procedures in a competitive society. Right now, labor is cheap and plentiful, and, putting first things first, we must recognize that it is extremely important to put these people to work earning a better livelihood and constantly improving their standards of living.

To one who has lived all his life in a highly developed nation, it may seem almost incredible that others whose forebears have spent generations in an area, and who have relied for the most part on an agricultural economy, do not yet have the proper tools even for agriculture. Throughout all of the Asian subcontinent, for instance, plowing is done with a wooden plow, called a *hoel*, which is capable of plowing only a two-inch furrow. It takes a local farmer from one to two days to plow a one-acre plot. With a plowshare, common in America more than seventy years ago, the same farmer with the same pair of oxen could plow his field in one-quarter of the time—but the plowshares are not available.

The evolution to the use of more modern tools and equipment must necessarily be gradual, because the problems of maintenance and equipment repair are tremendous. Much of the modern transportation equipment (buses, etc.) supplied to these areas through various foreign aid programs has fallen into disuse because suitable repair facilities are lacking. It is essential, therefore, that maintenance and repair facilities be able to keep pace with an ever-increasing rate of technological progress. It is also essential that this progress be at a rate far above the birth rate in order to accomplish the primary objective of increased standards of living in a reasonable period of time.

One of the most serious roadblocks in the way of progress is the lack of a distribution system or complex; yet apparently little attention is being given to this problem. Suppose we created a factory in one of the developing nations to produce much-needed farm implements. How would we get them to the farmer? How would he know they were available? Where would he buy them? There are no distributors or dealers, no farm implement houses, not even stores as we know them.

Traveling through these areas, one detects a feeling, even in educated circles, that distribution is of secondary importance—the most important thing is to make the products available, and the customers will automatically beat a path to the factory door. Experienced businessmen know this to be a fallacy which has been demonstrated time and again, but the "better mousetrap" idea, which was accepted in the United States until well into this century, is still common in some countries. Hence if the overall objective of increased standards of living is to be attained, the important problems of marketing, including sales promotion, selling, and distribution, must be solved concurrently, else we will have the peculiar paradox of overproduction in a land which actually needs even more of the products.

Where would the United States be today without the aggressive merchandising activities of the door-to-door salesman, the mail-order house, the department store, the many specialty stores—all supplemented by tremendous advertising campaigns? Generally speaking, goods locally made or imported in many instances today do not provide sufficient profit margins to support the selling effort needed to create a major market or to support an ever-increasing flow of products, but internal production of properly selected items *can* support such marketing efforts and must have them in order to survive.

Where would the United States be today if not for our installment buying system? How many people would own automobiles, refrigerators, TV sets, etc., if they were unable to buy these items on the installment plan? Even our large department stores, mail-order houses, discount houses, etc., buy on 30-, 60-, and 90-day credit, but such credit facilities are virtually nonexistent in the developing nations of the world. True, there are moneylenders in almost every area, but the cost of this kind of credit is prohibitive. If a farmer, for instance, borrows from a moneylender in order to purchase a pair of oxen, he may be indebted to that moneylender for the rest of his life. If one of the oxen dies, his situation is almost hopeless. There is a false conviction in many quarters that the peoples of developing nations are not always strictly honest and upright in their business dealings and cannot be extended the same kind of credit facilities which we of the highly developed nations enjoy. This generalization has no foundation whatsoever. We may assume, on the contrary, that the peoples of these nations are all endowed with the same honesty and the same potential brainpower as the rest of us. What is necessary is that an atmosphere be created in which these credit accommodations can, and will, be extended to all who deserve them. The element of credit is another factor which must be developed on an evolutionary basis along with all the factors which contribute to higher standards of living.

In merchandising under these conditions, do we strive for large volume with low markup, or for small volume with high markup? Experience suggests that a middle course is indicated, because at the start neither the market nor the distribution system will support a really large production volume, while the disposable income of the customers will not enable them to pay prices which might normally be justified by a relatively low rate of production. As has been demonstrated in some countries already, both of those retarding factors can be remedied fairly rapidly, but there has to be a period of buildup, and the governments concerned are helping the starters in these programs by granting special privileges mentioned elsewhere. During this period, an atmosphere must be created which will encourage the establishment of mail-order houses, specialty stores, department stores, direct selling activities, and all the other methods which have made the United States the strong industrial complex it now is.

Other Considerations Which Complicate the Problem. There are many other considerations which must be looked into before a new industrial establishment can be undertaken in a developing nation.

First of all, there is the important consideration of feasibility. What industry should be selected? Where should it be located? How big should it be? Each of these factors requires careful consideration, but for the most part, unfortunately, only inadequate basic information will be available. In most developing nations the intelligentsia have given some consideration to these problems, sometimes on their own and sometimes with the collaboration of consultants furnished by the governments of the more highly developed nations, but the information available will still be inadequate to form the basis of sound conclusions. Even such basic data as statistics on imports can be very misleading, because they may be either incomplete or inaccurate, yet some reasonable and economical way must be found to get at the factors which must be considered to determine feasibility.

Once a determination has been made that a given project is worthy of exploitation, there are other problems to consider.

The problem can be simple in the case of license agreements, because after all they will revolve around a contractual arrangement equitable to both sides. However, if a joint venture is being considered under which entrepreneurs from two or more countries will have equity interests, the situation can become very complex. For instance, what type of corporate setup can be arranged in which a foreign investor might have something less than 50 percent of the equity interest? What kind of protection can be afforded to him for his know-how and his investment? Can he control its management, at least in the early years of information and implementation? What happens if there is a serious disagreement between the two partners? These are among the basic questions that must be considered.

There are many other additional management concepts to be implemented by agreement, including those relating to marketing in its broadest sense. The lack of attention given to this important function even by the more highly educated entrepreneurs has already been mentioned.

A case history will point up this situation, one which concerns the marketing of shotgun shells. Incredible as it may seem, a facility located in a developing nation was making shotgun shells to a finer standard and a higher quality than in the United States, but they were not being sold in sufficient quantities to justify the investment already made. It turned out that the shells were being sold through "bazaar stores," many of which existed throughout the nation. The bazaar stores were contacted (or supposed to have been contacted) by a factory salesman who earned the huge sum of 1 percent of net sales! Worse than that, the bazaar store proprietor was allowed a discount of only 7 percent. When this entrepreneur was told about the American way of marketing such products, he was not only astounded, but seemed to doubt whether it could work even for the American counterpart of the bazaar store—the hardware store. That an American hardware store would expect a minimum of 40 percent discount from the retail selling price, that the distributor or jobber would expect another 10 to 15 percent, that the factory salesman selling the product to the wholesale house would get commissions varying from 4 to 5 percent, and, on top of this, that advertising and sales promotion materials must be provided—all this seemed unbelievable.

The next problem of major importance has to do with wholesale and retail credit. Some success may be realized in the early days of the venture when the availability of the products becomes known to the citizenry at large, but sooner or later consideration must be given to wholesale and retail credit, else progress will stagnate. An example from Southeast Asia illustrates how important this is. In this particular case, a foreign manufacturer of motor scooters has licensed a local entrepreneur to manufacture and sell his line of scooters. Some of the component parts are still being made in the manufacturer's own country, but an assembly line has been set up to assemble the motor scooters from components partly made locally, partly from abroad. The assembly line is very efficient, presently turning out about twenty motor scooters daily, but it could produce many more if they could be sold. The scooters could be sold if there were a finance plan available to local would-be buyers. An installment purchase plan could, in the words of the entrepreneur, triple or quadruple his sales in one year.

What about the financing of the capital structure of the proposed undertaking? In most developing nations there are a host of entrepreneurs who have large deposits of local funds, but they are unable to get foreign exchange to purchase, for instance, U.S. equipment from American manufacturers who, from necessity, would have to be paid U.S. dollars. There are many foreign investors who could become partners with the local entrepreneurs, but they too may lack the resources to make the investment in a joint venture, or they may not desire to risk so much money in any one particular venture. In many cases, however, they are not aware of the many sources of loan funds available to them to assist in the establishment of such ventures.

There are other questions to consider: What kind of organizational setup can be established which will be fair and equitable to both sides? Will one party dominate management, and for how long? What safeguards can be instituted to protect both sides in the event of a serious disagreement? In addition to all the foregoing, there are many problems involving taxes, insurance, labor rules and regulations, fringe benefits, and other items too numerous to mention, none of which can be safely ignored even in the initial feasibility decision.

In summary, the problems are many and varied. They all seem very complicated—as indeed they are—but with competent advice and planning, the complexity begins to dissolve. When we approach the problem soundly, we find that doing business in developing nations can be no more complex than in the United States, and the key is *planning* based on carefully predetermined facts.

Suggested Approach to Problem Solution. No hard and fast rules can be set forth to guide foreign entrepreneurs in attaining their full potential success in the developing nations of the world because, in effect, almost every individual transaction will be different. In addition, there are different rules and regulations for doing business in the various developing nations. However, here are some of the ways and means which have been and are now being used to solve these problems.

There are certain basic facts which every foreign manufacturer must consider when he plans to exploit his overseas potential.

The international business climate has changed considerably in the last decade. No longer can manufacturers in highly developed nations expect to export finished items to developing nations, because, even if the peoples of these developing nations desire to purchase finished goods made abroad, they can no longer get the necessary foreign exchange to complete such transactions, except in a very limited way. Their governments will guard very carefully their available foreign exchange in order to reserve this for the purchase of raw materials and other components needed to support their own developing industrial complexes. This is a very necessary move if they are in fact to increase employment within their own countries and thus raise their standards of living—the ultimate desire of every nation throughout the civilized world.

This changing aspect of the international situation dictates that if a manufacturer in a highly developed nation is intent on exploiting his whole potential in the developing nations, he must discard old concepts and plan for some kind of joint venture or licensing agreement, else he may find that his chances of doing business in the area will be nil.

Generally speaking, even the intelligentsia of developing nations are suspicious of foreigners. This is only natural, because over the centuries they have been exploited in many areas by the more highly developed nations, who all too often extracted their resources and sold finished goods in return, with no thought of encouraging the creation of a self-supporting economy. They now wonder what to expect, and with what motives the peoples of the Free World are coming to them. They want to be, and they must be, convinced of our sincerity. Our joint venture and/or license agreements, therefore, must be *mutually beneficial.*

With proper motivation, and a reasonable opportunity, the developing nations can attain, in probably little more than one generation, the economic and industrial progress which the United States and others attained only very slowly over a period of many generations. The developing nations already have available to them the managerial principles and technological stepping-stones which the present industrial nations had to build laboriously before they could climb. Technology in being, added to the advice and other assistance made available from various sources, provides the opportunity. The motivation comes from the acute and increasing awareness on the part of developing nations of the benefits gained by other peoples, only recently in similar situations, who have already made progress up the steps.

Japanese progress since the end of World War II, though not directly comparable to some situations in the developing nations, is nevertheless a classic example of what can be done in a relatively short time. Even before that war, Japan had undergone an amazing transition, jumping to the stature of a world power in about seven decades from a standing start rooted in twenty-five centuries of medieval-type feudalism.

At first Japan merely copied not only foreign products but also some ideas and institutions. Even then, as is well proved in commercial history, Japan made great inroads on many cherished markets of the world. But Japan's more impressive, more lasting accomplishment of the prewar period was its emergence from feudalism to an economic, social, and political order capable of fitting in and competing with modern industrial nations. That made possible, but not less amazing, the last stage of the process, in which the Japanese are no longer copying but are creating and leading in many areas.

In less than two decades since 1945, Japan has become a fully modern industrial nation in the best sense of the term. She is now among the world leaders, capable of helping other nations and already actively doing so.

Japan has achieved all this in a period which is amazingly short in relation to the "time of climb" of other industrial nations. Developing nations still farther down the road can take heart from the Japanese example, but they have a higher springboard from which to depart.

There are still some businessmen and others who take the shortsighted position that programs being followed to assist developing nations will create commercial and industrial chaos. "Why," they ask, "should a businessman help build competition for himself?" In some cases, the question stems from an ostrich attitude which refuses to recognize that the world has turned a long way from the era when world markets were open to exploitation by outside interests. It also fails to recognize that, even under the best prior conditions, the market in a given country was only a fraction of what it might have been had it included the whole population and not just a narrow segment. The age of exploitation is past. Instead, the accelerated progress of developing nations is creating new markets which will bring almost incredible opportunities to businessmen who are able to understand and act on the facts. First, however, a businessman who would share in this growth must discard the thought of simply making and selling, either directly or through wholly owned subsidiaries. Rather, he must investigate thoroughly and then adopt the particular procedures or concepts, including joint venture arrangements, which are suitable under the conditions that exist today.

Where and How Do We Start?

A foreigner considering the possibility of going into business in one of the developing countries would be wise to follow a meticulous approach. In one sense, launching any new business, even under familiar circumstances at home, is fraught with risks. To set up a successful new business in the less well known environment of a developing nation calls for a business counterpart of the space age "countdown."

Each step, no matter how obvious or basic it may seem in the home environment, must be singled out for specific examination in the context of the contemplated environment. The businessman will find information and advice available to him, though he may have some searching to do. But his first step is to recognize the need for preplanned thoroughness before he even begins to search for the data he needs.

The Feasibility Countdown. While it is not possible to spell out the specific steps needed to analyze every situation in every country, answers to the following questions, illustrating typical steps along the way, will be needed to some extent in every situation:

1. Which country appears most desirable as the one in which to start?

2. Does that country seem to have a potential market for my product line? Or what alternative product lines am I prepared to consider for a joint venture?

3. What is the business climate in the country I have tentatively chosen? For example: What about taxes? Required permits and concessions? Import licenses for equipment and materials?

4. What is the initial market? The ultimate market? How long will it take

to attain the necessary market? What price structure would be acceptable for initial and ultimate markets?

5. Where should the enterprise be based?

6. What raw materials, hardware, and components may be purchased locally? Which ones must be imported? From where? At what delivered cost?

7. What technical and managerial skills are already available in the country, and how can the skills that are lacking be provided?

8. What parts and assemblies can be made in the country?

9. Can the necessary marketing concepts be implemented without insurmountable obstacles from customs and traditions? How long will that take?

10. What size and type of plant will be necessary and feasible?

11. What capital equipment will be needed? Where will it come from? At what delivered cost?

12. What will be the production and operating costs, both direct and indirect?

13. What will be the break-even production volume, and how long will it take to attain that volume?

14. In the light of tentative answers to the foregoing questions, what amount of capital will be needed to establish the enterprise soundly? How much working capital is needed?

15. What guarantees are available with respect to investment against political and commercial risks—as well as the removal of profits in U.S. dollars?

16. What capital is available in the country, and how is it to be located?

17. What financial structure is necessary and feasible?

18. What degree of control may be exercised by each party?

19. What type of organization will be feasible?

20. How should a complete and specific feasibility study be made, and at what cost?

After reading those questions, the sophisticated businessman may consider them too elementary. Yet the wise chief executive would seek answers to most of these (and many other) questions before starting a new venture even at home. Because the factors vary so much from those at home, and also because conditions and attitudes have been changing so radically even in fairly recent years, the detailed "countdown procedure" is the only safe process for launching a new enterprise. If the answer all along is "go," all is well. But if there is even a minor snag, time should be taken to find and correct the cause before venturing ahead.

This does not mean that there are always hidden pitfalls, or that such ventures are inherently more dangerous than domestic ones. It only means that unique conditions exist and must be recognized. While conventional American solutions may not always work, common business sense will still prevail; but that common sense must be applied against a background of detailed knowledge that takes into account all circumstances—few of which are in the textbooks or in the usual economic reports. Still, the company or individual financier interested in the possibility of participating in a joint venture in a developing country has ample information and assistance available to him.

Getting the Facts. The most obvious first step is to contact the several governmental or international agencies which are active in various aspects of industrial and economic development throughout the world. Although some needed information is readily available from such sources, a great deal more has to be searched out, analyzed, and related to the requirements of the particular venture.

Suitable answers to the previously suggested list of questions are the end products of a comprehensive "feasibility study," which can be expensive, whether it is carried out by the investor's staff or by outside consultants employed for the purpose. If it is to be done properly, it calls for the highest-quality research and analysis by varied types of expects whom few companies have on their regular staffs. The costs involved have undoubtedly deterred many potential investors from seriously considering their possibilities in the developing nations. With the special AID (Agency for International Development) arrangement to reduce the amount of risk involved in making the necessary preinvestment survey or feasibility study in qualified cases, it may be worthwhile for more companies or investors to become seriously interested in their prospects in a developing nation.

Planning the Venture. If the feasibility of the project has been favorably established, including the matter of capital requirements, then the problems of corporate financial structure, sources of local capital, and the relationships between joint venture participants must be resolved. The way will have been paved for a good part of this if the feasibility study was comprehensive enough. Even so, it is now necessary to be more specific about questions such as:

1. Who furnishes how much capital and in what form?
2. Where does control rest and for how long?
3. What safeguards can be provided for the minority interests?
4. What form of corporate organization should be adopted?

Financing the Venture. In general, it is probable that the American investor may be permitted to have no more than 50 percent of the equity interest. Though he may have to put up, in effect, more than 50 percent of the capital, it is possible that a good part of his contribution can be in the form of capital equipment, tools, and dies shipped from the United States. In addition, patents, licenses, and know-how (both technical and managerial) may have to be provided by the American partner. In some cases already considered, this type of capital contribution can be almost enough to cover the American partner's share of the obligation, but considerable cash may be required in many other instances.

The portion of required capital which comes from within the developing country will generally be in local currency. A sufficiently comprehensive feasibility study will at least have discovered leads to a number of suitable local sources. The local government may also be able to help find partners within the country.

Protecting Minority Interests. The next questions concern control and provision for protecting the interests of the minority participant, who is probably the foreign investor. This is not easy, but neither is it impossible if approached intelligently, particularly in the light of guarantees available from local governments as well as from other investment insurance programs. A definite and sufficiently binding understanding is needed, however, and it certainly should not be treated lightly. Again, nothing should be taken for granted, assumed, or "understood." Everything should be spelled out, such as, for example, a possible "last resort" provision for one side to buy the interests of the other side on specified terms in the event of irreconcilable differences. In any event, suitable understandings have been developed in the past, and they should be easier under present circumstances, which include the fairly new types of guarantees from official sources.

Spelling Out Policies. Though not necessarily in the same document as the needed understanding mentioned above, there must also be clear prior agreements on such matters as policies relating to labor and management personnel and to marketing plans, including sales, pricing, and distribution. Another policy which must be firmly spelled out relates to the disposition of earnings: What portion of earnings will be plowed back into the business, and for how long? What portion may be distributed to equity interests, and in what form?

When such questions arise in an American company, they may be left for a board of directors to decide. When they arise in connection with a foreign venture, however, they may easily be neglected as points on which firm agreement must be reached before a final commitment is made. The lack of a suitable and binding understanding on these very points can cause serious difficulty. Only when everything relating to the future operation has been spelled out prior to final commitment can both parties comfortably sit down together to make it work.

Perhaps this approach sounds formidable, but there is no need for concern. Even if all the details of agreement were spelled out instead of being briefed, the list would generally be only a little longer than one required when starting a business in this country.

Thoroughness Is the Key. The main difference between considering the feasibility of a new business in a developing nation and that of one in the United States is in the thoroughness with which all factors are to be considered. Even in the United States, fewer new businesses would fail if similar thoroughness were exercised. The strange environment merely stresses this need for thoroughness; it does not necessarily mean that the danger is greater or that the process is too difficult. In fact, with available official safeguards, a properly planned venture in a developing country can be even safer than a similar venture at home, and the profit potential may be greater. This should be a matter of great interest to both large and small investors, because the potentials are immense and the risks are less than they have ever been before.

THE CONTROLLER'S CONTRIBUTION TO ORGANIZED INTERNATIONALISM

Herbert C. Knortz, M.B.A.; B.B.A.; C.P.A.

The decade of the 1960s will be characterized by a vigorous international surge in business affairs. This new international development will be as unique in its own way as were those of the Venetian traders, the Hanseatic League, the British colonizers, or the oil imperialists. An essential characteristic of the new era will be an international reliance upon local industrial competence and upon a mutually profitable trade between developing nations and those which have reached industrial maturity. The controllership function will contribute significantly to the effective development of this organized internationalism.

International Controllership

Controllership is essentially a communication function which has as its basic objectives the facilitation of accurate decision making and the inducement of effective action. Over the years it has shown a remarkable ability to adapt to the changing needs of the business environment. At various times in its chronologic development, controllership has emphasized the demands of the commercial traders, the viewpoints of the small industrialists, the requirements of consolidated enterprises, and, more recently, the needs of international trade and finance.

As a communication function, controllership must arrange to assimilate masses of data and tabulate them into appropriate classes for presentation as meaningful economic relationships. Other business functions attempt analysis of various activity segments (e.g., quality control, market statistics, personnel data), but only in controllership is the full panorama of business placed under logical surveillance.

Mr. Knortz is Vice President and Comptroller of the International Telephone and Telegraph Corporation.

As a consequence, controllership stands as the integrating force which gives perspective to the decisions of the management group and analyzes the group's success in comparison with other periods of time and other economic units. It integrates because it comprehends

1. The utilization of various economic resources
2. The processes by which performance is achieved
3. The nature of the completed production

It gives true perspective because it applies objective and unbiased criteria within a framework of practical (not idealistic) accuracy. It measures areas of accomplishment as absolute values and as compared with other economic alternatives.

As an internationalist, the controller is faced with certain special challenges which do not concern his colleague working in the purely domestic environment. He must adapt the technique of his procedure so as to recognize the needs of the local controller in a developing nation while at the same time encompassing the sophisticated requirements of a parent company financial group. Barriers to common understanding inevitably exist and must be eliminated. Time delays must be minimized. Professional standards and practices must be appropriately reconciled. Above all, the controller must apply in the wider sphere of international activity the acid test of all business accomplishment—"available profit over the long term."

Staffing the Controllership Function

The international controller requires unusual skill as a manager and as a professional financial man. Whether he works in the international headquarters or in the environment of the developing nation, the controller must accept the responsibility of being the most informed financial man in his geographic area. Since he is relied upon to know the intricacies of financial practice within his particular environment, he must constantly improve his skills and broaden his acquaintance.

Furthermore, he cannot rely on a specialization in systems, audit, market pricing, and cost accounting, as could his colleague in domestic practice. Instead, he must constantly deal with the problems of raw material restrictions, export guarantees, fluctuating currencies, changing political environments, local financing, and language and social complications. In concept, the scope of the job is inestimably greater than that of domestic work, and it is made easier for the local operator only by the smaller size of most foreign subsidiaries.

In recruiting the staff of a new subsidiary in a developing country, every possible attempt should be made to find a well-trained local man who can establish the financial function. Experience indicates, however, that these men are seldom available. Consequently, it usually becomes necessary to recruit a competent man from outside the local borders.

This new man may be an experienced member of the parent company staff or a newly employed person with broad international experience. In either case, he must have proficient business use of the languages spoken in the local area and in the home office. It is a serious mistake to expect a vigorous installation activity out of a "noncommunicator."

Whenever possible the new controller should recruit his own staff, and it is important that he insist on rigorous employee selection, even at the expense of paying high initial salaries. He must set very strict standards for the new group, since the early habits of the new company will do much to set the pace for later years. Above all, he must insist upon a professional viewpoint and must begin from the start to emphasize the unit's basic obligation to its stockholders.

In all probability the new controller will be hired at a liberal salary to ensure his availability. Since he will subsequently be replaced by a local man, it is desirable to separate his total compensation into salary, special allowances, and local allowances. The salary can reflect the value of the job, and, in theory, it should represent the pay which would be earned by the local replacement. The special allowances should reflect the parent company policy on overseas living allowances or tax adjustments, and the local allowances should represent special privileges made available to the job (e.g., car and chauffeur, quarters, club rights).

Obviously, it is more expensive to import professional skills, and it is important, therefore, that every possible step be taken to train adequate local replacements for the top jobs and for the supporting supervisory positions. This staff development will prove particularly helpful when new economic and political forces disturb the normal continuity of corporate relationships.

Timeliness and Clarity in Reporting

An international operation is seldom relieved of the customary need for well-coordinated reporting. As a rule, the financial reporting date of the international headquarters is governed by the timing of its press releases to the financial community. This date is normally established as the "tenth working day of the following month" for interim reports, and added time is allowed for the more complete reporting at the end of the year.

The expansion of an enterprise to encompass a foreign area will not usually be allowed to alter the customary deadlines. It is important, therefore, that a policy be formulated which will permit coordinated reporting. Several alternatives are possible:

1. To avoid consolidating the new subsidiary and thus to relieve the pressure for timeliness. This solution is useful when the foreign operations are not material in significance.

2. To accept the reports of foreign subsidiaries on a one-month-lag basis (inclusion of subsidiary's November with parent's December). This procedure is not inconvenient if prompt control of operations is assured by other measures and if the net income of the subsidiary is relatively constant in amount.

3. To gear the subsidiary reports to the corporate reporting cycles, and by proper communications and methods work to assure reliable compliance. This policy requires some leeway for special delays due to local holidays, political situations, unusual clearance of special transactions, and air or cable traffic problems.

In achieving a sound reporting structure, it is important that the report schedule be well publicized and that emergency procedures be ready to cope with unusual situations. Where possible the data should feed directly into an automated data processing system at headquarters. Similarly, the data should be the logical summary of information developed on the local books so as to minimize unnecessary delays caused by the restatement of information.

"Clarity" is as important as "timing" in achieving a sound reporting system. In international practice clarity presents a special problem. Three aspects seem particularly significant:

1. *The language problem.* Where multiple subsidiaries exist, it is impractical to expect the head office manager to learn several foreign languages. Instead, a "corporate" language should be identified, so that no one person needs to know more than one language in addition to his native tongue. In almost all cases, translation into the corporate language is best accomplished in the field.

2. *Preprinted formats.* Nuances of meaning inevitably creep into reporting practice. These can be minimized if standard preprinted formats are used. In addition, matters relating to particular data can be made more definitive in cable or telephone communications if reference is made to lines and columns identified by number.

3. *Monthly letters.* A supplementary written report from each foreign controller can permit the home office staff to "flesh out" the bare data represented by the financial tabulations. The letter should cover all items of interest having an effect on the financial affairs of the subsidiary. It may deal with rates of exchange, national budgets, insurance rates, availability of money, labor rates, inventory levels, quotas, tax matters, lease terms, etc. It is not intended to replace the letter usually written by the managing director, but it should try to keep the corporate controller fully apprised of local developments.

Reliability of Data

It is important that the international headquarters have full confidence in the ability, intent, and accomplishment of the controllership representatives in the foreign subsidiaries. This confidence is facilitated by the employment of qualified people. However, a basic confidence in the ability of the local people must be bolstered by a continuing review through technical staffs.

Customarily each local group wishes to remain as autonomous as possible and thus prefers to maintain its own control, perform its own audit, and develop its own systems. Unfortunately, very few subsidiaries in developing nations can afford to employ skilled specialists in the financial fields. Of necessity, therefore, the international headquarters must arrange to make these services available. Even more fundamentally, the headquarters unit can be assured that it is getting reliable information if it provides certain services on a centralized basis.

System Work. The integrated needs of the total control system require that compatible procedures and equipment be employed. Only through a centralization of the creative methods group can effective interworking be assured. Furthermore, technical specialization in forms control, equipment selection, and procedures writing can permit the hiring of highly skilled technicians. Naturally, if the local operation is large enough, it may also be permitted to hire an expert to assist in local applications.

Audit Coverage. Only through independent coverage can the international headquarters be reasonably assured of the reliability of data submitted by local groups. For official purposes, such as tax filing and year-end closings, reliance can properly be placed upon the audit by public accountants having a complete awareness of local practices. At the same time, the local audit firms must be prepared to conform to the minimum audit standards of the headquarters country, so that an effective consolidated "certificate" can be obtained. In American practice it is customary for the auditor to observe physical inventory counts and to verify receivable balances by direct mailing to the debtor. Even though this is not the requirement of the local country, the independent firm must be prepared to accept the international standard.

For assurance on interim operating plans and reports and on compliance with announced managerial policies, it is essential that an internal audit be performed regularly. The examination of this internal audit group should concern itself with more than the existence of assets and the realization of income. If conducted as a broad scale examination of operations, the reviews will easily pay their own costs by measurable savings. In addition, they constitute a valuable technique for maintaining headquarters awareness of local conditions.

Financial Controls. Subsidiaries should gear their financial controls to a standard manual of accounts, and in appropriate circumstances to a uniform cost system and budgetary planning technique. This ensures a correct interpretation of reported data. The local controllers usually welcome standardized instructions which keep them coordinated with their home office. However, consistent vigilance is required to ensure that the local reports realistically penetrate the details of the foreign operation while leading logically to the home office data. Overlapping reporting structures inevitably become frustrating, confusing, and expensive.

A foreign subsidiary is concerned with many problems that are distinct from those of its domestic colleagues. To ensure that the specialized circumstances are dealt with realistically, it is useful to have financial supervision of the subsidiary assigned to a particular financial executive. This executive should visit the subsidiary regularly and should represent it at headquarters meetings.

The above-mentioned special financial services must be provided to ensure a reliable and efficient controllership function. Most companies feel that the subsidiary should bear the cost of such service. From the functional viewpoint it does not matter whether this assessment is made on the basis of specific services rendered, on the basis of a management fee, or as an implicit part of the dividend remittance. The first approach is easier to defend before local tax authorities, while the third method tends to increase the tax withholdings on dividends. In any event, the cost of special services constitutes a proper charge against the income earned by the foreign subsidiary.

Techniques of Analysis

The early success of a business enterprise may be the accidental result of a superior product or of a peculiar market condition. The achievement of the *maximum success possible* depends upon hard work guided by effective measurement. The local controller must accept a responsibility for the professional review and measurement of his company's operations. In many ways his reporting can reveal new aspects of the commercial data and stimulate effective action.

The format and objective of any reporting program must be individually adjusted to the operations, problems, and recipients. It is impossible, therefore, to suggest any universal series of analytic reports. However, as an addition to the customary balance sheet and income statements and the foreign exchange report, which is dealt with subsequently, the following list defines items that might form an illustrative group of special reports:

Inventory measures, in terms of days of future sales, the volume of inventory on hand. It should identify obsolete stock and any appropriate reserves.

Receivable measures, in terms of days of past sales, the value of uncollected customer receivables. It should identify balances not currently collectable and any appropriate reserves.

Cash flow reflects the need for cash, the supply of such cash, and the throw-off of extra cash, in terms of remittances to the home office.

Margin trends compare the price trends of unit cost data with unit sales data so as to isolate the opportunities for future profit.

Outstanding orders list the dollar value of the backlog of unfilled orders and should identify the gross profit expected on such orders.

Wage cost reviews the per hour cost of work performed by the average employee. In addition to the basic wage payment, it should show the voluntary and required fringe benefits made available to the employee.

Value added roughly measures the productivity of the average employee. It deducts the purchased inventories from the sales and divides the remainder by the number of employees to establish the value added per employee.

Market penetration measures the share of the market won by the subsidiary as compared with its competitors and the unabsorbed potential.

Break-even point measures the effect of volume on unit costs and the profitability of the business as it reflects fixed and variable costs.

Return on assets measures the effectiveness of the total employment of the economic resources. Where the subsidiary does not control its own equity and borrowed debt ratios, this effectively substitutes for "return on investment."

Quantitative statistics records in appropriate classifications the number of people, the floor space, the working hours, the units of products, the units of fuel, etc.

Economic statistics lists certain data related to the economic climate of a developing nation. It encompasses the gross national product, employment, wage rates, price trends, money supply, balance of trade, and the national budget.

The above reports, of course, are only the guideposts which point out developing trends and relationships. Once a significant indication is identified, the real job of interpretive analysis begins. It is then that the controller must organize for the financial review of various alternative courses of action. In due course he must also induce management to act upon his analysis. An accurate and professional report is ineffective if it remains "usable" rather than "used."

Weak-currency Considerations

Among the most frustrating of those problems encountered in doing business in developing nations are those related to weak currency. Too often the financial reports expressed in local currency have an appearance of acceptability until the results are converted to the currency of the international parent. At that time the general feeling of satisfaction engendered by higher sales levels and lower margins is replaced by a home office conviction that "something" is wrong.

Perhaps it is an oversimplification to state that weak currencies develop because people want more economic improvement than they have earned by increased productivity, but that seems to be the fundamental cause. In satisfying their economic wants, people and institutions tend to expand their credit resources until they become overly strained. At that time money costs rise in order to induce new funds into the market, and demands for higher wages become irresistible. Prices are raised to cover the new costs, and an inflationary situation develops.

A continued inflationary trend soon forces an increase in export prices. This in turn leads to a contraction in the number of customers. Unless imports are curtailed, an unfavorable balance of international payments is created. Local gold supplies shrink, and in comparison with other currencies the local money becomes less valuable.

The international controller is expected to measure the losses experienced as a result of changes in currency. He does this in the following manner:

Income Statement Effect. When the current rate of exchange varies during the course of the year, "the average rate of exchange" is used in translating income and expense items (with special treatments of certain items such as depreciation). Thus a decrease in the exchange rate will adversely affect the income as converted for reporting to the international headquarters.

Balance Sheet Effect. Within the balance sheet the current conversion rate will be used to translate the net working capital, and historical rates will be used to translate the plant and property accounts. The "surplus account" will be used to balance the converted statement.

Unstated Loss. It is not customary to convert the plant to a replacement value, but it is certainly true that, in a devalued currency situation, it will require more funds to replace the fixed assets than those paid for them before devaluation. Only the original cost is recovered through the customary accounting techniques.

In order to deal properly with the weak-currency problem, the local controller should be completely informed as to the corporate viewpoint on foreign exchange. He must be prepared to cooperate actively in minimizing the losses inherent in the devaluation situation. He must be fully aware of the procedures that can be taken to minimize potential losses.

He should take action, to the extent authorized, along the following lines:

1. Measure continuously the amount of his net exposed assets (current assets less current liabilities).

2. Minimize the company's investment in receivables, inventories, and cash by finding the means to small balances and quick turnover.

3. Borrow funds in the local money markets. In some cases it is wise to finance plant by local borrowing of a short-term nature.
4. Make prompt remittance of dividends so as to avoid the devaluation of excess cash.
5. Insist on a prompt adjustment of sales prices to reflect costs and maintain the percentage of margin.
6. Be prepared to use swaps, forward exchange contracts, dollar loans, and barter deals in order to avoid currency loss.
7. Ensure that the buildup of surplus is sufficient to permit the replacement of plant and equipment, despite an inadequate accumulation of depreciation.

The above listing is not intended to be complete, but it indicates some of the steps that an energetic controller can take in protecting the realizable profit and economic soundness of his local company.

Economic Planning and Evaluation

The principal contribution of the internationally oriented controller lies in his ability to assist in the selection of economic alternatives. In the main, this selection will be incorporated in the long-term planning of the company and will reflect itself in the proper choice of location, legal format, product line, market area, and market approach.

The controller's group should be extremely alert in identifying the various advantages and disadvantages of basic courses of action. A current cheap labor cost should be challenged in respect to the effect of future consumer price trends and size of labor force. The potential balance of trade should be considered from the viewpoint of its effect on future exchange rates. Tax subsidies and investment funds should be considered from the viewpoint of the long-term and the near-term operating margins. Quotas, duties, and freight rates should be evaluated in respect to their influence on supply and prices. The probable availability of funds for remittance to the parent company must be equated with their profitability in other potential uses. No opportunity should go unchallenged—no penalty should be unexpectedly incurred.

The controller is not the only management person who will be evaluating the situations coming to light in the developing nations. Nevertheless, he seems to be the man most qualified to tabulate the effects of a given deal and to compare the total results with the results of possible other courses of action or inaction. Directed planning, objective analysis, sound evaluation, and vigorous action can maximize the potential strengths of the local organization.

In addition to his action in his local environment, the international controller should seek to enhance the worth of the whole corporate system by cooperation with other subsidiaries. In this connection the international group should parcel its activities throughout the world so as to make the most of local advantages, while maintaining the virtues of large-scale production and marketing. Just as the European Common Market has broken down some old national restraints, so is it possible for an international corporate system to avoid the evils of localism.

Assembly work should be done where labor cost is low, bulky items should be produced near their market, refining should take place near the source of raws, and laboratories should be near engineers or places where engineers will go. An integrated program can make the most efficient use of available resources—and the controller can assist in measuring the financial results and risks of each corporate policy or possible alternative. The appraisal cannot be exact, but it will be useful.

Conclusion

Controllership must be organized as a completely coordinated financial function if it is to operate successfully in the international environment. At the international headquarters appropriate steps must be taken to clarify corporate policy, to promote proper planning, to issue useful forms and manuals, and to ensure that skilled supervision and review of international actions will maximize the protection and profit of the ultimate shareholders.

On the other hand, the local controller must accept responsibility for finding ways to advance the consolidated interests. At times this responsibility may not correspond with the social or economic preferences of the local area. Despite this, the controller must keep the final objective in mind. He is relied upon to install adequate and helpful controls for the subsidiary, to suggest methods of providing or remitting funds, to explore and identify possible tax advantages, and to protect the local company from the worst consequences of devaluation or inflation.

All the above services are essential and quite significant in a technical way, but the controller's contribution transcends his role as a professional. By contributing to a wise development of the basic economic advantages of a nation, he serves to maximize the usefulness of that nation as a part of the international family. By controlling certain aspects of business policy, he minimizes the strains and dislocations that develop in unsettled environments. By advising against the exploitation of areas in which minimal advantages exist, he does much to curtail social and political difficulties.

Controllership can measure the existing production skills and marketing abilities in developing areas. By communicating an understanding of the intrinsic national strengths, the financial representatives can give direction to the activities of international managers. By sound planning, they can successfully integrate the activities of a far-flung corporate operation. With constant energy and vigilance, the controller can indeed make a significant contribution to organized internationalism.

MANAGING A LATIN AMERICAN MANUFACTURING SUBSIDIARY

Harold R. Ohlheiser

Introduction

Observations and suggested procedures described in this article are based on the author's experiences with two large international United States firms during the period of establishing new subsidiaries in Brazil and Argentina. In one company consumer end products are manufactured, whereas the other firm is a supplier of products to automotive vehicle manufacturers. In two cases the foreign subsidiaries established were wholly owned by the U.S. parent, and in another case, majority-owned. Machinery and equipment were sent from the United States to the foreign country.

In the past twelve years tremendous industrial advances have been made in some Latin American countries, such as Brazil. It should be recognized that management methods and procedures must remain flexible in order that they can be readily adapted to local customs as well as to changes as they develop. In this sense, the term "developing nations" is descriptive of exactly what is taking place and indicates the need for the flexibility just mentioned.

It should also be stated that in any given project or operation, there will always be certain conditions which apply specifically to that project. The observations and procedures here recorded, however, are believed to be sufficiently broad and general in character to serve as a reference for many types of manufacturing and for most Latin American countries.

The establishment of foreign subsidiaries of the general type described involves a broad spectrum of management problems. These problems are readily related to work required to be done in the U.S. parent firm and to the

---

Mr. Ohlheiser is Regional Director–Latin America, International Operations, The Bendix Corporation, New York.

management of the foreign subsidiary. Consequently, the remarks which follow are recorded under two main headings, "Management of the Project in the U.S. Parent Firm" and "Management of the Foreign Subsidiary."

Management of the Project in the U.S. Parent Firm

A great diversity of matters must be considered and many decisions made in the parent firm when it has been decided to establish a foreign operation. Knowledge must be obtainable concerning conditions in the foreign country which bear on these matters. For instance, if a certain machine is required, it would be a mistake to assume that it is available in the foreign country. Conversely, it cannot be assumed that a country will permit importation of any given machine. In general, the matters requiring consideration and decision can be divided into three main areas—personnel, manufacturing, and financial. Under each of these headings are tabulated certain actions required, decisions needed, and cautions to be considered.

The area of sales and distribution will not be discussed. Methods and problems in this field vary widely with type of product and country. It is felt, therefore, that a discussion of product sales could not be made sufficiently broad to be of general interest.

Personnel. *Domestic Employees to Be Assigned to Work in the Foreign Country for an Extended Period of Time*

1. Decide on the management organization required for the new foreign company, and determine qualifications and experience necessary for each position.

2. Choose as early as possible the man who will have chief responsibility to the parent company for the foreign operation. He will hereafter be designated as general manager. Establish lines of authority and communication for the general manager.

3. The general manager should have an opportunity to visit the foreign country to look into business and personal details before final assignment to the project.

4. With the help of others, the general manager should choose each staff man required for the management of the foreign organization. This should be accomplished as early as possible.

5. Each man who is seriously considered for assignment to a foreign country should be given a careful and detailed briefing to cover all phases of living and working there. Preferably, this should be done by someone who has actually lived and worked in that country.

6. Each man should be familiar in detail with the personnel policy applying to the foreign country concerned before final transfer is made to the new organization. If no personnel policy exists, one should be written immediately. In addition, a personal letter should be addressed to each man covering any details not included in the policy and to be discussed with him before departure.

7. Assign the general manager and staff men to full-time work on the new project as soon as possible.

8. After definite assignment has been made, basic instruction in the conversational language of the foreign country should be a requirement.

9. Considerable time and effort should be given by all concerned to the choosing of personnel for foreign assignment. First of all, a man must satisfy the technical requirements for the work. It is just as important to employ various means to determine whether the man and his wife are likely to be compatible with life in the foreign country. Characteristics of integrity, emotional stability, and social habits should all be evaluated as carefully as possible. Something happens to many people when transferred to a foreign environment which adversely affects their effectiveness to the company.

Domestic Employees to Be Assigned to Work in the Foreign Country for Relatively Short Periods of Time. Certain trainers or "know-how" men are usually required for varying periods of time in starting up an operation. With the assistance of others, the general manager should decide on the skills required, the number of men needed, and the specific persons for this work. Where practicable, language instruction should be provided for this group also.

Timetables. The general manager should make up a timetable covering approximate dates when various personnel will be required. In addition, he should make up a broader "schedule of events" showing estimated dates for all important phases of the project. This should be revised and refined as conditions warrant.

Domestic Staff. Immediately a decision has been taken to go ahead with a project, form a group of employees to be assigned full time to the work involved. This group of employees would be drawn from, and work in, the parent factory. Persons in this group would normally revert to their regular assignment upon completion of the project.

This group should be assigned as required and will vary in number and composition according to the project. Normally it would consist of one man or more in the areas of accounting, product design and engineering, processing and tool design, and machine and equipment procurement.

Manufacturing. *Products.* Carefully clarify and determine the exact products to be manufactured and the quantities contemplated at the earliest possible time. This is the basis for all manufacturing information to be compiled.

Drawings and Records. Provide for complete detailed manufacturing information such as drawings, routing sheets, specifications, manufacturing procedures, and parts lists. It is very important that all written information and drawings be clear and legible. One special reason for this is the probability of language problems.

Processing and Tool Design. This work should be complete and detailed, based on the tools and equipment to be used for manufacturing in the foreign country. The man who does the processing should be available to go to the foreign country to put methods into satisfactory operation there.

Tool design should take into account degree of skills available as well as actual machining equipment to be used. Furthermore, it is very important to try out all tooling as completely as possible before sending it from the United States in order to ensure that all "bugs" have been eliminated. This applies to perishable tools as well as to durable ones such as stamping die sets. Care in detailed tryout of all tooling cannot be overemphasized.

Domestic Procurement. Experienced domestic personnel should purchase the required machinery, equipment, and tooling. Durable tooling purchased on the outside must be carefully examined and tried out.

In the early stages of manufacturing an end product in the foreign country, some parts of that product may be required initially from the U.S. parent company. A clear written procedure should be developed covering all details of handling such requirements, indicating responsibility for all steps in the procedure.

Shipments to the Foreign Country. Considerable care and tremendous detail are required in preparing and shipping all items. Detailed information regarding documentation, both domestic and foreign, should be obtained at an early date. In order to develop these details, visits should be made to the appropriate consular office which will approve documentation for shipments to the country concerned.

Boxing and crating should be closely supervised to ensure its adequacy. Detailed listing of the contents of each box is very important. Protection against salt air and spray must be taken into account.

Those in charge must investigate transportation routes, problems which might occur between port and foreign factory site (e.g., roads, bridges, tunnels), and the availability of transportation equipment. Thought should be given to the order of shipment of the various items. Normally, any lift trucks or similar equipment for handling boxes and machines should be included in the first shipment. Toolroom equipment should be installed first, so as to have available the means to repair damaged machines, to make items overlooked in the planning, and to make any other items required quickly.

Liaison between Parent Company and Subsidiary. Clearly define liaison channels and responsibilities, and establish procedures for keeping the subsidiary abreast of the latest product engineering changes or of faulty designs. This is in addition to the normal channels of management responsibility.

Financial. Forecasts. From the beginning, estimates and forecasts should be made covering total costs, sales, and profit for the project, and these should be related to a specific manufacturing program. While such estimates may not at first be highly accurate, it is important to make them.

Domestic Accounting. Establish a detailed written accounting procedure for the control and accumulation of all domestic expenditures and their allocation to proper accounts in the parent company.

Refined Forecasts. Periodically revise and refine estimated total costs, sales, and income and expense statements.

Periodic Reports. Establish type and frequency of periodic statements and reports desired by the parent firm.

License Contracts. Examine all license contracts carefully. For arriving at dates when royalties are due, note especially the details concerning manner and time of converting foreign money to dollars. Provide for a flexible date for the start of royalty payments, since the time when profits will be realized is usually unknown.

Management of the Foreign Subsidiary

In this section we shall assume that the general manager and his staff are in the foreign country and that the start-up and early operating phases of the subsidiary are in progress. An incredible number of problems of a most diverse nature arise during this stage. The general manager must have very considerable authority to act on his own judgment in order to obtain effective and efficient results.

The various subjects to be discussed here will be grouped into the same three categories as in the second section, namely, personnel, manufacturing, and financial. Wherever the term "local" is used, it implies the locality of the subsidiary in the foreign country.

Personnel. *Men from the United States.* Much has been written about the reactions of U.S. employees who are transferred to a foreign country and are first exposed to "culture shock." This experience undoubtedly creates different problems for different people, and these problems become very serious in some cases. It is common for firms to find that 10 to 15 percent of a group going to a foreign country for the first time cannot, or do not wish to, adjust to the new conditions. It should be expected that this will happen during the first year or two of a new operation, even though considerable care has been exercised in choosing personnel.

The general manager should engage a local bilingual person to handle most of the detail work in locating suitable housing and in helping with the many problems relative to arrival, living, and working in the foreign country. There are local requirements for identity and working documents. Local patterns of rental and living should be known and adhered to where reasonable. Instruction in the language should be started at once. Arranging for all these matters requires considerable time.

Normally men from the United States will find that they have a wider range of responsibility than at home. This arises from the need to restrict the number of U.S. personnel to the minimum possible. The philosophy of "make do" with what is available requires versatility and initiative on the part of all supervisors. This philosophy comes into effect automatically and should be encouraged and developed early in the operation.

Trainers or "know-how" men should be requested from the United States only when circumstances have developed to the point where they can do effective work immediately upon arrival. Such men usually require the help of bilingual local personnel in order to perform their tasks and give effective training. The time period for which such men are required varies considerably with the work or equipment concerned. Obviously, permanent locally hired employees should have been obtained and assigned to specific equipment in order that their training can begin immediately the trainer arrives. If well organized this phase of work will pay dividends, because the training period can be minimized, thus eliminating any unnecessary expense for the trainer and generating interest on the part of the local employees at an early date.

The responsibilities of all U.S. men, including trainers, should be clearly outlined to them as they report for work. The manager may well change these responsibilities from time to time during the early stages, resulting in misunderstandings if these changes are not clearly stated and properly handled.

Locally Employed Personnel. A competent personnel manager should be employed. The labor laws in most countries are very complex and detailed and are in some cases subject to local interpretation. A locally employed specialist in this field is most essential as early as possible in the operation.

For the U.S. general manager, probably one of his most important assistants is a competent bilingual secretary. Such a person can save the manager a great amount of time in a diversified field of work. Good secretaries often receive pay commensurate with higher-ranking foremen in the factory.

A study should be made with the aim of developing the local pattern of wages and then formulating labor grades and wage scales. In this area it is common to find a relationship between skills and labor grades completely different from that existing in the United States. For this reason it is very important to have the benefit of local experience and studies before establishing plant policies. It is particularly important not to start off a new operation by paying much higher wages than other established firms in the locality.

Training along many lines should be started early and maintained. Many training courses are available through semigovernmental agencies. When in full operation, training should extend through practically every field and type of work in the plant. English language courses should be fostered, since many employees are eager to learn English. The desire and determination to learn new and better skills is an outstanding characteristic common in all types of workers.

A final caution is worthy of note. In cases where the U.S. employee does not know the foreign language, he will have a tendency to employ local persons who speak English whether or not they seem to have other skills. This is a normal and natural situation which sometimes works out well.

In due time, however, such persons should be carefully evaluated to ensure that they have skills which warrant keeping them. Except for translators and interpreters, it is seldom necessary, after about a year of operation, to keep an employee only because he speaks English.

Language Problems. Every U.S. employee should be thoroughly cognizant of a double-edged problem related to the "language barrier." First of all, there is a very real problem in the simple lack of ability to convey thoughts because of not understanding a language. This may lead to many serious misunderstandings resulting in unnecessary expense.

In its most common form, the language barrier results in problems because either the U.S. employee or the locally employed person thinks he understands the other during a discussion when actually he does not. A variant of this is the normal tendency of most persons to indicate that they have understood something, knowing that it is not perfectly clear in detail even though understood in general.

Misunderstandings arise from another source which is not properly a language barrier problem but is often thought to be. For example, a local person is instructed to do something by a U.S. supervisor, and the words are completely understood. The two persons involved may have quite different backgrounds in the educational and social areas; the difference of greatest importance, however, is that of experience with the products at hand and with their manufacture. The locally employed person proceeds to do in good faith what his background dictates to him that he should do, but it may be completely wrong. Especially in the early training periods, all U.S. personnel must be extremely conscious of this possibility. Follow-up on instructions will often bring to light an error in the making, and correction can be made in time to minimize bad results and lost time.

Manufacturing. *Buildings.* Normal year-round weather conditions in the area must be taken into account when building a new plant or buying an existing plant or building. In many industrial areas, snow loads and very cold weather do not occur. In such areas buildings have a lighter overhead structure and a less "tight" construction allowing freer air movement. It is common not to have heating in factory production areas. Manufacturing requirements and local practice should control designs.

Plant Services. Few places in Latin America have ample and satisfactory public services such as electrical power, telephones, potable water, and sewage systems. An early study is required and decisions must be made regarding the need for power-generating equipment within the plant. Especially important are provisions to compensate for deviations from nominal power characteristics when public power supply is used. Low voltage, variable frequency, and power interruptions are very common. When hydroelectric power generation is used as a source, frequency or cycle variation and low voltage may depend on the time of the year. These conditions require special consideration in plant maintenance problems.

To acquire a proper telephone installation may be very costly. Potable water supply and sewage systems may be inadequate.

All these conditions will require proper investigation in order to minimize their effects on manufacturing programs.

Procurement of Supplies. This is a most difficult area because of the relatively recent industrial development. Basic raw materials of proper specifications are in short supply or completely missing from local sources. Local purchasing of semifinished or finished products is time-consuming and frustrating. Without doubt, however, these conditions are improving. The problems of procurement should first be met by making a survey of potential suppliers in as much detail as time permits.

In considerations of quality, much has yet to be learned by local suppliers. There are several products with excellent quality. In general, however, it is necessary to teach and assist local suppliers. In some cases, qualified technical men visit the factories of suppliers frequently in order to do this. Gauges and tools must often be supplied to vendors to give further assistance. In very few instances can it be assumed that placing an order with a supplier is sufficient to ensure the arrival of satisfactory products within the promised delivery time.

Delivery of purchased parts must be carefully followed up. In the great majority of cases, a long lead time is required because of the tendency for suppliers to underestimate difficulties in manufacturing a new product to proper quality specifications. There is also a tendency to accept orders knowing that delivery at the promised time will be impossible, or very late, because of a natural desire to take on as much business as possible. Production scheduling in the subsidiary plant must take into account all the uncertainties of supply.

Purchasing of special perishable tools, durable tools, and electrical and machine replacement parts presents special problems. Very frequently items of this nature are unavailable locally and must be imported. Sufficient stocks of such items, providing for possible interruption of delivery, must be established and carefully maintained.

In spite of the problems of procurement, it should be the objective eventually to obtain every required item of supply locally, even though initially many will have to be imported. Importing is generally a long, tedious process calling for much expensive documentation. Governmental requirements for import are constantly changing. It is important, also, that the subsidiary do its share to help in the industrial development of the country in which it is located. This is accomplished by helping in the development of local suppliers and minimizing import of products.

When importation of either machinery or production parts is required, the services of the best possible customs broker should be engaged very early in the project. When possible, it is beneficial to use a broker who has already had experience with the particular equipment and program to be handled. Depending on the size of the import program, fees can be negotiated.

Inventory. The inventory of supplies is a matter which justifiably receives careful attention in most industries. There is, however, a definite tendency to translate U.S. practice to the foreign subsidiary on exactly the same terms. Those with experience in managing a foreign enterprise generally agree this is not practicable. Because of the problems in procurement, it is not possible in the early years of a new operation to count on regular deliveries according to schedule. It should be accepted as part of the cost of operating in the foreign field that larger inventories are inevitable. In the future, with continued industrial development, this condition will be alleviated.

Factory Operators. In recent years there has been a great increase in the number of workers who have developed the advanced skills required in an industrial country. The great majority of factory operators are ready and anxious to learn, and they have notably improved their skills in operating complicated and precise machine tools and equipment. Some of the larger subsidiaries of foreign firms operate regular trade schools. It is a mistake to feel that present-day industrial equipment cannot be operated by factory workers in the subsidiary. Only the highly sophisticated type of equipment requiring unusual skills in service and maintenance might be considered unsuitable so far as the local operation is concerned.

It is interesting to note that some countries have very strict rules regulating the importation of used machinery. Foreign countries generally feel that it is best for them to have modern, up-to-date manufacturing facilities.

Factory Costs. Related to the item just discussed, considerations of investment and production quantities may well dictate the type of machines and equipment to be used by a subsidiary. The cost of manufacturing is influenced by the type of equipment as well as by labor costs, and the two should be balanced, one against the other. In cases where the machine controls feeds and speeds, the output per man hour will usually compare favorably with that in the parent plant. In general, however, the overall output will be somewhat less than in the home plant.

Care should be exercised in discussing local labor rates and comparing them with parent plant rates. The local direct hourly rates of pay are very much less than in the United States, but there are many social and fringe benefits accruing to the workers which must be paid for by the company. These benefits vary considerably in different countries but may be 40 to 75 percent of the direct hourly wage. Even with these benefits, labor costs in general are appreciably lower than in the U.S. plant for comparable work.

Factory layouts and methods should take into account the fact just stated. For example, expensive equipment for handling materials, along with other laborsaving devices and equipment, is often not warranted.

Labor laws restrict the amount of overtime work. Detailed regulations cover additional pay for overtime and for night-shift work. These premiums, however, are much less than usual in U.S. practice.

Poor quality of materials and unreliable delivery contribute to increasing factory costs. There is a tendency for higher scrap, decreased output, increased number of machine setups, and larger quantities of stock to be reworked.

Material costs are, in general, greater than in the United States for industrial products of a reasonably high quality. The need to import, lower volume of production, higher interest rates, and less efficient methods are among the factors contributing to higher material costs.

Financial. *Legal Aspects.* It is important to choose a high-quality local law firm as soon as the decision has been made to form a subsidiary. The usual law firm will have specialists available for legal problems related to corporation matters, tax liabilities, and treatment of the labor laws. In these areas, differences from American home office experience are substantial. In the field of complex labor laws especially, not only are the services of an excellent local personnel man required, but expert legal advice must also be available.

General Accounting. Government requirements as to legal accounting books must be learned. In actual practice, deviations from exact regulations are permitted. Legal requirements are adaptable to modern methods of machine accounting, and many firms use such methods. An experienced general accountant should be employed, preferably one from the same governmental tax district in which the subsidiary is located.

Factory Accounting. Factory accounting as known in the parent company is very uncommon in local firms, except in those cases where foreign parents have initiated such practices. Generally, it is necessary to train locally employed persons in the methods of factory and cost accounting desired by the parent company.

Banking Practices. Banking practices are quite different in many respects from those familiar to the parent company. In a city of 200,000 population there may be thirty banks, and a firm in that city may have accounts in twenty to twenty-five of these banks. Considerable movement in a bank account appears very desirable, even though the size of transaction may be small. Special services are offered for the discounting of invoices. Rates of interest are very high in comparison with U.S. rates. Under constantly changing local economic conditions, it is impossible to predict with any certainty whether or not local short-term borrowing or discounting may be advisable or possible. Local long-term borrowing is not often available. The parent company should be prepared to finance the local subsidiary until such time as it is in a profit position.

Inflation. Rapid inflation is in many countries a fact of life. Currency devaluation may vary from 20 to 40 percent per year, depending on the time and place, and must be considered very carefully in all financial planning and pricing. This condition creates special problems in inventory pricing.

Remittance of Funds. Sending profits and royalties to the parent company is most difficult in many countries of Latin America. It is subject to politico-economic winds which may blow hot or cold. At times there are no restrictions, and during other periods rules and regulations effectively preclude fund transfer. During periods when profits cannot be sent to the parent company, inflation becomes even more of a financial danger than normally. At such times the subsidiary must watch helplessly while the profits earned diminish in value as related to the dollar.

There are some financial techniques for hedging against inflation, essentially through acquisition of assets other than money. The effects of inflation can be alleviated by reinvesting in the local business when this is considered desirable. Sometimes excess funds can be loaned. In some countries, subject to treaties between governments, convertibility and guarantee of repatriation of funds can be ensured through the U.S. government.

It is hoped that with further political and economic development conditions will become stabilized and restrictions will no longer be placed on the sending out from the foreign country of reasonable profits and royalties to stockholders of a subsidiary.

Conclusion

Management will have to utilize to the fullest its initiative and imagination in solving the problems of establishing and operating a foreign subsidiary. For this reason it is very important that the management consist of sufficient competent personnel to supervise and control efficiently the main areas of operation, namely, manufacturing, finance, and sales.

We do not want to conclude without referring briefly to what might be termed social responsibilities. The establishment of a new foreign enterprise in a community is accompanied by certain obligations if the operation is to be considered completely successful. The personal character of the general manager and of the company policies which he controls will be reflected in the community in a very short time.

The objectives of the new firm should be to become a respectable part of the community, to help and work for improvement, and to assure fair and equitable treatment in all business and personnel matters. In smaller communities, contact with government officials is helpful and desirable for many reasons. Cooperation with government at all levels in plans and objectives of a democratic and equitable nature should be the rule.

It is a most gratifying experience to witness at first hand the establishment of a new enterprise in a community. Direct, tangible benefits to individuals can be observed. The new firm is a source of funds and knowledge which directly improve people's lives and, indirectly, the life of the whole community. In many cases the persons concerned fully recognize and appreciate the opportunity for personal improvement.

It is difficult to think of a more direct and more effective way for the United States to help its neighbors in Latin America achieve a better life than through private foreign investment in a subsidiary.

WHAT TO DO WHEN A FOREIGN MARKET CLOSES— STARTING A FACTORY IN INDIA

Gilbert T. Bowman

One of the favorite devices for stimulating the development of domestic manufacturing in underdeveloped nations is simply to shut off imports. This is done in any of several ways—by high tariffs, by banning the importing of products already manufactured in a country, by requirements that 50, 60, or even 90 percent of a product's content be produced locally, and by a number of other means.

When an underdeveloped nation takes such steps, it effectively halts imports and closes its market to American and other foreign manufacturers. India provides a classic example of the closing of a substantial market for one of the major product lines of the Rockwell Manufacturing Company—in this case, metalworking and woodworking power tools. It is an interesting case history illustrating what U.S. industry now faces in many underdeveloped areas of the world.

For many years, the Rockwell Manufacturing Company had been represented in India by agents. We have gradually seen our sales to India drop to a fraction of their one-time volume—and this in years when our foreign sales were generally growing. The reasons are familiar—a lack of foreign exchange plus the Indian Government's desire to encourage development of local manufacturing, which has virtually eliminated Indian demand for many items of not only U.S. but any foreign manufacture.

Since many factors ruled out the acquisition of an existing Indian company and government restrictions prohibited establishment of a wholly owned subsidiary, we chose to set up a subsidiary in which our long-time Indian distributors would be minority stockholders. Our Indian distributors are well

---

Mr. Bowman is Vice President of Rockwell Manufacturing Company.

established and well financed. When they first suggested to us the possibility of a partnership, we were intrigued by the idea.

We soon learned, however, that our initial plan of majority ownership by Rockwell was doomed by governmental restrictions. Ultimately, after many months of negotiations, we settled on a joint venture with Rockwell and our Indian partners sharing equal ownership.

This plan of corporate formation, the third approach we tried, was approved by the Indian Government in 1963, and our plant is now in limited operation at Udhna, a suburb of Surat, located some 150 miles north of Bombay.

The company, Rockwell India Private Ltd., will initially manufacture woodworking and metalworking power tools, products previously sold in India by our partners in this joint venture. Once production of the power tool line is well under way, we hope to add a number of other Rockwell products, beginning with small gasoline engines.

Our aim is to manufacture for sale in India and for export to other nations in the Middle East and Far East. With India fighting an overwhelming balance of payments problem, the government is particularly receptive to proposals that promise simultaneously to cut imports and boost exports.

When Surveys May Not Work

Normally, a U.S. company investigating the possibilities of a foreign investment makes a market survey as a first step in developing a pro forma profit and loss statement. If the picture looks favorable, the company proceeds to work out agreements with local partners, enter negotiations with the government, and attend to the myriad of details associated with such a venture. We practically dispensed with the market survey in India after reviewing the records of all Indian imports of anything resembling our products over the last several years.

The preliminary figures we came up with had no relationship, we felt, to what is a market of imposing potential for our products. On the basis of such figures we could never have justified any investment. But we were sure enough of ourselves to throw out our preliminary research and proceed on what we call an "experiment in hope."

Our decision was, of course, influenced by a variety of Indian domestic factors, not the least of which was the knowledge that our proposed venture would almost certainly qualify as one of the sixteen "essential industries" designated by the Government of India. Machine tools "on a selective basis" had been earmarked as an essential industry on the government's priority list, and, fortunately, the power tool line we will produce qualifies under this heading.

The importance of this cannot be overestimated. The Government of India has said it will not assume responsibility for allocation of foreign exchange or supply of fuel, electric power, and essential raw materials to any manufacturer who fails to meet the "essential industry" requirements. Without government aid in obtaining these essential commodities, it is impossible to do business under anything like normal conditions. Indeed, it is barely possible to do business at all.

Production Machinery Problems

Some discussion of our experience in obtaining tooling and other equipment for the new plant seems appropriate. The Government of India flatly refused us permission to import production machinery from the United States, although we did ultimately win a concession on tooling.

Because of India's acute shortage of foreign exchange, it is impossible for any manufacturer—domestic or foreign-based—to import machinery from countries that do not accept rupee payments. This, of course, means all manufacturers in India are obligated to do business with such Communist Bloc nations as Hungary, Poland, and Czechoslovakia if they are to obtain the production machinery essential to their business. It is possible to avoid patronizing Iron Curtain suppliers only in those rare cases where the needed machinery is manufactured in India. If the needed machinery is not available in India or in any country that accepts rupee payments, special authorization to import it is required. In such cases, the Indian Government will provide foreign exchange for the purchase.

In our own case, we were able to import seven essential machines from the United States, but fifteen others had to be purchased from Czechoslovakia. Americans are instinctively repelled by the thought of having to buy from Iron Curtain countries, but there is no alternative if one expects to manufacture in India.

We were able to import the needed tooling only because it was already available from stocks of the Rockwell Manufacturing in the United States. We had purchased such tooling previously for use in our domestic operations, but the conversion of many of our U.S. manufacturing processes to automatic machinery and other laborsaving devices had eliminated the need for the sort of tooling previously used in this country and now required for our Indian operations. Our manufacturing license was approved by the Government of India on the basis that needed tooling would be supplied from the United States by Rockwell Manufacturing. Still, an import license for the tooling was required.

Special Considerations

Doing business abroad involves one particular technical problem that U.S. manufacturers sometimes overlook, that is, converting to metric dimensions. There are two aspects to this problem. One can either convert dimensions directly into the metric system or compromise design and dimensions to conform to local conditions and local materials.

Obviously, economical conversion to metric dimensions is not as easy as it sounds. Anyone can take a slide rule, convert inches into metric measurements, and mark these on an American blueprint, but to do the job correctly requires an engineer with an intimate knowledge of local standards. As an example, the American blueprint might show a 1-in. hole into which a 1-in. rod is to be inserted. The metric equivalent of 1 in. is 25.40 mm. It would be easy to order a 25.40-mm drill to drill the hole, and also some 25.40-mm rod stock. However, both items would be quite scarce in India and, therefore, very expensive.

The alternative to the conversion problem is to keep the same shape, function, and approximate size of the component and "round off" the metric dimensions to the nearest common Indian size or dimension. In this example the nearest standard size would be 25 mm. The engineer who does the converting must be very careful when changing any dimensions into a standard, because there are contributing pieces, such as the rod that has to go into the hole. All the dimensions have to be changed to meet standards if the product is to be manufactured at a reasonable cost.

Another consideration involving the basic design of the product is availability of materials. Rockwell's U.S.-made power tools have cast aluminum housings, but those to be produced in India will employ cast zinc because zinc is more readily available than aluminum in India. Moreover, we feel Indian-made aluminum alloys do not have all the desirable properties found in the aluminum alloys we use for housings in the United States.

We have also converted from steel stampings to iron castings for certain of our components for the Indian tools. The iron and steel castings industry is one of the sixteen essential industries designated by the Government of India, and we feel relatively certain of the continued availability of cast components, while the future of stamped parts is less certain. In our particular case, we are very fortunate to have next door to our own plant a foundry that can supply good quality gray iron castings.

Production Techniques

Unemployment and low per capita income continue as major problems in India. For these reasons, the government frowns on the use of automatic machinery. Even if this were not so, manufacturers would seldom be able to justify the added cost of automatic equipment because of the low labor rates. As an indication of the difference in Indian and American production methods, we find the labor content in a typical product is 2½ times greater in India than in the United States. Even so, overall labor costs are lower in India.

Another factor to be considered in establishing production methods is that skilled labor to operate complex machines is extremely scarce in India. This is true also of maintenance personnel, where skilled labor is, if anything, even rarer. One steel mill recently reported that its inability to operate at anywhere near the rated capacity stems largely from the lack of skilled labor and the "total lack" of adequate maintenance personnel and procedures.

Under these conditions, it is obvious that the American manufacturer in India must accept responsibility for training native laborers. While our plant, as of this writing, has not reached the stage where we have the equipment in place for training factory workers, we long ago embarked on a program to train key Indian personnel in basic U.S. production methods with particular emphasis on Rockwell procedures.

U.S. Internship

Our management cadre consisted of two Americans and three Indians. Once production processes had been established and Indian laborers had been trained, we recalled the two American technicians, leaving the day-to-day operation of the plant completely to the Indians.

When we decided to go into India, we made the selection and training of key personnel a priority matter. We picked two engineers and one administrator for Rockwell India and brought them to this country for intensive on-the-job training.

One of the hazards encountered in training foreigners in this country is also found by educators conducting student exchange programs. Sometimes the foreigner who comes here to train will find influences much stronger than his inherent national pride and will end up staying in the United States. Our hand-picked administrator found an American bride, so we had to find another Indian to take the job originally earmarked for him.

Two engineers, both of whom were educated in India and did graduate work in the United States, were put through a thorough eighteen-month indoctrination program at our Tupelo, Mississippi, plant, which manufactures Rockwell-Delta and Walker-Turner power tools. They now qualify as experts in machine operation, maintenance, production methods, design and tooling drawings, personnel training, and all the other skills they will need to supervise the engineering and production end of our Indian operation. Two others are presently in training at our German engine factory.

When the time came to hire and train production workers, we made arrangements with a technical school located near our plant to supply a large number of qualified young people as job candidates. This school is comparable to U.S. vocational high schools and will be able to provide for most of our skilled labor needs.

While on the subject of training, it is worth noting that our initial training costs have been much higher than those incurred in establishing European operations. We also expect the cost of training production workers to exceed the European average. On top of this, progress in reaching peak production capacity will very likely be slower than normal.

Choosing a Plant Site

Plant site location was most interesting. We found that electric power is not always available in India. We found that labor absenteeism, while prevalent everywhere, is worse in some places than in others. We learned that the national and state governments are much more favorably disposed toward helping an industry located in an undeveloped area. And we learned much about living and working conditions that differ markedly from normal U.S. and European practice.

Our plant is located in a developing industrial area that can best be compared to the "industrial parks" established in many parts of the United States. The Government of India is currently developing several such sites, but we are building in a privately owned area. At present, government-sponsored projects are open only to companies with fewer than fifty employees and annual sales of less than 500,000 rupees ($106,500).

The particular site we are using is one previously owned by our Indian partners, but that was only one of several factors considered in our selection. While it may be surprising to many people, real estate costs in India are exceptionally high. The nation is still largely agrarian, and much of the land is devoted to farming. When real estate is available in an area suitable for industrial development, costs are fantastic.

Our site has every advantage we could expect in India. While the electric power shortage is severe in some parts of the country, the supply is adequate in the vicinity of our chosen site near Surat. Since ours is a light industry, our power requirements are not as great as many companies might have, and we experienced no difficulty in contracting with the government for the necessary power. To encourage industrial development still further, the Government has announced plans to construct a new power plant within 35 miles of our site. This plant is expected to be in operation by 1965 and will probably generate about 30,000 kw annually.

Current regulations require that most new or expanding companies negotiate with the appropriate state government for power demands exceeding 2,000 kw annually and with the Coal Commissioner for the necessary coal supply.

Water power, another sometimes scarce commodity, is also readily available in the vicinity of Surat, as is reliable rail transportation. It is rare to find good north-south and east-west rail connections in India, but our site has both.

As indicated previously, suppliers of many raw materials and components, e.g., gray iron castings, are located conveniently to the plant, thus solving another major problem for manufacturers in India.

Government Negotiations

Despite the unusual personnel, equipment, and site selection problems we encountered our task was on the whole relatively simple until we opened the necessary negotiations with the various Indian Government agencies involved in approving the corporate formation and in the licensing and financing of the project. We were told that Indian Government approval procedures have been successfully fought through in as little as six months. A year and a half is probably more like "par," and in our case it took twenty months before final approval was obtained.

Generally, there are five different Government agencies to be seen, and they all take time—not only in negotiations, but more particularly in preparation.

They are (1) the Secretary of the Ministry of Commerce and Industry, who decides that the project generally conforms or does not conform with the needs of India's growth patterns; (2) the Chief Controller of Imports and Exports, who gives, or does not give, permission to import machinery and auxiliary equipment; (3) the Controller of Capital Issues, who reviews the proposed corporate setup, the foreign equity share of the project, any license or patent of know-how agreements, and the capital repatriation plans of the foreign investor; (4) the Industrial Policy Section of the Ministry of Commerce and Industry, which reviews the feasibility of the whole project; and (5) the Exchange Control Department of the Reserve Bank of India, which gives explicit permission to issue shares to the foreign investor, remit profits, and repatriate capital.

India's economy is divided into private and public sectors and, typical of all the developing nations, is basically a controlled economy. Whenever such a condition exists, stringent government regulations and the red tape characteristic of a bureaucracy are to be expected.

One governmental agency will approve an application from industry conditional on concurrence from a second agency. The second agency makes the same conditional approval or, worse, refuses to consider the application until a third agency has approved.

As a result, private business completely depends on government action and permits. Labor laws are much stricter than in the United States, and government approval is required for importing, exporting, allocation of raw materials, plant expansions, addition of new product lines, etc.

Conclusion

In such countries it takes a great deal of perseverance to get the job done and a great deal of confidence in one's judgment of the market to undertake a manufacturing operation in the first place. The company unwilling to face these frustrations would be well advised to stay away from investment in the less developed areas of the world.

While our knowledge of the less developed, non-European countries is limited, we have undertaken investment programs in South America as well as India. As a result, we feel our experience in India is typical of what U.S. companies will face as they move into such countries.

Without any question, the establishment of manufacturing operations is expensive, time-consuming, and often frustrating in these developing nations . . . but we honestly feel it is worth the considerable effort involved, once it is ascertained that the market and the growth potential exist in a given country.

HIRING EMPLOYEES FOR FOREIGN ASSIGNMENTS

Robert C. Zuehlke, M.A.

The hiring of persons in one country to work in another which is markedly different from their own is a particularly difficult task. This article is written with the purpose of offering some suggestions which may help to simplify the problems. The observations made are the result of experience in selecting candidates for middle management and high-level technical and executive assignments in nonmetropolitan areas of Central America; however, the same principles should be applicable to most situations involving the employment of expatriates to work in underdeveloped parts of the world.

No infallible techniques exist to seek out candidates who would be certain to succeed in overseas positions. There are, however, a number of common-sense precautions that can be taken to ensure that persons with the best chance of success are selected. Actually, the techniques involved in choosing employees for foreign service are essentially the same as those used by experienced personnel administrators to fill domestic positions. The difference is mainly in the more intensive use of such preemployment tools as the physical examination, the background and reference check, the depth interview, and possibly psychological testing and the psychiatric interview. In addition, in considering applicants for foreign employment, the wife and other members of the candidate's immediate family must also be evaluated.

A very effective approach to the matter is the use of a set of key factors against which every prospective applicant for a foreign assignment is matched. All available means of obtaining information about the candidate's experience, personality, and background should be used to give the personnel administrator the information he needs to make the comparison. The following factors have been found by the author to be the most important points to be considered in screening applicants:

Mr. Zuehlke is Personnel Manager of Standard Fruit and Steamship Company.

Position Qualifications

The ability to do the job in question is, of course, the first factor to be considered. In a sense, good technical qualifications are even more important in selecting an employee for foreign service than in hiring a person for a domestic position. The need for job proficiency is great, not only because of the cost of placing an employee in a far-off location, but also because of the extra critical scrutiny he will receive from nationals. This stress on superior qualifications is not to imply that the candidate for an overseas position must necessarily be the top man in his profession, but it is definitely important to determine in advance that the prospective employee has the training and experience to do the work.

Investigating a candidate's qualifications for a position is more or less routine for all types of employment, but when a foreign position is involved a perfunctory check is not enough. Former employers should be contacted as far back as practical for verification of data furnished by the applicant. Personal references from close friends and relatives are of little help. The candidate should be required to supply the names of authorities in his field and former supervisors who are able to report on his past work performance. If possible, these persons should be reached by telephone or personal interview, but a well-constructed letter explaining the demands of the position can be used satisfactorily. In any case, the individual being contacted should be asked to comment on the candidate's weaknesses as well as his strong points. (Quite understandably, many people hesitate to mention shortcomings of others, unless they are specifically requested to do so.) Naturally, the more important the position, the more thorough should be the check of the candidate's job qualifications.

In studying a candidate's fitness for a position, it is also important for the employer to furnish the applicant factual information about the job and the working conditions in the foreign location. This is the other side of the coin which is often overlooked. An individual who is completely capable from a technical point of view is of little value if it is discovered after his arrival that he cannot operate under the conditions present or that the position is not what he had been led to believe back in the hiring location.

Personal Traits

Although sometimes the exception is the rule, there seem to be several personal traits commonly shared by employees whose adjustment to a foreign location is most successful. The happiest expatriate is usually the one who can quickly adapt his personal life to his new surroundings. An open-minded, unprejudiced attitude toward other people, their customs, and their way of life appears to be the trait most helpful in making this adjustment. Rigid, strongly conventional persons who are critical or suspicious of anything differing from their life back home are obviously not likely to be happy in a foreign country for any length of time. In other words, flexibility is a highly desirable—if not essential—quality in a candidate.

Unfortunately, an individual's flexibility, or lack of it, may not be apparent until he is placed in the new situation. In interviewing a prospective employee, an attempt should be made to note clues concerning this trait from the applicant's present life. His attitudes toward new ideas and toward persons differing from his own background should be examined. His spare-time activities, reading habits, and personal philosophy can also supply indications of his approach to life. Signs of a moderate degree of nonconformity (or acceptance of such) usually suggest sufficient flexibility to make a good adjustment. At the same time, the interviewer should beware of the too strongly individualistic or the radically unconventional person. It is, of course, possible to be too flexible.

Another important trait might be called "social sense." This term is meant to describe the quality of being able to mix well with people while at the same time knowing how to respect the dignity and privacy of others. The person who has good social sense gets along well with others because he is interested in people in general and is wise enough to avoid tactless criticism, bragging, or poor taste in his words and actions. Since he must work with not only his expatriate associates but also with nationals inside and outside the company, he should be able to get along with persons at varying social levels and cultural backgrounds. He does not need to be a paragon of virtue, but he should be as different as possible from the self-centered, boorish, and superior-acting type who is so often criticized in discussions regarding the behavior of some expatriate employees. The interview can again provide insight as to whether or not a candidate and his wife have the necessary amount of good social sense. Careful reference checks and background information reports from private agencies specializing in this service can also furnish valuable information about this factor.

Another quality which may help a person to make a good adjustment while living in a foreign country is his self-sufficiency. This refers to one's ability to function without a great deal of dependence on others or on material things. Self-sufficiency does not mean that the person does not enjoy the company of other people or appreciate modern conveniences, but rather that he does not need television, big-league baseball, Broadway shows, and the like to be happy. Usually, the self-sufficient person is able to make his own entertainment. He is an active rather than a passive participant in life, with his own hobbies or other interests which keep him busy. A sort of accompanying trait seems to be that this type of person is not easily bothered by external factors like the weather or unpaved streets. In investigating these twin traits, the best approach is to find out how the candidate and his wife feel about the luxuries of life. Do they view them as nice to have or absolute necessities? The way a person spends his leisure time is also revealing. If their entertainment is devoted to activities which will not be available in the new location, then there may very likely be serious adjustment problems.

Health

The complete physical checkup should be a part of the selection procedure. The more isolated the post or more rugged the climate, the greater the importance of the candidate's being in good physical and mental health. It is also advisable to at least review the medical history of the applicant's wife and other members of his family. The examining physician should be on the lookout for past illnesses or current problems such as allergies which might present difficulties in the foreign location. In addition to the usual components of the physical examination (X rays, blood tests, etc.), certain positions may warrant an interview by a psychiatrist or clinical psychologist. Even if a formal psychiatric appraisal is not deemed appropriate, some attention must be paid to the applicant's mental health. In this respect, the applicant's stability should be carefully evaluated. Although an individual's adjustment may have been adequate in his own country, he must be stable and mature enough so that he will be able to handle the greater stress of operating in a foreign environment. Closely related is the person's motivation. While there are apparently a number of satisfactory reasons for seeking foreign employment, in so far as possible an effort should be made to find out why the applicant wants to work overseas. Overly romantic, impractical, or immature reasoning and expectations should be regarded as serious warning signals. If the physician who handles the physical examination is alerted to the fact that the person is being considered for a foreign job, he can assist in screening out candidates who would be mental risks. The experienced interviewer, aided if necessary by properly administered psychological tests, should also be able to spot those whose mental adjustment would make their success in a foreign position doubtful.

Language Facility

The ability to speak the language of the foreign location is an extremely important factor when considering an applicant; however, it is also one that can be overstressed. Someone who possesses both the proper technical and personal attributes plus the necessary bilingual ability certainly has a tremendous advantage. On the other hand, a candidate should not be hired merely because he speaks the language of the country where the position is located. Language facility without other qualifications is meaningless. As evident as this seems, applications are frequently received from persons who insist that there must be some position available for them because they "speak the language." In other cases where the candidate does have some measure of job qualification, so attractive is the prospect of finding an applicant fluent in the necessary language that glaring personal short-comings are often overlooked.

Obviously, preference is for the person who is personally and technically qualified and also speaks the language. In lieu of the language ability, however, the prudent course is to select the best otherwise qualified person who gives indication of being able and willing to learn another language. Admittedly, there is no precise way to measure this facility, but a sincere desire to learn and a willingness to practice seem to be fairly good predictors. Because of the unquestioned importance of an expatriate employee's being able to converse in the national tongue, language instruction should be a "must" for newcomers who arrive without this ability. A good orientation program for new expatriates should also include a course on local customs as well as background information about the area.

The above four key factors should provide a good guide for selecting candidates for foreign assignments in most situations. As in most things, the ideal may not always be attained, but it should be strived for. In hiring persons for overseas positions, prospective candidates should measure up reasonably well against all four factors. Unfortunately, in view of the difficulty in locating qualified persons willing to leave their homes and work in underdeveloped areas, there is always a temptation to overlook shortcomings. In some cases a person who speaks the right language or seems to be the "right type" may be chosen without sufficient regard for his qualifications. On the other hand, there are instances when a prospective employee who appears to possess all the technical qualifications will be selected even though there is doubt about his personal qualities. Actually, the only truly qualified candidates for foreign assignments are those who meet both job *and* personal specifications.

THE PURCHASING ORGANIZATION IN AN EMERGING ECONOMY

Neil E. Firestone

Introduction

In most emerging economies, some basic obstacles distort the normal supplier relationships. The primary difficulties are:

1. Untrained vendors and personnel
2. Marginal-quality raw materials obtainable locally
3. Lack of experience in understanding the profit motive and the efficient multiplication of human effort by organization
4. Inexperienced buying personnel

These obstacles must be overcome by shedding the traditional competitive-bidding purchasing methods and adopting a radical and patriarchal approach to the potential vendors. A guiding principle must be, "There is nothing more costly than an uninformed vendor."

Evaluating the Prospective Vendor

Exchange of know-how requires a two-way flow of information. The evaluation of a vendor progresses simultaneously with the education of the buyer. While the first meeting may take place in the buyer's location, it is essential that subsequent discussions take place at the seller's office.

This is where the buyer can best assess the vendor's competence. Before any serious discussions take place about the prospective procurement, an inspection of the vendor's facilities should be made. Depending on the product being purchased, he should look for the following elements:

1. An organization that is functioning on a day-to-day basis
2. Stability and dedication of personnel

Mr. Firestone is Vice President of the International Telephone and Telegraph Corporation.

3. Degree of orderliness and reasonable cleanliness
4. A nonbelligerent attitude toward a foreign newcomer
5. Reasonable quality of product standards
6. Access to raw material and end-product transportation facilities
7. Some evidence of manufacturing ingenuity

Since preliminary negotiations will be carried on at the vendor's location, this gives the buyer an opportunity to evaluate the vendor's organization in actual operation. Any questions can be answered without delay, and the buyer obtains a firsthand impression of how the management is able to respond to new manufacturing problems.

Concentrate the major portion of preliminary discussions on educating the vendor in exactly what is required of his organization. While respecting the customs of the country and the ambiguous nuances of the language, do not accept the vendor's "Yes, I know," or "Certainly, we can do that" replies. The affirmative reply is always the easy answer for the vendor. Such replies, if accepted unreservedly, can be costly to both parties. Question, with polite suspicion, these "affirmatives."

Language Barrier

Negotiations in two languages through translators can be a vexing experience. Delays in communication and misinterpretation irritate both sides. Patience, combined with a sense of humor which accepts this slow pace of communication, is a basic requirement.

When a language barrier exists, a trained translator in your employ is of the utmost importance. Hire a translator who has been given a specific education in translating if you can. Put him on your payroll full-time. Insist that he be present at all discussions. This simple tactic not only keeps the two-way communication flow moving but also gives the buyer open access to the side remarks and conversations which invariably take place. If he is without a translator, the buyer is automatically excluded from these asides, which can be more revealing than all the formal replies put together.

As the educational process continues, the vendor's translator will acquire a better comprehension of what is being misunderstood by either side. These areas can be given more careful attention in future conversations with better results.

A word of caution . . . the buyer should do the thinking and the talking, and the translator should translate. This is the only way the buyer can retain control of the conversation. Limit the translator to explaining the complications and difficulties to you, and let him tell you only what the vendor has misunderstood. Then it is up to the buyer to correct these deficiencies, *not* the translator supplying his own interpretation of the situation.

Time Required

Following this principle of educating the vendor in what is required of him means that the manpower hours normally allotted to the buyer for the solicitation, negotiation, and contract award must be multiplied by a factor of 10. In some cases, for example, where the language or business customs barriers cause additional delays, even this factor will fall short. When the success of a new enterprise depends upon purchases made in an emerging economy, the excessive time required to place an order must be recognized.

Product Manufacturing Specifications

Since this may be the vendor's first attempt at more complicated manufacturing, it is essential that he have a complete understanding of the manufacturing specifications required. Nothing should be taken for granted at this stage. He must know what raw materials will be used and where they can be obtained. The tools required must be reviewed in complete detail. Even the tool repair and maintenance facilities should be examined. Quality control requirements must be evaluated so that adequate inspections are included in this scrutiny.

Concurrently, the buyer should obtain the following information:

What is the vendor's reputation?
Does he honor his commitments?
Are his sources of raw material reliable?
Will these materials be available each month, or are there possible weather delays at certain times of the year?
Has he demonstrated the ability to train personnel?
Does he have adequate capital?
Does he have accurate financial data?
Will the proposed work load fit his productive capacity?

The critical question is: Can the vendor equip his plant to do a satisfactory job and train his people properly in the required time?

Price Discussions and Negotiations

Here is where the buyer's normal methods of stimulating active competition must be discarded for a new technique. First, abandoning the "trinity concept" of three bids for each procurement is essential. One prospective vendor who understands what you need, has a clear idea of how to supply it, and has demonstrated an ability to meet price, quality, and delivery schedules is as precious as the discovery of a new diamond mine. He is worth three vendors whose ambitions camouflage their lack of competence.

Usually the abnormal amount of time required to educate a vendor in an emerging economy automatically eliminates multiple-source solicitation in depth. It is better to be selective in the early educational stages. Drop those who cannot qualify as quickly as possible. Once you have taken the time to inform a vendor, plan to follow through with him unless something unusual happens.

As the industrialization of the country expands, these preferred vendors then can be exposed to the competitive situation. This must come later. The first assignment is to develop one reliable source for the part required.

The buyer must also abandon the practice of asking for a quotation. However time-honored the custom is of making no reference to price until the vendor submits a formal quotation, it will only consume precious time and result in unrealistic prices—prices that are usually defensive and, as a consequence, too high.

When approached by the buyer, the vendor has some idea of what is expected of his manufacturing operation, but he has little to go on when it comes to costs and cost calculations. Anxieties press in on every side. The end result is either a price too low, which can be disastrous to the vendor at this point, or a price too high, which is equally bad for both buyer and seller. Consequently, the buyer must be prepared to set in advance a reasonable price which he is willing to pay.

This price is offered by the buyer saying, "If your company can supply us these materials at this price, we will work out a purchase agreement with you." It will contain the basic elements of cost, such as materials, labor, and overhead. In an emerging economy, these cost elements must be well thought out in advance. Sources for this information will include the Ministry of Commerce and Industry, Chambers of Commerce, banks, local businesses, and equivalent organizations in surrounding territories.

It is important that the labor costs be set at an appropriate level. It is just as serious to overstate the labor rates as it is to understate them. Finally, these cost elements must be identified so that the vendor fully comprehends their importance.

A natural inclination to bargain over the price may crop up at this stage. Suppress it. Assuming the price is fair and the vendor agrees to the cost breakdown, this should preclude any search for the proper price level. Certainly this should apply to at least the initial order.

Progressive Procurement

In order to benefit from evolution rather than to suffer from revolution, it is preferable to have the vendor progress step by step with his production program. Therefore, the buyer may elect to furnish some semifinished material which will permit the vendor to train his employees one group at a time. A crash training program in all departments can be disastrous.

Furnishing the vendor with parts which require only manual assembly skills permits him to concentrate on his training program for final assembly. While his labor cost will be high at this stage, it compensates by minimizing his capital investment. However, since his employees must be paid, even while being trained, he may need additional financial assistance from the local banks. These start-up expenses can cause the same financial anxieties in Africa as they do on Seventh Avenue in metropolitan New York.

Two safeguards should be considered at this stage:

1. The financial safeguard of working with the local banks to ensure that the required working capital is available. If it can be explained that additional money is not needed, assuming all goes according to schedule, so much the better. A limited line of credit for payroll needs is still the final objective.

If the local banks are not enthusiastic about making money available to assist the vendor, the buyer's company may be required to do this interim financing on its own. Reconvertibility of the funds in foreign currency applied to any credit before it is offered to the vendor is a vital consideration. Permission must be obtained from the proper authorities in order to guarantee the reconversion of the credit into dollars at a later date. It is equally important that an express authorization be obtained to export the dollars no longer used for credits to vendors out of the country when they are no longer required.

2. The help of the bankers can be enlisted in working with the customs authorities. Permits will be required to import the raw materials, parts, and subassemblies on a duty-free basis. The bankers, combined with the vendor's interest in obtaining these assembly materials, become a formidable combination in successfully meeting the customs authorities' requirements for duty-free importation.

Our progressive procurement program actually works best when the normal purchasing routines are reversed. The vendor who plans to start this manufacturing operation does not begin with the part in traditional fashion and go from part design to tools, to fabrication, to assembly, to inspection. Actually, inspection is the reverse starting point. While quality cannot be inspected into a product, full knowledge of how the inspection is to be done safeguards the quality of the end product. The vendor should be provided with whatever tools, fixtures, or gauges are required to make the physical inspection. He should be provided with a complete inspection procedure. If the product is one which can be worn out by too much inspection, or if the final inspection is adequate only when a destructive test is employed, it may not be too early to discuss inspection by sampling or other simplified statistical quality-control techniques.

Once the inspection techniques have been mastered, it is time to move in reverse order to the assembly methods. This assembly routine follows the basic logic of any final assembly operation, but it is best understood in the light of how the final product is to be inspected. Reverse concentration on the inspection and then on the assembly operations will reduce the learning time and make the instruction task an easier one.

Lead Times and Transportation Costs

When delivery schedules are discussed, extra consideration must be given to the question of lead times for imported materials. This lead time calculation must include adequate transportation time as well as a generous allowance for the required customs clearance. The extra cost of these additional handling operations must be recognized. These add-on expenses, plus the unusual transportation costs involved, are a significant cost item and must be included in the total cost estimate for the final product.

Scheduling must also take into account the number and frequency of local, civic, and religious holidays. These holidays cannot be ignored or overlooked. When they are an integral part of the local mores, it is useless to plan for any production at such times. A complete knowledge of the holiday patterns must be part of purchasing's scheduling calculations. It is equally valuable to understand the historical significance of these festival days. Some participation on the part of the local business community may be required on some holidays and completely out of place for other celebrations.

Purchase Contract Terms

When the price has been set and the delivery schedule calculated, all the terms of the purchase contract should be fully discussed. Every effort should be made to have open communication at this stage. The vendor must have a complete understanding of his obligations under the contract. Naturally, this contract must be written as simply as possible. Remember, it may be the vendor's first purchase contract. Even simple contracts must be understood before they are effective. A copy translated into the native language and submitted to the vendor for advance study facilitates these negotiations.

Incentive Scrap Contracts

When the vendor is provided with material for additional processing, the safest course from a financial point of view is to have the vendor purchase these materials outright. This automatically makes the vendor responsible to his own bank balance for any subsequent scrap losses. These scrap losses can result from a variety of causes, ranging from improper tools or untrained labor to petty theft. When the vendor pays for such materials, this is sufficient incentive for him to control the situation and, whenever possible, is the safest arrangement.

This prudent approach may not always be possible. When the vendor needs financial assistance, the first recourse is to the use of parts and materials furnished by the buyer on a "no charge" basis. While the accounting and paper work still attempts to hold the vendor responsible, on a basis of arithmetic, for so many pieces delivered less the number shipped, it does not solve the problem. The problem is more than asking the vendor to be responsible for your property; it is to recognize that there will be unavoidable scrap losses. Once this is understood, some formula for repayment by the vendor for these scrap losses can be devised. This brings the financial incentive back into play with satisfactory results on both sides.

The incentive scrap plan simply works as follows. A scrap allowance expressed as a percentage is agreed upon. This allowance should be set generously and at a level that both buyer and vendor feel will cover any potential losses. At the same time, the piece cost of the parts furnished by the buyer under this plan must be clearly identified.

As the buyer furnishes various quantities of parts, the scrap percentage is applied. If 1,000 pieces are furnished and the scrap percentage is 8%, 80 parts will be within the scrap allowance. If the vendor returns 920 parts, no charge will be made for the scrap. Of course, the vendor is paid only for his work on the number of good parts delivered. He has the incentive to deliver all 1,000 parts, if this is possible.

The scrap allowance is then accumulated on a quarterly basis. In this example, if 1,000 parts are furnished each month with a total of 3,000, and the vendor delivers monthly 995, 990, and 780 (!), he is still within the allowance. The total of 2,765 is 5 larger than the 2,760 minimum quantity. If the vendor delivered a total of only 2,700 pieces, he would be required to pay 60 times the agreed-upon piece cost. Whenever small amounts are deducted from the last invoice of the quarter, the desired results are obtained. The vendor finds out what is causing the excessive scrap and corrects it.

Payment of Invoices

Each invoice should be paid promptly. These payments usually represent a major portion of the vendor's working capital, and the prompt return of this money is crucial to his financial position. To ensure that the vendor does receive his payment promptly, investigate fully the local banking practices. They are frequently different from yours.

Handling of Rejections

Most procurement difficulties develop when the buyer rejects the vendor's product. These rejections should be anticipated by both parties and an adequate plan of attack worked out well in advance. When they do occur, rejections should be handled promptly. As the defects are discovered, pieces should be returned with a complete explanation followed by a visit to the vendor's place of business. A satisfactory solution is to have a final inspection and *final acceptance made in the vendor's plant*. This shortens the communication chain, with remarkable results. It prevents delays and avoids costly transportation expenses.

As technical problems occur, the quick availability of parent company assistance via telephone or jet transport should not be overlooked. While the distance may be great, the time required to get on-the-spot aid is short. As engineering, technical, and manufacturing skills are in short supply in these countries, do not hesitate to obtain this assistance when required.

Purchase of Outside Services

In an emerging economy, most services which in developed economies are normally purchased from outside suppliers are just not available. Technical services, such as tool maintenance and repair, may have to be supplied internally. When services are available from outside suppliers, special procurement techniques fitting these emerging economies must be applied.

A few of the problems associated with procurement of special services such as painting, maintenance, or roof repairs are:

1. Inadequate liability insurance coverage
2. Lack of adequate tools
3. Insufficient knowledge of required materials, building codes, or specifications
4. Inadequate financial backing

Insurance. If insurance is required in order to protect the company against third-party liability claims, the company will normally accept the risk and self-insure. If this is felt to be unwise, then the company must accept the responsibility of providing such liability insurance. It must also be prepared to pay this cost initially and include it as part of the total cost of having the services performed.

Tools. The same is true for tools. Whenever the services to be performed require a special set of tools or even an unusual quantity of tools, the company must have a method established for providing them to the vendor. The most satisfactory method is to provide the tools at actual cost to the vendor. Payment should be made in equal installments deducted from the vendor's monthly invoice. The least satisfactory method is to provide the tools on a no-charge basis with the hope that they will be returned when the service contract is completed.

Financing. Financing the service vendor's labor costs and unusual material expenses may also be required. If the local bank can be encouraged to do this under a private guarantee of the company, the money problems can be overcome without the company finding itself involved in operating a local finance office.

Personal Liability. Knowledge of the local personal liability law is helpful. When service employees are in your plant, should an injury occur the key question is: Who is legally responsible? If there are hazardous areas in your company, this should be pointed out in advance to the service vendor. He should agree, in writing, to take all necessary precautions. He should agree that his men will use whatever safety equipment is normally provided to the regular plant employees. It should be made clear to the service vendor that if any of his employees are treated by the plant first-aid staff for injuries received while working in the plant, the company does not incur any unusual responsibilities.

Use of Distributors

When an economy is just getting on its feet, greater use is made of distributors than is normally the case. The distributor or "stockist," as termed by the British, may become a key link in the supply chain for many purchased items. In other more developed countries, parts acquired from the distribution would normally be purchased directly from the manufacturer.

Faced with the same problems as the rest of the local business community, the distributor tends to be cautious in making his inventory decisions just at a time when the buyer will need his maximum support. Under these limiting conditions, if this support is going to be effective, it must be intelligent.

To be effective in supplying the requirements of his customer, a distributor must know what the customer plans to use in detail. He should know the monthly usage, the type of item, and what safety stocks will be required. It is normal for a distributor to ask for this type of information, but not for the customer to take the time and effort to provide these details.

When the distributor becomes the sole source of supply for some critical items, the situation is reversed. Now the buyer must not only inform the distributor in complete detail as to his plans, but also learn all he can about the distributor and his supply and inventory problems. In so doing, the buyer will take an active and constructive interest in the total lead times required. "Lead time" is defined as the time elapsed between the writing of a requisition and the receipt of material ready for use. The buyer's next step is to work with the distributor to reduce these lead times wherever possible.

Many times, after this careful analysis, it becomes apparent that a large proportion of the lead time is consumed by the paper-work routines within the distributor's own company. Where this is so, reductions in time can be made immediately. The distributor needs only to agree that he will place an order with his supplier, for specified parts, on the day when he receives notification from the buyer.

Similar attention must be paid by the buyer to the other key steps in the distributor's ordering, stocking, and shipping operations. When the distributor finally has what you want, when you need it, it is well worth the effort made, and it can be safely said that he has earned his commission.

Customs and Excise Tariff Regulations

Purchasing must be familiar with the workings of the local customs authorities and have firsthand knowledge of alternative procedures, the individuals concerned, and even the vernacular used within the department of customs.

A direct responsibility of the purchasing personnel is to be currently informed on all customs procedures. Purchasing staffs should keep up to date on customs regulations and revisions. If any of these revisions restrict the planned procurement, corrective action must be taken immediately by going to the banks or government trade agencies.

Those responsible for purchasing must know the whereabouts of each shipment being processed by customs. They must identify the reason for any delay and take corrective action before a shipment is lost in the local red tape. This pattern of taking immediate action will pay dividends in the long run, particularly in the more "relaxed" countries.

Local Business Ethics

The normal guideposts for standards of how to do business are usually missing in an emerging economy. The best policy to follow is to stay with the tried and tested methods of doing business—puritanical as they may be. Ample justification will be found locally for changing the method and doing things differently, but most of these suggestions will move one closer to the boundaries of questionable conduct.

There is nothing wrong, per se, in doing things differently. Whenever the new situation requires any actions that are felt to be instinctively wrong, plan in advance not to get involved. The practical method is to remember that the only group which needs to be impressed is the parent organization. Naturally, it is impressed only with results, but these should be results accomplished by the standard honest methods of doing business. While it may be trite, avoid the compromising situation.

The rules of conduct for employees of a publicly held corporation are quite simple. Any person acting as an agent of the company shall not profit personally as a result of business transactions performed on behalf of the company. A more sophisticated way of stating it is that there shall be no "conflict of interest." These policy statements should be clearly and forcibly stated, in writing, to all of the employees.

If the companies acting as your vendors are privately owned, the problem may be more acute. A single proprietor may do many things and make many offers on his own initiative that are completely unacceptable from the point of view of an agent of a publicly held corporation. These offers may be made in innocence, but they can be politely refused, nevertheless.

These positions must be made equally clear to any local nationals in your employ, particularly those who work in the purchasing function. They, too, may have strange ideas on how American businessmen operate. Erroneous impressions created by the movies' land of make believe are hard to erase. Start at the beginning and make your "no nonsense" position clear to the entire department. Any hint of gratuities or special favors being offered to the purchasing personnel must be quashed at once. If the standard of doing business on a merit basis is firmly established from the first, it will prosper.

Conclusion

Purchasing in an emerging economy requires imagination—enough, that is, to anticipate the vendor's problems before they cause loss of precious time. Money can buy many things, and while the buyer may be an expert, he cannot buy time. Applying his imagination, the buyer must drop his passive role of merely analyzing quotations, placing orders, and waiting for delivery. His new role in this particular situation is an active one. He must anticipate the full scope of his vendor's activities.

In this active role, the buyer brings the resources of his own organization to parallel the vendor's facilities, and, as required, the parent organization can assist the vendor when difficulties occur. Both buyer and vendor must be prepared to put this assistance mechanism into operation while there is still time to recover the situation. Part of the preparedness program is being alert to any delays as they develop. Vendors attempting a new venture will self-excuse most of these interruptions automatically. The buyer must probe extensively to learn the causes and dimensions of any potential slowdowns.

As the difficulties are encountered, there are certain to be unusual stresses on the buyer-seller relationship. Out of meeting these difficulties will come a much better understanding of the vendor and his organization than could be learned, conversely, from an unblemished record of successes. If the vendor meets his problems with candor and contributes his share of ideas willingly when called upon to do so, stay with him. When a successful relationship has been created, and that means one which is mutually profitable, both can say with pride, "Remember the fun we had in the early days when we were both getting started."

ESTABLISHING A MANUFACTURING BUSINESS IN BRAZIL

Colonel Earl Haefner

Introduction

This is a management case history of problems and solutions encountered in setting up a successful automotive parts manufacturing plant in Brazil. These problems, and the solutions applied, point up the contrasts between operating conditions in a less industrialized nation and those in Europe or the United States.

The business structure was formed in 1956; pilot line production began late in 1957, and a profitable level of operation was reached in March, 1958. The unprecedented growth of the business has required three expansion programs, including a new factory which was occupied in July, 1962. In perspective, it can be noted that unit output in 1962 was fifteen times the 1958 production rate. Nonetheless, Borg-Warner experience in other Latin American countries and other less industrialized nations around the world has demonstrated a remarkable similarity in the problems and solutions to be found when setting up operations in developing countries.

Outline of Operations. Foreign investment proposals submitted to the Borg-Warner Corporation operating committee by divisions and subsidiaries include a pro forma profit and loss statement, balance sheet, market forecast, assessment of management capability, and information on the political and economic situation of the country under consideration. An accompanying "Reason Sheet" summarizes significant facts, conclusions, and recommendations essential for management decisions.

The problem of finding a capable manager for the Brazilian operation was solved through affiliation with a local group, who furnished the man. Among other Borg-Warner operations around the world, some are managed by local nationals and some by Americans.

Colonel Haefner is Vice President of Borg-Warner International Corporation.

Problems related to laws and customs regulations required legal liaison with the licensing authorities and the services of a capable customs broker to deal with the port authorities. (Additional details are given in the case examples.)

Evaluation of the Brazilian market was relatively uncomplicated, since International's sales records provided a wealth of data giving an accurate picture of product mix and a statistical base for sales forecasting. However, regardless of how market information is acquired it is paramount to the success of a foreign venture that the content and the potential of the market be accurately analyzed and assessed.

The concept of product standardization proved to be one of the most important innovations contributing to the manufacturing excellence and profitability of the Brazilian business. Moreover, this program is now finding profitable application in other countries of the world.

Problems related to materials and processes will be described later in detail. These explain the valuable help of Stateside suppliers in furnishing technical assistance for solving local problems.

Coordination and control of the project was most vital to its success. Our initial planning was premised on a statement of the objectives and assumptions we considered essential to our basic strategy. As our plans took form, we delegated task responsibility for the various functions to be performed. We assigned target dates and imposed a system of control which enabled us to measure progress daily and to take command over the results we wanted.

The importance of export packing in delivering machinery and equipment to the factory site damage-free can hardly be overemphasized in the light of government red tape for obtaining replacements. One serious mishap to a vital machine might conceivably delay the production start-up for six to eight months.

Some start-up problems are not foreseen in spite of previous experience in establishing overseas operations. Generally, these are best solved through local ingenuity, resourcefulness, and determination to meet the program schedule.

Manpower and related problems are primarily solved at the local level. This is a function of management leadership which has been ably performed in our Brazilian operation. The importance of production planning and control is cited among the case examples, since problems in this area have greater implications in many South American operations than in Europe or the United States.

The long Stateside role of Borg-Warner as a supplier of vital parts to original equipment manufacturers has carried over into fifteen countries of the world. Consistent with this background of service, the Brazilian subsidiary kept pace with the rapid growth of the local auto industry. This was accomplished via three expansion programs closely coordinated with Stateside management through an effective system of liaison control. The following examples elaborate on how this was done.

Case History Examples

Foreign Investment Proposals. The policy of Borg-Warner Corporation is to promote overseas expansion whenever evaluation of foreign opportunity indicates a potentially profitable situation, due consideration being given to overall risk factors. The proposed investment is expected to yield a higher return than domestic investment, in order to compensate for the greater risks generally involved in foreign operations.

Normally, reliance is placed upon the Borg-Warner International Corporation to seek out and initially evaluate a foreign opportunity. This is because International operates through a world-wide distribution network and is charged with the responsibility of keeping abreast of significant changes in foreign markets which create both threats and opportunities at home and abroad.

After International has screened the potential opportunity, coordination is effected with the Stateside manufacturing division for further studies to determine market potential, operating margins, and such data as are necessary to decide whether the project should be undertaken. Considering that some forty divisions and subsidiaries engineer and produce over 2,000 diverse products, it is apparent that technical problems alone require a major assistance contribution by each division concerned with an overseas operation.

Operational experience suggests that problems of producing and marketing widely diversified products have been best solved through decentralization of operations, which are closely monitored through a system of liaison control by the Stateside management group responsible for the foreign operation.

The presentation of an overseas investment proposal for approval by top management involves painstaking fact finding, particularly in the area of market potential. From the voluminous raw material collected must be culled the essential and significant data for presentation in summarized form as a basis for management risk-taking decisions. The data should include a projected pro forma profit and loss statement, balance sheet, market forecast, assessment of management capability, and information on the political and economic situation in the country.

Political and Economic Problems. The depreciation of the Brazilian currency in relation to the dollar has exceeded 90 percent in the past six years. To meet this problem, all surplus operating income was promptly converted to inventories, land, plant facilities, etc., with at least temporarily good results. It is hoped that Brazil will continue to exercise its reason and restraint in meeting the present economic crises.

The Problem of Management Performance. Probably the greatest single deterrent to overseas investment opportunity is the dearth of management talent capable of getting economic results from the proposed enterprise.

For our Brazilian project, the vital factor of management was a most important consideration, and, without going into details, it influenced us to associate with a Brazilian group who were interested in bringing new industry to the country. They were willing to accept a minority interest and to provide the services of an American executive with excellent qualifications for managing the prospective undertaking. Our partners contributed the land, factory buildings, and the initial funds for raw materials and starting expenses. Later, after the factory was operating profitably, they gave us the opportunity to acquire full ownership on an equitable basis. We accepted this offer in October, 1958, and retained the managing director whom they had furnished.

Laws and Customs Problems. As an incentive to foreign investment, Brazilian Instruction 113 authorized the importation of machinery and equipment on a relatively duty-free basis if such machinery and equipment came in as a capital contribution for establishing an enterprise deemed essential to the nation's development. This government policy was instrumental in establishing in Brazil an automotive industry which, in a period of five years, attained a productive capacity of 200,000 vehicles annually, fabricated almost wholly from Brazilian-made components and assemblies.

The most troublesome feature of the duty-free provision was that net weights of the machinery and equipment listed on the import license should be within 5 percent, plus or minus, of the weight stated on the license. Through a strict system of liaison and control with the machine tool vendors, we were able to minimize these difficulties, but only after we learned by earlier mistakes that the net weights furnished by vendors were not always accurate.

We also found it advantageous to have a law firm in Rio (then the seat of the Brazilian Government) to act as liaison with the bureaus and agencies having authority over import licenses. In several instances, the customs authorities at the port contended that a certain machine in the shipment was available in Brazil and therefore subject to duty charges, even though the import license presumably would not have been granted in the first place if a local machine were available. In all cases the conflict hinged on interpretation of the equipment classification. In these instances we relied upon our Rio law firm to clarify the issue with the license authorities, who in turn notified the customs officers at the port to release the goods.

One experience taught us that a saving in paper work and forwarder fees could actually penalize clearance at the port. We covered one large shipment of special equipment contained in several cases by a single consular invoice. As a result, it took approximately three weeks longer to clear this shipment from the port because all the items were on one invoice. The examining inspector would not release any part of the shipment until each case had been inspected. After that, we furnished a separate invoice for each box of equipment, which considerably expedited delivery.

In another instance, a vendor shipped an incorrect machine which was useless to us in Brazil. We assumed that we could explain this to the Brazilian authorities and obtain an amendment to our project license to permit shipment of the correct machine and return of the incorrect machine. Our customs broker pointed out to us that if we pursued this course, we would immediately place the examining engineer at the port on the spot, since he had certified that the item delivered to us was in accordance with the license. A compromise solution to this problem was negotiated with the Stateside vendor which included recovery of penalty costs. It was not feasible to rectify the error through replacement under the original license provision.

Market Analysis. Brazil was first considered for clutch manufacturing operations in 1953, when a sharp decline in clutch exports occurred owing to dollar shortages arising from the coffee situation. Brazil was our largest service replacement market for clutches in the world, since the vehicle population consisted primarily of U.S. makes. Moreover, the possibility of developing a local auto industry was then being discussed by U.S. vehicle manufacturers and the

Brazilian Government. As this interest developed, we undertook a thorough survey of the market potential in Brazil, including a detailed analysis of our own sales records. Evaluation of our market data, including the status of local competition, convinced us that a modest manufacturing operation could be established which would prove profitable even if confined to after-market demand.

Our studies indicated that the Brazilian vehicle population included approximately 85 percent American-made vehicles. Ford and Chevrolet represented about 63 percent of the passenger and truck vehicles in Brazil—equally divided. In contrast to the U.S. vehicle population, the truck registrations in Brazil represented over 50 percent of the vehicles in operation, and this in turn increased the overall service replacement rate of clutches. Our studies indicated that the average life expectancy of a clutch disk in a passenger vehicle operating in Brazil was about 2½ years, compared with six years or more in the States. In trucks, the life expectancy was indicated at approximately one year. In developing estimates for our program, we used the 2½-year life expectancy for both cars and trucks. Fortunately, the sales of clutches which we had made over the years to Brazil provided us with reliable data as to the clutch models sold in Brazil. This information proved to be invaluable when we reached the stage of determining tooling costs and equipment requirements.

Product Standardization. Our market data revealed that 166 different models were sold in the Brazilian market, which in turn were manufactured by the three clutch divisions of Borg-Warner in the States. Each division had its own engineering design and methods of production to meet the requirements of its OEM[1] customers. As a preliminary step, each division was requested to prepare machinery, equipment, and tooling estimates for a given number of its clutch models required in the Brazilian market. When these estimates were correlated, it became evident that the cost of special equipment and tooling was exceedingly high in the light of the estimated sales volume in Brazil. As a solution to this problem, the Borg & Beck Division was given the task of standardizing its clutch design to meet the various vehicle makes and applications. Through this program of standardization, it was possible to cover 92 percent of the market with some fifty standardized models. This resulted in equipment and tooling savings which amounted to $217,000.

Materials and Other Problems. At the outset, because of dollar shortage threats, we aimed for an operation that would be as nearly self-sufficient as possible. We investigated the availability of raw, semifinished, and purchase-finished materials, including the serious problem of variable quality from local suppliers in meeting our material specifications.

Our preliminary survey of materials availability did not disclose any unusual problems in this area. Samples of the more critical raw materials and of several purchased finished parts were procured, sent to the States for evaluation tests, and found generally acceptable. Later, we were to learn as pilot production got under way that the erratic quality of items furnished by our suppliers would create serious problems for us. This experience taught us an

[1] Original Equipment Manufacturers (OEM) are such manufacturers of end products as Ford, General Motors, Chrysler in the motor vehicle industry; General Electric, Norge, Philco, etc., in the home appliances industry.

important lesson—never evaluate the quality level of a raw material or a finished part on the basis of a few samples. Since then, we have demanded and received samples from separate and intermittently spaced production runs by the supplier before accepting his product.

One item which was initially approved and later created a problem was a small brass tubular rivet. When quantity deliveries began, we experienced difficulty with our automatic riveting machine, which would not feed the rivets because of their irregular quality. This problem was finally resolved by purchasing a cold-header machine from the States which enabled us to make these rivets in our own factory. Since we had no provisions for a cold-header on the original import license, we faced a serious cost penalty in getting the machine into Brazil. Nonetheless, there was no alternative for us, since it was impossible to begin production without acceptable rivets, and, because of import restrictions, it was not feasible to rely upon imported rivets for any period of time.

Similarly, locally made friction facings were tested and approved by our Borg-Warner laboratories in advance of our decision to establish operations in Brazil. The favorable results from these earlier tests seemed plausible, since several of the local facing producers had good plants and turned out a product fairly acceptable for the local service replacement market. However, through other information which we had gathered, we suspected that possibly we had not tested enough samples to really determine the average quality level. Additional samples were requested, and the Stateside test results confirmed our doubts. We felt it was imperative to maintain the level of quality associated with the Borg-Warner name and, consequently, proceeded to import semi-finished facings from the States at a huge cost. The problem with friction facings continued to plague us until, finally, we were compelled to set up the necessary facilities to produce our own friction materials under a license arrangement with a leading U.S. manufacturer in this field.

Another critical material problem was related to locally drawn steel wire for clutch springs, which are comparable in quality to engine valve springs. In Europe and the United States the technology for producing such springs is well advanced, and these items are purchased by clutch manufacturers from outside suppliers as finished parts. Here again, preliminary tests on the wire samples indicated a quality level meeting our requirements, but during the pilot production runs we found that a high percentage of the springs did not comply with our standards for fatigue life. The deficiences were traced back to the Brazilian steel and to the rod rolling mill. Although the wire supplier had an excellent equipment setup, he could not produce finished wire of a quality better than the steel furnished by the mill. As a result, we were compelled to import springs from the States at an extremely high cost because of duty and dollar exchange penalties. We worked on this problem for several months in liaison with our Brazilian manager and in cooperation with the foremost producers of high-carbon steel wire in the United States. As an outgrowth of these activities, the wire processor in Brazil was persuaded to send his technical chief here for firsthand study of production facilities and technical know-how. This visit convinced him of the need to import wire material regardless of cost until such time as local mills could produce the required quality. Consequently, with the raw material now imported from Sweden, our plant is producing quality springs well below the cost of imported springs and with a fatigue life as good as or better than any similar spring produced in Europe or in the States.

One other small part, an eyebolt, was to be purchased in Brazil. After several months of trial and error, the prospective supplier gave up, since all his efforts to produce a satisfactory bolt had been futile. As a result, we were forced to import eyebolts from the United States. The purchased cost of the eyebolt in the States was 8 cents, However, the landed cost in Brazil varied from 42 to 50 cents each, and since three bolts were used in each clutch assembly, the aggregate cost represented 10 percent of the clutch assembly, which was intolerable by any standard. To make this seemingly simple part correctly required a good deal of technology, which was chiefly held and guarded by one principal supplier in the States. Through the helpful cooperation of this supplier, we were able to acquire the know-how and cold-forge the bolt in our own plant, after installing special equipment at a landed cost of $50,000. The savings have already recovered the cost of the investment required to solve this problem.

Coordination and Control. After acceptance of the product standardization concept, it was necessary to develop new revised requirements for machinery, equipment, and tooling. These requirements were determined in coordination with the Borg & Beck Division. At this stage, our managing director in Brazil came to the States to review the equipment and tooling requirements and to participate in the final decisions as to what should be purchased.

With this final determination of machine and tool requirements, we presented our appropriation request to the central office. They approved the request almost immediately. We then faced the fact that although we had the authorization for funds, we did not yet have a license from the Brazilian Government to import the machinery and equipment. Under the provisions of Instruction 113, our equipment requirements had to be final and fixed and presented with our manufacturing proposal to the Government as a basis for obtaining the import license.

Our Brazilian manager estimated that it would require sixty to ninety days to obtain the license. At about this time, machine tool manufacturers were advancing their prices and were requiring lead times of six to twelve months on machine tool deliveries. Consequently, we decided to take a calculated risk and place purchase orders for all major items involving price increases and long lead times before receiving the license from Brazil. Purchase orders were issued by telephone and confirmed, with detailed specifications involving some two hundred items of machinery, equipment, and special tools. Accrued savings of $25,000 resulted from this decision and the prompt action taken.

We obligated 57 percent of the authorized appropriation by telephone in one week, and within five weeks 75 percent of the funds had been obligated. When the Brazilian import license was received five months later, many of the items were ready for shipment. Consequently, 92 percent of the items were released for shipment in the next two months. The value of the items released in the two-month period represented 88 percent of the total Brazilian project. We set up a master control and status record covering eighteen significant

Project Control and Status Record

Item No.	Description	PO No.	Vendor	FOB Pt.	Lic. Net Wt.	Vendor Net Wt.	Ack.	Sched. Del.	Aux. Equip. Del.	Consol. Ship and Re-lease	Sea Shipped	Boat	Clear Port Santos	Tech. Lit. Sent	PO Amount	Cum. PO Amount	Appro. Amount	Cum. Appro. Amount
1	#311 Press	56-302	Hyman	Phila.	100,000	120,000	9/7	2/5		2/7	2/10	Teal	3/15	10/10	17,750	17,750	20,000	20,000
a.	Cushion	56-302A	Hyman	Phila.			9/20	2/5						10/10	2,050	19,800	2,000	22,000
b.	Spare Parts	56-511	Bliss	Toledo			10/15	12/10	12/15						1,732	21,532	1,500	23,500
c.	Safe Gd.	56-504	Univ.	Cleve.			10/55	11/15	11/18					W/S	150	21,682	150	23,650
d.	Lubric. Syst.	56-512	Alemite	Phila.			10/16	10/28	10/26					W/S	388	22,070	400	24,050
e.	V-Belts	56-520	Suppl. Inc.	Chi.			10/28	11/20	11/15						130	22,200	130	24,180

Note: The above entries, taken from the actual record, illustrate the coordination required and consolidation effected for shipping one major item and its auxiliary equipment, often procured from diverse sources. The license net weight was based on vendor estimates, but actual vendor weights substantially exceeded the original estimates. Brazilian regulations require that license net weights and shipping net weights be within 5%. In the above example, it was necessary to obtain a weight amendment from the license authorities in Brazil, which involved a time lapse of two months.

factors related to machinery procurement, license requirements, follow-up, and shipments, which provided daily information as to project progress. Special tooling requirements, spare parts, and perishable tools required a great deal of coordination to meet delivery schedules and to effect delivery of these items with the proper machine in accordance with the Brazilian import license provisions. The license description for each machine included accessories, spare parts, and tools, and this made it necessary that these items go with the designated machine.

In most cases, we found that, where special tooling was required for a machine, a machine tool manufacturer placed such a high price on this tooling that we found it profitable to consider outside sources. In some instances, the special tooling was procured in Michigan and shipped to New England to be boxed with the machine. A case in point involved some double-splined arbors for use with an automatic lathe. The machine tool vendor quoted $450 per arbor, but we procured them through a known and reliable source in Michigan for approximately $120 each. A total of twenty arbors were involved, and the $6,600 saving which we effected was well worth the coordination efforts on our part.

Export Packing Problems. For a project of this kind it is paramount that the machinery and equipment arrive at the factory in good condition. Damaged equipment is useless and involves many months of time in obtaining replacement parts from the States, because of licence problems. We had no fear of packing problems for new equipment, since most machine tool vendors learn through costly experience how to pack their equipment safely for shipment to all parts of the world.

We did have some serious misgivings about the competence of independent packing contractors to take used machinery and box it for shipment so that it would arrive intact. Several years ago, we shipped a complete plant from Detroit to England, and the breakage in transit rose to alarming proportions. This time we decided to take every precaution. As an example, we had one large press weighing over sixty tons on which we had obtained two estimates for export packing. The difference in the quotations caused us to question whether the low bidder knew what he was about, even though he had a good reputation in this field. He assured us that we had nothing to worry about, but we took the added precaution of having our insurance agent keep an eye on the job. It was fortunate that we did so, because the insurance inspector discovered that the skids were cracked on some of the larger pieces when delivered to the pier for loading. We took this evidence seriously, demanded that the entire job be reassessed, and agreed to an increase in the packing charge for added factors. The press arrived in Brazil in good condition, undoubtedly as a result of the extra precautions which were taken. For the rest of our used equipment, we employed an export packer who had done a great deal of work in accordance with army specifications, and while his overall costs were somewhat higher, we did not have a single case of damage on some sixty items of used machines and equipment.

Start-up Problems. At the time our project program was firmed up, we worked out a schedule of target dates for the things to be accomplished in Brazil concurrently with our activities in the States. When these target dates were established, it was assumed that certain phases of the tooling would be accomplished in Brazil through the use of local facilities. Unfortunately, these facilities did not produce the results we had anticipated, and it became apparent that the tool and die work was falling behind schedule. Although our studies had shown that we could produce the tools in Brazil at a cost of roughly one-third what they would cost in the States, we found it expedient to transfer some of the tooling responsibility back to the States at a higher cost but at considerable saving in time. This failure to keep pace with the initial program schedule retarded progress three to four months in meeting some of our special tooling requirements.

Another factor which slowed progress was the final acquisition of the factory building. When our negotiations first started, it was assumed that we would occupy a building which was then under construction. Later, for reasons not foreseen, it was decided that another building should be erected for our operation. Because of this, our time schedule fell behind. Our project planning specified that all machine foundations would be prepared prior to the arrival of machines and equipment. All machine tool vendors had been required months in advance to furnish foundation specifications and other technical data, which, in turn, were forwarded to Brazil. However, because of the delay in occupancy of the building there had not been time to install any of the foundations prior to the machinery arrivals.

To bring our installation program back on schedule, we formed two task groups consisting of three workmen in each group. One team was assigned to daytime installation activities and the other to night tasks. By this means we regained the lost time, although at a higher cost than we first estimated. As a result, a number of "bug-free" components were produced within eleven months after our Stateside appropriation request was approved.

While we failed to achieve our start-up target date 100 percent, we did set a record in getting under way—at least, that is the verdict of other manufacturers who faced similar start-up problems in Brazil. We attribute our success to good luck, liaison between Stateside and Brazilian management, and last, but not least, a mission concept that had no place in the *modus operandi* for elaborate personnel requirements bearing overtones of Professor Parkinson's law.

For an American, accustomed to telephone communication as we have it in the States, one of the most frustrating experiences encountered in Brazil is the inability to grab the telephone and make prompt calls to adjacent communities. A telephone call between our city office in São Paulo and our factory at San Bernardo, a distance of fifteen miles, required placing the call at eight o'clock in the morning to get through sometime by early afternoon. Recently, this has been largely rectified through a new telephone exchange center in San Bernardo which permits direct dialing to São Paulo.

Communication at the factory level can be greatly facilitated if the key personnel are bilingual. At the outset, we were not too well prepared along this line. Our managing director speaks Portuguese fluently, but the staff of key people whom he recruited hardly spoke English, although they read and understood it. This deficiency has been partially corrected through night-school English classes for the key personnel.

To provide on-the-job technical assistance to our new subsidiary, we arranged for a retired vice president in charge of manufacturing of the Borg & Beck Division to go to Brazil. His thirty-seven years of experience in making the Borg & Beck clutch product have been invaluable to our manufacturing operations.

Manpower and Related Problems. Personnel training and turnover form a common topic of discussion at management levels in Brazil, since there is always the possibility of losing an employee after he has acquired training and experience valuable to another manufacturer. The situation is a by-product of the steady inflationary pressures which have escalated the cost of living, and of the industrial expansion which has increased the demand for workers. Until the basic problem of inflation is brought under control, there will undoubtedly continue to be a high rate of turnover for skilled labor and technical personnel. Among both American and Brazilian firms it is quite common to bid openly or under cover for the services of technical people. Sometimes these activities take the form of outright pirating, as between vendor and customer or vice versa.

Transportation of employees between home and factory is still a problem for us because of inadequate public transportation. However, this is a problem which nearly all manufacturers in the area must contend with. Public transportation in the São Paulo area has not kept pace with local industrial expansion. Many facilities have been added, but these have not matched the rapid growth in outlying areas. We expect that many more years will pass before we can relieve ourselves of the responsibility of transporting at least some of our personnel. In contrast, manufacturing plants located within the São Paulo city limits seldom have to provide transportation for employees. Nevertheless, on baalnce, we consider the advantages of our outlying location have more than offset the disadvantages of the transportation problem.

One last word on personnel needs in the area of production planning and control. I would emphasize the importance of setting up a well-qualified production planning and control unit charged with the responsibility for procurement functions and the maintenance of balanced inventories. These are difficult functions to perform under the average conditions of foreign operations. As an example, some steel mills operate on a production cycle basis and produce a certain type and grade of steel during that run, then they switch over to another type and grade for a cycle run. This requires that procurement lead time be phased with both the steel mill and the manufacturer's production schedules. Any malfunction in this area may cause production line stoppage or excess inventories.

Our experience has proved that competent people for performing production planning and control functions are not easy to find. A partial solution to this problem has been through on-the-job training of carefully screened and selected personnel having aptitudes and traits considered essential to success in this field. The job training includes the use of texts, articles, and case examples based upon U.S. technical know-how in administrating production planning and control principles and procedures, including some familiarity with linear programming methods.

Original Equipment Manufacturers' (OEM) Expansion Problems. Our initial project was primarily planned for production of clutch disk assemblies, since, at the time of inception, there was no assurance that original equipment business would be forthcoming. As a precaution we took in sufficient heavy equipment, less tooling, to produce complete clutch sets for original equipment manufacturers at modest production rates. Some months after our decision was made and the program started, the government executive group of the automobile industry in Brazil, known as G.E.I.A., issued a decree which required that by 1960 vehicle manufacture in Brazil must be fabricated 85 to 90 percent by weight of locally made components.

The sharp rise in OEM requirements for components under the G.E.I.A. program dictated that we substantially increase our manufacturing facilities. We began planning for this within six months after our initial start-up date. The urgency of demand arising from the OEM business gave our project high priority. To meet our target dates we initiated a "crash" procurement program, and six months later most of the additional machinery and tooling was in production. Our manufacturing volume soared 50 percent above the previous level, and presaged an upward trend which has continued unabated despite the political situation in Brazil.

Fortunately, as OEM customer purchase orders increased far beyond earlier expectations, our plant was able to meet their tooling requirements largely because excellent toolroom facilities were included in the original project in keeping with our policy of local self-sufficiency. How this policy paid off can be seen by citing an example. One leading foreign vehicle maker was dissatisfied with his local source of supply. He offered to place an order for a sizable part of his requirements, provided tooling and pilot run production could be completed within four months. Our general manager accomplished this feat through superb personal leadership and the fact that he had available the necessary equipment and trained manpower to meet the target date required.

Early in 1961 it was apparent that manufacturing space was fast becoming inadequate. An on-the-spot study and evaluation were made by the author, in collaboration with the local general manager, to determine whether the existing facilities should be expanded or whether a new land site should be acquired which would accommodate all future expansions for many years to come. The decision was reached to relocate and erect a new plant with a floor area more than double that of the old premises. The construction details, processing layout, time schedule for building, and additional equipment requirements were closely coordinated by liaison with Stateside management. The new plant was occupied in July, 1962. The move from the old plant to the new was accomplished by the local management without loss of production or other significant detriment. The new modern facilities have increased appreciably the overall productivity of both administrative and factory employees. However, the continued growth of market demand has already required a 25 percent increase in manufacturing area, completed in 1964.

THE ENTREPRENEURIAL ELEMENT IN ECONOMIC DEVELOPMENT

Bert F. Hoselitz

This paper attempts to examine the role played by the exercise of entrepreneurship in the process of economic development. In the literature on economic growth much has been written on entrepreneurship, a variable customarily designated as an important contributing factor to economic development. Though there have been some case studies on the emergence of entrepreneurs in several developing countries, generalizations in the field of entrepreneurial roles and contributions have been rare, and there is even some uncertainty as to the proper definition of the concept. It is proposed to suggest here some general principles relating to the performance of entrepreneurial functions in the process of economic growth in general, and in the developing countries in particular.

The definition of entrepreneurship, like that of many other crucial concepts in economics, is not uniform. Some think of entrepreneurs primarily as innovators, some chiefly as managers of enterprises, some as bearers of risks, and others place major emphasis on their function as mobilizers and allocators of capital. The idea that the specific role of entrepreneurs is the carrying out of innovations goes back to Joseph Schumpeter, who expressed this view originally in 1912, at a time when most entrepreneurial performance was in the hands of private individuals acting on their own account, and when governmental and private bureaucracies still played a relatively subordinate and limited role in the running of economically significant enterprises. In the fifty years that have elapsed since Schumpeter's views were first expressed, the corporation and other highly structured business units have come to perform the main entrepreneurial functions in the economically advanced countries, and

---

Dr. Hoselitz is Professor of Economics and Social Sciences at the University of Chicago, Illinois. This article is reprinted from *The Economic Weekly,* Bombay.

public officials working in government enterprises or government-controlled corporations have come to carry it in the Socialist countries and in many important branches of production in the developing countries.[1] Hence the individual, "irrational," visionary entrepreneur whom Schumpeter saw as the main carrier of economic progress has been replaced by a private or public "business leader," whose action is based largely on known and predictable principles, whose risk taking has been greatly reduced, and whose activities are supported by a large corporate or governmental bureaucracy among which many functions have become thoroughly routinized so as to make the performance of the typical entrepreneurial function stipulated by Schumpeter either impossible or superfluous.[2]

New Concept of Entrepreneurship

It is not intended to belittle the contribution of Joseph Schumpeter, but rather to suggest that his conception of entrepreneurship must be modified in the light of concrete developments in the last few decades, especially in the less advanced countries of Asia and Africa. Most of the business leadership in these countries is, or may be, carried out by managers of large private or public enterprises or by small and medium-scale private entrepreneurs. Scarcely any of these are innovators in Schumpeter's sense, and none of them are visionaries who strike out for previously unexplored territory. All of them are imitators, adapters of experiences gained in the economically more advanced countries to the conditions of their own. The technology they apply is usually borrowed from abroad, the legal and marketing practices they employ are adaptations of those developed in more advanced countries, and often the commodities they produce and sell are selected because of the operation of the "demonstration effect" through which consumption goods of the more advanced countries become popularized and enter general demand in the developing nations.

In the light of these considerations, it is necessary to change our description of entrepreneurship and the entrepreneurial function from that originally postulated by Schumpeter. The person who typically performs this function in developing countries today is either a manager or an imitative entrepreneur, i.e., a man who adopts and adapts new methods, new products, new sources

[1] Among the more interesting case studies see, for Asia, James J. Berna, *Industrial Entrepreneurship in Madras State,* Asia Publishing House, Bombay, 1960; for Africa, Peter C. Garlick, *African Traders in Kumasi,* University College of Ghana, Accra, 1959; for the Middle East, Y. A. Sayigh, *Entrepreneurs of Lebanon: The Role of the Business Leader in a Developing Economy,* Harvard University Press, Cambridge, Mass., 1962.

[2] See Joseph Schumpeter, *The Theory of Economic Development,* Harvard University Press, Cambridge, Mass., 1934, pp. 74ff. This book was originally published in Vienna in 1912; the preface to the German edition is dated July, 1911.

This transformation of the exercise of entrepreneurial functions from a single personal business leader to a corporate bureaucracy and the subsequent decline of genuine entrepreneurship have often been commented upon. See, for example, the passage from Werner Sombart, cited in B. F. Hoselitz, *Sociological Aspects of Economic Growth,* The Free Press of Glencoe, New York, 1960, pp. 144–145.

of supply, or new markets to the needs and conditions prevailing in the newly developing country in which he lives. In the subsequent discussion we will be concerned primarily with these "imitative" entrepreneurs, i.e., with individuals who are active as business leaders in the private sector. Most of the public or quasi-public servants who run the large government-owned or government-sponsored enterprises are part of the body of so-called high-level manpower about whom there is widespread discussion these days. Yet the actual facts of economic development in Asia and Africa seem to indicate that an important role in this process may be played by small and medium-scale plants, provided a private enterprise sector is at all in existence and provided that, within the framework of government plans for economic development, it is intended to develop a "mixed" economy, i.e., one in which public and private enterprise combine for the mutual improvement of the level of economic performance or economic welfare.

Role of Small Business

In short, we will be concerned in this paper primarily with private entrepreneurs who are active in the many small and medium-sized industrial, commercial, and financial enterprises which are developing or are bound to develop in the economically less advanced nations. Many of the characteristics, especially those relating to personality variables, will also apply to persons in positions of business leadership in the public sector, and others will be applicable to them provided the different scope and conditions of their functioning is taken into account. Thus, although we will discuss explicitly only the development of private entrepreneurs, we will bear in mind the parallel needs of public servants who perform business leadership roles, and in some cases we will be able to point to differences resulting from private and public business leaders being subject to different influences and responding in different ways.

Lest it be thought that, in concentrating on small and medium-scale private entrepreneurs, we are dealing with a group of persons who are of little significance in the process of industrialization and general economic growth, it might be useful to cite a few figures indicating the general significance these persons may have. If we classify industrial establishments in terms of the number of workers employed and designate enterprises employing fewer than 50 workers as belonging to the class of small and medium-scale plants, we find the following data from the economic experiences of Western European countries: in Austria, in 1930, 57.7 percent of the total labor force in secondary production (manufacturing, mining, and construction) was in firms employing fewer than 50 workers. The corresponding figures for other countries were as follows: in France, in 1906, the percentage was 70.6; in Germany, in 1907, it was 54.5; in Japan, in 1955, it was 50.6; in Switzerland, in 1955, it was 43.7; in Norway, in 1953, it was 51.3.[4] From these figures it becomes apparent that small and medium-sized plants have played an important part in industrial countries, and that even long after the onset of the industrialization process the majority of workers in secondary production

[4] See Bert F. Hoselitz, "Small Industry in Underdeveloped Countries," *Journal of Economic History*, vol. 19, pp. 601–602, 1959.

were employed in these "small" firms. The corresponding proportions for commercial activities, especially retail trade, and for financial activities, except investment banking and modern types of insurance, are probably much higher than those in secondary industries. In brief, the small and medium-scale firms can be said to have played an important role in the more highly developed countries and may, for this reason alone, be expected to play an important role in the process of economic growth in the developing countries.

But there is still another reason why we may assign an important role to these enterprises in developing countries, especially those with dense populations and extensive labor supply. It is quite customary, when we think of industrial development in the new nations, to evoke the picture of a large-scale industrial plant, e.g., in steel or cement production. But the existing markets, demand patterns, and conditions of comparative advantage in developing countries are such as to make the establishment of small plants, mainly those producing light consumer goods, most attractive.[5] Hence industrialization must be thought of in the next two or three decades not so much as the growth of the Pittsburghs or Birminghams in the developing nations of Asia and Africa, but rather as a process in which small capitals get allocated in various industrial and commercial fields, gradually growing to increasing size but remaining—from a world point of view—confined to fairly small and at best medium-sized industrial, commercial, and financial units rather than becoming giants in their fields of economic activity. The reason for this is mainly the very different relative supply of labor and capital in the developing countries as compared with the more highly developed nations. Labor, as has been pointed out by competent students before, is in "unlimited supply," and capital, particularly capital to be invested on a long-term basis, is in very short supply and often altogether unavailable through ordinary channels.[6] In other words, banks will ration credit to small entrepreneurs who would wish to grow rapidly, and this means that many enterprises will begin with meager capital funds and grow only to the extent to which they can reinvest their profits. But this means that, especially in the industrial field, we must count upon the long-run persistence of small and medium-scale enterprises in the developing countries. Coupled with the historical experiences of Western Europe, it appears to be safe to assume that small and medium-scale entrepreneurs are likely to play an important role in developing nations for several decades, provided these developing nations permit a private sector of enterprise in the industrial, commercial, and financial fields at all.

Financial versus Industrial Entrepreneurship

Up to this point no distinction has been made between the different areas of economic activity in which entrepreneurship is exercised. Moreover, in the literature on entrepreneurship, usually little or no distinction is made as to

[5] See Walter Elkan, "Criteria for Industrial Development in Uganda," *East African Economic Review*. vol. 5, pp. 50–57, 1959; and H. W. Singer, "Problems of Small-scale Industry," paper submitted at the International Economy Association Regional Conference on Economic Development South of the Sahara, Addis Ababa, July 17–29, 1961 (mimeographed).

[6] See A. W. Lewis, "Economic Development with Unlimited Supplies of Labour," *The Manchester School of Economic and Social Studies*, no. 22, pp. 139–191, 1954.

whether this activity is exercised in the commercial, financial, or industrial field. Yet even a superficial study of business leaders in many developing countries shows that industrial entrepreneurship is not exercised to anywhere near the degree to which commercial and financial entrepreneurship flourishes. Why do we find in so many developing countries no dearth of moneylenders and traders—either of native stock or originating in other nearby developing countries—and so few industrialists belonging to the same ethnic category? For example, we find in almost all the new nations of West Africa extended networks of trade in which Africans, persons of Middle Eastern origin, and other Mediterraneans participate. Yet few of these persons engage in industrial pursuits. The same could be said about African, Indian, and Pakistani traders in several East African countries, of the Chinese in various parts of Southeastern Asia, and of the other indigenous or non-European immigrant groups elsewhere in the world of developing nations.

Various arguments have been put forth to explain this phenomenon, and since developing countries are interested in industrial development, these arguments may be of importance. Among them is principally the proposition that indigenous industrialists, especially in former colonial areas, were unable to compete with the powerful industrial enterprises set up by Europeans. A similar argument may be made for developing countries which were politically independent but whose native potential entrepreneurs faced the overwhelming competition of foreign investors. But this argument is hardly convincing, since, in the first place, most European foreign investments were concentrated in such basic industries as mining, transport, and power, and only small proportions of private foreign capital flowed into manufacturing in developing countries or colonies; and in the second place, whatever competition was exercised by large-scale and economically powerful enterprises in industry, this competition was equally severe in commerce and banking. If we look at the kind of enterprises which indigenous entrepreneurs did establish in the trading and moneylending fields, we find that they were often supplementary to similar activities exercised by European firms. Native traders and moneylenders found a place in the interstices of the economic system left unoccupied by the larger foreign firms. They mediated between the major urban centers and the countryside, they provisioned small and even minute retailers, they serviced the financial needs of rural and semirural populations unable to offer bankable securities, and they distributed commodities on a scale which would have been uneconomical for the large foreign enterprises. This role has been often noted for the Chinese in the former Netherlands Indies, for Africans in Nigeria, and for many other indigenous or other non-European entrepreneurial groups elsewhere.[7]

Factors Inhibiting Industrial Enterprise

Why do we not witness a plethora of similar developments in the industrial field? Clearly we should not expect that the small indigenous entrepreneurs

[7] In addition to the work by Garlick, *op. cit.*, see Astrid Nypan, *Market Trade: A Sample Survey of Market Traders in Accra*, University College of Ghana, Accra, 1960; and R. D. Lambert and B. F. Hoselitz (eds.), *The Role of Savings and Wealth in Southern Asia and the West,* UNESCO, Paris 1962.

would have competed with the large foreign mining or transport companies. But there were and still are numerous industrial branches in which ample opportunities appear to exist for the establishment of small and medium-scale plants which would play a similar "interstitial" role, vis-à-vis the larger foreign-financial industrial enterprises, to that of the native trader and moneylender with regard to the foreign import houses, wholesalers, and bankers. This difference in behavior in different economic fields by indigenous entrepreneurs appears to be of importance, mainly because economic development everywhere is tied to a significant degree to the growth of industry. And, as was pointed out earlier, in mixed economies industrial growth is not confined to a few large establishments mainly in the field of heavy industry, but also applies substantially to the rapid growth of many small and medium-scale firms in consumer goods and service industries, and even in the production of various more highly specialized capital goods which serve the needs of the larger enterprises. Hence the gaining of a clearer insight into the different conditions under which industrial, as against commercial and financial, entrepreneurship may flourish in a developing country may be an important guide for overall economic policies.

One of the reasons for the sluggishness of industrial entrepreneurship in developing countries may be the fact that the talents required to guide an industrial enterprise differ from those needed for successful commercial or financial entrepreneurship. The small trader or moneylender can operate successfully with only few, and often even without any, permanently employed assistants, whereas the industrial entrepreneur—provided he is more than a craftsman or artisan—typically must hire a group of men or women whose work he must organize and guide. Hence, in addition to being motivated by the expectation of profit and the capacity of applying innovation—even if these are imitations of practices used in the economically more advanced countries—he must have managerial abilities, particularly the ability to command and organize. In short, we may presume that an industrial entrepreneur must have a wider set of personal abilities than a moneylender or trader. Even more important than being venturesome and profit-oriented, he must be a person who can lead others in a common enterprise and must have extensive technical skills and knowledge in his branch of production, for in the small enterprises which are so common in developing countries the head of an enterprise combines technical and economic leadership.

Another aspect of the distinction between industrial entrepreneurs, on the one hand, and financial or commercial entrepreneurs, on the other, is the depth of commitment of assets in the production process. A trader may carry on his business without ever attaining property rights to the objects he deals with. If he is a broker or commission agent, he may merely lose his earnings from a transaction, but not the capital invested in it. In addition, the capital that a trader or moneylender does invest in his business normally turns over much faster than that invested in an industrial establishment. A moneylender or banker, moreover, deals in a commodity that has the widest currency, that is accepted by anyone, that can easily be transported, hidden, or converted into other assets, and that, if need should arise, can be employed for bribery or other illegal acts. An industrial entrepreneur has usually a much larger proportion of his assets tied up in fixed capital; he depends on an often imperfect market for the sale of his output; he may sometimes be able to become only a subcontractor and thus be exposed to monopolistic pressures, his property is exposed to a series of dangers—destruction by fire or other accidents—which moneylenders or traders escape. Other things being equal, the risks and uncertainties of transforming a given amount of capital into industrial assets are much greater than those involved in trading or financial operations. This means, however, that a commitment of one's property to investment in industry implies normally a longer-term commitment, which also increases the uncertainties of one's action. For there is less flexibility in an operation once capital has taken the form of fixed assets, and the prospective profitability of an enterprise is more directly influenced by changes in tastes and fluctuations in demand than is true for capital invested in commerce or finance.

Climate for Entrepreneurship

The preceding discussion has brought out the fact that entrepreneurship depends in part upon the appearance of persons with a certain psychological makeup favorable for entrepreneurial activity and, in part, upon the social and economic environment in which individuals with the proper personal inclinations will find it attractive to apply them to the appropriate economic ends. Since many developing nations have the desire to create a climate favorable for the rapid development of entrepreneurship, especially industrial entrepreneurship, it may be useful to discuss in greater detail the ways in which these personal and environmental conditions can be enhanced. Let us turn, therefore, to a brief discussion of the conditions in the social and economic environment and the qualities in the persons concerned that must be created in order to produce a corps of entrepreneurs adequate for the needs of economically developing nations. The significance of psychological disposition for entrepreneurial activity is quite clear from the discussion in the preceding paragraphs, and some writers have made these personality factors the fully determining conditions of economic innovation and economic growth.[8] This appears perhaps too extreme a position, and there is little doubt that many features in the environment, which can be manipulated with much more predictable outcomes than the shaping of personality development, also have an important bearing on the growth of entrepreneurship in developing nations. In other words, we may quite appropriately consider certain conditions in the economy and society which will make possible the successful exercise of entrepreneurial functions, regardless of the relative abundance or scarcity of certain personality types.

These conditions of the economy may be classified as consisting on the one hand of certain forms of social and economic overhead capital, and, on the other, as being composed of certain governmental services which are placed at the disposal of entrepreneurs. One of these environmental conditions, the precise impact of which is not often examined in detail, is the maintenance

[8] See, above all, D. C. McClelland, *The Achieving Society*, D. Van Nostrand Company, Inc., Princeton, N.J., 1961.

of law and order. A somewhat deeper examination of this point reveals that the problem may much more usefully be discussed in terms of the distribution of status and political power in a society, of the way it affects the exercise of entrepreneurial functions, and of the role that the business community plays in the political decision-making process. A system of private enterprise can exist only if the following basic conditions in the legal-political field are met:

1. What is required is not complete nonintervention, but rather governmental action designed not to deny actually or implicitly any kind of autonomous decision making in the economic field to private persons.
2. A minimum provision of legal and legally enforceable institutional rules according to which private economic decisions can be made and implemented.
3. Protection of the assets owned by an enterprise against expropriation by others either with high social status or with political influence, and protection of the contractual relationships entered into by business leaders with one another or with outsiders.

Historical Experience

If we consider these conditions, we will find that in some historical situations they were forced upon governments by the political action of business leaders and their political allies. The meaning of the "industrial revolution," whether it arose gradually through a process of legal and political reform, as in Britain, or whether it was strongly supported by a political revolution, as in France in 1789, had precisely the impact upon the legal and political system described in the previous paragraphs: no more arbitrary privileges in the economic area for the aristocracy, no more special treatment of certain privileged groups, such as the church, wider access to the elite from the ranks of the business community, and a platform—in Parliament or some less visible arena—from which pressures could be exerted by business leaders for legislation in support of their most important needs. In other countries, the process by which this greater participation and protection of the entrepreneurial community was achieved differed. In Germany, for example, we find that a political alliance was concluded between the aristocratic junkers and the interests of industrial enterprise; in many of the ex-colonial countries the development of entrepreneurship by nonindigenous elements deriving from other colonial or non-Western countries—the pattern which Max Weber called "pariah entrepreneurship"—may be explained by the fact that a European system of legal security and predictability was imposed upon these countries. In Japan, finally, it appears that the attainment of this system was brought about with a minimum modification of the external aspects of social structure and primarily through the reorientation of a part of the existing elite in the direction of meeting the overall needs of the nation, not through political isolation from the rest of the world, but through the adoption of Western technology and economic organization.[9]

[9] The British and French developments are too well known to require explicit documentation. For Germany, see Alexander Gerschenkron, *Bread and Democracy in Germany*, University of California Press, Berkeley, Calif., 1943; for Japan, see E. E. Hagen, *On the Theory of Social Change*, The Dorsey Press, Richard D. Irwin, Inc., Homewood, Ill., 1962.

The crucial lesson to be derived from these instances is that private entrepreneurship will develop only if the legal order provides the necessary accommodation for the needs and protection of entrepreneurial activity. But this means not merely the inauguration of a "neutral" system of laws, but also the shaping of a set of social institutions through which pressure can be exerted by entrepreneurs upon the actions of the state and especially upon legislation, and in consequence of this the raising of entrepreneurial performance to a level where it can provide not merely wealth, but also social status and some form of political influence. In the absence of the creation of these conditions, various alternative outcomes are possible. One is the socialization of all enterprise and the willingness by the government to make all decisions in the economic realm. In brief, one alternative is the establishment of a fully planned economy, with complete abolition of private enterprise. A second alternative is the establishment of a system of statism, such as existed in Turkey in the interwar period, in which private enterprise exists nominally but functions under the full tutelage of the government. A third is the neglect of enterprise altogether and the subsequent stagnation of the economy. Thus the creation of a "climate of entrepreneurship" has not only an economic and social but also a political dimension, and disregard of this fact may force alternative policies leading either to entrepreneurial functions being exercised or fully controlled by the government or to the abandonment of the economy to economic stagnation.

Necessary Economic Overheads

If the establishment of a legal order and the resolution of the political and status roles of entrepreneurs may be considered as one part of the social environment conducive to the development of entrepreneurship, there are also some obvious features of economic overhead capital the provision of which influences the development of entrepreneurship in a positive direction. Most important among these are the provision of transport facilities and the provision of power for industry and allied types of economic activity. These are perhaps the two most important single items among the vast variety of economic overhead capital features whose presence in relative abundance encourages the growth of industrial and commercial enterprise. It is not necessary to enlarge upon the utility of power, since without it all modern productive processes are impossible. But transport facilities, roads or railways, and the rolling equipment by means of which commodities may be shipped easily, safely, and cheaply over some distance are of equal importance, for one of the characteristics which have led to severely limited markets and have prevented the establishment of some firms is the absence of a wide enough, conveniently accessible sales area. The more underdeveloped a given region is, the more important is a good transport network, for one of the main variables in the creation of a new orientation which will attract individuals to participate in entrepreneurial activity is the wider extension of the exchange economy and of conscious production for the market. The growth of transport facilities exerts a stimulus both in situations where commercial and industrial exchange networks are already in existence, and in those where the exchange economy has only just begun to attain a foothold and the development of entrepreneurship in all fields is contingent upon the rapid and effective extension of an exchange economy.

We have moved in this discussion from suggesting first those features of the socioeconomic environment which are most important, but also most difficult to provide, to those which are somewhat easier to make available. Most significant, and yet most difficult, is the creation of an appropriate climate for entrepreneurial effort; power and transport are slightly less important, but their provision is easier, provided the necessary financial resources can be raised. An even easier set of tasks, though a much less important set, is the establishment of various government agencies offering, either without charge or at low cost, a number of services of importance to an entrepreneurial community. Among these services are, above all, various forms of information on markets, sources of supply, technical innovations, internal organization and layout of a plant and flow of works, and innovations in design, also various other items of technical and market information which the small and medium-scale entrepreneur in a developing country normally cannot obtain on his own or would have great difficulty in obtaining. In advanced countries there exists a plethora of trade journals and technical magazines in which a small industrialist or merchant can obtain much of this information. But markets in most developing countries are as yet too small and confined to too limited areas to make the publication of these journals and magazines attractive, and thus business leaders must, and often do, rely upon the government to provide this information. This role was assigned to government even by such a confirmed "classical liberal" as Jeremy Bentham. In an essay[10] in which he considered the proper sphere of government action in the economic realm, he argued:

> There are cases in which, for the benefit of the public at large, it may be in the power of government to cause this or that portion of knowledge to be produced and diffused, which, without the demand for it produced by the government, would either not have been produced, or would not have been diffused.

Government and the Entrepreneur

But in addition to information on markets, technology, and related matters of utility to entrepreneurs, the government may also offer or cause to be offered additional services either at low cost, or, as a subsidy to the growth of rational entrepreneurship, free of charge—at least for a limited initial time period. These services consist, above all, in assistance with accounting, including cost accounting, in the provision of cheap credit, notably long-term credit, and in the provision of various types of technical education which are primarily of importance to small and medium-scale entrepreneurs in a large number of branches of industry. The need for all three types of services has been widely recognized, and in several developing countries appropriate institutions have been created which do supply them, usually at especially low cost—which, as already pointed out, constitutes essentially a subsidy for the new industrial and other establishments. The agencies charged with providing

[10] Jeremy Bentham, *Economic Writings*, George Allen & Unwin, Ltd., London, 1954, vol. 3, p. 337.

these services bear different names, but have normally been designated collectively as development banks or development corporations. It would lead us too far to enter here into a detailed discussion of all the kinds of activities, forms of organization, and spheres of operation of development corporations. There exist fortunately a number of useful descriptions of these institutions.[11] They all participate in credit operations for industry and other enterprises, and it was for this purpose that many were originally formed. But just as it was found that the provision of agricultural credit to peasants in developing countries had to be supplemented by extension services if the credit operations were to have their optimum impact, so it is gradually found that the extension of long credit to nonagricultural enterprises in developing countries must be supported by analogous educational and related services if the new industrial and commercial enterprises are to have a maximum chance to survive.

It may not be inopportune to discuss in somewhat greater detail certain aspects of the activity of development banks serving private entrepreneurs. The best-known aspect of these operations is the provision of credit, particularly for the long-term investment needs of a new enterprise. But, in addition, a development corporation which does provide financing for new industrial or related investment by entrepreneurs in a developing country should provide also all the technical and economic information which would be helpful to the new entrepreneur in the early phases of his activity. The development bank has better facilities to find out where the most suitable machinery can be bought, and, in fact, what the most suitable machinery for a given type of productive enterprise is. It will have better and more up-to-date information on markets, freight, charges, insurance costs, and other expenses incurred in establishing and running a new business than most traders and industrialists. It will have staff persons who can, after due examination of the productive processes to be applied, develop a system of accounting which will be both relatively simple and accurate and meet the current needs for financial information of the entrepreneur. It may even, as does the Small Industries Corporation in India, establish a department which acquires industrial and other machinery likely to be of use to new firms and sells these machines on a hire-purchase plan to new entrepreneurs. Finally, it may collaborate with new firms in finding suitable locations, possibly in industrial estates, and in designing work procedures, factory, and related patterns of practical operations which will further production rationality and reduce the costs of productive operations.

In many developing countries where industrial development banks or similar financing agencies have been established, their activities are confined to larger-scale enterprises. This is understandable, since the assistance that these firms need upon their establishment is proportionally smaller, especially if measured against their financial credit needs, than that required by the smaller firms. In other words, whereas in larger establishments the chief assistance needed by entrepreneurs is long-term credit, and whereas the training of persons performing entrepreneurial functions in larger firms is identical with that instituted for the creation of high-talent manpower in general, in smaller firms

[11] Perhaps the most informative account of these institutions is the book by William Diamond, *Development Banks,* The Johns Hopkins Press, Baltimore, 1957.

the chief requirement is for advisory services of various kinds, in addition to credit, and the training required by the smaller entrepreneurs is less extensive than that of managers of large private or public corporations but more explicitly oriented toward the economic, organizational, and technological processes on which their enterprises are likely to concentrate. All this suggests that the development of commercial, financial, and especially industrial entrepreneurship, on a wider basis, requires different approaches not only by banks and governmental information services, but also by the educational system. For we encounter the common belief that the basic propositions on the development of high-level manpower, as expressed, for example, by Frederick Harbison, find general applicability in the formation of entrepreneurs in all cases.[12] But this is a misinterpretation of the role and capacity of the many small and medium-scale entrepreneurs who form, numerically speaking, the bulk of the business leaders in developing countries.

Personality Characteristics

As has already been repeatedly argued in this paper, entrepreneurship implies the exercise of leadership. It is aided by maturity of character and by a sense of personal security, and this is enhanced by information on relevant matters. It means that a person in an entrepreneurial position must be able to read and write and must have knowledge of accounting and related skills. It is helpful in some lines, and imperative in others, that he know something about the technical aspects of production. But the entrepreneur is principally a "generalist," not a technical or economic specialist. In this he is distinguished from the expert manager of a large private or public corporate enterprise. This latter is employed because of his specialized knowledge. He is in charge of some technical aspect of a productive enterprise, of purchasing, labor relations, or some other precisely circumscribed sphere of action. Hence his special skill is of value. But the entrepreneur in a small or medium plant must be not only a man with some knowledge of the productive techniques employed in the plant he owns, but a person who makes the chief decisions relating to sales, supplies, production processes, relations with workers, and numerous other matters. In the case of the entrepreneur the relative weight is the reverse. Though information and skill level are not unimportant, the small entrepreneur must primarily display the required characteristics of personality and leadership, the willingness to take some risks, and the desire to innovate and experiment in order to perform his role properly.

But although these personality characteristics are assigned first rank, the education and training of an entrepreneur is not a matter of complete insignificance. This is true especially of industrial entrepreneurs who—as was pointed out earlier—must possess a good deal of technical information on the production processes which they guide. This experience, which must be eminently practical, can best be acquired by some on-the-job training program in establishments already in operation, even in a foreign country. For example,

[12] See Frederick Harbison, "The Development of Human Resources in the Newly Developing Countries," in J. D. Brown and F. Harbison, *High-talent Manpower for Science and Industry*, Princeton University Press, Princeton, N.J., 1957, pp. 61–90.

an entrepreneur who wishes to start a foundry should be enabled to obtain access to such an enterprise in his own country, if foundries there are already in operation, and in a nearby developing country which has foundries, if his own country has as yet none. Similarly the would-be entrepreneur in textiles or leather work, food processing, or any other industrial operation should gain access to establishments in that branch of production. After spending some time in such an on-the-job training program he will be in a much better position to run his own factory. These training programs for industrial entrepreneurs may have to be supported by governments, and, in cases where an international exchange of persons is required by governmental agreements, the travel and subsistence funds of trainees should preferably be supplied from public funds.

Psychological Aspects

Up to this point we have been concerned with an enumeration and analysis of all the external factors which may conceivably influence, in some fashion or other, the growth and encouragement of entrepreneurship in developing countries. But, in the last resort, the appearance of entrepreneurs is a matter of changing human effort and human action, and hence we must look also to the more narrowly human aspects of recruiting and promoting a corps of entrepreneurs in developing countries. In dealing with this problem we are in one of the most disputed and uncertain areas of social research relating to developing countries. Opinions expressed on the human factor in entrepreneurship range all the way from sheer resignation at the impossibility of dealing with this factor meaningfully and purposively to the prescription of elaborate schooling and training programs. In this paper the value of a general elementary and at least rudimentary secondary and vocational training for entrepreneurs has not been questioned. But rather than pursue the well-trodden path of educational programs for entrepreneurship to its ultimate end, we will turn to the more difficult and even less fully explored question of the psychological aspects of entrepreneurial action. For if this factor has the influence which some students ascribe to it, all the changes in environment and all the adjustments in education and public services are of no avail, unless the proper entrepreneurial personality traits can be fostered.

The psychological aspects of entrepreneurship have been stressed principally by E. E. Hagen and D. C. McClelland, though each has stressed somewhat different characteristics.[13] In brief, the generally accepted viewpoint on the psychological dimension in entrepreneurial action may be summarized as follows: The industrial entrepreneur, and in fact the innovating entrepreneur in general, is a distinct personality type. He must be persuaded that change can occur and that it can be brought about by individual action. He must also be motivated to bring about this change by his own activity. There probably exists a limited number of persons in all societies with these beliefs and motivations, who, though acting in part on the basis of pecuniary motives, usually have other ambitions and objectives as well. For example, they may use the acquisition of gain to rise in social status, to acquire political influence, or to preserve an existing prestige position originally stemming from their

[13] See E. E. Hagen, *op. cit.*, and D. C. McClelland, *op. cit.*

membership in certain ascriptively determined groups. This is the reason why—as we have maintained earlier—the general standards of a society must allow persons with newly acquired wealth some access to power and/or prestige. If social obstacles to deriving these gains from the exercise of entrepreneurial action are overwhelming, persons with the appropriate personality disposition will fail, will seek other careers, or will attempt to emigrate.

This sketch of the psychological conditions of entrepreneurship has followed so far largely in the footsteps of Schumpeter and those influenced by his views on the role of innovating entrepreneurs in economic development.[14] The argument raised by Hagen and McClelland turns around the view that economic growth will occur only if individuals with characteristic entrepreneurial personalities appear in sufficient number, that is if the appropriate motivations affect not merely a handful of persons, but penetrate more deeply into all layers of society, and if the persons who perform entrepreneurial roles belong to some social class or group which enjoyed a higher level of power or prestige in the past, has lost it, and attempts to regain it not by traditional paths of upward social mobility, but by the acquisition of wealth instead.

Entrepreneurship on Mass Basis

According to this theory, the appearance of entrepreneurship on a mass basis can be explained as the result of two factors. First, it flows from a special historical situation in which motivations and new paths to higher social status are sought through economic achievement. Secondly, it is the result of the appearance in a society, with more than ordinary frequency, of persons with special personality traits, i.e., persons with unusually high achievement motivation. It is sometimes argued that these two developments have been related to one another in all cases in which entrepreneurial activity flourished autonomously and vigorously. Thus, whatever may be said of the change in values and motivations as a precondition for entrepreneurship, the relationship between successful business leadership and certain prevalent personality patterns appears plausible, and even substantially confirmed by empirical research in the economically advanced countries. A timid person, a person who has a great need for cordial and friendly attachments with others, a person who wants power over other men, will not become an entrepreneur—the first because he lacks venturesomeness, the second because he will sacrifice achievement for the sake of friendship, and the third because he wants to control and dominate others, not lead them in a mutually profitable enterprise. But a person who has a high achievement orientation, that is, a man who sets a goal for himself which he strives to attain, who is willing to take a calculated risk, and who is eager to exploit a new and potentially challenging situation and use it to his best advantage, this is a man who may become an entrepreneur and who may be very successful in this career.

[14] The two most authoritative treatments of entrepreneurial personality deriving from Schumpeter's views are L. H. Jenks, "The Role Structure of Entrepreneurial Personality," in *Change and the Entrepreneur*, Research Center in Entrepreneurial History at Harvard University, Harvard University Press, Cambridge, Mass., 1949, pp. 108–152; and Arthur H. Cole, *Business Enterprise in Its Social Setting*, Harvard University Press, Cambridge, Mass., 1959.

McClelland and his students have shown that such persons existed at various periods in history when societies did undergo rapid economic development, and that not only these persons but the whole value system of a society adopted a more intensive preoccupation with achievement.[15] This group of scholars has also shown that the appearance of these persons is a result of the way they have been raised by their parents. But the very fact that a substantial number of entrepreneurs appeared in societies where a short time ago little or no such talent seemed to be available makes one suspect that individuals with the required achievement orientation exist in all human societies, though they may not always make their impact felt with the same intensity. If economic development and industrialization are planned as goals of a society as a whole, would-be entrepreneurs step into a very different environment from that which prevailed in the historical epochs which McClelland and his students, Hagen, and even Schumpeter had investigated. These men are concerned with the explanation of the appearance of entrepreneurs as an autonomous social process and with the growth of economic achievement motivation as an alternative path to upward social mobility in an environment where the acquisition of wealth was not a preferred or even customary avenue for those who tried to rise in the social scale. In these situations a much higher than average frequency of achievement-oriented individuals may be a prerequisite for economic development.

In developing countries, however, we are confronted with nations which have placed the slogan of economic growth on their banners and are prepared to provide the most extensive accommodation to persons who wish to, and who can, step into positions of entrepreneurship. Moreover, from the great number of traders (though many of them are merely small peddlers) who are found scattered about the urban and rural areas of almost all developing countries, we may deduce that individuals exhibiting achievement-oriented personalities are available in sizable numbers in developing societies, and that what is required is not so much the creation of new personality types, but rather the opening up of opportunities in the social, economic, and political environment, in the scale and impact of government services, and in the intellectual equipment and training of the persons concerned to push them into new and potentially successful entrepreneurial roles.

It may well be that those concerned with the encouragement of entrepreneurship in developing countries should study the work of McClelland and his students and should attempt to influence child-rearing practices in a direction which will make the appearance of achievement-oriented persons more likely. But these practices will have their full effect only in the next generation, and, long before the present children are grown to maturity, entrepreneurial roles must be filled by persons who presumably have acquired the needed personality traits in the past. The experience recorded by G. Papanek from Pakistan is encouraging.[16] He showed that the Moslem population of British

[15] See N. N. Bradburn and D. E. Berlew, "Need for Achievement and English Economic Growth," *Economic Development and Cultural Change,* vol. 10, pp. 8–20, 1961; and J. B. Cortes, "The Achievement Motive in the Spanish Economy," *ibid.,* vol. 9, pp. 144–163, 1961.

[16] See G. F. Papanek, "The Development of Entrepreneurship," *American Economic Review,* vol. 52, pp. 48–58, 1962.

India, which exhibited remarkably little entrepreneurial talent, has produced, particularly in certain of its subgroups, quite a sizable number of able business leaders. With the development of new and protected markets, a sufficient number of persons with the appropriate personality characteristics were coming forward to meet the challenge which the emerging situation presented. These men emerged in a population which half a generation ago displayed an almost proverbial lack of business leadership. It cannot be doubted that a similar appearance of new opportunities in other developing nations may be an important, if not the most important, factor calling forth a similar outburst of new entrepreneurial talent.

Some of these opportunities may be created by education, others by policies which were outlined in previous paragraphs of this paper. Given the widespread desire to apply rational principles of planning to the fostering of economic growth, the resulting socioeconomic system would be one commonly designated as a "mixed economy." A mixed economy is one in which the government and private interests undertake parallel and combined efforts for the overall economic growth of a nation. This pattern of cooperation and division of functions is appropriate to developing countries, because an underdeveloped economy cannot afford to be doctrinaire. It faces serious shortages of all kinds and must, in order to experience economic growth, confront the serious business of getting things done, i.e., of getting capital accumulated and invested in the most useful directions for economic growth. Given the widespread backwardness among large masses of the population and the urgency with which economic development is desired, the leadership of the government is essential to an economy which otherwise might remain almost completely stationary.[17] This cooperation between public and private interests may have the result that, on the one hand, all available means are employed to encourage and enhance the rate and amount of saving in the economy, and that, on the other, the most efficient channels are used to allocate these savings among those branches of production in which their overall net return to the economy will be greatest.

A New Economic System

It is within this context that a centrally prepared plan has manifold uses, and if such a plan is well thought out and based upon the existing moral and political rules of the society, it may have a crucial role in the overall growth of the economy. But if the general moral and political rules of a nation recognize the right and, in fact, the necessity of private enterprise, the plan will be successful only if it makes due allowance for the exercise of private initiative in all or a large number of fields of economic action.

Thus it is not impossible to combine an overall economic development plan with the simultaneous encouragement of private enterprise and the fostering of an entrepreneurial class. There are too many cases on record in developed and less-advanced countries which prove this. It does not mean that friction cannot arise between the business community and the planners—friction often caused by differences in overall objectives between different groups of persons. Some may prefer short-run gains at the expense of lower growth rates in the

[17] Alexander Eckstein, "Individualism and the Role of the State in Economic Growth," *Economic Development and Cultural Change,* vol. 6, pp. 81–87, 1958.

long run, whereas others may be willing to acquiesce in many short-run sacrifices in order to ensure the maximum rate of growth in the long run. Conflicts may also arise as to the division of decision-making functions between public and private agencies and the precise limits of what industrial functions have been reserved for government. Though—as was pointed out earlier—the business leaders will want and must be given some greater degree of access to the realm of political decision making, they must learn, on their part, that a governmental development plan is not an instrument which robs them of all freedom of action. It merely designates, from the point of view of overall economic considerations embracing the society as a whole, the paths of progress and the primary patterns of investment which are considered most conducive to the progress of the economic performance of a society.

These remarks are intended to reconfirm the fact that entrepreneurship can play a vital role in the planned economy of a developing country, provided that the development plan is drawn up in such a way as to provide room for the operations of private entrepreneurs, and provided that these entrepreneurs are not dismayed or frightened away from making independent decisions, even though many decisions relating to production and investment are reserved for or regulated by government. It is quite conceivable that the mixed economy, as it takes shape in many developing countries, may grow gradually into a new form of "economic system" with its own distinctive characteristics, one of which would be the fruitful and constructive collaboration between public officials and private entrepreneurs in the development of the economy. The ultimate outcome most highly prized by both public officials and business leaders in a developing nation is economic development. For the growth and improvement in the performance of the public sector stimulates demand for the output of private entrepreneurs, and the increase in output and improvement in the quality of goods and services supplied by private firms adds to the standard of living and the material welfare of the population at large. Hence, from a secular viewpoint, the interests of government, the newly emerging entrepreneurial class, and the mass of the population in a developing nation are closely parallel. The main problem is to find a formula by means of which this parallelism of interests can be put into effect with least friction and greatest likelihood of success.

CAPITAL INTENSITY IN INDUSTRY IN UNDERDEVELOPED COUNTRIES

Prepared by the United Nations Bureau of Economic Affairs on the Basis of Reports by United Nations Technical Assistance Administration Experts

The scarcity of capital and abundance of labor in underdeveloped countries have given rise in various quarters to the contention that, in the industrialization of these countries, preference should be given to industries and techniques tending to employ relatively less capital and more labor; in other words, that industrialization should largely follow labor-intensive lines. On the other hand, it is also sometimes maintained that, although capital may be scarce, it should by priority be invested in industries using capital-intensive techniques; large-scale resorption of the structural unemployment existing in some countries would, in this case, have to be deferred.

The determination of the appropriate capital intensity—that is, the right combination of factors of production—in the industry of an underdeveloped country is one of the key issues involved in formulating a program of industrialization. It arises in respect of both the "macroeconomic" aspect of planning for the industrial sector as a whole and the "microeconomic" aspect of designing a given plant or project. At the general planning level, it may involve a choice between overall objectives—such as maximizing employment or maximizing income—in assigning priorities as between individual industries. It may involve decisions on the relative importance to be given to long-run and short-run considerations in setting up industrialization targets, the emphasis to be given to "heavy" or "light" industry, and the tempo of industrialization itself. At the level of actual plant design, it may involve a choice—if a choice is technologically possible—between alternative techniques allowing different combinations of machinery and manpower. At both levels, decisions may be influenced by noneconomic as well as economic considerations.

From *Industrialization and Productivity*, Bulletin 1, April, 1958, pp. 5–23.

General Policy Recommendations

In a number of reports on industrial development presented by United Nations Technical Assistance Administration experts, the relevant policy recommendations are founded essentially on an assessment of the basic resources and potentialities of the countries concerned. Such a criterion often entirely overshadows other considerations of an economic or social nature. Thus, in the case of a relatively small, semidesert African country, the experts concluded that its poverty in industrial raw materials, the smallness of its market, the high fuel, power, and transportation costs, the shortage of credit, and scarcity of skilled labor entirely preclude industrial development "of the kind that is commonly assumed to play a central role in development"; in another small country of the same area, a similar assessment of conditions led to the analogous—though more guarded—conclusion that "there is little immediate prospect for industrial development." Accordingly, the experts recommended only the development of handicraft and cottage industries. In still another case, a small country in Central America, an appraisal of domestic resources and potentialities and of foreign trade prospects led the experts to the conclusion that "the development of a heavy industry is impossible and the only path to industrailization is through the establishment of light industries." The experts recommended establishing or expanding a number of small-scale, little-mechanized consumer goods factories processing indigenous agricultural products partly for domestic consumption and partly for export. In a few other cases, experts recommended, also on the basis of an appraisal of resources only, the establishment of various types of suitable industries, both "light" and "heavy," of appropriate size and level of mechanization.

In the majority of cases, however, the criterion of resources was not the overriding one. Different and sometimes divergent policies of industrial development were proposed by experts for countries with similar endowment in natural resources and factors of production, and even for the same country. This was not necessarily due to conflicting views on the best use of natural resources, but very frequently to differences of opinion among experts as to the type of industrialization which they considered most appropriate, particularly as regards the "best" use of factors of production. It is this type of policy recommendation which is now reviewed.

The Case of Labor-intensive Policies. In its report to the government of a small, densely populated Asian country with a predominantly agricultural economy, a technical assistance mission states its basic position in the following terms:

> The desired increase in the product of industry can only be brought about by the combined use of various factors of production. . . . Problems arise, however, more particularly . . . at the time of planning, [concerning] the relative proportions of capital and labour which should be used in the setting up of any particular industrial undertaking. . . . Any consideration of this problem must start with the fact that there is a large volume of unemployment and of under-employment; the policy of industrial development is being pursued largely with a view to bringing a partial remedy to this situation. In addition, the amount of capital available in the country for creating employment opportunities

> through investment in industry is limited. It is, therefore, clearly advantageous to spread the available capital thinly over the labour force which can be employed by it. On these grounds, it is desirable to promote the application of relatively labour-intensive methods of production, and to place the emphasis in selecting industries rather on those manufacturing products which can suitably be made by more labour-intensive methods.
>
> This policy is justified on both social and economic grounds. It provides more employment. It distributes purchasing power among a sector of the population which will spend nearly all of it immediately, mainly on current consumer goods. But even more important is the fact that if a worker produces something, he is contributing more to the community than he would if he were unemployed. If more labour-intensive methods of production are used, the community gains by the fact that capital is saved by the use of labour which would otherwise have remained unproductive; this capital can then be used for the production of other goods and the employment of still more labour. Total output and income will thus be higher than they would have been if more highly mechanized production methods had been used.

The mission considers that "the criterion for the selection of the type and size of industries is not merely the growth of income but the absorption of labour." It recommends that, as a general policy, the government should promote the development of numerous decentralized small-scale undertakings of "acceptable" efficiency, in industries which allow for a relatively low degree of mechanization. The mission considers that in between large-scale mechanized mass production and small-scale handicraft production lies a considerable range of techniques superior in efficiency to those of the traditional cottage industry, but inferior to the latest techniques in industrial countries, and points out that "it is in this zone that the main solution to [the country's] industrial development must be sought."

According to these experts, such a course would present for the country they are advising appreciable advantages from economic, social, and practical standpoints. From an economic point of view, small-scale labor-intensive production has the advantage of better corresponding to the limited size of the country's present and foreseeable market, both domestic and foreign, which imposes a limit on the possible increase in volume of output. It also corresponds better to the factor price relationship prevailing there. Because of low wage rates, many operations do not warrant introduction of the "last word" in mechanization. On the other hand, the price of capital, as reflected in the current rate of interest in the country concerned, does not necessarily reflect its real overall scarcity.

> This arises mainly out of institutional factors, including the good credit standing of the Government, the country's satisfactory situation as regards balance of payments, the extension of government support for certain projects and the organization of the banking system. The main value in saving capital resides, therefore, not in reducing the cost to the producer, but in limiting the extent to which the Government would need to seek outside capital for other developmental purposes.

Another advantage for the country is that drawing on foreign exchange reserves would be limited. Also, from a social point of view, the establishment of small-scale, labor-intensive industries would not give rise to an undesirable increase in urban population and a concomitant rise in social overhead expenses.

Finally, the practical advantages of such industries and processes are that they require relatively simple skills, maintenance facilities, machinery and techniques, management, and organization, which would minimize breakdowns, waste, inefficient use of machinery, and low degree of utilization. Furthermore, such industries could be rapidly and easily established and could soon yield appreciable returns. Their establishment would be likely to stimulate the economic development of rural areas, attract the interest of local entrepreneurs, produce a relatively large pool of skilled people, and have other favorable effects.

The mission considers that labor-intensive development is also consonant with normal development patterns. The highly industrialized countries have themselves passed through different stages of growth, in the course of which different principles and practices have prevailed. Though the process of growth in underdeveloped countries could and should be accelerated, it still involves a series of steps, each presenting its own special problems, the solution of which cannot be achieved by a mere transfer of techniques and institutions from industrial economies.

> Small-scale industry is the natural precursor to large-scale industry, in that it provides the necessary "know-how" and markets for the latter. Large-scale industry has made and will continue to make its contribution to development, but in many respects it makes a lesser contribution than small-scale industry in reducing unemployment and in providing a momentum for further development.

Large-scale industry may be established under more favorable conditions at a later stage; as is often the case in advanced countries, small-scale undertakings not only may exist successfully alongside large-scale enterprises, but may also account for a substantial proportion of total output.

The mission, however, stresses the fact that a rise in production resulting from the increased employment brought about by labor-intensive policies must also be accompanied by higher labor productivity, and recommends in this connection that industries and techniques be selected which permit at the same time a maximum absorption of excess labor and use of efficient technology. Such a combination will admittedly still be less productive than one of higher capital intensity, but both output per worker and output per unit of invested capital will be much higher than before. Apart from the adoption of mechanized techniques, substantial results may be achieved in improving labor productivity, in existing as well as in proposed undertakings, by a more efficient use of plant and equipment, better organization and management, and training.

The mission stresses in this connection that inefficient techniques and activities should not be condoned simply because they provide additional employment; in other words, labor-intensive activities need not be in the nature of an unemployment relief scheme nor an uneconomic "make work" process. In fact, the mission emphasizes the importance of the cost factor in the policy it advocates: investment

> . . . would only be undertaken after a true assessment has been made of its cost. It should not be pushed to the extent that the additional cost of the locally made article compared to that of the imported article is so great as seriously to reduce the standard of living of the . . . purchaser. Further, even though the additional cost may not be great for an individual article, account must be taken of how far this policy affects the costs of a number of manufactured goods which are necessary to the nonindustrial consumer.

Cost is thus considered as an important criterion for deciding whether to establish an industry and for determining its relative size (within the range favored by the mission, that is, small to medium size) and the nature of its equipment. The mission insists, however, that it must be balanced by other considerations: a given industry may be of national interest in spite of high cost and may justify protection—through subsidies, for example—to make it competitive in the long run; and lower cost of production, which is the principal advantage of large-scale production, may have to be forgone because of economic and social considerations, such as those listed above, and preference given to smaller-scale industries producing at a higher cost.

Other experts take it for granted that only the development of small-scale, labor-intensive industries would be appropriate for the countries they advise. A mission to a small Latin American country where agriculture and mining are the principal economic activities points out that scarcity of capital and abundance of labor "render it *natural*[1] to encourage small, or medium-scale, little-mechanized industrial establishments rather than large, highly mechanized ones," the more so since the substitution of electrical for steam power has tended to render small plants more economical. This mission also introduces sociological considerations and warns against concentration of industry in large plants; such concentration brings about agglomeration of population in large urban areas, making necessary heavy "social" investment in housing, public utilities, and sanitation; it also brings about great and sudden changes in social organization and habits of life among large numbers of people. "On the other hand, small-scale industry, utilizing local village labour and producing for a local, and thus relatively stable, market, is likely to offer a higher degree of security to the workers, and . . . to effect . . . savings to the State in respect of expenditure on social welfare and relief."

A more extreme position is taken on similar grounds by an expert on industrial development advising the government of a small Middle Eastern country with a predominantly agricultural and pastoral economy. In order to avoid formation of an "industrial proletariat," the expert recommends, as a general policy, the development not only of small-scale industries but also of handicrafts and workshops which might gradually be expanded into small industrial undertakings. It may be pointed out in this connection that many experts favor maintaining or even expanding handicrafts and cottage industries, while developing at the same time manufacturing production. One of them

[1] Italics supplied.

points out, however, that the development of handicrafts and cottage industries "should not be confused with industrialization, which is based on the introduction of factory techniques." The expert cautions "against trying to move true cottage handicraft production methods into central shops or factories and expecting them to pay."

An expert on industrial development advising a Far Eastern country with rich, largely unexploited resources considers that certain conditions prevailing there at the present time are contrary to its best interests, as they tend to direct investment toward capital-intensive, laborsaving industrial activities. The main economic activities are concentrated in the plantation, mining, and industrial sectors; these sectors are capital-intensive or have a level of capital intensity (as measured by ratio of land and capital to labor, for instance) which is relatively fixed or at least is "regarded as such." The expert points out that managers and engineers, particularly those trained in highly industrialized countries, are often so convinced of the superiority of mechanized techniques that they do not seek labor-intensive ones although alternative methods may be technically available. New investment in the country is directed toward industries such as those producing fertilizer or iron and steel and certain others processing domestic raw materials, which have a high capital cost per additional job; few jobs are thus provided in relation to the amount of capital invested. On the other hand, the price of labor is, in the expert's opinion, at an excessively high level, which does not correspond to the country's real factor endowment; this is partly due to the minimum wage law, which "in so far as it is enforced . . . reduces the total level of private investment by making some ventures unprofitable, and . . . provides an . . . incentive for introduction of labour-saving devices." This situation, which tends to maximize the rate of increase in income, has prevailed in the country concerned throughout the postwar period, during which a substantial rise in unemployment has taken place. The expert's explanation is that investment in the capital-intensive sectors was unable to absorb the surplus manpower and, as the rate of population growth exceeded the rate of capital accumulation in the labor-intensive sectors, labor in the latter soon became redundant, adding to the country's disguised unemployment.

Under the circumstances, the expert considers that it is wrong to base industrial planning on conventional considerations of market cost.

> For economic development, engineering concepts of efficiency are almost irrelevant. Maximization of output per man-hour employed is of little use in an economy where labour is redundant and capital is scarce. . . . Cost per unit of output is an unreliable guide where minimum wage legislation distorts the wage structure and exchange control distorts the price structure for raw materials and capital goods. For social accounting and planning purposes one might try to revise wages and prices of raw materials and capital goods according to an estimate of true opportunity costs.

The expert considers that, even if factor proportions were determined by opportunity costs, labor-intensive methods would be used only when "as efficient economically as capital-intensive methods, but not otherwise," and concludes that "since individual employers cannot be expected to do their accounting in terms of opportunity costs, it is necessary for the planning authorities to do so, and to design policies that will induce entrepreneurs to adopt techniques and choose projects appropriate to the factor endowment of the country." It may be presumed that the expert has in view government policies which, on the one hand, would aim at correcting the existing factor price relationship (for example, by means of wage subsidies to entrepreneurs) and, on the other hand, would permit a level of entrepreneurial profits adequate to induce investment in labor-intensive industries. In the expert's opinion, the factor endowment of the country warrants a development policy giving priority to labor-intensive projects and use of techniques "as efficient, in terms of cost-benefit ratios, as capital-intensive ones," which will substantially increase both income and employment. The expert considers that, at this stage, a choice between maximizing income and maximizing employment is not necessarily required. Indeed, a decision to maximize output would, "with known techniques and limited capital, involve a degree of mechanization which would not permit absorption of all the unemployed," while a decision to maximize employment may mean, as an extreme case, giving priority to make-work projects, or, more generally, expressing preference for labor-intensive techniques or projects even when it is recognized that a higher output could be reached by more mechanization. The expert implies that certain combinations of development projects and techniques might be achieved; while he does not specify their exact nature, he suggests that public investment in labor-intensive projects "could be more efficiently done if studies of labour patterns were available," and recommends that "research on the amount of employment created directly or indirectly by various types of development projects" be carried out by competent government services. By the time predominantly labor-intensive projects of this type are exhausted, the country may have to choose between higher income and higher employment; the question would then be "one of policy, not of technical analysis" and could not "be settled at the advisory level."

The Case for Capital-intensive Policies. An expert advising the government of a large Asian country on economic planning for national development takes a strong stand in favor of industrialization along capital-intensive lines. His position can be summarized as follows.

No country has ever succeeded in solving its economic problems by favoring low efficiency. It is necessary to achieve higher and continuously increasing labor productivity in order to bring about a cumulative process of increased production, national income, savings, and investment. In turn, higher productivity can result only from the use of increasingly efficient techniques involving capital-intensive processes. As a result of its higher productivity, industrialization along capital-intensive lines will yield a larger surplus of product over consumption, which will be available for capital formation and in the long run lead to higher employment than would be possible with labor-intensive methods of production. It will also have, in the long run, more favorable effects on the balance of payments. These views deserve examination in more detail.

If it is assumed that a given output can be produced by alternative combinations of labor and capital, the more capital-intensive production will yield in a given period of time a smaller net product per unit of capital, but a larger net product per worker, than the less capital-intensive combination. Consequently, the surplus available for reinvestment, per worker—that is, the difference between the product and the wage per worker—will be larger per unit of time in the more capital-intensive industry than in the less intensive one; this would hold true even if the wage rate were higher in the former than in the latter, as long as the difference in wages was less than the difference in productivity.

If the surplus is continually reinvested, the net product generated by it in the more capital-intensive alternative will grow at a higher rate, and faster, than in the less intensive one, and the employment and consumption to which it gives rise, while lower during the early years, will soon equal the levels attained in the labor-intensive industry and shortly thereafter expand faster. It is true that the surplus achieved in the labor-intensive process could also be increased through an appropriate price and wage policy tending to reduce real wages and consumption; however, real wages being already low, such curtailment might result in social discontent and tensions which would hamper further development. It should be mentioned here that the expert takes the view that, as a rule, low wages constitute for private enterprise a disincentive rather than an incentive to invest, so that in an economy with a large private sector, little or no planning, and a backlog of unemployed or underemployed population, savings capital is not automatically invested, and the process of intensively enlarged production does not take place; this results in a low growth of the economy or in economic stagnation.

The expert also points out that, in the early stages of industrial develop-tively early stage of industrial development and has a large surplus of unemployed and underemployed labor, the planning of investment should aim essentially at raising productive capacity; this can be achieved in a fast and cumulative way by establishing capital goods industries. While in the short run the effect of such investment on new employment will be relatively modest, it will soon gather momentum and lead in the long run toward full employment. The expert recognizes that industrialization along labor-intensive lines would bring about, in the short run, a greater amount of employment per unit of investment and thus larger total employment; however, he argues, since the process is not self-accelerating, the result would be that the economy would merely stagnate at a somewhat higher level of employment.

The expert also points out that, in the early stages of industrial development, as little investment capital as possible should be used to replace worn-out or obsolete equipment with more efficient production facilities, as this would result in lower costs rather than addition to capacity; a reorientation of new investment in the direction of modernization and improved efficiency will have to take place at a later stage as full employment is being achieved.

With regard to the effect of the alternative policies on the balance of payments, the expert considers that a labor-intensive policy of industrialization which results in little if any increase in labor productivity is likely to lead to greater balance of payments difficulties, which, in turn, will hamper further development. He argues that as employment and, consequently, consumption will grow at the same pace as production, imports of consumer goods will have to grow at the same rate, their share in national income remaining the same. Since the productivity of producer goods industries is also assumed to remain unchanged, imports of capital goods will also grow in absolute amounts with the increase in investment which will accompany the growth of national income; they will have to increase even more, if the share of investment in national income is to increase. Since productivity in the export sector is also assumed to be unchanged, no increase in exports through a reduction of export prices will be possible. All this in combination will lead to balance of payments difficulties. A reduction of imports would, of course, be possible through substitution of domestically produced goods, but this would involve new investments. Thus, to quote the expert, "the apparently capital-saving techniques may not be capital-saving at all." This is all the more true as the production of goods to replace imports would require in many cases a technology—hence a level of capital intensity—similar to that of foreign production.

The expert admits, on the other hand, that in the short run a capital-intensive policy may exert a greater pressure on imports, since domestic production focused on capital goods is likely, in spite of a smaller initial increase in employment and consumption, to require larger imports of consumer goods at the same time as substantial imports of investment goods. In the longer run, however, the more efficient production process will make it possible first to balance, and subsequently to exceed, the rise in imports through increased production available for export at competitive prices. In addition, because of higher productivity of domestic output, the import content of the addition to the national product will decline. In order to achieve this stage of economic development as rapidly as possible, it is necessary that production of producer goods receive the highest priority in any plan of development. Production of consumer goods will accordingly have to increase more slowly.

Not only is development of this type considered advantageous, but the expert also believes it to be in conformity with the requirements of balanced economic growth. In order to achieve balanced growth, production in the various sectors has to increase at different rates. At a given level of income, prices, and costs, consumers distribute their consumption expenditure in a given way; it would therefore be useless to increase production of certain consumer goods if certain other goods are not available in required proportions. The rate of increase in production of consumer goods will thus be governed by the possible rate of increase in output of those consumer goods whose production is particularly inelastic in the short run. In many underdeveloped countries, where the bulk of consumer expenditure is on agricultural products, the rate of increase in industrial production of consumer goods will thus have to be geared to the rate of increase in production of food, which, for economic and technical reasons, is usually rather low. This, in the opinion of the expert, is also an argument in favor of massive capital-intensive investment in basic industries producing equipment goods, which in turn will make possible, at a later stage, a more rapid increase in the production of agricultural and industrial consumer goods.

A "Neutral" Position. Another expert on economic planning presents recommendations which do not proceed from any preconceived position in favor of one or the other alternative. This expert—who advised the government of the same Asian country to which the recommendations discussed in the preceding section were presented—considers that there is no a priori solution to the problem of appropriate capital intensity in a program of economic development or industrialization. In his view, the recommendations of the technicians in charge of planning can only be a function of the overall objectives or goals, formulation of which is the political responsibility of the government; the alternative goals set by the government's economic policies call for alternative optimum solutions. Consequently, this expert does not advocate any particular policy, since he considers that for each particular set of goals there is a corresponding combination of both labor-intensive and capital-intensive processes.

In practice, the drafting of a program will begin by formulating a set of basic policy decisions defining the desired ends. The means to achieve these ends—the economic plan—are then determined by a mathematical solution of a system of variables linked together in a certain number of functional relationships. The basic decisions would relate to such matters as whether the emphasis of economic policy is on rapid absorption of the unemployed, or, alternatively, on a rapid raising of the overall consumption level. The goals, expressed numerically, would include the following: annual percentage increase in consumption; maximum tolerated amount of unemployment; maximum allowable foreign exchange deficit; maximum tolerated excess demand for certain products. The basic principles having been formulated and expressed mathematically by a system of equations, the next step—the operational part of planning—would consist in aggregating the relevant economic and technical information in a programming matrix; the system would then be "solved" for those variables which it is sought to evaluate.

Presumably to simplify construction of the programming matrix at an early stage, the expert assumes that factor proportions in each industrial sector are given, in the form of constant coefficients corresponding to given techniques. The model presented by the expert is based throughout on aggregative concepts: output is measured in units of "product mix," when individual commodities are not specified; techniques of production are composite magnitudes inasmuch as they are defined with respect to product mixes; the "factor mix" or capital intensity of an individual industrial sector is also, therefore, an aggregate. Operational analysis by means of the programming matrix will make it possible to find the optimum overall combination of capital-intensive and labor-intensive industries—as defined above—corresponding to a given set of overall targets. Alternative factor combinations for a given industry could, however, be introduced, instead of constant production coefficients, in a more complex model.

The expert takes it for granted that, in the country he advises, the development of some activities will be required along both capital-intensive and labor-intensive lines.

> Certain features of a development policy in an under-developed country are of such a conspicuous nature that one can see offhand and without any calculation that *some* activity in these directions will be useful and within reach. In [the country considered], for instance, it is obvious that some development of heavy industries will be useful and feasible, for example, in steel, aluminum, cement, fertilizers, heavy machine tools, etc. Similarly, for certain schemes of power development and irrigation . . .

Also, the uncertainty of the world situation and of international trade, along with, in many countries, failure to maintain full employment, would justify attempts to increase national self-sufficiency.

However, the establishment or expansion of producer goods industries with high capital requirements and long maturity periods requires the simultaneous development of certain consumer goods industries with shorter maturity periods. Otherwise, the rise in income generated in the producer goods industries will create consumer demands which cannot be met; this will cause either price increases or pressure upon price controls, and, in both cases, political unrest may follow. The expert considers that, in the country he advises, where labor is a factor of production in practically unlimited supply, where capital is scarce and rich natural resources have been discovered, the experience of countries with abundant capital equipment and relatively scarce labor is not applicable at present; in fact, methods may prove successful that would not be economical in industrially advanced countries. Thus, the expert suggests, the cottage industry type of production—that is, handicraft production combined with agricultural occupations—not only should continue to exist but should be expanded at the same time as mechanization is introduced in industry. "As judged by standards from other countries," adds the expert, "this kind of production may seem irrational, but I feel convinced that in the [country's] situation, it is, at least for the time being, a really economic proposition to introduce . . . such a craft as [hand-loom] weaving. . . . Spinning, on the contrary, must be [done] in factories."

The Interindustry and Intraindustry Aspects of the Problem of Capital Intensity

Some of the reports reviewed in the preceding section also discuss, in the light of the overall principles set forth with respect to capital intensity, the more specific problem of selecting industries for development. A few of them also consider the question of the appropriate degree of mechanization in individual industries. The latter type of problem, however, is dealt with mainly by engineering experts working at the industry and plant levels. The recommendations relating to selection of industries and degree of mechanization, which may be called the "interindustry" and "intraindustry" aspects of the problem of capital intensity, are here examined.

The Interindustry Aspect. As a rule, labor-intensive industrialization is considered by experts to be synonymous with development of consumer goods industries and, as far as size is concerned, with development of small-scale or medium-scale establishments. Capital-intensive industrialization, on the other hand, is generally associated with development of capital goods industries. The association is usually implicit, and no attempt is made to justify it either on theoretical or statistical grounds. When labor-intensive policies are advocated, these assumptions are generally coupled with other considerations not necessarily related to such policies, such as giving priority to small consumer goods industries using local raw materials or producing goods replacing imports; preference is also given to projects outside urban areas, with a view to absorbing the surplus labor in rural areas and avoiding the concentration of population in large cities.

As an example of such selection, the following industrial activities were recommended by the mission whose views favoring labor-intensive industrialization in an Asian country have been discussed above.

Rice Milling. The proposal provides for a ten-year expansion plan, starting with a pilot plant. The existing facilities are to be replaced gradually by a large number of small, simple, and inexpensive milling plants.

Coir-fiber Manufacturing. The recommendations provide, inter alia, for replacing the hand process of bristle-fiber extraction through the use of simple mechanized equipment. Other recommendations are that coir spinning and weaving of bristle mats be mechanized with a view to reducing labor cost, so that a better product can be offered which can compete in world markets. "Such mechanization," adds the report, "should not result in a reduction in employment, as lower prices, made possible by mechanization, should open up substantially larger markets, particularly in the export field."

Production of Cotton Textiles. Domestic production in the country under consideration amounts to less than 10 percent of consumption, with hand-loom production about 35 percent of total output. The mission notes that "it is the desire of the Government that the country should produce as high a proportion of its needs in cotton textiles as possible" and that "in view of the low price of the imported cloth and the high costs of production of the small amount now woven in the country, it will obviously not be easy to achieve this aim." The mission recognizes that a "fairly large and vertically integrated spinning and weaving mill would produce cloth more cheaply than by recourse to any other method." It considers, nevertheless, that other economic as well as social reasons make it imperative to encourage the development wherever possible of small-scale production, and expresses the hope that

> . . . the possibilities of small-scale production will be fully explored before embarking upon a programme of encouraging greater mill production. If, however, experience with small-scale units demonstrates, after a period of trial, that costs are not competitive enough, and that small-scale production is not making the country self-sufficient enough in textiles, consideration should be given to the encouragement of larger mills.

Even in this event, the mission advises that decentralized, medium-size units with yearly capacity of 10 to 12 million yards be established rather than a few integrated large-scale plants. It further recommends that, in the proposed small-scale units, two shifts be worked in order to provide more employment per unit of capital invested. As regards hand-loom production, the mission suggests concentrating it on the more expensive types of cloth, where the advantages of the power loom are not as great. However, the spinning of all cotton yarn (destined for both hand-loom and mechanical weaving) should be developed as large-scale mill manufacture, because "hand spinning is quite uneconomic, particularly when it does not arise out of past practice, and . . . very small decentralized units are not viable."

Screen Printing of Textiles. This work "is particularly suitable for small- to medium-scale industry, as its output, relative to capital cost, is very great."

Manufacture of Footwear. National production in the country under consideration amounts to about 35 percent of total demand, and the mission estimates that it can be expanded ultimately to cover all domestic requirements. As a first step, the mission recommends expanding the output of existing establishments, through purchase of additional equipment and by using imported leather; later on "at some stage in the course of the expansion of the industry, consideration should be given to the relative merits of further development through large-scale manufacture or through expansion or extension of small units."

Metal and Metalworking Industries. Such industries should be established only when they lend themselves to small-scale operation: for example, jobbing foundries of small capacity for producing simple grey-iron castings; later on, the possibility should be considered of establishing a small rerolling mill, combined with an electric scrap furnace using off-load hydroelectric power, to produce simple steel products.

Among other industries selected by the mission for early development are the following: kaolin; sawmilling; woodworking, including plywood; making tanning extracts; ceramics (tiles, bricks, crockery, industrial wares) and glassware; making agricultural implements, building materials and hardware, brass products and aluminum ware; galvanizing and electroplating. All these industries are to be established as small-scale units. In addition, kapok processing, food preserving, including meat packing, and tanning are recommended, as well as the making of plastic ware, paints and varnishes, bicycles, umbrellas, and other products.

The mission previously mentioned, which favors labor-intensive development of the industry of a Latin American country, states that

> . . . in view of the particular needs and limitations of the [country's] economy during its initial stages of economic development . . . policy should aim at the encouragement of decentralized small-scale industry supplying the simple needs of everyday consumption and the raw materials needed for construction of roads, industrial buildings, housing, etc. The mission believes further that priority should be given to projects which will reduce the need for foreign exchange, thus freeing it for economic development in general.

Its report gives as examples of such industries and plants: sugar and oil refineries; sawmills; cotton and wool spinning mills; textile, shoe, furniture, and household goods factories; cement, brick, and tile factories, and others. While mining is one of its most important economic activities, the country possesses practically no smelting or refining facilities; its entire mineral output is exported as ore or concentrates, and all mining equipment and supplies must be imported, there being no domestic manufacture of such articles. While the mission suggests that the possibility of domestic refining of ores should be considered, it states that, in view of the scarcity of high-grade ores, the smelting and refining of low-grade ores within the country "is at present considered unlikely to become economically possible."

The question of choice between manufacturing, cottage, and handicraft industries is often determined primarily by the expert's basic position in matters of social policy. One expert, who advocates promoting handicraft industries in a Middle Eastern country with a view to avoiding the formation of an industrial proletariat, urges the establishment, whenever possible, of an integrated complex of small-scale and handicraft industries. Thus, for the country's textile industry he recommends that spinning, dyeing, and finishing of cotton be carried out by factory techniques, and that sizing, weaving, and knitting be done by handicraft, cottage-industry methods.

Another expert sent to the same country takes a similar attitude and, in order to avoid the social effects of "big conglomerations of industrial working population," suggests building three or four small textile units in villages some 15 or 20 kilometers distant from each other. "With proper telephone and road connections between the factories, these could be run as easily by one management and one technical service as one big factory. . . . The extremely heavy labour turnover at the [existing textile] factory, notwithstanding free housing and many other advantages to the workers, should be a warning." The expert further draws attention to the "desirability of a careful determination of the optimum level of mechanization, taking into account the specific conditions of this country." He observes, "on the one hand, an attitude of letting everything be carried out by hand because labour is cheap and the procurement of machines from abroad is difficult and troublesome; on the other hand, there is the inclination not to be content with anything less than the latest type of European or American machinery," and concludes that "of course, neither of these extremes is wise." The expert is thus led to

> . . . wonder whether it would not be wise . . . to revise the plans for the new factory [an integrated spinning and weaving factory envisaged by the government] so as to drop mechanical weaving almost altogether and to sell all the yarn for weaving in village workshop or cottage industry. This would open the way to make use of the spare labour during winter time, provide an opportunity to farmers to earn some badly needed extra income, and solve partly the problem of major concentrations of industrial working population referred to above.

The same reasons lead the expert to recommend expanding carpet weaving as a cottage industry.

On the other hand, the expert advocating capital-intensive industrialization in an Asian country, whose views have been discussed earlier, recommends that special emphasis be laid on development of large-scale capital goods industries—in particular, heavy machinery. He considers that such development is favored by the country's economic situation. Among the favorable factors he mentions the relatively high level reached in food production; a satisfactory foreign trade position and absence of balance of payments difficulties; the existence of a large reserve of manpower permitting production and employment to be increased in the basic industries without curtailing production in other sectors; and a relatively large amount of idle productive capacity in many industries, which, if used, would permit a higher rate of increase in production than would be possible through current investment only. As to consumer goods industries, the expert has no objection to their decentralization nor to their establishment on a small or medium scale, provided investment in these industries is not made in "backward technologies" on the assumption that techniques involving lower labor productivity would generate more employment than more advanced methods. He objects, however, to a proposal to increase employment through expanding cottage industries. Inasmuch as the creation of such additional employment involves subsidies to cottage industries, while at the same time restrictive output quotas are imposed on the larger-scale industries producing competing products, he considers it to be equivalent to disguising unemployment by way of measures of social relief.

This expert also disputes the view that, as an alternative to investment in capital goods industries, priority might be given to export goods industries with a view to importing more producer goods. He admits that such investment "can have the same long-run effects as investment in capital goods industry, with the advantage that here the capital-output ratio will probably be lower and the time lag shorter." But he points out that, in practice, there is not much scope for such a policy. "Most of the industries characterized by low capital-output ratios are consumer goods industries for which there seem to be not very large prospects for expansion [in foreign demand] in the near future." The expert sees no point in expanding existing consumer goods export industries, as he deems it more advisable to diversify the country's export trade, though an effort should be made to promote expansion of output in industries of this type having excess capacity, which are fairly numerous, so that exports might be increased without new investment. Efforts should also be made to locate industries with low capital-output ratios which have had an expanding export market in recent years; at the same time, the possibility of establishing an internal market for part of their output should be explored, as "it is generally unsound to develop 'pure' exporting industries." The expert cites as likely candidates the so-called "new" industries, such as special branches of light engineering industry and electronics, and considers that "although their time lags will probably not be very short, because they require new 'know-how,' " the effort can be worthwhile.

As to raw material–producing industries, the expert raises objections to a policy of developing them beyond the needs of the national economy in order to create exportable surpluses for the reason that raw material prices are unstable and that total proceeds from raw material exports fluctuate even more than prices. Such a policy is, in his opinion, inadvisable in the absence of international commodity agreements or long-term bilateral contracts guaranteeing price stability.

In a more general way, this expert objects to a policy of channeling industrialization into export industries—whether of consumer goods or raw materials—on grounds that it would weaken the country's economic independence. On the other hand, industrialization oriented toward capital goods industries should not lead to a smaller volume but to a change in the structure of the country's foreign trade.

> With progressive industrialization, in the long run, the trade patttern of [the country] has to be of the same type as the trade pattern of other industrialized countries; exports of primary products and of consumer goods will have, in the long run, to grow less rapidly than exports of other manufactured products, including equipment goods, light equipment goods to begin with and, after some time, heavy equipment goods.

The Intraindustry Aspect. The question of capital intensity within a given industry is mainly raised in reports by engineering experts sent out under the

United Nations technical assistance programs to advise on the establishment, operation, or reorganization of specific industries or plants.

Before entering into an examination of such recommendations, a few words might be said concerning the more general problem concerning the adaptation of industrial techniques used in the more developed countries to conditions prevailing in the underdeveloped areas. This problem has been discussed by an expert working in a large Far Eastern country. He considers that "there are certain industries the [Western] 'blueprints' for which can be used almost without change. This applies particularly to the chemical process industries requiring equipment that cannot be operated efficiently on a small scale," such as caustic soda, sulfuric acid, and the nitrogenous fertilizer and cement industries. "The small units now operating in highly industrialized countries can be copied with relatively few changes," with the qualification that highly trained engineers are required to erect and operate such plants. The expert continues, however:

> Another type of industry can be established . . . by a process of adaptation from the West. It may be desirable to reduce the size of the equipment, de-mechanize it, and in general simplify the operation to make possible a reduction in the capital expenditure and reduce the length of training required to obtain managers and highly skilled operators. In this category fall many of the mechanized industries as well as some based on chemical processes.

The expert also suggests that, apart from copying or adapting existing Western installations and methods, fresh thinking should be devoted to the specific requirements of industry in underdeveloped countries. Some very advanced industries may be established in this way, and in fact certain underdeveloped countries already have industries using processes as advanced as in the United States or European countries.

The expert is convinced that "all the stages . . . followed by certain industries in the West over the past centuries need not be followed. In fact, a direct jump into the twentieth century is not only possible but in many cases desirable." Thus, the "normally expected railroad age" is being skipped in many countries; instead, air and highway transport are used. Also, extensive cable and wire systems are made unnecessary by radio communications. However, while the basic new knowledge can be put to use in most cases, the techniques cannot be applied with the high degree of capitalization, specialization, and integration that are characteristic of industrial operation in advanced countries. The expert concludes that the factories to be established in the country he advises "will almost always be small-scale and labour-intensive, but can be 'modern' in the sense that they will apply the latest technical information to the economic and social conditions prevailing in the country."

While this conclusion is undoubtedly shared by most of the experts advocating industrialization along labor-intensive lines, the extent to which these general principles have actually been applied in the recommendations of the experts—that is, the extent to which the proposed installations have been adapted as regards size and capital intensity to the conditions of the country—is beyond the scope of the present article and might be the subject of a separate technical inquiry.

The engineering advisers sent out under the technical assistance programs of the United Nations are as a rule primarily interested in solving the practical technical problems involved in raising production and improving productivity in industrial plants. Mechanization, which may extend from use of hand tools to fully automated factories, is perhaps the most important of these problems. Even though the engineers' recommendations are generally made without taking explicitly into consideration overall criteria regarding the appropriate capital intensity, they have a bearing on the subject of the present article. Their reports generally contain estimates of investment and manpower requirements, also cost schedules for the industries involved. In a number of cases, they contain plans for gradual mechanization of certain industries. In very few cases do they contain alternative proposals in regard to equipment.

The general pattern that seems to emerge from their recommendations is a ready resort to mechanization. The type and extent of the proposed mechanization vary considerably, for reasons which are usually technical in nature. What these experts primarily seek to achieve is to increase the volume of output, improve the quality and uniformity of product, and reduce unit costs. The effect on employment, as can be expected, is seldom dealt with as such, though attention is sometimes paid to it, particularly when the result of the suggested changes is a displacement of labor. In such cases, while considerations of engineering efficiency are given preference, concern is expressed regarding reemployment of the labor laid off. Employment of labor thus emerges as a variable determined by the type of equipment and techniques selected rather than as a factor determining the latter. Deliberate recommendations to limit mechanization on grounds of avoiding technological unemployment are seldom made. When a relatively low degree of mechanization is recommended, this is generally caused by the fact that the expert's terms of reference call for advice on partial or gradual mechanization only, by a shortage of financing or power, by insufficient skilled labor, or by other limiting factors. The question of alternative techniques involving different factor combinations is seldom discussed, if at all.

The following examples are thought to be representative. An expert in a Far Eastern country, helping to implement a program of partial mechanization of industry, recommends methods of production in a school slate factory which would result in the dismissal of ten employees; the expert adds that these will be reemployed in another factory. In a factory producing shrimp biscuit, the same expert recommends installation of several slicing and mixing machines to replace hand operations; shelling the shrimp is, however, still to be done by hand, and when the machines recommended are installed, their higher output will require twenty-four more workers for the shelling operation. In this case, introduction of mechanized operations results in an increase in employment. The overall capital-labor ratio may thus have remained constant or even declined as a result. The same expert recommends, on several occasions, introduction of a second shift as a further means of increasing production, which would result in a proportionate reduction of capital intensity.

Another expert in the same country observes that, in the making of brass products, all the shaping operations are performed entirely by hand, with the use of hammer, chisel, and files. To increase the rate of production and improve quality, he suggests installing a certain number of machines. In making this proposal, the expert stresses that owing to the great demand for brass products no unemployment need result from the introduction of this machinery, as total output will be multiplied many times and the demand for labor will increase. In another case, an expert proposes that a large tile plant using modern equipment be established in an area where it would compete with existing small establishments using locally made, hand-operated tile presses. The expert justifies his proposal by pointing out that, although production is slow in the small plants, demand for tiles is so great that they could continue operating.

The concern on the part of these experts with the effect of proposed mechanization on employment is partly due to the general directives which they had received from the country's government to have regard to the need for increasing rather than decreasing employment. Other directives declared that "the technical structure and the economic capacity of each locality studied with reference to the industrial production will determine what method of production (small, large, mechanical, by hand) offers most opportunity for development; where the economic possibilities are equal, preference is to be given to manual industry and small business."

In the same Far Eastern country, engineering advisers working in certain sparsely populated areas go beyond partial mechanization and recommend a high degree of mechanization and even "full" mechanization because of local scarcity of labor and its high cost. Thus, an expert writes: "The woodworking industries . . . could undoubtedly be expanded to the benefit of the country as a whole. Those at present operating have a seller's market and claim very high prices for inferior products. It is essential that, due to the high cost of labour, all future industries of this type be completely mechanized. . . ." Elsewhere in his report, the expert states that brick and tile plants "would have to be fully mechanized, due to the high cost of labour." Another expert mentions that "the very high wages demanded . . . make more imperative the mechanization of the woodworking plants." Another writes that "in the erection of factories, one has to take into account that [this part of the country] is rather thinly inhabited so that the plants should be mechanized as much as possible." Consequently, he submits plans for the establishment of certain industries on a completely mechanized basis.

That the same situation may lead to completely different conclusions is shown in the following statement by another expert who visited this area later: "[the area] at present lacks the prerequisites for any major degree of industrialization. There is little local capital, the population is sparse and unskilled, and managerial talent for even medium-scale enterprises has yet to be developed. The plans made in the [previous] report are overly optimistic under present conditions." His conclusion is that only a few preliminary measures of mechanization and modernization of existing small-scale industries are advisable at this stage.

In many cases, experts recommend the use of high-cost, highly productive—sometimes fully automated—machinery, even in light industries. Such proposals are usually justified on grounds of technical efficiency; their direct or indirect effects on employment seem either to be ignored or discounted as the inevitable price of technical progress; in a few extreme cases, the resulting saving of labor is even considered a net advantage, although severe unemployment and underemployment may exist. Thus, recommendations are often made for the establishment of fully automated and probably highly capital-intensive textile factories, glass plants, and other industries, or for the introduction of highly mechanized techniques of production in existing plants.

As was mentioned previously, the problem of alternative techniques involving different degrees of mechanization has been given little recognition by engineering experts. One instance, however, is found in the recommendations of an expert in connection with a plan to achieve self-sufficiency in cotton textiles in an Asian country. He submits alternative estimates of loom requirements for the cotton weaving industry: one estimate gives the number of power looms on a three-shift operation basis, which would be required if hand looms were to be eliminated; another gives the equivalent number of hand looms, either on a three-shift or a two-shift basis, which would be required to match the output of the power looms. Estimates of the number of weaving establishments, looms per establishment, and required sizing centers are also given. The expert makes no suggestion as to the proportions in which power looms and hand looms should be combined, but submits his estimates "for convenience of calculations only . . . ; in actual practice, further discussions and decisions may be necessary according to the policy of the Government."

A related problem sometimes dealt with by experts concerns the minimum economic size of industrial units. Such estimates in terms of equipment, manpower, and cost vary appreciably, not only from industry to industry and from one country to another, but even for the same industry in the same country. This magnitude depends, indeed, on many considerations, among which are the engineering, technological, and production requirements, relative factor prices, and present and foreseeable domestic and foreign demand. It is not always possible to determine whether experts refer to minimum economic units, taking into consideration the economic and technical factors involved, or to absolute size of plant. The close association made by some of them between scale of plant and degree of capital intensity has been mentioned before.

Finally, it might be appropriate to refer to another type of recommendation made by engineers which has some bearing upon the problem discussed here. This relates to the use in underdeveloped countries of old or reconditioned machinery in order to save on the initial investment. While the question has seldom been raised, two conflicting views are found in the reports analyzed. An expert on production of ramie in a Far Eastern country suggests that second-hand decorticating machinery might be used: "While the [reconditioned] machines will not be as efficient as new models, first quality fibre can be produced with them. It is obviously important that every possible economy be practiced in order to conserve foreign currency funds." In another instance, the expert specifically recommends using old machinery because mixing the old equipment already installed with new machinery would "result in a serious imbalance in the flow of production." In contrast, an engineering expert in a Middle Eastern country, while discussing a proposal to use reconditioned textile machinery, states: "Old machinery . . . does not improve with age.

Merely changing a few bearings and putting on a new coat of paint does not improve performance very much. . . ." The expert considers that the earning capacity of an industry and its ability to compete with imports of similar products depend upon its efficiency in turning out products of good quality in large quantity. "Old machinery or even the best reconditioned machinery will produce only inferior goods." He considers that "there is no reason why the country should be handicapped with wornout theories and machinery which would only hamper its strides towards improvement and recovery."

Appraisal of Recommendations and Conclusions

Before evaluating the recommendations of the experts, it may be useful to discuss briefly the meaning they attach to the concept of capital intensity.

In a number of reports, this concept is used in an ambiguous way. Most experts mean by it the amount of capital per worker—presumably, fixed capital per man employed. Others refer to capital-output ratios, while still others refer to input of labor (or equipment) per unit of output. Some experts use alternatively several of these relationships.

Many experts refer not only to capital-intensive or labor-intensive *processes* but also to capital-intensive or labor-intensive *industries*. They apparently consider that there is an implicit correlation between capital per worker (or capital per unit of output) and type of industrial output. Thus, industries producing "light" consumer goods are generally identified with labor-intensive production and those producing "heavy" producer or capital goods with capital-intensive production.

In addition, capital intensity is also related by some experts to the scale of operation, "labor-intensive" production being largely identified with small- or medium-scale industries and "capital-intensive" production with large-scale industries.

It must be pointed out, as regards the concept of capital intensity, that various statistical measurements of it have been suggested in economic literature, none of which is generally accepted. A discussion of the relative merits of the definitions and measurements proposed by different authors would be beyond the scope of the present article. It may be observed here that not only is the economic significance of the indicators still uncertain and their mutual relationship imprecise, but that actual statistical data are relatively scarce. Further research on the conceptual and statistical aspects of the problem is desirable if the usefulness of these tools in economic analysis and in economic planning is to be enhanced.

As regards the concept of capital-intensive or labor-intensive industries and the relation between capital intensity and scale of operation, it is true that some industrial activities lend themselves better than others to more capital-intensive techniques of production and larger scale of operation, and vice versa. Thus, in heavy industry, the use of techniques and scale of operation of the former type is the general rule. However, these correlations are by no means general—as is evidenced, for example, by the trend toward the use of laborsaving techniques and larger-scale operation in light industries—and to postulate them as a basis for recommendations may be highly misleading.

Moreover, the qualitative way in which the concept of capital intensity is used introduces a basic weakness in the argument. Thus, when the same industry permits use of alternative techniques of different capital intensity, to define the industry as a whole as labor-intensive (or capital-intensive) can only mean that the range or average of capital intensity of the possible techniques is lower (or higher) than in other industries. The question may be asked whether increasing the capital intensity in a labor-intensive industry makes it capital-intensive, and if so, at what point the change in category takes place; whether, for instance, an industry such as textiles, in which the range of possible equipment may vary from a hand loom in a peasant's home to automatic looms in a modern factory, should still be classified, in the latter case, as a labor-intensive industry.

Both the recommendations of the experts for overall policy and those for individual projects reflect a wide variety of views on the appropriate capital intensity of investment in industry. Some arguments seem to proceed from somewhat dogmatic attitudes. Some positions are, in fact, clearly conflicting, when for instance an appraisal of conditions in the same country leads to quite opposite conclusions.

While all policy recommendations are based on economic considerations—to be discussed later—those for a general policy along labor-intensive lines lay considerable emphasis on the social aspects of the problem. The proposals for a capital-intensive policy pay less attention to these aspects. The recommendations of engineers proceed essentially from technological considerations. They evidence in many cases a ready and sometimes indiscriminate resort to mechanization. The potential labor-displacing effect of the latter is seldom paid attention to, and techniques are rarely chosen with the specific aim of creating employment. Among the proposals by engineers there are few, if any, which entail alternative factor combinations.

In many cases, no overall policy directives have been formulated by the governments. In other cases, government policies exist expressing the desirability of preventing the labor-displacing effect of mechanization, but these do not appear to have percolated to the technical level. Even when government policies have been formalized in an economic plan, they may not be explicit enough to guide technicians in the field. There is thus often little, if any, link between the "macroeconomic" policy directives and the action of technicians in charge of carrying out individual projects. This aspect is important—particularly in planning—since general policy decisions can be meaningful and effective only if correctly implemented on the project level.

As pointed out by one expert, the adoption of objectives or planning targets, which precedes and determines the choice of means to achieve them, is to a large extent a political problem. National authorities have to decide whether to strive for self-sufficiency or rely on international interchange; what weights to attach to the social, economic, technical, or even strategic considerations involved in setting up certain types of industry, and the extent to which the government finds it desirable or feasible to intervene in the process of development; in particular, what controls it is prepared to impose—whether it should emphasize long-run or, alternatively, short-run measures of development and a faster, or slower, tempo of industrialization. While the present conditions and foreseeable developments in resources, in prices of raw materials and factors of production, and in domestic and foreign markets affecting the country concerned may limit the scope of possible alternative policies, there exists in most cases a measure of choice between basic objectives which may be expressed by different systems of priorities in allocating resources. Such a choice depends not only upon an evaluation of economic and technical conditions and potentialities, but on the political and social order that a country may wish to achieve in the course of its development.

It will be noted that both labor-intensive and capital-intensive industrialization policies advocated by experts have certain common economic objectives. Both aim at raising the level of output and income through developing the industrial sector. Both recognize the importance of solving the problem of chronic underemployment which exists in most underdeveloped countries. Both agree that industrialization requires an increase in labor productivity. A major divergence between the two views arises through the fact that proponents of labor-intensive industrialization would achieve these results through obtaining the largest amount of employment per unit of invested capital, while the others would from the outset concentrate the investment resources of the country in industrial branches yielding a high productivity regardless of the labor-absorptive capacity of such investment. Proponents of the latter view readily recognize that labor-intensive development would, in the short run, bring about larger employment for the same invested capital, but point out that little if any cumulative increases in income and employment would be attained in the long run. In their view, resorption of the unemployed is a second priority goal, to be achieved only after an adequate rate of investment in basic productive capacity has been reached; from then on, both income and employment will rise more, and faster. It is the higher productivity and correspondingly higher surpluses available for capital formation generated by capital-intensive investment that proponents of such industrialization emphasize.

There is no doubt that most experts advocating labor-intensive industrialization policies lay emphasis on short-run rather than long-run aspects. They stress primarily the employment-creating effect and, while recommending that labor productivity should also be increased, do not make clear how an adequate rate of capital formation—which should solve the problem of full utilization of the country's manpower in the long run—is to be achieved.

In the absence of external sources of financing, the accumulation of an adequate amount of such surpluses for capital formation is unquestionably a basic requisite to a rapid and cumulative process of growth of production and employment over the years. Some supporters of labor-intensive policies recognize that surpluses can be generated in adequate amounts only through raising productivity of labor sufficiently in excess of its real wages; that capital-intensive techniques do yield higher productivity and, in the long run, result in a faster tempo of industrialization. They point out, however, that labor productivity is affected not only by the quantity of physical capital per worker, but also by the nature and quality of the equipment and its appropriateness to conditions in underdeveloped countries, and by such factors as a better rate of utilization of plant capacity, proficiency of management, and worker efficiency in terms of skill and effort. They are confident than an appreciable rise in productivity may be achieved in labor-intensive industries, which, together with the increase in employment, will slowly but gradually enlarge incomes and investment resources. This will make possible, later on, the establishment of more capital-intensive industries, if necessary.

Under either policy, it is thus implicitly assumed, first, that a surplus will be generated and, second, that savings out of this surplus will somehow be consistently channeled into further investment. With regard to the first point, it will be noted that the magnitude of the surplus depends on the number of workers employed, the productivity of labor, which is in turn a function of capital per worker employed, and the level of real wages. All these magnitudes are interrelated. All other things being equal, a rise in wages would clearly reduce the surplus. Pressure on wages will increase with the rise in productivity and will be likely to be stronger under conditions of industrialization along capital-intensive lines. Controls to restrict consumption and encourage capital formation may have to be used, whatever the form of the industrialization process; to be effective, such controls might need to be particularly severe under a capital-intensive type of industrial development, the more so as the requirements of an accelerated rate of capital formation are bound to give rise to heavier inflationary pressures. This is often one of the reasons for which, in spite of the slower tempo of industrialization of the labor-intensive type, preference is given to the latter by some experts.

As regards the second point, many experts consider that the fact that redundant labor and scarce capital entail low wages and high interest rates constitutes not only a basic argument in favor of government policies of labor-intensive industrialization, but also a strong incentive for private investment in industries allowing the use of labor-intensive techniques. It must be borne in mind, however, that while a price relationship favoring labor-intensive industrialization may often exist, the market prices of the factors may not always reflect their relative endowment, and the relationship may be adversely affected. Because of structural and other rigidities in the economy, the market prices of factors may diverge considerably from the levels they would reach under competitive conditions; the price of labor may be above, and that of capital below, the respective equilibrium levels. In such cases, labor-intensive industrialization may be inhibited. Several experts mention instances where lack of mobility of labor, trade union activities, or wage and social security legislation exert a pressure on wages which raises the factor price ratio in favor of labor and constitutes an incentive to private enterprise to substitute capital for labor; some experts justify proposals for full mechanization on such grounds. A similar effect obtains when the price of capital, as reflected in the rate of interest, is kept below the equilibrium level by government credit and foreign-exchange policies, in particular by the use of preferential rates. Also mentioned by some experts—or implicit in their recommendations—is the tendency of engineers and industrialists to use highly capital-intensive methods following current practices in industrial countries even when alternative technical possibilities of lower capital intensity exist. In some cases, this tendency is not altogether irrational even though it is not reducible to purely economic calculus.

Although some of the government measures discussed above result in disincentives to private investment in labor-intensive undertakings, it could hardly be expected that they would be modified in order to promote a policy of labor-intensive private investment, as they aim at furthering other purposes which may be equally important. Savings may have to be stimulated and channeled into private or public investment, or both, by other measures.

The important problem of the effect of industrialization under either of the two policies on the balance of payments of the respective countries has received very little attention in the experts' reports. Thus, although labor-intensive industrialization implies resort to imports of the required capital goods—which are not likely to be produced in the country—and, in several cases, also to imports of consumer goods, the experts advocating such a policy have completely neglected to discuss its balance of payments effects. Some reference to this problem is made by the expert favoring capital-intensive industrialization. He mentions that both methods of industrialization are likely to lead in the short run to balance of payments difficulties, as they involve an increase in imports of capital or consumer goods, or both, which cannot be met by a corresponding rise in exports. His conclusion that such difficulties would be alleviated, over a number of years, under a capital-intensive process of industrialization—while they would persist under a labor-intensive method—does not seem to be demonstrated, nor perhaps to be demonstrable in a general way, because of the many internal and external factors affecting both the process of industrialization and the balance of payments situation, and the uncertain course of their development.

The problem of alternative techniques for a given industrial process remains to be considered. In many cases, the choice may in fact be nonexistent or at least severely limited. As is well known, certain industrial operations can be carried out only by standard processes of relatively high capital intensity, so that more labor-intensive techniques are inapplicable. This accounts for the fact that in many industrial sectors in underdeveloped countries highly capitalized techniques are used in spite of the existence of abundant manpower available at low wages. Still, in such industries, certain ancillary operations—for instance, materials handling, packaging, and the like—may lend themselves to alternative techniques. Aside from industries where basic processes are technologically inflexible, there are a large number of industries where alternative factor combinations are applicable in major processing operations.

To reveal such technological alternatives, and make possible the determination of a power "factor mix" in specific industrial operations, a great deal of research is required in a new and relatively little-explored field. The macroeconomic tools of the economist who measures capital intensity in terms of statistical aggregates are inadequate for that purpose. As stated in a recent article, it is necessary, in order to reveal the possible technological combinations, to achieve "a much higher degree of disaggregation . . . than is currently practised or appears feasible." A method for studying factor proportions, derived from research on coefficients for input-output tables, is suggested in that article. Two approaches are proposed: a *product analysis* method, which involves a census in each plant studied of the amounts of each type of factor of production used in expanding the output of a particular product; and a *process analysis* method, which involves determining the combinations of factors used by firms to perform certain standardized operations.

Research of this type might be undertaken at first in respect to a certain number of selected industries where there is a strong suggestion that alternative techniques are possible, with a view to evolving a number of general principles regarding the appropriate selection and combination of techniques in industrial operations. The scope of the investigation could then be widened to cover a large number of industries. Such research would permit determining, for any given industrial process, the highest level of productivity compatible with maximum employment of labor, an objective which should meet with the approval of both those who favor labor-intensive policies and those who support capital-intensive ones. In many cases, various forms of partial mechanization would probably be adopted. Further research along these lines would also make possible a rational adaptation of advanced techniques to the needs of less developed economies; the problem would then be approached in a qualitative way as well as in a quantitative one.

The information which would gradually be evolved through such research would facilitate the task of planning authorities and help in the preparation of programs of industrial development; in particular, it might be combined with and enhance the value of the planning techniques based on linear programming earlier. It would help to establish a more direct link between general policy directives at the planning level and their implementation in individual projects; thus, the target of maximizing employment of labor to the extent consistent with achievement of an acceptable level of productivity could, in many cases, be translated in practical terms at the actual project level. As mentioned earlier, such a link is at the present time rarely in evidence. Conversely, such information should make it possible for planning authorities better to appraise proposals by engineers for the establishment of new industries or the expansion of existing ones, from the point of view of the general objectives of the plan. The magnitude of the effort involved in developing and carrying out an adequate program of research along the proposed lines is by no means underestimated; it is considered, however, that the results would be at least commensurate with the effort involved.

POTENTIAL TO PRODUCTIVITY

Paul Gray Hoffman

The Chronic Crisis

This is the richest of all centuries. Yet there is a vast segment of the modern world where:

- Thirty thousand children die each day from lack of food and medical care.
- Some 800 million people are completely illiterate.
- Hundreds of millions have an income of $100 a year or less.

These statistics are drawn from the facts of life in more than one hundred countries associated with the United Nations. They illuminate not only a vast and largely needless tragedy, but a chronic and dangerous politico-economic crisis of global proportions.

The world's wealth of material resources, human resourcefulness, and technical know-how is potentially adequate to alleviate—and some day to eradicate—the hunger, disease, illiteracy, and destitution that now shadow and shorten the lives of well over a billion people. For humanitarian reasons alone we should be moving against these problems with far greater speed than is presently the case.

The economic arguments for a global attack on want are similarly sound and compelling. Only a healthy and expanding world economy can provide the industrialized countries with outlets for their explosively increasing productivity. And only in such an economy can the low-income countries hope to find adequate sources of the foreign exchange they so desperately need to raise domestic standards of living. An increasing interdependence gives all nations a strong self-interest in relieving the poverty that now afflicts so many of their number.

Mr. Hoffman is Managing Director of the United Nations Special Fund.

But political considerations are perhaps the most urgent of all. For the peoples of the developing countries are today caught up in what has been aptly termed "the revolution of rising expectancy"—a great subsurface stirring that may well be the most important movement of our times. As a result of vastly improved communications and transport, unprecedented numbers of men and women throughout Asia, Africa, and Latin America are coming to realize that misery is not mandatory. They see that a better life exists; they are determined to create such a life for themselves; and they will not brook undue delay. If their hopes for a future of decency and dignity can be realized, the world will have taken a giant step toward stability and peace. If, on the other hand, these peoples are denied the chance to make rapid and significant progress, explosive outbreaks of discontent—occurring ever more frequently—may edge humanity closer to the nuclear brink.

Thus, from many points of view, the alleviation of chronic world poverty is an acute concern for the United Nations.

Internationalizing Assistance

Fortunately, the United Nations and its associated agencies have accumulated a vast amount of experience in helping emerging countries speed their social and economic progress. Most of this experience has been gained during the fifteen years' existence of the UN family's technical assistance program—a coordinated broad-spectrum effort covering industry, agriculture, education, technical and managerial training, communications, transport, health, social welfare, national planning, and a variety of related fields. The UN has also been long involved in the financing of development, through the work of the World Bank, the International Development Association, and the International Finance Corporation in providing investment capital, and through the currency-stabilization activities of the International Monetary Fund.

The United Nations Special Fund

The inauguration of the United Nations Special Fund in January, 1959, marked the beginning of a new and critical phase in our world organization's assistance to the low-income countries. For the Special Fund was specifically established to help these countries remove what is perhaps the most important roadblock on their path to progress.

The developing lands are in a position much like that of the mythical King Tantalus, who sat starving while surrounded by fruit he could not touch. These countries are rich in natural and human resources, often extraordinarily so. Brazil, for example, possesses the third-largest expanse of arable land in the world, over thirty per cent of the earth's known iron ore, huge deposits of bauxite, and a hydroelectric potential estimated to exceed that of any other nation. Libya has proved petroleum reserves so great that, although development is still in its early stages, she can already export a million barrels of oil a day. The waters of East Asia's Mekong River Basin, if harnessed for irrigation, could make millions and millions of presently low-yield acres into a far more bountiful "rice basket." Such instances could be multiplied almost indefinitely, for there is probably no nation or region so *basically* poor as to be without substantial and economically exploitable physical assets. Furthermore, the developing world is largely a *youthful* world, with more than half its population in or entering the potentially most productive age group.

But as of now, the emerging countries cannot convert their latent potential into anything like full productivity. They cannot substantially increase the present output of their farms and factories, forests and fisheries, mines and mills and business enterprises—because they lack the *investment capital* and the *trained personnel* required for this purpose. The mission of the Special Fund is to provide the kind of assistance that will help them remedy both these lacks.

The Practice of Preinvestment

The Special Fund is essentially a "partnership for progress." Working through the United Nations and nine related agencies,[1] the Fund gives aid to well-defined and well-supported local or regional projects whose fundamental importance and reasonably rapid benefits are clearly evident.

These projects fall into three basic categories:

1. Surveys of available resources and their potential for economic development
2. Facilities for training nationals in the effective use of these resources
3. Research institutes for applying modern technology to development needs

The concept behind such projects is one which, many years ago, I christened "preinvestment assistance," since its aim is to help developing nations create conditions that will allow them to attract capital investment in sizable amounts and use that investment with maximum effectiveness for speeding social and economic progress.

The low-income nations have responded to this "self-help" approach with such enthusiasm that by January, 1965, 485 large-scale projects in 130 countries and territories had been approved by the Fund's Governing Council, with the large majority already operational. The program's cost is now over 1 billion dollars, some 60 percent of which is borne by the low-income countries themselves through the counterpart support they furnish for their own projects.

Equally significant is the fact that, at the Pledging Conference for 1964, 113 countries (many in the low-income bracket themselves) voluntarily promised contributions of well over 85 million dollars to the Fund's central resources. This represents a nearly fourfold increase from the Fund's first year; and the upward trend is continuing, with many nations very substantially increasing their pledges for 1965.

The number of international experts employed by the United Nations agencies to implement Special Fund-assisted projects has likewise shown spectacular growth, rising from 100 in 1960 to over 1,500 as of the present date.

[1] International Labor Organization; Food and Agriculture Organization; United Nations Educational, Scientific and Cultural Organization; World Health Organization; International Bank for Reconstruction and Development; International Civil Aviation Organization; International Telecommunications Union; World Meteorological Organization; International Atomic Energy Agency.

This money and manpower enable the Fund, *inter alia*, to assist 197 large-scale *surveys and feasibility studies.* Fund-assisted survey projects are helping 86 developing countries to make an inventory of certain key natural resources: what they are, where located, in what quantity and quality, of how much economic potential. Already they have triggered sizable and timely investments. Seventeen surveys costing some 17 million dollars have to date attracted local and external capital from both public and private sources totaling over three-quarters of a *billion* dollars. This is a fiftyfold return, and more is on the way.

The Special Fund is also helping 97 *research institutes* develop and disseminate methods for improving manufacturing techniques, raising productivity, and promoting better use of local raw materials. Located in 39 emerging countries, these institutes are also developing new low-cost manufactures for domestic use and new export markets with high earning potential. Their work, together with that of the Fund-assisted surveys, is helping many countries to construct the modern informational and technological base on which self-supporting economies can eventually be built.

No less vital is the fuller employment of *human resources* in the developing world, where, according to the best estimates, only some 10 percent of this critically important productive potential is now being brought to bear. Thus the Fund is aiding 191 *training projects* in 74 countries; and these projects have already equipped more than 56,000 nationals to play their part in hundreds of essential occupations. Of far-reaching importance and rapidly expanding impact, the majority are technical instructors whose contributions to development continually multiply as each, in turn, trains many times his own number of managers, supervisors, technicians, and line-production workers. The knowledge and skills on which self-sustaining progress depends are thus being home-grown.

In 1962, the Special Fund extended its activities at the request of five Latin American countries and helped establish a regional Institute for Economic Development Planning. This was rapidly followed by approval of a similar regional Institute for Asia, with a parallel African facility now getting into operation. Altogether, the Fund is, or will shortly be, contributing to the support of nine projects designed to aid individual countries and multinational areas map out comprehensive long-range programs for economic growth.

Special Fund-assisted projects are major undertakings in size, scope, and spread. Cost, on the average, is some 2 million dollars per project; and duration, some four years. A geographical breakdown shows 133 projects in Asia, 154 in Africa, 129 in the Americas, 28 in Europe, 40 in the Middle East, and 1 interregional.

Management Development as a Key to Progress

Significantly, almost 10 percent of all training activities assisted by the Fund are concerned with management and supervisory development. Total cost of the 15 projects currently operational in this area and of 3 new ones now in the planning stage runs close to 30 million dollars. But the importance of these projects is far more critical than such statistics indicate.

For of all the many shortages with which the developing nations must contend, none is more hobbling than the lack of skilled and experienced leadership at all levels of public and private enterprise—industrial, commercial, agricultural, and public service.

The economies of most of the emerging countries are well suited for small- and medium-scale manufacturing and retailing operations, and these, together with agricultural and industrial cooperatives, are badly needed to broaden and strengthen the economic base, provide new employment opportunities, accelerate the growth of domestic markets, and expand the presently limited range of exportable products. No less urgent is the need to enlarge and diversify basic heavy industry and to create or expand public utility networks. Yet progress in all these areas will continue to be severely retarded until the emerging nations can develop adequate numbers of knowledgeable entrepreneurs, administrators, upper- and middle-level managers, and first-line supervisory personnel.

Leadership in the Making

The management development and supervisory training projects assisted by the Special Fund are designed to help recipient countries fulfill some of their key needs for this type of leadership. A typical example is the Federation of Malaysia's National Productivity Center, established at Kuala Lumpur in February, 1962, with the International Labor Organization as executing agency.

The Center's work falls into two major categories: raising the standards of industrial management, including supervision at all levels, and improving efficiency in manufacturing, with particular emphasis on increased productivity, improved quality, lowered costs, and the development of constructive labor-management relations.

The Center has organized training courses for top and middle management staffs, supervisors, and trade union representatives. These courses cover such subjects as general administration, product development and standardization, modern production methods, quality and cost control, and personnel policies and practices. In addition, the Center furnishes consulting and technical information services to both government and private industry, thus carrying its work directly into the field. Finally, the Center's teaching staff is also available to give special courses and lectures at the University of Malaya's Technical College and Engineering Faculty, thus helping to prepare graduates for responsible management posts in industries throughout the Federation.

Among the recent results obtained from the Center's work is a 290 percent increase in the productivity of telephone-repair technicians, coupled with an annual savings of some $40,000 on repair costs. In another field, that of rubber processing, time reductions of nearly 30 percent were achieved for certain key operations of a major sheeting factory; while a suggested layout for a rubber-packing plant will enable it to triple the daily poundage currently handled.

No less broad in scope are the operations of Iraq's Management Development and Supervisory Training Center set up in Baghdad under joint Special Fund and ILO auspices. The Iraqi Center is an autonomous, nongovernmental institution controlled by an administrative board, whose members include representatives from the Ministries of Industry, Planning, Finance, and Oil, together with officials of Baghdad University and the Federation of Iraqi Industries.

Since training was inaugurated in October, 1962, the Center has been contributing in a very direct and practical way to the success of Iraq's industrial development plan. Trainees are drawn directly from the working management staffs of various companies, and they bring to the classroom their day-to-day problems and attempted methods of solution. Subjects they discuss under the guidance of international experts range over a broad spectrum from general and production management to management accounting, foreman training, marketing, sales, and distribution.

After several weeks of intensive instruction in up-to-date management techniques, combined with a full and free exchange of practical working ideas, participants go back to their own plants, there to put into effect a variety of newly learned skills. In addition, each is assigned a specific project important to improving operations of the company in which he works. After some two months, during which he is aided in the implementation of his project by experts from the Center, each returns to the Center for a review of results and follow-up training.

Recently, the Center has also established an information service aimed at keeping industrial management personnel throughout the country abreast of the latest developments in their specialized fields. A research service to assist in further improving industrial productivity is also being planned to round out the Center's services.

Projects for the development of managerial, supervisory, and entrepreneurship skills—with specific activities tailored to specific national needs—are now also being assisted by the Special Fund in Argentina, Cyprus, India, Iran, Korea, Pakistan, the Sudan, Syria, Tanganyika, Thailand, Trinidad, Uganda, and Venezuela.

Management development in its broadest, most practical applications constitutes an expanding and challenging field of opportunity for the Special Fund. For this particular method of enriching human resources shows notably rapid and far-reaching results in translating potential into productivity. Furthermore, it is directly consonant with the basic aim of the Special Fund program: to help the emerging countries attack poverty at its root causes and to develop the institutions that can further extend and perpetuate progress after the Fund's assistance comes to an end.

EXPROPRIATION OF FOREIGN INVESTMENT: RIGHTS AND REMEDIES OF THE PRIVATE INVESTOR

Raymond L. Brittenham, A.B., LL.B.

Introduction

The Resolution on Permanent Sovereignty over Natural Resources, adopted by the Seventeenth General Assembly of the United Nations, brings into focus a problem of major concern to potential investors in developing nations: the possibility of expropriation of foreign-owned property by the local sovereign. The UN resolution, as the title indicates, emphasizes the "right of peoples and nations to permanent sovereignty over their natural wealth and resources." In the exercise of this right, the sovereign may expropriate property "on grounds or reasons of public utility." The only duty to the owner of the expropriated property is the payment of "appropriate compensation . . . in accordance with international law. . . ." While the resolution states that "foreign investment agreements freely entered into by or between sovereign states shall be observed in good faith," the emphasis on the principle of national sovereignty over natural wealth and resources remains its key feature.

Despite the flood of official and unofficial studies and statements recognizing the great need of developing countries for foreign investment, it nevertheless appears, as this paper is being written in late 1964, that the developing nations have thrust into the forefront their inherent sovereign power over natural resources rather than their willingness to protect the foreign investor. Aware of this fact, potential corporate investors may ask whether more widespread expropriations may be anticipated. In any case, it is imperative that a corporation considering investment in a developing country acquaint itself

Mr. Brittenham is Senior Vice-President and General Counsel of the International Telephone and Telegraph Corporation.

with the measures it may take to prevent expropriations and with the remedies available to it following expropriation.

Expropriation: National and International Law

The right of a government, whether it be *de facto* or *de jure,* to appropriate private property for public use is an inherent attribute of sovereign power superior to all property rights of private persons. Neither the principle of sovereignty nor the power of the sovereign to appropriate private property is at issue. The question at hand is whether just compensation must accompany the appropriation.

The Fifth Amendment to the United States Constitution requires that "just compensation" be paid to owners of private property taken for a public use. A property owner claiming that he is not being justly compensated by the appropriating authority may have the courts determine the correctness of his plea. However, a foreign nation's constitutional guarantee of just compensation to the owner of the appropriated property may not actually ensure a judicial determination of the adequacy of the compensation. The late President Vargas of Brazil once issued a decree-law contradicting the condemnation compensation provisions of the 1937 Brazilian constitution. At least one writer commented that the Brazilian Chief Executive was able to supersede his country's constitution because the same hand that signed the decree on expropriation could also amend the constitution. If this were to become the standard, constitutional compensation guarantees to the owners of appropriated property would be mere chimeras.

There is a diversity of view on the question of whether the legality of an expropriation under international law depends upon payment of just compensation to the former property owner. According to the view espoused by many of the developed Western countries, international law sanctions appropriation of alien-owned property only when the payment to the property owner is "prompt, adequate, and effective." However, some of the African states, some of the Latin American states, and the Eastern bloc countries view any taking by the sovereign for a public purpose, whether or not the private owner is in any manner compensated, as sanctioned by international law. As a result of these conflicting views, it is necessary to look beyond the customary sources of international law to determine whether just compensation will be forthcoming.

The United States has signed many friendship, commerce, and navigation treaties with foreign countries. Many of these treaties require expropriation to be for a public purpose and with immediate provision for payment of adequate and effective compensation to the deprived property owner. These treaties often contain clauses committing both nations to give force and effect to contractual arbitration provisions. A breach of the provisions of such treaties would be a violation of international law. Therefore a breach of the arbitration provision between a government and a private investor would violate international law. However, the international-law sanction depends for its effectiveness on the willingness of the parties to fulfill their obligations. Consequently, when amity between the contracting nations is broken, the private investor, who generally has no status under international law, may find his treaty rights to be a phantom protection against expropriation.

The Techniques of Taking

Takings with Compensation. In this situation, a government takes and provides for just compensation to the injured property owner. In deciding what compensation is "just," the administrative or judicial tribunal must determine the difficult question of the fair value of the property taken. Intangible losses, such as the destruction of a shopkeeper's trade because of forced relocation, are hard to prove and harder to value. Therefore the businessman must be aware that even "just" compensation may not fit his notions of full compensation. However, any individual misfortune results not from discrimination based on class or nationality, but from defects embedded in the orderly process of the law.

Takings without Adequate Compensation. In this situation, the government takes private property for a purportedly public use, but does not provide compensation to the private owners, or if compensation is provided, it is grossly inadequate. The sovereign normally issues a decree declaring the need for and the methods of expropriation.

The Eastern European Communist governments followed this procedure when they appropriated private property for public use shortly after World War II. For example, the Czechoslavakian government issued general decrees listing the industries affected and the size of the enterprises in each industry subject to expropriation. Later government pronouncements specified, usually by name, the particular enterprises now denominated the property of the state. An expropriation along these lines may have the appearance of lawfulness even to Americans. This image of lawfulness is heightened by the establishment of judicial appeal machinery in the expropriatory decree. However, there is little indication that such appeals could have been effectively pursued in the Eastern European Communist nations.

Soviet expropriation techniques in the post–World War II period generally conformed to the same pattern of taking. Expropriation decrees affected particular enterprises because of the nationality or wartime records of the owners. The decrees provided compensation in some cases, but not in others. Furthermore, when the cold war thawed, negotiations on various subjects, including compensation payments to former owners of expropriated property, were entered into with the Western nations. Varying schemes were arranged which compensated individual property owners in direct proportion to the bargaining power of their national governments. Other Soviet Bloc countries followed the same procedure of expropriation and subsequent negotiation of the compensation issue on the national level.

Seizures. While all takings are seizures in one form or another, the term here refers to a physical confiscation of private property without the benefit of a prior executive or legislative decree of expropriation. The "agrarian reformers" of Red China were exponents of this method of taking. The People's Army would physically occupy the privately owned property, while Party activists gained *de facto* control of the plant operation. Subsequently, the tangible assets of the expropriated property would be integrated into the

Communist industrial complex. If this "integration" were accomplished by physical relocation of the seized machinery and inventory, the former owner would seldom be able to identify the seized assets for valuation purposes even if compensation were offered.

Such seizures must be differentiated from action taken by a state in order to reach enemy assets when a state of actual hostilities exists. The United States thought its actions justified in passing the wartime alien property acts. However, legal questions may arise as to the justifiable basis of the action when the property, although in enemy hands, is claimed to be owned by neutral or allied interests. Thus serious controversy was caused by the Allied seizure of the German General Aniline and Film Corporation in the light of the ownership claim of the Swiss corporation Interhandel and by the Russian removal of the assets of German subsidiaries of Allied corporations. (A curious twist to this situation is found in the action of a Japanese corporation which, throughout the war, credited the account of its American licensor, although the Japanese regime had seized the licensee company's entire assets.) In any case, international law and order would appear to be better served by a posthostilities settlement of claims arising from such wartime acts.

More Imaginative Techniques of Taking. A foreign-owned enterprise in a country turned hostile for political or economic reasons is very much at the mercy of its host. Recent years have seen the development of many techniques of property taking unknown in less sophisticated eras. Many of the postwar Eastern Communist regimes imposed a "millionaire's tax" on capital-producing property, predicated on the theory that any increase in assets during the years of German occupation was immoral and therefore should be forfeited. If it be any consolation, national enterprises were subject to this tax to the same extent as enterprises owned by foreign investors.

Takings for less overtly punitive reasons can also be carried out under varied guises. Where foreign capital alone has developed a country's natural resources, a tax levied on underground reserves or on the extraction of a particular mineral might well be considered discriminatory and confiscatory. Other indirect measures available to the local government include the harassment of local managers, the delay in the customs clearance of essential imports, and the fomentation of labor strife. Some governmental activities, such as refusal to permit foreign public utilities to increase their rates in the face of an inflationary economy, or the imposition of social laws that vastly increase labor costs while at the same time prohibiting a price increase, may so deplete a foreign-owned enterprise that the investor can only abandon control and ownership of the undertaking to the host government.

All in all, if a government wants to take over the foreign investment in its country, it can, and only the form of taking will vary.

Postexpropriation Remedies Available to the Private Investor

The Role of the State Department. In this day and age, when so much attention is paid to world opinion, a private investor in foreign countries cannot depend on the armed might of the U.S. government to protect his investment. Since a corporation or a private individual is not a state, the general assumption is that the corporation or individual has no standing under international law to protest a government's action. Consequently, once his property has been expropriated by a foreign sovereign, the investor's primary remedy is often an appeal to the State Department, which may negotiate his claim of a violation of international law on a nation-to-nation basis. Recently, the State Department was instrumental in obtaining an interim compensation settlement after the Brazilian Government took over a public utility owned by Americans in Brazil. In 1963, the State Department curtailed U.S. foreign aid to Ceylon because of Ceylon's unwillingness to guarantee prompt and adequate compensation to the American oil companies whose facilities the Ceylonese government expropriated.

These actions by the State Department may prophesy a change in the Department's view of the protection of American assets abroad. Previous to these actions, a large portion of the business community was of the opinion that European governments and their representatives were much more active than the U.S. government and its representatives in protecting the foreign investment of their citizens. Perhaps the Hickenlooper-Adair amendment to the Foreign Assistance Act of 1961, which requires denial of foreign-aid financial assistance to countries expropriating the assets of U.S. citizens or corporations without payment of compensation equivalent to full value of the asset seized, will lead the State Department to a more vigorous policy of protection of American foreign investment.

Lex Talionis and Other Forms of Self-help. The most obvious countermeasure to an uncompensated expropriation is the seizure of assets owned by nationals of the expropriating country and located within the boundaries of the victim's country. This measure was taken by the United States in retribution for the expropriation of assets of United States nationals or companies by several of the Eastern Communist regimes. However, in today's economic pattern, often the countries most likely to expropriate foreign-owned assets have the least property within the United States. For example, because of the meager available assets, claimants receiving a Foreign Claims Settlement Commission award as compensation for property expropriated in Hungary realized only pennies on each dollar claimed. The developing nations are not likely to have many assets in the United States.

Perhaps of more value than affirmative payment from foreign-country assets blocked in the United States is the demand for payment of past-due expropriation debts as a condition of entry into future economic programs. This weapon is equally available to the government official or the private investor. The U.S. government coupled a program of reparation to American investors with a pledge of aid to Poland. In addition, it is widely known that certain large American companies have conditioned future economic relations with a foreign sovereign on the liquidation of obligations to the companies arising from previous expropriations. Of course, the possibility of either the government or the private investor successfully demanding payment of expropriation compensation before future business relationships are agreed upon will depend on the political or economic climate of the moment. When U.S. trade is booming in many markets, the feasibility of withholding products from any one market is much greater than it would be if the trade situation were less favorable. Of course, the more deteriorated the nationalizing government's economy at bargaining time, the more receptive it will be to demands for compensation as a condition for the infusion of new economic blood.

Act of State Doctrine. If a private investor is not in a position to take advantage of economic pressures to secure retribution, his prime concern is whether he may expect aid from the courts of the expropriating country or from the courts of any country where he may locate products made with the expropriated assets. It is usually futile to seek redress within the judicial system of an expropriating Communist country. Experience indicates that the act of its sovereign will always be declared legal. Whether aid may be forthcoming from the courts of another country within whose borders the investor is able to find the products of his expropriated assets depends on that country's view of the act of state doctrine.

In *Banco Nacional de Cuba v. Sabbatino*, 376 U.S. 398 (1964), a case arising from the seizure by the Cuban government of a load of sugar in Havana harbor, the United States Supreme Court declared the act of state doctrine to be a rule of decision in the courts in the United States. The Court there defined the act of state doctrine as meaning that the

> judicial branch will not examine the validity of a taking of property within its own territory by a foreign sovereign government, extant and recognized by this country at the time of the suit, in the absence of a treaty or other unambiguous agreement regarding controlling legal principles even if the complaint alleges that the taking violates customary international law.

The Court founded its decision on the separation of powers between the three branches of government. The conduct of the nation's foreign relations belongs to the Executive. Therefore, if the State Department does not affirmatively assent to court action, or at least expressly declare its indifference to court action, the U.S. courts, both state and Federal, may not declare the act of a foreign sovereign done within its own territory as invalid. It is doubtful that the act of state doctrine will be applied when the foreign sovereign's act is merely executory, that is, when the assets supposedly nationalized are not within the territory of the nationalizing state at the time of the nationalization decree. When this situation was presented prior to *Sabbatino*, courts in the United States often refused to apply the act of state doctrine and found the foreign sovereign's acts to violate U.S. public policy and thus to be unenforceable in U.S. courts. Nothing in *Sabbatino* indicates that the Supreme Court would extend the application of the act of state doctrine to this situation.

In reaction to the decision in the *Sabbatino* case, the Congress of the United States, in October of 1964, passed legislation declaring that:

> . . . no court in the United States shall decline on the ground of the federal act of state doctrine to make a determination on the merits giving effect to the principles of international law in a case in which a claim of title or other right is asserted by any party including a foreign state (or a party claiming through such state) based upon (or traced through) a confiscation or other taking after January 1, 1959, by an act of that state in violation of the principles of international law, including the principles of compensation. . . . P.L. 88-663, 78 Stat. 1009, Part III, Ch. 1, Sec. 301(e) (Oct. 2, 1964).

Further, this statute allows the President to determine that the application of the act of state doctrine by the courts is in the best interests of the United States in a particular case. Such a determination by the President, when filed with the court, allows the court to override the statute and to apply the doctrine. More importantly, perhaps, the statute does not apply to any case commenced after January 1, 1966. This does not mean, though, that the statute may not then be renewed. Representative Adair of Indiana stated to the House that adoption of this amendment to the Foreign Assistance Act.

> now requires the State Department, which opposed it, to give the amendment a fair chance to operate in practice, and puts the burden on them in our hearings next year of showing how the amendment's Presidential waiver provision does not amply meet any problems that may arise in the actual conduct of foreign affairs. 110 Cong. Rec. 22849 (daily ed. Oct. 2, 1964).

Consequently, the application of the act of state doctrine is narrowly limited in courts of the United States, and they must determine, on the merits, the validity of the act of a foreign sovereign in the light of U.S. public policy and the general principles of international law. Thus, by statute, at the present time, the courts of the United States must find that expropriation decrees grant adequate compensation in order to sustain the expropriation as lawful.

Other Western countries do not always interpret the act of state doctrine with the strictness of the United States Supreme Court in the *Sabbatino* case. When tobacco, grown in plantations nationalized by the Indonesian government, was seized in Germany and Holland by the former plantation owner, the German courts disallowed the attachment of the tobacco, while the Dutch courts gave effect to the former owner's claim. Consequently, choice of forum may be extremely important in situations where the act of state doctrine is claimed to apply.

Perhaps, as a corollary to the rigorous application of the act of state doctrine, the states applying this doctrine in the national interest should indemnify the property owners for their loss. In this way, national policy could be served without infringing individual claims of right. The United States, to a degree, compensates nationalization victims. Often it creates a pool of blocked assets of the expropriating nation's assets in the United States and proportionately pays U.S. victims from this pool.

U.S. Tax Relief. Tax relief would be one method of providing some help to U.S. corporations which suffer foreign expropriation losses. Section 165(a) of the Internal Revenue Code of 1954 provides for the deductibility of losses sustained by taxpayers which are not compensated for by insurance or otherwise. Illusory compensation promises with little or no possibility of actual payment do not deprive a corporation of the benefit of this Section. Generally, for corporations, the expropriation losses are capital losses which may only be set off against capital gains. Section 165(g)(3) of the Code accords ordinary loss treatment to expropriation losses only when the security which has become worthless, through expropriation or otherwise, has been issued by a corporation in which 95% of the shares are held by a domestic affiliated corporation. In addition, it must be noted that there are other conditions set forth in this section, not relevant to the present discussion, which must be met before the sufferer of such losses may appropriately take such a deduction.

It is arguable that if the tax laws were changed to allow ordinary loss treatment, including loss carryback provisions, for all expropriation losses, the inhibitions on investment abroad by U.S. corporations to which the possibility of expropriation or seizure without compensation give rise would be lessened. While ordinary loss treatment would tend to shift the burden of the loss to all the taxpayers generally, instead of placing it on one specific taxpayer, such treatment would appear to be basically fair. Many taxpayers benefit from increased foreign trade, and it is national policy to encourage such trade. Therefore the nation might appropriately share the risk of foreign investment.

Preexpropriation Protective Measures Available to the Investor

In the face of the risk of expropriation and in the absence of effective countermeasures in the event of loss, business practices and procedures have been developed to offer a measure of preventive protection to the investor in foreign markets. All these, however, hold disadvantages either for the investor, the host country, or the U.S. government.

Limited Commitment. One of the better protections against expropriation that can be devised is a foreign investment which is limited so as to leave as little property worth expropriating in a foreign country as possible. Such a mode of investment favored today is the low-capitalization company formed under the foreign nation's laws as a sales outlet for imported goods. The loss of such a company by expropriation would seldom be great, for the initial investment is small and the company assets are ambulatory. The only inventory lost would be that stored within the foreign country. Contrast this with the vulnerability to expropriation of a foreign-owned public utility. Not only is a public utility such as a railroad subject to extensive public regulation, but a railroad caught in a political, economic, or social squeeze cannot shift its tracks to a friendlier environment. The utility's movable assets represent but a small portion of its historic investment in the expropriating country. The natural effect of political and social uncertainty is to discourage investment, in many of the developing nations, of the capital necessary to establish heavy industry. Unhappily, yesterday's investment opportunities often become today's political crises. Consequently, limited investment in certain small projects is a popular foreign-investment method.

Patent Licensing and Know-how Agreements. A variation of the technique of limiting the exposure to expropriation by limiting the capital invested is the technique of participating in a nation's development through patent and technical-information, or know-how, licensing. But the protection provided by such devices may be limited.

Patents established in a country which subsequently becomes unfriendly are unenforceable and therefore valueless in that country to the foreign patent owner. However, patents in other countries to which the nationalizing country may wish to export the patented products perhaps can be utilized to block imports of the patented goods. In this way the competitive advantage of the patent violator may be minimized.

Know-how agreements can have a commercial value subsequent to nationalization. However, this value to the expropriator may be limited where the know-how licensee must continually receive new information in order to remain productive or competitive and the know-how supplier ceases to transmit further technical information after nationalization. Although the licensee may be established in a low-cost labor area and therefore can perhaps be more competitive in world markets than the licensor, his advantage may be only temporary as a result of his lack of current technical information.

Patent licenses and know-how agreements have the disadvantage of not giving to the U.S. investor the same rewards as an equity share in a growing business. At the same time, the foreign government loses the advantage of adding additional foreign capital to its industrial base. Consequently, such arrangements, while protective, leave much to be desired from the point of view of the investor as well as the foreign government.

Joint Ventures with Foreign Nationals as Partners. An investment method rapidly gaining favor in underdeveloped countries is the joint venture between local and foreign capital. The foreign investor frequently adds know-how, training, and management to his capital contribution. The foreign investor forgoes an immediate return of capital and counts instead on the future prosperity of the joint enterprise. Where the joint venture establishes a technically complex industry, at the outset, the U.S. partner generally supplies components produced in the United States to the joint venture. It is generally contemplated that as the skills and experience acquired by the joint venture increase, they will increase the scope of the manufacturing carried out and ultimately produce all the product components locally.

The joint-enterprise method of investment relieves the local government of a foreign-currency drain and consequently helps stabilize the local economy. A recent U.N. report on the international flow of private capital indicates an increasing use of joint ventures. It also sets out examples of contractual devices employed to transfer managerial and technical know-how to the developing countries.

Host-country Financing. Raising capital locally, by either equity or debt financing, is often an effective hedge against both expropriation and landslide inflation. Of course, raising capital by the sale of stock dilutes the equity of the foreign investor. Further, local minority shareholders in a foreign-based enterprise can impinge upon management decisions. For example, the freedom to shift an operation from one country to another for economic or other reasons may be lessened by the presence of a large minority of local shareholders who are opposed to any transfer of the operation from their country.

Debt financing in developing countries can be very expensive by U.S. standards. Interest rates on business loans in underdeveloped nations can range from 9 to 40% per annum. On the other hand, owners of an enterprise which has been nationalized need not be concerned with the payment of the enterprise's debts, at least in the absence of parent-company guarantees to creditors which are enforceable extraterritorially. Further, borrowing, large in terms of the local currency, may dwindle rapidly in terms of U.S. dollars when the local currency is faced with runaway local inflation.

Host-country Guarantees. It is not unusual for developing countries, in order to attract foreign capital, unilaterally to "guarantee" foreign investments in their countries. This guarantee may be expressed in the constitution, in a legislative pronouncement, or in an executive decree. Understandably, the worth of such guarantees depends on the attitude of the government in power. Many businessmen are of the opinion that the violent shifts of the developing nations between alliance with the West and allegiance to the East make a unilateral government guarantee of foreign investment a thin reed upon which to base substantial foreign capital investment.

Bilateral treaties providing reciprocal promises to make "adequate and effective compensation" to the owners of expropriated property have proved more beneficial to the private investor than a unilateral guarantee. A violation of a treaty obligation is everywhere understood to be a violation of international law. Even the 1962 U.N. Resolution emphasizing the rights of the sovereign over natural resources stated that "foreign investment agreements freely entered into by, or between, sovereign States shall be observed in good faith." Unfortunately, few such treaties are in effect today between the United States and important Latin American countries.

Country of Export Guarantees. Guarantee against investment risks offered by the government of a developed country to increase foreign trade presents sound protection to the international investor. Western European governments have for a long time provided insurance and guarantees to minimize the risk of loss to investors in foreign enterprises. The German, Belgian, French, and British governments offer low-cost insurance against foreign economic and political risks.

Following the European lead, the U.S. government has developed a broad, low-cost Specific Risk Investment Guarantee Program under the Foreign Assistance Act of 1961, as amended. This program, administered by the Agency for International Development, is intended to increase the investment of U.S. capital in the developing countries by guaranteeing investors against specific investment hazards. The program covers (1) the risk of impossibility of conversion of foreign currency received as earnings from or returns on an investment in a developing country, (2) the risk of loss due to expropriation or confiscation of property in the developing countries, and (3) the risk of loss due to war, revolution, or insurrection in the developing country. In addition, there is no ceiling on the amount of the guarantee. Coverage in a particular country depends on the willingness of that country's government, even though it is not a coguarantor, to agree to U.S. guaranty coverage of investment in the country. Agreements have been reached with a good number of the developing countries, allowing projects within their countries to come within the scope of one or more of the guarantees provided by the program.

It must be kept in mind that the program does not provide guarantees against the risk of currency devaluation or against any investment risk in developed countries, although the underdeveloped dependencies of such countries come within the program's coverage. Further, each foreign investment project must be approved by the local government before the United States will guarantee the investment.

In addition to the Specific Risk Investment Guarantee Program, private investors may be eligible to receive investment guarantees from several national or international organizations. The Export-Import Bank, the Inter-American Development Fund, and the Inter-American Social Progress Fund are prepared to guarantee the private investment of domestic corporations which meet their criteria. In addition, investment guarantees for certain projects, such as low-cost housing in the Latin and South American countries, may be available. Any corporation or individual about to invest in a developing nation should inquire about the various U.S. and international guarantee programs and, if convenient, tailor the project to meet the criteria. The guarantee may be worth the bother.

Conclusion

Many steps are being taken by both capital-exporting and capital-importing countries to attract private investment to the underdeveloped nations of the world. Investment guarantees by the sending and receiving states as well as by international organizations are intended to calm the fears of the potential international investor concerning the risk of loss of his foreign-based capital. The private enterprises themselves have created business practices meant to minimize possible loss of foreign-based assets. However, the power of the sovereign to restrict ownership and management, to limit the repatriation of capital, to regulate many enterprises, and to tax at will must leave the potential investor in a developing country in a position of risk. Perhaps the most successful inducement to foreign capital is a local government with a history of fairness to foreign investors engaged in local enterprises. Governments and private enterprises must cooperate to a considerably greater degree if the goal of increased international trade creating higher worldwide standards of living is ever to be attained.

A BLUEPRINT FOR BANKING IN DEVELOPING NATIONS

W. A. Muriale

Background of Modern Banking

For centuries the expansion of trade, explorations to the far corners of the earth, military campaigns, even explorations into space, as well as many other domestic or international major undertakings by the nations of the civilized world, have been possible only when strong and adequate banking support has been available. The absence of it has altered the course of history in many instances and certainly has contributed to the changes that have been made on the map of the world.

Our modern banking system had its origin in the Republic of Venice during the eleventh and twelfth centuries. Born in an environment of trade and exploration, banking has never abandoned its legacy but rather has added to it by providing the new and broader services dictated by changing economic conditions and a rapidly changing world.

Today the need for adequate banking support and assistance is, if anything, more essential than ever—to the individual, to the corporation, and to the nation. This is particularly true in the case of emerging and developing nations, those who for the first time must face the realities of independent statehood in the competitive arena of world affairs without the protective shelter of a major power.

Independence and the right of self-determination are two of life's most cherished possessions. No price, whatever it may be, would be too high to pay in acquiring them; and so the developing nations cope with the problems which they have accepted as part of the price paid for their newly acquired place in the community of nations.

One of the major problems confronting developing nations is the creation of a banking structure capable of meeting the needs of the country, both in the public and private sector, and in the domestic and international field.

Mr. Muriale is Vice President of the Bank of America, San Francisco.

Planning or Developing the Banking Structure

Some of the new nations, fortunately, have at least inherited a modern banking framework from the former colonial powers—the British, the French, the Belgians. This has served in most cases to reduce the problem but not to eliminate it, since the indigenous personnel of the colonial banks, generally speaking, were not adequately prepared for assuming the management role in the financial institutions of the country. So, in many instances, while administrative and operational technicians were available, the executive or managerial level presented a void that had to be filled. In short, it may well be said that practically all developing nations are confronted with the same problem, at the executive or policy-making level, in supplying the banking needs for their respective countries.

In determining banking needs and in planning the banking structure of any given country, there are important factors, purely national in character and scope, which the architects of the system must consider in their planning.

Basic Factors Influencing Planning

Some of the basic factors which should influence planning would be:

1. The geography of the country: Is it a maritime or mountainous area, or both? Does it border on one or a number of other countries? Is accessibility into the country from the outside world such as to encourage or discourage travel in both directions?

2. The economy of the country will also weigh heavily in determining the banking needs. If the economy is basically an agricultural one, certainly the needs will differ substantially from one whose industry influences the economy to a major extent. These differences will be set forth later.

3. The living habits and characteristics of the people vary from country to country. The banking needs again will differ for those who tend to have large concentrations of people—such as India and Pakistan—and those whose people tend to live in the scattered villages or towns of the tribal or rural complex, as is often found in Africa.

The language factor is also a matter to be considered. In some areas of the developing world language barriers arise at relatively small distances. While a country may have an official language, not infrequently a majority of the people are unable to speak it, being familiar only with one of a dozen or more dialects spoken by the vast majority of the people of the country. As a result there is often the inability to communicate among people beyond a radius of forty or fifty miles. This, too, can have an effect on a branch banking system.

4. The educational system and the related institutions must of necessity provide the major portion of the management talents and technical skills of the banking complex for both short- and long-range planning. In this age of specialists a banking industry that cannot draw on the resources of a sound educational system and the institutions of higher learning cannot progress and prosper.

5. The government of any country, to a large measure, sets the tone for the banking structure of the country, both directly and indirectly. Its measure

of stability is, of course, of paramount importance. Without government stability one can hardly look for economic, monetary, or fiscal stability or responsibility.

The government's attitude creates the climate under which commerce, industry, and agriculture must survive, grow, and prosper. A government that is favorably disposed toward a free enterprise system tends to encourage private investment and initiative.

6. The resources of the country should be accurately assessed and inventoried as part of the planning. These resources can be classified in three major groups, each of vital importance.

a. *Natural resources.* The availability of natural resources will have an important bearing on the direction in which the foreign relations of the country and its banking system are oriented.

It is inevitable that those countries which are limited in natural resources must, of necessity, resort to importing to a greater extent than those countries which are rich in natural resources. This invariably creates problems and difficulties in trade balances which must be met by drawing on their foreign exchange reserves, which are generally lacking. As a result exchange control regulations, import licensing, and other restrictions are inevitable. These will be touched upon again later in this article.

Those countries having a wealth of natural resources, that is, in excess of their own internal needs, may export these in the form of raw materials, thereby creating the foreign exchange necessary for the purchase of those essential products or commodities not grown or produced domestically which must be imported.

b. *Monetary resources.* The monetary resources of a country are essentially the stock in trade of the banking complex. The capital requirements of commerce, industry, and agriculture, even of government, must be nourished and satisfied in large measure from the capital flow through banks. Resources available for this purpose are heavily influenced by gross national product, per capita income, and external financial aid received by the country.

In the developing nations, practically without exception, monetary resources are wholly inadequate to meet capital demands because of low per capita income and gross national product. As a result external financial aid is becoming a major factor.

c. *Manpower resources.* The progress and development of any nation, its natural or monetary resources, are determined by and dependent upon its manpower resources. Without an adequate pool of manpower in the skilled, semiskilled, and unskilled sectors, all other resources of a nation cannot be developed or utilized to maximum advantage.

We have clear evidence of this today in some of the most highly developed and industrialized countries of the world, where an imbalance has developed between manpower resources and other segments of the economy. In some countries this condition has been at least relieved, if not corrected, by importing labor as a commodity. This has been true in West Germany, Switzerland, and other parts of Europe.

The Communist Bloc countries, too, notwithstanding their vast populations, have felt an adverse impact on their economies as a result of the imbalance in their manpower resources. Here the problem has not been one of numbers but rather one of a lack of proper proportions between skilled and unskilled and agrarian and industrial workers.

7. The economic development plans of the developing nations will greatly influence their banking structure. This planning must of necessity indicate whether the emphasis will be on public or private ownership and should also give a clear indication of government policy toward nationalization of utilities, transportation, and financial institutions.

Developing nations, almost without exception, are parched for capital. The prevailing shortage of savings and of foreign exchange is often further aggravated by the lack of debt instruments and a debt instrument market. The inability to obtain venture capital or investment capital through the media of stock or bond issues renders the procurement of adequate capital rather difficult. In such cases a market for commercial paper is generally also lacking. Without such a market, capital flow is restricted. Thus, either the capital needs which cannot be found in the marketplace must be provided from external sources, if possible, or the economic development of the country must be nourished with the limited capital available.

8. The existence of a sound central bank is indispensable to the creation of a sound banking and monetary structure in any developing nation.

The powers and attitude of the central bank have a tremendous influence on the policy and procedure of the commercial banks of the country; as a regulatory body, such a bank in effect lays down the ground rules under which the commercial banks are to function. Being government or quasi-government organizations, central banks generally exercise very broad powers which may have an important impact on the credit structure of the country. They generally have the authority to establish and adjust reserve requirements of the banks of the country and to adjust the discount rates. By so doing they may expand or contract the amount of credit that flows through the commercial arteries of the nation. The manipulation of these "valves" not only enables the central bank to control credit but also enables it to exercise a strong measure of control over the inflationary forces which can deteriorate the currency value, thereby undermining the economy of the country. Credit and credit instruments, like the fires that feed the furnaces of industry, if not properly controlled, may well become forces of destruction rather than of benefit.

Much of the central bank legislation of the 1920s and early thirties was tied to the gold standard concept, and central banks tended to have more concern for form rather than purpose.

In the postwar years, central bank legislation in many countries was standardized. The influence of the International Monetary Fund contributed much to this standardization, and its technical missions abroad provided invaluable assistance in this direction.

The International Monetary Fund, which was born of the Bretton Woods Conference, was created for the purpose of promoting international monetary cooperation and a balanced growth of world trade.

As a result of this postwar standardization, central banks developed more flexibility, and the application and interpretation of regulations was done in a more liberal light. There was a trend toward viewing credit requirements in the light of their contribution to the economic development of the country rather than favoring primarily short-term, self-liquidating loans.

Under IMF cooperation, exchange regulations and restrictions have been relaxed considerably, and exchange rates have shown a higher degree of stability than might otherwise have been the case.

Today central banks may induce or encourage the flow of capital into diverse sectors of the economy by the application of variations in reserve requirements. While a conservative banker may, for example, have a preference for extension of short-term credit to the import-export fraternity, with the attendant collateral benefits, the application of variations of central bank reserve requirements may, and often does, encourage him to extend credit to the agricultural or other segments of the economy.

Domestic Banking Requirements

The domestic banking needs of a country may be satisfied by banks that are purely local or regional in character. However, generally speaking, such banks cannot satisfy them with the same degree of flexibility or in the same full measure which an extensive branch banking system might provide. For example, a local bank in an agricultural area may find itself hard pressed for, or unable to meet, the seasonal credit needs of its clients if a substantial number of them are engaged in the same activity, possibly raising the same crops, and all needing funds at the same time.

The local bank located in the city may very well be confronted with the same problem, with only the demand period differing, according to seasonal peak activity.

The branch bank, on the other hand, having a better mix of deposits, is generally better able to meet the varying regional seasonal demands. Loanable funds from the low-demand areas may be channeled and utilized to meet high seasonal demand in other areas. Thus the branch bank may, within its own framework, accomplish that which a local bank may do only through arrangements with correspondent banks in other areas, or discounting arrangements which may affect its profitability, or other arrangements limiting its fulfillment of local needs.

The flexibility of the branch banking system has some built-in advantages which are deserving of mention. The mobility and seasonal availability of loanable funds will usually tend to enable the bank to view requests for credit on the basis of credit worthiness, free of a natural reluctance to "put all its eggs in one basket." Consequently, there is a greater willingness and ability to meet local needs.

The branch bank, by lending in the various areas of the country, is better able to spread its risk factor, thus making for greater security and stability for its depositors. While failure of a crop or low prices for a single commodity in a given area might have a seriously adverse effect on a local bank, the branch bank, with its diversification, can usually weather such a storm without serious effect.

The development and progress of any nation, even at the domestic level, today makes greater demands upon its banks than ever before. The small-unit banks which adequately provided the banking services of the community during the early part of the century have practically disappeared from the scene by merger, expansion, or liquidation. The depression of the thirties was probably the biggest single factor in bringing this about. The trend was further emphasized during the war years, when the demands of the war effort caused commerce, industry, and agriculture to seek working capital in unprecedented volume.

International Banking Requirements

The end of hostilities did not bring about a decline in the demand, as might have been expected. Instead we witnessed a shifting from war production to production to meet the consumer demands that had gone unsatisfied for several years.

While these domestic demands were being met by nations such as the United States and Canada whose industries had not suffered the ravages of war, it was also necessary for the industry of those countries to produce the goods and services essential to the rebuilding of a war-torn Europe and Asia. This was to continue for quite some time after the end of hostilities. Thus the demand for capital, instead of declining, tended to increase.

In the postwar period, therefore, we see the resurgence of foreign trade and witness its growth to proportions never before equaled in the history of the world.

No nation, developing or developed, is self-sufficient. All must engage in foreign trade to a greater or lesser degree, in order to procure those raw materials essential to the economy of the country which are not produced domestically. Consequently, international banking services must provide the channels through which the flow of goods and services must pass.

Essential International Banking Services

The international banking sector of the banking organization plays as vital a role as any other department in the modern scheme of things. The shrinking world, the increasing importance of foreign trade, and the increase in travel and tourism have created a tremendous increase in demand, on a very broad base, for international banking services.

The client engaging in importing and/or exporting will require a variety of international banking services. These activities are generally undertaken on the basis of commercial letters of credit, documentary collection, or open account. So the bank must be able to provide import or export letters of credit as a means of protecting the buyer or the seller. A usance import letter of credit may also provide the short-term postimport financing required for the transaction.

For clients buying or selling on a draft basis, in lieu of the letter of credit, the bank must provide prompt and efficient handling of documentary collections to or from all parts of the world. Where necessary, the bank may find it advantageous to provide financing to its exporter clients by means of advances under the outgoing documentary collections. This procedure has the advantage of tying the bank's advance to a specific transaction, while at the same time it provides the bank with some measure of collateral in that, by controlling the documents, it in effect has control of the merchandise.

For transactions which its clients handle on an open account basis, the bank must be prepared to arrange to buy or sell foreign exchange arising from the incoming or outgoing transaction, as the case may be, and it must be prepared to do so at rates that are favorable with the market. A competent foreign exchange trading section is indispensable to a bank operating in foreign trade, as well as to its clients. By assisting the clientele in covering its foreign exchange commitments, either on a spot or forward basis, a good foreign exchange trader can eliminate the element of speculation from their normal business transactions. This he normally does for a very nominal commission or spread in the rates.

For its nationals traveling abroad, the bank should be in a position to supply them with the necessary means of exchange which they may safely carry in lieu of cash. There would be traveler's checks, traveler's letters of credit, or foreign drafts payable abroad. These modern methods of carrying funds in lieu of cash are not only more convenient but also offer the traveler maximum protection against the loss or theft of his funds.

The bank must also be able, through its contacts abroad, to assist its clients in finding new sources of supply or raw materials, or new outlets for its goods in other parts of the world. This foreign trade service has become increasingly important. Such contacts developed through the bank may in many instances obviate the necessity of a trip abroad by the merchant, or at least considerably reduce the time spent abroad, by laying the groundwork for his contacts by preliminary inquiries.

In establishing commercial relationships with a foreign firm abroad the merchant ought to investigate the moral and financial responsibility of the foreign organization. He is entitled to know that he may deal with the firm with confidence and that it will fulfill its commitments to him. The necessary credit checkings to supply the merchant with essential information for a sound evaluation must be provided quickly and accurately by the bank.

Foreign Correspondent Bank Relationships

The above are some of the international services which a bank must be able to offer its customers over and above the normal financing or depository services.

They can be provided in a prompt and efficient manner only if the bank has an adequate network of correspondent bank relationships in the principal countries and cities of the world.

In a broad sense, the correspondent bank network is an extension of the domestic banking organization beyond its national borders. These relationships should be established carefully, selecting foreign banks which are best able to meet the needs, provide technical assistance when requested, and channel reciprocal business to the domestic bank commensurate with the relationship.

Naturally, among the correspondent banks with whom relationships are established it is always wise to give preference to those possessing a well-developed international banking department and a name that is internationally prominent and respected.

The Foreign Bank on the Domestic Scene

In rounding out the banking structure of the country, a developing nation should certainly give consideration to the inclusion of foreign banking interests within its overall complex—preferably a foreign bank of the country whose capital market and foreign trade with the developing nation are most important. This could be done by inviting a carefully selected, prominent foreign bank to establish a branch or branches in one or more of the principal cities of the country or by arranging for it to join with domestic interests in establishing or acquiring a domestic bank in joint ownership. Another common approach has been through the medium of minority participation in the ownership of a domestic bank by a bank or banks from several foreign countries. This participation may be direct or through a subsidiary.

The presence of such foreign interests may be of considerable assistance to the domestic bank by facilitating its access to important capital markets abroad, by aiding in the development of its indigenous management talents, and by creating important close working relationships with banking interests abroad.

Developing the Plan for Banking

While many developing nations may pursue the same course in determining their banking needs and requirements and may all consider the same factors in arriving at a decision, it is hardly likely that many of them will come up with the same combination of local unit banking, branch banking, international banking, and foreign interest banking. This is natural and correct, inasmuch as each will weigh the various factors in accordance with their respective importance to the particular nation.

Whatever the decision, it must be remembered that banking is a living, growing thing. The pattern of the banking structure, whatever it may be, must have built-in flexibility in its makeup to enable it to continue to offer the nation and its people new and improved services in keeping with the changing times and economic conditions in a rapidly changing world.

INSURANCE FOR INTERNATIONAL MANAGEMENT

Robert W. Self

In recent years there has been a major industrial development in countries which were previously noted only for agriculture, the supply of raw materials, or, perhaps, hand-crafted items.

With this increase in trade and manufacture has come the problem, familiar to the industrialized country but new to the developing nation, of securing protection against loss of concentrated financial values as well as earning power by means of purchased insurance.

Insurance coverages available in any particular country vary widely in scope; when the peculiarities of each country are multiplied in present-day world-wide operations, the situation becomes almost unbelievably complex. A better understanding of the basic principles of insurance will enable the buyer to evaluate the facilities of local and international markets in the light of his own particular situation and, thereby, to make informed decisions.

The Nature of Insurance Risks

Risk is uncertainty of loss, either personal or resulting from business activities. Many business risks are insurable. Certain types of risk, however, do not lend themselves to the application of the insurance principle of shifting the loss from the individual to an insurer. This group includes risk of loss due to depression, business judgments, speculation, and currency or market fluctuations.

The insurable risks, those which lend themselves to shifting and to group participation generally, may be divided into three categories:

1. Damage or destruction of physical assets
2. Loss of income or earnings
3. Loss arising from legal liability to third parties

Mr. Self is Senior Consultant of the Insurance Counseling Services, Management Consulting Division, EBS Management Consultants Incorporated, New York.

Each of these categories comprises risks of loss which are confronted both in the personal activities of individuals and in the operations of business enterprises, whether conducted by individuals, partnerships, or corporate organizations. The degree of their relative importance will, however, vary considerably as between individuals and as between specific business enterprises. Therefore, in all instances the nature of the exposure to loss and its magnitude and application to the specific individual or business enterprise must be considered jointly in evaluating the risk involved.

Methods of Protecting against Insurable Risks

Self-retention of Risk of Loss. In dealing with the matter of providing protection against an insurable risk, the individual or business firm is normally free to decide whether to accept and shoulder the financial loss involved or to shift the burden to a professional risk bearer in the form of purchased insurance coverage. The principal exception to this is that under the regulation of some national jurisdictions certain types of exposure to loss, mainly in the social insurance and third party liability fields, and also to a limited extent in the physical damage field, are closely regulated as to insurance coverage requirements which make it mandatory to purchase coverage either from a governmental agency or an approved insurance company.

Aside from this limitation, however, the person or firm confronted with the risks of loss is free to retain the burden of loss either through outright self-assumption as a personal or business expense, or by means of self-insurance. Both methods contemplate predetermination of the amount of financial risk and loss which can be self-retained and protective measures to limit the self-retained portion of the loss within this limit. They differ in that self-insurance contemplates an insurance company approach through the establishment of reserve funds sufficient to meet the maximum self-retained loss should it occur, while self-assumption contemplates dealing with a loss as if it were an unrecoverable expense.

It is apparent, therefore, that self-assumption can be safely utilized either by individuals or business enterprises only with respect to exposures presenting a relatively minor financial loss potential. If it is followed in connection with a risk of large financial potential, as it often is in the case of earthquake and flood exposures, the occurrence of a loss not provided for by reserves may seriously tax financial resources, tie up borrowing power otherwise needed for operational purposes, or even prove financially disastrous.

The Purchase of Insurance Coverage. Having decided upon protection in the form of purchased insurance, the business manager must then seek an insurance carrier. This does not usually present a difficult task, for insurance is traditionally more sold than bought, in the sense that the industry itself has had to go out and sell its product. Insurance salesmen, therefore, abound on every hand, each with his own plan for the broadest coverages at the very lowest of rates.

It will often be found, however, that despite assurances the local market simply cannot provide proper protection at equitable rates, and it then becomes necessary to go to the international market. Many insurance companies from the United States, England, Germany, and France, to mention a few, are pushing hard for markets overseas and are most anxious to do business wherever local regulations permit. Adequate insurance, with rare exceptions, is available anywhere in the world today.

The Insurance Policy as a Contract. An insurance policy is simply a contract between two parties. The essential elements, as of any contract, are:

1. Agreement—a meeting of the minds
2. Competent contracting parties
3. Legal objective
4. Consideration

One of the first steps in the preparation of a contract is the reaching of an agreement between the contracting parties. One of the parties offers to act, or to refrain from acting, in a certain prescribed manner if the other party will act or refrain from acting as agreed.

Contracts which are in violation of the law are invalid. Wagering contracts are in some countries considered illegal and, therefore, unenforceable except as may be specifically provided by law. An insurance contract, although in a sense a wager, is considered to be in the public good and therefore becomes an exception to the general rule concerning wagers.

In every valid contract there must be a consideration, the waiving or promising to waive of a legal right at the request of another. It is the price which the offerer demands for carrying out his part of the contract. In insurance the premium is the consideration.

It is important that an insurance contract cover an insurable interest in the life or property that is insured. A person cannot collect on a fire insurance policy unless he has a provable financial stake in the property insured and is then limited in his recovery to the amount of that interest.

The Insurance Market Media

It is important that the buyer entering the insurance market to purchase protection against loss be well acquainted with the general nature of the market and cognizant of the fact that several types of sellers operate therein. This is important because the different types of sellers offer different types of services, and, depending upon the specific operational and exposure conditions in individual instances, considerable advantage from the aspects of service, coverage, and premium cost is to be gained from dealing with the seller offering the organizational setup and type of contract that is best suited to the situation.

Likewise, the exploration of the market, the arrangement of proper policy contracts, and the maximum utilization of the service offered by the various types of insurers involve experience in the market and technical skills that are not normally possessed by the average insurance buyer. The buyer must therefore rely upon the services of purchasing media offered by the market in the form of representatives or agents of the insurers, or brokers who offer professional marketing services as representatives of the buyer.

Some knowledge of the basic similarities and differences existing between the various types of insurers and the relative positions of agents and brokers is advantageous to the insurance buyer.

Types of Insurers

There are two general types of insurance organizations or risk bearers. These are:

1. The proprietary organization, providing no membership and returning all profits to its investors.

2. The membership organization, operated in theory for the benefit of its members.

Capital Stock Companies. Any insurer must have adequate resources out of which to pay losses in the event that premiums collected prove inadequate. It is the capital which is invested in the stock company that provides a guaranty for the payment of these losses. In order that investors may be persuaded to bear a risk of this type, there must be an expectation of profit. This profit is in the form of a dividend which is paid on the capital stock if the operation is successful, that is, if the premiums received exceed the losses paid and the expenses incurred. Laws usually limit the activities of such companies, provide the conditions under which they may be organized, and prescribe the amount of capital required for various lines of insurance. The capital stock principle is quite suitable for insurance companies because it provides an inherently stable financial structure with exceptional ability to pay unexpected and catastrophic losses.

Lloyd's Associations. The membership of Lloyd's associations consists principally of subscribing individuals who carry on an insurance business and operate in syndicates which, in turn, are controlled by an underwriting agent who actually carries on the insurance business. The insurance written by the underwriting agent is divided up among the members of the syndicate he represents in accordance with a predetermined ratio. The proportion of the risk assumed by any individual underwriting member may vary considerably, depending upon that member's financial resources and individual wishes.

The makeup of Lloyd's permits extreme flexibility in the writing of insurance and provides a market for insurance that cannot be placed elsewhere or that requires special individual treatment. Admission to membership in Lloyd's is subject to a searching examination into the member's financial capability and requires a substantial deposit. Close control is afforded thereafter in the form of an annual audit into the affairs of each syndicate.

Insurance is placed at Lloyd's only by brokers designated by Lloyd's to represent them. The insurance written here not only comprises all ordinary forms of coverage but also caters to the unique and unusual demands of the insuring public as well. Lloyd's associations operate throughout the world and have an enviable record for fair and prompt claims adjustment.

Mutual Insurers. There are three types of mutual insurance carriers:

1. Full advance premium mutuals
2. Class or trade mutuals
3. Pure assessment mutuals

The advance premium mutual requires the full term premium in advance, with any premium remaining, after paying losses and costs of operation, being returned to the policyholder in the form of dividends. Depending upon the financial resources of the individual mutual association, nonassessable policies may be written. Many large life insurance companies are advance premium mutuals.

The class or trade mutual is organized for the purpose of interesting certain specialty trades, such as lumber dealers or farmers, in purchasing insurance from that association. The original concept of the Factory Mutual Group in the United States was that of a class mutual insuring only factories. These class mutuals have pioneered in developing safety and fire protection standards designed to prevent the occurrence of accidents and fires.

The pure assessment mutual, not commonly found outside the United States, is very simple in operation, being based upon the premise that every policyholder is a member of the association and the losses of the association are assessed upon each individual member in proportion to the amount of insurance that each member carries. The larger associations of this type maintain a reserve fund equivalent to the amount of claims expected and levy assessments adequate to maintain this fund at the established level.

Reciprocals. Although a reciprocal is similar in many ways, it is not identical with a mutual. Each policyholder insures each of the other policyholders; in other words, each is liable to the other. The reciprocal is managed by an "attorney-in-fact" whose powers are described in the power-of-attorney given him by each of the policyholders. A part of the premium for the insurance policy goes to the attorney-in-fact as pay for his services in managing the operations of the reciprocal and in developing new business; the balance of the premium is credited to the account of the policyholder. At the end of the year the losses paid and the reserve set aside to cover unpaid losses are charged against each policyholder in accordance with his proportionate share. In general, no dividends are actually paid the policyholder until the reserve funds reach a certain amount, which must be left with the reciprocal so long as that particular insurance is carried.

The reciprocal is a uniquely American institution seldom found outside the continental United States.

Agents and Brokers. Prior to the emergence of direct writing as an important factor in the selling of insurance, the contact between an insurer and the insured was through the agent or broker. Today, many insurance companies write business directly through representatives who are employees of the company and are paid a salary or commission, or both.

The function of agents and brokers varies in accordance with the laws of the country in which they operate, but in general an agent represents his principal, the insurance company, and is compensated by a commission which is a stipulated portion of the policy premium. The broker on the other hand is normally defined as representing the insurance buyer in the negotiation of the insurance contract. A broker usually deals directly with the company, and, despite the fact that he represents the buyer of insurance, his compensation also is paid as a percentage of the premium for the insurance policy.

The authority of an agent is limited by the "agency contract" between him and the company which he represents. The broker's authority, on the other hand, is much more strictly limited, since he is soliciting business on his own account, and a contract can exist only when he has placed the business with the insuring company.

There is a very wide range of competence and objectivity in the service part of the insurance business, and every agent or broker must, to some degree, perform in this respect. When an insured (or self-insured) desires the most effective insurance counseling or engineering attention, a top-grade consultant, who never acts as either broker or agent, is often brought into the picture. This is especially true where the company has competent and experienced insurance department personnel who are desirous of obtaining objectivity and independence in securing the best and most economical insurance program.

Local and World-wide Insurance Markets

Once the decision is made to protect an insurable risk by means of purchased insurance, it becomes necessary to select a market and to determine the forms of coverage and premium rates that are available. There are two major markets available to the purchaser of insurance:

Local Markets. These consist of insurance companies that are domiciled in the particular country where the risk is located and are licensed to write that particular form of coverage, as well as those insurance companies domiciled elsewhere but admitted to do business there. An "admitted" insurance company is one that has official governmental sanction and writes its policies in the language of the local country in accordance with local forms and at local rates, with premiums and losses payable in the local currency.

In some countries, such as Brazil and Argentina, only certain "national" companies may write the statutory coverages that are required by the social security or workmen's compensation laws of the country. Quite often the national government itself sets up and operates an insurance company in the form of a monopolistic system or as a combined reinsurance and/or coinsurance arrangement, whereby the governmental body shares in the premiums and losses on a predetermined and compulsory basis. These governmental bodies invariably regulate the rest of the industry and promulgate rules and rates governing its actions.

Foreign (International) Markets. To the buyer of insurance with a risk located outside the United States or England, these markets with their broad coverage forms may be attractive, particularly when these coverages are competitive, cost-wise, with locally obtained insurances. The London market is well known all over the world and, as has been seen in the above discussion of types of insurers, consists primarily of Lloyd's syndicates together with English companies. London is an excellent market for unusual forms of insurance, for "catastrophe" types of coverage, and for large-premium risks which can be written on a nontariff basis.

The United States foreign market consists primarily of two underwriting groups, the American Foreign Insurance Association (AFIA) and the American International Underwriters (AIU). The Insurance Company of North America has extensive overseas operations, and even some smaller U.S. companies have entered specialized fields, the American Motorists Insurance Company writing a general line, including boiler and machinery insurance, in Brazil, for example.

Although United States companies are likely to be "admitted" in the country in which they are doing business, the London Lloyd's group of syndicates is not likely to be "admitted" in the sense that it is specifically sanctioned by the government. Most countries do have laws permitting access to foreign markets under certain circumstances, some permitting insurance to be written freely, others drastically limiting the conditions under which foreign insurance may be bought.

In some countries only "admitted" insurance is tax-deductible as a business expense; this point should be checked before purchasing such insurance. In countries where workmen's compensation and/or automobile insurance are mandatory there may well be filing and premium tax requirements.

Types of Insurance Contracts

As indicated above, an insurance policy is a contract between the insured and the insurer. Accordingly, to effect a binding contract the terms of the agreement must be clear and understandable and express precisely the intent of the parties. Because the policies are subject to both legal interpretation as to meaning and regulatory definition as to scope, the terms of any policy must be in accord with the legal interpretations and regulations of the jurisdiction in which the coverage is to apply. This, of course, necessitates certain variations in policy forms in different governmental jurisdictions. Therefore, both in order to meet regulatory requirements and to avoid litigation, the insurance industry has developed standard forms of policy contracts for the major lines of coverage. Many of these are so drawn that in general terms they meet the requirements in most national jurisdictions. In other jurisdictions insurance is normally provided in a manner to meet local regulations and legal interpretations by appropriate modification of these standard contracts.

Therefore, in procuring coverage for the more common exposures to loss, the buyer of insurance normally has recourse to policies standardized either in the local jurisdiction or in the international insurance market. In practically all jurisdictions, modification or extension of these contracts is permitted to meet individual exposure situations. Where the desired result cannot be realized in this way, certain less standardized contracts may be used, or individually tailored contracts may be worked out between the insurer and insured.

On the basis of the division of insurable risks above outlined between damage or destruction of physical assets, loss of income, and legal liability to third parties, the available insurance contracts for personal and corporate protection generally include the following:

Damage or Destruction of Physical Assets. The more or less standard contracts in this category are:

Fire insurance
Ocean-Marine insurance
Machinery breakdown insurance
Crime insurance

These coverages can normally be extended or modified to meet individual exposure situations by including, e.g., various closely related exposures (such as explosion, collapse of building, vandalism, malicious mischief, and water damage) in the fire policy; various individual perils in the marine coverage; various types of coverage, such as explosion or breakdown, under the machinery policy; and individual coverages such as employee dishonesty, theft, burglary, or robbery under the crime coverage, or a limitation to money and securities or merchandise.

Fire and ocean-marine insurance are two of the oldest lines of coverage in existence, and since these exposures to loss are world-wide, standard forms of almost universal application have been developed. A brief discussion of these two coverages will, therefore, exemplify the type of standard coverage which can be obtained.

Fire Insurance. The standard basic fire insurance policy, as written in most countries, indemnifies the insured for all direct loss to the insured property by fire and lightning. The basic contract may be extended by an endorsement to cover many other perils. Other coverages commonly added to a fire insurance policy by endorsement include:

1. Explosion (by endorsement may include loss by explosion to boiler and pressure vessels and loss by explosion to the object itself)
2. Strike, riot, and civil commotion, including ensuing fire
3. Falling aircraft and objects falling therefrom
4. Vehicles, windstorm, hail, and smoke
5. Fire loss as the result of the burning of forests, prairies, and jungles
6. Earthquakes, including ensuing fire
7. Vandalism and malicious mischief (usually added only in connection with strike, riot, and civil commotion)

Losses due directly or indirectly to war and related causes are usually excluded from the coverage under the fire insurance policy and endorsements thereto. Losses due to spontaneous combustion, fermentation, and inherent defect are ordinarily excluded, as well as those arising from subterranean fire and burning by order of public authority.

Fire insurance coverage can normally be arranged under two types of coverage arrangements—specific and blanket.

Specific insurance is a form of coverage wherein a stipulated amount of insurance is applied to each structure, its contents, or part of its contents, and the amount of recovery in the event of loss is limited to the amount of insurance carried on the structure or contents items.

Blanket insurance is a form of coverage wherein two or more properties or other subjects of insurance are insured under a single item for one total amount of insurance. In the event of loss, the total amount of blanket insurance is applied to any one or more of the subjects insured. Therefore, even though the total amount of blanket insurance may be less than the total value of all the insured property, complete loss recovery at individual loss locations up to the total amount of insurance is possible, as the loss on any one item of property is only a partial loss under the entire contract.

Blanket insurance also has several other advantages. When a large number of policies are obtained from numerous insurance companies supplying specific insurance on buildings or contents at several locations, a great deal of effort is required to supervise the insurance properly. A blanket form of policy permits the insurance to be divided up among various companies by means of their participation in the same policy through their issuing identical contributing policies in various amounts covering the same property. Blanket insurance is especially valuable as a replacement to specific insurance on contents, as it permits the transfer of property from one location to another without affecting the insurance, thus eliminating some of the need to carry any excess insurance on the individual locations to cover fluctuations of value. In addition, with regard to insurance subject to the conditions of a coinsurance clause, it reduces to a minimum any serious consequence which might result from an error or omission in determining the value at any individual location, for although such error may represent a substantial proportion of an individual location value, it would represent a smaller portion of the total value of all locations.

Limited to the amount of the policy, fire insurance companies or underwriters are liable in the event of loss for the actual cash value of the insured property at the time of the loss, not exceeding the cost of repairing or replacing the property with comparable material within a reasonable time after loss. The value of property for loss adjustment and coinsurance purposes is normally the actual replacement cost of the property at the time of the loss less a reasonable amount of depreciation based on age and general physical condition.

In consideration of a reduced premium or special features in an insurance contract, the policy is frequently made subject to a coinsurance clause or its equivalent. Coinsurance clauses are policy conditions whereby the insured is required to carry insurance in an amount equal to a specified percentage of the actual cash value of the property insured at the time of loss or be penalized in the amount recovered. In the event that the insured fails to carry sufficient insurance to comply with this percentage, all partial losses are settled on the following basis:

$$\frac{\text{Amount of insurance carried}}{\text{Amount of insurance required}} \times \text{amount of loss} = \text{payment}$$

If sufficient insurance is carried, all losses are paid up to the amount of insurance in effect, with no coinsurance penalty.

In some countries the word "coinsurance" takes on slightly different meanings in addition to the customary interpretation of a coinsurance clause as being a method of compelling the purchaser to insure to a predetermined percentage of actual cash value or be penalized at the time of loss settlement for his failure to do so. Coinsurance, for example, can mean the contribution made by each of several insurers to the total amount insured. It can also mean the compulsory percentage of any loss (in effect a percentage deductible) which an insured must bear in many countries where insurance regulations prohibit insurance to full value and, consequently, full loss recovery.

Repair or replacement coverage, sometimes described as "new for old," is quite common in the United States, where it eliminates depreciation as a factor in loss settlement. In many other countries, however, such coverage is specifically prohibited by law, on the theory that insurance which could conceivably improve the financial status of the policyholder would be against the public interest; insurance should make the policyholder whole only in the sense that he was in the same relative position after settlement of the loss as he was before the loss occurred.

There are many common extensions of coverage that can be considered when exposure to loss warrants them.

Some of these extensions of coverage are:

1. Property in the open
2. Property of others
3. Debris removal
4. Loss clause
5. Subrogation waiver
6. Permit for alterations or additions
7. Liberalization clause
8. Vacancy and unoccupancy permit
9. Permit for removal of property
10. No control clause
11. Waiver of fallen building clause
12. Permit for other insurance
13. Waiver of written communications requirement

The provisions and terms of individual fire policies necessarily vary widely from country to country, but in general the aforementioned provisions apply.

Ocean-Marine Transportation Insurance. The purpose of a marine open cargo policy is to provide automatic coverage on all goods imported and/or exported. The basic section of the policy provides a limited type of coverage commonly supplemented by forms and endorsements setting forth more specifically the shipments of merchandise covered, perils insured against, the geographical limits, limits of liability, and other provisions designed to fit the specific need to the policyholder. The basic policy covers a limited number of causes of loss, for example, the perils of the sea, such as sinking, stranding, collision, fire, rovers sailing the seas, jettison, and criminal barratry of the master or mariners. General average and salvage charges are also covered. If the insured cargo is assessed to make up the loss or expense incurred in the effort to save a vessel or other cargo, the insurers will respond on behalf of the insured.

While the goods are on docks, wharves, or elsewhere on shore, and during land transportation, the policy covers the perils of collision, derailment, overturning of or other accidents to the carrying conveyance, fire, lightning, sprinkler leakage, aircraft damage, cyclones, hurricanes, earthquakes, floods, and collapse or subsidence of docks or wharves.

If desired by the insured, and if the underwriters are willing, coverage may be broadened to include additional risks such as theft, pilferage, nondelivery, and breakage. Commonly cargo insurance is provided against all risk of physical loss or damage from any external cause, subject to certain exclusions, such as loss due to delay, inherent vice, loss of market, war and related causes, strikes, riots, and civil commotion.

To supplement the marine cargo policy it is a general practice to issue a separate open policy insuring against risk of capture, seizure, destruction, or damage caused by war, warlike operations, or the prosecution of hostilities, or caused in the operation of sanctions under international agreement, whether before or after declaration of war and whether by a belligerent or otherwise, including the risk of aerial bombardment, floating or stationary mines, and stray or derelict torpedoes. A standard strike riot clause may be added to the policy to cover these otherwise excluded perils.

Other Less Standardized Policies. In many other lines of physical damage insurance, because of their limited usage and because individual localities and individual risks present less similarity in extent of exposure and coverage requirements, certain less standardized policy forms have been developed. Among these are earthquake and flood insurance; transportation insurance; insurance on automotive and contracting equipment; tidal wave insurance; protection and indemnity insurance, and similar lines. In many jurisdictions local markets are unable to handle the major exposures, and the major source of coverage is therefore the international market. In this market, although general guide policy forms exist, extensive tailoring of coverage conditions can normally be made to suit individual needs. In this category might also be mentioned expropriation insurance, which is coverage issued to reimburse for loss due to governmental expropriation of property. This insurance, however, is not normally available to a firm chartered and opening in a given jurisdiction. It is mainly used by a foreign firm establishing branches or subsidiaries in a jurisdiction where such exposure is felt to exist.

Difference of Conditions Coverage. In many instances neither the standard policies nor the less standard forms can be set up or adjusted so that they will fully meet the exposure potential of an individual insured. This may be due to local regulations or to the fact that certain categories of coverage are entirely unavailable in the local market. To meet this situation, the international market has made available a type of coverage known as "difference of conditions" insurance, which serves as a supplemental coverage to the basic insurance procured under the available policies by filling in the missing coverage for the exposures which could not be procured in the basic contracts. It is readily apparent that this type of coverage is valuable for the purpose of obtaining complete protection for the specific individual exposures where coverage under available normal contracts cannot be procured.

Loss of Income. The risk of loss of income is an insurable exposure which falls with great impact upon both personal and business activities.

The oldest of the specialized lines of insurance is that covering the loss of life. However, insurance covering accidental injury, physical disability, or sickness is also a long-established line of coverage which largely originated in the category of personal insurance. With the trend toward social insurance in recent years, however, there has been a marked tendency to link basic needs of protection against these exposures with business activities and with national social insurance legislation. Thus in most areas these formerly strictly personal insurance coverages have become an integral part of business insurance programs, with the business entity required to see that a certain minimum coverage is provided to workmen and their families either by the direct purchase of such coverage in the insurance market or by a contribution to the cost of such protection provided and handled by governmental bureaus. The degree to which this is practiced varies considerably by national jurisdiction, some requiring protection to the worker in only basic categories, others following a "cradle to grave" philosophy, under which benefits extend from accidental injury and hospital, medical, and surgical expenses to maternity, sickness, and death benefits, including not only the workman but his entire family. Recent developments in this field have been in its extension to cover loss of wages due to unemployment and its provision for old age retirement by means of pension plans. Even in jurisdictions where little or no positive requirements of social-type protection are set up by government legislation, labor organizations in the interest of the worker, and employers in the interest of employer-employee relationships and the retaining of personnel in competitive employment markets, have been instrumental in fostering the advance of coverage in these areas.

It can be seen, therefore, that in setting up its insurance program a business entity must carefully review local requirements in these personnel insurance fields and guide its insurance philosophy by legal requirements, employer-employee relationships, local practices, and its position in the employment market.

The trend of both government regulation and business practice toward arranging basic coverages for loss of income by workers has a very direct bearing on the matter of the worker's arrangement of his personally purchased insurance coverage in these lines. In arranging his own personal insurance he must first consider the extent and nature of the coverage provided to him by his employer and by the governmental social security. Normally such benefits are marginal, and, if he is in an economic position to do so, he can use those coverages as a base, supplementing them to adequacy by insurance purchased on his own behalf. In practically all lines of unemployment coverage, the insurance market offers policies designed to supplement the social or employer-furnished coverage.

Apart from the above, business entities must consider possible loss of income resulting from damage or destruction of physical operating properties. In this category, coverage can be purchased for loss of profits during shutdown caused by fire, boiler explosion, or machinery breakdown, and for most of the perils discussed above as physical damage exposures. This coverage is known by various names in the insurance markets, such as business interruption, earnings insurance, use and occupancy, or profits insurance. Basically, however, these vary only slightly, being designed to reimburse for loss of earnings during a period of physical disability of operating properties.

Along much the same lines, insurance coverage is available to cover extra expenses involved in continuing business activities during a period of disability of operating properties. This is commonly known as extra expense insurance.

Business entities may also protect themselves from loss arising from the death of valuable key employees by arranging life insurance on such employees with the business named as the beneficiary. This type is known as key man insurance. Partnerships also often find it advantageous to arrange life insurance on individual partners, with the other partners as beneficiaries, to the extent of providing them with funds to purchase the deceased partner's interest in the business in case of his death.

Loss Arising from Legal Liability to Third Parties. In all jurisdictions there exists a basic concept that one who negligently causes injury to the person of another, or damage to his property, is liable for restitution in the form of damage payments. In some jurisdictions the doctrine of damages is carried further to a point where liability for damages exists merely on the fact that damage was done, with little or no consideration being given to the negligence involved.

This condition, of course, gives rise to an insurable exposure to loss commonly known as third party liability.

As in the case of exposure to loss of earnings, social trends have greatly influenced the insurance of third party liability exposures. It has been recognized that the ability of the one causing the injury to pay the proper damage assessment has important social implications. Accordingly in most jurisdictions, it has been made mandatory that either certain exposures be insured through governmental agencies, included as a part of the national social insurance system, or purchased insurance be arranged by those whose operations have a recognized element of such third party liability exposure. Thus, in most jurisdictions, insurance coverage, or the establishment of financial responsibility to pay losses, is required for work injuries to employees (workmen's compensation) and for the operation of automotive equipment (automobile public liability). In arranging coverage in these categories, therefore, the insurance buyer must acquaint himself with, and give full recognition to, local requirements and regulations.

In instances where the required benefits or scope of coverage are marginal, supplementary coverage to raise the level of protection may be arranged in either local or international markets.

In those categories where regulations do not require the purchase of coverage for the third party liability exposure, the importance of providing voluntary protection against the financial loss inherent in such exposure cannot be overstressed. Practically every business action taken and every physical property owned produces its own source of liability. The realization of any one of these potentialities may have a crippling effect upon the entire future of the business. A judgment for damages can produce severe financial hardship upon any enterprise, no matter how large, and insurance against loss from a potential source of liability is usually considered to be even more important than insurance against loss to physical property.

Standardized third party liability policies intended to cover all such liability arising out of business operations, other than liability to injured workmen (workmen's compensation) and liability under the social security laws, have been designed and are widely used.

These standard policies normally contemplate coverage against all types of third party liability, except those specifically excluded, and may normally be extended to include liability assumed under contract, claims based upon occurrences as well as accidents, personal as well as bodily injuries, and other coverage refinements. In addition they generally provide defense facilities and expenses (apart from policy coverage limits) for all suits against the insured, whether justified or unjustified. This is an important benefit, since even suits with a favorable outcome require considerable time in preparation as well as annoyance and expense.

Because such policies are primarily designed for industry in general, they must be carefully examined in each instance and fitted to the insurable exposure needs and operational practices of the individual purchaser as well as to the local insurance requirements and regulations. If the first of these cannot be accomplished, the buyer normally has the opportunity of arranging separate individual contracts to insure exposures not covered, or of arranging "difference of conditions" coverage of the same nature as that discussed above under the physical damage exposures.

In the field of personal insurance, automobile liability coverage is normally and prudently purchased, even if not required by local regulatory statutes. It is usually readily available, therefore, in the insurance markets under standardized policy contracts. Coverage for other personal third party liabilities, however, is by no means so universally purchased. Thus, although standard forms and markets for such liabilities have been arranged in many jurisdictions, insurance protection on an individual level is difficult to obtain in others. It can, however, be normally obtained under special policy forms either in the local or international market. Since the incidence of high-valued third party liability loss is as pertinent to the individual as to the business enterprise, this phase of insurance protection should be very carefully considered in arranging a personal insurance program in any jurisdiction.

As in the case of the physical damage insurance discussed above, individual exposures of an unusual type, and those for which insurance coverage is not widely written in this field, can normally be covered either in the local or in the international insurance market by specially drawn contracts or the use of less standardized policy forms.

Additional Insurance Coverages to Be Considered. In addition to the three major divisions of insurance coverage described above, a company operating exclusively in a given country, trading between countries or having branch or divisional operations in a number of countries, must give consideration to certain lines of insurance required or regulated by local governmental units. It must also consider specialized types of coverage which, although not required by local regulations, may be valuable for the protection of company financial and physical assets, or necessary for contractual arrangements.

In this general category, the following coverages are important but by no means all-inclusive: social insurance, subject to local regulations and requirements; key man insurance; export credit insurance; and bonds required as security for contractual performance.

Social Insurance. In many countries, an employer's liability for injury of employees and workmen in the course of their work is a part of the social security system administered by the various national or state governments—not to be confused with the American social security system. In most areas where this system applies, subscription to the social security provisions is obligatory for both employer and employees, and no alternative for providing basic benefits for work accidents or occupational diseases is available.

The obligatory social security system in some countries is divided into two parts, (1) illness-maternity insurance, and (2) insurance of accidental injuries and occupational illnesses.

The illness-maternity portion of the fund is usually on a contributory basis, being proportioned in some manner between employer and employee with benefits provided for the employee and his immediate family. Contributions to the accident and occupational illness portion of the fund are assessed against the employer alone. In many countries, an employer's liability for the injury of employees and workmen in the course of their work may be insured by certain "national" insurance companies.

The provisions of workmen's compensation and social security laws vary so widely by country that specific statements cannot be made. In general, it can be said that the coverage is of a statutory nature and the requirements of the various state and national laws are quite specific in detail.

Key Man Insurance. A business relies heavily upon the manager of its overseas branches and often upon other overseas personnel as well. These key men are in positions of responsibility where their continued existence may mean the success of the business; their death or permanent disability may result in serious financial problems. These men may have special skills, knowledge, or experience peculiar to the business employing them, and as such they represent an asset of considerable insurance value. Insurance on the lives of these key personnel is used to offset in part the financial loss to the corporation which would result from their untimely death or total disability.

Export Credit Insurance. Exporters in the United States are able to purchase insurance covering credit shipments abroad. Policies covering both political and commercial export credit risks are available from a group of private insurance companies forming the Foreign Credit Insurance Association and working closely with the Export-Import Bank. The Export Bank assumes the political risk and shares in the commercial risk with the insurance carriers. Similar protection against political and commercial risk is offered by institutions of most European nations.

Bonds. An expanding market for surety bonds has resulted directly from the increase in construction in newly industrialized countries. This coverage, hardly available at all until just recently, is finding ready acceptance and has resulted in several carriers developing the facilities for writing this very specialized line.

A surety bond is simply a guarantee that he who contracts to perform in a certain prescribed manner will perform his duties as promised, the guarantee being made by a third party, usually a professional bonding company, for a fee or premium. The bond in no way reduces the responsibility of the contracting parties; it merely serves to guarantee performance in the form of money reimbursement in the event of failure to perform as specified.

Regulations

Regulations relating to the conduct of the insurance business exist in practically all governmental jurisdictions. Regulations are necessary because the insurance business supplies an essential service to the economy and furnishes protection to the economic status of the insured. Thus, it follows that its usefulness will be increased in proportion to the degree to which the benefits of insurance protection can be extended to all industry in the economy and all members of the population. Regulations designed primarily to certify the solvency of the insurance companies and protect the policyholders must also have the supplemental feature of encouraging the extension of insurance services to the greatest possible segment of the industry and population.

The first and greatest service which legislative regulations and administrative procedures can accomplish toward this result is that of developing the confidence of the population in the insurance carriers by making certain that all insurers organized within the jurisdiction or admitted to do business therein are financially solvent. It is essential to have strong companies in the insurance industry. An insurance policy has no intrinsic value; it is merely a promise to pay, and this promise is of no value if the firm making it is unable or unwilling to make payment. Many insurance buyers are unable to distinguish good contracts offered by good companies from poor contracts offered by poor companies. Regulation of insurance companies thus goes a long way toward assuring the buyer of insurance that the company he selects will be able to meet his just losses.

Any regulatory activities which assist in the prompt settlement of all legitimate claims and resist the payment of any fraudulent or unfounded claims will tend to increase the public confidence in the commodity of insurance and to encourage its purchase. It can probably be safely stated that no single element will tend to disturb the spread of the insurance business more than the insolvency of an insurance company or a general tendency among companies to resist the payment of just claims. The regulatory authorities assist in the spread in the use of insurance facilities by their policy of licensing insurance agents and brokers in the territory they serve.

If the administrative regulations are so drawn that only companies of sound financial standing are permitted and only persons of high character who have demonstrated their knowledge of insurance coverages by proper examinations are allowed to act as insurance solicitors and agents, unsound practices and misunderstandings concerning the extent and nature of the insurance coverage, which tend to destroy the confidence of the public in insurance companies, will be eliminated.

It becomes important, therefore, for the buyer of insurance to ascertain the degree to which insurance companies and insurance practices in general are regulated in the area where he is contemplating the purchase of insurance, for the proper regulation of rates and policy forms tends to promote the healthy growth of the insurance industry. Regulation, on the other hand, which is overly political or dictatorial tends to stifle the insurance industry by suppressing competition and discouraging the development of broader forms of coverage at more equitable rates.

Considerations in Setting up an Insurance Program

Every businessman needs insurance. All too often the purchase of insurance is not given the careful consideration it requires. Any businessman owes it to himself and to his company to determine exactly what kind of insurance he needs, why, and in what quantity. A business stands to lose so much in so many ways that it is courting bankruptcy if it underinsures. On the other hand, if it is overinsured or does not get the best premium rates, its cost of operation will be so high that its competitive situation with respect to other companies offering a similar product is worsened. There are four principal points to consider in seeking adequate insurance:

1. The kind of hazards to which the business or the individual is exposed
2. The degree to which these hazards can be controlled or reduced
3. What losses can be taken as business risks; what the business can accumulate for a reserve fund of its own; and what it must cover by purchased insurance
4. How to buy insurance at the lowest cost for those losses the business cannot assume or insure itself

As stated above, the risks normally faced divide generally into these categories:

1. Damage to, or destruction of, owned buildings, machinery, and equipment
2. Loss of earnings or extra expenses resulting from production equipment down time
3. Liability to third parties for personal injury or for damage to, or destruction of, their property (including operation of equipment, workmen's compensation, and property of others under the insured's care, custody, or control)
4. Political risks
5. Commercial credit risks

The buildings, structures, and equipment a business depends upon are in constant danger of damage or destruction. Hazards include fire, windstorm, flood, earthquake, vandalism, machinery breakdown, and many others. The calculation of insurable values of property is a relatively simple matter; the matter of calculating the extent of financial loss which claims and accidents may produce is entirely different. There is no way to determine beforehand how much a third party will be awarded for bodily or personal injury, nor can the cost of damage or destruction of another's property be accurately assessed. Courts in many countries are granting increasingly higher awards for bodily injury, and property values (including loss of use) continue to rise. Therefore, in arranging an insurance program, the following analysis should be undertaken:

1. Prepare a schedule of all physical properties, indicating type of construction, location, and exposure to hazards. Each item should include an estimate of the cost to replace it and the extent to which it is depreciated. Appraisals made for tax purposes are also valuable in preparing this schedule.
2. A second list should be prepared showing all inventories, bank deposits, and other liquid assets which present an exposure to loss not only by physical destruction but also arising from employee dishonesty, burglary, robbery, and similar "crime" exposures.
3. A third list should be made showing possible exposure to loss of company assets resulting from the payment of liability claims arising out of damage to property of others and bodily injury resulting from the operations of the company or acts of its employees. This will include injury to employees sustained in the course of their employment.
4. Any company engaged in export trade with foreign countries faces both political and export credit risks. An evaluation should be made of this exposure

to loss, and if it is found significant, arrangements should be made to insure it wherever it is feasible to do so. Both United States and European Common Market exporters are able to insure medium-term (one to five years) as well as short-term (up to one year) credit risks.

When properly completed, the above three lists will indicate the type and severity of important losses. It is important to analyze each risk carefully and then decide in which of the following three ways it should be handled:

1. Accepted as a business risk
2. Self-insured, with a reserve set aside to meet any losses
3. Insurance purchased to cover it

Normally it is best to deal with certain small recurring losses in the first way. Insurance companies normally operate on a permissible loss ratio only a little in excess of 50 percent, the balance being required to pay commissions and overhead expense and allow a small margin of profit. It is therefore reasonable to expect that the loss payments will average about one-half of the premium, so it is not economically feasible to insure against small losses. For example, the hazard of fire is generally insured against, but damage from burnout and breakdown of small machine tools, electric motors, and so forth is assumed as a business expense.

The second case covers those potential losses which are too large to assume as a business expense but, because it may cost too much or may not be available to cover them, purchased insurance is not feasible. Many catastrophes which result in loss of property, such as earthquake, floods, hailstorms, and other hazards in certain geographical areas, thus do not lend themselves to the economical purchase of insurance. They are of sufficient magnitude, however, to preclude assumption without self-insurance reserve funds. To a large extent the availability of liability coverages varies with the exposures inherent in the type of business operation being conducted. These types of exposures can be handled prudently on a self-insurance basis by building reserves which are set up in accordance with expected frequency and severity of loss tables.

For other risks, the possibility of coverage by means of purchased insurance should be considered.

INTERNATIONAL BASIC ECONOMY CORPORATION—A PATTERN IN INTERNATIONAL DEVELOPMENT

Robert W. Purcell

The Problem

A characteristic of almost all developing countries is that living standards for the bulk of the people are low. To bring them up to the level enjoyed in the mature nations of the Free World would, of course, be a tremendous task involving broad social, political, and economic advances that would take years to accomplish.

The fact remains, however, that something can be done, and by private enterprise, to improve these living standards appreciably. Supplant outmoded, inefficient methods of producing and distributing food with the modern techniques we take for granted, introduce new ways of building low- and medium-cost homes, bring savings out of mattresses and real estate speculation and channel them into productive investment—do these things, and the result will be a better life for millions.

What is needed is a combination of capital, management, and technical knowledge often lacking in whole or in part in developing lands. It was to provide this combination that the International Basic Economy Corporation (IBEC) of New York was established.

The IBEC Approach

The idea that there was a place for a company like IBEC can be traced to the experience of Nelson A. Rockefeller, first as a businessman dealing with Latin American interests and then, during the war, as Coordinator of Inter-American Affairs in Washington. It seemed to him that Latin American

Mr. Purcell is Board Chairman of International Basic Economy Corporation.

efforts toward progress could be accelerated if U.S. capital, management, and techniques could be introduced in such basic fields as food and housing. The proper vehicle, he felt, would be a company set up specifically for this purpose, and operated on a businesslike, profit-making basis.

Thus in 1947 Mr. Rockefeller and his brothers joined in the establishment of IBEC. Initial investments were in food production and were concentrated in Venezuela and Brazil. In the years that followed, the company's investments spread to other fields and to some three dozen countries.

In starting a business or making an investment, IBEC's policy has always been to seek sound, profit-producing ventures that fit into the basic economy of the country concerned. IBEC considers basic economy to be that part which is closest to the public, such as food and shelter.

There are other policies that should be mentioned:

• Wherever feasible, it is desirable to invite local investors in the country concerned to participate in a new investment. Experience has shown that such investors can make an important contribution through their knowledge of local conditions. It is also good public relations. Similarly, it is IBEC policy to employ nationals of the foreign country involved to the fullest extent possible.

• It is desirable to hold a majority interest in a new investment. This ensures management remaining in IBEC hands, permits greater flexibility, and minimizes controversy.

• Where a new investment calls for highly specialized technical know-how, a company having this knowledge may be invited to participate, thus providing a three-way ownership—IBEC, another U.S. or foreign company, and local investors.

• There is nothing sacred about a successful investment—or an unsuccessful one. If a subsidiary or investment is doing well and an opportunity arises for a capital gain, it may be taken in whole or in part. On the other hand, the parent company is prepared to cut its losses in an unsatisfactory investment and put the money into something else. Thus, nonrecurring gains and losses are a way of life for IBEC.

• While the emphasis remains on investing in developing areas, it is proper to enter more mature countries with enterprises that fill an obvious need—hence, for example, poultry-breeding farms and plants to make automation devices in Western Europe.

• Finally, IBEC at present is confining itself mainly to the fields of food production, processing, and distribution; poultry breeding; housing; mutual funds; and manufacturing. Those are the businesses that IBEC knows best. But it does not necessarily close the door to anything else that fits its philosophy of investing in basic economy at a profit.

IBEC at Work

Company activities may be summarized as follows:

Food Processing and Distribution. IBEC had, at the end of 1964, 24 supermarkets in Venezuela, 11 in Argentina, and 3 in Peru; it also was still managing a supermarket chain in Italy, which it founded and sold.

In Brazil, IBEC has Latin America's largest hybrid seed corn producer. It controls a tuna-packing plant in Puerto Rico, a sugar mill and plantation in Peru, and a coffee-processing company in Venezuela, while holding a half interest in a soluble coffee plant in El Salvador. It has a minority investment in a Venezuelan milk company.

Poultry. In 1964, IBEC completed acquisition of Arbor Acres Farm, Inc., one of the largest poultry-breeding companies of the United States, with subsidiaries and affiliates in many countries of South America, Europe, Asia, and Africa.

Housing. The company is a major builder of low- and medium-cost housing outside the continental United States. In Puerto Rico, IBEC has built and sold more than 10,000 homes. Additional projects are under way there, and large housing developments are being built in Peru and Chile. IBEC also operates shopping centers in Puerto Rico and Venezuela.

Mutual Funds. IBEC established and manages mutual funds in Brazil, Colombia, Argentina, and Chile. The company is a partner in a growing insurance brokerage business overseas.

Industrial. IBEC's Bellows-Valvair Division, headquartered in Akron, Ohio, is a leading producer of hydraulic and pneumatic devices and valves used in automation. Plants are located in many areas of the United States, Canada, and Europe. The V. D. Anderson Company Division in Cleveland manufactures vegetable oil mill machinery and equipment for the chemical and rubber industries. Other substantial IBEC investments in the industrial field are in Industrias Integradas, manufacturing household appliances in Venezuela, and Trimak, producer of a unique lightweight three-wheel transport vehicle in Spain. In Thailand, one IBEC subsidiary manufactures and designs original textiles, and another, using part of this material, designs and manufactures clothing; some of IBEC's Design-Thai women's wear is sold in U.S. stores.

The selection of a project for investment may come in any number of ways. IBEC's decision to enter the supermarket business abroad was an outgrowth of an early project involving the wholesaling of food in Venezuela. Because the wholesale operation was not achieving its objective of paring food costs, the decision was made to move into the retail area to ensure lower food costs to the consumer. The success of the first operation led to the establishment of what is today a nationwide chain of food stores.

The achievements of the supermarket operation in Venezuela led IBEC to look to other areas of the world where food merchandising would obviously benefit by the introduction of new techniques. A consultant was dispatched to survey Western Europe in 1956, and he returned with the recommendation that one of the most likely areas was Northern Italy. The result was the establishment of Supermarket Italiani S.p.A. in Milan.

IBEC's role in building up a modern dairy industry in Venezuela may also be traced to its early days. Together with an American milk company, IBEC was surveying Venezuela with the idea of entering the reconstituted milk business. It encountered a group of Venezuelan dairymen operating a small plant in Valencia. As a result of discussions with this group, the reconstituted milk plan was shelved, and a new company was formed to enter the fresh milk business.

IBEC went into the low-cost housing business as an obvious way to achieve its objective of raising living standards. A method for the mass production of homes was developed by IBEC, using precast concrete walls and roof, and the building operation was begun in several areas.

The introduction of the mutual-fund concept overseas was a natural extension of know-how of IBEC people who had engaged in the business in the United States. It was obvious that in many of the underdeveloped countries, a large percentage of savings was not being put to productive use and that a mutual fund could channel much of this money into local development, to the benefit of all.

Ideas leading to investments are sometimes brought to IBEC by outsiders, but in large measure they are the result of recommendations by staff members on the scene in foreign countries or a logical extension of an interest already pursued by the company.

In IBEC's present organizational structure there are, just below the chairman of the board and the president, nine vice presidents. Five of these are the operating heads of the various groups: food and agriculture, poultry, housing, mutual funds, and manufacturing. The Bellows-Valvair and the V. D. Anderson Company Divisions, which fall into the industrial group, also are led by vice presidents. There are, furthermore, vice presidents for finance and miscellaneous projects. Overseas there were, at the end of 1964, seven regional vice presidents.

Directly beneath the operating vice presidents are one or more assistants who have become thoroughly conversant with the field involved and are thus able to deal with many of the day-to-day affairs of the section and to handle the work in the absence of the vice president. Often, these young assistants are selected, after sufficient grounding, to head IBEC offices abroad.

Able administrators for overseas spots are sometimes inherited by IBEC through the acquisition of a company. In cases such as supermarkets, where specialized training is required, a number of approaches are used. Promising young men, both Americans and nationals of the country involved, may be sent to a Massachusetts supermarket chain. Sometimes, as in Buenos Aires, selected people will be sent to another IBEC food operation, perhaps in Peru or Italy, to acquire on-the-job experience. The fact is that the company has had remarkable success in making efficient employees of local people. When the Milan supermarkets were opened, a number of key spots were filled with former waiters whom the American manager had come to know during the period when the company was being organized.

Finding top men to undertake the organization of a supermarket chain abroad—which calls for everything from site selection to the procurement of inventory—is not easy. When the Milan company was established, the manager brought with him an American without previous supermarket experience who subsequently proved himself so well that he was placed in charge of setting up the Supermarkets Italiani chain in Florence. A new American manager then took charge in Milan, and the former manager moved on to Buenos Aires.

In the poultry operation, new personnel receive training at Glastonbury, Connecticut, by Arbor Acres Farm. As for mutual funds, the operation in Brazil has served as a training ground for a number of men now assigned to work with funds in other countries. New personnel hired by the housing division are normally groomed in Puerto Rico.

Benefits for All

In many cases, the achievements of IBEC—the benefits to the local economy from its efforts—have been easy to measure. In Venezuela, retail food prices declined approximately 15 percent after the opening of the supermarkets. In Italy, the cost to the housewife of many foods dipped as much as 25 percent. The same pattern is discernible elsewhere. It is also to be noted that supermarkets, providing as they do an assured mass market for foodstuffs, serve to stimulate local food production and processing. When IBEC opened its first store in Venezuela in 1949, for instance, some 80 percent of a long list of foods had to be imported. Today, the great bulk of these items are produced in Venezuela.

The Venezuelan milk operation, in addition to making fresh milk available to tens of thousands of Venezuelans, likewise provided farmers with an important outlet for their production. The company has played a significant role in encouraging the use of modern methods of milk production, testing, and distribution. It pioneered the use in Venezuela of the paraffinated milk carton and the idea of home delivery.

The startling growth in the use of hybrid corn seed in Brazil demonstrates the job that has been done by the IBEC subsidiary there. While seed production has risen steadily, supply consistently runs behind demand as more and more farmers learn of the yields that are possible with special seed.

While the poultry operations are still quite new, it is readily apparent that their effect overseas will be striking. The farms set up by IBEC and Arbor Acres are stocked exclusively with the finest strains of fowl developed in the United States for the production of laying hens and meat-type birds. As these farms sell day-old chicks or fertile eggs to local farmers, the result is the building up of flocks of chickens vastly superior to those formerly available. With increased production, an important new source of protein is becoming available to people for whom poultry has been a luxury.

The benefits to be derived from making low- and medium-cost housing available to meet the enormous demand in developing countries are obvious. Of paramount importance is this fact: provide a people with good housing and you have taken a giant step toward strengthening a whole nation. Speaking of the need for housing in Latin America, Rodman C. Rockefeller, vice president in charge of the housing group, has said: "The middle class in Latin America has been denied the normal material rewards that the middle class expects in the United States. While the Latin American middle class is loyal to the Western concept of government, this puts a tremendous strain on its loyalty."

The mutual fund approach to investing offers large and small investors the opportunity to participate in a diversified, professionally managed portfolio of securities and thus to share in the growth of the economy. Recognizing that the establishment of mutual funds in countries overseas would provide an effective means of mobilizing savings, IBEC launched its first fund in Brazil in

1957 and followed up with similar ones in Argentina, Chile, and Colombia. The growth of these funds demonstrates that they are achieving their purpose. It should be noted that, in addition to investing in local securities, the funds may assist in financing new industries through the purchase of convertible debentures and preferred stock. Also, an important result of fund operations is that ownership of local industry is broadened, with special emphasis on the small investor.

IBEC's industrial activities are far-flung and serve countless manufacturing and processing fields. As the sale of Bellows-Valvair devices is extended to more and more countries, it is plain that manufacturing productivity will rise, and with increased efficiency will come lower prices. V. D. Anderson equipment is used in scores of countries, making available the newest developments in specialized food processing.

The Economic Climate

While investing abroad can be profitable and can accomplish much that is good, it can also be a hazardous business. Foreign exchange fluctuations, political developments, the outcries of Communists and ultranationalists, the difficulties in breaking down traditional, old-fashioned ways of doing business, the question of finding financing in countries where capital is tight, and the shortage of mortgage money in nations desperately in need of housing—all of these are things a foreign investor must try to cope with. Some of them may be anticipated, while others simply cannot.

The economic climate for overseas investment, in sum, is scarcely ever just right. Nevertheless, IBEC has learned to live in varying climates, the job made easier because, demonstrably, its projects are of benefit to the countries concerned.

FINANCING NEW VENTURES IN THE DEVELOPING ECONOMY OF MEXICO

Bruno Pagliai

The Basic Problem: Scarcity of Equity Capital

Entrepreneurs in Mexico are faced with a shortage of equity money. Although there are about one hundred industrial stocks listed on the Mexico City Stock Exchange, fewer than twenty are actively traded. Historically, Mexican capitalists have preferred land as an investment. Those who invest in securities often prefer bonds to common stocks. The growing middle class has not yet recognized the advantages of channeling savings into common stocks, and so the market is narrow and thin.

A very high proportion of Mexican corporations is closely held. Consequently, there is no floating supply of the majority of common stocks. These circumstances create a vicious circle which we recognize and which we are trying to break. Without a large following and a broad market, many entrepreneur-capitalists see no personal advantage in making a public offering of common stock in order to create a floating supply. Without a floating supply available, it is impossible to get a large following of investors and create a broad, orderly security market.

In contrast to practices prevailing in Mexico, my associates and I have chosen in the cases of two industrial Mexican companies to make stock available to the investing public. We do not regard this as pure altruism. We *do* think it is enlightened self-interest, which is also in the best interests of the Mexican economy and the Mexican investor. Ours, however, is still a minority opinion.

The common pattern in Mexico is for an entrepreneur to finance his new venture with his own capital together with what equity money he can obtain

Mr. Pagliai is an industrialist and banker.

from relatives, friends, and business associates. It is safe to assert that many Mexican firms lack adequate equity capital. In order to meet their needs, they are often forced to resort to short-term loans. With all liquid capital in short supply, which is characteristic of rapidly developing economies, lenders who supply this disguised equity money in the form of short- and intermediate-term loans demand and get high interest and stringent guarantees of payment. My associates and I consider this short-sighted and believe that it retards the development of the necessary securities market and of the economy.

Bond Financing Can Play a Very Useful Role

The National Securities Commission of Mexico discourages, as being excessive, leverage beyond 50 percent. That is, it prefers that the total funded debt and long-term loans do not exceed the amount of the capital and reserve (i.e., surplus) accounts. Inasmuch as the typical Mexican securities buyer is more interested in income from interest and dividends than in eventual capital gains through the plowback of earnings, this is probably a sound rule under Mexican conditions, though obviously it tends to inhibit market movement and reduce the interest in the market.

Although coupon rates of 8, 9, 10, and even 12 percent are paid on bonds, which makes bond financing expensive compared to stock issuance, earnings in a rapidly developing economy for a well-managed company can and should be high enough to cover the interest, amortization, and service charges without posing an insuperable problem of managing cash flow. It is common practice in Mexico to issue bonds with a ten-year maturity and with a provision for amortizing them by lot during their term, so that there is a declining balance outstanding. If the proceeds of the bond issue are invested in slowly wasting earning assets having a long useful life, bond financing, despite the high temporary cost, can often be the method that is in the best interest of the stockholders in the long run.

Private placement of long-term notes with international or governmental lending institutions, or with foreign banks or insurance companies, is formally different from selling a bond issue through an underwriting, but it is effectively equivalent. Provided the proceeds are invested in long-lived earning assets, the borrowing corporation, even if the local currency has a long record of devaluations, does not seriously endanger itself by promising to pay interest and principal in U.S. dollars. The reason this is safe in a developing economy is somewhat complex, but it can be stated quite simply. Inflation is endemic in both developed and developing countries and has been since about 1500 A.D. There is little in the policy of modern governments, or in the philosophy of most labor leaders and many schools of economists who are influential advisers to governments and labor unions, to support a belief that an enduring trend toward deflation is in near-term prospect. Consequently, it is reasonable to suppose that both the replacement cost and the residual earning power of the assets will be greater in both local currency and dollars than the declining balance of the loan, even if made in dollars. This explains, at least partially, why the historical record shows that seasoned Mexican stocks of industrial companies have increased in value in *constant pesos* despite internal inflation, and in *constant dollars* despite devaluations of the peso vis-à-vis the U.S.

dollar and the erosion of the purchasing power of the dollar in the United States. That is, they have performed their investment function of providing a complete hedge against devaluation and inflation and of providing a rising real income and real capital. In nominal, or current, pesos and dollars, which are what we earn and spend day after day, results have been excellent.

The Evolution of Tubos de Acero de México, S.A.

Some years after the conclusion of World War II, we systematically analyzed the attractiveness of new and necessary Mexican industries. We concluded that one of the most immediate needs was for seamless steel pipe used in the expanding petroleum, petrochemical, and process industries. With Mexican and some foreign, chiefly Italian, capital, we incorporated TAMSA on January 30, 1952. Compagnia Tecnica Internazionale, S.P.A., Milan, Italy, were employed as construction engineers and remain as technical advisers. Manufacturing commenced on a pilot basis in August, 1954. Table I gives appropriate statistics.

TABLE 1. PRODUCTION, SALES, AND EARNINGS, 1955–1961

Year	Production, metric tons	Sales, $	Net profit, $
1955	35,886	8,107,200	592,837
1956	49,664	12,149,200	724,497
1957	73,058	19,829,600	1,783,783
1958	98,570	27,190,480	2,416,232
1959	108,872	28,277,040	3,151,700
1960	123,181	30,754,400	4,237,228
1961	109,043	28,260,000	4,139,821
1962	120,150	31,558,800	4,549,440
1963	127,140	35,562,960	4,302,720

Because TAMSA could qualify as a new and necessary industry, it was granted certain tax exemptions. Among them were exemption from the Mexican Federal Government share of the 3 percent gross sales tax; exemption from import duties; and partial exemption from the corporation income tax. These tax savings permitted plowing back a larger share of gross profit than would otherwise have been possible. Such savings are important to new ventures in a developing economy because of the high cost of money, as are the maximum permissible rates of depreciation of equipment.

It is apparent from Table 1 above that the growth production could not have been financed out of retained earnings in a country in which the investment public is relatively small and current-income–minded. TAMSA management has followed a financing policy which it believes to be consistent with local conditions and also enlightened in the sense that it is designed to help create a money market that Mexican entrepreneurs sorely need. One of the problems has been that the company has had to play the role of banker to its customers, extending credit on very liberal terms to purchasers. Consequently, it has had to borrow short-term money from *financieras* (a type of industrial bank) at rates as high as 12 percent. While it will probably always find it wise to meet temporary needs by commercial borrowing operations, the time is approaching when a further increase in capitalization can reduce or eliminate what amounts to dependence on renewals of commercial loans for financing receivables.

TABLE 2. EARNINGS AND TOTAL LIABILITIES OF TAMSA
In U.S. dollars

	1955	1957	1959	1961	1962	1963
Total current liabilities	5,779,088	13,927,727	15,604,517	15,496,848	19,865,277	21,383,803
Long-term debt	3,000,000	10,818,525	10,406,501	8,451,436	4,778,117	6,207,820
Common stock	9,280,000	13,600,000	16,000,000	22,080,000	22,080,000	22,080,000
Surplus accounts reserves	564,261	883,203	1,459,771	2,388,346	3,865,176	5,251,784
Net earnings	592,837	1,783,783	3,151,701	4,139,822	4,549,459	4,510,735*

* This figure is after deduction of US$419,760 provision for employee profit sharing, which went into effect for the first time in December, 1963.

The first of the major pioneering operations was the offer in 1957 of US$3 million six-year 5 percent dollar bonds, amortized by the drawing by lot of $750,000 principal amount on June 30, in each year 1960–1962, and callable at a descending premium in whole or part on December 31, 1958, or any subsequent year. These bonds participate in earnings up to a maximum interest rate of 9 percent per annum, based upon a sliding scale, when earnings exceed 5 percent per annum on the common stock, as they consistently have. This yield has naturally made them attractive to American investors, who expect no such return on well-secured mortgage bonds of profitable domestic companies.

Mexican law forbids the issuance of bonds or other securities in foreign currencies. (The stocks of the Mexican Light and Power Company pay their cash dividends in Canadian currency, and the preferred is callable in Canadian dollars, but this is a Canadian corporation.) Yet, in 1957, memories of the 1954 devaluation were fresh, and fears were widespread that another devaluation might occur. Nevertheless, the company secured the necessary approvals to base the payment of the interest and principal and participation in profits in U.S. dollars at the rate of $1 to 12.50 pesos, irrespective of what the actual market value of the peso or official exchange rate might be during the life of the issue. As it happens, no devaluation has occurred, and none is expected. Nevertheless, even if we had had a devaluation, the holders would have been secure, for, as I have pointed out, our plant can produce and sell its products profitably at or below world prices.

From the beginning of operations, we had listed our shares on the Bolsa de Valores in Mexico City and Monterrey, and when the Guadalajara Bolsa was formed we also listed them there. There was a limited amount of trading, but the floating supply was small. We felt that this was bad for Mexico, bad for the financial and investing community, and bad for the company, which would have to go to the public from time to time to finance expansion. It was therefore determined in 1960 that the time had come when we should make a reasonable floating supply available. In July, 1960, we offered 100,000 shares of TAMSA common at 190 pesos per share through a syndicate headed by Intercontinental, S.A. This was the first secondary offering of shares made in Mexico, the shares having been released from the portfolios of our larger stockholders, who were convinced that this was a prudent action, even though it might cost them some future capital gains. The offering itself was successful. More important, this example has now been followed by a number of other companies, so that more securities are now available to investors. If imitation is the sincerest form of flattery, we have indeed been flattered. Because of the interest of Americans in our stock. we also arranged in 1960 to issue American depositary receipts for our shares, with Morgan Guaranty Trust and Banco Nacional de México acting as our agents.

Our most recent move has been to make the first true stock split in Mexico. It has long been the practice, followed by TAMSA itself, to capitalize earned surplus and pay a stock dividend in lieu of or supplementary to cash dividends. These, however, are not splits. In 1962, we split each outstanding 100-peso par value share into one Class A and one Class B share each of 50 pesos par value. The Class A is what Americans would regard as a true common stock, having full voting power and residual rights to assets and earnings after the rights of the Class B have been satisfied. The Class B (without going into the technicalities of Mexican law) can be regarded as a preferred stock or a preference common with limited voting rights, a cumulative 9 percent dividend, and a right to share equally with the Class A in any further distribution.

We have, of course, done the usual things in a developing country. As mentioned, we borrow against our receivables and make commercial loans against our general credit. We have also sold securities and long-term paper to government financial agencies and to institutional securities, for we qualify all our issues for the "Legal List."

If some of the things we have done have been innovations in Mexico, they have been carefully worked out in advance, and when setting about the execution of our plans we have been very careful to follow through in details. We have, of course, our specific problems of complying with Mexican law, Mexican customs, and Mexican money market conditions. While differing in detail, these are no different in principle from those of entrepreneurs in other countries. We believe that TAMSA is an important demonstration that it is possible to raise venture and later loan capital for a new firm.

The Joint Venture Road to New Venture Financing

Among the industries that Mexico has wanted and needed is aluminum refining. My associates and I decided to supply this need. However, it was obvious to us that we had neither the amount of capital nor the technical knowledge to do the job alone. Mexican mining law, which applies to aluminum refining as well as to mere mining and mineral extraction in raw state, makes Mexican majority control mandatory for all practical purposes. Hence, we had to find partners who could and would accept a minority ownership and furnish both money and knowledge.

The American and Foreign Power Company, Inc. had recently sold its Mexican operations to the Mexican Nacional Financiera and was seeking investment opportunities in Mexico. The Aluminum Company of America was also willing to come into Mexico on a minority basis, as required by law. It would be very difficult indeed to find partners with greater knowledge than that possessed by these two firms of electric power generation and of aluminum technology and marketing. (Owing to the trivalence and low atomic weight of aluminum, efficient power generation and utilization are essential.)

We concluded mutually satisfactory agreements with both companies whereby American and Foreign Power would take a 14 percent interest and extend loans to the new venture, Aluminio, S.A. de C.V.; Aluminum Company of America could take a 35 percent interest; and we would finance the remaining 51 percent. Obviously, in developing countries entrepreneurs have a moral, though not a legal, obligation to put their eggs in as many baskets as they can carry without breaking the eggs. We and our foreign partners agreed wholeheartedly that a public offering was in the interests of all concerned—the partners, the financial and investing community, and the economy as a whole.

It is the general custom in Mexico for publicly owned corporations to issue stock in bearer form. Yet, to ensure permanent retention of majority ownership by Mexican citizens, the appropriate authorities ruled that we must issue registered common stock. We had hoped and tried to obtain permission to waive Mexican ownership of preferred shares offered to the public, but this permission was not granted, although effective control resides solely in the common stock.

We met this problem by making a public offering of 100,000 units each consisting of two shares of registered preferred stock and one share of registered common stock at a unit price of 310 pesos. The units may be split and the shares traded and transferred on the books of the company separately, as long as each new buyer is a Mexican citizen. The initial offering was a success, and there were 180 subscribers. Had we been able to accept subscriptions from the foreign colonies in Mexico, this number could have been materially greater.

Summary and Conclusions

There are problems in financing industrial ventures in developing economies, but they are surmountable problems. It is the business of entrepreneurs to weigh existing possibilities and to seek the best available choice. Too often, instead of doing so, they take the easy way out. They contribute what equity capital they can readily command from their own resources and rely for the rest on loans at high cost. Loan money is essential, and we never hesitate to borrow for purposes that are properly and justifiably financed with fixed obligations. We are, however, very reluctant to use loans, particularly short-term loans, as a substitute for equity money.

This is our selfish, but enlightened, reason for going out of our way to get a broad money market established in Mexico. We of course recognize the importance of getting foreign equity capital, foreign loans, foreign licenses, and technical assistance agreements—any foreign help we can profitably use. Personally, I am a great believer in international business cooperation on a businesslike and mutually profitable basis. I would like to see more of it, and we have taken the initiative in forming a Council of Private Enterprise for Mexico which is devoted to promoting understanding of Mexican private enterprise abroad.

Yet God still helps those who help themselves. There is no way in which a developing country can develop soundly and swiftly without generating as much capital as it can by working hard and saving wisely. Foreign capital and foreign know-how are very important, but they cannot and should not be substitutes for self-help.

Consequently, it is my considered opinion that every entrepreneur owes it to himself and to the developing country in which he chooses to live and work to do all in his power to create a broad, active money market and, especially, a market for common stocks. This is not easy, but it must be done. There is no substitute for widespread stock ownership to provide new money for new ventures and for the expansion of old ones, or to help promote capital formation and political stability. Since developing economies are necessarily expanding economies that are almost explosive in their growth, they are the countries in which opportunities are greatest and the need for capital markets greatest. The best way to finance a new venture, in my opinion, is to finance it in a way that educates the middle class to save and invest in common and preferred stocks in order to reap the entrepreneurial benefit of supplying equity money.

THE REVOLVING LOAN FUND AS A DEVELOPMENT DEVICE: A CARE SELF-HELP PROGRAM

E. Gordon Alderfer

The Need for Credit Facilities

The CARE Revolving Loan Fund for needy fishermen in Hong Kong represents a unique and significant experiment in credit financing as a self-help program.

The establishment of this fund in October, 1957, sought to solve a constant problem faced by the fishermen of Hong Kong: shortage of capital, one of the most serious problems faced by the majority of fishermen, small farmers, laborers, and tradesmen throughout Asia and, indeed, throughout the less developed economies of the world. Unable to put up the collateral required for loans by local banks, these marginal producers are generally forced to turn to the private moneylender, who, because of the high risk involved, charges interest rates which often reach astronomical proportions, sometimes as high as 150% per annum. The moneylender, often a village tradesman himself, is able to perpetuate his ancient profession by refusing to accept complete repayment of the principal and interest of a loan, with the result that village farmers often spend the better part of their lives repaying not only their own debts, but also those which they inherit from their fathers and grandfathers.

The magnitude of this problem is apparent in an unofficial study made two years ago by the U.S. Agency for International Development in several countries of Asia. It was then estimated that approximately 55% of the loans obtained by farmers in that area of the world are from private moneylenders,

---

Mr. Alderfer is on leave as Assistant Executive Director of CARE, Inc. (Co-operative for American Relief Everywhere), a nonprofit organization for relief, rehabilitation, and reconstruction. He is currently Director of the Center for Research and Education at Estes Park, Colorado. He is also Book Editor of the *International Development Review.*

whose rates can vary anywhere between 20 and 400%, with an estimated average of 55 to 60% interest per annum.

Other primary sources of credit for marginal producers, it was found, are relatives, credit societies (particularly in Japan and the Philippines, average interest of 6 to 10%), government agricultural banks, and commercial banks, but the distribution of these facilities is generally inadequate, and in many areas they cannot be extended to the people who are in greatest need of loan capital, because of the high risk involved.

One approach to this problem has been taken by the governments of several Asian countries, notably India, Pakistan, Iran, Japan, and the Crown Colony of Hong Kong, which have established special funds to be used specifically for loans to farmers and fishermen unable to obtain them from other sources. The disbursement of these funds is generally supervised by a land revenue agent, or an agricultural or fisheries extension officer, who works closely with the marginal producers in his area and knows them well. Operated on a non-profit basis and backed by commercial banks, these "revolving loan funds," as they are called, charge 6 to 10% interest and ensure repayment of the loans through the cosignature of at least two guarantors and, where applicable, a cooperative society on every loan. Interest on the principal is used to enlarge the fund.

Prior to 1957, CARE's experience with revolving funds had been limited to individual community projects. It was CARE's policy then—as it is now—to suggest that agricultural, fishing, small-trades cooperatives, or similar community enterprises receiving CARE tools and equipment should set aside a portion of their increased income to establish a revolving fund for the purchase of additional equipment and to make loans to their members. By the use of this system, dependence upon outside help can be more rapidly eliminated.

Hong Kong: Credit for Fishermen

Recognizing the value of such a system on a larger scale to meet the needs of the crowded Hong Kong fishing industry, its members already swelled by the stream of refugees from Communist China, CARE began discussions with the Crown Colony's Fish Marketing Organization (FMO) during the summer of 1957. This government agency, which has paid out 5,820 low-interest (6 to 7%) loans totaling $1,700,000 (HK$10 million) to Hong Kong fishermen from its own special fund since 1946, knows the fishermen and their problems, helps them market their catch, taking a 6% commission to pay its own expenses, advises them in the formation and management of cooperative and credit societies.

The FMO loan fund, however, is limited by regulation to offering low-interest loans only to those fishermen who have established sufficient catch records to show that they can borrow against anticipated catches. CARE therefore sought to establish a similar fund which would be available to needy fishermen who had not built up catch records adequate enough to qualify for the FMO loans. It was found that in order to purchase the necessary nets, sails, and fishing gear, or to pay wages to their men, these fishermen were often forced to deal with private moneylenders whose interest rates varied between 100 and 150%, or to return to Communist China and accept the seasonal rate of 20% offered there. As a result, many of these fishermen, more interested in following the catch and the lower interest rates than the currents of political ideology, would maintain both Communist Chinese and Hong Kong fishing registrations for their boats. Reports in 1956 indicated that whenever the catch was plentiful in the Aberdeen fishing areas of the Colony, the Communist regime would lower even further its interest rates on loans to the fishermen in order to discourage their departure. But as soon as the fish moved back into the area off the Communist Chinese coast, the interest rates would return to their 20% level. In retaliation, the Nationalist Chinese Government in Taiwan, realizing that the high interest rates of private moneylenders in the Colony discouraged emigration from Communist China, offered a $20 reward to any fisherman "fleeing" Communist China for the first time.

As might be expected, the fishermen played both ends against the middle. Following the catch, they would arrive in the Colony, stay long enough to do some fishing, collect the $20 reward offered by the Nationalist representatives, and then return to Communist China ahead of the fish to cash in on the lower interest rates. During the six-month period from June to December, 1956, for example, it was estimated that of the 170 boats arriving at Cheung Chau Island, the main port of entry into the Colony, 140 would return to Communist China, and that the majority of these would again return to Hong Kong.

A Revolving Loan Fund

To meet this need for low-interest capital, the CARE Revolving Loan Fund was established in October, 1957, with the initial sum of $5,000. The fund was placed under the administration of the Fish Marketing Organization, in the hope that this would also reduce the risk of nonrepayment on the part of fishermen.

The CARE fund, then, was to benefit the general category of "needy" fishermen and was to be placed under the close and careful scrutiny of the FMO in the following manner:[1]

1. CARE turned over the sum of $5,000 to the FMO for its administration of a special CARE Revolving Loan Fund.
2. The FMO, in turn, investigates the individual needs of the applicants, their family histories, and their ability to repay, just as it does in the administration of its own fund. Less emphasis is placed, however, on previous catch records.
3. In order to obtain a loan, each fisherman has to have two guarantors, each of whom receives a small remuneration from the fisherman. The guarantors are subject to investigation by the FMO. In the event of a default, the FMO is responsible for recovering the loan from the two guarantors.
4. The FMO establishes the terms of repayment with each applicant. The loans are to be either short-term (one year), or medium-term (two years), with deductions of 15 to 25% made from the proceeds of the catch each year to ensure repayment. Interest varies from 6% for members of cooperative so-

[1] See the two questionnaires, "Loan Application" and "Loan Guarantor Investigation Form," on pages 320 and 321.

cieties to 10% per annum for individual fishermen who are not members of cooperatives. Of the 6% interest, 3% is used to enlarge the CARE fund and 3% is paid back to the fisherman's cooperative society, creating capital that can be used for either productive or nonproductive loans.

5. The FMO issues monthly and quarterly financial reports to CARE on the status of the fund.

Fund Performance Record

On October 10, 1957, fisherman Kwok Tai Fook was the first beneficiary of a $260 loan from the CARE fund, enabling him to purchase nets and gear, make a semiannual advance to his hands, and pay the maintenance costs on his boat. In February, 1960, Kwok Tai Fook completed repayment of his loan with $45 interest, averaging 7.2% per annum. Monthly and quarterly reports from the FMO now show that the CARE fund, which began at $5,000 (HK$31,375) had, by December, 1962, expanded to $6,230 through interest payments. Since its inception, over $40,000 (H.K.$249,190) has been paid out in a total of 93 loans averaging $466 apiece to individual fishermen and fishing cooperatives, so that the initial fund has, in effect, "revolved" eight times.

A few difficulties were encountered at first in the administration of the program, primarily in extended periods of repayment, but these were largely due to the fact that many of the recipient fishermen were at that time unfamiliar with the FMO, and the FMO was not familiar with their fishing abilities, living standards, abilities to repay, and their basic honesty. In the first six months, for example (October, 1957, to April, 1958), a total of $3,850 had been made available to twelve applicants. Of this amount, and including interest, only $1,461 had been repaid. The situation began to improve, however, as the fishermen made greater efforts to repay according to the established terms. Many were able to complete their repayment schedule in half the time, and to date there has been no record of default in repayment.

The success of this initial fund can be illustrated by a specific example. During Typhoon Wanda in September, 1962, the fishing vessels of four fishermen—Lo Leung Yau, So Leung Hing, Shek Kam Lee, and So Kam—were completely destroyed. Loans ranging from $175 (HK$1,000) to $260 were immediately made available to them. Putting this money to good use, they have not only recovered their vessels and resumed fishing with an increased catch, but they have been able to make repayments ahead of schedule. Similarly there is the case of So Tai Wah, a trawler fisherman in Tai Po. Hard pressed and unable to support his family because of his poor fishing equipment, he obtained a $520 loan from the CARE fund in January, 1961, purchased the new equipment he needed to increase his catch, repaid the loan in half the time, and through his own savings is now planning to build another vessel for the further expansion of his business. Purse-seiner fishermen Cheng Kam Shing and Wong Shap Pak were on the verge of bankruptcy in the fall of 1961, due to the poor condition of their boats. Using loans of $350 and $520 respectively, obtained from the CARE loan fund, they mechanized their

HONG KONG FISH MARKETING ORGANIZATION

LOAN APPLICATION

..............*Market/Depot*

Ref. ....

Applicant	Name	Chinese	Age
		English	Identity card No.
		Other names used	Junk licence No.
			Usual anchorage

Type of fishing

Income	Year	Catch through F.M.O.		A. Value of catch not through F.M.O. and B. Other income	Total
		Quantity	Value		
				A.	
				B.	
				A.	
				B.	
				A.	
				B.	

Indebtedness			
	Name of creditor		
	Address		
	Date of loan		
	Amount		
	Interest		
	Purpose		
	Outstanding balance		
	Condition of loan		

Past record of F.M.O. loan	Amount	Date of loan issued	Date of final repayment

Loan applied	
	Amount of loan required
	Terms of repayment
	Purpose(s)

Proposed guarantor(s)

Remarks

Date:.............................. *Signature of applicant*..............

LOAN GUARANTOR INVESTIGATION FORM

Name | Occupation

Address

Assets amount	Loan received from Fish Marketing Organization				
	Date	Amount	Date of last installment	Repayment	Overdue

Relationship with applicant

Financial position

Remarks

Previous guranteed for

Name	Type of boat	Date	Amount	Date of last installment	Repayment	Outstanding

Remarks

Opinion of investigator

Opinion

Date | Place | Investigator | Market Liaison Officer, Depot Manager/I/C Post vessels and used the increased income from the catch to repair them, build two new sampans, and send their children to school.

Fund Expansion and Cooperative Societies

Realizing, however, that the potential success of this program was limited by the size of the initial revolving loan fund, CARE decided in 1958 to expand its assistance to the fishermen of Hong Kong through the cooperative societies which they had formed with the help of the FMO. CARE felt that if it could provide fishing gear and equipment directly to the cooperative societies, the funds generated by the increased income of the members could produce expanded loan facilities within the cooperatives themselves, thereby reducing the drain upon the CARE loan fund. Thus, early in 1959, CARE provided $17,000 worth of nets, sails, lines, lamps, hooks, anchors, thread, oars, and sampans directly to eighteen cooperative societies falling under the FMO's jurisdiction. The cooperatives loaned these materials to their members and set up loan funds in CARE's name which were audited periodically by the FMO. The latest report from the FMO indicates that CARE's original presentation has now been repaid more than twice over, and that the $17,000 in fishing gear has generated $36,000 (HK$206,000) in loan capital and has benefited over 3,500 fishermen.

The third phase of CARE's venture into credit finance for fishermen in Hong Kong was inaugurated in December, 1962, with an additional $10,000 investment in the CARE Revolving Loan Fund, bringing it up to $16,230 (HK$92,400). This was done to accommodate the needs of the shrimp fishing industry, which now forms a substantial part of the Hong Kong fishing fleet, comprising over 2,000 vessels that are trying to meet not only a local demand for the product but also a growing export trade, particularly with the demand for frozen shrimp in the United States. The Fish Marketing Organization was limited in its operation to marine fish and could not always extend its marketing and credit facilities to crustacea—or shrimp—fishermen. In the few loans which the FMO did extend to the shrimp fishermen, however, it was noted that they had no record of bad debts.

In the three months during which shrimp fishermen and shrimping cooperatives have benefited from the CARE loan fund, the results have been good. By way of example, loans of $240 and $170 respectively were given to shrimp fishermen So Shing Tai and So Fat in February, 1963, whose homes, previously destroyed by Typhoon Wanda last September, were rebuilt and then completely destroyed again by a fire which broke out during a Chinese New Year's Eve celebration. Through the purchase of additional fishing gear, both families have saved up enough money now to rebuild their homes at Kam-shan. Fisherman Lee Sang of Tai Po, who lost his shrimping vessel during Typhoon Wanda, was granted a $1,900 loan from the CARE fund in March, 1963, and has already rebuilt a mechanized trawler more powerful than the one he formerly owned. His income is now increased and steady. Although the combined efforts of the CARE and FMO loan funds have not eliminated the private moneylender from the fishing industry in Hong Kong, several thousand fishermen are no longer forced to turn to him for capital.

Other Similar Revolving Loan Funds

The success of this revolving loan fund over the past six years has led CARE to undertake similar programs in other countries, notably Panama, India, and Colombia. Under the sponsorship of the Nationwide Insurance Company a $2,000 revolving loan fund has been established for students at the National Agricultural Institute in Divisa, Panama, in June, 1960. Providing low-interest (6%) loans to student farmers, this fund enabled them to purchase seed, breeding equipment, livestock, and fertilizer for in-school projects. The initial fund revolved four times, paying out $8,000 in loans which by August, 1962, had helped the students bring their working capital up to $35,000. Through CARE the Nationwide Insurance Company then boosted its initial investment in this fund by $15,000 in March, 1963, in order to make development loans available to recent graduates of the Divisa Institute.

Furthermore, university cooperatives in India at present have access to a $50,000 Cooperative Development Loan Fund approved by CARE in March, 1963, to be administered by the World University Service. Most of the loans made from this fund will be interest-free and will be used to provide low-cost accommodations, cafeterias, community centers, and scholarships and to establish credit societies for students throughout India.

Smaller in scope but perhaps equally significant is the sum of $834, approved by CARE in March, 1963, to be used as a loan fund in the development of a fique—or hemp—manufacturing cooperative in the Colombian village of San Joaquin, under the guidance of a Peace Corps volunteer.

In Hong Kong, CARE established a revolving loan fund with $17,000 to be administered by the Hong Kong Federation of Pig-Raising Cooperative Societies in providing low-cost loans for the construction of pigsties throughout the Crown Colony. A smaller revolving loan fund was established for the members of two fishing cooperatives in the villages of El Higo and El Farallon.

CARE's total involvement in revolving loan funds is over $100,000, a significant investment in a self-help venture that has already produced encouraging results.

THE STRATEGY OF INDUSTRIAL DEVELOPMENT

William A. W. Krebs, LL.B.

Introduction

In the perspective of history the belief that man can remake his economic environment to the image that he desires is a new idea. That he can do so without sacrificing the political freedom of individual citizens is controversial. Combining these notions in a program of action is an act of faith and daring. The remarkable fact is that so many of the nations of the world have embarked on such an adventurous course in this generation.

The battle for economic development thus joined is fought on many fronts, of which the industrial is only one, and, in most nations at this stage of the battle, statistically the least significant. In this decade the greatest advance in per capita income in most of the developing nations will arise from increasing the productivity of agriculture. The symbolic importance of industry is so great, however, that progress in industry is a political necessity in the development battle, quite apart from the important role that the processing and supply industries play in supporting the growth of agriculture everywhere and the promise of rapid industrial advance on a broad front in certain countries.

Industrial development, in appropriate balance with other development effort, is thus indispensable, and a strategy especially designed for the industrial sector must be a part of each country's larger strategy of economic development. The design of such a strategy, however, must remain for many years to come more art than science. Industrial development programs in enterprise economies outside the continental United States or Western Europe are of recent origin, with the notable exception of Puerto Rico, whose twenty years of intensive industrial development provide a rich store of experience. Facts about such programs are inadequately available; analysis of their meaning has scarcely begun. Twenty years from today, one may hope a social

Mr. Krebs is Vice President of Arthur D. Little, Inc.

science of industrial development may have emerged. For the present, we must work with much less—but work we must.

Fortunately it is possible to distill from even limited experience a body of principles which may be regarded as the elements of a strategy for industrial development having general applicability to the needs of the less developed areas of the world. These elements may be classified as institutional, procedural, and substantive.

Institutional Elements of an Industrial Development Strategy

The key institutional element in successful industrial development strategy is a central executive organization having high professional competence and political power. In some underdeveloped countries such an institution already exists; in others, its functions are present but are being exercised in a variety of political and economic organizations scattered through the governmental structure of the private economy. Successful programming requires that these functions be centralized, placed in competent hands, and backed to the hilt with political power.

The mere establishment of such an institution—whether it is called an industrial development corporation, an industrial development center, or some other name—has symbolic importance inside and outside its country. It demonstrates that the country is serious about industrial development. It shows that the acceleration of industrial development is recognized as something that is not expected to happen without major concentrated effort, and that it is seen as a key task which ministries having their normal work to do cannot be expected to perform adequately, and as something which a few key individuals, no matter how highly placed, cannot do without adequate budget, technical staff, and capacity to follow through.

The role of the industrial development organization is primarily to give leadership in mobilizing the resources of the country for industrial development. This means working closely with both government agencies and representatives of the private sector. It also means making full use of the increasingly wide range of resources available from outside the country, from international agencies, from foreign governments, and from foreign industries and investment organizations. Another major task is to act as the government's adviser on a wide variety of important policy questions affecting industrial development, including taxation, tariffs, labor laws, education, and financial policy. The organization must monitor the economic climate, from the point of view of industrial development, to identify the barriers which are holding development back and to take action to see that something is done about them. Many such barriers can be broken, but often after months or years of study, steady and intelligently applied pressure, and long campaigns. The organization should also be the center for information of interest to potential investors in industry, both foreign and local. This involves maintaining adequate statistics and library reference material and carrying on research to obtain information not readily available. Publication of basic information of interest to prospective investors is usually also necessary.

The conditions which are essential to the success of the key executive organization for industrial development include continuity of basic personnel and policy, strong leadership, highly qualified staff, full support of the key ministries, and the respect of the private sector. Continuity can often best be achieved by establishing such an organization at a position midway between government and the private economy, with a mixed government-private board or governing body. It can then better survive the changing tides of political fortune while remaining responsive to the changes of policy which must come with changes in government.

Strong leadership requires that the head of the organization be a person who commands the respect of the ministries of the government, of the bankers and industrialists, of foreign businessmen and government officials, and—in many countries—of labor leaders and the press. This is a large order in any country, but failure to meet it is likely to lead to failure of the program.

Backing such an individual with highly qualified staff is equally essential and perhaps even more difficult in view of the shortage of such persons in most developing economies. Fortunately, if the policies of the country will permit it, the use of expatriate specialists, either as individuals or through contract with the increasingly large number of foreign organizations, both public and private, which now operate in this field, can fill the gap while nationals are being trained to execute the duties of staff.

Full support of the key ministries is important, because industrial development depends so heavily on preconditions and services which are the responsibility of government almost everywhere in the world. For example, the design of highway systems can have a stimulating or stultifying effect on regional dispersion of industry; decisions on tariff policy spell for many industrial projects the difference between survival or failure; labor laws affect competitive position.

The same conditions which lead to continuity and strong leadership are likely to earn for the organization the other essential ingredient for its success, the respect of the private sector of the economy, without which, in the mixed economy characteristic of so much of the developing world, little can be done. Winning the confidence of those with the private investment resources and managerial skills necessary for industrial development, like winning the confidence of the ministries, is an essential prerequisite for the success of the executive organization in building strong industrial development programs.

Around or within the key executive organization for industrial development must be clustered a range of ancillary specialized institutions. Like the concept of the central organization itself, the ideas expressed in many of these have emerged only recently. As tools of industrial development, they are still experimental and evolving. They include development banks, technical assistance institutes, industrial development consulting centers, and managed industrial districts. Each of them has a unique contribution to make to a program of industrial development. If institutions of these kinds do not exist in a developing economy, one of the first tasks of the central industrial development organization is likely to be to create them or bring about their creation.

The development bank in one form or another, normally a quasi-governmental corporation charged with responsibility for mobilizing capital for economic development programs, is by now a common phenomenon in the developing economies. The number of such institutions around the world today is close to a hundred, and more are appearing as new programs of development are launched. Historical studies have shown that such institutions, in various forms, normally operating as private investment banks, have been an essential component of economic development in Western Europe and the United States since the beginning of the Industrial Revolution. The basic difference between a development bank and a commercial bank is that, while the latter engages in financing trade and commerce through loans usually limited to one year, a development bank provides medium- and long-term "soft" loans and, more important, invests in equity securities of new enterprises. This is normally the least easily available form of capital in a developing economy. Of almost equal importance in contributing to the success of new industrial projects is the practice of the better-run development banks of making careful technical and financial analyses of new ventures as well as rendering consulting assistance to management during early stages of operations. Fortunately, there are relatively plentiful sources of capital for development banks today from international institutions, from the foreign assistance programs of the industrialized countries, and from the governments of developing countries themselves.

A further contribution that a well-managed development bank can make is to stimulate the creation of a capital market for securities of industrial enterprises, thus channeling local capital away from relatively unproductive uses into the mainstream of industrial development. If such a bank also participates actively in cooperation with the central executive organization for industrial development in searching out and analyzing the merits of investable industrial projects, it can effectively catalyze the growth of industry. In economies where this kind of institution is not present, or where its effectiveness has been limited for any of a variety of reasons, early attention to strengthening it is an element of industrial development strategy that will pay dividends.

The technical assistance institute is another specialized institution for the support of industrial development which may have to be created or enlarged to accelerate industrial growth. Such an organization ideally will provide at least the following services at a high level of skill and low level of cost relative to value: management counsel, product and process development, market research, technical troubleshooting, and applied research and development. In at least a portion of its program, such an institute must be in a position to maintain the proprietary confidences of its industrial clientele. It follows that, although it must almost always be subsidized by the government in its early stages, it must be so organized as to give it substantial independence at the earliest practicable date.

Somewhat like the technical assistance institute, and overlapping it in function in the management field, is the industrial development consulting center. Of particular value in those economies with a thin layer of trained business management or with poorly developed small and medium-scale enterprises, this institution—of which increasing numbers of prototypes have recently been appearing—concentrates its services on the business management problems of industrial enterprise and extends, in effect, a subsidized management consulting service. In some forms this service has been coupled with the provision of a wide range of training programs, both at the headquarters of the institution and on the job, and with an information service designed to bring to the attention of industrial managers the most useful and current knowledge of their professional field and the industry within which they function.

The planned and managed industrial district represents still another institutional device called into being by the special needs of industrial development programs. Experience with the industrial district—variously called industrial estate and industrial park—goes back to the nineteenth century in the United Kingdom and the United States, in both of which it has been spectacularly successful. More recently Puerto Rico and India have experimented in the field with good results. Fundamentally, an industrial district is an area prepared with sites, roads, utilities, a communication network, service facilities, and in some cases shell buildings or even completed simple factories, ready for occupancy, with internally consistent legal and management arrangements specialized to meet the needs of industrial tenants or cooperative owners. Prearranged financing for equipment or even working capital is sometimes provided, together with advisory services, assistance in meshing into the community, and other amenities designed to ease the entrance onto the scene of foreign or new indigenous industrial enterprises. Economies of scale in planning and construction and the immense value of "readiness" are the significant advantages offered by this approach to expanding enterprise. Recently, the planned industrial district has been experimentally used in an effort to make national policies for decentralization and regionalization of industrial development more effective.

Another group of ancillary institutions must be of concern to the central executive organization responsible for industrial development—those necessary in the creation of the intellectual infrastructure of an industrial society: the vocational training schools, the centers for management education, and the universities, which supply the leaders of the service professions of law, accounting, and finance. Obviously the techniques for stimulating activity in this quarter must be more subtle, more indirect, and in some ways more imaginative than those applicable to other parts of the institutional problem. In the long run, however, the quality of these independent institutions will govern the quality of the development program. In many developing countries the pattern of education has been classical or oriented to the supply of civil servants rather than industrialists, engineers, and businessmen. Redressing this imbalance, consistent with the limitations of the culture and the economy, requires long and costly effort, but it must be done. One technique which has proved effective is fostering linkages between indigenous centers of learning and foreign institutions prominent in technology, management education, and vocational training. In some countries, ambitious experiments are under way which include the creation of new institutions of learning emphasizing these aspects of education, sponsored by foreign institutions and sharing their faculties during the early years.

Each of the ancillary institutions described must be designed for the special circumstances of each national or regional setting into which it is to be fitted. Fortunately, however, experience with all of them is accumulating, and in recent years the literature of experience is becoming more widely available. A successful strategy for industrial development will draw heavily on such experience while adapting it flexibly to local requirements.

Procedural Elements of an Industrial Development Strategy

So far as experience may be relied upon as a guide, it suggests the importance of four procedural elements in a successful industrial development strategy:

1. Early formulation and use of quantitative objectives
2. Adherence to a system of priorities for development
3. Reliance on sound economic research to illuminate decisions of policy
4. Energetic promotion of investment

That finite goals are important means for mobilizing effort is a fact of human nature. An industrial development program requires a timetable and quantitative objectives. In the most successful programs these have been expressed in the number of industrial jobs to be added to the economy in some fixed period of time, in units of production of key commodities, in numbers of industrial establishments to be created, and in monetary wages. Experience suggests that the danger of setting too modest a target is greater than that of unrealistically reaching beyond reasonable capacity. The most successful programs of industrialization have been dramatized in terms which caught the imagination and awakened the enthusiasm of the whole community and, often by contagion, of industrialists and investors in foreign countries.

Since industrial development is most effective when carried out in the context of a broad and comprehensive economic development plan for all sectors, sound strategy requires consistency between industrial plans and those for the other parts of the economy. The recent emphasis on intermediate-range national economic planning for development in many countries is a welcome phenomenon and permits industrial development to be both more orderly and more realistic. Critics of planning who express concern that it leads to destruction of private initiative in economic affairs miss the point. On the contrary, a well-defined set of objectives and realistic procedures for moving toward them is evocative of the best efforts of the entrepreneur, as experience testifies in Puerto Rico—certainly an enterprise economy.

Of nearly equal importance to quantitative objectives is adherence to a system of priorities in making the key decisions. Everything cannot be done at once with limited resources. An explicit framework of priorities for development, honestly constructed and consistently adhered to, will take the heat out of difficult decisions which will otherwise be made on grounds of political expediency, thoughtless enthusiasm, or other unsound bases.

Both objectives and priorities can arise—if they are to be sound—only out of careful and conscientious economic and sometimes technical research. The time and money spent in obtaining a clear and complete view of the circumstances within which the development program is to proceed are the least costly investment that can be made, even though the process may require hundreds of thousands of dollars and months of painstaking effort. Nor is research something to be done once and filed away. The pace and complexity of change mean that every decision must be regarded as open to revision in the light of changed circumstances, so that a strong economic research staff must be continuously addressing itself to the production of new information and insights into the continuing process.

In danger of being overlooked, but critically important for success, is the use of investment promotion in industrial development. Fundamentally, promotion of investment is required because of the imperfect knowledge about opportunity and risk which exists in even the most sophisticated investment community. In the case of a developing economy, the imperfections are enormously greater. Promotion is the communications function which connects investor with opportunity and gives him the knowledge and the confidence to risk capital in industrial development. For most developing economies promotion of investment from abroad is the most critical task. Foreign investors usually have little knowledge of the developing country, its laws, or its people. Accordingly they lack confidence in their ability to enter successfully, even if their attention has been attracted by general favorable publicity. A system must therefore be devised to overcome this lack of confidence and lead the desirable prospective investor virtually by the hand through the stages of early investigation to decision making and, later, through start-up and early stages of operation. The most highly successful investment promotion programs, like the most highly successful industrial development programs (and they have to date been largely the same ones), have been both massive and highly personalized, with great emphasis on research and the communication of accurate factual data to carefully selected prospects. A failure to budget adequate funds or plan sufficient effort for the promotional phases of development can waste all the other expensive gains of a fine industrial development program.

Substantive Elements of an Industrial Development Strategy

The substantive elements of an industrial development strategy are the most diverse, specialized to each situation and controversial. Even here, however, experience has begun to yield lessons which validate principles of general applicability.

The Importance of Market Analysis. It is likely that more waste has been caused in industrial development programs from decisions made with inadequate knowledge of the market for production than from any other single cause. This is a particularly common phenomenon where a substantial portion of the capital for the project comes from public agencies or from a large number of private investors no one of whom has actual experience in the operation of the particular industry. On the other hand, a careful examination of present and potential markets for the products of industry and the selection of projects on this basis can be the touchstone of success. Like so many other aspects of management "science," market research has developed a methodology and principles which can best be applied by experienced professionals. At the same time, no specialist in marketing can possibly be sufficiently familiar with all sectors of industry and factors affecting markets for a wide range of products. Thus a successful program of market research requires both the marketing expert and the industry specialist. The selection for emphasis in an industrial development program of those industrial sectors in which market analysis indicates opportunity, not only for the present but through the foreseeable future, can be a key substantive element for success.

A Policy of Integrated Development. The extent to which the selection of industrial projects to be emphasized in a development program can be guided through analysis of the degree to which they mutually support and stimulate one another is a controversial matter. It is clear, at least, that industrial projects can be linked to one another in the sense that one provides the raw material or the market for the other. There is a growing body of theory which suggests that certain types of industry tend to induce or stimulate complementary industrial activity to a higher degree than others. Thus the much-maligned iron and steel industry is seen as having a high degree of interdependence with other sectors both in terms of purchases from them and sales to them, while such activities as fishing, transport, services, and trade have relatively low interdependence characteristics and therefore, presumably, low priority in development programs, at least for that reason. Of course, the importance of such an activity as fishing for the supply of protein in low-protein diets represents the kind of qualification for such a priority selection that illustrates its basic complexity. To the extent that analysis can carry the load, however, it appears important that attention be paid in formulating development strategy to the stimulus-creating aspects of new projects or, in other terms, how well they will "mesh into" the growing economy.

Application of the Test of National Benefit. The analysis of an industrial project to test the costs it will place upon the economy, as well as the benefits it can be expected to produce, is an essential but sometimes neglected step of industrial development programming. While in many cases an industrial project which is sufficiently promising to attract investment capital will without question represent a net gain to the national economy, there are also situations in which there may be a great difference between the value of a project to its private owners and its value to the economy as a whole. For example, because a project may use labor which is unemployed otherwise, it may be more valuable to the national economy than would be shown by a simple tabulation of the wages to be paid, for purposes of private analysis of the soundness of the investment. Similarly a project using natural resources which would otherwise be wasted, such as forest products, may have a greater value to the economy than to the private company which must pay for the resources at regular prices. A project which can make a valuable contribution through training labor or in providing services or goods needed by other new industries, thus serving as a stepping-stone in the process of industrialization, may have a surplus of value to the economy that will not show up in the entrepreneur's calculation of commercial profitability.

The converse may also be true. A project to substitute local production for imports may be commercially profitable only because, through tariff protection, it can sell its product to the local market at protected higher prices. The difference between the protected price and the price at which the competitive import would be available represents a cost to the economy which should be made explicit by analysis.

To show such national costs and benefits separately from commercial profitability is not to answer the questions of policy to which they are related, such as: "How much tariff protection is justified?" But to fail to break them out for consideration is to run the risk of making decisions which will later prove to have been faulty because of failure to recognize and consider all the consequences.

Application of the Test of Commercial Viability. Strange as it may seem, industrial projects sometimes receive the benefit of national subsidy, tax concessions, and even investment of public funds, when careful analysis would have shown that for technical or commercial reasons they could never be financially successful. There are many interested parties whose return from the initiation of a project will be secured before the early years of operation have passed and whose support of the project is given without concern for its long-term success. Protecting the program from the influence of such special interests can be achieved only through painstaking analysis of the commercial feasibility of each significant industrial project at a high level of competence. One way of securing such analysis is by arranging for the participation of substantial industrial or banking interests under terms that will make certain that the investment is not fully paid out until commercial viability has been demonstrated. Another is to provide the technically qualified staff directly or through securing competent independent advisers. Regardless of method, the function is an indispensable substantive element of successful industrial development strategy.

Creative Use of Technology. It is hard to imagine a successful industrial development program which does not make use of a wide range of technical analysis. Even in the preliminary screening of an economy for identification of sectors of industrial opportunity, the insights of an experienced team of industrial specialists, trained in the engineering and management sciences, can enrich and illuminate the judgments of administrators, economists, and managers. The possibilities for adaptation of processes practiced in the earlier stages of the more advanced economies for application under current, usually more limiting requirements of scale and complexity in a developing economy can best be analyzed by the experienced technologist. Furthermore, the wide range of industrial operations and processes to be analyzed in the course of project feasibility studies demands the availability of a similarly wide range of technically qualified industrial specialists. Fortunately, conditions of transportation and communication in today's world make available such services from the resources of the more highly industrialized economies through a variety of institutions and firms. Wise use of such resources is another key to a successful industrial development program.

Respect for the Capacity of Research and Recognition of Its Limitations. Most successful industrial development programs put great reliance on both economic and technical research to illuminate problems which must be resolved by the decision maker. Experienced managers and administrators, whether in industry or government, know the value of a cold shower of facts in a heated controversy over plant location, level of subsidy, competition among suppliers, or project selection. The countervailing principle—that all technical analysis falls short of the subtle but overwhelmingly important intangibles of politics, human relations, taste, and "hunch"—is of at least equal importance and perhaps in more danger of being overlooked in the increasingly professionalized field of industrial development. A nice balance is of the essence of success.

A Climate for Enterprise. Finally, an industrial development strategy for an enterprise economy will most certainly fail unless it provides the preconditions which evoke enterprise: civil order and good government, reasonable economic stability, laws which encourage risk taking, and a physical infrastructure—transportation and utilities—capable of supporting an industrial effort. More subtle, but more far-reaching and fundamental than any of these, is the creation and sustenance of an attitude in society which sees in the man of enterprise a symbol of what the society values. To the extent that this occurs, all other measures will be facilitated.

To catalogue the institutional, procedural, and substantive elements which comprise a successful industrial development strategy is not equivalent to designing it. Designing a strategy is not equivalent to executing it. As in all human affairs, the link in the chain of circumstance supplied by the administrator is indispensable if desire is to culminate in achievement. Nonetheless, sound theory maximizes potential and minimizes risk. It can be disregarded only at peril.

ENCOURAGING PRODUCTIVITY IN INTERNATIONAL MANAGEMENT

Keith Davis, Ph.D.

In South America recently, a consultant from the United States was called in to discover why the West German machinery in a cellophane plant owned by South Americans was not operating properly. (This single preliminary sentence gives insight into the complications of international management in showing that already three different cultures were involved in the problem.) When the consultant arrived, he studied the situation for several weeks, and his conclusion was that there was nothing at all wrong with the machinery. It was of excellent quality and in perfect adjustment; the raw materials and other supporting factors were entirely satisfactory.

The real problem was caused by the supervisors, who had a "father image" of the mill manager and were unable to make operating decisions without his approval. They deferred to him as their elder and superior. When something in the mill was out of adjustment, they waited indefinitely for his decision before they would correct the problem. Since he had other business interests and was frequently out of the mill for part of the day, or even for two or three days, they permitted the continuous-production mill to produce scrap cellophane for hours or even days because of some minor maladjustment which they could have corrected. The mill manager tried to delegate decision making on these control matters to his supervisors, but neither he nor they were able to overcome this custom of deference to authority which existed in their culture. As the consultant finally summed up, "The problem is the men, not the machines."

Dr. Davis is Professor of Management at Arizona State University, Tempe, Arizona. Some of the illustrations in this article were first used in his book, *Human Relations at Work*, 2d ed., McGraw-Hill Book Company, New York, copyright, 1962; and in his article, "Managing Productivity in Developing Countries," *Management International*, vol. 4, no. 2, 1964.

International management offers many new situations of this type which involve a blending of various cultures and require new adjustments by all persons involved. A manager who enters an underdeveloped country to install advanced technological equipment and get it operating will have to make adjustments in the leadership habits which he employed in the advanced country from which he came. Also, the native employees in this new installation will find that they can no longer follow the ways of their old, less productive culture. In other words, each must change. There must be a blending of cultures in which both parties adjust to the new situation of seeking greater productivity for the benefit of both the enterprise and the citizens of the country in which it operates.

Almost every civilized country of the Free World has established as one of its national goals an increase in the productivity of its people. To accomplish this goal, its own people will have to adjust to new ways of doing things as determined by modern technology and scientific management. These conditions require an international manager to have a greater understanding of human relations and social systems than he would need in his own country to accomplish equal results. Since he knows less about the native culture, he must know more about good management in order to be successful. In the example just given, it is evident that the machinery was built to operate in an advanced industrial culture, but now it must operate in an underdeveloped one. Neither the machinery nor the supervisors could be quickly changed to meet this new situation. Re-engineering of machinery would be costly and time-consuming, and in this case it might reduce the machinery's productivity. Retraining would likewise be time consuming. The solution offered by the consultant was an effective compromise to the effect that the general manager should appoint one person as "acting general manager" during his absence and should work closely with that person to build up his image of authority with the supervisors. Then there would always be someone at the plant to make decisions quickly.

There are four major areas which need to be understood in order to encourage productivity in international management. These areas are social systems, change, productivity, and motivation. Let us discuss each in some detail.

Integrating Social Systems

The overriding factor in all international management is that it operates within different social systems. These social systems affect the responses of all persons to the machinery and the management which is offered. In many cases, a native social system has had little experience with modern concepts of productivity and so is either blind to the idea or antagonistic to it. For example, in some cultures of the world the idea exists that the more education one has, the less work he should do. An educated man may surround himself with aides whose primary job is to do errands for him rather than to work as a team toward productivity. In some instances, an educated man looks upon work as degrading, which certainly does not endear it to those subordinates who should be becoming more productive.

Sometimes social caste and rank interfere with teamwork and communication. In India, in some retail stores, when a cashier finds that a clerk has made an error in a sales check, he will not correct it himself or tell her what is wrong. He simply returns it to her while the customer waits for her to try to find the error.

On other occasions, social customs interfere with understanding. In the United States, a supervisor feels that when he is talking to a man, that man should look him in the eye. In fact, if an employee evades his direct glance, a supervisor judges that the man is "shifty," and may be trying to hide something. In some other countries, however, it is a long-established habit for a person never to look an elder or superior in the eye. To do so is considered impertinent. Consequently, a supervisor from the United States who tries to deal directly with his men in this manner may find that he cannot establish good human relations with them.

Similarly, culture in the United States emphasizes face-to-face thrashing out of differences. Hence, companies in the United States have been able to develop bargaining systems which, in most industries, are built around local face-to-face negotiations by the persons directly involved. In Latin America, where status differences and authority are more significant, it is more difficult to deal directly with an employer. Hence, bargaining is more dependent upon an intermediate role by government. Workers have no difficulty telling an intermediary—the government—how they feel about management, but they are not culturally prepared to tell management directly.

Making Changes

The second point concerns change, which is the effective device by which different cultures are integrated. Culture changes slowly, and in so doing it gives stability and security to society. This is an advantage. However, there is the balancing disadvantage that culture makes change more difficult for each of us. The international manager's job is to try to retain in his management practices the essential elements of both old and new cultures so that his group may work with the security of some old practices, but also wiith greater productivity than the old culture has normally accomplished.

As we have learned in both experience and research, change is a human relations problem as well as a technological one. The technological part of change can usually be solved by the logics of science, but the human relations part is dependent upon the art and skill of supervision. The following story will indicate how change may be made acceptable through a simple adjustment.

On the plains of Texas at the beginning of World War II, one of the first blackout aircraft factories was constructed. As was the pattern in those days, this factory had no windows or skylights, so that it could be operated at night without showing lights to attract enemy aircraft. The building was air-conditioned by the latest equipment to control temperature, humidity, and air circulation. Since the ceiling was over fifty feet high, most of the air exits were high on the walls and ceilings.

As soon as the first group of employees started work, they began to complain about inadequacy of the air conditioning—the factory was too humid, too hot, and too close-feeling. Air-conditioning engineers were called to check the equipment and the temperature, humidity, and circulation of air throughout the building. They reported that the air conditioning was excellent—providing exactly the air conditions that scientific studies showed the human body needed. Still the complaints persisted; in fact, they grew worse until they were definitely undermining morale and productivity.

Finally, one alert manager recognized the problem. He reasoned that most of the workers were rural people who were new to both industry and air conditioning. They were used to an outdoor life and felt restricted in a windowless plant where they could neither feel a breeze nor see it blowing. Since the vents were too high for employees to *feel* the air, they needed to *see* that it was stirring. This manager simply had tissue streamers tied to the ventilators high on the walls. Anyone who felt uncomfortable could look up to see the paper fluttering in the breeze and be assured that he was getting plenty of air. The result was that employee complaints soon became negligible. That which was technically right was finally made *humanly* right.

The paper-streamer device was later used many times in areas where air conditioning was new. It is rarely seen today in the United States because people are adjusted to air conditioning, but it can be seen in other parts of the world. A few years ago, when teaching in a South American executive program, I mentioned the paper-streamer incident to participants. A few days later, we visited a new factory and observed the streamers in use. I was told that employees claimed that there was insufficient fresh air in the new building, and management had used the streamers to demonstrate that there *was* fresh air. This action was a simple demonstration of good international management—a recognition of the human factors in a technological change and an effort to apply human tools to achieve a workable result.

Gaining Employee Support for Changes

Since management initiates most changes, it has primary responsibility for handling them in such a way that there will be satisfactory adjustment. Though management initiates change, the employee controls the final decision to accept it or reject it, and he is the one who actually accomplishes it. Under these conditions, employee support becomes essential.

Management has developed a number of ways to encourage employee support of changes. One of these is to set up various pledges to protect employees from economic loss or from decreases in status and personal dignity. Each worker needs to feel that he personally will not suffer from the change or, better yet, that he will gain from it. In fact, if workers can be assured that they will share the benefits of a particular change, this will be their positive motivation toward acceptance. Sometimes, when supervisors introduce changes which may be resisted, they attempt also to introduce personal conveniences at that time, such as floor mats, chairs, ventilators, and better lighting, thereby showing that they are interested in the whole job process, including the worker.

Communication is another essential element for reducing resistance to change. People tend to fear that which they do not understand; consequently, the full meaning of a change should be communicated even though some aspects of it may be bad. Naturally, positive aspects should be emphasized as much as possible. Since people resist change for both logical and emotional reasons, communication should deal with both logical and emotional viewpoints of the employee. *Logic alone is not an effective way of influencing attitudes.*

A manager also reduces resistance to change by preventing trivial and unnecessary changes. Individuals can tolerate only so much change, and if they are bombarded with irritating small changes, they will be less apt to accept major changes that occur later. If a group can be encouraged to participate in recognition of the need for a change, then change will be even more supported. Since change requires unlearning of old habits, attention should be devoted to this process. Take the situation of a supervisor who is taught by an overseas management new ways of leading employees. What sometimes happens is that he retains most of his old approach also, so that now he has a strange mixture of newer, positive practices which are substantially offset by practices held over from his old habit patterns. As a consequence, there is little net benefit from his new practices. If he does not substantially believe in them, he tends gradually to return to the old ways of doing things because they are more secure. Even when he does believe in his new practices, he may become frustrated because his old habits (and those of his manager) interfere.

Change should be made on the basis of the *impersonal* requirement of a situation rather than on personal grounds. A supervisor who says, "I want this done," is less likely to gain acceptance than a supervisor who says, "Men, this is a need of ours which we can solve by doing it in this way."

Old habits can be changed only through long-run creation of new conditions rather than by short-run temporary adjustments in a management effort. Consider the smoking habit of a man who usually smokes two packs of cigarettes a day. There are times when he smokes less, such as near the end of the month when he is running short of money to purchase cigarettes, or when he reads an advertisement or receives a warning from his doctor about the possibility that cigarettes will cause cancer. At other times he smokes more, such as when he is nervous or worried. However, he generally returns to his old habit of two packs a day. These temporary pressures have not been effective in changing his long-run habit patterns. Neither will a temporary lecture or reprimand by a supervisor be effective in changing the habit patterns long established by his men in their different social system. There must be a long-run effort based upon long-run new conditions.

Likewise, the supervisor himself must make some adjustment. In the United States, for example, it is the custom for people in face-to-face conversation to maintain some physical distance between them, perhaps a foot or two feet. In some cultures, however, it is the custom for people who talk face-to-face to do so quite closely, at perhaps six inches' distance. A supervisor from the United States may be uncomfortable in a conversation of this type. I observed one supervisor overseas who, by the end of a short conversation, had backed halfway across the room trying to increase the distance between himself and the other person, who, of course, kept following him in order to keep the cultural distance of six to nine inches with which he was familiar. Under these conditions, it is difficult to develop good human relations with subordinates because the supervisor appears uncomfortable in their presence.

Communicating the Idea of Productivity

A third important idea in improving overseas supervision is to communicate the real meaning of "productivity" to the people involved. The modern industrial concept of productivity is not really understood in many cultures of the world. Even when people are able to *talk* about productivity in an intelligent way, they still may not be able actually to *apply* the concept in their day-to-day work. In other words, productivity does not get priority over other cultural values which are inconsistent with it.

In one country, I observed a crew of seven men unloading half-inch steel rods from a flat-bed truck. I watched them for nearly a whole day. In normal circumstances, this job should have been accomplished in an hour or more, but in this case it took more than one day. On the truck bed, there were four men. Three men lifted the rods one by one and threw them to the ground. A fourth man on the bed counted the rods. On the ground, two men picked up the rods and moved them about five feet to a stack. A third man in a coat supervised the entire operation.

Of particular interest to me was the fact that one man on the truck bed always picked up a rod on the wrong side of it. Two men were on one side of the rod and he was on the other, so that when they stopped to the edge of the truck bed to throw off the rod, his head always was in the way! At that point, he had to turn the rod loose, stoop under it, and grasp it on the other side before it could be thrown off the truck. The foreman watched this odd operation all day without offering any suggestion for improvement in productivity. Furthermore, the truck could have been driven adjacent to the stack so that the rods could be thrown onto it. However, this was not done. It would appear in this case that the supervisor as well as his men did not have an abiding interest in productivity; consequently, they were unable to discover means to improve their productivity as they worked.

It is possible to make large increases in productivity while still keeping enough of the old culture to maintain security for the persons involved. In other words, the old culture is blended with the new. Oil companies in the Moslem East have been effective in blending culture and yet accomplishing considerable productivity. Similarly, Japanese industry has been able to retain much of its old culture and yet to be competitively productive. Japanese workers are hired virtually for life, and managerial promotions are mostly by seniority. However, within this cultural context, most of the technological improvements of modern industry have been introduced. What the Japanese factory misses in rationality and efficiency, it seems to gain back in stability and employee loyalty. Culture is used to reinforce production needs rather than to interfere with them.

Motivating People

A fourth point in improving international management is to apply concepts of motivation in terms of the environment of the people supervised rather than in terms of an advanced industrial economy. What is effective in one environment may not be so in another.

In a South American factory, for example, the accident rate was high. The six native superintendents were not following management's instructions for accident prevention. They seemed agreeable but somehow failed to sell accident prevention throughout the organization. The overseas top management of the company then tried a high-powered safety publicity program of the type used in its own home plants. This was to no avail. Finally, a wise staff man offered an effective solution. Papier-mâché heads of the six superintendents were molded and colored, with the idea that each week these heads would be arranged on a "totem pole" at the front gate in the order of the weekly safety rank of each department. No superintendent wanted to see himself as low man on the safety totem pole, so the accident problem was quickly corrected. In this case, management used existing cultural values of this country in order to accomplish the desired result of better safety.

Modern psychology reports that new human needs take priority whenever former needs are reasonably satisfied. In other words, man is motivated more by what he is seeking than by what he already has. Priority of human needs is generally recognized to be in order from physiological needs to security needs to social needs to ego needs. In underdeveloped countries, most employees are still seeking basic physiological and security needs. Hence, some of the more sophisticated and elaborate motivational devices of modern industrial management may not be appropriate in these countries. The needs of their workers at this time may be more simply reached by direct motivation. In some instances, they have worked in economic systems which had little direct connection between how effectively they worked and how well their needs were satisfied. Therefore, they need management to show them simple, direct evidence that if they work more effectively, they will receive more. In other words, work needs to be interpreted in terms of their immediate needs, rather than waiting for indirect results through a complex economic system. Accordingly, action which would sometimes be inappropriate in an advanced country may be effective in the underdeveloped country, as illustrated by the following example.

In South America, an international petroleum company employed about twenty natives in an oil well perforation team managed by a nonnative executive. In spite of management efforts, each perforation job averaged nine days. Since a similar job with similar equipment was done in the United States in 1½ days, management reasoned that—even considering the more primitive operating conditions in South America—the job could surely be done in six days or less. Since the job did require genuine teamwork and the men worked in isolated locations less subject to direct supervision, management decided on a drastic step to break the cultural pattern. It offered nine days' pay for each job regardless of actual work days. This dramatic economic incentive proved sufficient to alter long-standing cultural habits.

The employees' attitudes changed rather quickly. Within four years, they had reduced perforation time to 1½ days, the same as in other efficient countries. Team members readily offered suggestions to improve teamwork and adapt technology to the special conditions of that area. On two occasions, the team encouraged transfer of men who would not change their habits and were thus holding back the team.

In summary, international management is filled with many inconsistencies and difficulties if one approaches it from the culture of an advanced industrial economy, but if the situation is approached with the view of integrating the best of modern technology and scientific management with the best culture of the underdeveloped country, then better productivity is sure to follow. In the accomplishment of this better productivity, the wise international manager will pay particular attention to understanding social systems, making changes carefully, communicating the idea of productivity, and motivating people.

COOPERATIVES IN ECONOMIC DEVELOPMENT

Dr. Victor B. Sullam

Basic Principles of Cooperation

Definition. A cooperative is "a form of organization wherein persons voluntarily associate together as human beings on a basis of equality for the promotion of the economic interests of themselves." (See H. Calvert, *The Law and Principles of Co-operation*, 4th ed., Thacker, Spink and Co., Calcutta, 1933, p. 13.) This definition embodies the main principles and major problems of cooperation:

1. A cooperative is an association of human beings rather than of capital. Accordingly, the human element (qualities of leadership, orderliness, foresight, personal integrity, respect for engagements entered into, etc.) plays the dominant role. This is true even for quasi-cooperative associations or organizations in which the membership is essentially comprised of landholdings rather than of individuals (drainage districts, irrigation districts, pest control districts).

2. The members of the association are equal both as to rights and as to obligations. Equality of rights is usually formalized in the by-laws of the cooperatives, the accepted principle being one member, one vote. Equality of obligations implies equal good faith among members.

3. The act of association is voluntary. Even in the industrialized West, however, cooperatives did not spring spontaneously from the people but were the fruit of the initiative and dedication of a few enlightened individuals. In underdeveloped areas it is considered "virtually impossible for a cooperative movement to grow and develop without active government assistance, supervision, and (at least in the initial stages) direction."[1]

Dr. Sullam is U.S. representative of the Italian Federation of Farmers' Co-operatives.

[1] United Nations, *Special Study on Economic Conditions and Development in Non-self-governing Territories*, New York, 1962, p. 187.

4. The implicit common weal of the members impels them to work together to attain the objectives of the association. Cooperation then requires the awareness of an explicit economic need which can be satisfied through the contribution of each member of the association. In practice, cooperatives have been introduced with success where individuals have sought to improve their position by banding together when they found themselves exploited either in obtaining goods and services they require or in the disposition of their production.

5. The range of needs which can be satisfied through cooperative associations may be wider in underdeveloped countries than in the West. As stated by John H. Heckman,[2]

> Cooperatives have a place in the economic area of the United States but they have a far greater role in the economic progress of developing countries. In the United States, protective laws and effective competition are assuring factors of quality, ethics and adapted services. In developing countries, either or both of these may be lacking. Cooperatives have an opportunity to bridge this gap.

Social, Ethical, and Political Tasks. Cooperatives, then, are organizations of individuals created to perform certain economic tasks. Yet the origin of cooperatives must not obscure a basic fact: the tasks performed by cooperatives, "the marketing of produce, the channeling of savings, the purchasing of supplies, and so on could in many cases be done just as efficiently by private enterprise or by public agencies."[3] The cooperative movement, however, is fostered as a way of life with high moral values and as a school for democracy:[4]

> Experience has shown that among backward populations cooperative societies, simply through their working and independently of their economic results, have contributed to the intellectual, moral and civic training of their members. The cooperative movement frees its members . . . from themselves and their bad habits. . . . By placing them without distinction of class or sex within a simple framework of self-government in which they become familiar with democratic procedures, it trains them in their civic duties.

According to Heckman,[5]

> Cooperatives have two additional opportunities in developing countries. These are to stimulate the pride and stability that goes with the feeling of ownership and to serve as laboratories of democracy. . . . The feeling of ownership and belonging which goes with their cooperative can be a strong stabilizing ballast to citizenship. Cooperatives are economic and social democracies and grass root democracies at that. Thus, a country covered with local cooperatives and their members understanding owners of them, has a strong foundation for national democracy.

[2] John H. Heckman, *A.I.D. Cooperative Programs and Policy,* remarks made at Taipei, Taiwan, on Nov. 23, 1962, Agency for International Development, Office of Material Resources, Washington, D.C., p. 2 (mimeographed).

[3] Arthur W. Lewis, *The Theory of Economic Growth,* Richard D. Irwin, Inc., Homewood, Ill., 1955, p. 200.

[4] Maurice Colombain, *Cooperatives and Fundamental Education,* Paris, UNESCO, 1950, quoted in United Nations *Special Study,* op. cit., p. 187.

[5] Heckman, *op. cit.,* p. 3.

The cooperative movement is also looked upon as a way of easing the transition from a society based on the extended family, the tribe, or the local community to the individualism of a market economy. Cooperatives are viewed as an instrument for preserving the principles of mutual aid, so often encountered in primitive societies, throughout the painful process of modernization. There are indeed numerous instances of cooperative organizations which have been grafted onto traditional, and especially communal, structures: for example, cooperative sawmills processing the lumber and timber of community-owned forests, and cooperative dairy plants handling the output of individually owned livestock that grazes communal pastures. In those cases, however, communal ownership was firmly established in law and, for this very reason, could not be affected by contacts with the outside world. In most other cases communal or tribal arrangements are likely to be destroyed in the process of modernization long before cooperation can be established.

The recognition of the social, ethical, and political contributions of cooperatives, while essential, must not interfere with a realistic appraisal of the economic role of the cooperative movement in less developed countries. Cooperatives can be socially and politically fruitful only when they are successful business enterprises. While this tenet is fully recognized in advanced countries, it is at times overlooked in the case of newly developing areas. It is therefore essential that the role of cooperatives in economic development be discussed in strictly economic terms.

Cooperatives in Economic Development

Cooperatives and Economies of Scale. Cooperatives must be viewed as a means of offsetting the economic disadvantages of small-scale production units, such as pocket-size farms and one-man handicraft shops, and of applying modern technology to increase the productivity of traditional societies and societies in the transition stage. The results of experimentation and research conducted in industrialized countries, along with the technological improvements introduced in their agriculture and manufacturing industries, can be usefully applied in the physical environment of less developed countries to a much greater extent than is generally indicated even in authoritative treatises on economic development. Such is the case, for instance, for farm chemicals, hybrid corn, and hybrid sorghum, as well as for industrial equipment. Knowledge of appropriate techniques and methods for extending modern technology to farmers and artisans has grown rapidly during the last two decades. Much of the modern technology that can be applied in developing countries does not necessarily require large-scale production units. It requires, however, additional inputs of capital and the consensus of a relatively large number of producers, regardless of the size of their farms or shops. Thus, for instance, artificial insemination is an ideal tool for increasing livestock productivity, but it is economic only where enough dams are made available to permit full utilization of the services of a superior sire (i.e., at least thirty or forty times as many dams as would be required with natural insemination). Similar considerations apply to rural electrification, farm mechanization, seed production, crop storage, and so on.

While the size of production units tends to increase in industrialized countries, less developed countries often show an opposite trend. Enterprises of all kinds are often subdivided through inheritance. Farm holdings are also split by voluntary transfers and by land reform. Cooperative organizations may be a means of preserving some of the advantages of large-scale production. P. T. Bauer points out, for instance, that economies of scale exist in the creation of plantations. Once plantations are established, they can be operated as small units, provided the small entrepreneurs are willing to maintain the production standards and practices of the past.[6] This highly desirable result may be secured through the organization of cooperatives. In fact, countries adopting land reform legislation have often taken steps to promote cooperative associations among the newly created small landholders.

Cooperatives as Schools of Management. A number of devices may be used in place of cooperative organizations to offset disadvantages of scale. They range from voluntary organizations, such as marketing agencies, to coercive regulation of credit, production, and commerce. Because of their unique nature, however, cooperatives perform an additional role in economic development, and a most essential one withal, namely, they serve as a training ground for management. Regardless of the purpose of the organization, the people who supply the capital and organize the activities of the cooperatives are also its suppliers and/or its customers. "The cooperative member is both a part-owner and a customer of his society. It is this duality of role which is typical of cooperatives and serves to differentiate them economically from corporations or partnerships."[7] The fact that every member has a financial interest in his cooperative gives the membership an insight into business problems and some experience, direct or indirect, of business management. Sooner or later every member understands "the importance of selecting as his representative on the management committee a man who is known for his probity as well as for his intellectual attainments."[8]

Single-purpose versus Multipurpose Cooperatives. Cooperatives may be organized for a wide variety of purposes, such as credit, marketing, or purchasing, or for a combination of activities and purposes. Opinions differ on the relative merits of the single-purpose versus the multipurpose cooperative. In some advanced countries much stress is placed on single-purpose cooperatives, and an individual often belongs to several of them. In underdeveloped countries the contrary is often true, principally because the problems of village families are viewed as an inseparable whole.

Promotion of multipurpose cooperatives also reflects the effort to utilize as fully as possible whatever is available in the way of efficient management and organization. The advantages of single- or multipurpose cooperatives vary with local conditions, and cases of highly successful multipurpose cooperative

[6] Peter T. Bauer, *Economic Analysis and Policy in Underdeveloped Countries,* Duke University Press, Durham, N.C., 1957, p. 110.

[7] Peter T. Bauer and Basil S. Yamey, *The Economics of Under-developed Countries,* The University of Chicago Press, Chicago, 1962, p. 223.

[8] J. H. West, "The Cooperative Movement in the Federation of Rhodesia and Nyasaland," *The South African Journal of Economics,* vol. 25, no. 1 p. 55, March, 1957.

organizations are by no means rare. However, experience suggests that success may be more likely if cooperation begins on a small scale with a single clear-cut purpose or with few closely related purposes. A multipurpose cooperative requires qualities of management and a measure of mutual understanding among members which are not usually available at the start, especially in less advanced countries. The same applies to cooperatives that begin by taking in too wide a geographical area.

Importance of Purpose. The purpose for which a cooperative may be organized is closely connected with its prospects for success. Cooperatives tend to be fragile, especially in their early years. It is therefore essential to refrain from organizing a cooperative simply because there is a demonstrated need or an evil to eliminate, but rather to concentrate on the type of cooperative which is "most likely to succeed." In addition, the promotion of cooperatives is often a government undertaking. It is therefore vitally important for government agencies and their advisers to know which cooperative should be encouraged with a reasonable expectation of success and where approaches other than the creation of cooperatives are more likely to yield the desired results. Thus the danger of starting a cooperative solely because there is an obvious need for lower-interest credit or for better marketing methods cannot be overstated. This danger is forever present even when one starts with feasibility surveys designed to provide essential background information on the present credit system, land tenure and land uses, marketing facilities, and so on. Recognition of needs and identification of problems must be attended by a constant awareness of the root causes of the successes and failures of different types of cooperatives.

Role of Government. Whatever their purpose or purposes, cooperatives in developing countries require a large measure of government intervention. Basic laws on cooperatives have been enacted in most newly emerging countries, together with model by-laws. Quite often the government is the sole source of credit for cooperative societies. In addition, government supervision and control of cooperatives are often needed to protect less sophisticated members from unscrupulous minorities and to cope with the shortage or lack of trained and capable leaders. Government assistance, however, often goes far beyond regulatory and credit activities to include[9]

> . . . outright financial contributions or subsidised loans, preferential treatment in the allocation of controlled commodities for distribution, the provision without charges of the services of special government departments or the use of cooperative societies as the sole channels for the distribution of official loans or of other forms of assistance.

Compulsory cooperation is often adopted, especially in the marketing of crops. At times, government control of and interference with the activities of cooperatives, while avoiding financial disaster, has hindered the development of sound leadership and management.

[9] Bauer and Yamey, *op. cit.*, pp. 224–225. For examples of extraordinary assistance to cooperatives, cf. A. J. Meyer, *The Economy of Cyprus,* Harvard University Press, Cambridge, Mass., 1962.

Organizing Agricultural Cooperatives

Purposes of Farm Cooperatives. Any discussion of cooperative organizations in underdeveloped countries may well start from agricultural cooperatives because of the preponderant role of agriculture as a source of employment and income in less developed economies. Moreover, most of the considerations, problems, and techniques of organization that apply to agricultural cooperatives are also applicable to handicraft and cottage industries.

Agricultural cooperatives may be established for a wide variety of purposes or combination of purposes, with the general aim of obtaining advantages of scale or of increasing the bargaining power of the members with regard to their suppliers or customers. Thus, farmers may band into cooperatives to encourage thrift and to secure credit; to pool, store, grade, and sell their products; to process crops and livestock products; to obtain consumer goods and services; to transport farm requisites and products; to improve land tenure arrangements; to pool the use of machinery and breeding stock; to obtain seeds and agricultural chemicals; to provide insurance, or for a combination of these activities and purposes.

Credit Cooperatives. W. K. H. Campbell, one of the leading authorities on practical cooperation in underdeveloped areas, deems the *credit society* the most desirable type with which to start a cooperative movement. This view is predicated on a number of considerations. First of all, credit cooperatives encourage small farmers to save. Small-scale savings can play a very important role in capital formation, as illustrated by the case of Japan. Secondly, in many underdeveloped countries, usury is prevalent in farm areas. Thirdly, the cost of credit for small borrowers is high, even in the case of a government-operated loan system. Fourthly, the control exerted by moneylenders over the output of their debtors is often viewed as a major obstacle to productivity improvement which must be destroyed if the economy is to grow. Moreover, the fixed costs of evaluating the credit standing of the potential borrower, collecting installments, etc., are much smaller for a village cooperative than for a commercial bank.

Among the most widespread and effective forms of credit societies are the Raiffeisen unlimited liability societies, where each member pledges his entire assets to cover the debts of the organization. Creation of a credit society requires first of all an understanding of the risks involved. In underdeveloped countries, agricultural production is often subject to major disasters (droughts, floods, pestilences) which are likely to affect the entire membership and thus cause the collapse of the society. Moreover, the society must be both large enough to defray overhead costs and yet small enough to enable all members to know one another well and to follow what is going on. Loan applications must be scrutinized impartially and thoroughly, and compliance with repayment terms must be enforced.

The question of the purposes for which loans may be granted deserves special consideration. In theory, loans should be extended only for essential purposes (i.e., to increase production) and in the minimum amounts required for their achievement. In practice, developing societies are exposed to the "demonstration effect" and crave all sorts of consumer goods. Thus, loans obtained for productivity purposes may actually be used to buy a bicycle or a camera. Advocates of credit societies state that their success depends upon qualities of character which exist even in the smallest village. These qualities in today's world may well be offset by the widespread desire for higher levels of consumption, which makes credit societies more dangerous than in the past.

Farmers in most newly developed countries are likely to need much more capital than they can afford to save. Recourse to outside capital may also be necessary to alleviate the impact of community-wide crop failures. The credit cooperatives may be an excellent channel to convey outside capital to the farmers. Yet the provision of outside financing—especially from government sources—on generous terms may well encourage irresponsible behavior on the part of borrowers. Moreover, under inflationary conditions, agricultural credit may be used to finance the hoarding of essential commodities.

In short, credit cooperatives may play an essential role in freeing farmers from their thralldom to moneylenders and enabling them to dispose of their output. However, they entail substantial risks which increase steadily with the rise of consumption standards and the disappearance of traditional values.

Landholding Cooperatives. The establishment of cooperatives that operate farmland as owners or tenants is often advocated as a way of improving land tenure systems. The nature of land-operating cooperatives is determined by the basis on which the land is actually controlled, either jointly or in family-size units or allotments. The latter may be the case where large estates are usually leased to individual operators through a chain of intermediaries (large tenants, large subtenants, etc.). Here the sole function of the cooperative is to replace all intermediaries and to rent the land directly from the landlord. The members become subtenants of the cooperative for their individual plots. This system has been used with success in some sections of the Mediterranean Basin.

Where the holdings are operated jointly as single units, two of the major problems of cooperatives, incentives and authority, come to the fore. Recalling that in a cooperative each member must rely on the good faith of the other and that any member may malinger without reducing his share of the earnings, methods must be found to penalize the idlers and to reward superior efforts. In addition, while the members are equal partners, they cannot have equal authority; decisions must be delegated to a managing committee or a manager. Success is possible in a farming cooperative when all the members participate in group tasks—such as the harvesting of crops—or where they can be organized according to their skills in easily supervised work crews or teams and be rewarded on the same basis. Otherwise, landholding cooperatives are likely to succeed only where there are strong ideological or religious ties among the members (for example, Israeli communal farms, some cooperative farms in northern Italy, some small religious communities in various parts of the world) or where vigorous outside management can be obtained. Obviously enough, these considerations apply also to other kinds of rural cooperatives where production is carried on as a joint and cooperative undertaking.

On the whole, the difficulties encountered by landholding cooperatives are so great that caution should be exercised in their promotion. One must not expect that cooperatives of this type can offset the adverse consequences of a drastic land reform. Nor is there any reason to rely on cooperative organizations to carry out the exceedingly difficult task of recomposition of overfragmented holdings.

Machinery Cooperatives. The importance of farm machinery for better soil preparations, speedier harvesting of crops, and more efficient crop processing, along with the advantages offered by large-scale farming with regard to the efficient use of machinery and equipment, have all resulted in many efforts to establish cooperative ownership of tractors, threshers, and other major implements. These arrangements seem to succeed only where the timing of the operation is not essential or where the ties of membership are sufficiently strong to alleviate conflicts among the cooperative owners. In any event, the success of machinery cooperatives also depends upon adequate provisions for accounting, amortization, and maintenance.

Purchasing Cooperatives. Cooperative marketing societies for the procurement of farm supplies and for the sale of produce (eventually after grading and standardization) offer several significant advantages in developing countries. In the first place, bulk purchase of supplies permits very significant savings for the members. Purchasing cooperatives may also be able to obtain farm supplies more adapted to local needs. Finally, they may exercise qualitative controls (e.g., on the quality of fertilizers and feedstuffs) that may otherwise be lacking in societies where *caveat emptor* is the rule. From the standpoint of the economy as a whole, purchasing cooperatives may effect substantial savings of foreign exchange by more efficient procurement abroad. They may also engage in some processing of farm supplies, such as the formulation of pesticides, and thereby stimulate the growth of minor industries within the country. Finally, cooperative procurement and distribution of seeds and other propagating material may facilitate the standardization of crops.

In a number of countries, merchants have become the major vehicle for the introduction of improved methods of production, simply because farmers reject the unsolicited advice of extension workers but understand the merchant's efforts to peddle his wares. Purchasing cooperatives may well become major instruments of agricultural extension.

Marketing Cooperatives. Producers may also band into cooperatives to handle the marketing of their cash crops. Marketing cooperatives or producers' cooperatives can make all the contributions possible with purchasing cooperatives. Growing evidence suggests that the improvement of farm practices is much easier with the introduction of new cash crops than with traditional subsistence crops. This being true, marketing cooperatives may well become a major tool and an essential component of agricultural development.

Most authorities on cooperation recognize the essential role of purchasing and marketing cooperatives, as shown, for instance, by the coffee growers' cooperatives of Tanganyika. They also acknowledge that prospects for the success of such cooperatives may be easier to ascertain. Experts on underdeveloped areas, however, believe that the problem of credit must be solved first, because farmers are otherwise bound to the moneylenders both as sources of supplies and as customers for their crops. Where this is true, it may still be wiser to solve credit problems through noncooperative means and start the cooperative movement in the purchasing or in the produce marketing field.

Organizing Cooperatives for Handicraft and Rural Industries

Economic development requires a drastic reorientation of the activities of artisans and cottage industries. Mass demand for their traditional products (textiles, pottery, footwear, metal goods, etc.) shifts to the factories. Thus the craftsman must find new markets or a new trade. This may mean either the reorganization of old trades to produce artistic work for tourists and the export market (as was done in Sardinia and Indonesia) or the organization of new trades on a cottage industry basis, as in Japan.

In any case, cooperatives can play a key role in the improvement of production techniques, the standardization of products, and the organization of procurement, marketing, and finance. Cooperatives can reduce production costs by pooling the production facilities and inventories of individual craftsmen and by bulk purchases of materials, along lines similar to those obtaining for farm organizations. There are, however, important differences between agricultural and industrial cooperatives. First of all, the latter must bring together producers who heretofore engaged in highly individualistic activities and derived both income and satisfaction from differences in their products. In the new circumstances, standardization of production is the key requirement both in the case of artistic goods for export and with parts and components for industry. Secondly, while the risk of physical losses is much smaller in handicraft and cottage industries, major financial losses may accrue from lack of standardization and failure to meet specifications. Thirdly, even otherwise competent leaders and managers are unlikely to understand the problems posed by new markets.

Local leadership cannot be relied upon, consequently, to supply design and specifications for new products or to handle the surveying and development of markets. These tasks should be left to outside organizations, public or private. Cooperatives, instead, should be the channel through which raw materials are distributed, credit is provided, and output is allocated. Since the success or failure of these activities depends upon the salability of the products, cooperatives in handicraft and cottage industries must be multipurpose organizations which combine production, procurement, marketing, and credit. The provision of credit may be used as a device to start a cooperative organization, but from its very outset the cooperative, once established, must engage in all other activities designed to secure the desired volume and quality of output. This does not mean, however, that in areas where most of the craftsmen are also engaged in farming, the artisan cooperative should extend its activities to encompass agriculture. On the contrary, it must confine itself to its industrial tasks.

Given the variety of tasks, the selection of suitable leaders is exceedingly difficult. The community will naturally look to the outstanding craftsmen as the natural leaders. Yet, and precisely because of their high level of skill, the best artisans may be those least suited to change the patterns of production and to understand the requirements of new markets.

Problems and Pitfalls

Especially at their beginning, cooperatives are extremely fragile organizations. Much has been written, in fact, on the failure of cooperatives. At first glance, the immediate causes of failure appear to be inefficient, dishonest, or incompetent management, insufficient cohesion and unity of purpose of their members, lack of loyalty, excessive competition, operation on too small a scale, *inadequate* study of the physical, economic, social, and cultural environment, and improper assessment of potentials.

Both the local pioneers of cooperation and the government officials concerned with the cooperative movement are at the outset fired with a zeal and enthusiasm which often interfere with realistic assessment of conditions and, at times, make it impossible. Government intervention, in the form of credits, subsidies, and special privileges, may lead to the formation of purely artificial cooperatives. Pioneers and local officials may look to cooperatives as the means to solve utterly impossible problems, such as those of an exceedingly adverse physical environment, the overfragmentation or pulverization of farm holdings, and the disappearance of markets for the products of artisans and cottage industries.

This is why the promotion and establishment of cooperatives must be preceded by an impartial assessment of local conditions and potentials by specialists *not* connected with the cooperative movement. The training of such specialists, in turn, must be based on the study of carefully selected, thoroughly reliable case studies of cooperatives in a wide range of countries, grouped in accordance with their purpose. The problem does not differ basically from the broader one of forecasting responses to public and private investment and to technical assistance. Where, for instance, the physical environment makes agricultural production very risky, no amount of cooperative effort can ensure stability and growth. Nor can any amount of cooperation turn crude products of handicraft into goods highly coveted by tourists and other foreigners.

It is impossible, at the present stage of our knowledge, to formulate an overall theory of cooperative organization. For practical purposes, what is needed and what may be sufficient is to gather enough empirical information to provide at least some benchmarks for the assessment of prospects in a new area or in a new field of endeavor.

It is often suggested that pilot projects are "an effective means of determining the applicability of a particular type of cooperative to a given local situation."[10] Pilot projects do offer a number of advantages, such as manageability, flexibility, opportunities for thorough analytical evaluation, and limited repercussions in case of failures. They may, however, give rise to much friction when assistance is given to only a small segment of the population. Above all, there is the great danger of making pilot projects into showcases, with concentration of managerial skill and technical and financial assistance, and with levels of overhead costs utterly impossible in an operation of wider scope. In other words, as is often the case with technical assistance projects and with demonstration projects, their lessons, if any, may not be applicable to operations on a larger scale. Pilot projects must then be handled as experimental material, with due regard to conditions as representative as possible of the overall situation, and with a careful assessment of exceptional, nonrecurring factors.

[10] *Cooperatives: Democratic Institutions for Economic and Social Development,* Agency for International Development, Washington, D.C., Nov. 1, 1961, p. 21.

Special attention should be given to what Heckman calls the Achilles' heel of cooperation both in feasibility surveys and in the setting up of pilot projects,[11] namely, the lack of basic understanding among members and of capable and competitive management. The mere recognition of a felt need does not necessarily imply a full understanding of the role of cooperatives, nor does enthusiasm for cooperation necessarily breed competent managers. Pilot projects may promote understanding, but they are likely to be managed, in fact if not in name, by outside promoters.

Two additional problems and pitfalls of cooperation deserve special consideration: the role of youth movements and the question of federations or unions of cooperatives. As to the first, cooperatives are essentially instruments and elements of change. As such, they are likely to meet with resistance on the part of the older age groups in the population, including the community leaders. And yet it is within these groups that the traditional virtues, so essential for the success of cooperation—thrift and integrity, for instance—are more likely to be found. Recent experience suggests that youth, because of its intense interest in change, may play a major role in the establishment of cooperatives. Farm youth movements patterned after the 4-H Clubs and the Future Farmers of America have become important starting points for cooperation. The classical "projects" of farm youth movements teach the members the techniques and benefits of record keeping and accounting. Projects also reveal the need for additional physical facilities and organizations that can be obtained only through a cooperative effort. A specific project may, for instance, prove the advantages of mechanical plowing and thus stimulate the formation of a cooperative for the operation of a tractor. Another project may point to the need for joint marketing or bulk purchasing. This has been proved again and again in a number of countries, especially in Italy. Finally, not least of all, attachment to the movement may provide those ties of cohesion so essential for the success of cooperatives.

Problems of scale may at times be solved by banding cooperatives into federations or unions to strengthen their competitive position and to provide joint services (e.g., accounting, auditing, technical information, standards) and credit. This step is likely to prove essential as the cooperative movement grows. Yet a large union of cooperatives soon loses contact with the individual members of its affiliates and becomes indistinguishable from any other form of enterprise of comparable size. In the long run, then, cooperatives work themselves out of a job in so far as noneconomic tasks are concerned—and should aim to do so. One final comment cannot be avoided: Traditionally, the cooperative movement was developed to promote thrift and to increase production rather than to give immediate encouragement to a rise in consumption. Thus old hands in this field tend to frown at initiatives based upon "luxury and frills." Yet viable cooperatives may sprout and grow precisely to cater to the new demands of a society in transition. In some highly individualistic communities of southern Italy, for instance, the cooperative movement had failed but proved a success when peasants formed cooperative societies to procure and operate a TV set, which brought to their village the images of a more

[11] John H. Heckman, *Achilles' Heels of Cooperation*, Kurukshetra, December, 1960

affluent society. What was originally a "frivolous" purpose became the foundation of more obviously constructive undertakings. The general lesson seems to be that in underdeveloped areas the stern traditional standards of the past may, and should be, made more flexible if the seeds of cooperation are to be planted and to thrive.

ADDITIONAL REFERENCES

Campbell, W. K. H.: *Practical Co-operation in Asia and Africa,* W. Heffer & Sons, Ltd., Cambridge, England, 1951.

Food and Agricultural Organization of the United Nations: *Co-operative Thrift Credit and Marketing in Economically Underdeveloped Countries,* Rome, 1959.

Government of Tanganyika: *Tanganyika: A Review of Its Resources and Development,* Government Printer, Dar-es-Salaam, 1955.

International Labor Office: *An Introduction to Cooperative Practice,* Geneva, 1954.

THE ENGINEER'S TASK IN THE UNDERDEVELOPED COUNTRY

Francis L. Brown

The Problem

The engineer in a new country cannot estimate a cost or develop a professionally competent engineering concept without some knowledge of local conditions and customs, any more than he can design a water treatment plant without a knowledge of sanitary engineering. It is not that he is faced with new technical problems; his education has given him the basic facts of design regardless of the location in the world where his new venture takes him. However, he will meet point-blank new customs, concepts of approach, and conditions which are often so strange that his equilibrium is completely destroyed.

For example, there is the matter of preconceived notions. Recently, an engineering executive was asked to submit his list of requirements for a field study of a highway bridge deep in the heart of Africa. The list included pith helmets and gear for head porters. The influence of a movie safari had cropped up, and it would not take long to discover that the pith helmet and shorts went out with Colonel Blimp and the colonial days. A small item, perhaps, but a combination of many such small items can throw a logistics cost estimate off by 50%.

The lack of ability by new administrators to write engineering specifications except in the broadest generalities makes it necessary to hedge each proposal with variations in every direction. Typical of this was a request to furnish a price for a single survey party of four to eight men over a period of one year

---

Mr. Brown, of Brown Engineers, New York, is an executive in several engineering firms. His work has included many highway, bridge, airport, water supply, and other engineering projects, in the United States and abroad.

in the rainforest jungle, the "lump sum" price to include all costs, such as transportation to the site, food, camp, all equipment, local transportation, the engineering work required, demobilization, and return transportation. As a result of submitting a proposal which was subjected to a competitive bidding evaluation, a contract was awarded that eventually lasted four years and had twenty-one engineers and seventy locally hired personnel working the entire time.

How far and how fast do the changing times require the engineer to go? The transition from the oxcart to the superhighway took two thousand years. It is not sufficient to envisage a future growth that makes the usual standard in a highly developed country suitable for the new theater of operation to achieve in one jump. A gradual transition will more often be the most economical and in fact the only practical approach. In other words, opening up new land in Burma or Sierra Leone does not need an expressway—a farm-to-market road is more practical; yet hundreds of thousands of design dollars have been spent on the "expressway approach" to just such problems.

Even the matter of a home or camp requires a new approach. Each area of the globe has developed a way of living that at first seems crude, but a little study will indicate a purpose leading to maximum comfort. In the high-rainfall areas of the tropics good ventilation is more important than air conditioning because high rainfall means high cloud cover, therefore the temperatures are not necessarily extreme, but drying is important. Conversely, an air-conditioning system quickly brings the humidity to 100%, and the result is a cold, damp feeling not always comfortable. Thus the variation in climate is important, and customs can dictate good design features.

One of the most difficult characteristics to assess is the degree of complexity new installations should have. On the one hand, the lack of local technicians may make it desirable to use only the most simple and manually controlled machinery; on the other, the situation may require more complex machinery as being more economical and efficient. No degree of simplification can eliminate the need for importing skilled technicians, however. In one example concerning a water purification plant, the use of slow sand filters did not prevent the need for outside technicians, and the low efficiency could not compare with that of rapid filters of more modern design for which the same technicians would have been required.

In the final analysis, cost is always important. There is a never-ending need for new facilities. Even in a highly developed country like the United States, there is always the question of affording the necessities. The less the country is developed, the more the problem exists. To the engineer, his ability to get more per unit of money is a measure of his ability for a job. Without precise knowledge of all factors, economy cannot be real.

Maximum use of local effort, materials, and skill is the key to economy, and if their availability is not studied, lack of economy results. The measure of injecting more advanced techniques, materials, and skills tests the best of engineering talent to produce the optimum of economies in design. A highway with a price tag of $250,000 per mile, a house for $25,000, or a precision tool that fails completely after one year of inferior maintenance do not solve problems, but create them; such is the responsibility of the engineer in his new assignment.

The engineer quickly realizes that life abroad is not too different from life at home. He must still design and build, with money as the test of his design. He must live with people, and although they have customs strange to him, these may have purpose and reason. He must be the skilled manipulator of old and new, and, regardless of his decisions, he will be subject to review by officials who must accept his work based upon confidence. If the reader finds his own approach confirmed in the light of these examples, then the underdeveloped country will present no problem to him.

Pitfalls of the Inexperienced

The common faults of the engineer at the start of a contract in a new land are for the most part easily avoidable, being caused by failure to adjust to a strange environment. Too much self-assurance may easily lead to trouble. Conversely, getting to know everyone connected with your activity and listening to good advice is a cheap price for saving headaches.

One of the first people an American should get to know in a new country is the U.S. Ambassador, then his staff. The American Embassy will not become a salesman for the new arrival, as some of the Western European Embassies do for their commercial adventurers, but nevertheless there is basic knowledge and information available, with a fair appraisal of local conditions.

Each U.S. Embassy has an operations mission housing the foreign aid personnel. These people know more clearly the exact projects which are to be undertaken if aid is to be a factor.

Unlike at home, competitors of American nationality in the foreign field can and do help each other extensively. They know that a failure by one hurts all Americans, and therefore the creed has been created to help each other as long as everyone is trying to do a good job.

The official in a foregin country is usually more easy to reach than his counterpart in the United States. Therefore, it is good business to get to know him quickly. If a proper relationship is established, he can be of the utmost help.

Last, and certainly not least of the factors influencing the fate of a project, is the local business community. In most countries there are in the big cities businessmen who are well educated and have traveled extensively. While these men are in business and resent local competition from the outsider, naturally among them are those whose business will be assisted by a relationship with the new arrival, whether his venture is complementary or remote by nature.

While getting to know as many members of the local business community as possible is one way to avoid pitfalls, its corollary is just as important, namely, that the inexperienced must realize and know that there will be many a "fast promoter" looking for a new arrival. This takes many different forms. Unlike in the United States, many businessmen will be government officials while at the same time holding large outside interests. It would be indiscreet to generalize, but a warning should be given that many will permit their dual interest to become a factor in their decision process, so that the innocent can find himself in deep trouble by ignoring this fact of life.

Another dangerous factor in some countries is that knowledge is salable; and the way in which the sales operate is intriguing. It is not unusual for a secretary to sell copies of the boss's letters, or for the cablegram messenger to see that a copy gets into a competitor's hands. There have been cases of a letter in the mails being duplicated before delivery. Each country has its problems, and if you do not know them, you may be the victim.

The promoter of new business suggesting projects to you is often quite a difficult friend to handle. No one in business will turn down a good new deal. However, the "pot of gold at the end of the rainbow" more often than not becomes a sticky mess. It is true that some promoters are sound and good salesmen, but it takes a little caution and a great deal of patience to be sure before it is too late. Generally, it is easy to meet people in new countries, but it is good business to be sure that a friend is just that—a friend.

A strange new problem to the American engineer in a new country is the competition of the Western European and the Far Eastern countries. In the United States, with its complete services available, foreign competition does not make heavy inroads; but in the newly developed country this competition is keen and very powerful. Depending upon the client, the American can find himself ever at a disadvantage. From such simple factors as familiarity with systems of measurement to such complex problems as terms of credit, foreign competition will make itself felt. To many officials trained in Europe, the metric system is basic, therefore a lack of knowledge of standards and values in kilograms, meters, or marks, for example, will put the American at a disadvantage.

To the European engineer, a design may be our concept of a preliminary plan; consequently, differences in concepts may influence cost estimates. In the rating of machinery, our conservative approach may result in cost estimates that are too high. On the basis of lower European standards, cost will be only one-half as much. In other words, a 5-hp motor, American standard, may be 7½ to 10 hp by other standards. In price comparisons the American must therefore appear too expensive.

Another wide difference of approach concerns the credit facilities available. The European and, in particular, the Japanese have the services of their Embassies behind them. It is not strange for a foreign Embassy to entertain at a party all the potential business associates that a new arrival from the Ambassador's country wishes to contact. For some reason, U.S. government officials do not support the U.S. businessman as effectively. In the matter of credits, each European country has a government credit guaranty program that makes it easy to extend credits. Although the door has been cracked open in this field by the U.S. government, there is plenty of room for improvement. An example of this problem came recently, when bids were taken for power plant equipment. The approach by the Export-Import Bank allows a manufacturer to get credit terms on three-quarters of his risk, after deducting 15% coming from the manufacturer's profit and other items not considered risk by the United States. This leaves a large gap for the U.S. manufacturer. In the case in point, the German ambassador not only offered 100% guaranties and credit facilities for the German manufacturer, but also an aid program to the country if the German manufacturer's products were purchased under the bid. The American unaware of such competition can spin his wheels of business frequently with no results.

Problems of Logistics

The logistics of a foreign operation are very complex. On one hand the local labor may be available for 15 cents a day, while on the other hand an American mechanic will cost the price of a vice president at home. Each item of supply has its variations. On one construction operation, a contractor's superintendent boasted of how well he cared for his men—and this he did. It was a startling revelation when the auditors disclosed his camp was costing $6.50 per man per meal; in other words almost $20 a day just to feed a man. Needless to say, some changes were made. It is also possible for a man wise to the ways of the desert or the forest to support himself with only a minimum of added items. While being a hermit or ascetic is not advocated, there is a happy medium.

For construction and engineering, the base establishment always presents difficulties. Mention was made earlier of adaptation to local conventions. In this area logistics can vary tremendously. The wise use of screening and a minimum of aluminum structural sections, along with the native's methods of hut construction and the use of local block or brick, can make very comfortable and economical offices and housing in many countries. In cold countries, local convention will also show the way, with minor introduction of structural elements, insulation, and modern heating equipment. I have seen a native building transferred into a most livable unit in southwestern Iran with a minimum of modern lighting and air conditioning, plus a great deal of cleanliness—standard elbow grease and whitewash.

Public Relations

Public relations is a pitfall full of snares and traps. Several instances come to mind quickly of the unsuspecting newcomer creating major public relations problems. One case concerns a new project manager who was almost instantaneously involved, after being in a country only two days. A few drinks, a few careless words with a woman at a bar, and the still more careless slip of allowing the woman to follow him to quarters—it took the skill of the whole staff two weeks to redeem this man's public image. It is unnecessary to say that his value to the firm decreased to zero, yet he was for the most part innocent of any intentional wrongdoing.

The city with only a small foreign element is a gossip shop. It takes very little for poor public relations to get a head start, and it always affects an operation adversely. To keep ahead of such danger requires constant vigilance, a tightfisted discipline, and plenty of positive public relations effort.

Good workmanship requires good employees and good employee relationships. These are standardized to a great extent in the United States. In a newly developing country, they are not. Usually there are complicated labor laws, made more complex to the foreigner by variants in social theories. The rights of an employee, the large number of holidays, the allowances for terminal pay, vacation, sick leave, etc., are usually baffling in the beginning. What is more baffling is the man himself. Like all people, some are good and some are bad; some are bright and some are slow; some are kind and gentle, and some are hard and hostile. One cannot give tests or conduct interviews to find these characteristics. Therefore the selection, discipline, training, and turnover of labor constitute a constant economic problem. In the end, only experience, wise counsel, and mature intelligence will cope with these challenges. If the routine is not learned quickly, it is expensive and sobering. One may be dealing with a man who is only a year or two away from primitive life, not two thousand or more, as in one's own case.

Suggestions for an Approach to New Business

Being unable to conquer the world, one should try to keep within limits. Select an area for an effort, then learn by visit, study, and research what there is to know. It is important, of course, not only to know about the people and their customs, but also to make acquaintance with a few well-selected ones.

Once the area has been selected and visited, then promotion of a project is the logical step. Acquaintance with a good agent, the Embassy, or a businessman may lead to a project. Projects are not usually hard to find. Those that are properly conceived, well supported, and have immediate feasibility may be a little more difficult to discover. One with proper finances, or capable of sound financing, is what you are looking for.

After a project has been planned and sufficiently explored, the negotiation of a proper contract is the next step. As stated before, officials of new countries often think in the broadest of generalities, and contracts come out looking very much alike. To insist on a book for a contract with all the "boiler plate" common to U.S. contracts is futile, but there is a balance, and often the choice of a word can mean much in the way of effort and money at a later date. Contracts should be precise documents, stating clearly the scope of the project, exact methods of survey and control, the quality of plans, and the extent of detailing. The submission of an endless variety of preliminary plans from which a final one will be selected can be costly. The amount of specifications and their quality must be delineated in harmony with the intention upon which the parties agree. The following incident will illustrate the value of this detail: On one project four preliminary designs were required for a bridge design contract, but the client asked for more. Because the number had been clearly stated, an extra fee of $90,000 was obtained. Without this precision of expression, collection of the extra amount would have been doubtful.

The organization of a project differs from that usually encountered in the States. In the first place, many projects require the establishment of camps on the project, with all of the logistics involved. Even though they may work in a city, quarters must be established for the American personnel, offices for the operation, and a liaison system with local officials, local personnel, and the business community must be created. All of this requires time, patience, and good judgment. Two project managers on one job developed offices for the project. The first contract was $11,000 per annum; the successor obtained the same service for $3,000. Every item has this potentiality for variance.

In the selection of personnel, one possibility should never be overlooked. A large number of European technicians are available in many countries, and these are excellent staff personnel requiring lower wages than most Americans. In the Middle East and Southern Asia there are also many locally trained engineers. This is true in most nations, but the number and quality vary from country to country.

The wise engineer will therefore find that his most economical solution is the adaptation of local buildings or building materials and the judicious use of imported materials to make his headquarters and housing livable and useful. His personnel will be a wise balance of American, European, and local men. With proper discipline, the operation can then utilize the tested efficiency of American methods, with lower-salaried personnel trained in these procedures. A combination properly conceived and executed will result in astonishingly economical performance and high-quality workmanship.

The logistics of an engineering operation depend a great deal upon the contract, its organization, and the policy of the engineer-manager. Each item must be thought through to a conclusion. The failure to requisition every nail, bolt, or sheet of paper needed can actually hold a project up for days, since usually there is no store to which you can go for a missing item. Radio communication between a camp or survey operation and the principal city near a project is a necessity. Single side-band transmitters for two-way conversation, with ranges up to 500 miles, are not expensive. Food is always a problem. If reliance is placed upon imported refrigerated foods, the food bill will become high; however, most project areas have local foods which can, by wise selection, reduce food costs. Careful and wise purchasing will result if a local chef of more than ordinary intelligence is allowed to cooperate with the purchasing manager. As important as the purchase and serving of food is the maintenance of proper morale. At a forward camp I once heard one of the survey party chiefs comment on a meal of roast turkey, fresh vegetable salad, mashed potatoes and gravy, dressing, ice cream, cake, and coffee: "When are they ever going to stop feeding us this trash?" A Thanksgiving Day dinner good enough for anyone was "trash" to this man, who had lost his sense of proportion.

Transportation is a most important item in any operation. Accidents are common if control and discipline are loose. The maintenance of spare part requirements is difficult, yet if not available may result in an important vehicle being out of service for a long period of time. The selection of equipment must take into consideration the need for service, the local availability of service, and, finally, the ability of the available mechanics.

On large operations many miles from a central supply point, the use of small planes can become a necessity. In these cases, the plant provides quick service for needs such as refrigerated foods and supply parts, cutting down the inventory requirements, and supplies emergency exits for personnel in cases of accident or surgery. All these uses reduce the needs of the camp and pay for the plane many times over.

Clarity of Concept

A project organized and supported properly has its major battles over. Once established, the engineering problem is geared to the concept of design and then its execution. More dollars are wasted in the failure to think through a design problem before a line is drawn than in any other way. In one case in point, an entire design report which cost half a million dollars was not used because its concept was wrong before it was started. It is therefore advisable that the concept of any project be clearly established and approved in writing by all review agencies before a line is drawn or a word written in final draft.

Some of the concept problems will be outlined:

1. Unit cost
2. Use of local materials versus imported materials
3. Degree of complicity of units requiring maintenance
4. Efficiency of operation
5. Availability of technical operating personnel
6. Utility of end product
7. Stages of construction

One of the problems in American governmental foreign aid programs has been the cost of facilities higher than preliminary estimates have indicated. This has led to congressional investigations and all types of criticism. Such criticism can be avoided in most instances through a thoughtful concept of design. Proper concept will tie the cost to the contemplated figures or point out the fallacy of preliminary estimates before the result is disastrous.

Recently, a project which had been estimated at $15 million was taken under design contract. Immediately the concept of design fluctuated as officials talked first of concrete pavement, then of no pavement; first of 100,000 cm^3 of excavation per km, then of 60,000 cm^3 of excavation per km. In the end, all such problems must be resolved in order to eliminate uncertainties from cost variations of 200 to 300%.

When the concept has been established, the budgeting of the project can be refined in sufficient detail for a final cost control. Accurate delineation of control and approval procedure then becomes desirable. The budget provides answers to such questions as: How many, what size, and what quality drawings shall there be? What specifications shall be written? What standards shall specifications include, U.S., European, other? Outline specifications or detailed specifications? Number of copies of plans required? A good example of the complexity that lack of specific budget details can cause was study of a project for a railroad 500 miles long. The contract stated that fifty copies of the plans were required. In an attempt to delineate the requirement, the railroad committee was asked, "Do you want fifty copies of the cross sections?" Quickly, the answer was "Yes." When it was pointed out that each set of cross sections consisted of 950 sheets, the answer became indefinite. Eventually, only one set was filed with the client. The reader can imagine what the blueprinting bill might have been.

In the execution of the design, continued care must be exercised to get approvals at each stage of the design. Failure to keep the client responsible for his own project will result in disagreements at every stage, and changes in concept or detail can upset any budget control.

While the execution of a design is under way, the problems of public relations and liaison between American and local officials continue unabated. The success of the project in no small way depends on the acceptance of the effort in an atmosphere of trust and client satisfaction.

A project well conceived and well executed must be properly presented. Quality of final presentation is good public relations. A well-prepared set of plans or report is the monument which will remain for the engineer as testimony to his initial effort. Except for the final execution of the construction, his reputation has been established by his design as submitted. While the layman will await the finished results, the official with whom the engineer must work can predict the results from his report.

ELECTRIC ENERGY FOR DEVELOPING NATIONS

Walker L. Cisler

In recent years it has become increasingly well recognized that the use of electric energy is an important yardstick for measuring economic progress. In the issue of Jan. 5, 1963, the magazine *Business Week*, discussing electric power, states: "This is one of the broadest and best measures of the nation's progress, a commodity that cannot be stockpiled economically. Electricity is produced for immediate use in factories, offices, stores, homes, farms, highways, and streets. Industry alone consumes half of the electric power generated in the United States. Another 10 percent goes into commercial establishments. Thus two-thirds of power output is used in American business activity in one way or another." While *Business Week* refers primarily to the United States, long experience there and elsewhere clearly indicates that electric power occupies an equally important, or perhaps even more important, position in the economic advancement of most of the newer nations.

We should hasten to add, however, that electric power is only one of many components which enter into economic advancement and that power facilities for every nation must be planned to fit properly into the broad development program. Progress requires investment in many sectors of an economy. When funds are limited, an overinvestment in any one sector limits the ability to meet necessary investment needs elsewhere.

In planning an electric power development program that is appropriate for a given nation, two tools are of proved value: (1) the electric power survey and (2) the broad energy resource study.

Electric Power Survey

It is not difficult to make an electric power survey for a nation. The compilation of this information is required:

Mr. Cisler is Chairman of the Board of Directors of The Detroit Edison Company, Detroit, Michigan.

1. Extent and capabilities of existing electric power generating facilities
2. Power loads actually being supplied by existing facilities
3. Power loads expected in future years
4. New facilities definitely planned now to meet future power requirements

Let us examine each item separately.

Existing Electric Power Generating Facilities

The capability of existing electric power generating facilities is known by those responsible for their operation. The compilation is largely a matter of arithmetic—that is, listing the various facilities and finding the totals as to capability and units available for the country as a whole and for well-defined subsections or power regions.

It is necessary to use judgment in listing such capabilities. One must be sure that the facilities are capable of carrying loads at all times and that they are rated at their highest load-carrying capabilities. In this way one can determine what power facilities are already available within a country, where they are located, and what service they are capable of performing. In compiling this information no deductions should be made for maintenance requirements or other outages.

Power Loads

Let us consider now the power loads that are actually being supplied from the existing generating facilities. To provide adequate electric service, power must be available for use whenever the customer so requires. The power loads that are to be tabulated represent the peak loads which the customers may demand at any time to meet their requirements.

Here again a considerable knowledge of electric power operations is necessary. In some instances facilities may not be available to carry full load, but the problem is to determine what the peak loads would be if there *were* sufficient generating facilities able to carry such loads at the time when they might reasonably occur.

In the United States, for example, peak loads generally occur in December, the darkest and often the coldest time of the year. Nevertheless in certain warm sections of the country we are now finding that the peak loads occur during the summer period, when extensive use is made of air-conditioning equipment and, in some cases, pumps for irrigation water. So in each situation it is necessary to determine what peak loads would occur if facilities were adequate, and when they would occur.

Forecasts of Future Loads

Forecasting future power loads is a more difficult problem, but it is possible to determine quite closely what the future customer requirements will be by surveying the types of facilities under construction for manufacturing, housing, and other purposes. In the United States various methods are used in determining such power loads, and we find that by working closely with the major customers who will be using the power we can determine the schedule of probable load growth by studying their plans for expansion.

For example, a large steel mill requires some two or three years to construct. The designers of the mill are well acquainted with the power loads that it may develop. It is possible, then, to determine how great an additional load will be applied to the electric power system by a certain date.

There is also the increasing use of electricity by existing customers. Most power systems in the United States find that residences increase their electricity consumption each year by 2, 3, or 4 percent. In figuring the future peak load of a power system it is necessary to take into account these small increments of load.

At the present time there has been enough experience throughout the world in dealing with the electric power problems of emerging nations to forecast the load increases that apply to uses in the home, in small business, in commerce, and in industry. In this way it is possible to determine, for the near future at least, the power loads to be expected.

The problem is more complicated when we consider the longer range in forecasting, but generally in the emerging nations today the plans are developed for economic improvement for many years in the future, and out of these plans can come reasonably good statistics or forecasts concerning the power loads which may develop in five, ten, or even twenty-five years.

Since 1948 this has been done quite successfully in Greece, where load forecasts for ten and twenty years ahead were made. Ten years later, in 1958–1959, it was found that the forecasts were very close to the actual loads developed by that time.

New Generating Facilities

Our final item in the power survey has to do with the new facilities definitely planned or proposed for the future to meet power requirements. This also is a fairly simple compilation of the plans of the various power systems throughout the country to meet increasing power loads.

In the United States we find that new thermal power plants can be designed, built, and prepared for operation in three or four years. If an extensive amount of site preparation is in prospect, the job may take longer than four years, even for a thermal plant. For hydraulic power plants, where there is a vast amount of civil work including large dams and the construction of long tunnels, more time is required for design and construction, and they must be planned five, six, or even seven years ahead.

Rationalization of Generating Facilities and Power Loads

Once planning is started, it is possible to determine what facilities are needed to carry the peak loads in the immediate future and what additional plants may be required in the more distant future.

As these determinations are made, and as financing, engineering, and other problems are worked out, the new facilities go from planning into construction and then into use, to provide on schedule for the anticipated increase in power load.

This kind of planning can be carried through quite accurately in relation to the entire picture. Once the facts are at hand, we can summarize the capability of the power facilities as programmed for either a few years or for a long period ahead. This will show the power loads which the available facilities can be expected to carry. Then by putting together the statistics which we have discussed, we can determine, year by year, the peak power loads that may develop.

In the United States, where this program of power surveys has been in use for some eighteen years, it is well recognized that to carry all power loads without interruption power systems must have some capability in excess of the loads themselves. This, of course, is to provide for the outages of some machines which are bound to occur and for unexpected variations in the load applied to the system by customers.

In countries where the economy is just beginning to develop, it will be found from time to time that the loads which can be expected will exceed the capability of the generating facilities. There is but one answer to this—power loads must be curtailed because generating facilities are not adequate to meet requirements.

Experience in the United States has indicated that, under ideal circumstances, power systems have operated successfully and without curtailment of load when the capability exceeded the load by as little as 5 percent. Under most circumstances, however, it appears that good operation can be assured only when the capability of the power system exceeds the peak load by 10, 12, or even as much as 15 percent, depending to a large extent upon the nature of the power systems involved and the extent of interconnection.

In some countries where there are comparatively small, isolated systems, the margin of reserve must be substantially higher than that necessary where the generating facilities are well interconnected. Decisions must be based upon actual situations. Thus the compilation of capabilities and loads provides the basis for judgment. When it is found that the existing facilities are not enough to carry the load without difficulty, then the installation of more equipment is indicated. The exact nature of the new equipment and where it should be installed depend, in turn, upon the individual situation.

In the United States, where electric power systems are highly developed, there are areas where thermal generation is the only reasonable means of providing electricity. Companies plan many years ahead to obtain sites where new stations can be installed economically. When new facilities then become necessary, these companies are in a position to move ahead rapidly with decisions concerning the size of the machines that should be installed and the location and type of fuel that should be used, whether it be coal, oil, gas, or nuclear.

A power survey of this kind, although it was not so labeled, was made in Greece during 1948 and 1949 and served, as I have said, as the basis for the development of the nationwide power system. Based upon the loads which were determined, power facilities were approved, both hydraulic and thermal, to carry the loads which it was believed would develop during the next ten years. Three hydro plants and one thermal plant were installed quite close to schedule and found the loads which had been anticipated ready to use power. Through the years the load has increased, additional power plants have been built, and the system has worked out satisfactorily.

In 1952, a power survey program was undertaken in Japan, and it has served remarkably well there to bring out the fact that power loads were growing at a tremendous rate and that a very large program of new power plant construction was needed to meet the demand. An electric power survey has been made in Tunisia and is being used in carrying out the program for economic development there. This type of survey is made with little difficulty by any nation that wants to plan its electric power program in a rational manner to fit the development of the economy.

Energy Resources for Power and Generation

In contemporary civilization, energy is extremely important to industry, commerce, and even to our homes. For example, the production of steel requires vast amounts of energy, supplied perhaps by electric furnaces or by the burning of oil or gas. Even the coke which is used in steel furnaces burns and supplies heat which is required for the processing.

The chemical industry requires tremendous amounts of energy. Electricity is used for the production of caustic, and heat in various forms enters into the manufacture of many other chemicals.

At home electricity is needed for lighting, cooking, and frequently for space heating. It is possible for gas or oil to serve for heating. Thus energy becomes an extremely important item in the economic development or advancement of any nation.

Let us look at the various kinds of energy that may be involved and note how they may enter into the planning for economic development.

Hydroelectric Power Resources

Perhaps one of the best-known sources of energy in many areas is falling water, which generates hydraulic energy. In some parts of the world there are vast amounts of water power that can be developed, while in other parts there is none. In some countries the water power may be in remote areas, as in the Rocky Mountain section of the United States, making it necessary to transmit the generated electric energy long distances to points of use.

In an energy survey it is important to know quite accurately the amount of hydraulic power that can be developed, regardless of the location of the sources. This requires detailed study of river characteristics, the heads which may be developed, the use of the land along the riverbanks, and the like. Such studies are important to a comprehensive energy resources survey.

Fossil Fuels

Fuels, of course, are our most important source of energy. We can burn them to make the heat used directly in industrial processes. They can also be used for direct-heating purposes in homes and other buildings. They can be burned to supply the heat needed in the fuel industries themselves. Let us consider briefly the three main sources—coal, petroleum, and natural gas.

Coal deposits are scattered all over the world, and our knowledge is still incomplete in some localities, particularly concerning the extent of the deposits. Nevertheless it is generally known where the deposits may be found, and their extent can be determined through comparatively simple core-drilling operations. Because there are wide differences in quality, it is necessary to determine the nature of the fuel.

In some instances, as in Ireland, the coal, generally called "sod," is of low-quality, mainly vegetable, matter that has only begun the long process of conversion into coals. In other parts of the world, such as Korea, the coal deposits are extremely old, and the transformation process has progressed to the point of producing low-grade graphite. In other countries, of course, as in the United States, where there are vast deposits of coal ranging from lignites up to the anthracites, there are large, easily mined deposits of the better grades, with a heat value of about 12,000 Btu per pound. Such coals can be burned very readily for nearly all purposes.

Petroleum is generally found at much deeper levels than coal. Exploration is now going on in many parts of the world, and within the past twenty years vast new deposits of petroleum have been discovered in many parts of the globe and production begun. Because petroleum can be burned almost as it is brought from the ground for steam-raising purposes, it becomes an important item in the generation of electricity in thermal stations.

Through refining, a part of the petroleum can be stripped off and used as a fuel which remains liquid under very low pressure but gasifies readily at atmospheric pressure (low-pressure gas). Such gases are widely used in many parts of the world and enter into the energy picture in a significant way. Petroleum is also used for the manufacture of gasolines and fuel oil for many types of internal combustion engines—and here again the availability of petroleum becomes one of the key considerations in a nation's energy study.

Natural gas has been found in many areas in vast quantities. This is a higher-quality fuel and may be substituted for coal and for most uses of petroleum. Therefore a sound determination of the availability of fossil fuels and their cost is a key item in the study of the use of energy for any country.

Because of the large world resources of fossil fuels, they are available for import into almost any country. Vast amounts of coal have been transported at various times from the United States to Europe and into other countries suffering temporary or extensive shortages. Currently the transportation of petroleum is a major undertaking. Very large tankers have been built which range the waters of the world. Any country close to water can enjoy an unlimited supply of imported petroleum products. Even though fossil fuels are not indigenous to a nation, it can obtain adequate supplies through importation.

There is, of course, the cost problem. Transportation is an expense, and when it becomes necessary to transport fuel over long distances, the cost of the energy may become higher than can be justified economically.

Nuclear Fuels

During the past fifteen years nuclear energy has become a most important item among the energy resources. It is not clear at the present time, however, exactly how nuclear fuels will fit into the energy situation in many countries. The research and development program which has been in progress for some ten or twelve years, in the endeavor to develop the uses of nuclear fuels for power generation, has advanced unusually well. It is now known that, technically, nuclear reactors can be built which will operate in a highly satisfactory manner for power generation, and the major endeavor is directed toward the solution of economic problems of nuclear energy.

The major problems seem to be the cost of such reactors, the cost of the nuclear fuels that must be used, and the cost of the power produced by such reactors. It is clear that to achieve nuclear power economically, it will be necessary to utilize very large production units for some years, at least. By late 1964 it was announced that 24 nuclear power projects with capacities ranging from 4,300 to 800,000 kilowatts would be built in the United States for operation in the late 1960s. It is believed that these stations will have good operating characteristics and will produce power at costs which will be competitive with conventional fuel-burning power stations, or nearly so.

It has been demonstrated that technical knowledge of a high order is required for the design, construction, and operation of nuclear plants. Therefore for some years to come it would appear that the smaller nations and those not thoroughly experienced in exotic mechanical, physical, and electrical problems should first devote their endeavors to the gaining of experience in the design, technology, and use of nuclear power plants, rather than in the actual construction of small projects for commercial use. The author nevertheless believes that nuclear power plants will be developed in time which can be used successfully anywhere in the world, provided that correct operating procedures are followed. All the evidence points toward nuclear power assuming a key role in the energy patterns of all nations in the future.

Economics, Economic Development, and Financial Considerations

As indicated earlier, many and varied problems exist in the development of any nation. Electric power is simply one of the facets. It is presumed that qualified economists would plan the development of industry and other resources in accordance with the finances and advancements anticipated.

With information on energy resources, it becomes possible to plan for the long-term development of a country and particularly for those industries which are large users of energy. Knowing the hydraulic resources, the fossil fuel resources, the availability of imported fuels, and the conditions related to the use of nuclear fuels, it becomes possible to plan for the proper development and use of such resources.

It may be found, incidentally, that whereas hydraulic resources are available, it is more advantageous from the standpoint of finances and other matters to develop the use of fossil fuels. In Greece, for example, while there were many hydraulic power sites available for development, it was finally decided that the first plant to be built should be a fairly large thermal plant close to a coal-mining area. This provided both the much-needed electric power and the rehabilitation of an extensive mining operation, and also created jobs for some two thousand men. This plant proved so successful that others have been built and are now being extended. As part of the overall program, it has been found possible, subsequent to the initial program, to undertake the construction of additional hydroelectric projects. The entire program has been worked out to provide the most desirable economic conditions within the country.

Similar plans can be made for other nations. They require careful study of the resources and careful planning for the economic development of the country and the utilization of its financial resources.

THE PLANNING OF FERTILIZER MANUFACTURING PROJECTS

Dr. L. M. Qureshi

An essential step in planning a fertilizer manufacturing project is the selection of the fertilizer or fertilizers to be manufactured. A number of compounds can act as chemical fertilizers; ammonium nitrate, ammonium sulfate, sodium nitrate, cyanamide, etc., can supply the nitrogen required by plants, and superphosphates can supply the required phosphorus.

Many factors have to be taken into consideration for the selection of the fertilizer. These include the chemical composition of the soils, the response of the principal crops to the use of the various fertilizers, and the availability of raw materials. A knowledge of the chemical composition of the soils is necessary for determining in what respect the soils are deficient, in order to produce the chemical or chemicals that would correct this deficiency. If the soils are deficient in nitrogen, there is no point in producing phosphatic fertilizers; similarly, if they are deficient in phosphorus, the addition of nitrogenous fertilizers will not make up the deficiency. Thus it is essential to make an extensive chemical survey of the soils in the various parts of the country where the fertilizer is intended to be used.

A knowledge of the response of various crops to the use of the fertilizers is also necessary. One cannot rely only on the chemical composition of the soil. It is possible that the addition of a nitrogenous fertilizer to a soil deficient in nitrogen may not result in such increased yields as would make its use an economic proposition. So it is necessary to know whether or not the crops on which the fertilizer is intended to be used will respond favorably. This calls for extensive experiments on different crops under various climatic and other conditions prevailing in the country.

Dr. Qureshi is a Consultant at the United Nations. This article is from his "Planning of Fertilizer Manufacturing Projects," in *Formulation and Economic Appraisal of Development Projects,* 1961, vol. II, pt. XI, pp. 685–690.

The availability of raw materials is obviously another important factor. If the production of a particular fertilizer is indicated on other grounds, but the necessary raw materials are not available locally, its manufacture from imported raw materials may turn out to be a wasteful operation. This consideration may necessitate a geological survey of the country to be sure about the availability of the raw materials required.

All these factors must be taken into consideration before a correct decision on the matter can be taken. This may take considerable time if the necessary research work has not already been done.

Another essential step in planning the project is the selection of the manufacturing process. A fertilizer can be made by different methods and from different raw materials. Let us take nitrogenous fertilizers as an illustration. There are many possible ways for preparing them. One method consists in the direct combination of nitrogen and oxygen at the temperature of the electric arc. The materials formed as a result of this combination can easily be converted into a fertilizer. The principal raw materials, namely, nitrogen and oxygen, are derived from the air at practically no cost, but it requires the use of enormous quantities of electricity. The conversion of 1 ton of atmospheric nitrogen into a chemical fertilizer may require as much as 67,000 kwhr of electricity. This method would be a practical proposition only in countries where electricity is extremely cheap.

Another method is the combination of nitrogen and hydrogen under high temperature and pressure and the conversion of the ammonia so formed into ammonium sulfate. Nitrogen can be easily obtained from the atmosphere. Hydrogen is the costlier raw material, and it is the preparation of this element which is sometimes the main problem in the manufacture of ammonium sulfate. It can be obtained from water with the help of electricity, but here again the cost of electricity is a very vital factor. It can also be produced with the help of coal, coke, charcoal, and wood. There are different methods for its preparation even with the help of coal. The conversion of ammonia into ammonium sulfate requires another raw material, namely, sulfur, which may be available in the elementary form or as a sulfate such as gypsum; this conversion can also be brought about by more than one method.

This brief account indicates the complexity of the problem in the selection of the processes to be used for the manufacture of the required fertilizer. It is a highly technical question and requires a careful examination of the availability and costs of different raw materials and of the capital and operating costs of the equipment required. A wrong decision in this matter would result in higher costs of production than might be alternatively possible.

The next step in the planning of the project is a decision about the size of the plant. Fertilizer manufacture is an industry in which the economies of large-scale production are very great. For example, the Technical Mission to Advise on the Production of Artificial Fertilizers in India, appointed by the Government of India in the early forties, estimated that if 350,000 tons of ammonium sulfate were to be manufactured annually in one factory, the capital investment would be about one-half of what it would be if the same quantity were manufactured in six smaller factories. For obvious reasons, the unit costs of production in smaller factories are bound to be much higher than in the bigger ones. In a small country the fertilizer requirements may not be sufficiently large to justify production on a scale at which the unit costs of production are the lowest. It is therefore necessary that the country should know the difference in the capital costs and unit costs of production in the case of bigger and smaller factories in order to decide whether it should go in for fertilizer production at all, or whether it would be worthwhile and practicable to enter into an arrangement with some neighboring country for meeting the requirements of more than one country from a common source. This calls for the preparation of detailed estimates of capital costs and unit costs of production for factories of various sizes under the conditions prevailing in each country. It is possible, however, that in a big country with raw materials available in various districts it may be more economical to have a few smaller factories than one big factory, if the economies in transport are greater than the economies of large-scale production.

Another important decision which has to be taken in the course of planning the project concerns the location of the factory. Factors which determine this include the location of raw materials and fuel and of the consuming areas, transport costs being a substantial part of the total costs of production. Raw materials and fuel have to be transported from their sources to the factory, and the fertilizer produced has to be transported from the factory to the consuming areas. In the case of the manufacture of ammonium sulfate from coal and gypsum, for example, the raw materials are approximately three times the weight of the finished product. This indicates that the nearness of the raw materials and fuel is more important than that of the consuming areas. A map of the country should be prepared indicating the location of the raw materials and of the consuming areas, and the location of the factory should be determined so as to minimize the total transport costs, that is, the transport costs of the raw materials to the factory and of the finished article to the consuming areas. Other factors which have to be taken into consideration in determining factory location are general climatic conditions and the availability of power, water, and other facilities.

The importance of raw materials and fuel has already been mentioned. One must ensure that they are available not only now or for the next five or ten years, but also for the next forty or fifty years. If the raw materials are exhausted, say, after ten years, it will result in great losses, for it will no longer be possible to make proper use of the fertilizer plant. The sources of raw material and fuel should therefore be geologically surveyed and estimates of available quantities prepared. The manufacture of fertilizer is an economic proposition only if the raw materials and fuel are sufficient to last for the lifetime of the manufacturing plant.

The mere existence of the raw materials in the country is not sufficient. It is possible that some development work may be necessary before they can become available. A mine may have to be developed in order to extract the raw materials, so the fertilizer manufacturing project should include detailed plans for such development, if it is necessary. These plans should also indicate how long it will take to produce the raw materials in the quantities required, in order to ensure that the operation of the fertilizer plant after it has been installed is not held up for want of raw materials.

Comparing the estimated local costs of production and the estimated costs of imports is an essential part of the planning of the project. If the estimated local costs are higher, it is necessary to consider whether the country should manufacture fertilizer at all or should import the required materials from abroad. It is possible that, for considerations other than purely economic ones, a country may find it advantageous to be self-sufficient in respect of its fertilizer requirements; but in that case it is absolutely necessary to know in advance the price that must be paid for self-sufficiency, so that the question may be decided in full awareness of what is involved.

Estimating the costs of future imports is not an easy matter. These costs are dependent on a number of factors which may be completely unpredictable. All the same, the past can sometimes be a useful guide for the future. Information should be collected about the costs of the imported fertilizers during the last ten to twenty years. If a country has not been importing chemical fertilizers in the past, information about the f.o.b. costs in the principal producing countries can be utilized in calculating the c.i.f. costs for the country concerned. An examination of the costs of imported fertilizers for a sufficiently long period in the past is likely to be useful in so far as it indicates whether or not the current prices of the imported fertilizers are influenced by any extraordinary world factors which may not be lasting in character.

An estimation of the future demand for the fertilizer is another essential part of the planning. Among other things, the demand for a fertilizer is dependent on its price and on the prices of the crops to be raised with its help. If the latter are high, the demand for the fertilizer can be great even if its price is rather high, but if the prices of the crops are low, the demand for the fertilizer can be large only if it is available at very cheap prices. Thus the future prices of the crops to be raised with the help of the fertilizer must be estimated. This is a very difficult task and may be no more than mere speculation, for the prices of agricultural commodities which enter the world market are dependent on a number of world factors which cannot be foreseen. Still, an examination of the fluctuation in local prices of the various crops in the past ten to twenty years can be a useful indication of future prices. In any case, estimates of the demand for the fertilizer at various prices of crops should be prepared on the basis of the estimated local costs of its production. These estimates would be helpful in indicating the amount of the subsidy required to ensure full utilization of the fertilizer in the event of a fall in crop prices.

If the current consumption of the fertilizer in a country is small and it is intended to encourage its use, the project should include detailed plans for the extension services necessary for ensuring greater use of the fertilizer by agriculturists.

Experiments on an extensive scale must precede its actual use if the best results are to be obtained. The agriculturists must know the optimum conditions for the application of the fertilizer, including, if necessary, the addition of other chemicals and organic manures, taking into consideration climate, chemical composition of the soil, and other factors. This would necessitate a considerable extension of agricultural research.

The importance of costs in the utilization of fertilizer has already been emphasized. In the case of many commodities, the prices paid by agriculturists are much higher than the wholesale prices; the setting up of a special marketing organization may therefore be necessary to ensure that the distribution costs are kept at a minimum and that the fertilizer is delivered to the agriculturists at the lowest possible price.

Fertilizer manufacture is an extremely complex industrial undertaking requiring a large number of technical personnel with the highest degree of skill in their respective fields, so an estimate of the staff requirements should be made. In an underdeveloped country, most of the high-grade technicians may at first have to be imported from abroad. Plans should, however, be prepared for training the nationals of the country to replace the imported staff in the course of time. As it usually takes a number of years for the manufacturing plant to be set up, a sufficient number of students may be sent abroad for training, so that they may be available for service when the plant goes into production. Simultaneously, arrangements should be made for training the staff locally, to ensure that the operation of the plant is not held up for lack of technical personnel and that the cost of keeping the foreign technical staff is kept to a minimum.

As has already been pointed out, the completion of a fertilizer project takes a number of years, India, for example, started planning the manufacture of fertilizers in 1944, expecting to go into production in 1951. A timetable for the completion of the project should be prepared, including estimates of the funds required during the entire period, so that the necessary financial arrangements may be made in advance. The obstacles to be encountered and the causes for delay might also be anticipated, so as perhaps to eliminate some of the causes for delay. Besides, it would enable the training of the staff to be properly coordinated with the execution of the project.

The importance of transport in the production and distribution of chemical fertilizers has already been referred to. The increased agricultural produce resulting from the use of the fertilizer may need additional transport. An examination of the existing transport system of the country is therefore necessary in order to determine whether or not it can handle the additional traffic brought about by the transport of the raw materials, fuel, fertilizer, and the increased agricultural output. If the existing transport services are not adequate for these additional burdens, the fertilizer project should also include plans for an extension of these services.

It is possible that the agriculturists may not be able to use the fertilizer for lack of finance; it may have to be paid for immediately, whereas the increased yield of the crop from which this payment can be conveniently made will be realized after the harvest. If the existing credit facilities for the agriculturists are inadequate, some means will have to be devised for making the necessary credit available. This would call for a careful examination of the existing system of agricultural credit of the country. Otherwise, it is possible that the fertilizer may be produced in the quantities required and that the agriculturists may be anxious to use it, yet that it may remain unused for lack of the necessary credit facilities.

The system of land tenure in a country has an important bearing on the use of fertilizer by tenant cultivators. If the tenant is required to pay rent in the form of a fixed percentage of the gross produce, there may be no economic incentive for the use of the fertilizer by the tenant, for the cost of the fertilizer may have to be borne by him alone, while the increased yield resulting from its use is shared with the landlord. It is therefore possible that a reform of the existing land tenure system may be necessary. In any case, a careful examination of the system is essential for a proper appreciation of its effects on the use of fertilizers by tenant cultivators.

It should be borne in mind that a fertilizer project is a long-term undertaking that starts yielding returns only after a number of years. Thus, for a long time, the expenditure incurred, in so far as the disbursements are made in the local currency, continues to generate incomes without producing corresponding goods and services available for consumption, causing inflationary effects. The country concerned should be prepared for this development.

The manufacture and utilization of chemical fertilizers calls for a very large investment of a country's resources and has far-reaching effects on its economy. Technically it is one of the most complex industrial enterprises, and its planning is by no means an easy task. It requires the pooling together of the knowledge and experience of a large number of experts in many fields. It may require a fairly large organization having adequate resources. It is definitely economical in the long run to obtain the best available technical advice on the various aspects of the project; expenditure on planning should be regarded as money well spent, for if some wrong decisions are made owing to defective planning, the country concerned may be involved in heavy losses later.

THE IRON AND STEEL INDUSTRY IN A DEVELOPING ECONOMY

E. K. Sandbach

Introduction

The establishment of an integrated iron and steel industry in a developing economy creates a great new driving force which, experience demonstrates, provides the basis for rapid economic, industrial, and social growth. The decision by a developing nation to create such an industry begins a long chain of events which require the most careful and professional planning in a large number of fields.

Before a decision of this magnitude is made, responsible officials need to weigh carefully the many considerations involved. This paper is intended to be of assistance in this regard, and it is divided into three parts, first, prerequisites for building an iron and steel plant; second, the benefits which accrue to the economy when a basic iron and steel industry is established; and third, the step-by-step evolution of such a project.

Prerequisites for Building an Iron and Steel Plant

Despite the attractiveness of the idea of creating an iron and steel facility, there are definite prerequisites, listed below, which must be fulfilled before any steel mill project can be wisely undertaken. This cannot be overemphasized. Whether or not these prerequisites can be fulfilled, however, can be determined only through a very careful survey and analysis by specialists in a number of key areas.

1. Adequate markets—based on present consumption and predictable growth to support a minimum economic-sized plant
2. Adequate raw materials at reasonable cost

Mr. Sandbach is Vice President of Koppers International, C.A.

3. Adequate transportation at reasonable cost for raw materials and finished products
4. Good site location accessible to raw materials (including water), markets, and labor supply
5. A satisfactory financial plan for construction and operation of the plant

Adequate Markets. None of the benefits of an iron and steel industry is possible unless there is a sufficient internal market for steel products to support an economical-sized steel-producing facility. Therefore, the first step to be taken in determining the economic feasibility of establishing a steel industry is a well-planned market survey. Quantities of iron and steel imported in the past serve as a convenient starting point.

If the statistics available in the country are inadequate to establish this point, then information can be obtained from the records of importers of these products. To predict the future growth is sometimes difficult because, in a rapidly developing economy, previous economic history is not indicative of future growth after steel products become available locally at steady prices. Prediction of future trends depends upon a study of conventional indices such as the gross national product, population growth, and combinations of statistical facts which may seem reasonable and relevant in the light of present conditions. Of special significance here is the use of information on trends in other developing nations comparing what happened before and after the building of a steel plant.

Once total steel consumption has been established, it is necessary to spell out the various end uses of the products. These end uses include reinforcing rod for concrete construction; round rods for wire and nails; small angles and channels for construction; pig iron for independent foundries; structural shapes for construction of buildings and machinery; and flat sheets for siding and roofing, utensils, hollow enamelware, containers, and tinplate.

The quantity of each product must then be carefully estimated. This information is used to determine the size of mill to be designed in order to satisfy both markets immediately available and those projected for the immediate future. It is important to understand that it is seldom practical to propose a plant that will make all the sizes or all the types of steel products that have been imported in the past. It would not be economic to make a small quantity of a given product, particularly if the market forecast for this product were also small. Therefore, it is necessary to design the plant to produce the greatest number of products which it can make most economically.

It is interesting to note that in steel plant projects in developing economies there is a pattern of growth which usually begins with the production of merchant products required for construction applications, such as concrete reinforcing bars and angles, and then proceeds eventually to the flat steel products necessary to a more highly industrialized economy.

Consideration of all these factors will result in an estimate, by classification of products and individual sizes, of the total iron and steel requirements for the next ten years, which is about as far ahead as one can make a reasonable prediction.

Raw Materials. Accessibility of adequate raw materials at a reasonable cost is vital to the development of the plant. As it will be necessary to have proved reserves of assured sources of the various raw materials available to serve the plant for a period of twenty to twenty-five years, a scientific program of drilling and testing under competent supervision must therefore be undertaken. This program must prove not only the quantity of the raw materials available, but also their physical and chemical characteristics. The costs of mining and transporting these raw materials to the plant site must also be established, and these costs *must* be reasonable, or the economic soundness of the entire project may be jeopardized. If insufficient quantities are available or poor qualities of raw materials are encountered, it may be necessary to consider importing such materials, or at least importing a portion of the total requirements, if the economics justify doing so.

A firm commitment for adequate supplies of raw materials must be obtained at definite prices on which to base the economic viability and financial projection of the project.

Transportation. Next comes accessibility and transportability of raw materials at a reasonable cost. Also, consideration must be given simultaneously to the cost of moving the finished products of the plant to consuming markets. Excessive costs here, even with all other factors favorable, could defeat the project.

The most desirable and cheapest form of transport is by water, that is, river, lake, or ocean. Other methods of transport are railroad, aerial ropeway, and highway. Each method has its own "pros and cons" as compared with the others, so a thorough investigation should be made of the cost of transporting materials to and from the various plant sites selected for investigation.

Plant Location. Plant location can often make the difference between profit and loss in steel plant operation. In addition to the obvious factors of accessibility to raw materials and markets, and the cost of transportation, the land must be obtainable at a reasonable cost. It must also have good soil-bearing conditions to carry the heavy loads and not require extensive piling or other site preparation costs. In addition, the site must provide adequate supplies of potable and process water and be situated so that it will be easily served by good housing, schools, hospitals, utilities, and other facilities for workers and their families. Highways, roads, airports, waterways, and transportation services into the plant are also required for a good location.

Should the plant have to be located in an undeveloped part of the country, it may be necessary to construct a complete town site and provide all the necessities of a town or village. When this happens, it adds to the economic burden of the steel plant project, if the cost of these facilities must be charged to it. Experience indicates, however, that local governments are often willing to subsidize the town site development in order to make the project possible, decentralize their industries, and bring about the development of a new portion of the country. In this event, the iron and steel plant is relieved of a financial and administrative burden.

Financial Plan. Sufficient funds must be provided on reasonable terms to finance the construction and initial operation of the plant. The loans must be on a long enough term and at low enough interest rates to permit the plant to be economically viable.

With satisfactory answers to these five prerequisites, possible benefits may now be evaluated and the characteristics of the project determined in terms of plant design, capital cost, financing, and plan of operation.

Benefits

It is well known that the consumption of iron and steel products is a barometer of economic, technical, and social growth. Examples could be cited showing that the advent of an iron and steel plant in some of the recently developing nations resulted in economic advancement. In addition, the development of an iron and steel industry promotes certain other immediate benefits, which include local availability of steel products as compared with imports, large-scale employment of local labor, and conservation of foreign exchange.

While the primary benefits created by the introduction of an iron and steel industry are of great importance, the other benefits which are in turn created play a very significant role in spurring economic growth. For instance, it has been learned by experience that for each individual employed directly in an iron and steel mill approximately eight to ten persons will find employment in supporting industries, such as the mining of iron ore, coal, and limestone, and in the transportation services associated with the plant. A tertiary effect is the generation of other smaller servicing businesses that find their mainstay of support in the industries created. In addition to this, as a result of local availability of steel at steady prices, a wide variety of consuming industries come into being for converting the steel mill products into finished and semifinished goods. The local steel mill provides a basis for confidence among people who desire to go into business, because they are assured of a steady supply of these steel products.

Because of their need to import a large number of finished products, many developing countries find themselves with a major problem of conserving foreign exchange. Hence the introduction of an iron and steel industry and the substantial reduction of iron and steel imports which this brings about make it possible to conserve foreign exchange and bring the economy of the country into better balance. The full realization of this saving is made possible when the raw materials for the production of steel are indigenous. Quite obviously, if a steel mill were built on the premise of importing some or most of its raw materials, the advantage which would accrue to the country would be correspondingly reduced.

Because the greatest quantity of products needed initially by a developing economy follow a pattern, it can be stated that even a small steel plant with a capacity of 150,000 metric tons per year, producing only a partial range of steel products well selected according to the local market demand, may be able to supply a very large percentage of the local finished steel requirements.

Thus we find that in most cases the creation of an iron and steel industry in a developing country introduces a dynamic, driving force that provides a real basis for rapid economic, industrial, and social growth.

Evolution of an Iron and Steel Plant

Size of Plant. Using the information furnished in the market survey, it is possible to determine the size of plant which should be built to satisfy the market for the various products required by the economy. It may be that the required quantities of one product are insufficient to justify expenditure of huge sums for the specialized equipment necessary for its production; for example, if a country had a market for a small quantity of high-quality tin-plate for its canning industry, say 20,000 tons of electrolytic grade, and had no use for other flat products, it would be impractical, cost-wise, to build a good flat-product mill to produce such small tonnages of this high-quality product. The same would be true if a small quantity (say, 5,000 tons) of large structural members or a small quantity of railroad rails were required. Providing the facilities for such small-scale production would increase costs beyond the point of economic feasibility.

It is therefore necessary to decide on a plant of such size as to produce economically the greatest possible number of products required by the growing economy.

The Iron-making Process. Once the size of plant has been determined, and the raw material costs and availability established, it then becomes necessary to select the iron-making process best suited to that size of plant and those raw materials. In some developing countries the selection of a suitable iron-making process is much more complex than in the highly industrialized nations of the world, generally owing to the small plant capacity required coupled with the lack of one or more of the basic materials in the quality and quantity usually considered acceptable. Subject to the availability of raw materials and the planned size of plant, any of the following processes may be adopted:

Blast Furnace. The conventional blast furnace normally operates with high-grade lump iron ore (or sintered or pelletized iron ore), which is low in contaminants, such as titanium, zinc, nickel, chrome, copper, and the like. A good grade of metallurgical coke must be used. This highly efficient type of furnace is preferred when the capacity required is sufficiently high and high grades of iron ore and coking coals are available. It is ideally suited to continuous operation at larger tonnages. If small tonnages are required, however, if good grades of iron ore and coking coal are available, and if electric power can be furnished at reasonable rates, then consideration might be given to the iron-making process described below.

Submerged-arc Electric Smelting. The submerged-arc electric smelting furnace may be built for capacities as low as 100 metric tons of pig iron per day. The advantages of this furnace over the blast furnace described above are that it can give acceptable economies at smaller tonnages and that it uses electricity, which may be more available and cheaper than other sources of heat. The major disadvantage is that, in the larger sizes, it costs more to produce pig iron by this method than by the blast furnace under normal conditions.

Electric Reduction Processes. For many years a process has been needed that can treat off-grade iron ores or can use noncoking coals with low- or high-grade iron ores. A number of such electrical reduction processes (often referred to as direct reduction processes), offering certain technical and economic advantages, have recently evolved. After an exhaustive study of those developed in the past ten years, Koppers Company decided that the Strategic-Udy process is the best of these processes applicable to the above conditions. The Strategic-Udy iron-making process heats and partially reduces the iron ore, coal, and limestone in a rotary kiln. This heated and partially reduced mixture is then introduced as a free-flowing sinter into an electric furnace, where the final reduction takes place. It is not able to compete with the blast furnace when tonnages are large and other conditions are proper for that type of operation. However, if the capacity of the plant is small, if the available iron ore contains copper, nickel, chrome, titanium, or the like in substantial quantities, or if only noncoking coal, anthracite, or lignite is available, the Strategic-Udy process can produce pig iron under conditions which are technically and/or economically unsuitable for the blast furnace or the submerged-arc electric furnace. The significant advantage to a developing economy of using the Strategic-Udy process is that it may use the locally available source of noncoking coals and off-grades of iron ore. The same coals (whether lignite, anthracite, or noncoking bituminous) may be used also to produce comparatively low-cost electric power. Especially significant to developing nations is the fact that this process, operating at a capacity of approximately 100,000 metric tons per year, can produce pig iron more cheaply than the conventional processes operating at this capacity. In addition, it can make full use of fine iron ores without sintering.

Scrap Melting. Still another alternative exists for the developing nation, namely, the melting of available scrap. However, a scrap-melting operation generally serves as only the beginning of a steel plant, since such an installation is dependent upon the continued availability of scrap. In some nations there exists initially sufficient scrap to support such a facility, but the scrap gradually disappears and imports are required, depleting the foreign exchange which most developing nations are attempting to conserve. The process unit in which the scrap melting can take place depends upon many factors, the most important being the source of heat. A cold-charge open-hearth furnace may be used, fired by either oil or gas. If there is reasonably priced electric power, an electric melting furnace is ideal, followed by the usual metal-processing facilities as dictated by economics. If electric power is not readily available in sufficient quantities, then the hot-blast cupola offers certain advantages for the production of pig iron. The hot-blast cupola, however, requires the use of metallurgical-grade coke. In some developing nations, pending development of a market sufficiently large to support an integrated steel plant, it may be advantageous to start with a scrap-melting operation to be expanded later to include more basic metal-producing facilities. However, because of the need to furnish scrap iron from local sources on a continuing basis, the plant would have to be small in size and would therefore be capable of producing only a limited line of products. If the initial requirements were small enough, however, the initial plant could be designed for later expansion into an integrated iron and steel plant.

Steelmaking Process. The selection of the process for converting the pig iron or molten iron to steel is also a vital decision. It is dependent on the type of iron produced from the raw materials and the capacity of the installation under consideration. Each of the various available processes has unique advantages and disadvantages.

About sixty years ago most of the world's steel was manufactured by the so-called "Bessemer process," which consisted of blowing air through the bottom of a refractory-lined vessel containing molten iron. In the United States, Bessemer steel was all made in acid or siliceous refractory-lined vessels, and it was necessary that the molten iron be low in contaminants such as phosphorus and sulfur, since neither was removed in the process. In some parts of Europe, a similar pneumatic process became widely used with vessels having a basic refractory lining, necessary because of large amounts of phosphorus in the molten iron which had to be removed by means of a basic flux, such as lime. The process of making steel by this method from high-phosphorus iron came to be known as the "Thomas process." Both of these pneumatic processes produce steels limited in their useful application since they are relatively high in nitrogen picked up from the air blast.

About 1870 the open-hearth steelmaking process was invented by Siemens. Its adoption in the United States was very rapid, and by 1905 about half of all steel ingots produced in the United States were made by this method. Use of the process continued to spread, and by 1951 it accounted for approximately 87 percent of the steel-producing capacity of the United States. It permits a wider range of quality steels than the Bessemer process.

Some years ago steel manufacturers began using relatively pure oxygen as the oxidizing agent, the iron being contained in a vessel similar to a Bessemer shell. Oxygen at high pressure was applied to the molten iron by means of a top lance. This process has gained increasing favor in the past ten years because it makes steel of as high a grade as the open hearth and because, for a new installation, the initial capital investment is likely to be lower.

If reasonably priced electric power is available, electric refining furnaces may be economical to use, owing to their inherent flexibility and adaptability to comparatively low capacities.

There are other generally accepted and widely used methods of refining pig iron into steel, but, for the purposes of this paper, the discussion has been narrowed to the better-known and more widely used processes.

Billets and Slabs. The selection of method for the production of billets and slabs is of vital significance. Billets are normally square bars, varying in size from 2 by 2 inches to 8 by 8 inches, from which merchant products are made; slabs, rolled to produce flat products such as sheets and plate, vary in thickness up to 12 inches and in width up to 75 inches. The type of process used to produce these billets and slabs has a direct bearing on the cost of producing the finished products as well as on the initial capital investment.

In small-size plants where large capital investment cannot be supported, a method of producing billets and slabs directly from the molten steel has been developed—the continuous-casting process. In such a process the slabs and billets are continuously cast and cut into the desired lengths by means of an oxygen acetylene torch.

By eliminating the need for ingot molds, soaking pits, blooming and slabbing mills, and billet mills, initial capital investment and production costs are reduced. It is probable that the continuous-casting process would be more appropriate for a developing nation whose market is in the process of expanding.

Rolling Mills. It is necessary to determine which combination of rolling mills will most economically produce the immediate requirements and, at the same time, have inherent excess capacity to take care of the future demand predicted by the market study. Normally in a developing economy smaller merchant products, such as rods for concrete reinforcing, small angles and channels for building construction, and round rods for wire nails, constitute the bulk of the initial demand. These items can be produced economically, if nothing more is needed, in a smaller merchant mill. Next, the economy begins to demand larger steel sections and shapes. However, a much larger capital investment is required, and a greater demand for these products is necessary to justify the additional facilities.

As the economy continues to develop, a market is created for flat products—sheets and plate. The market study will have determined current and future demand for the types of flat products required. Many countries embarking on an industrialization program require a small quantity of flat products—sheets and plate for corrugated roofing and siding, and black sheet for hollow enamelware, barrels and cans, and tinplate. This need may amount to only 40,000 or 50,000 metric tons, and therefore a large reversing hot-strip mill or the even larger capacity continuous hot-strip mill could not be justified.

A possible solution to this situation which has been used in many countries is the hand sheet mill, which, as its name implies, uses more manual labor in its application and less highly automated machinery. The hand sheet mill has the advantage of a lower economic break-even point and is consequently well suited to fulfill the requirements of a smaller market. Unit cost of production of the hand sheet mill will be higher than that of continuous hot-strip mill producing above its break-even point, but the unit cost could be far less than that of the larger mill if the latter were producing only 40,000 to 50,000 tons of product.

It is necessary, therefore, to design the rolling mills to take care of the immediate needs of the market, as projected to the end of the first five years of operation (this will normally be eight to ten years after it has been decided to build the plant), so as to give the most product for the least capital and operating cost.

Source of Electric Power. The source and cost of electric power are important to the steelmaking facility whether it is based on the conventional iron- and steelmaking processes or based on electrical reduction and refining processes. In the latter cases, it is more important and forms a larger part of the cost—supplanting the coal or coke in part. But whatever the processes, the cost of electric power is important to the operation of the rolling mills and the multitude of auxiliaries used throughout the plant. In many nations sufficient local power exists in the form of hydroelectric or thermal plants. The use of these particular sources is, to a large part, dependent upon the availability of power in adequate quantities and the dependability of the supply.

In many instances, owing to the unusually large demands and an already overloaded grid, it has been found both practical and economical to construct captive power plants. This has the added advantage of giving complete control of the power source to the steel plant management, and the source is not subject to power interruptions due to breakdowns in the distribution system outside the plant boundaries.

General Facilities. Provision must be made within the plant boundaries for other utilities such as potable and process water, electric lighting and power, and sewage, as well as roads, railroads, repair shops, warehouses, first aid stations, and the like. If the steel plant is located in a remote area, it may be necessary to build shops capable of repairing almost any of the equipment in use in the plant. This will necessitate the establishment of the following maintenance departments:

1. Mechanical
2. Electrical
3. Mason
4. Blacksmith and welding
5. Carpentry
6. Instrument repair
7. Locomotive and car repair
8. Auto and truck garage

The utility department controls the supply of water, power, steam, oxygen, compressed air, etc. It is responsible for the maintenance of all potable and process water lines, as well as fire lines, and for the operation and maintenance of power generation and distribution facilities, as well as tie-ins with other utilities.

Adequacy of Infrastructure. In selecting the location for a steel plant, consideration must be given to the availability (or lack) of all facilities (the infrastructure) needed to support such a plant. In general, these facilities may be divided into those required for the people working in the plant and those required to support the plant itself. The workers and their families need housing, schools, churches, hospitals, stores, water, lights, sewage, transportation, etc.; the plant requires developed highways, railroads, and/or waterways for low-cost transport of raw materials and supplies to the plant and of finished products to the consuming market. Potable and process water must be brought to the plant and effluent taken from it. Electric power, fuel oil, natural gas, or other power sources must be made available.

Before any plan can be finalized for the construction of a steel plant, all infrastructure problems must be solved—who will furnish the services, or the money to supply them. Whenever possible, it is highly desirable that all supporting facilities be supplied to the steel plant, so that it is not burdened with their cost or their administration. The steel plant is then left to its primary task of making steel.

Profitability. Because of the heavy initial investment required for a steel plant, large capital loans are needed to finance the construction and operation of the plant. These loans, obtained from private and public financing institutions, must be repaid with interest. In addition, shareholders will demand that they be given a fair return on their investment. Therefore, the steel plant must be designed to hold all costs to the minimum so as to make it a profitable operation.

Private enterprise, working in cooperation with government, mindful of its duties to produce efficiently and for profit, should be the goal for the majority ownership of the steel plant. Many governments have stated their intention of supporting private enterprise by agreeing to sell their interests to the private sector as and when private investment capital becomes available.

Profit, of course, is the difference between income (which is the total value of the steel products sold) and cost (which is the sum of the direct operating cost, the overhead expense, and the financing charges). Therefore, the selling prices of steel products which create income deserve our consideration. In most instances, it has been found that prices being paid for steel by non-steel-producing countries are high enough to justify construction of local steel plants (provided raw materials, power, and other necessities are available). If the plant is small, steel products cannot be provided as cheaply as they can be produced in the huge mills in Europe or America. It may require, therefore, that the new small plant be given a modicum of protection by the government during its formative years. It will not normally be necessary to raise tariffs, but it may be necessary to continue existing tariffs for a period of years. In addition, provision may have to be made to prevent the sale of steel products in the local market at exceptionally low prices during periods of overproduction in the larger mills abroad. This protection may take the form of a program of import licensing for the products of the new local steel mill.

It is therefore essential to the economic viability of a project that decisions as to raw materials, location of the plant, source and cost of electric power, and methods of transport be made strictly on the basis of economics. This is true because a small new mill, with its high capital charges, newly trained operating and management personnel, and newly developed sources of raw materials and services, must be given every possible assistance to stand on its own feet without subsidy—and to make a profit for its owners, public or private, so that it may grow, expand, and assist in the industrialization of the nation.

Corporate and Capital Structure. The corporate structure of the steel plant will depend on the source of capital and the policy of the government. In most developing countries there are insufficient funds in the private sector to finance the development of a steel mill, and the local government may furnish some or all of the funds. In such cases, the local government may either pledge itself to take a subordinate position to private owners or offer to sell its shareholdings to private owners in the future. The capital required to build and operate the plant normally comes from two sources—the shareholders or owners of the business, and long-term loans from private and public lending institutions.

Although steel is a basic industry, it is not one in which high profits can be expected. At the same time it is an industry in which capital requirements are high. It is desirable, therefore, that loans provide a substantial part of the capital required to build the plant, that these loans be long-term, and that the interest rate be reasonably low.

A medium-sized steel plant producing an adequate mixture of steel products has an excellent chance of success, provided the following conditions exist:

1. Adequate market for its output
2. Suitable long-term debt financing
3. Reasonably established sales prices for its products

4. Adequate raw materials and reasonably priced power
5. A mutual determination by government and business for its success

An important source of long-term loan capital has been the various lending institutions in Europe and the United States, both public and private. Another source of financial assistance has come from the equipment suppliers, who are often willing to extend long-term credits for the purchase of their equipment. In some instances these suppliers have assumed a financial interest in the operation by purchasing shares of stock in the company.

The raising of capital within the borders of the nation through the sale of stock to insurance companies, banks and other lending institutions, and the general public is recommended, since this ensures the active participation of those most affected by the results of the steel plant. At the same time, it helps to develop the private sector as a moving force in developing the industrial strength of the nation.

Technical and Management Assistance. The management and operation of a steel plant is a complex task requiring many highly trained specialists in many different fields. It is not to be expected that all these qualified specialists will be available in a developing country, and it will therefore be necessary to import additional specialists. The number of such imported technicians and managers will depend on the local availability of skilled technicians and managers and on the number of local employees who can be trained during the period of plant construction. However, specialists have to be imported at the start to inaugurate an interim program for training local personnel immediately—training them in all phases of plant operation and maintenance, including management and administration, not only on the job but also abroad. The president, sales manager, plant manager, plant superintendent, safety director, superintendent of various departments, the chief of the laboratory, the operators of furnaces and rolling mills, the superintendents of electrical and mechanical maintenance, all must be trained to assume their responsibilities. As soon as they are qualified, the imported specialists are released.

It is therefore vitally important that the company selected to furnish the technical and management assistance to the new steel plant be one with a background and history of achievement in this field, where unusual technical ability and previous experience are so vital. The objectives of the technical and management assistance group must be to obtain the most efficient and economical operation of the steel plant and to complete the training of the local employees of the plant at the earliest possible date so that they themselves can progressively assume in the shortest possible time all the management, administrative, and technical positions in the plant.

If competent personnel are available for the management, administrative, and supervisory positions in the office and in the plant, then the technical assistance group will furnish only advice and guidance in the execution of their duties. If, on the other hand, such personnel are not available locally, the technical assistance group will help the steel plant recruit adequate talent from abroad and supervise the training of local personnel to take over these responsibilities after a period of training. The technical and management assistance group should align themselves with the steel plant on a long-term, continuing basis, because it takes many years to bring a steel plant into full and efficient operation. When that point has been reached, the plant will undoubtedly have to be expanded in order to take care of a market for steel products that has been growing rapidly thanks to the availability of locally produced products at steady prices.

Conclusion

And so, as emphasized at the opening of the discussion, when a developing country has economically and technically usable raw materials and a sufficient market for the products of a steel plant, building its own iron and steel industry will usually benefit its entire economy, expand its industrial base, and accelerate its social progress.

THE PURCHASE OF KNOW-HOW FROM ABROAD

Claude McMillan, Ph.D.

Imported Know-how: Its Source and Importance

A large part of the technological know-how utilized in business and industry in the developing nations is imported know-how. Part of this imported know-how is acquired through international scientific and engineering symposia, trade conventions, industry fairs, and trade and professional journals. Part of it is inherent in machinery and equipment purchased abroad. Much of it is exported by firms which operate their own subsidiaries or branches abroad and implement in these subsidiaries and branches techniques and practices which they employ at home. Today a major part of this know-how is traded in international commerce through business alliances which have as their chief purpose the exchange of technological and managerial knowledge and skills.

The principal suppliers of that know-how which is imported by the developing nations are the large industrial firms of the advanced nations. No country has a monopoly on innovation, and most have contributed to the world's rich store of knowledge. Yet the fact is that the bulk of the innovation which is of particular value to business management is the contribution of the United States, the larger and more highly industrialized nations of Western Europe, and Japan. These nations are therefore heavy exporters of know-how, while the developing nations are net know-how importers.

Concomitantly, while the developing nations are net importers of know-how, as they advance they become even heavier know-how importers. Studies have shown that while the advanced nations are heavy exporters of know-how, they are also heavy importers. Thus, while West Germany is a source

---

Dr. McMillan is Professor of Management at Michigan State University, Graduate School of Business Administration, East Lansing, Michigan.

of know-how for export, there is some evidence that Germany imports more know-how than all of Latin America combined. As nations progress industrially, they find imported know-how of greater usefulness, and, rather than becoming "technologically independent," they become more internationally interdependent.

This condition of increasing interdependence can be expected to continue and to accelerate. There is under way today a revolution of research and technological innovation. Its implications for an alert and resourceful management are clear: success and even survival will depend upon whether the individual firm can keep pace with changes which reduce costs, improve quality, and raise productivity. At the base of these changes is innovation; and at the base of innovation is research. Therefore, as the research revolution progresses, business enterprises will become ever more dependent upon one another, and imported know-how will become more important.

Some managers have argued that the technology of the advanced nations is not optimal for the developing nations; that many of the tools, techniques, and practices of the very advanced nations are simply too sophisticated for the less advanced, smaller-volume firms of developing nations; and that imported know-how is therefore of only very limited value. The facts do not bear this out. Clearly, as a nation or an industry advances and grows in volume, the know-how of the advanced nation becomes more useful and requires less adaptation. But experience proves that the great bulk of the technology of the advanced nations can be adapted to use in the developing nations; it also shows that the pace with which imported know-how can be usefully employed is limited chiefly by the perceptiveness of the importing manager and by the speed with which he can accumulate the capital and human resources required for exploiting know-how which is already available.

Thus, while no responsible manager can afford to depend solely on imported know-how, he must nevertheless expect that, as his business operations grow in volume and expand in depth and breadth of product line and customer service, he will have to look with increasing diligence toward foreign sources of know-how.

Imported Know-how: Its Nature

Know-how is a broad term, covering many kinds of knowledge. It ranges from the highly specific and "specifiable," to the very general and "unspecifiable." At one extreme we find specifications covering material components in metal alloys, petrochemicals, and pharmaceutical products. This may be know-how which can be expressed clearly in written engineering specifications. At the other extreme we have knowledge of man-machine and operations-time configurations and of organizational methods and procedures. This type of know-how defies precise written specification; it is elusive and sometimes vague. And yet, this latter know-how can be a major determinant of efficiency, and it forms an increasing part of the know-how traded today in world commerce. Between these two extremes we find a wide variety of technological, engineering, and managerial knowledge now traded more than ever before in history.

Most managers are aware of the value of patentable trade secrets and fully appreciate the fact that to gain access to knowledge of this type a price must be paid. But few managers are aware of the magnitude of the importance of that know-how which is not patentable: engineering methodology, processing techniques, programming and control procedures—know-how which may not be essential to the manufacture of many products, but without which no product can be manufactured at competitive prices.

Henceforth the term "know-how" will be used to embrace a wide variety of knowledge, technological to managerial, which is indispensable to the efficient operation of modern industrial enterprise.

Alliances for Know-how Exchange

As suggested above, a certain amount of know-how is acquired with the importation of machinery, equipment, components, and materials. Most business firms trading in world commerce recognize that long-run success requires an extensive effort to make certain that the buyer is provided with the product optimum for his needs, that the product is adapted to suit his unique environment, and that it is properly utilized. To achieve these objectives the vendor is obliged to offer a variety of consultative services along with his product. The skillful and perceptive buyer can generally exploit these opportunities for maximum useful know-how import. Payment for this know-how import is a part of the purchase price of the equipment.

Other sources of beneficial know-how are also important. Among these are research and product development institutes, especially in the advanced nations, which rent their services; consulting firms, which do a world-wide business and offer a wide array of technical and managerial services; and "turnkey" contractors, who design, build, and even finance and manage, for a time, industrial plants for customers abroad. Payment for know-how from these sources is generally on a fixed fee or cost plus basis, negotiated at the time the agreement is made.

The above kinds of know-how sources are important, but they tend to be one-time affairs and are not the major vehicle for the international transfer of know-how today. The bulk of contemporary know-how transfer is that which arises out of "alliances" of a more intimate character. These alliances go by a variety of names—technical assistance agreements, licensing agreements, technical service or exchange agreements, or management contracts. These agreements may or may not involve the exchange of equity interest and hence may or may not involve joint ownership ventures between know-how importer and exporter. They may involve a parent firm and a wholly or partially owned subsidiary or branch abroad. They frequently involve an alliance between a foreign subsidiary or branch and a host-country national firm. More commonly they involve the host-country national firm in alliance with a firm in a foreign country which may or may not have subsidiary or branch operations in the country of the know-how importer.

The term "license agreement" is employed more commonly when the relationship between know-how importer and exporter involves no sharing of ownership. When ownership is shared, the terms "technical assistance" and "technical exchange" are more prevalent, and when the know-how exporter assumes a significant role in sharing the management of the venture, the term "management contract" is more prevalent. The general term "licensing" will henceforth be employed to represent all these types of agreements.

Two or more firms may ally themselves in a series of agreements involving several license, technical assistance, or management contracts covering various areas of operation which are of mutual interest to them. Similarly, one firm may be the licensor or the licensee of a number of other firms, and the agreements may provide for cross-licensing, wherein all parties become both importers and exporters of know-how.

Advantages and Disadvantages of Know-how Licensing. Commerce is never successful unless it is mutually advantageous to both parties in a transaction. Where trading is not successful, it can usually be traced to errors on the part of one or both parties involved, and these errors are generally caused by ignorance.

License agreements, like joint ownership ventures, are rather long-term alliances, and it is doubly important that the parties to long-term alliances are fully appraised of the advantages and disadvantages, problems, and pitfalls that can be expected. Each party to a know-how alliance should be as aware of the problems which are responsible for apprehension on the part of his partner as he is of his own problems.

Advantages: To the Licensee. The consideration which the licensee acquires in the know-how agreement depends on what is specified in the license contract. Know-how alliances commonly provide for several of the following:

1. Right to the use of patents, trademarks, models, design specifications, formulas, and other trade secrets
2. Technical and engineering services, including assistance in layout, process design, material lists, quality and cost control methodology, assistance in selection and purchase of equipment and components, and training of licensee personnel
3. Assistance in sales promotion, advertising, and the determination of marketing strategy
4. Supervisory and managerial assistance in organization building and manpower development

In addition to the above the licensee may acquire rights to future innovation of the licensor firm, exclusive rights to sell the imported products of the licensor firm, and, commonly, an intangible element of prestige which has value in establishing new marketing contacts, acquiring financing, and attracting qualified managerial personnel. Finally, by becoming a licensee, one can sometimes preclude competition with his licensor, who, but for the license agreement, might sell his own products in the licensee's market through a direct manufacturing investment.

Advantages: To the Licensor. As before, the advantages to the licensor depend on the nature of the agreement. Among the more important are the following:

1. Acquisition of additional revenue from company-owned know-how and the spreading of the cost of research and development
2. Acquisition of a strategic advantage in marketing products abroad, especially where total loss of a market is threatened by trade restrictions
3. Protection of proprietary rights abroad—particularly through efforts of the licensee to prevent infringement

4. Entry into an expanding market with a minimum of capital investment and no obligation to deal with restrictions and regulations in an unfamiliar environment
5. Provision of service for large industrial customers operating in the country of the licensee
6. Development of sources of materials and components for other operations

Disadvantages: To the Licensee. Except in cross-licensing agreements, the licensee's consideration is almost always a monetary payment—usually a percentage of the sales revenue from the products to which the agreement applies. Very frequently the licensor also demands an initial fee for setting up the agreement and as a manifestation of good faith. Meanwhile, since effecting the know-how transfer may take some time, the licensee sometimes finds himself paying for a considerable period in advance of the time that he begins to enjoy a payoff from the know-how import.

The amount of the periodic royalty fee varies. It may be as low as 2 or 3% of sales in the applicable product line, or as high as 18%. Generally royalty fees are about 7 or 8% of sales. In addition to these charges, the licensee is commonly obliged to pay expenses involved in visits by technical personnel from the offices of the licensor.

Disadvantages: To the Licensor. While licensing holds advantages for the licensor, it is not the most profitable way of exploiting foreign markets. For the duration of the license agreement the licensor is commonly precluded from making a direct investment, except through some agreement with the licensee. As time passes, making a direct investment may become more difficult, as a result of government restrictions, increasing competition, and the improved competence of the licensee.

Licensing deprives the licensor of real control over his product; quality may suffer, and if the licensee fails to promote sales in the applicable product line with real vigor, the licensor may enjoy almost no exploitation of the available market opportunity. Finally, the licensor may develop, in the licensee, a future competitor.

Exploratory Inquiry Preceding the Agreement. The bulk of the mistakes which lead to unsuccessful licensing can be traced to misunderstanding during the negotiation of the agreement or during the exploratory communication which precedes it.

There are a number of media through which a firm can find prospective licensor firms abroad. These include export-import journals, the trade bureaus and international trade associations of foreign countries, the commercial offices of foreign embassies and consulates, and direct contact with local firms, especially banking enterprises, which have some affiliation with firms in countries where prospective licensors might be expected to reside. Most manufacturers are already acquainted with the leading producers and innovators in their field of specialization, and many license agreements grow out of initiative taken by the prospective licensee with a known leader in his field.

It is important that both prospective licensor and licensee explore fully their mutual compatibility. During the exploratory stage the prospective licensee would do well to seek answers to the following questions:

1. Is the alliance being considered of mutual advantage to both parties?

2. How much experience has the prospective licensor had in foreign operations, or in licensing abroad? Is the licensor being contemplated the best choice among a number of possible licensors?

3. Does the prospective licensor possess both the know-how desired and the ability and will to make it available?

4. Is the prospective licensor a promising source of future innovation? (Licensing is successful only when there is a continuous flow of know-how.)

5. Is the prospective licensor interesting as a potential equity partner? (License agreements tend to lead to a more intimate affiliation. While equity sharing is not essential, if licensor and licensee firms have no interest in a more intimate possible future association, the chances are that the degree of compatibility which is essential for successful licensing is lacking.)

Negotiating the Agreement. Once general agreement has been reached that an alliance would be mutually interesting, serious negotiations can begin. These may involve intermediaries. There are a number of agencies which hold themselves forth as intermediaries between prospective licensor and licensee. These may be law firms, consulting organizations, commercial banks, and other licensees or subsidiaries of a licensor. While there is a place for intermediaries, they are usually of limited value, and at some stage in the negotiation the top management officials of both licensor and licensee should become involved before an agreement is made.

In negotiating the agreement, the following should particularly be kept in mind:

1. Communication with representatives of the prospective licensor should be extensive and as unequivocal as possible. In some cases this will require one or more visits abroad by representatives of both prospective licensor and licensee, but in many cases this should not be necessary. By a variety of means the prospective licensee should endeavor to acquaint himself fully with the types of services which the prospective licensor is capable of offering, now and in the future, and the means by which these services can be made available.

2. The prospective licensor will want to know a good deal about his prospective licensee. While the licensor or his representatives will probably conduct his own investigation of the licensee's facilities, his particular areas of competence, his place in the industry of which he is a part, and the like, he will also look to the licensee for specific information. The following are representative of the types of data the licensor is likely to request:

a. Annual sales volume over the past several years
b. Licensee's estimate of future market potential
c. Summary cost data, including a breakdown by product lines (of considerable importance, since inability to provide it has sometimes led licensors to discontinue further negotiations)
d. Identification of the licensee's place in the market and of the names and estimated volume of business of principal competitors
e. Financial condition of the licensee and possible credit and business references

f. Quality and magnitude of licensee's physical plant and the availability of space and capital for expansion

g. Ownership structure of the licensee, and his affiliations (such as existing licensee or joint venture agreements with other firms)

In addition to being prepared to provide the above data, the prospective licensee would do well to prepare a brochure including photographs of his physical plant, product catalogues and specifications, and financial statements for examination by the prospective licensor. Each party will do well to secure information about the other through commercial information agencies.

The License Agreement. The licensor generally takes the initiative in proposing the formal agreement itself. The specific terms of the agreement are then negotiated, usually with the help of the legal counsel representing both parties. The contract generally involves the following, in addition to the customary legal provisions:

1. Dates of beginning and terminating the agreement, with provision for earlier termination by either party
2. Present and future proprietary rights to be made available by the licensor and the means for communicating these
3. Exclusivity or nonexclusivity as to products, product lines, sales territories, and rights to sublicense
4. Provision for adaptation to the needs of the licensee
5. Terms of payment for know-how and proprietary rights of the licensor
6. Provision for enforcement of the contract and settlement of disputes
7. Miscellaneous terms, including the means for dealing with problems of international currency exchange, compliance with laws and regulations of both governments, and the rights of both parties after termination of the agreement

The larger and more experienced licensor firms generally administer their licensing alliances through special staff groups which concern themselves only with international operations. However, the bulk of the licensor's know-how resides in his domestic operating units. The know-how transfer, therefore, generally involves direct communication between the licensee and the operating units of the licensor, through the coordinating efforts of the licensor's international operations staff. Provision in the license contract is generally made for this involvement on a periodic or as-called-for basis.

Problems and Pitfalls in Licensing. Where licensing has been most successful, its success can usually be traced to three basic factors, namely, that (1) the license relationship has enjoyed serious top management support from both licensor and licensee; (2) both managements have taken a long-term view of the license relationship; and (3) managements of each have had full and abiding respect for the interests and objectives of the other and have had a flexible, adaptive attitude toward implementation of the agreement.

The Need for Serious Top Management Support. To the early leaders of the scientific management movement basic management functions include the provision of resources, the determination of work methods, the setting of standards, and the evaluation of performance. These early theorists argued that methods were of major importance in determining productivity. Recent economic studies have substantiated the view that only about 20% of the increase in productivity in the advanced nations of the world during the past half-century can be attributed to the accumulation of capital, and that *improved know-how is responsible for the remainder.*

Thus we see the magnitude of the importance of know-how as a productive resource. Its provision is as surely a responsibility of management as is the provision of materials, labor, and capital. If the potential usefulness of a license agreement is to be fully exploited, the serious support of top management is required.

The Long-term View. License agreements sometimes prove unsuccessful to the licensor and/or licensee because a short-term view has been taken. If the licensee enters into the agreement chiefly to acquire the right to use a trademark, or for the purpose of excluding a competitor, or simply to acquire a patent right which will some day expire, the agreement will be only a marginal success. If the licensee chooses his licensor with care, he will have associated himself with an innovating, creative organization whose future know-how is of major interest. Licensors frequently complain, with justification, that their former licensee entered into a licensing agreement simply to acquire some specific know-how right, and that as soon as this right had been acquired, the agreement was terminated, with the former licensee now enjoying the benefits of the know-how acquired and giving no consideration in exchange for it. This condition suggests that (1) the licensor was not a continual source of innovation, maintaining a lead in his field, or (2) the licensee had no interest in the longer-term benefits to be acquired through association with an innovator. In either case a short-term interest on the part of the licensee is implied, and the consequences are unfortunate. *Know-how must be looked upon in the same way as any other productive resource.* In a world of rapidly changing technology one must develop sources for its continuous supply.

The Flexible, Adaptive Attitude. Know-how, like any other productive resource, cannot be employed without adaptation or modification. The specific methodology of the licensor will often have to be modified if it is to be optimally employed by the licensee; the scale of operations of the licensor is generally larger, and, with labor costs higher in the licensor's country, equipment is likely to be more developed and more highly automatic. The licensor can generally be expected to play an active role in the process of adaptation, but the initiative for this effort may have to come from the licensee. Without an equity interest in the operations of the licensee, the licensor has no managerial authority over them. Hence the licensor only makes suggestions; the decisions as to what shall be done rest with the licensee. The extent to which the available know-how is exploited, therefore, depends substantially upon the perceptiveness and initiative of the licensee. Too frequently the licensee, less familiar perhaps with some of the complexities of an advanced industrial system, fails to recognize fully the extent to which the methodology of the licensor *can* be adapted for his use and rejects truly promising opportunities. If the licensor shares in the management, his voice is given greater decision-making weight, and such opportunities are less likely to be missed.

In any know-how alliance, and especially in those alliances involving no sharing of ownershp, a major responsibility for initiative rests with the know-how importer if the usefulness of the alliance is to be fully exploited.

MEASURING THE IMPACT OF A BUSINESS INVESTMENT ON A DEVELOPING SOCIETY

Richard D. Robinson, M.B.A., Ph.D.

The reason for an analysis of what one's firm proposes to do in an underdeveloped country within the context of the national interests of that country lies in the near certainty that the host government will analyze its activity in these terms—if not sooner, then later. Thus, the Western businessman is well advised to be prepared to defend the social value of his local enterprise, also his relationship with it. If he cannot, he compounds his risks to the point of jeopardizing his entire business position. The fact that he may get away with such disregard for the time being is beside the point; in the long run, by ignoring the social impact of his venture he may help to dig the grave of the free enterprise concept, whatever his immediate profit may be. Social responsibility is inherent in the concept of freedom, whether it be free speech or free enterprise.

National interest in the developing non-Western states may be equated with sustained material improvement under a modernizing sovereign national government. So our inquiry is twofold: (1) How does a Western business affect the long-run economic growth rate? (2) How does a Western business affect the modernization of a sovereign national government? The two are related because it is unlikely that growth in the physical well-being of a people can long proceed without parallel development of political functions. The reverse is equally unlikely. Hence, when speaking of national growth, I refer to both economic growth (sustained increase in real, per capita, national product) and political modernization (sustained increase in the degree to which political

---

Dr. Robinson is a Senior Lecturer in International Business at Massachusetts Institute of Technology, Alfred P. Sloan School of Management, Cambridge, Massachusetts. This article is adapted from his recent book, *International Business Policy,* Holt, Rinehart and Winston, Inc., New York, 1964.

functions are affectively neutral, collectively oriented, universalistic, specific, and achievement-oriented). I cannot envision the two apart. (See Gabriel A. Almond and James S. Coleman (eds.), *The Politics of the Developing Areas,* Princeton University Press, Princeton, N.J., 1960, especially pages 3 to 64.)

Impact on Economic Growth

The first measure of economic growth is the direct effect of the operation of an enterprise on the per capita national income of the host society, hence the *national income effect.* The experience of many underdeveloped countries points to foreign exchange strangulation as a serious—probably chronic—deterrent to sustained rapid growth. Consequently, the *balance of payments effect* is a second important measure, a measure having to do really with a nation's external economic balance in a structural sense, a factor partially determining a nation's ability to sustain growth. Inasmuch as increase in directly productive investment requires a higher level of social overhead investment, often only available from public sources, the *public revenue effect* is a third measure, one which concerns us with internal economic balance and is likewise a measure of a nation's growth capability.

But all three of these concepts provide only relatively short-run measures, for economic growth is sustained in the long run by continuous innovation, as Everett Hagen has so convincingly demonstrated in his recent book.[1] Our fourth measure, then, has to do with the *innovational effect,* which leads one into the political area.

At the outset, let me underscore one important difficulty in using many of these measures in specific situations: the measures are relative, not absolute. That is, although a given project may be judged to have a positive effect on per capita national product, the commitment of scarce resources to that project may be judged contrary to the national interest for the reason that some other project would make a larger contribution. The mere proof that a given project is of benefit is inadequate so long as any scarce factors are involved, unless it can be demonstrated that these factors are not likely to contribute to greater growth if employed in other uses. This observation is equally relevant to discussion of the balance of payment effect, the public revenue effect, and the innovation effect.

It should also be borne in mind that for virtually every project in which Western enterprise may be involved something of value will be destroyed or expended. One cannot simply add up the benefits, as many writers have done, and thereby derive the measure of impact.

Furthermore, any quantitative statement of the national income effect, balance of payments effect, or public revenue effect of a given enterprise necessarily assumes a price system, for one works in money terms—given the need to aggregate. If these effects are used to determine the "desirability" of a given enterprise from the point of view of economic growth, prices must be assumed to represent (1) the relative contributions of the various factors and products to the growth process, and (2) the relative availabilities of these factors and products. There are several reasons why current prices may not

[1] Everett E. Hagen, *On the Theory of Social Change,* The Dorsey Press, Richard D. Irwin, Inc., Homewood, Ill., 1962.

reflect these relationships even approximately, namely, that (1) market organization may be so poorly developed as to affect supply-price and demand-price elasticities (i.e., elasticities may change simply by improving market organization); (2) factor supply—and prices—may not be responsive to supply-and-demand forces; (3) demand may be determined by factors other than long-term growth considerations; and (4) price relationships may change over time, perhaps by reason of the proposed enterprise itself, general economic growth, or structural change. Therefore, in measuring the impact of a given project, assumptions about present and future prices should be made explicit.

Some economists have observed that the contribution to economic growth of individual projects cannot be measured meaningfully,[2] so interdependent is a national economy. In terms of precise quantification, this claim is undoubtedly correct. But it is likewise true that the development of precise measures for an *entire* development program is likewise an unrewarding objective, even if one postulates perfect knowledge about the intentions of all state agencies and private entrepreneurs. National growth is not an impersonal economic process. It is, first of all, a human process generated out of the battle waged endlessly in man's personality between desire and innovation on the one hand and lassitude and traditionalism, on the other. How will individuals react to given situations? One can only make informed guesses. Secondly, the growth process can be measured only in part by economic concepts, for political modernization is an important component, a component lending itself even less well to quantification. Therefore, one should be forewarned not to lean too heavily on economic measures alone. In the final analysis, judgment based on knowledge and experience must govern, not mathematical formulas.

[It should be emphasized that the guidelines suggested below are for the management of an individual firm considering a specific project in an underdeveloped country.]

Further, I suggest that a management look at what it proposes to do as a group of separate processes, rather than as a given package of processes (i.e., a plant), in reaching a decision in reference to the degree of integration or the size of plant that is optimal. If it does, management may find that its assumptions as to what constitutes a "plant" or "enterprise" are culture-bound. Admittedly, to examine a project in this way assumes a degree of technical and organizational ability which is not always present in the firm.

National Income Effect

> The national product (or consumption) test of a certain investment project is a calculation of the contribution of that project to present and future national product or consumption.
>
> The calculation must be based on an accurate assessment of the project's consequences, estimated for each of a succession of years, as to value of production and costs. This assessment should include direct as well as indirect consequence and possibly secondary ones.[3]

[2] Siro Lombardini, "Quantitative Analysis in the Determination of the Efficiency of Investment in Underdeveloped Areas," *International Economic Papers*, The Macmillan Company, New York, 1959, p. 134.

[3] Jan Tinbergen, *The Design of Development*, Johns Hopkins Press, Baltimore, 1958, p. 41.

The point of departure is provided by the projected profit and loss statements and balance sheets of the proposed enterprise. (Although dependent on the nature of the enterprise, relevant test periods might be years one, five, ten, fifteen, and twenty.) From this material, one can derive the first approximation of the net value that will be added by the project, which—in the traditional accounting sense—is equated with the sum of the shares of the five factors of production[4] within the income of the firm, specifically:

1. Labor—consisting of salaries and wages, bonuses, and commissions received by the employees and wage earners of the firm
2. Land—rent of land and buildings used by the firm in production
3. Entrepreneur—net return
4. Capital—interest payments on loans
5. Government—taxes paid

Taken collectively, these shares comprise the national income. In point of fact, however, the remuneration paid to labor, land, entrepreneur, and capital constitutes net value added by a new enterprise only to the extent that these factors are currently unemployed or underemployed. Also, to the extent that the remuneration paid to scarce factors—perhaps to skilled labor, entrepreneurs, capital, certain resources—understates their marginal yields, the cost to be charged against gross income to derive net value added should be greater than that shown on the firm's books. For example, the "interest rate to be applied should express the real scarcity of capital, to be derived from the marginal yield of projects as well as the marginal rate to be paid for foreign loans."[5] Taxes paid to government contribute to net value added only in so far as those taxes exceed the taxes paid by reason of the present employment of the resources to be used.

On the other hand, certain costs not usually included in net value added should, under some conditions, be included. If a firm plans to engage in training programs to upgrade its labor, the present discounted value of the increased annual output expected by reason of that training should be included in net value added. To the extent that domestically produced raw materials would not otherwise be used, their total cost should likewise be included. If they would be used for less valuable purposes, the difference between present cost and their estimated marginal product in the new use should be added in.

Closely related is the problem of assessing the external economies and diseconomies of the firm's proposed operation (at present discounted values).

Plus Items

1. The net value that will be added by economic enterprises likely to be stimulated by reason of the project under consideration
2. Lowered costs of external goods and services by reason of the firm's added demand for them (e.g., power, transport, component parts, raw materials, etc.)
3. The increased efficiency accruing to other enterprises to the extent that the product price does not fully compensate the firm for these external benefits

[4] I feel that it is useful conceptually to consider government (including private nonprofit welfare institutions, e.g., private schools) as the fifth factor of production.

[5] Tinbergen, *op. cit.*, p. 41.

4. The cost of social overhead investment by the firm in the development of services that would be required whether the enterprise were undertaken or not (i.e., those available for use by others without full payment)

Minus Items

1. The net value added by economic enterprises that would be replaced by the project under consideration
2. Increased costs of external goods and services by reason of the firm's added demand for them
3. Increased inefficiency accruing to others, to the extent that the product price more than fully compensates the firm
4. The cost of social overhead investment by public or other agencies made necessary by the enterprise (housing, urban facilities, transport, etc.)

Granted, these items are not subject to easy or exact measures, but approximations can be derived through examination of the host economy, engineering data of the input-output type, and the nature of the processes and products involved. In so doing, management should not assume the same relationships or benefits as may exist within the United States.

Inasmuch as the host government tends to look at a given project from the point of view of net *domestic* value added, other adjustments should be made. Items to be excluded are the cost of imported goods and services; foreign currency salaries and other payments made to foreign employees; and interest, dividends, fees, and royalties paid in foreign currencies to foreign persons or entities. (I assume that local currency paid to foreign nationals for these purposes would be spent locally. To the extent that it would not, but would be converted into foreign currency, this amount should likewise be excluded.) Payments made in the production of exports, of course, constitute part of the national income and are included in figuring the net domestic value to be added by a projected enterprise.

A further adjustment is required because the price of imports and exports is measured by means of an exchange rate which, more often than not, is pegged at some official value. At best, an exchange rate at any given moment represents only the *marginal* value of the two currencies in the minds of those in the market that day. Therefore, an investment which results in exports or a reduction in imports may in fact contribute more or less to the national product than would be measured at the official rate. If, for example, the foreign currency were undervalued in terms of the local currency, both import costs and export earnings would be unduly low. In such cases, the value added by export earnings should be increased by a percentage and the deductions made by reason of import costs likewise increased. An example will clarify the point:

Suppose a firm in country X imports $1,000 worth of parts from the United States. In country X, given the domestic price level and import duties, they sell for 4,000 dinars. But the official rate of exchange is only 3.0 dinars to the dollar, so the firm actually pays only 3,000 dinars for the dollars with which to pay for the parts, locally worth 4,000 dinars. The economy, in effect, subsidizes the firm to the extent of 1,000 dinars.

Suppose another firm exports products worth domestically 4,000 dinars for $1,000. It does so because domestic prices are relatively high and it cannot find a buyer at a higher price. In other words, its foreign exchange earnings are only $1,000, for which it would receive 3,000 dinars. In effect, this firm is subsidizing the economy to the extent of 1,000 dinars.

In the first case, 1,000 dinars should be added to the imported cost of the product and the firm's net value added adjusted accordingly. In the second case, 1,000 dinars should be added to the earnings of the firm and its net value added similarly adjusted. Similar adjustment should be made for other enterprises with which the one under question will be linked via external economies and diseconomies.

Implicit in the foregoing is the concept of an equilibrium exchange rate. In so far as I know, no one has provided a satisfactory formula for establishing such an equilibrium exchange rate against which the actual rate is to be compared to determine whether the local currency is under- or overvalued. In fact, to assume that there is *one* equilibrium rate is to beg many questions.[6] Rather, I suggest, an equilibrium rate might better be established for each project or process. Such a rate may be derived by calculating (in local monetary units) the annual net domestic value added (as defined) by a project over, say, a twenty-year period, discounted to the present by the rate of interest at which the host country may borrow foreign exchange of the variety to be used, and dividing the result by the foreign exchange to be committed. This figure would be a rough measure of the marginal product of the foreign investment (i.e., of the foreign resources to be used).

Summary. Net value that may be added by a new enterprise can be approximated by:

1. Making maximum-minimum assumptions as to demand-price elasticities for factors and supply-price elasticities for products. (In so doing, one should eliminate the effect of all public subsidies, i.e., price supports, export premiums, and import tariffs.)
2. Projecting sales and costs and setting up profit and loss statements for as long a period as management feels that it must maintain a given equity-debt-contractual relationship with the foreign enterprise in order to assure itself of an adequate return.
3. Calculating the net value added by summing up the amounts to be paid to the factors used in production, plus the before-tax profit.
4. Adjusting net value added so derived by:
   a. Subtracting that share of factor cost representing only a shift in factors from one activity to another (i.e., include only the value of the incremental product of the factor in its new use)

[6] The problem has been stated and analyzed by A. Nove, "The United States National Income à la Russe," *Economica* vol. 23, 1956; by M. Gilbert, *Comparative National Products and Price Levels: A Study of Western Europe and the United States*, OEEC, Paris, 1958; by M. Gilbert and I. B. Kravis, *An International Comparison of National Products and the Purchasing Power of Currencies*, OEEC, Paris, 1954; and by A. S. Becker, "Comparison of United States and USSR National Output: Some Rules of the Game," in *World Politics*, vol. 13, no. 1, October, 1960.

b. Adding to factor costs to the extent that they understate the marginal yields of these factors by reason of market imperfections
c. Adding the present discounted value of increased annual output expected by reason of company-financed training and other social welfare expenditures
d. Adding the cost of domestic raw materials that would not otherwise be exploited
e. Subtracting other external diseconomies and adding other external economies
f. Excluding the income derived from products or services that free resources, which will then remain unemployed (i.e., mere substitution)

5. Adjusting the foregoing calculations by:
a. Excluding the cost of imported factors (including foreign personnel paid in foreign currencies)
b. Excluding interest, dividends, fees, and royalties paid in foreign currencies to nonnationals
c. Modifying import costs and export earnings to reflect the marginal value of the foreign currency used

Granted, these calculations are exceedingly difficult and at best represent only an approximation, but reasonable assumptions make it possible for management to determine at the very least whether what it proposes to do falls at one extreme or the other in terms of the net value one can validly expect a project to add to the national income.

Balance of Payments Effect. Equilibrium in balance of payments, which is essentially an annual cash flow concept, is considered by some to be a prerequisite for sustained economic growth, such equilibrium being defined as "stable balance of payments over the relevant time period to maintain an open economy [i.e., uninhibited flow of capital and goods] on a continuing basis."[7] It is seen as a self-perpetuating system, that is, one not consuming its capital resources nor dependent upon the largesse or emergency help from politically allied states. (When one looks upon military—and perhaps economic—aid as payment for services rendered, i.e., political and military support, this latter qualification becomes somewhat fuzzy.)

What one has in mind, I suppose, is a balance between national and world economies which permits national growth at a politically acceptable level and international trade at an economically acceptable level. Behind that equilibrium lies an international exchange rate system, money supply, interest rates, production functions, income levels, liquidity preferences, price and wage levels, supply and demand elasticities, and a variety of political factors (e.g., fiscal and trade policies, effectiveness of government administrative machinery, degree of national political leverage). Changes in any one of these variables may affect the balance of payments. Both planners and managements should be aware that the traditional balance of payments concept is stated generally in annual terms. For long-run development, a year is not the

[7] C. Kindleberger, in a seminar at Massachusetts Institute of Technology, Cambridge, Mass., spring, 1962. For a relevant discussion, see F. Machlup, "Equilibrium and Disequilibrium," *Economic Journal,* vol. 68, pp. 1–24, March, 1958.

relevant time period, but something substantially longer—long enough to wash out short-run variations in inventories of imports and exportables, to eliminate the effect of weather and other disasters or windfalls, to permit an investment to set up a reverse flow, to allow induced secondary effects to appear, to balance out autonomous short-term capital movements, and to flatten out cyclical changes. Therefore, when using the term "balance of payments effect," I mean the anticipated average annual effect over time. This comes closer to what is called structural in explaining persistent disequilibrium. It may be, of course, that in a given situation future gains may be so heavily discounted that only the immediate effect (referring to the current year) is taken into consideration by the local authorities. However, if a country may still borrow abroad on reasonable terms, this should not be the case. Therefore, I believe that it is in terms of the longer-run balance of payments effect that most host governments are likely to view the problem.

Given perfect mobility of factors, the balance of payments effect cannot be differentiated completely from the net domestic value added in the dynamic and modified sense in which I have used these terms above. The one is part of the other, in that the direction of international transactions generated by an enterprise helps determine the level of net domestic value added by that enterprise. But factors are not perfectly fluid; both time and money attend the shifting. And many, given their specialized or localized nature, cannot be shifted at all. Furthermore, a persistent balance of payments drag may be sustained by a structural disequilibrium, to which a foreign-inspired enterprise may contribute. An example would be the channeling of local resources, including foreign exchange, into a skewed development so that the economy rests to a larger extent on a single product or a few products the supply of which is inelastic, except over the very long run, and the demand conditions for which are subject to changes beyond the influence of the producing country.

Therefore, I suggest that it is appropriate to consider the balance of payments effect separately over the moderate run—say five to ten years—as representing a distinct gain or loss. And quite apparently, it is so considered by many governments. Even though a project may release resources, increase investment, raise incomes, and eventually lead to a net credit on the balance of payments (depending on export and import income elasticities), loss may nonetheless occur in terms of the present nonavailability of the foreign exchange consumed to purchase the substance of alternative investment projects that would contribute to foreign exchange earnings in the shorter run. The cost of borrowing that foreign exchange lost should thus be charged to the using enterprise, for it is a rare underdeveloped country that does not suffer from a chronic foreign exchange shortage.

That the balance of payments effect may well take time to work out is demonstrated in the following: Consider a foreign exchange–using enterprise that will produce a commodity or service sold entirely to the domestic market. The product is not an import substitution in that present domestic supply is adequate for essential domestic consumption and imports are blocked.

What may happen to produce a long-run credit impact on the balance of payments?

1. More efficient use of scarce resources may eventually release exportable resources, or resources usable in producing exportable products. Examples:
   - More efficient use of local fuels for power generation, thereby releasing fuels for export
   - More efficient use of land for production of a locally consumed crop, say wheat, thereby releasing land suitable for the production of a crop that can be processed into an exportable product, say sugar beets
   - More efficient use of scarce skilled labor through automation, thereby releasing it for use in the production of an exchange-earning industry
   - More efficient use of capital, by shortening the time of production or reducing inventories, thereby releasing it for use in developing exchange-earning industry
2. Resource development may make possible the establishment of other enterprises which are exchange earners or exchange savers. Examples:
   - Production of a nonexportable perishable product, say, fish, thereby making possible the manufacture of an exportable processed product, e.g., fish meal
   - Production of a bulky resource on which freight is high (too high to export successfully), say, a mineral ore, thereby making possible an exportable concentrate
   - Production from a nontradable resource, say, hydroelectric power, thereby making possible externally competitive industry
3. Lowered service costs, thereby making other production externally competitive. Examples:
   - Improved domestic transport
   - Improved storage, etc.
   - Improved market organization
4. Lowered product costs, thereby making using industries externally competitive.
5. Increased incomes, thereby increasing the propensity to save and leading to investment in exchange-earning or exchange-saving activities.
6. Lowered factor costs by reason of increased demand, thereby making factor price externally competitive (in a decreasing-cost competitive situation).
7. Production of a popular consumer product in which the income-demand elasticity is positive—a "superior good"—thereby producing a deflationary effect which lowers the prices of certain exportable goods into the externally competitive range (e.g., soft drinks in some countries).
8. Direct stimulation of other industries producing exchange-earning or exchange-saving products. Example:
   - Technical assistance and purchase contracts given by a firm to stimulate local suppliers, thereby generating the production of new products which are exchange earners or exchange savers
9. Encouragement of diversification into industries in which product supply is less vulnerable to weather and is more elastic in respect to price and/or overseas demand conditions are more elastic in respect to price decreases, less elastic in respect to price increases, and less elastic in respect to level of national income of the importing country. Examples:

- Increased demand for a locally manufactured good, thereby causing a shift of resources, e.g., diversion of local investment in rubber plantations to rubber products manufacture
- Increased demand for annual crops, thereby causing a shift out of perennial crops, e.g., from a tree crop to vegetables

It can be seen that even though an enterprise be directly responsible for a net outgo of foreign exchange, its induced impact could be such as to reverse its rating; or a net foreign exchange earner might generate a long-run drag. The difference between an enterprise producing an immediate and direct *plus* impact on the balance of payments and one that does so only at some later date, given a chronic foreign exchange shortage, is the cost of borrowing over the interim. But, even taking into consideration the possibility of these time-delayed and indirect balance of payments effects, if management cannot establish beyond reasonable doubt that what it proposes to do will, at the very least, have a neutral balance of payments effect, the project is likely to be of a nature such as to contribute to a structural imbalance in respect to the international economic relations of the host country. If this be the case, the project will one day be vulnerable even though it might now be permitted.

Three Important Rules. A safe rule is that foreign ownership which capitalizes locally available resources—or imports resources for which local substitutes are feasible (even though development of these resources be required)—should examine its project with particular care and should do so periodically. Once it is suspected that the same activity could be carried on with available local resources, including human skills, the foreign equity may be challenged. At this point, the host society is making available foreign exchange to pay the foreign owners without any economic justification. The marginal product of the foreign exchange in this particular use has been reduced to zero.

A second rule is that if the firm's activity constitutes a significant part of the total economy of the host country, it should be wary of creating undue dependence upon a single activity or product, or a group of related ones. Such concentration may lead to structural imbalance and persistent balance of payments deficits. Geographical and/or industry diversification is then in order. What is "a significant part" in this context? This query may be answered by asking what would have happened if the local resources used by the firm had been otherwise employed. Would the result have been significantly different?

A third rule is that a firm should make certain that all the foreign exchange arising out of a foreign operation is made available to the host country. In a country where foreign exchange controls operate, foreign exchange transactions are generally undertaken by a public agency, although in some cases authority is given to a private interest to export and retain part or all of the foreign exchange earnings, perhaps as an export incentive device. Even in the absence of such authority, when the foreign company is exporting to an associated U.S. company, it becomes virtually impossible for the host government to be sure that it is receiving all the foreign exchange earnings in fact generated by the export. The foreign company can sell to the associated U.S. company at an abnormally low price, and the latter can sell at a much higher price. Meanwhile, the product may have been processed or mixed with other goods. A scarce resource—foreign exchange—may thus be lost, and the host government can be expected to react vigorously whenever it sees any alternative or effective leverage at hand.[8] A firm owned by nationals of the country of reference can be expected—unless capital flight or overseas investment is intended—to repatriate these foreign currency earnings in the form of imported goods and services, the selection of which may be controlled by the government. But there is no reason to expect that the foreign-owned firm will do so unless it has a deliberate policy of using foreign currency earnings, over and above those required for repatriation of profit and capital (often subject to governmental agreement), for the purchase of needed capital imports.

Public Revenue Effect. As with the balance of payments effect, the public revenue effect, as I have defined it, cannot really be separated from the criteria for net value added. Contributions to public revenue, as well as public costs set up by an enterprise, are included in the calculations. However, in the same way that international structural imbalance may be created by projects that set up a sustained drain, projects which set up a persistent drain on public resources may lead to a domestic structural imbalance as between soical overhead and direct productive facilities.

To determine the public revenue effect, management should consider not only the taxes it pays—or indirectly induces others to pay—but also the following:

1. The firm's share in the losses, a negative effect (or profits, a positive effect) incurred by public services which it buys
2. The costs that a firm incurs for services provided by the firm itself which are of far-reaching consequence and would otherwise be undertaken by a public agency (e.g., basic education, generalized technical training, public health, housing, provision of urban facilities, maintenance of law and order)—a positive effect
3. The cost of public housing, social welfare, and urban facilities required of public authority by reason of the firm's operation—a negative effect
4. The relative ease of taxing the net value added by the firm (e.g., a capital-intensive enterprise in general may be taxed more easily—tax collection being less costly—than a labor-intensive one, since the bulk of the tax is collected from fewer persons)
5. Dividends paid to public owners (a positive effect), or license, management, and royalty fees paid by the government to private owners (a negative effect)
6. Profit on the sale of the firm's product or services to public agencies—a negative effect.

If it cannot be established beyond reasonable doubt that the projected enterprise will have at least a neutral public revenue effect, it seems likely that it will consume more social overhead than it will supply, thereby pushing in the direction of imbalance. If the host government finds difficulty, as many do, in capturing adequate resources to provide what seem to be minimum social

[8] The many disputes between foreign oil companies and oil-producing countries constitute examples.

overhead requirements, management can anticipate difficulty once the situation is noted—perhaps in the form of services denied or higher taxes. In the former case, the firm itself may have to provide social overhead services whose cost may be nearly prohibitive, unless it wishes to integrate horizontally on a grand scale. Power, housing, and general technical training are three possible areas of concern.

If forewarned that its enterprise will be a net consumer of publicly financed services, a management is well advised to accept at least part ownership by a public agency. External social economies and diseconomies are thus internalized in the sense that they form part of the calculus for investment and policy decisions.

Additionally, a U.S. firm should stand ready to prove beyond reasonable doubt that its associated foreign firms are profiting from the relationship to the same extent that would be true were the transactions conducted between entirely unrelated enterprises. Through cost and price manipulations it is simple to minimize the profits shown by foreign associates, thereby reducing the tax base of the foreign government. So long as the foreign tax percentage is less than that charged to the parent enterprise at home (and the foreign taxes qualify as tax credits), there is rarely any purpose in reducing foreign profits by intercompany transactions carrying subnormal margins. However, if the foreign company be a tax-haven subsidiary of the United States parent, profits untaxed in the country of origin (because of subnormal transfer prices) may be invested by the parent elsewhere, likewise with little or no tax erosion.

Innovational Effect. In estimating the national income effect, balance of payments effect, and public revenue effect of a given enterprise, the time span that one chooses is both relevant and material. It may be so in reference to product usage, to industrial linkage effects, and to social welfare effects. The production of good A may lift the national income more in the short run than would the production of good B, even if the calculation of net value added by the two were modified as indicated in the preceding discussion. In the longer run, it is perfectly possible that the larger gain in national income would flow from good B. The same might be said of foreign exchange and of public revenues. A classic case in point would be the comparison between a cosmetic project and a pharmaceutical enterprise. The full impact on national income of the latter—via improved health and energy level—might take a fairly long time to work itself out but eventually be greater, even if discounted, than that of the former project. Another case in point: Assume equal amounts spent on soft drinks and on agricultural or industrial research. Which contributes most to national income? Now? Five years from now? Twenty years later? Obviously, even the suggested modifications to the concepts of net value added, balance of payments, and public revenue do not make them truly dynamic measures of the impact on the *growth* process, which in the long run has to do with placing resources in the hands of innovating entrepreneurs, thereby augmenting the productive capability of local innovators.

It should be borne in mind that the governing elites of many underdeveloped societies are primarily concerned with accelerated and sustained growth, only secondarily with short-term additions to consumers' real incomes. In other words, future income (or consumption) is discounted at very low rates—if, indeed, at all. This fact is relevant to the selection of appropriate discount rates to use in making the estimates previously suggested.

Furthermore, if long-run growth be the major concern, it becomes important, then, *who* receives the incremental income, the foreign exchange, and the public revenues, and what is done with these resources. Take the incremental income, or net value added: if most goes to labor, say in a labor-intensive project, the propensity to consume the added income may be relatively high. If, on the other hand, the bulk goes to entrepreneurs and financiers—as would tend to be the case in the more capital-intensive enterprises—the propensity to save this added income and invest in productive enterprises may be relatively high. (Also, it may be more difficult and costly to tax away the incremental income in labor-intensive enterprises than in capital-intensive ones.)

One can anticipate a cross fire between the *political* interest in maximizing the number of persons employed, distributing income more equally, and increasing immediate consumption and the *economic* interest in maximizing the net value added *over time* by the investment of a given amount of capital (which in a capital-poor country tends to lead to more capital-intensive enterprise). The political interest—in driving toward maximum employment, a more equal distribution of income, and higher immediate consumption—tends to emphasize labor-intensive enterprise. The second, the economic interest (which pushes in the direction of a more skewed income distribution and a higher level of saving), tends to encourage capital-intensive industry.[9] "Failure to introduce capital-intensive techniques at the outset of the industrialization process may create insurmountable institutional barriers to modernization."[10]

Another point relevant to the capital intensity–labor intensity controversy: among the most capital-intensive activities of all are various public welfare enterprises (education, housing, resource conservation, public health, pioneer power, and communications) in which the payoff is far removed in time from the period of heaviest investment. Resources development, including agriculture, would probably come next, then basic industry, intermediate industry, and finally consumer goods industry, which in the aggregate is the most labor-intensive of all.[11]

Whether capital-intensive or labor-intensive undertakings receive priority depends very largely upon whether the emphasis placed by a society is on short-run income (and consumption) or on long-run development. Where the emphasis falls depends on the extent to which the society discounts future consumption. The question is, who acts for society?

[9] A similar view is expressed by Walter Galenson and Harvey Leibenstein, "Investment Criteria, Productivity and Economic Development," *Quarterly Journal of Economics,* vol. 69, p. 358, August, 1955, although they did not make explicit the full implications of these two points of view.

[10] *Ibid.,* p. 359.

[11] V. Leontief, "Factor Proportions and the Structure of American Trade: Further Theoretical and Empirical Analysis," *Review of Economics and Statistics,* vol. 38, no. 4, pp. 386–407, November, 1956. With the exception of public welfare activities, with which he does not deal, Leontief ranks these activities in this order.

The evidence seems quite clear that within the foreseeable future the principal social actors will be strongly authoritarian elite groups, often with a military tinge, which will emphasize growth rather than immediate consumption. Hence, the foreign enterprise that can identify itself solidly with the long-run growth of the host society will occupy the most secure position, but it will do so only as long as the foreign interest is seen as contributing something at least equal in worth to what is being taken out of the economy.

As many economists and sociologists recognize, there is no neat correspondence between sustained growth and savings. Implicit in the foregoing discussion is that the savings generated can and will be invested in *productive* enterprise. Characteristic of the underdeveloped society is massive investment of savings (i.e., equated with incomes more than adequate to sustain a socially or politically acceptable consumption level) in nonproductive activities—war, ostentation, ceremonials, inventories of nonessentials. Saving in this sense is no assurance of future growth. The central question is: Does an enterprise induce greater domestic investment in *productive* enterprise? Or, put another way, does the enterprise tend to expand and support the technically and economically innovating elements among the local population? Possible measures are the degree to which it

1. Expands and upgrades the social recognition of local technical and organizational skills (e.g., training of local nationals and their employment in responsible positions)
2. Places resources in the hands of local innovating elements, whether public or private (e.g., encouraging local equity participation)
3. Induces a recognition of the value of literacy (e.g., via hiring policies, promotion, bonuses)
4. Induces the physical mobility of individuals (e.g., labor concentration)
5. Induces dissatisfaction with traditional agricultural methods (e.g., via demonstration of improved methods)
6. Induces locally oriented research and resource exploration
7. Stimulates the expansion of a local middle class (e.g., via development of local supplies of goods and services)
8. Stimulates the growth of a cash economy (e.g., increased demand for cash crops), thereby expanding market communication

These things do not lend themselves to precise mathematical measures, but approximations can be made. If a firm finds itself weak in these several respects, it would be well advised either to alter its policies and structure or to anticipate powerful pressures once another manner of operating is envisioned by the local authorities.

Impact on Political Development

A foreign firm which does not measure up in economic terms to what the local political authority expects, or feels is desirable, may anticipate political pressure against its interests. In addition, and quite apart from these economically induced political feedbacks, the firm should be aware of the more direct political consequences of its entry into a non-Western environment.

Modern Nationalism and Western Enterprise. Inasmuch as the rise of nationalism, both economic and political, in the newly independent nations characterizes the postwar era, it is useful to look closely at its rationale. The true meaning of nationalism in this context has to do with the criteria on which basic decisions are made. Consideration of national interest (i.e., universalistic norms within the nation), however well or ill defined, tends to predominate—not consideration of personal interest or that of specific interest groups. Political functions thus verge toward the more universalistic and affectively neutral norms in the national sense, though not yet in the international, and the process of political socialization (i.e., identification with a given political culture) expands to include the entire indigenous population of the nation-state. At the same time, the process of political recruitment (i.e., participation in the process of legitimizing political authority) often remains inadequately developed, which means that political change appears sporadic and disorderly, if not violent. Writing of Latin America, one analyst observed,[12]

> What seems to worsen the investment climate and to deter new investment is not the hostility of [local] businessmen or governmental corruption, but the coming to power of radical reform governments. Since Latin American radicalism is not only likely to stay but is also a noisy and often harsh instrument for institutional changes which many of these countries need if they are to develop solid cohesion and economic dynamism, this reaction of American investors, though understandable, is unfortunate.

Perhaps precisely because of past interference by Western governments and Western enterprise in the evolutionary process of political modernization, political change in many of the newer nations is inescapably equated with violent revolution and the emergence of charismatic leaders. In the modern context, a successful revolutionary leader must ultimately gain acceptance by appearing to embody the nation within his own personality and convictions, for interest-aggregating and interest-communicating functions are only inadequately differentiated. Rather, they tend to be exercised by powerful and appealing political personalities, and, partly because of the collaborationist record (in respect to former colonial regimes) of a large number of bureaucrats, the charismatic leader tends to be suspicious of them and to retain virtually all decision-making authority in his own hands. Indeed, where the process of political recruitment is so unstable that political leadership can be changed only by violent, extralegal means, it is perhaps unreasonable to expect the development of effective, differentiated rule-enforcing and rule-adjudicating functions. The administrator is understandably disinclined to make decisions or identify too closely with the rule-making authority. His survival may depend on his ability *not* to act independently, or perhaps not to act at all.

Government thus remains personal, and political functions remain nonspecific (i.e., not differentiated, diffuse), which renders it exceedingly difficult for the political authority to cope effectively with the complex problems of internal development and international relations thrust upon it with independence. The frustration and emotional outbursts against those seen as responsible for the problems—namely, the foreigner—may be more violent than would otherwise have been the case. Western enterprise not infrequently be-

[12] *United States Business and Labor in Latin America*, University of Chicago Research Center in Economic Development and Cultural Change, Committee on Foreign Relations, United States Senate, 86th Congress, 2d Sess., January, 1960, p. xi.

comes the convenient scapegoat against which to spend the pent-up fury of both social discontent and national frustration, for Western enterprise remains on the scene after Western governments have withdrawn and can no longer be attacked directly.

Western business efforts to maintain control of overseas activities after the withdrawal of Western political power have often led to a deliberate structuring of enterprises so as to assure control either by limiting information, by restricting access to decision-making centers within management, or by making the foreign enterprise a captive of the home industry by limiting its function to intermediate activities, such as assembly or other processing of foreign-supplied materials. Therefore, managerial and organizational skills were not transmitted in the measure needed to sustain development. Only of recent years, since World War II, has there been a serious effort by Western enterprise to develop local managements and highly skilled local technicians. Possibly, previous effort would have been doomed to failure in any event in view of the relatively low level of achievement motivation in the traditional societies.

Nonetheless, there now seems to be a politically compelling national need in non-Western countries to close the gap in material well-being. The sense of national inferiority, generated in part by the closed-door policy of Western enterprise, must be assuaged. It appears likely that "the sacrifices which economic growth requires, particularly in the early stages of economic development, can only be imposed and borne in the name of powerful ideologies: nationalism, in the sense of rising national consciousness and solidarity, has often proven capable of calling forth such sacrifices."[13]

In some cases the charismatic leader has deliberatively elevated accelerated economic development to the level of a political ideology and merged it with the nationalistic ideology itself, thereby substituting nonmaterial motivation for the material reward of increased consumption which such a society must temporarily forgo. A responsible leader of this type necessarily undertakes a vigorous effort of nation building, inherent in which are two major tasks: (1) a deepening of political socialization (identity with a political culture), and (2) a broadening of political recruitment (legitimizing of political authority). To be successful he must concentrate on elements of cohesion and similarity and de-emphasize all politically significant symbols of internal difference. Western enterprise tends to be a victim unless it succeeds in so thoroughly building itself into the local society as to be effectively localized—that is, nationalized in the sense of being so closely identified with national political and economic interests as to be indistinguishable from them.

Social Change Induced by Western Enterprise. It is quite apparent that Western enterprise, both deliberately and otherwise, tended in the past to draw about it local nationals who had already withdrawn from the traditional culture (the "modernists") or were in the process of so doing (the "transitionalists").[14] One writer reported,[15]

[13] *Ibid.*, p. 61.

[14] These terms are borrowed from Daniel Lerner, *The Passing of Traditional Society*, The Free Press of Glencoe, New York, 1958.

[15] J. S. Fforde, *An International Trade in Managerial Skills*, Basil Blackwell & Mott, Ltd., Oxford, 1957, p. 107.

> In many of the underdeveloped countries, foreign firms are almost unique in being able to offer a well-paid career in private business which is socially rewarding, respectable, and usually better paid than the Civil Service or armed forces. . . . Moreover, a career in [such] . . . enterprise is one with full opportunity. This contrasts favorably with that in the communal, family-dominated, local business whose practices in any case are often not considered respectable by the old or newly-emerging professional class.

The danger is that Western enterprise may isolate itself from effective communication with the traditional culture and, in so doing, bring hostility upon itself. For example, "Latin American businessmen, as a rule, prefer [to accept] foreign enterprises which do not enter into serious competition with them or radically upset existing business practices and labor policies."[16] At the same time, Western enterprise may be interfering with the political recruitment process by pulling many of the most competent "modernists" and "transitionalists" out of the traditional society and thus alienating them from the local political culture. Not only are these firms likely to be more achievement-oriented, but they can often offer higher salaries and more cosmopolitan careers.

One way around this dilemma, utilized by such enterprises as Arabian American Oil Company and Sears, Roebuck de México, has been to undertake to surround the enterprise with a variety of local, *independent* ancillary services and industries. The result is the creation of a modern, indigenous middle class. Possibly it would have been cheaper and easier for these companies to have provided the goods and services themselves—as similar companies elsewhere had done and are doing—or to employ foreign contractors. But by this policy of *local* contracting, they induced an internalizing of new values by a new middle class which identified with the interests of the firm but was not part of it. By remaining personally independent of the foreign company, such individuals are not blocked from performing effectively in political roles within the necessarily nationalistic environment, nor are they as likely to become alienated from their own culture.

One study of the Latin American scene has recommended that:[17]

> United States firms and their subsidiaries in Latin America should continue their activities in health and sanitation, education and training, and related fields to improve the productivity of employees and the welfare of their families. Where public programs serving their employees in these fields are underway, the business firms should participate in them, and if feasible seek to achieve integration of the public and private activities.

From the point of view of political development, the above may be very poor advice. Too many foreign concerns have usurped local government function, in line with traditional practice carrying over from the previous era. Granted, it is often less time- and money-consuming to continue the obligations of the paternalistic employer rather than to rely on others. But once a nationally responsible political authority emerges and some semblance of specific, differentiated political institutions develop, the Western enterprise should

[16] *United States Business and Labor in Latin America,* p. 51.

[17] *Technical Cooperation in Latin America,* National Planning Association, Washington, D.C., 1956, p. 132.

probably undertake a concerted effort to rid itself of all these extrabusiness activities. Public health and basic education should be a function of the public authority. If the Western enterprise is seen as competing for public favor with the local government in these fields, it becomes vulnerable to political reprisal and opens itself to the charge of interference with the process of national political development. The wiser policy would be the exercise of subtle pressure on local individuals, local groups, and the local government to assume responsibilities for these activities. Perhaps technical assistance, loans, and other forms of support might be given, as Aramco has done in Saudi Arabia and Sears Roebuck in Mexico.[18]

The Problem of Role Conflict. It is revealing to examine the roles presently occupied by the Western businessman in the newly emerging states and the conflict among those roles. First, he represents a Western management. As such, he is required to structure the foreign enterprise so as to yield maximum profit. Being on the ground and hence frequently significantly more knowledgeable of the local political culture than those at a higher level in the home office, he is acutely aware that practices yielding the highest profit in the short run may endanger the company's assets in the long run. The longer many of the more modern, professionally trained businessmen remain abroad, the more deeply they become aware of the genuine interests of the country in which they are employed, sometimes more so than national political leaders themselves. And so, at least in emotional terms, they become involved in local political choices. As foreign nationals they are also unofficial representatives of their own country's foreign policy. As a professional manager or technician, each is concerned with his own standing in the profession. To maintain that standing, he may be restless about remaining overseas too long. His various roles may be summarized thus:

Role	*Measure of success*
Stockholders' representative	Maximum profit, short term
Management's representative	Conformity with policy, low-cost operation
Management's country specialist	Maximum profit, long run (i.e., security of assets and market position)
Resident in a foreign country	Identification with national interests of host country
Innovator, modernizer	Local acceptance
Foreign citizen	Identification with national interests of home government
Member of a professional group	Prominence in professional associations, principally at home
Member of local business	Identification with interests of that community
Member of a local foreign community	Identification with interests of that community

Many cases could be cited of serious conflict between American managers abroad and their home offices, or between those in charge of organizing a

[18] The ramifications of the Sears development in Mexico are outlined by Richardson Wood and Virginia Keyser, *Sears, Roebuck de México,* S. A. National Planning Association, Washington, D.C., 1953.

foreign project and top management. One instance was the organization of the Merck project in India, during which the American team sent to India to study and negotiate came to feel very strongly that the company should enter into a joint manufacturing venture with the Indian Government. Top American management refused, apparently on almost doctrinaire grounds that indicated little sensitivity to the differences in the Indian situation from the American—i.e., the critical nature of the products involved, the inadequacy of supply, and the resulting need for public control of distribution.[19]

Such conflicts as these may seriously interfere with the effective transmission of skills and values. A further problem, now challenging some of the more thoughtful members of the international business community, is the suspicion that certain values long held in at least verbal awe in professional management circles may not, in fact, be universally valid. The concept of complete neutrality in interpersonal relations may not, after all, be conducive to the most effective communication within a large organization. The Japanese experience would indicate that at least some modification of the neutral and achievement norms may generate greater efficiency, at least under the same circumstances. In short, there is a growing awareness that additional research is needed before proceeding any further in the attempt to "modernize" foreign business associates.

Local Integration. A way to obviate some of these conflicts may be to combine roles through a variety of devices designed to bring about a high degree of local integration. Some Western firms have moved far in this direction. By so doing, the foreign associate is more likely to be cast in the role of a transmitter, that is, one who moves from one culture to another and *consciously* tries to change both. Such a role is in contrast with the amalgant role, which is assumed by one who is at home in both cultural worlds, but makes no attempt to try to change either.

Local integration may take a variety of forms, many of which are not necessarily mutually exclusive:

1. Intensified public relations to stress the importance of the enterprise to national development
2. Assistance to local public authorities (i.e., loans, technical assistance, use of facilities, etc.)
3. The employment of local nationals in specialized and supervisory roles
4. Contracting for all possible ancillary services with independent local businessmen, who may or may not be assisted by the company
5. Processing of locally procured materials and production for the local market
6. Organization of joint ventures in which local capital participates on a minority basis or a widely held majority basis (thus securing control for the minority foreign interest)
7. Local management, but with continued foreign financial and policy control
8. Local majority ownership, but with a management contract held by the foreign associated company

[19] Richard D. Robinson, "Merck & Co., Inc., in India," Harvard Graduate School of Business Administration, Boston, 1959, business cases ICR 183 and ICR 184. A shorter version appears in R. D. Robinson, *Cases in International Business,* Holt, Rinehart & Winston, Inc., New York, 1962, p. 100.

9. Local ownership and management, with only a minority ownership held by the associated foreign concern, together with perhaps some form of contractual relationship (license, technical assistance, sales, etc.)

10. Representation in the parent foreign firm by members of the associated local group (i.e., board membership)

11. Participation by the local group in the ownership of the parent foreign firm

It will be noted that as we move up the ladder of integration, roles tend to be combined and to change in character from the amalgant to the transmitter. True integration involves the deliberate structuring of the relationship so as to encourage a feedback from the host culture into the management of the firm, preferably at the parent-firm level. Obviously, many practical commercial, financial, legal, and national political factors enter in the judgment as to what is *now* practicable and desirable under specific circumstances. But generally, the greater the feedback into the associated Western enterprise at its home headquarters, the greater will be its constructive impact on the host culture and the greater will be the security of its assets and market position. If individuals at policy-making levels are thus identified with both cultures, they are much more likely to open up effective communications and to change attitudes and practices at both ends so as to eliminate conflict and enhance efficiency.

Some managements are sensitive to this need. Within such a firm, the attitude of both the local and foreign managements tends to become increasingly *de*national, for they no longer identify completely with either national culture. The pressure in this direction will, one suspects, be substantially intensified by technical developments now clearly on the horizon.

Political Vulnerability: A Summary. An enterprise may be politically vulnerable for a variety of economic reasons. To summarize, these reasons are:

1. The capitalization of locally available resources in the foreign equity

2. The insistence by foreign owners of an ownership share larger than the proportional contribution made by them (measured against the *potential* local contribution)

3. A net drain on public revenues and services (as previously defined), coupled with a management refusal to enter into a joint venture with a public agency

4. A net drain on foreign exchange resources (as previously defined)

5. A weak or neutral effect on national economic growth (as previously defined)

Closely associated with these causes of adverse political pressure is the injury to a local enterprise by the incursion of more efficient, foreign enterprise—even though the displacement may mean a net gain in national product.

> Sometimes American investors, exercising free enterprise, drive the local firms out of business by their superior methods and know-how. This is not a triumph for American technology. The local firms might have done as well if we sent technicians and advanced the capital. Foreign capital that displaces internal capital is not welcome.[20]

[20] H. L. Matthews, "Diplomatic Relations," in *The United States and Latin America*, 2d ed. American Assembly, Columbia University, New York, 1963, p. 150.

Other, essentially *noneconomic,* measures of political vulnerability relate to the sheer size of an enterprise as projected against the total economy of the host society. In event of large relative size, these factors become blown up:

1. Seat of decision making (also nationality of decision maker)
2. Public awareness of the firm's activities (i.e., degree of pervasiveness)
3. Relation with previous, now unpopular, political regimes
4. Relation with U.S. political interests and activities
5. Size of payroll (e.g., capital-intensive projects may be somewhat less vulnerable politically)
6. The amount and sort of local resources used (e.g., land is particularly vulnerable)

An additional set of criteria, relating to the product, are suggested by the following questions:[21]

1. Is the product ever the subject of important political debates in respect to adequacy of supply? (Sugar, salt, kerosene, gasoline, foodstuffs, transport facilities, public utilities, tires, medicines, etc.)
2. Is the product one on which other industries rest? (Cement, steel, power, machine tools, construction machinery, etc.)
3. Is the product one in which effective competition is difficult in small national markets?
4. Is the product one held to be essential, either economically or socially? (Key drugs and medicines, laboratory equipment.)
5. Is the product important to agriculture? (Farm tools and machinery, pumps, fertilizers, seed, etc.)
6. Is the product of national defense significance? (Communications equipment, transport equipment, etc.)
7. Does the product include important components that would be available from local sources? (Labor, skills, materials.)
8. Is the product one for which competition from local manufacture may be reasonably expected in the foreseeable future?
9. Does the product relate to channels of mass communication media? (Newsprint, radio equipment, etc.)
10. Is the product primarily a service?
11. Does the use of the product, or its design, rest upon some legal requirement?
12. Is the product potentially dangerous to the user? (Explosives, drugs.)

If each of these questions were answered on a 1-to-10 scale, from a strong "yes" to a strong "no," the lowest-scoring products would be among those most vulnerable to political pressures. (It is often useful to ask how foreign ownership of a given industry or product source would be treated in the United States.)

Political vulnerability may lead to labor agitation; public regulation (price fixing, allocation quotas, etc.); nationalization (in the sense of restricting ownership to local nationals); socialization (public ownership) on the one hand,

[21] Discussion of political vulnerability of product is taken from Richard D. Robinson, "The Challenge of the Underdeveloped National Market," *Journal of Marketing,"* vol. 25, no. 6, pp. 24–25, October, 1961.

or, on the other hand, favoritism and protection. The way the pendulum swings depends largely upon the sensitivity and foresight of management in responding to political pressures before they become irresistible, also upon the effort management makes to relate its product to the specific needs of the market in respect to both design and impact.

Goods deemed to be essential (for example, high scores in questions 2, 4, 5, 6, and 9) often receive first claim to scarce foreign exchange in respect to importing. Likewise, these same products, if made within the country, often receive a high degree of encouragement and protection, up to and including government guarantees for the repatriation of profits and capital and an official prohibition against competing imports. Therefore, other than the possibility of nationalization or socialization, the risk of investment abroad in the production of essential products is substantially less than that incurred in the case of less essential products.

This entire discussion is predicated upon the assumption that management possesses the willingness and ability to:

1. Look at and evaluate foreign projects in business terms
2. Consider these projects in terms of the interests of the host societies
3. Adapt processes and products to the foreign environment
4. Search out and examine a variety of alternative projects simultaneously
5. Structure overseas enterprises in the most appropriate manner (i.e., avoidance of inflexible policies regarding ownership, control, financing, choice of foreign associates, etc.)

In the absence of these qualities, an overseas venture is something of a shot in the dark in that management is likely to be taken completely by surprise when its enterprise becomes politically vulnerable. Mounting regulation, "discrimination," loss of effective control, and even total expropriation are likely to follow.

ASSISTANCE TO SMALL-SCALE INDUSTRY

Willem Brand, Ph.D.

Role of Small-scale Industry

Characteristics. By "small-scale industry" we understand firms employing a relatively small number of workers. As is known, comparisons between countries are difficult to make on this point because varying numbers of workers may be used to classify small-scale industry, while in other instances value of output, capital investment, or the use of electricity have been employed as criteria. Generally, we have in mind firms where there is only one director, or perhaps two, not engaged in actual production, but performing all managerial functions, i.e., supervision of production, buying and selling, bookkeeping and costing, training of workers, etc. Thus the organizational structure will consist of few levels between top and bottom, with no branches or special staff off the line of command. As a rule, the ratio of people engaged in indirect productive work to the total number of employees will be lower in small-scale than in large-scale industry. We are not concerned with handicraft production, where the owner devotes most of his time to actual production. In small-scale industry, however, there will be little specialization, line and staff functions may be combined in one person, and the director(s) will have close contact with workers as well as suppliers and customers.

Position. It can be observed that as a result of industrial development the average size of plant, in terms of output or even of the number of persons engaged, tends to increase. On the other hand, it can also be seen that the proportion of small-scale industry in the total of all manufacturing plants remains more or less the same. In certain sectors, it may disappear or be largely replaced by large-scale industry; then, as a result of a growing or more diversi-

---

Dr. Brand is Professor of Economics at the University of Leyden, Netherlands. He is also adviser to the Research Institute for Management Science at Delft, whose staff helped in the preparation of this article.

fied demand, new opportunities for its emergence seem to arise. Small firms may

1. Manufacture their own products
2. Make products for other firms on a subcontracting basis
3. Offer maintenance and repair services
4. Supply other services

One of the advantages of small-scale industry lies in the fact that it can produce small quantities of special dimensions or with a personal touch. It can often provide on order a great number of models or types of the same product in quantities which would be unattractive to large-scale industry. Further, it can sometimes serve a restricted market where, owing to a limited number of customers, large-scale industry cannot compete on account of transport or service costs. Large-scale industry has discovered that it pays to subcontract to small-scale industry such articles, parts, components, or operations which do not utilize its own more specialized skills or machines to optimum capacity. On the other hand, by catering to the needs of various large enterprises in the same line, small-scale industry often acquires a higher special skill at a lower cost than the individual large-scale firm. Repair, which is a service based on short-term delivery, points to the need for decentralization or nearness to the customer, qualifications fulfilled by small-scale industry. In short, small-scale industry owes its viability in part to its degree of adaptation to the requirements of its clients and its location vis-à-vis its markets. Though the subject warrants further investigation, experience in the Netherlands seems to prove that small-scale industry in many fields is very well able to compete price- and quality-wise with large-scale industry. From a study conducted some years ago, it was learned that in the Netherlands 60% of a sample of small firms in the metal industry exported part of its output, thus being able to stand on its own even in the international market. The table on page 420 shows the significance of small-scale industry in a number of countries in varying stages of development. We have purposely excluded establishments with one to five employees, as they comprise largely craftsmen and do not concern us.

It can be seen that small-scale industry is and remains important even after a country has attained a certain maturity in its industrial structure. This fact is confirmed by country statistics showing the share of small-scale industry in the total number of enterprises employing more than 10 persons. In the United States and the Netherlands, for example, 64 and 68% respectively of all such establishments are in the class employing 10 to 40 workers, while in India and Japan this share reaches even 87%. Table 1 does not confirm that the size of the average firm tends to increase as a result of economic growth. This tendency may be disguised by the manner in which the information regarding industrial firms is compiled or by historical circumstances. However, statistics available for some industrial countries do show that small-scale industry as a source of employment tends to decline percentage-wise over a long period. Further, it would appear, as can be seen from Table 2, that in certain developing countries the small factory has often a substantially lower output per man than the large factory, while in the industrial countries productivity in small and larger factories is about the same. This may be attributable to the fact that in such developing countries small-scale industry still embraces

TABLE 1. DISTRIBUTION OF EMPLOYMENT BY SIZE OF ESTABLISHMENT IN MANUFACTURING INDUSTRY, RECENT CENSUS YEAR*

(*In percent*)

<table>
<tr><th rowspan="2">Country</th><th rowspan="2">Census year</th><th colspan="3">Size of establishment</th><th rowspan="2">Total</th></tr>
<tr><th>5–50 employees</th><th>50–250 employees</th><th>Over 250 employees</th></tr>
<tr><td>Brazil</td><td>1950</td><td>31</td><td>26</td><td>43</td><td>100</td></tr>
<tr><td>China (Taiwan)</td><td>1954</td><td>56</td><td>23</td><td>20</td><td>100</td></tr>
<tr><td>Greece</td><td>1958</td><td>57</td><td>43</td><td></td><td>100</td></tr>
<tr><td>India</td><td>1956†</td><td>43</td><td>15</td><td>42</td><td>100</td></tr>
<tr><td>Iraq</td><td>1954</td><td>37</td><td>25</td><td>37</td><td>100</td></tr>
<tr><td>United Arab Republic</td><td>1950</td><td>30</td><td>18</td><td>52</td><td>100</td></tr>
<tr><td>Denmark</td><td>1948</td><td>46</td><td colspan="2">54</td><td>100</td></tr>
<tr><td>Japan</td><td>1955</td><td>45</td><td>25</td><td>30</td><td>100</td></tr>
<tr><td>Sweden</td><td>1951</td><td>27</td><td colspan="2">73</td><td>100</td></tr>
<tr><td>United States</td><td>1954</td><td>15</td><td>26</td><td>59</td><td>100</td></tr>
</table>

* For China (Taiwan) and Japan the lower limit is 4 not 5 persons engaged; for these countries, the upper limit of medium-scale industry is 300, so that large-scale industry starts with 300 workers.

† P. N. Dhar and H. F. Lydall, *Small Enterprise in Economic Development*, New Delhi, 1961.

TABLE 2. DISTRIBUTION OF EMPLOYMENT AND VALUE ADDED BY SIZE OF ESTABLISHMENT IN MANUFACTURING INDUSTRY, RECENT CENSUS YEAR*

(*In percent*)

<table>
<tr><th rowspan="2">Country</th><th colspan="3">Size of establishment</th><th rowspan="2">Total</th></tr>
<tr><th>5–50 employees</th><th>50–250 employees</th><th>Over 250 employees</th></tr>
<tr><td>Lebanon</td><td></td><td></td><td></td><td></td></tr>
<tr><td>Persons engaged</td><td>57</td><td colspan="2">43</td><td>100</td></tr>
<tr><td>Value added</td><td>41</td><td colspan="2">59</td><td>100</td></tr>
<tr><td>Philippines</td><td></td><td></td><td></td><td></td></tr>
<tr><td>Persons engaged</td><td>40</td><td>35</td><td>25</td><td>100</td></tr>
<tr><td>Value added</td><td>19</td><td>46</td><td>35</td><td>100</td></tr>
<tr><td>Finland</td><td></td><td></td><td></td><td></td></tr>
<tr><td>Persons engaged</td><td>23</td><td>49</td><td>25</td><td>100</td></tr>
<tr><td>Value added</td><td>21</td><td>46</td><td>35</td><td>100</td></tr>
<tr><td>Sweden</td><td></td><td></td><td></td><td></td></tr>
<tr><td>Persons engaged</td><td>27</td><td colspan="2">73</td><td>100</td></tr>
<tr><td>Value added</td><td>24</td><td colspan="2">76</td><td>100</td></tr>
<tr><td>United States</td><td></td><td></td><td></td><td></td></tr>
<tr><td>Persons engaged</td><td>15</td><td>26</td><td>59</td><td>100</td></tr>
<tr><td>Value added</td><td>12</td><td>23</td><td>65</td><td>100</td></tr>
</table>

* Only establishments engaging 5 or more persons have been included in this table.

a large number of traditional handicrafts. In any case, the table would seem to indicate that in these countries there is considerable scope for raising the efficiency of small-scale industry.

Needs and Assistance

Needs. The advantages of small-scale industry form at the same time some of its limitations. Though conditions differ in countries in varying stages of development, some generalizations seem in order. The manager or owner of a small firm is usually so engrossed in his daily chore of activities that he lacks the time to analyze his present operations or his future prospects. Often he possesses a rather narrow outlook, which makes him somewhat impervious to external advice. Especially, the need for training a successor, whether a son or an outsider, remains in many cases unnoticed, causing the downfall of many small-scale enterprises after the second or third generation has taken over. Another tendency is that when his business grows, the manager generally keeps to himself a particular field of action depending upon his interest or aptitude, while he transfers other functions to another person without giving him enough freedom to work effectively. Scarcity of financial resources besets practically all small-scale industry, partly as a result of insufficient equity capital or unwillingness to attract outside financing which may imply partial surrendering of control by the owner.

Assistance. The above short summary of requirements indicates in what respects small-scale industry needs to be helped. Though there is no substitute for visiting individual firms to solve their problems, no country can afford services catering to all small-scale industry in all respects. Because by nature these small establishments are numerous and widely dispersed, a choice has to be made between assistance provided through centralized or decentralized agencies, through efforts by the state or voluntary organizations, and through group or individual approach. Financial limitations and the caliber of the persons available for consultancy work determine in general the system which is set up. In most countries, banking institutions have been created to provide for the need of obtaining adequate short-, medium-, and long-term credit for small-scale industry. Such specialized banks with a more or less extended network of branches have in many cases also helped in developing minimum cost accounting and budgetary and financial control schedules. More recently, hire-purchase facilities have often been offered through these channels for the acquisition of better machinery and tools. To facilitate the supervision of credits to their diverse clients, such banks have sometimes been instrumental in establishing associations (or cooperatives) of branch-wise organizations of small firms which know their members and the conditions under which they work. Such associations have also sprung up independently in order that small-scale industry through joint buying or selling may obtain some of the advantages of large-scale organization. In the Netherlands, for example, some of such associations are subsidized by the state in order that they may be enabled to widen their scope of work. Thus, they are distributing technical and commercial information to their members and have set up services which can give individual advice in these and similar fields, such as legislation and taxation. They have also been instrumental in making interfirm comparisons from which it is possible for each participating member to have an idea of the efficiency of his firm regarding certain work methods or processes in relation to other members within the same branch.

Governments have in many countries founded technical consulting services. Originally, they have started out by offering advice on, say, choice of equipment, costing systems, and improvement of layout in small factories, but gradually their work has been embracing almost every detail of small-scale industry operations. Improvement of working methods, training of workers, research on raw materials, equipment, maintenance, etc., have been included. In addition, they keep up-to-date libraries and connections with institutions in other countries, enabling them to answer any inquiries which may reach them from the field.

In developing countries, governments have usually gone even further in assisting small-scale industry. They have, for example, held fairs, provided permanent showrooms, or even assigned or reserved a certain quota of its purchases for small-scale industry to augment its sales possibilities.

Pamphlets regarding the setting up of a particular industry have been issued to visualize for the potential entrepreneur the amount of capital, equipment, labor skills, raw materials, etc., required for establishing an enterprise. Demonstration plants have even been erected for the same purpose. Statistics of imports have been properly presented, giving a clue to interested parties as to what part of domestic demand small-scale industry may fulfill. If domestic supply is forthcoming, import quotas have sometimes been established for a limited period in order that small-scale industry can overcome some of the difficulties inevitably encountered in a new field. Foreign exchange has been set aside especially for importing raw materials and equipment. In nonindustrial countries, it has generally been noted that special measures have to be taken to instruct owners of small-scale industry about adequate maintenance of equipment. Further, repair services (including a sufficient supply of spare parts) have often to be established to avoid having new machinery out of production for prolonged periods.

It should be emphasized that the service to be rendered to small-scale industry depends to a large extent upon the quality of the extension workers involved. They must be practical persons who can obtain the facts, diagnose weaknesses, and offer solutions in the language understood by managers of small-scale industry. In order to inspire confidence, they must also be able to help in implementing the recommendations which they have proposed. Furthermore, they need to be constantly given refresher courses in order that they may keep abreast of recent developments. Though their work is by nature confidential, they are apt to discover that certain problems are similar in all small-scale industry. Thus group lectures or discussion groups may be organized which, based on actual experience, will bring home to managers or their potential successors the practical application of new methods to increase the productivity of their enterprises.

In view of the width of the field and the impossibility of covering it entirely by existing organizations, university and college students in the Netherlands who have followed courses in industrial management have been given assignments of three to four months' duration in small-scale industry.

Under the supervision of an experienced consultant, they have thus been able to see many aspects of management in a concentrated form and have contributed to acquainting small-scale industry with new developments in management science. We may now give some details about some recently used methods for assisting small-scale industry.

Integrated Plant Survey. The above method has been developed in the Netherlands in order to make a diagnosis of the position of a small-scale enterprise, to evaluate the efficiency of the various sectors, and to indicate a certain priority as to improvements which may be necessary. In the first stage, data are gathered covering the sectors of production, marketing, financing, and personnel.

Regarding production, for example, a check is made to see whether work stations are situated in the right sequence of operations and whether the capacities of the various stations are adequately balanced. In addition, attention is paid to the flow of materials in process and the changeover of jobs by operators. The different items of production are listed, and an analytical distribution of costs of production for each is made. Further, the ratio between direct and indirect work and the time utilization of individual workers and machines are established. As for marketing, the items recorded are location of and amount sold to regular and occasional customers, delivery times, visiting sequences of salesmen, some information on the potential market, etc. In the financial sector, the main data used are the balance sheet and the profit and loss account, preferably over the last three years, while the liquidity position of the firm is also looked into. For the personnel sector, an organization chart is drawn up, as well as a turnover diagram and a table comparing the performance of the various workers with the actual and future labor needs of the firm.

This entire survey can be carried out in two or three man days if the firm can be encouraged to assemble some of the required data in advance. The above information, quantified to the greatest possible extent, makes it possible to assign ratings to the standing of the firm in each sector, indicating whether for certain aspects improvement is necessary or desirable or whether the situation is reasonable or satisfactory. The findings are presented in an evaluation diagram with some text which can be read in about fifteen minutes.

It may be pointed out that, in the Netherlands, improvement appears to be most needed in the financial and marketing spheres. Too often firms are short of equity capital or long-term loans (thus indicating too much short-term credit), or are unaware of the high cost of small orders or the decrease of their market share while total demand is growing. From the analysis will follow which shortcomings can be handled by management or, after some training, by a staff member, and which deficiencies need further investigation by outside assistance. The method (which may be compared with a medical checkup) would appear to be especially valuable in developing countries to judge the credit worthiness of firms and diagnose common weaknesses which can be combated through training courses in certain fields.

Industrial Estates. In many countries in recent years new small firms have been concentrated in industrial estates, i.e., improved sites with good access to transport facilities and water and power connections. Thus from the outset certain economies of scale in construction and maintenance are obtained. By not having to invest in land and building, but only paying a monthly rental, the owner of a small-scale enterprise can utilize a larger share of his funds for working capital and thus finance his future growth more easily. The management of the estate can further provide a repair and training workshop or a canteen, either on its own initiative or through joint action by the tenants' association.

Cooperation in shipment or transport of workers may give additional advantages. The grouping together of several industries facilitates advising them on selection of machinery, satisfactory layout, and the utilization of proper management methods. In several cases, the firms in an industrial estate have proved to be model plants whose operations can have a beneficial spread effect on other enterprises in the neighborhood.

The site for the estate has to be carefully selected with a view to availability of raw materials and labor, the marketability of the articles to be produced, and a potential supply of entrepreneurs. Exploratory surveys of the appropriate industries to be included in the estate and their likely expansion should precede any construction work.

Management Training. Recent economic literature has emphasized the importance of organization apart from the input of labor and machinery in raising output. Thus, it is necessary to develop special channels to transfer organizational knowledge to management. This may be done by teaching the principles of organization in vocational, technical, and commercial schools from which future managers may graduate. Such curricula should include certain techniques for recording the situation of a small enterprise and show simple solutions to various contingencies arising in a changing society.

However, a wider group needs to be involved. Managers, future extension workers, and university students and other persons likely to be concerned with assisting small-scale industry are to be approached. Evening and daytime classes at varying levels, depending upon the background of the participants, can be provided for them, but in addition training in industry should be given to increasing numbers. It has been shown in the Netherlands and probably elsewhere that, though the theory of management can be easily appreciated, the application of its methods and techniques to the practical problems arising daily in the factory is a more difficult matter.

In-plant training programs provide a partial answer to this problem. Through such training the student learns to synthesize the knowledge gained by recording and analyzing into an integrated judgment the various elements which combine to make a firm work. The development of this ability will simultaneously lead to the discovery of possible improvements and their translation into suggestions and recommendations which appear likely to be implemented under the particular circumstances prevailing in each firm.

Thus, in-plant training, necessarily under expert guidance, will make apparent the suitability of technicians of different caliber for consultancy work. Though in industrial countries the subject has hardly yet been approached in a systematic manner, it would appear that developing countries would be wise to devote some of their resources to this type of training in order to accelerate their economic growth.

Promotion of Small-scale Industry

Objectives and Policies. The objective of all developing countries is to raise the living standards of their inhabitants. Industrialization is seen as a main lever in the process of development because of the already existing overpopulation in the agricultural sector or the likelihood of an outflow of agricultural labor as a result of foreseen improvements in the primary sphere. It is, however, recognized that the expansion of industrial production is conditioned by increases in output of raw materials, extension of transportation, more electric power, etc. Thus, development programming has lately come to the fore to take into account the interdependency of the various economic sectors or attain a balanced economic growth. After a desirable rate of development has been determined, calculations are made to decide what investments are required to reach the targets for the different sectors. Subsequently, within each sector, the most productive projects based on cost-benefit calculations are established to obtain the targets envisaged.

As regards industrial projects, in recent years considerable attention has been given to the factors which should be weighed in the choice of the proper technology or the relative proportions of capital and labor. Though there appears no doubt that for certain forms of manufacturing (chemical, heavy engineering, and building materials industries) capital-intensive and large-scale production is indicated, most authors seem to agree that developing countries should place special stress on supporting small-scale industry. As such countries are more or less by definition characterized by an underdeveloped transport network and a scarcity of capital, the promotion of small-scale industry is considered to be even more important than in already industrialized countries. It is recognized that tools and implements for small-scale industry can often be produced from locally available materials, thus saving foreign exchange.

Additional investment in "overhead" facilities (power, buildings, housing) is less expensive in smaller conglomerations, and decentralized industrialization will have the effect of diverting the flow of migrants to the larger towns, where facilities are usually already overburdened. As small-scale industry provides more employment per unit of capital, it has the further advantage that purchasing power tends to rise more evenly (in comparison with large-scale industry) with an increase in production.

Before any development plan is put into action, an evaluation of the skills of the labor force is essential, as the execution of the different projects is dependent upon the quality of the personnel available. Here again, the establishment of small- and medium-size industry is generally recommended as it requires less technical and organizational skills than large-scale industry. It will, however, be apparent from the foregoing that an array of interrelated services, either by the government or through private sources, will be needed to assure that viable enterprises are erected and maintained.

In deciding by whom the various parts of the program are to be implemented, the government should be led by the principle of social efficiency, which entails that projects should be entrusted to those who are best able to handle them. The economic policy to be initiated should also take into account that a proper climate must be created in order that the motivation or incentive for developing entrepreneurial characteristics will be encouraged. Generally, it is again pointed out that one advantage of small-scale industry is that it leads to a larger diffusion of the managerial and supervisory skills which are so important for further industrial development. It is a well-known fact in industrial countries that many medium- and large-scale industries arose out of small firms. This aspect should of course be supported by a constantly expanding system of technical and commercial education from which an increasing flow of skilled workers and managers will emerge.

Technical and Capital Aid. After a careful assessment of domestic resources, developing programming will also reveal what technical assistance and capital aid is to be attracted from abroad in order to reach the goals established. Individual experts may be required to assist in overcoming technical and organizational bottlenecks in particular industries. Nationals need to be sent to more advanced countries to learn particular skills which will help solve the problems faced in the execution of certain projects. Joint ventures, i.e., participation by foreign firms in local enterprises, may be encouraged especially to expand and diversify export trade in view of the largely inelastic world demand for the traditional commodities of the developing countries.

The International Bank for Reconstruction and Development has in the past been helpful in providing foreign exchange for national industrial banks erected to provide credit to small-scale industry. Also the United Nations Special Fund has contributed to the cost of institutes or laboratories for industrial research or services set up to improve techniques, select equipment, and study raw materials or survey markets for small-scale industry. It has also provided assistance to pilot plants and demonstration units after satisfying itself as to the adequacy of a previous investigation of raw materials, technical skills, factory design, production flows, and other elements requisite to successful industrial production.

However, it appears that at present not enough lines of communication exist to raise the techniques of production and improve the quality of the labor force engaged in small-scale industry in developing countries. Foreign investment fulfills the role only to a limited extent, as it is not usually interested in manufacturing industries in less advanced countries. Although through its input of capital, experience, and the application of modern techniques in its enterprises it can indeed stimulate the copying of its method of conducting business by national entrepreneurs in secondary activities, this will not be the main objective.

Foreign investors do at present show willingness to contribute, for example, to the training of local technicians and higher personnel, even if they are not to be employed in their enterprises, but the effort remains necessarily below what is required. In view of the manner in which industry is organized in the West, it would seem that agencies are needed which bring more private entrepreneurs in our countries in contact with governments or interested groups in the developing countries. In our opinion, it would be advisable to reserve for this purpose some of the larger aid funds which are likely to flow into underdeveloped areas in the coming decade. Subsidies to existing managerial organizations in an industrial country to encourage interest in management techniques and facilitate the dissemination of information concerning them in developing countries could be another means of achieving this goal, but we think that there is no alternative to sending larger numbers of qualified persons from the more advanced countries to increase efficiency standards. Such persons may be attached to productivity centers or schools where students are trained for consultatory functions. Little research has yet been devoted to the subject of how to accelerate the introduction of modern management techniques in developing countries, but we feel that a systematic attempt to improve the transfer of knowledge in the managerial field could be one of the most fruitful solutions in narrowing the gap in levels of living between rich and poor countries.

BIBLIOGRAPHY

Alexander-Frutschi, M. C.: *Small Industry: An International Annotated Bibliography,* New York, 1960.

International Labor Office: *Services for Small-scale Industry,* Geneva, 1961.

United Nations: *Establishment of Industrial Estates in Underdeveloped Countries,* New York, 1961.

Recent information on the subject may be found, for example, in *Asian Productivity* (a publication issued by the Asian Productivity Organization, Tokyo) and certain United Nations publications emanating from New York or the regional commissions.

SERVICES FOR THE DEVELOPMENT OF SUBSOIL RESOURCES IN THE IVORY COAST

John Allen

Thomas A. Mead

This article describes the association between a private American company—Development and Resources Corporation— and the government of a newly independent and developing country—the Republic of the Ivory Coast—in the planning and carrying out of a mineral resources development program.

D & R's relationship with the Government of the Ivory Coast goes back more than four years and presents one or two rather unusual aspects. In the first place, it rests upon an agreement which was negotiated on the Government's initiative and has been financed entirely from the Government's own resources. In the second place, the relationship has not been a static one, rigidly adhering to particular contractual provisions, but is readily adaptable to the changing circumstances and to the expanding capabilities of the client country. Third, and most important perhaps, the effort has not been limited to the provision of those technical skills which are the common deficiencies of all the developing nations; it has been directed in addition, and very deliberately so, to the cultivation in the Ivory Coast of institutional and organizational strength, without which no amount of foreign technical assistance is capable of producing lastingly beneficial results.

In what the United Nations has named the Decade of Development (and after nearly two decades of earnest and expensive effort), the results of many technical assistance programs (both bilateral and multilateral) still seem to

---

Mr. Allen was formerly assistant to D & R's Vice President for Industrial Development, by whom the company's services to the Ivory Coast have been directed.

Mr. Mead was D & R's resident representative in the Ivory Coast from 1960 to 1963.

fall short of the intensions of those who give and the expectations of those who receive. We of the affluent nations cannot yet say with confidence that we have mastered the mystery of applying our own profuse knowledge and resources to the betterment of our less fortunate relations in the tropics. We may have come too readily to the conclusion that technological skills and money are the obvious deficiencies and that, if these are supplied, economic development will follow. Method and purpose, more elusive, are equally important, and the experience described in this article may illustrate opportunities and problems and suggest solutions to other American enterprises which seek to assist the developing nations.

The Republic of the Ivory Coast

Formerly one of the territories that made up the Federation of French West Africa, the Ivory Coast became a fully independent and sovereign republic on August 7, 1960, and, sponsored by France, it was admitted to membership in the United Nations shortly afterward. It is a compact state of some 125,000 square miles—about the size of New Mexico—with a population which was estimated at 3,200,000 in 1960 and is increasing at a rate of 2.5 percent a year. Situated on the Gulf of Guinea, with an Atlantic shoreline of 340 miles, its frontiers lie with Ghana to the east, Mali and Upper Volta to the north, and Guinea and Liberia to the west.

The territory of the Ivory Coast falls into two clearly marked geographical zones, with a belt of tropical rain forest in the south and savannah in the center and north. Immediately behind the coast there is an extensive system of lagoons.

Ninety percent of the population is still dependent for its living on the various branches of agriculture, but in recent years light industry has made progress, especially in the principal centers of Abidjan and Bouake, and there is some production of minerals, notably diamonds and manganese, with a little columbotantalite. Until recent years there was also a little gold, won by small individual operators.

The Ivory Coast is determined to expand its economy in a free enterprise system. Lack of local investment capital, the shortage of professional and technical workers, and deficiencies in managerial expertise are obstacles to be overcome, as they are in most developing countries, though the Ivory Coast is somewhat better off in these respects than many of its neighbors. The need to import know-how is evident, and, refreshingly, it is recognized.

The United States is a good and valued client of the Ivory Coast, buying appreciable quantities of its coffee, cocoa, timber, manganese, and diamonds. At the same time Ivory Coast is buying American managerial and technical services to promote an important feature of its economic development program, the investigation and exploitation of its subsoil resources.

Problems of Geological Exploration

The Ivory Coast acquired a geological survey service of its own comparatively recently, only a year before independence, with the creation in July, 1959, of the Direction de la Géologie et de la Prospection Minière. Geological exploration had previously been undertaken in the context of

French West Africa as a whole, and while much excellent work was done, it was not, for obvious reasons, done to promote the well-being of any particular territory of the former Federation.

The new department had much to contend with. Apart from the natural difficulties of the terrain (the geology of large areas of West Africa is concealed by heavy vegetational cover), it suffered from severe shortages of equipment and personnel, and there were no geological laboratory facilities of any kind in the country. Dependence on laboratories overseas—in Dakar and Paris—delayed the confirmation or orientation of field work in accordance with laboratory results. In terms of the national budget, the department, a newcomer to the Ivory Coast's administration, found itself in competition with the older and better-established agencies of government, and the means placed at its disposal never corresponded with its needs.

The Direction de la Géologie et de la Prospection Minière encountered difficulty in setting up a working program which recommended itself to the Government and would command the Government's approval and therefore the necessary financing. In October, 1959, the department, with the help of the Bureau de Recherches Géologiques et Minières, submitted a program of exploration scheduled for a three-year period. The program provided for (1) airborne geophysical surveys over 150,000 square kilometers, about half the total area of the country; (2) detailed surface investigations of the very large number of anomalies expected to be revealed by these surveys; (3) wholesale alluvial prospection of some 10,000 kilometers of major and minor water courses; and (4) studies of a limited number of specific known occurrences. The cost of this program was to be considerable in terms of the Ivory Coast's total resources and was variously estimated at between $12 and $16 million. The Government took no action on these proposals and instead, in May, 1960, asked D & R, a consulting firm of New York, to review them on its behalf and present recommendations. The Government emphasized the Republic's need for practical results in terms of prompt and sound development of commercially significant mineral deposits.

Preliminary Study by Development and Resources Corporation

In response to this request, two representatives of the corporation visited the Ivory Coast in June–July, 1960. They were provided with all existing data relevant to a program of minerals development; they participated in frank discussions with geologists of the Direction de la Géologie et de la Prospection Minière; they understook field trips to familiarize themselves with the conditions in which geological field parties would be working; and they were given information on other aspects of Ivory Coast industrial development which seemed pertinent to the geological program. On the basis of their report and subsequent discussion in the New York office of D & R, D & R's recommendations were submitted to the Minister of Finance, Economic Affairs and Planning on July 25, 1960.

In the judgment of D & R, the proposals of the Direction de la Géologie et de la Prospection Minière and the Bureau de Recherches Géologiques et Minières were not necessarily calculated to produce the result the Ivory Coast Government had asked for—economic exploitation of its mineral resources, with the shortest possible delay and at the most reasonable cost. The corporation was obliged to question whether the Ivory Coast would be wise to depend so heavily on a method—airborne geophysical surveys—with which it had had little (and at that unsatisfactory) experience and which had not yet been proved to be of value under West African conditions. The corporation considered that the proposed program had drawn less than it should have done upon the far from negligible quantities of geological information already available. It suggested instead that:

1. In the next three years the Ivory Coast should confine its attention to fifteen to twenty known occurrences and areas in which, on the basis of present knowledge, mineralization was most likely.

2. These areas and occurrences should also be selected with regard to (*a*) the present international market situation and the probable future demand for particular minerals and (*b*) the requirements of the country's development plan as a whole.

The second of these recommendations is by no means as obvious as it may sound. First, there is a disposition in some of the developing countries to assume that, simply because a commodity exists, overseas markets will dutifully and eagerly compete for it and that demand will automatically correspond to supply. Disappointment and disillusionment are very often the result. Second, as a corollary of the above, the same countries tend to think of subsoil resources in terms of the heavy and precious metals which they can sell to foreign clients, ignoring as a result the great potential value to their own economies of underground water resources and the nonmetallic industrially useful materials, for which an urgent need and an excellent market very often exist on their own doorstep.

D & R added its opinion that a satisfactory program could be designed and undertaken in accordance with these general recommendations at a cost which, including construction and equipment of a modern analytical laboratory, would fall well below that of the previous proposals.

In submitting its recommendations, D & R took the occasion to stress one aspect of this kind of program, often ignored because it does not appear related to the immediate economic purpose—the opportunity it provides to build up local institutions of enduring strength. In present circumstances in the developing countries, programs such as this cannot be undertaken at all without calling in outside help; but the methods by which help is applied may be just as important as the economic purpose it is intended to serve. Such help should encourage the establishment of increasingly self-reliant local agencies and diminution of dependence on assistance from overseas.

Design of a Geological Exploration Program

On consideration of the D & R report, the Ivory Coast Government requested D & R to assume responsibility for the detailed design of the kind of program it had recommended. An agreement between the Government and D & R was executed on October 4, 1960.

The agreement provided that, while the program was to be designed with the help of D & R, it was to be carried out by the Ivory Coast's own agency, the Direction de la Géologie et de la Prospection Minière, with D & R's continuing support and guidance; that D & R was to provide the Direction de la Géologie et de la Prospection Minière with specialist services—geophysicists, photogeologists, metallurgists, etc.—such as it might not be economical or practicable for the Direction to employ full time; and the D & R would assist the Government, as occasion arose, in securing the development in the Ivory Coast's interests of any deposits discovered. In order to administer the services to be furnished under the agreement, D & R was to establish a representative office in Abidjan, and this was done within two weeks of the agreement's being executed.

A mission consisting of two outstanding consultants, a geologist and a geophysicist, was dispatched to the Ivory Coast in November, 1960, and a three-year program for geological exploration and minerals development was submitted to the Minister of Finance, Economic Affairs and Planning in March, 1961.

D & R's findings were that, at that time and on existing knowledge, manganese, diamonds, gold, beryllium, and lithium had primary potentiality for Ivory Coast industry and that, of these, manganese was the most promising for rapid development, while secondary potentiality existed in chromium, nickel, platinum, cobalt, tin, graphite, iron, and rare earths. The program provided for the investigation of these possibilities in the three-year period 1961 to 1963 and listed the areas in which prospection was likely to be most rewarding. It provided also for the systematic study of ground-water resources and, in the vicinity of the larger centers of population, for the cataloguing of industrially useful materials such as sands, gravels, clays, feldspars, and micas. The employment of twenty-two geological and prospecting field parties was foreseen, and their assignment to particular subjects and areas was laid down. For the sake of flexibility, however, and in order to meet suddenly arising needs, two of the parties were not specifically assigned.

A detailed estimate of the cost of the recommended program was included, amounting to $4.5 million over the three-year period. This figure was inclusive of constructing and equipping a modern analytical laboratory employing X-ray beyond the term of the present three-year program, for instance, the cost of constructing and equipping a modern analytical laboratory employing x-ray diffraction and fluorescence as well as the more traditional methods of analysis.

In substance, the program rested upon a theoretical concept of the Ivory Coast's geological origins and structure, drawing of course upon the work done by a number of geologists over a considerable period of time, but never previously expressed as the basis for systematic exploration of mineral resources. While such a concept was essential to the definition of areas and subjects capable of yielding economically interesting results, the circumstances in which it was developed were also important; it was the result of mutual study and harmonious discussion by the Government's and the company's geologists, and so established a pattern for the kind of relationship which has since emerged.

The recommendations which D & R presented in March, 1961, did not set out to comprehend all the various aspects of geological research. The Ivory Coast Government intended, for instance, to undertake simultaneously basic geological mapping of the country's less well known areas, and also intended to proceed (though only in limited areas) with certain airborne geophysical surveys for which contractual arrangements had already been negotiated before D & R's recommendations were delivered. Neither of these activities was taken into account in the cost estimates presented by D & R, but D & R presented, with its program, specifications to be applied to the airborne surveys in the hope of making their results meaningful and useful. As mentioned above, the Ivory Coast's previous experience of airborne geophysical work had cast some doubt upon the usefulness of this exploration method in present conditions in the Ivory Coast; however, D & R had also found itself obliged to criticize the procedures adopted by contracting companies and recognized the advantage of giving the method a fairer trial than it had yet had. The specifications were intended to serve this purpose.

For a variety of reasons, the preparation of the program did not immediately result in the launching of field operations on anything like the scale intended. The submission of D & R's report coincided with the Government's involvement in important international negotiations, including those affecting the Ivory Coast's treaty relation with France. The nature and the conditions of France's aid to the Ivory Coast's development plan (of which the geological program was part) were not known pending the outcome of these negotiations, and the latter constituted the Government's principal preoccupation in 1961. As a result, the development projects originally scheduled for 1961 were deferred until 1962.

Second, doubt soon arose concerning the capacity of the Direction de la Géologie et de la Prospection Minière, a government department, and therefore subject to governmental regulations controlling recruitment, salaries, and purchasing, to mount the effort called for by a program of such dimensions.

At an early stage of its relations with the Ivory Coast, D & R had suggested to its client that a company-type organization, possessing financial and administrative autonomy, might prove to be a more suitable instrument for achieving its economic ends, but D & R did not make a precise recommendation involving matters of administrative principle. Toward the end of 1961, the Government found it necessary to give serious attention to the organizational problem. The ability of the Direction de la Géologie et de la Prospection Minière to provide geologists and prospectors in the field was diminishing rather than increasing; its agreements with its principal contractor, the Bureau de Recherches Géologiques et Minières, expired, and in the absence of any decision for financing, no new agreements could be negotiated; and while D & R's consultants continued, in 1961, to provide geophysical interpretations and photogeological studies of strategic areas, there were not nearly enough men on the ground to apply the results. By the end of the year the field work actually in process was insignificant.

Finally, the existence of more than one program and the not very clear relationship between the various proposed and existing programs were a constant source of confusion. By and large, the work done in 1961, though extremely limited in scope, was in accordance with the recommendations made by D & R at the beginning of the year; but more energy than was advisable was spent on the fruitless investigation of anomalies noted in one of the early airborne geophysical surveys carried out without benefit of D & R specifications. No attention was given to geological mapping, and there was no formal notification of the Government's approval of the recommendations it had received, so that the status of the program itself remained uncertain.

The advantages of a single, well-coordinated, and comprehensible program, combining both long-term and short-term aspects, were by this time becoming obvious, and a joint recommendation to this effect was made to the Minister by D & R, Direction de la Géologie et de la Prospection Minière, and Bureau de Recherches Géologiques et Minières, after discussions held at the Minister's request. In the meantime, the D & R program had attracted favorable attention and an offer of financial assistance (for the equipment of the laboratory) from the Technical Assistance Administration of the United Nations. Some significant and very encouraging decisions were made shortly afterward. The Minister first requested D & R to expand its recommendations and revise its estimates of cost so as to provide in one program for both D & R's own proposals and the geological mapping of the country's comparatively unknown southwest region. At the same time, he announced the Government's intention to establish a publicly owned company (with the operational freedom which D & R had suggested) to carry out the program, with D & R as its consultant. He also reaffirmed the Government's intention to finance the undertaking of the revised program, if necessary, from its own resources; external assistance would obviously be welcomed, but the execution of the program was not to be conditional upon it.

Implementation of the Program

These decisions were implemented. The Société pour le Développement Minier de la Côte d'Ivoire (SODEMI) was created by government decree in April, 1962. A three-year revised program and a revised budget, now amounting to $7.9 million, were prepared by D & R, and received the formally expressed approval of the Government in the following month. SODEMI's technical committee (presided over by D & R's chief geological consultant and with its membership drawn from D & R and from the Bureau de Recherches Géologiques et Minières) met in June and laid down a work plan for the remainder of 1962. SODEMI was authorized to recruit the staff recommended by the committee, and was successful in attracting qualified men; satisfactory contracts were negotiated with the Bureau de Recherches Géologiques et Minières and other companies; and within two months of the technical committee's meeting, field operations were launched on a satisfactory scale. Thirty-two exploration and mapping parties were operating in the field by January, 1963.

Two years have now[1] passed since the three-year program went into effective operation. During this period interesting industrial possibilities have been revealed by the location and study of ceramic clays, glass sands, and construction gravel; a complete inventory has been established of the Ivory Coast's resources in subsoil water; airborne and surface geophysical methods of exploration have been tested under proper controls in three areas and, interpreted for SODEMI by D & R's consultant geophysicist, have brought to

[1] November, 1964.

light potentially useful deposits of iron ore and also the existence of mineralized basic and ultrabasic rocks which warrant further exploration; and additional opportunities have recently come to light in small but sufficiently high-grade deposits of alluvial gold, bauxite, and tantalite.

Apart from these material gains, the fact of a detailed, accepted, and well-designed program and the existence of a competent organization charged with its execution have led to other results.

First, in spite of the Ivory Coast's original modest expectations on this score, the program has attracted interest and considerable financial support from overseas. Thus the Fonds d'Aide et Cooperation of the French Government has met the cost of basic geological mapping in the Southwest region and of the services of French companies employed by SODEMI under contract for hydrogeological and airborne geophysical surveys. The Technical Assistance Board of the United Nations has paid the entire cost of the equipment required for SODEMI's analytical laboratory and has also supplied foreign technicians to staff it (the laboratory is in full operation and is probably the best equipped and most efficient establishment of its kind anywhere in West Africa). More recently the United Nations Special Fund has approved generous help for an intensive project of prospection, involving airborne and surface geophysical surveys, geological and geochemical studies, and drilling, in two significant areas of the country.

Equally encouraging has been the awakening interest of private companies in minerals exploration in the Ivory Coast, especially for diamonds. The rights SODEMI enjoys as an official agency for minerals exploration are by no means exclusive: the activity of private interests in this sector of the economy is encouraged and welcomed, private prospectors have received the full cooperation of the public company, and in certain instances arrangements have been established between SODEMI and private overseas enterprises for the pooling of resources in a common exploration effort.

Second, the Société pour le Développement Minier de la Côte d'Ivoire is an established fact. In spite of continuing dependence on overseas recruitment for professionally qualified staff (which will diminish as Ivory Coast geologists complete their training), this is an Ivory Coast agency whose policy and operations are directed by a board consisting of Ivory Coast citizens and officials. SODEMI has achieved recognition by other public authorities; it has, for instance, assumed entire responsibility for hydrogeological surveys previously entrusted to the Ministry of Public Works—and by private companies—as witnessed by its association with the WASTON organization in diamond exploration and the assistance it has given the Mokta el Hadid Company in locating extensions of its manganese deposits near Grand Lahou.

The relationship between D & R and its Ivory Coast client has inevitably and gratifyingly changed as a result. Upon the establishment of SODEMI, a supplementary agreement was entered into, providing for continuing services by D & R beyond the term of the original agreement, and also for D & R's assistance in the preparation of a second three-year program upon expiration of the present one. Only one year later a second supplementary agreement recognized that it would no longer be necessary for D & R to maintain a representative office in Abidjan solely to serve SODEMI's interests. While D & R continues, through its membership on the Technical Committee, to provide technical direction of SODEMI's operations, and also to provide expert services for particular features of the exploration program as requested by SODEMI, its activities are becoming increasingly directed toward the opportunities for industrial exploitation revealed by the resource investigations of the Ivory Coast agency. This is precisely what the parties anticipated when the agreement for D & R's services was first negotiated.

Summary and Some Reflections

In late 1960, Development and Resources Corporation was asked by the Ivory Coast Government to assist it in designing and carrying out a three-year program of geological exploration and minerals development. Early administrative and organizational problems were encountered, which were eventually met by the establishment of an autonomous publicly owned company for minerals development, thus creating the conditions in which genuine progress was possible. Execution of the three-year program, though not yet complete, is well advanced, and some interesting economic possibilities have already been revealed. While substantial financing has been made available from the Ivory Coast Government's own resources, the program has also attracted considerable support from overseas.

The obvious measure of the success of a resource development program is the economic result, and ultimately the success of this particular program will be expressed in terms of the mineral ores shipped from Ivory Coast ports, the water supplied to its people and its industries, the cost of building materials delivered to construction sites in the growing cities, and the raw materials supplied to its factories. Although these results are still to come, what has been achieved in the first two years of effective program operation provides good reason to believe that the Ivory Coast will derive substantial economic benefits from this work.

It is submitted that there are, however, other measures of success. The Société pour le Développement Minier de la Côte d'Ivoire, established to undertake the program recommended by D & R—and other similar programs which will follow it—represents a solid and permanent increase in the Ivory Coast's institutional strength. This is important; competent indigenous enterprises of this kind are not easily come by in the developing countries today, and no opportunity to create and foster them should be missed. (In the anxiety to get rapid technical results, it nevertheless very often is.) Part—perhaps a large part—of the present promise of this particular program is that it is being carried out by an agency which is an Ivory Coast native, not an imported exotic, and has, therefore, excellent chances of survival in the testing West African climate. It is already showing signs of vigorous growth.

The experience of D & R in the Ivory Coast since 1960 suggests some other general observations which may be relevant to resource development programs carried out by U.S. enterprises in the developing countries.

There is only one reason for D & R's presence in the Ivory Coast, and for its continuing presence, well after the term of its original agreement has expired—the fact that it was asked to go there. The Ivory Coast's need for assistance in its geological exploration and minerals development program was not prompted by external suggestion, but spontaneously expressed by the party principally concerned, the Ivory Coast Government. The original Agreement providing for D & R's services to the Ivory Coast was drafted by the client, not the contractor; the program which eventually emerged was very definitely an Ivory Coast program, comprehending not merely the contractor's recommendations, but also the wishes which the Government developed and expressed after those recommendations were submitted; responsibility for carrying out the work included in the program is vested in an Ivory Coast agency, which draws upon D & R's assistance in specific matters only by specific request and to the extent it needs in each particular case; and although generous financial support has been forthcoming from overseas for certain features of the program, SODEMI's own operations and the cost of D & R's services have throughout been financed entirely from the Ivory Coast's own resources. This too is important, and even remarkable, for the instances in which foreign contractors are engaged in the developing countries without any bilateral or multilateral financing of their activities are regrettably rare.

In establishing a program which met the client country's principal requirement—early economic results—D & R drew upon the good, sometimes excellent, work that had already been done in the Ivory Coast before independence. The field it came to was not a scientific desert, and although the materials it offered required collation and skillful interpretation, at least they were there. This is probably true of many other countries besides the Ivory Coast. Aerial photographic cover, for instance, is practically complete, throughout former French West Africa, and there has been some high-quality topographic mapping. There has been much valuable and painstaking geological research. Foreign organizations assisting these countries do not, therefore, need to start from scratch, provided they are prepared to dig for documents which may have become buried and to accommodate themselves to the languages used. It is fallacious to suppose that nothing whatever has happened in these areas before the foreign contractor arrived on the scene, and equally fallacious to imagine that the client Government will be willing and equipped to talk to the contractor in anything but the official language of the country. The Ivory Coast was certainly not, and French has been the consistent medium of communication between D & R and the Government.

While D & R established its offices, dispatched its experts, and presented its recommendations within five months of the agreement's being executed, work in the field did not get off to an early start, nor in the year that followed did it make rapid progress. It may be as well to recognize that, in the beginning, the administrative, organizational, and financial problems will nearly always stand in the way of technical progress and that there cannot be a great deal of the latter until solutions have been found to the former. There is, in fact, far more to the undertaking of resource development programs than simply putting parties of geologists or any other specialists into the field.

It may also be well to recognize that the governments of the developing countries have more than one preoccupation and could not afford, even if they wished, to devote a monopoly of their attention to a project which is a particular contractor's one and only concern. Because of this, and because, frequently, of administrative inadequacies in many newly independent countries, the word "frustration" is in increasingly frequent usage. Since it reflects upon the user as well as upon the circumstances in which he finds himself—and also since it does no good—it would be better avoided. Given patience, understanding, a readiness to accept and build upon what work has already been done, and sufficient flexibility to adapt oneself to changing needs and circumstances, good work can be done and lasting results obtained.

PSYCHOLOGICAL TESTING IN A DEVELOPING ECONOMY

Dr. Achim H. Fuerstenthal

Introduction

The Background of Testing. In Latin American countries with developing economies, psychological testing and other psychological techniques have become a fairly well established activity during the last twenty years. Two circumstances seem primarily responsible for this trend: the influx of European psychologists who left their home countries as political refugees and the influence of American industrial philosophy and organizational thinking. Among the immigrants were clinical psychologists and psychoanalysts, former professors of psychology, and directors of psychological laboratories, some of whom had worked on industrial problems. In their new environment the most capable obtained university posts and subsequently trained psychologists of the clinical, experimental, and industrial type.

At the same time the use of psychology in business was stimulated by the upsurge of American enterprise, the financial and technical participation of U.S. industry in national enterprise, and the influence of advanced managerial thinking on industrialists and executives in general.

The assessment of human productivity is an important feature of industrial organization anywhere. In a highly structured industrial society this assessment does not necessarily have to rely on psychological methods. Records of a person's past performance are plentiful and reliable; references to an individual's character and personality can be obtained from most of the institutions through which he has passed (schools, army, etc.).

In a developing economy, for a multitude of reasons, such information is rarely available and hardly ever reliable. Schools and universities, for instance, are generally far removed from the needs of the machine age, and their intellectual and behavioral standards have little application to the emerging

Dr. Fuerstenthal is managing director of a consulting firm in São Paulo, Brazil.

industrial pattern of life. Previous work records do not mean as much as in a fully developed society. Supervisory judgment of employees is more often than not tinged by emotion, prejudiced by bias, or distorted by concern with authority, or else it is the result of poor observation, comprehension, or cooperativeness. At times labor laws and union interference confuse the issue still further.

One of the characteristics of developing societies is the heterogeneity of industrial organization, implying the coexistence of varying degrees of technological progress and variations in equipment, procedures, and the demands made upon operating personnel. People who are valuable in certain functions within one organization may fail completely in related functions within another because of divergent approaches to the same production problem.

In developing economies most enterprise finds itself, justly or unjustly, geared to a policy of short-term profits. Testing is accepted as a time- and expense-saving device but not as a research program. Most test material is imported on the strength of its reputation, i.e., on the basis of validations carried out in the country of origin. In the following chapters we shall try to analyze various types of tests in their applicability to developing economies. It should be understood beforehand that only validation done on the spot has been accepted. The author suggests that the test itself should be conceived in the area of application, although general internationally accepted principles will have to be incorporated.

The Role of Apparatus Testing

Reaction Time. Apparatus for testing reaction time is as old as experimental psychology. Within developing economies it has had a revival, being most commonly used to screen rural workers for industrial jobs and identify those fit for technical training. Whatever the equipment used, the results of reaction time testing are likely to be confusing. This confusion springs from the fact that there is hardly ever a significant correlation between reaction speed and later production. The administration, scoring, and interpretation of such tests call for the experience of trained psychologists.

To control results, testees should be divided into three groups, namely delayed reactors, medium reactors, and prompt reactors. With a few exceptions, delayed reactors are a poor choice for industrial work. Yet it will be found that some effective older workers and even foremen react much more slowly to the test stimulus than one would expect from their work. These are victims of "exhausted adaptability." It is a completely different matter if young testees whose reactions are not set in any way score poorly in reaction time. In this case delayed reactions may be an indication of physiological, emotional, or mental disturbance. On the other hand, there are problems with prompt reactors as well. Particularly quick and facile reactions often go hand in hand with a peculiar uninhibitedness which tends to spread into the moral field.

Multiple Reaction. Most industrial functions require the right choice among several possible reactions rather than particularly quick ones. To test for this purpose, apparatus has been devised which requires different muscular responses to different signals, usually engaging both hands as well as legs and feet.

Again no simple reading of scores referring to reaction speed, error avoidance, or perseverance (breakdown avoidance) is as yielding as one might surmise. Performance in such experiments proves to be strongly influenced by present physical and mental state, disposition to comply with rules, and previous acquaintance with similar tasks and situations, as well as other accidental conditions.

There are testees who show something like a natural talent for multiple response, but these are not necessarily the quickest learners of actual work routine, nor are they generally the most reliable operators. In fact, a pronounced facility in dealing with stimuli seems somewhat conducive to treating stimuli with half attention, which leads to errors in the long run. Here again the mediocre testees seem to be the most likely to succeed in a work situation, a fact which renders classical test validation impossible.

On the other hand, choice reaction tests, if carried out over a considerable span of time, such as ten minutes or more, become an actual working proposition and provide innumerable clues to the testee's working disposition, his resistance to fatigue and distraction, his cooperativeness and willingness to overcome obstacles, and his tendency to improve with practice rather than to relax his efforts. In short, such tests measure little in terms of working skill but much in terms of working personality.

***Manual Skill and Personality:* A Case History.** Electrical engineers who applied at a light and power company were required to perform a wire-bending task which was part of the test used by the company's personnel department to screen technicians. Experience had shown that in the course of day-to-day operations there always emerged situations which required the active interference of people who possessed both competence and manual skill. In such situations the desk type of engineer would give advice but would not dirty his hands. The operating personnel, feeling that they knew better, would act independently, often with disastrous results. Since the introduction of the wire-bending task, this kind of mishap had been avoided, and therefore the selection experts felt strongly that they had found a good thing.

In accordance with the rules, an engineer who had failed in this wire-bending test was declared unqualified. However, the electrical department, claiming to have excellent references regarding the candidate's professional past, overruled the decision, suggesting that when it came to electricity the psychologists in the personnel department might still have something to learn, etc.

The engineer joined the company, and a few days later he electrocuted himself and his auxiliary as a result of initiating work on a high-tension unit before receiving the clearance signal from the station superintendent.

The ensuing discussion between the personnel and electrical departments could fill volumes. Electrical pointed out that the man had been rejected by Personnel on the grounds of poor manual dexterity, while the accident had been caused by noncompliance with station rules. Personnel replied that it had warned against the man's admission because he had failed in a test whose significance was a proved fact, and that if an engineer lacked the degree of manual skill required for parts of his professional activity, this pointed to some kind of professional inadequacy and personality maladjustment. Maladjustment *might* lead to accidents, and it might not. Psychologists are not prophets; they do not claim to foresee what will actually occur but fulfill their function by indicating the probabilities of a man's success or failure in certain jobs. The rejoinder of the electrical department was that all this should have been made clear before the first test result was emitted. Personnel answered that it was not committed to teaching basic psychology to department heads. Electrical continued to argue the case, agreeing, however, that henceforth more attention should be paid to test results and concomitant interpretations.

Conclusion on Operational Tests. The testing of operational skill is a more complex proposition than is generally recognized. Hardly ever do test scores match actual work output. The test situation and work situation are far apart in their demands on the individual. Personality factors interfere with the formation and application of skills to a degree which is rarely appreciated and understood. Psychologists have a difficult job in selling management ideas which are, to say the least, untried and results that may forever lack the decision-inspiring hardness of accounting figures or engineering facts.

The Various Approaches to Mental Capacity

Scholastic Examinations. In areas of developing economy the quest for the man who can be upgraded to the next functional level is more intense than in the relatively more static developed areas. As might be expected, tests of mental capacity are often called upon to indicate such men.

The first instrument considered for this purpose is generally the scholastic examination, also called achievement test. Members of management are frequently of the opinion that employees who do not have a certain command of the language, do not know how to deal with certain arithmetical problems, and are oblivious of some facts in the historical and geographical sphere are not worth the money they earn.

This, however, is quickly proved to be an incorrect assumption. Once the examinations get under way, shocking ignorance is discovered in highly appreciated employees throughout the ranks, while the most accomplished intellectually get notoriously low ratings from their supervisors.

At this stage even conservative management starts considering a more psychological approach to mental capacity. Generally one of the more alert auxiliaries of the personnel department is asked to work out a battery of tests, intelligence quotients, or something of the sort. With all the books and test forms available, this is supposed to be a minor effort.

Nonverbal Tests. As far as areas of developing economy are concerned, there seem to be definite advantages in nonverbal testing of mental capacity. First, no translation of test material is necessary. Second, no divergences in cultural background between the countries of test origin and of test application need worry the examiner. Third, the educational level of the testee seems irrelevant. Nonverbal tests propose to go straight to the core of mental capacity, avoiding the passage through the verbal channel. And yet the authors of such tests claim high correlations with recognized verbal intelligence tests. All the odds seem favorable.

Among the nonverbal intelligence tests, Raven's Progressive Matrices are probably the best organized and therefore most widely accepted internationally.

Of course, correlation with other tests is one thing, and validity for selection purposes is another. To check on the latter, the author carried out an experiment involving 100 employees from six companies. Employees were taken in groups of ten and ranked by their supervisors, using man-to-man comparison on an overall effectiveness basis. The following correlations were obtained:

Financial and cost accountants	.23
General clerks	.31
Mechanical and electrical engineers	.42
Publicity designers	.38
Publicity account executives and copywriters	.43
Administrative assistants	.41
Salesmen (pharmaceuticals)	.11
Salesmen (textiles)	.33
Salesmen (typewriters)	.14
Bank apprentices (minors)	.07
	2.83

While the overall validity is .28, an inspection of the partial quotients may give more of an insight in such tests than the mere acceptance of the final figure.

As a group, salesmen do badly. The examiner provided the additional information that most salesmen had trouble sitting through the test and keeping their eyes and minds on the paper. A few of the textile salesmen were exceptions due to the fact that they became interested in the matrices as designs. The degree of this interest obviously correlated with their job performance. The same interest was observed in account executives and writers of a publicity agency while some of the best designers in the same agency had difficulty in accepting the matrices and working within the frame of the test. General clerks worked well and steadily, while some of the most proficient among the accountants entangled themselves with numbering the elements contained in the matrices, thus losing valuable time necessary for the correct completion. Administrative assistants drawn from all departments (sales, operations, finance, public relations, personnel) and rated by a board of department managers fared rather like the general clerks. More acute assessment was available in their case however, accounting for the higher correlation. Engineers' scores were spread from Highest to Very Poor, and performance was found to be very much in line with test results.

The author has seen the Raven and similar tests used, because of their easy availability and applicability, as sole selection instruments for all positions from mechanical apprentice to vice president of marketing. Such a procedure could ruin a company, as even the best correlation quotients above show. It will certainly ruin the reputation of the psychologists on the job.

Performance Tests. While progressive matrices, figure sequences, hidden cubes, and similar items require visualization and the inference of some kind of serial principle, there is a group of tests where some kind of design or spatial relation is involved as well but where the response consists not in the choice and pointing out of an element presented, but in actual pencil performance. Such tests are, for example, the Porteus Maze and the widely used digit-symbol substitution. Graphology can also be considered within this context.

Are such tests not really sensory-motor coordination tests, with paper and pencil assuming the role of an apparatus? One might say so; however, there are certain arguments against it. Factory workers who are at ease with industrial apparatus are disproportionately out of their depths when it comes to handling a pencil, while white-collar workers who have no problem with writing utensils are generally at a disadvantage in actual manual work. Paper and a pencil seem to constitute apparatus of a peculiar sort, intimately connected with education and a certain sensory-motor refinement and therefore more related to mental capacity than to manual skill.

Let us look at graphology, for instance. It is undeniable that a certain element of dexterity goes into our handwriting. Nobody writes with his untrained left hand as well as with his right. Yet graphologists prove that there are certain features common to a person's left- and right-hand writing. These features are expressions of mental and personality factors.

To demonstrate the intricacies of paper-and-pencil performance testing, the author's experience with a digit-symbol substitution test may be briefly described here. The item consists of a series of six meaningless symbols to be memorized by the testee in a given order. Then a table is presented composed of 250 squares irregularly numbered 1 to 6. The testee has to inscribe the symbols in the squares one by one in accordance with the numeration and as quickly as possible.

This test was devised to measure mental effort, i.e., it was thought that the repeated reproduction of the symbols in accordance with the upcoming digit required mental effort and that speed and accuracy in the task would be a measure of this factor, so important in many business functions.

Comparison with work records, however, showed something completely different. High scores, i.e., speed and accuracy in this test, did not mean anything as far as work was concerned. Low scores, however, did mean something. Slowness combined with accuracy turned out to be an indicator of inhibitedness. Slowness plus mistakes, on the other hand, coincided with laziness and indifference.

Some of the people classified as inhibited were successful in certain functions, primarily in accounting and control. But they were reported a failure in others, especially in sales. Some of the people eliminated from clerical positions for laziness worked out well in sales, especially when it was possible to put them on a commission basis. Others of the same group, test-wise and report-wise, could not be used in any function.

This throws a sharp light on the complexities connected with performance testing. There is always *some* psychological content in a test score. However, its application to actual work involves many factors and requires many considerations. The Porteus Maze in its simpler form turned out to be entirely insignificant in the author's validation attempts. In its more complicated form it still failed to correlate in any way with mental capacity, although there was some evidence that this test was an indicator of personality traits such as initiative, aggressiveness, resoluteness, freedom from inhibition, etc. One highly effective secretary never found her way out of one of the more complicated mazes, even after being shown the direction. This turned out to be a case of serious inhibitions in the psychosomatic area. This means that paper-and-pencil performance tests in their more demanding form are equal to projective techniques, a subject to which we shall return in a later context.

Numerical Tests. One of the traditionally accepted aspects of mental capacity is facility with numerical material. Here we have to distinguish between strictly numerical and numerical-operational tasks. An item of the first type would be the well-known clerical test which consists in the checking of repeating figures. A numerical operation is best exemplified by any arithmetical problem.

In areas of developing economy the exploitation of numerical facility leads to surprising results. Generally speaking, these areas are distinguished from others by a population which is relatively ineffective in dealing with numerical material. It may be suspected that behind this phenomenon there is less a lack of capacity, properly speaking, than a kind of emotional inhibition in relation to numbers. Dealing with figures is linked with objective-mindedness, and objective-mindedness seems to come with high-level social organization.

The results obtained in developing economies with numerical testing can be summed up as follows:

1. Correlations between various numerical test items are low. People may come out well in number checking and poorly in arithmetic; well in arithmetic and poorly in number series; well in number series and poorly in symbol series, etc.
2. Verbally presented problems are generally handled more successfully than pure number problems, even if the former are arithmetically more difficult than the latter. This proves that a certain emotional disposition is involved rather than capacity as such. Words ease some of the inhibition.
3. Testees who are professionally concerned with figures do not necessarily score highly in numerical tests. Accountants as well as engineers fail frequently in problems of elementary arithmetic, the first alluding to the fact that this kind of work is carried out by their auxiliaries, the second confessing that they feel helpless without their slide rule (the use of which implies operations of a considerably more complex nature).
4. Numerical operations are generally approached as something to remember from schooldays rather than as something to be reasoned out. Because of this tie-in with learning, distribution curves in numerical-operational items are often two-peaked. The first peak (minority) is formed by the people who remember, and the second (lower) peak is formed by the majority, who have forgotten but try to reconstruct.
5. High scores in pure arithmetic are sometimes accompanied by low scores in all other mental-capacity items. This has been found to be an almost infallible indication of poor social adjustment, although this rule may not apply at all in societies of developed economy.

In conclusion, one has to admit that numerical and numerical-operational tests are a poor measure of general mental capacity and of working effectiveness. Educational, occupational, emotional, and social factors are involved in determining a person's attitude toward numerical material and problems. There is a certain tradition of number blindness in developing societies of which one may find signs even in teachers of arithmetic. Arithmetic operations are rarely understood; even the people who seem to know how to handle formulas do it by memory. Graduate economists incapable of deriving the rules for the addition and subtraction of natural fractions were a frequent occurrence in the author's testroom.

Of course, numerical items cannot be excluded from mental capacity tests altogether. In spite of the absence of significant correlation with any kind of job performance, very low and very high scores always have some kind of meaning, i.e., point to some kind of factor which is worth knowing about.

Verbal Testing. Business in a developing economy, just as in any other economy, is mostly a matter of communication. This fact alone would be enough to justify an emphasis on verbal testing. So, in spite of the difficulties in obtaining verbal testing material which is geared to a developing economy, no testing program can be entirely devoid of verbal items.

Verbal test material cannot, of course, be translated without essentially changing its meaning. From developed to developing economy there is a complete variation of mental climate. Not only are other words used, but also other aspects of life are stressed, other facts known, other reasons given, other convictions shared.

Once this obstacle has been overcome, i.e., once verbal tests have been devised on the spot, a further problem arises. In business communication it is the spoken word which is most important, while in tests it is the written word that counts. Be it in sales talk, in supervisory orders, in a subordinate's question, in a vice president's address at a board meeting, in a discussion of marketing policy with a competitor, or in any other business situation, there is a need for improvisation, for split-second choice of terms, for convincingness, and for the mixing of conclusion and personal emphasis in a way which never applies to a test situation.

This poses a deep and complex problem, the solution of which would contribute considerably to a better appreciation of tests as a measure of business success. In order to attack this problem at least on the surface, the following experiment was carried out.

Of 2,000 job applicants, ranging from clerical to junior executive level, 400 individuals were chosen who could be distributed by uncontested agreement of three interviewers in equal numbers under the categories of prolix, informative, concise, and laconic.

As prolix (P) were classified 100 candidates who volunteered more information, comments, and general remarks than were required from them and who used more verbiage than necessary to make their points.

As informative (I) were classified 100 candidates whose answers to interviewing questions were ample and complete and who enjoyed the possession and use of a rich vocabulary.

As concise (C) were classified 100 candidates who never supplied information that was not explicitly requested and used only the minimum amount of words to complete their statements.

As laconic (L) were classified 100 candidates who had to be drawn out for the most elementary kind of information and were often at a loss for words to express themselves adequately.

These 400 candidates were submitted to a verbal test composed of four items called information, comments, omissions, and definitions. *Information* consisted of ten questions which required giving three independent answers. *Comments* consisted of ten doubtful statements which called for a conclusive counter-argument. These two items were termed "unstructured"[1] because of the freedom left for choice of words, length of statement, point of view, etc.

Omissions consisted of ten sentences each with two missing words which had to be found and inserted. *Definitions* consisted of ten definitions for which the corresponding concepts had to be found. These two items were called "structured" because of the narrow margin left for self-expression. The raw scores of the two unstructured items were combined, as were the raw scores of the structured items. Then the unstructured as well as the structured scores were divided into four classes with equal ranges called Highest, Medium, Poor, and Lowest.

The 400 candidates, split into the four groups (P, I, C, L) of 100 individuals, were then distributed in the four scoring classes. The resulting table is given below.

Range	Unstructured		Structured	
Highest	P 25	C 26	P 15	C 28
	I 31	L 9	I 32	L 19
Medium	P 23	C 39	P 23	C 32
	I 32	L 20	I 34	L 26
Poor	P 29	C 25	P 35	C 25
	I 18	L 31	I 22	L 23
Lowest	P 23	C 10	P 27	C 15
	I 19	L 40	I 12	L 32

The most obvious conclusions to be drawn are the following:

1. Abundance of the spoken word has no bearing on free written communication. The P group is spread almost equally over the four classes in unstructured items.

2. Abundance of the spoken word is almost inversely proportional to the command of precise written vocabulary. The P group is represented by 62% in the lower against 38% in the higher scoring classes in structured items, and it is 1.8 times more frequent in the lowest than in the highest class.

3. Facility in communication is fairly well carried over from the spoken to the written word. The I group is represented by 63% in the higher classes for unstructured items against 27% in the lower.

4. Facility in communication seems also to go with the command of precise vocabulary in writing. The I group occurs in 66% of the higher classes of structured items, against 34% in the lower. It is also 2.7 times more frequent in the highest than in the lowest bracket.

[1] "Unstructured" are tests that grant the testees a large margin of self-expression. "Structured" are the ones that impose a certain pattern within which the testee has to react.

5. Concise communicators as a group are the most successful in free written expression. A total of 64% is in the higher scoring class for unstructured items, while only 10% are in the lowest class, as against 19% of the I group.

6. Conciseness in spoken communication does not apparently carry over into conciseness in written communication. The C group is still represented by 60% in the higher class for structured items, but this means 6% less than the I group. Still it is in the two lower classes for structured written communication at 22% less than the P group.

7. Reticence in spoken communication carries over very largely to reticence in written free communication. The L group is represented by 71% in the lower classes of unstructured expression, and it is 4.4 times more frequent in the lowest than in the highest class.

8. In the precise use of the written word, laconic people as a group fare better than communicative people. Although they are represented as a majority of 55% in the lower classes for structured items, they are more frequent in the highest and medium classes than the P group. On the other hand, the L group has 32% in the lowest class, which means that roughly one-third of the people at a loss in spoken communication are equally at a loss in written.

9. The best all-round scores in verbal tests are obtained by people who are informative, that is, people with a marked facility of expression who make judicious use of it. The second-best group is composed of the individuals who use the spoken word strictly within the limits of necessity.

Depending upon the purpose for which the test is utilized, the table above yields further clues. A company looking for a controller may decide that it wants to employ a concise type. The most likely candidates are obviously to be found among the population with medium scores in unstructured items. If the aim is salesmen, the company might feel that prolix as well as informative communicators will do. One glance at the table reveals an alarming fact: looking for a P and I combination, neither the whole test nor any part of it yields any indication at any range. Similar percentages are obtained with excruciating precision whatever class of scoring is used and whatever item is consulted. The percentages for the combined P and I groups are: highest unstructured, 28%; highest structured, 23.5%; medium unstructured, 27.5%; medium structured, 28.5%; poor unstructured, 23.5%; poor structured, 28.5%; lowest unstructured, 21%; lowest structured, 19.5%. Admittedly, highest unstructured has a high yield. Here we seem to get 56 possible salesmen out of 400 candidates. However, there exist another 35 individuals in the same class who are definitely not salesmen, while at the same time there are 144 people in other classes who might possibly be salesmen. This should be a strong enough recommendation to select salesmen by interview in the first place.

There is an attractive feature in verbal tests which from a scientific viewpoint, however, is a disadvantage, namely, self-evidence. Inspecting a well-filled-out verbal test form, one is often impelled to say: "What an intelligent answer. It must be a bright fellow who wrote it. That is the kind of assistant I would like." In actual validation the picture is not quite so impressive. Cleverness on paper is not everything. However, as even a modest study like the above should show, valuable clues can be obtained from verbal testing if it is put to correct use.

Before closing this discussion a general word of warning may be in order. In the author's own service as well as in validation work carried out for the service of third parties, one fact has come to light again and again. The multiple choice type of verbal item, i.e., the most highly structured of all, has no validity whatsoever for any kind of industrial or commercial career. At least in areas of developing economy, the man who uses words as well as he can without worrying too much about little imprecisions seems to be the better businessman, the better industrial leader, the more natural mixer, and the more productive worker.

Personality

There is no need to repeat here the objections which have been raised by various international authorities against the so called personality test. From purely logical, statistical, and ethical points of view the value of any known technique of standardized personality assessment has been questioned.

In an experiment carried out with 100 junior and senior executives, the author found that 83% significantly revised their previously given replies to a personality questionnaire after a clarifying thirty-minute interview with one of the three psychologists working on the job. The interviewers had no opportunity to see the testees' first replies and thus to suggest modifications. They were confined to discussing in general terms the problems of recalling past experience, describing one's own actions, classifying one's attitudes, comparing one's feelings with those of others, etc. These general discussions were enough to lead the majority of testees to a different understanding of the questionnaire and to a different interpretation of their own experiences and attitudes.

In free associations and sentence completion the same group provided colorful material. However, it was found that the most telling clues were the result of recent intake (reading, conversation, movies, etc.) or of deliberate fabrication. There were two neurotics among the testees, both under treatment at the time of the experiment. These two handed in particularly noncommittal papers, yet again, they were not the most insipid of the group.

These results were similar to those obtained by a colleague using the Rorschach and Thematic Apperception Tests. Balanced people proved free to say what they wanted in response to verbal or pictorial stimulus. Whatever they did say had no deep root in their personality but was in the majority of cases sheer accident. Such evidence differentiates the so-called normal from the psychopath, who is driven by inner compulsion into determined actions and manifestations.

Mira's Myokinetic and Bender's Gestalt Tests[2] are in a way performance tests. Like graphology, they are based on the assumption that certain personality traits are reflected in certain muscular attitudes or motor tendencies. Experience shows that in many individuals this parallelism exists. In others, however, it is less developed, and in some cases the author has found it practically nonexistent. Furthermore, there are problems of a semantic nature. What, after

[2] See J. P. Guilford, *Personality*, McGraw-Hill Book Company, New York, 1959.

all, do terms like introversion or aggression mean when it comes to selecting a job candidate? Often an analysis is forthcoming which makes interesting reading, but then, so what? In pressing the testing experts for conclusions as to the employability of the man, the terms used in his personality chart start moving, their range enlarges and contracts, their applicability to practical tasks evokes whole philosophies of life and work, and in the end more doubt is generated than certainty.

As a shortcut through all such psychological meanderings, U.S. consultants have taken to the made-to-measure method, whereby a candidate is expected to approach in his habits and manifestations, as closely as possible, a pattern of response established by the successful individuals within a given company. Whatever the scientific and practical merits of this method, in areas of developing economy it has no application, simply because there are no patterns of response. In an environment of widely varying features, men of widely varying personalities come to the top. Success, even within the same company or on equivalent assignments, cannot be reduced to a common human denominator. Conformity means little, and this excludes the tests which aim at it.

Withal, the assessment of personality continues to be one of the aspects of a complete testing program. The author shares the view of many of his colleagues to the effect that personality *can* be tested, but not directly. Personality traits which are important from the viewpoint of personnel selection, namely, the ones which apply to work, almost invariably come to light during general testing. True, a test situation is never fully equivalent to a working situation. There are different emotional accents, different moral implications. Tests require a quick mental adaptation to manifold tasks in succession, work demands a tolerance for routine; tests produce more tension, work implies more responsibility; in tests the individual has to rely on himself, in work he has to coordinate his efforts with those of others. Yet, in spite of such differentiations, attitudes shown by an individual while taking a test, such as concentration or restlessness, interest or indifference, diligence or laziness, cooperativeness or antagonism, self-reliance or dependence, honesty or shiftiness, hesitance, impetuousness, or the like, are proved attitudes of this individual, They are likely to recur, if not permanently then occasionally, and an employer is well advised to take them into account along with the candidate's capacities.

Conclusion

One often hears that testing in areas of developing economy must be of a rudimentary character. The author hopes to have shown that, on the contrary, the need for testing in such areas is more intense and that its techniques should be more scrupulously applied than within industrialized societies, where a system of institutions, a network of communications, and a set of conventions assign a man to his niche almost automatically. In a developing society a psychologist can serve effectively only if he progresses with its social development; abiding by established procedures is not enough. With the development of an economy there is a development of manners, of mentalities, and, last but not least, of psychological methods. Thus, in the end, testing which accompanies this progress through its various stages may prove to be more versatile, more realistic, and more sensitive to the full range of human nature than it has been in areas of more advanced civilization.

Recommendations to Management. In areas of developing economy psychological testing fulfills an important function. It provides management with objective human data which otherwise would not be as available as in an economically developed society.

There are no insurmountable obstacles to psychological testing within developing economies. However, the mere application of "imported" test material, organized and validated in other areas, cannot be considered sound procedure. It may easily lead to erroneous human decisions which would then discredit psychological testing and related techniques altogether. In planning for the introduction of a testing program some essential points of divergence between populations of developing and developed areas should be taken into account:

In a developing society the distribution of knowledge is less uniform than in developed ones. There is not only a coexistence of illiteracy with supreme educational achievement, but also a sharp variance in knowledge at identical levels of formal education. Regional differences, daily experience, didactic disagreement among schools and among individual teachers, different degrees of family participation in the educational progress of children, frequent private tutoring, autodidactism, extracurricular indoctrination of a religious or political nature, and similar factors create conditions where no particular scholastic or general information can be taken for granted at any age or educational level. There are, for the psychological tester, no firm points of reference in the cultural scenery.

Official curricula lean on memorizing rather than on reasoning. Students get used to having pieces of knowledge ready for examination, never giving them a second thought thereafter. Nor do they develop the capacity for rediscovering forgotten data and rules through logical deduction. Since most mental testing relies on some basic information without the benefit of *ad hoc* study or exercise, test results are often demonstrations of abysmal ignorance. This, however, is neither as shocking nor as significant as an outsider might surmise, once the particular national or regional conditions of teaching and learning are understood.

Similar to the sharp social and economic differences existing in developing areas are sharp divergences in attitude toward education. Knowledge is highly valued by some and utterly scorned by others. Many pursue culture and academic degrees for the sake of social standing rather than for practical application. A graduate lawyer may decide after his first day in the courtroom to go into politics. Construction engineers are found as bank presidents and surgeons as dealers in gold bullion. Again, many of the individuals who study as a preparation for specific work find themselves left with a host of theories and no clues to practical application. Thus a graduate economist may be at a loss when he has to make out his first bank deposit.

On the other side of the picture there are the people who consider study a waste of time. Going to work at an early age, generally in sales or production, they often rise to important positions within a company. Yet, such personnel panic in the face of tests, while recently graduated sales and production trainees with brilliant test scores need surprisingly long periods of adaptation before getting down to real work

What, in view of this, is the relation between psychological tests and job performance? What, one might add, are the perspectives for other personnel techniques, such as performance rating and job evaluation?

One word contains the answer to such questions. This word is "flexibility." No technician working in areas of developing economy can expect to find things in accordance with the textbook. This refers to personnel, production, marketing, accounting, and even general management. Yet the rise of modern industry rests to a large extent on the application of modern administrative techniques. Psychological testing is such a technique. The more intelligently management assesses the human factor in connection with industrial expansion, the more it will realize the need for psychological counsel. Certainly there are difficulties in applying psychological measures and rules to a population which is in a process of transition from one form of existence to another. The evaluation of a new type of population meeting with a new set of occupational demands is not an assignment for somebody who has just learned how to apply a few standard tests. This is a job for a fully qualified professional with a maximum of methodological resources. Management will find that a competent psychologist, beyond providing test results, may contribute considerably to making a company's venture into a new human environment successful.

FREE TRADE ZONES

Andrew W. Weil

History

One of the oldest instruments of trade and marketing in the world is also one of the newest—new in the sense that it has been revived and redesigned to meet the requirements of modern economics, transportation, and distribution.
name *entrepô*, a French word which means *warehouse*.

It is the free zone, or, as it is known by other names, the free port, free trade area, or free perimeter. The history of such zones extends from ancient Mediterranean city-states and overland caravan routes to today's jet cargo flight and the nuclear-powered ship.

The concept of the international free trade zone is growing in significance. In a world where every center of population is a market, it offers governments and traders a haven free of duty, customs, and oppressive restrictions to which cargo can be sent for storage, processing, assembly, and transshipment to market. The goods that pass into and out of these zones give rise to the name *entrepôt*, a French word which means *warehouse*.

The modern, well-operated free trade area provides two important and fundamental services to management: (1) it reduces the burden on managers by providing essential facilities at forward distribution centers, and (2) it simplifies the manipulation (whether manufacture, labeling, processing, repacking, repackaging, or just storage) of merchandise.

While free trade zones were part of the community of ancient mankind, their origin is uncertain. They developed with man's mobility and his yearning to exchange goods. Variations of the free zone were established by the rulers of Tyre, Carthage, and Utica, trade cities of the Mediterranean, which turned to the sea for economic and political communications with other lands. Often, these areas were walled off. A portion of Carthage, which exerted control over three hundred cities and colonies, became a free port. In Greece, a stone wall

---

Mr. Weil is the United States Representative of Panama's Colon Free Zone.

surrounded a Piraeus harbor plot in which goods in transit were guarded, exempt from collection of revenue.

In the Roman era it was common to rent warehouses on shore where free port conditions prevailed. After the defect and decline of the Roman Empire it was not until the revival of trade from Europe to the Levant, stimulated largely by the Crusades, that the free port once more became an instrument of international commerce. In the seventeenth century Genoa established one of the earliest free ports as it is recognized today. It, too, was fenced off from residential quarters.

Emergence of Free Trade Zones as a Tool of Modern Management

Over the past four hundred years, as trade widened to include the world, free zones grew in numbers and significance, following the routes of colonial and international shipping to all continents and ultimately to air travel and cargo centers.

U.S. free ports were established by legislation in 1934. Emanuel Celler, a congressman who proposed the enabling law, defined a free zone as "a neutral, stockaded area where a shipper can put down his load, catch his breath and decide what to do next." There still may be an occasional entrepreneur who forwards goods to a free trade zone and casts about for buyers. But it is more likely to be a corporation dispatching bulk raw materials, auto parts, film, radios, textiles, telephones, drugs, toys, tools, and the like to an assembly, labeling, processing, or storage plant for transshipment.

There are more than one hundred free trade areas throughout the world, all of them established by executive decree, treaty, or legislative action. Some, like Hong Kong and Tangier, have a long tradition as free trade cities. Others are little more than fenced-in buildings near border towns. Still others are modern enclaves with a wide range of warehousing, administrative, manufacturing, and materials-handling services. These latter include such well-known free port areas as Colon, Panama; Shannon, Ireland; Antwerp, Belgium, and others in western and northern Europe. They are well managed in the modern manner, with staff and services that make it relatively simple to engage in foreign trade at a minimum cost with tangible rewards.

Trade Zone Advantages

Some of the denominators common to the best of the successful international free trade zones are:

1. Proximity to air and sea routes
   Easy access to deepwater port
   Dockside facilities for receiving and dispatching cargo
   Dependable labor for handling cargo
   Airport facilities for long-range jet planes
   Geographical proximity to expanding markets
2. Warehousing
   Air-conditioned, dehumidified, and heated warehousing, as required by climate

Variety of warehousing: open-air, roofed-over, fenced-in, space within enclosed buildings, office space, etc.
Guaranteed protection against pilferage and damage
Materials-handling equipment
Trained clerical and labor force
Experienced supervisory and managerial community

3. Clearly defined operating conditions
Stabilized tax procedures
Banking services
Guaranteed wage scales, rentals, fees, and the like
Well-defined management policy
Financing and building assistance from government (or zone)
Incentives for growth and expansion
4. Facilities for manufacturing and processing
Electric power and public utilities
Housing for workers
Transportation for workers
Sanitation controls

Few of the hundred or more free trade areas in the world are geographically located to provide all the conditions listed above. But aside from the question of proximity to transport lanes and markets, the management of many ports (or the governing authorities of port countries) does not appear to have a clear concept of the function of a free trade zone, or cannot develop agreement among diverse national interests on export and import policies. It is expected that the development of common markets and the enlightenment of free port managerial officials will, in the future, alleviate some of these shortcomings. The growth record of trade areas in which favorable policies have been stabilized will doubtless serve as an object lesson to produce improvement by imitation.

The Example of the Colon Free Zone

A clear demonstration of the use of a free trade zone for national economic development, and of goals attained both by the zone itself and by enterprising companies utilizing its facilities, has been made over the past twelve years by the International Free Trade Zone in the Republic of Panama.

Located on 100 acres of reclaimed swampland at Colon, near the Atlantic entrance to the Panama Canal, this free zone has shown an entrepôt volume growth of 20% almost every year since 1953. Established by the Panamanian legislature and built at an initial cost of $3 million, the zone attracted a few American companies and achieved a business volume of $14 million in its first year of operation.

By 1964, this volume had grown to $222,709,342. In that same year, 57,500 metric tons of cargo was dispatched into and out of the Colon Free Zone by some two hundred companies from all over the world. While the United States leads the other countries in terms of business volume achieved through the zone, commodities from the following countries are also reaching

Latin American markets through Colon facilities: Japan, England, West Germany, Sweden, Switzerland, Hong Kong, France, Italy, Spain, India, Canada, and the Philippines.

Exporting Leads to Manufacturing

Most of these foreign companies entered the zone as exporters, but changes in U.S. tax and trade legislation combined with increased marketing possibilities have resulted in a growing emphasis on manufacturing. An American publishing company has established a printing plant, a French textile mill has contracted to enter the zone, and a U.S. pharmaceutical company this year added manufacturing and packaging to its warehousing operation. The newest project of the Colon Free Zone, in addition to expanding dockside and warehousing facilities, is a transisthmian oil pipeline and pumping station, with oil storage tanks at terminals on both the Atlantic and Pacific Oceans.

Growing by volume and in range of activity, the Colon Free Zone is a showcase example of the benefits accruing both to the country and the companies using it. The zone has become in ten years second only to the Panama Canal as a source of service revenue to this country of 1,200,000 people. It is a particularly illuminating example, since Panama is a less developed country long vulnerable to the hazards of a depressed economy, lack of industrialization, and delayed social progress. Yet the country has accomplished something unparalleled among underdeveloped countries by taking advantage of its strategic location at the crossroads of Latin American and world markets where shipping and air lines from much of the world converge (Colon is served by 26 air lines). About 1,550 Panamanians are employed at the Colon Zone, and it is estimated that some five thousand other jobs in the country have been created as an outgrowth of this enterprise.

Experienced Managers and Trained Labor

A trained bilingual clerical and labor force, under the supervision of experienced managers, operates the facility and provides a wide variety of service. Many companies own their own buildings on leased land, and some were erected to specifications by the Colon Free Zone. Others rent warehouse space and contract with the zone management for storage and reshipment of goods to Latin American markets. Some contract with private management and forwarding firms which provide complete warehousing, distribution, and administrative services. They are thus enabled to engage in foreign trade without sending resident personnel to Panama.

A number of firms in England, on the Continent, and in the United States have developed over the years to help establish and expand companies seeking to export or manufacture in free trade areas. These firms have specialists and consultants familiar with tax and trade laws, labor practices, marketing, insurance and credit requirements, etc. These advise companies, exporting to a free trade zone, assist them in setting up overseas subsidiaries, and provide administrative services. Important sources of information and counsel are the ministries of trade and commerce of governments having jurisdiction over free trade ports. Attachés of consulates or legation officials are prepared to answer inquiries.

The table on pages 461 and 462 was prepared to show some cost comparisons and to indicate the kinds of services and facilities available in a sampling of free trade zones. Some of the best zones in the world are included in this sampling, but there are a number of perhaps equally well managed free ports not included.

Companies which have achieved notable success in building Latin American markets through the Colon Free Zone include Sweden's L. M. Ericsson, which acquired a large share of the expanding telephone and communications business; Canon Camera and Crown Radio, of Japan; Eastman Kodak, Pfizer, Bristol Laboratories, Parke Davis, Schering Corporation, The Upjohn Company, Sylvania Electric, and Victor Gasket Company, from the United States; Joseph Lucas, of the United Kingdom; and dozens of large and small companies from many other countries.

They benefit from the competitive advantage of bringing their products closer to market by using a cost-saving technique of bulk shipments by sea and repackaging at Colon to fill orders in a matter of hours by air. Their customers are able to free capital formerly tied up in inventories, since the inventory is, in effect, maintained for them by the supplier. A more important advantage is realized by customers in countries which, before granting an import license, require the entire value of a shipment in escrow to be held until the shipment arrives.

Shannon: Air Age Port

Another free port that has come into international prominence in the air age is at Shannon, Ireland. Operated by the Shannon Free Airport Development Company, this trading zone has provided more than two thousand jobs in a country plagued by underemployment. On 300 acres of land near Limerick, the operating company provides manufacturing facilities, low-cost labor, housing for workers, and a residential community; its revenue is derived from rentals and fees for services performed. Companies from the United Kingdom, from European Common Market countries, and the United States draw upon raw materials and components from their home countries and from Ireland itself in manufacturing and processing goods for distribution largely in Europe and the Americas.

The modern free zone at Shannon evolved from a curious history that began with the need for a fueling stop for piston airplanes when North Atlantic flights set down at Gander, Newfoundland, and at Shannon. The latter became the first customs-free airport and the locale of many a shopping spree for air passengers caught on a ground wait while enroute. When jet aircraft began hopping the oceans on nonstop flights, free port activity at Shannon declined. A company was formed to develop the 300-acre area into an industrial complex with free port advantages. The objective, of course, was to develop traffic in import and export cargo. By the mid-1950s, Shannon was earning $4 million for the Irish Government.

In 1958, with the introduction of jet planes threatening to isolate Shannon from the mainstream of air transport, the Government authorized construction of a jet runway and terminal buildings at a cost of $3 million. This decision was made in conjunction with the development of air cargo business and the free zone. The Government offered incentives to manufacturers, including tax deferments, the cost of training workers, and subsidized plants.

The Shannon development has worked well. The population drift toward Shannon has brought a fine labor pool to the nearby towns of Limerick and Ennis, where employees reside if they do not get housing in the zone. The Shannon port has grown concurrently with the Industrial Development Authority of Ireland, which estimates that new industries have created 15,000 new jobs throughout Ireland. Exports rose from $456 million in 1960 to $540 million in 1961 and were significantly higher in 1962. It is estimated that the Shannon free port will be generating 6 million kilos of cargo annually by 1965.

Unlike the Colon Free Zone, from which retail trade and residence are barred, Shannon is a complex of shops, new houses, apartments, and public services.

In addition to a growing number of Irish manufacturing companies and exporters, some of the companies occupying the Shannon site are General Electric Company, Jonathan Logan, Raytheon, and Standard Pressed Steel of the United States; Progress International, of the United Kingdom; Sony Corporation, Japan; Rippin, Limited, of Holland, one of Europe's largest piano manufacturers, and an Oppenheimer subsidiary from South Africa. These and other companies did a business volume of $34 million through the Shannon port in 1962.

Free Port Volume Estimated at $5,000 Million

Perhaps a score of the hundred or more free trade areas now operating in the world provide modern facilities and operate with sufficiently attractive liberal policies to benefit today's trader. All offer, of course, the traditional haven—a place to which a trader can dispatch cargo free of duties and taxes until it is transshipped to market. Some of the best-known ports in developed countries are located at Gibraltar, Copenhagen, Grand Bahama, Bermuda, Hong Kong, Antwerp, Amsterdam, Rotterdam, Singapore, Hamburg, Bremen, San Francisco, and New Orleans

No accurate figures are obtainable to report the total volume of business in all free ports of the world. In many countries, figures of free port business are not separated from reported general business totals. In March, 1963, the McGraw-Hill publication *International Management* estimated that trade valued at $5,000 million passed in and out of free zones in 1962. This was said to be twice the volume of 1955.

All evidence indicates that the free trade zone, if properly designed and managed, offers the trader cost-saving services while making foreign markets accessible. At the same time it offers the country of location, and especially strategically located underdeveloped countries, a chance to lure new jobs and industrial activity to their shores with a resultant growth in their economy.

World free ports, free zones, and foreign trade zones

Aden Protectorate	Aden: free port
Argentina	Buenos Aires and Rosario: entrepôts for Bolivia and Paraguay
Austria	Innsbruck and Linz: free zones; similar trade facilities in Vienna
Bahamas	Free trade zone at Hawksbill Greek, Grand Bahama
Belgium	Antwerp and Ghent: free trade facilities
Bolivia	Cobija, Puerto Suarez, and Yacuiba: free zones
Brazil	Santos: entrepôt for Bolivia and Paraguay
Canary Islands	Arecife, La Orotava, Las Palmas, Puerto Cabras, Santa Cruz de la Palma, Santa Cruz de Tenerife, San Sebastian de la Gomera, and Valverde: free ports
Chile	Antofagasta and Arica: entrepôts for Bolivia
Colombia	Providencia and San Andres: free ports
Denmark	Copenhagen: free port
Egypt	Alexandria and Port Said: free zones
Finland	Free trade zone at port of Hanko
France	Gex and Haute-Savoie: free zones
French West Indies	Marigot, French St. Martin, and Gustavia, St. Barthélemy: free ports
Germany (Federal Republic)	Bremen, Bremerhaven, Emden, and Hamburg: free zones
Gibraltar	Free port
Greece	Piraeus: free zone, and Salonika: free zone and entrepôt for Yugoslavia
Guadeloupe	Free ports at St. Martin and St. Barthélemy
Hong Kong	Free port
Indonesia	Riouw Archipelago: free ports
Ireland	Shannon Airport: free zone
Italy	Genoa, Leghorn, Naples, Trieste, and Venice: free zones
Lebanon	Beirut: free zone
Liberia	Monrovia: free port
Malaysia	Penang and Singapore: free ports
Mexico	Coatzacoalcos, Matias Romoro, Salina Cruz, and Topolobampo: free ports; all of Baja California, the northwestern tip of Sonora, Agua Prieta, Chetumal, Cozumel, Isla de Mujeres, Nogales, and Xcalak: free perimeters
Morocco	Free port at Tangier
Libya	Tripoli: free port
Mozambique	Beria: entrepôt for Rhodesia
Netherlands	Amsterdam and Rotterdam: free trade facilities
Netherlands Antilles	Free trade zones at Oranjestad, Aruba, Willemstad, Curaçao; free ports at St. Eustatius, Saba, and St. Martin
Panama	Colon: free zone
Spain	Barcelona, Cadiz, and Vigo: free zones; Aguilas, Algeciras, Alicante, Almeria, Aviles, Barcelona, Bilbao, Cadiz, Cartagena, Castellon, El Ferrol del Caudillo, Gijon, Huelva, La Coruna, Mahon,

World free ports, free zones, and foreign trade zones

	Malaga, Palamos, Palma de Mallorca, Pasajes, Ribadeo, San Sebastian, Santander, Seville, Tarragona, Valencia, Vigo, Villagarcia, and Vinaroz: free depots
Spanish Morocco	Ceuta, Chafarinas, Melilla, Penon Velez, and Villa Sanjurjo: free ports
Sweden	Goteborg, Malmo, and Stockholm: free zones
Switzerland	Aarau, Basel-Dreispitz, Basel-Rheinhafen, Basel-Swiss National Railway, Chiasso, Geneva-Cornavin Railway Station, Geneva-Rive, Geneva-Vernier, Lausanne, St. Gallen, and Zürich-Albisrieden: free zones
Syria	Latakia: free zone
Turkey	Free trade zone at Iskenderun
United States	New Orleans, New York, San Francisco, Seattle, Toledo, and Mayaguez, Puerto Rico: foreign trade zones

Areas under consideration for some type of free zone facility

British West Indies	Bridgetown, Barbados
Iraq	Basra
Israel	Haifa
Portugal	Setubal
Yugoslavia	Rijeka

SOURCE: U.S. Department of Commerce, Bureau of International Programs.

Location, Facilities and Services of a Selected Sampling of Seven Free Zones and Free Port Areas

(Prepared by Overseas Management Services, Inc., New York)

	Antwerp, Belgium	Bermuda	Willemstad, Curaçao	Grand Bahama Free Port	Colon Free Zone, Panama	Mayaguez, Puerto Rico	Shannon International Airport
Geographical location	Central north coast of Europe	Atlantic island, off U.S. east coast	South American north coast off Venezuela	Bahama Islands, Florida east coast	Crossroads of Atlantic-Pacific in Central America	Central Caribbean Sea	Limerick, Ireland
Principal area served	Western Europe to Iron Curtain and Italian border	U.S. east coast, Canada, Caribbean area	Northern South America, Central America, and Caribbean region	Caribbean Islands, U.S. east coast, Central America, some South America	Northern and western regions of South America, Caribbean, Central America, Mexico, Far East	Caribbean Islands, U.S. east coast, Central America	Western Europe, Scandinavia, Africa
Year founded	1946	1950	1956	1955	1948	1960	1958
Land area	12,000 acres	100 acres	20 acres	100 acres	100 acres (45 acres being added)	35 acres	300 acres
A. Transshipping and warehousing B. Assembling and processing C. Manufacturing	A B C	A B C	A B C	A B C	A B C	A B C	A B C
Principal transport service	Sea, air, rail, and truck	Sea and air	Sea and air	Sea and air	Sea, air, rail, and truck	Sea and air	Sea and air
Nearest port	On site	11 miles (30 minutes)	On site	On site	1,800 yards (5 minutes)	4.5 miles (15 minutes)	10 miles (30 minutes)
Nearest airport	40 miles (75 minutes)	15 miles (1 hour)	8 miles (20 minutes)	10 miles (25 minutes)	50 miles (75 minutes)	3.5 miles	On site

LOCATION, FACLIITIES AND SERVICES OF A SELECTED SAMPLING OF SEVEN FREE ZONES AND FREE PORT AREAS (*Continued*)

	Antwerp, Belgium	Bermuda	Willemstad, Curaçao	Grand Bahama Free Port	Colon Free Zone, Panama	Mayaguez, Puerto Rico	Shannon International Airport
Nearest railroad	On site	None	None	None	On site for trans-isthmian service	None	On site
Controlling agency	City of Antwerp Port Administration	Bermuda Crown Lands Corp.	Bureau of Economic Affairs	Grand Bahama Port Authority (pvt. corp.)	Colon Free Zone Authority (govt.)	Purto Rico Industrial Development Co.	(Govt.) Shannon Free Airport Development Co.
Government warehousing	No	Yes	No	Yes	Yes	No	No
Leased warehousing	Yes	Yes	Yes	Yes	Yes	Yes	Yes
Commercial warehousing	Yes	No	Yes	Yes	Yes	No	Possible
User-owned facilities	Yes	No (Crown Lands Corp. will alter buildings to specification)	Yes	Yes	Yes	Yes	Yes
Incentives							
Fiscal	Yes	Yes	Yes	No taxes	Yes	Yes	Yes
Investment*	Yes	Yes	Negotiable	Negotiable	Yes	Yes	Yes
Industrial†	Yes	Yes	Negotiable	Negotiable	Yes	Yes	Yes
Foreign base corp.	Yes	Yes	Yes	Yes	Yes	Yes	Yes
Minimum labor costs, $							
Unskilled (per hour)	0.85	1.06	0.48 to 0.74	Under U.S. rates	0.50	0.80	0.65
Skilled (per hour)	1.35	1.55	0.61 to 1.22	Under U.S. rates	1.00	1.40	1.00

* Investment incentives take various forms, not all of which are common to all free trade areas. They include repatriation of capital, tax relief, government grants against capital outlay, etc.

† The same applies to industrial incentives. In some cases, laws relating to locally owned industry may apply to manufacturing within the free trade zone—or they may not. Tax exemptions may also apply to certain industrial activity—noncompetitive within the country, for instance.

THE MAKING OF FEASIBILITY STUDIES

Dr. Ralph von Gersdorff

Need for Feasibility Study before Start of Project

Feasibility studies are needed by firms and institutions which want to expand old lines or start new production lines. Projects or the finding of suitable projects may be suggested by individuals (businessmen, bankers, officials, politicians, engineers, scientists) or by institutions (firms, private associations, development banks, governments, development boards, political parties, international institutions). Suggestions may be based on spontaneous discoveries of needs or demand, or existing studies and development plans, or simply on the desire for economic growth. Proposals for simple projects may already be accompanied by feasibility studies, e.g., profitability tests for expansion of an enterprise, but mostly feasibility studies will be made before a project is proposed, elaborated, and started. They are examined not only by the firm or institution concerned but also by engineering and management consultants, banks, and government officials, if financing and licences have to be applied for.

How to Collect Data for Feasibility Studies

The facts to be mentioned in such studies can be found mostly in statistical offices, trade information centers (such as chambers of commerce and trade fairs), university and other libraries, development boards, planning authorities, international institutions, professional associations and journals, research institutions, embassies and consulates, or management and engineering consulting

Dr. von Gersdorff is teaching economic development planning at the National Institute for Public Administration, Government of Lebanon, Beirut, on behalf of the United Nations Technical Assistance. The views expressed are the author's and not necessarily those of the UNTA.

and market research firms. The latter are often capable of carrying out the feasibility studies.

Feasibility studies are sometimes facilitated by available fact books and collections of data on various industries prepared, for example, by development boards or banks, planning units, and statistical services. They often contain indications of actual costs for the manufacturer (wages and salaries, social charges, worker productivity, taxes, power, transport, water rates, rents, insurance, banking charges, etc.) and figures concerning population, natural resources, and utilities and services, as well as information about incentives for industrialists, other government policies, company legislation, research institutions, and amenities. For market research, data are needed on foreign trade, on existing production, geographical distribution of purchasing power, consumption patterns, sales and inventories by branches of industry, turnover of enterprises, exchange controls, and import and export controls. By assessing and evaluating potentialities of labor, management, raw materials, and other assets, feasible industries can be identified by analyzing fact books.

Check List for the Collection of Data

Feasibility studies should start with a check list of data sought. This list can be broken down into six sections: (1) materials and supplies, (2) market factors, (3) economic and technical factors, (4) personnel, (5) financial factors, and (6) social factors.

Materials and Supplies

1. Are all materials and supplies available locally?
2. Is the local material market competitive?
3. Is satisfactory and prompt delivery of local materials assured at reasonable prices?
4. What materials and supplies must be imported?
5. Are they available in world markets at competitive prices?
6. Would prompt delivery of imported materials and supplies be assured so that large inventories will not be required?

Market Factors

1. Is there already a demand for the product? Who are the principal consumers? Who are possible new consumers?

2. How is the demand for the product now satisfied? By local production? If so, what is the volume and value of annual production? What percentage of total consumption is supplied by local production? By imports? If so, what is the volume and value of annual imports? What percentage of total consumption is met by imports? From what areas are imports derived?

3. What is the estimated annual increase in local consumption over the next five years? How were estimates made? By reference to official figures on population growth, family budgets, imports, etc.? By consultation with trade or industry, ministries, associations, bankers, commercial houses, wholesalers, retailers, industrial consumers, etc.?

4. If the product is already being manufactured, can the existing and estimated future local market absorb production of the new plant without price cutting or other dislocations?

5. Would the estimated sales price and quality of the new product make it competitive with an imported equivalent? After adjusting cost of local conditions, is the estimated sales price of the product so high that tariff protection is necessary to protect it from imports?

6. Could the product compete in export markets on the basis of price, quality, and dependability of supply?

7. Can export markets for the product be developed? If so, in what areas and in what annual volume and value?

8. What procedures would be necessary to develop export markets? What would it cost?

9. In calculating costs of the product, has adequate allowance been made for the expense of a sales department, advertising, and promotion that might be required?

10. Do consumer prejudices against locally manufactured products exist? If so, why? Would they apply to the new product? If so, how could they be overcome and what would it cost to do so?

11. Do marketing and distribution facilities for the product exist? If not, can they be set up? What would it cost to do so?

12. Will the product be sold to wholesalers? Retailers? Direct to the consumer? Other industries? Government?

Economic and Technical Factors

1. How much foreign exchange (and in what currency) is required to import machinery, equipment, and supplies? For annual interest payments and amortization of any loans contracted to import machinery and equipment, or for payment of royalties and technical services? For annual import of raw materials?

2. What are estimated annual foreign exchange earnings and in what currencies?

3. Has careful consideration been given to the possibility of depreciation in the foreign exchange value of the local currency? To the possibility of import controls, or restrictions on availabilities of foreign exchange necessary to operate the business?

4. What benefits would the new business bring to the economy in the use of local raw materials, in employment, and in technology?

5. Do dependable facilities exist for transportation, power, fuel, water, and sewage? If not, can existing deficiencies be eliminated satisfactorily? What would be the cost to do so?

6. Do existing labor laws, government regulations, laws, and taxes favor establishment of new business? If not, can existing obstacles be removed? If so, how and when?

7. In selecting the machinery and equipment for the new plant, have reputable and competent engineers and technicians been consulted? Have they been asked for advice on the most suitable types of machinery and

equipment for the process and locality? Have they carefully compared costs of various suppliers? Credit terms offered to purchasers?

Personnel

1. Is there an adequate labor supply near the plant location? If not, how can the problem be solved?
2. Can the problem of training competent management and supervisory personnel be solved? Also, the training of skilled labor?
3. Is technical advice available in the locality? If not, where can it be obtained and what will it cost?

Financial Factors

1. Has a definite plan to finance the project been worked out? Is sufficient capital available locally? If not, what is the plan to obtain the required capital?
2. In estimating the cost of the project, has careful consideration been given to the effect on costs of delays in construction schedules? In delivery and installation of machinery and equipment? In import of essential raw materials and supplies?
3. Has it been possible to make arrangements with local banks to finance short-term working capital requirements of the business?
4. In calculating cash flow and working capital requirements, has careful consideration been given to maintain adequate inventories of raw materials? Supplies and spare parts? Seasonal fluctuations in the business? The time required to liquidate credit sales to customers and bad debts? The period required to get the plant into production? Cash required to amortize its principal loans?
5. If the economy is in a period of inflation, has full allowance been made for the influence of rising prices and wages on the cost of the project and on working capital requirements?

Social Factors

1. Is there a hospital or dispensary in the vicinity of the project?
2. Are there sufficient schools, including professional schools, in the vicinity of the project?
3. Are there already a sufficient number of houses and apartments available for the personnel of the new enterprise, or should they be constructed? In the latter case, are potable water, sewerage, electricity, and telephone services already available?
4. What are the total social and overhead costs of the project (dispensary, schools, in-service-training, water, sewerage, power, telephone, transport, insurance, direct and indirect taxes, social security and own pension fund, housing, and incentives such as bonuses, prizes, and profit sharing)?

Technical versus Economic Feasibility

Market research should reveal the feasible production scale. Some industries are economically feasible only on a large scale (e.g., steel milling); some might be feasible on a medium (cement) or even small scale (oil refining). The proposed technical processes must be investigated. Availability of different production factors ascertained by economic feasibility studies should be confirmed by the technicians (raw materials, fuel, power, water, skilled labor, unskilled labor).

Governments of densely populated underdeveloped countries are interested in medium-sized and small-scale enterprises offering numerous employment opportunities and requiring relatively small capital investments. Techniques maximizing the effectiveness of investment and employment will be preferred; simple techniques should be used first and more complex ones introduced gradually. In thinly populated underdeveloped countries, capital-intensive techniques will be preferred. They achieve higher production levels which make possible higher rates of capital formation, larger output, and, in the long run, the creation of larger employment. Countries with big home markets give priority to producing substitutes for imported goods, protecting the market for the new products against the competition of foreign goods. Factor combinations permitting saving of foreign exchange are preferred in all the underdeveloped countries.

Determination of Technical and Economic Requirements

During the investigations on the technical feasibility of projects, technical *and* economic requirements should be considered. In many cases, especially where the type of activity involved is new to a country, or where an organization undertakes a major expansion involving a change in the scale of its operation, it may be necessary to employ consultants to assist those responsible for the engineering and commercial arrangements. The scope of the consultants' work may cover one or more of the following functions: design; preparation of specifications; drafting of invitations to bid; analysis of tenders and recommendation for placing contracts; arrangements for the payment of suppliers and contractors and for the transportation of equipment; inspection and expediting of equipment; supervision of construction and installation; training or arrangement for the training of staff; and sometimes the supervision of initial operations. In some countries cheap or even free consulting services may be obtainable from development boards or from development and/or central banks. As these services may often not be satisfactory or comprehensive enough, private local or foreign consultants should be employed, making sure, however, that the firm chosen has a good reputation and record, has adequate staff and organization, and has had ample experience in underdeveloped countries in the required techniques and business.

The objective of the economic appraisal is to discover whether a project is able to earn a reasonable return on the capital which must be invested. The answer to the question of what rate of return is reasonable may vary according to the type of project. Where market forces operate freely, it could be said that a new project should earn not less than the return from comparable enterprises in the country concerned. But in the case of projects which are subject to regulation because of their monopoly position, e.g., some public utilities and transport systems, this test tends to become indistinct, and resort must often be had to the application of pricing formulas to produce the desired results.

Determination of Manpower and Managerial Requirements

Most countries will have some population and labor statistics, but detailed information on people with particular skills, employed, unemployed, and underemployed will seldom be available. Inquiries will have to be made on the spot, in statistical offices, Ministries of Labor, labor exchanges, labor unions, technical institutes, and professional schools.

Densely populated areas usually have an abundance of unskilled workers, a great number of whom are unemployed (structural and seasonal unemployment). In most cases workers with the required skills will not be available in underdeveloped countries. Labor will therefore have to be trained before operations start or on the job, or both. Some governments provide assistance for training. Some governments sponsor apprentice organizations run by industrial and commercial associations as, for example, in Brazil (SENAI and SENAC).[1] In the initial stages of operations, on-the-job training will usually be marked by low productivity and difficulty in maintaining quality standards.[2]

The shortage of management experience and ability is one of the main difficulties standing in the way of economic development in many countries. This is compounded by the limited concept of the role of management in some countries, where it is not understood that management is much more than simply keeping a plant running, calling also for constant technical and market research (finding new products and markets) and care for workers and employees (profit sharing, housing, old age pensions, etc.). There is often an unwillingness to employ foreigners. It may be possible to arrange for a management contract with a foreign organization, or it may be practical to employ individuals from abroad. One of the objectives of such arrangements should be that the foreigners train local people to take their places as soon as practicable. But unless there is careful career planning by the parent companies for their overseas executives, these men are unlikely to be enthusiastic about preparing local manpower for their own replacement. Liberal immigration policies contribute greatly to the growth of a technical manpower reservoir on all levels of skill and thus to rapid formation of a local reservoir of managerial manpower favorable to industrialization.[3]

Problems of Enterprise Location

Feasibility studies will have to consider the choice of possible location of an enterprise, especially of one depending on a particular bulky raw material. Locations may be oriented for fuel, power, labor, or market. The proposed site

[1] Ralph von Gersdorff, *Saving, Credit and Insurance in Brazil: Their Contribution to Economic Development,* Government Printing Office, Barbados, West Indies, 1962, p. 72.

[2] Lincoln Gordon and Engelbert L. Grommers, *United States Manufacturing Investment in Brazil: The Impact of Brazilian Government Policies, 1946–1960,* Harvard University School of Business Administration, Boston, 1962, p. 110.

[3] John C. Shearer, *High-level Manpower in Overseas Subsidiaries: Experience in Brazil and Mexico,* Princeton University Press, Princeton, N.J., 1960, pp. 29, 50, 122, 123.

has to be considered in relation to the sources of the factors of production, to transportation, and to the markets where the products are to be sold. The layout of a project may also be very important, especially for future expansions. At present, movable power stations can overcome power bottlenecks (lack of hydroelectric power in drought periods), seasonal unemployment, and lack of power for cottage industries. Most plants in underdeveloped countries need their own power plants for protection against breakdowns of the public power supply.

Financial Projections of Outlay and Income

These usually fall into two parts:

1. Amount of money required to bring the project into operation, and money sources
2. Operating costs and revenue, and prospective liquidity in the operating phase

Money requirements will include the following items:

a. Cost of goods and services for the project itself
b. Allowances for escalation and contingencies
c. Interest on borrowed funds during construction

Allowance has to be made for the working capital required when the project starts operating. Many projects have experienced difficulties because of a lack of sufficient working capital. The requirements of this capital tend to be much larger in underdeveloped countries, because shipments are uneven and large inventories must be kept owing to the uncertainty of supply of raw materials, components, and spare parts. Customs administrations are uncertain; exchange control delays occur. Local suppliers often do not meet delivery schedules.

In many countries inflationary pressure on costs has also led to larger investments in inventory. One has to buy as far ahead as possible because of constantly increasing prices. Time lags occur in recovering increased costs from consumers. Short-term funds can usually be secured in underdeveloped countries with a stable currency but are difficult to obtain in inflationary countries. They are expensive in both cases, because owing to risk conditions debit rates are usually much higher than in developed countries. They are especially scarce because in inflationary countries depositors try to keep their accounts as small as possible, and deposits constitute the main source for lending. Distribution, consumer credit financing, and long delays of payments (lack of non–cash-payment facilities) also lead to very high accounts receivable.

The estimation of working capital requirements will take into account the terms on which products are sold (which will indicate the amount of receivables to be financed) and the amount necessary to take care of swings in payments and receipts (seasonal variation in production or sales).

Sources for financing will include funds generated from operations, e.g., depreciation and undistributed earnings, and also share capital issue proceeds, long- and short-term borrowings, and public funds from central or local budgetary sources. Investment of retained earnings enjoys tax relief in many countries. Regulated industries (e.g., electric power) are often unable to generate funds from their own operations, mainly in inflationary countries.

There should be two kinds of projections: (1) estimates of cash receipts and expenditures, which show if funds are available at the right time to meet expected requirements, and (2) periodical balance sheets showing the financial situation during the construction period. These projections and those of earnings are carried into the operating period, showing the likely results of the operations. Forecasts must take into account the time required to overcome initial operating difficulties; the rate at which the market may be able to absorb production; taxation, bank, private and social insurance charges;[4] and labor incentives. The latter are indispensable in order to achieve satisfactory industrial relations and labor productivity.

The cost estimates should be broken down according to the amounts to be spent locally and abroad, according to a *time schedule* and according to the different main elements of the project.

Estimates of Risks

There are political, social, monetary, commercial, technical, physical, and other risks which have to be taken into account, many of which cannot be easily insured or cannot be insured at all. The number and magnitude of the risks depend on the country chosen for production and the commodity to be produced. In the assessment of political risks, the form of government and its record are important, also its policies and attitudes toward private enterprise, "nationalizations," eventual defaults in the payment of debts, transfer restrictions, the type of foreign exchange and trade controls, occasional maladministration of public finance and enterprises, and inflationary trends.

In many countries the "social climate" asks for trouble because neither the employers nor the employed have a clear idea of their proper functions, duties, and rights. No lessons have been learned from disasters resulting from wrong or unfair industrial relations, or from strikes, riots, or revolutions calling for the abolition of free enterprise and for complete government control.

If it is proposed to produce a world market commodity or a product based on such a commodity, the risk of the usually large price fluctuations of these goods has to be taken into account.

Some countries suffer from periodical physical hazards, such as hurricanes, earthquakes, or floods. Projects which involve, for example, large earth-moving works are subject to geological hazards, for which provision has to be made. In such cases, there may be a substantial margin of error in the estimate of the work to be done, e.g., of the amount of earth and rock to be moved. There should always be a careful tabulation of favorable and unfavorable factors in a feasibility study.

Calculation of Safety Reserves in Projecting Financial Requirements

Cost estimates must include adequate allowances not only for physical contingencies but also for likely increases in the general level of costs (wages, prices, for example, owing to inflation) during the construction period, for

[4] For Brazil, see von Gersdorff, *op. cit.*, pp. 197–237.

seasonal variations in working conditions, and for interest on borrowed money during construction for initial working capital. The investigator has to judge whether the expected revenue from operations represents a reasonable return on the capital invested, whether there is an adequate margin in the funds generated by operations to meet fixed financial obligations, and, in many cases, whether revenue will be adequate to establish reserves needed for sound operation and possibly for future expansion.

Governments in underdeveloped countries usually provide tax relief, duty-free imports of raw material and capital goods, tariff protection, exchange benefits, and transfer facilities for foreign investors and entrepreneurs. With public utilities it will be necessary to obtain an undertaking that adequate rates will be sought, also in case of inflation, to meet the expenses of operations, financial obligations, and the provision of funds toward the cost of future construction.

Market Research: Stability of Markets and Trends as Basis of Economic Forecasting

Market studies are often made before other studies, such as those of manufacturing costs and facility requirements. Market studies provide information about the potential sales, what products should be manufactured, and what the product design should be; they also supply the basis for studies of facilities, costs, and profits. Marketing research can thus be applied before feasibility studies are made, indicating a range of products for which feasibility studies should then be undertaken. Development or export promotion boards and firms who cannot afford feasibility studies may contact great merchant firms such as department stores and mail-order houses, asking them to indicate items which they think should be produced in an underdeveloped country. Some of the big department store firms have departments of industrial experts who will set up a production enterprise in a country if they think that an item or various items can be produced more cheaply there than at their present place of manufacture.

Even where feasibility studies are undertaken before market studies are made, market research will be an essential part of the feasibility investigation and will therefore be undertaken in the course of feasibility research. Such research can be sponsored by a group of firms so that it can also be made available to smaller firms.

Statistics have shown that industrial products enjoy greater price stability than raw materials, which frequently experience violent price fluctuations in the world market. Therefore efforts have been made to stabilize these prices through international agreements. Only in a few cases, for example, in the past for tin and sugar, and today for coffee, do such agreements bring success. Therefore the underdeveloped countries seek to process as many raw materials as possible themselves and to add as much value to them as possible before they are exported. If countries are big enough, like Brazil, India, and Mexico, for example, they can force foreign exporters through the menace of import prohibitions to establish production inside the country rather than to supply manufactured articles from abroad. In Brazil the "Law of Similars" has been a most powerful incentive for foreign investors to move from importing to assembly, or from assembly to full-fledged manufacturing.[5] Economic forecasting has to take these factors into account. It is often not difficult to find considerable latent demand in developed countries for raw materials, such as meat and timber, and in underdeveloped countries for certain basic industrial products, such as steel, cement, and heavy chemicals, the latter becoming effective as soon as imports are replaced by local production. Indicators for unsatisfied demand are high prices and the existence of some type of control.

Availability of Maintenance, Transportation, and Distribution Services as Factors Influencing Feasibility

Maintenance costs are usually high in underdeveloped countries, owing to a lack of maintenance enterprises, absence of training (and resulting damage of machines through ignorance and neglect), and shortage of spare parts. Unduly high rates of depletion and waste of scarce capital assets are the rule rather than the exception. The need of smaller enterprises for adequate repair and maintenance facilities might be met by providing common repair facilities within an organizational framework. The device of industrial estates supplies some solutions to this problem, because such estates include repair shops for all the plants located there. Repair and maintenance service is essential for all industrial development and for the use of equipment in other development projects.

Although in most cases it will be advisable to provide effective competition between potential suppliers and contractors through international competitive bidding, it can also be most economic to standardize on the basis of existing equipment in order to reduce both the investment in spare parts and the cost of maintenance.

Many projects can be carried out only if other facilities are available or are provided at the same time. For instance, the establishment of an iron ore mine and/or a steel industry is practical only if there are adequate facilities to transport the raw materials and the finished products.

Feasibility studies must take into account not only the usual types of protection in force, such as imposition of import duties or quotas for infant industries, but also limitations on the freedom of road transport, for example, in order to protect a railway system.

Distribution services are often inadequate in underdeveloped countries. Profits are mostly made on exaggerated markups rather than on the expansion of turnover. There are many monopoly or quasi-monopoly positions which could be knocked out by efficient competition. Investigators should not only study the existing services and their costs and prices but also consider the possibility of establishing alternative services for a manufacturing project. It might be advisable, for instance, to establish a chain of hygienic, clean retail shops for a big meat packing plant. The establishment of marketing cooperatives or corporations may bring down prices of agricultural products by more efficient distribution.

[5] Gordon and Grommers, *op. cit.* 25 *et seq.*

How to Appraise the Influence of an Underdeveloped Environment

Each underdeveloped country has its own characteristics of underdevelopment or advanced development. During the collection of evidence for feasibility (e.g., collection of data on idle or underemployed human and natural resources), the influence of underdevelopment will be revealed. The worst bottlenecks are in the *infrastructure,* i.e., transport, power, water, education, and health services. As mentioned before, in most cases marketing itself is also poorly organized. Many underdeveloped countries suffer from the cancer of inflation caused mostly by "deficit financing" in public finance and by credit overexpansion. If inflation proceeds at a regular pace, it can be taken into account, and protective hedging is possible; but if its pace varies very much, proper calculations are virtually impossible. Any type of inflation is a serious inconvenience to current business operations, another factor of uncertainty in the planning of business and for the country as a whole. However, development in large countries such as Brazil occurs not because of but in spite of inflation.[6]

Commercial banking is well organized in most underdeveloped countries, but only for short-term financing of domestic and foreign trade. Working capital is more difficult to get. There is a big lack of long-term capital because of the lack of private and, in some cases, of public saving. In order to overcome the lack of financial institutions for long-term financing, development banks were established in most countries, usually financed with public funds.

Government services, with a few exceptions, are mostly slow and inefficient in underdeveloped countries (especially the statistical services, offering only late and deficient supply of data). Income tax holidays are granted for from seven to twenty-five years in some areas, such as the Caribbean and Mexico. Monopoly positions are granted by some countries for investors (Portuguese territories), and in many countries import and foreign exchange controls are applied for the promotion of economic development. In some cases controls hinder development rather than foster it. Projects are favored which contribute to reduction of imports (thus saving foreign exchange) or to the expansion of exports. The more or less positive net and indirect effect of a project on the balance of trade and payments and on the national income will be carefully studied. The investigator will have to elaborate and analyze these data carefully in order to get as much protection for his project from the authorities as possible.

Examples

In order to exemplify the making of feasibility studies, the author's experiences gained in five underdeveloped countries of different size, population, and natural resources are summarized below.

Brazil. Study for Harvard University Center of International Affairs of the roles and relationships of the public and private sectors in generating capital: *Studies for a Foreign Importer of Machines.*

[6] Gordon and Grommers, *op. cit.,* and von Gersdorff, *op. cit.;* see chapters on inflation and pertinent items in the index.

1. Feasibility of a meat packing plant in North Western Paraná. Meat has a good market in the big towns, where meat shortages occurred. Main problems: regular supply of cattle and pigs and location of plant.

2. Feasibility of a machine tool factory in the State of São Paulo. For a number of milling and planing machines (not yet produced in Brazil) tariff protection projected, if produced there.

3. Organization of an investment company in Rio. Although inflation is crippling, the capital market there seems to have good prospects.

India. Study of the economy of India and Goa. Capital- as well as labor-intensive industries are feasible. Market research for a foreign factory of sanitary fittings: because of increasing building activities, demand is expanding in the big towns. Production locally would get tariff protection.

Portugal.[7] Study of the economy. Study of the shoe industry for the Export Promotion Board in Lisbon: too many manufacturers producing too many models. Reorganization of production and marketing necessary, also for initiation of export drive.

Portuguese Africa.[8] Studies of possible measures for expanding exports by increasing agricultural production and processing.

Barbados, West Indies. Study of the economy on behalf of the United Nations Technical Assistance as Economic Advisor to the Government. Industries employing labor-intensive porcesses and establishment of a regional development bank suggested. Systematic approach beginning with available natural resources and their processing, continuing with the assembly of imported items, also for export to the Caribbean, and the import of raw materials and half-finished products, for adding as much value as possible to subsequent exports.

[7] R. von Gersdorff, *Measures to Promote Private Capital Formation in the Portuguese Territories: Saving Possibilities and Financing Methods in Underdeveloped Areas,* Polygraphischer Verlag, Zurich, 1958; *Public Finance in Portugal,* Verlag E. & W. Gieseking, Bielefeld, West Germany, 1961.

[8] R. von Gersdorff, *Angola and Mozambique,* German Africa Society, Bonn, 1958–1960, 2 vols.; *Economic Problems of Portuguese Africa,* Verlag E. & W. Gieseking, Bielefeld, West Germany, 1962.

PROBLEMS OF MANAGEMENT IN UNDERDEVELOPED COUNTRIES

Selected Readings from United Nations Papers, Compiled by Dr. Serge L. Levitsky

The Structure of Management

Industrial enterprises in underdeveloped countries often face problems similar to those which confronted industry in developed countries some fifty or even seventy-five years ago. One of the problems is that of transition from personal to functional management.

One of the inhibiting factors in industrial organization in underdeveloped countries is the tendency of entrepreneurs to be guided by experience gained in nonindustrial activities. It manifests itself in lack of familiarity with the nature of an industrial enterprise and results in an imbalance in the performance of the various managerial functions. Thus, the commercial aspect of a business might be emphasized as against production; in other cases—particularly when the owners come from mining or landholding activities—the opposite situation might arise. In the former case, the business policies of the enterprise are often likely to be guided by short-term considerations of immediate profit, while the long-term aspects, such as maintenance and modernization of the equipment and training of workers and foremen, are neglected. Entrepreneurs may be reluctant to exchange information and experience and undertake concerted action, a situation which prevents dissemination of knowledge and makes difficult the solution of problems best handled on a joint basis, such as improvement of marketing methods, promotion of sales, and training of labor.

Dr. Levitsky is Manager of Market Research of the Texas Gulf Sulphur Company.

The opening section, on the Structure of Management, is taken from "Management of Industrial Enterprises in Underdeveloped Countries," 1958, pages 4 to 8, passim.

It is considered that an effort should be made to impress upon entrepreneurs in underdeveloped countries the nature and advantages of functional management. As the various functions are taken over by professionals, it is likely that most of the deficiencies mentioned above will be eliminated. It is important, however, that the development of a functional organization should proceed in a gradual way and be kept within appropriate limits. If this development takes place without due regard to local conditions and the resources and requirements of the firm, it may defeat its purpose.

As regards the structure of lower-echelon management, the division of their functions also tends to lack precision in many cases. Thus, sales personnel may be burdened with legal and administrative duties, and maintenance departments may be assigned duties related to production; conversely, the responsibilities of a "staff" function may be scattered among various units of the "line" organization. Some of these defects stem from the scarcity of experienced personnel, which brings about accumulation of unrelated responsibilities in the same person, while in some cases certain functions may not be covered at all. In many undertakings, however, not enough thought has been given to the organizational problem, and there is a tendency toward the cumulation of functions and centralization of authority just mentioned. One result is the existence at lower levels of redundant staff with ill-defined functions, little responsibility, and inadequate incentives, while top management is overloaded with detailed matters of administration, to the detriment of its essential functions.

In this connection, it would appear that a major deficiency on the production side of industrial enterprise in underdeveloped countries is a shortage of competent foremen.

The training of foremen often omits proper indoctrination in elementary management techniques. While in the long run industrialization will result in the formation of a class of skilled technicians with a more widely accepted professional status, a serious effort appears to be necessary to solve the immediate problem by means of foremen training schemes. Furthermore, greater efficiency and better performance would be achieved if foremen were given higher pay and a larger measure of authority in such matters as wages and labor discipline. They should also be provided with the necessary control information on such items as budgets and performance records to guide their activities.

Recruitment and Training of Management Personnel[1]

Recruitment. *Top Management Personnel.* It is recognized that the recruitment and selection of top management personnel presents a different problem from that of recruiting personnel on lower management levels. The functions of the latter require a greater measure of specialized technical knowledge; the former require a broader background of training and experience, with greater emphasis on initiative, foresight, and willingness to assume responsibility.

[1] From "Management of Industrial Enterprises in Underdeveloped Countries," 1958, pp. 8–14, passim; "Public Industrial Management in Asia and the Far East," 1960, pp. 39–40.

Large-scale Enterprises. Lower-echelon specialized personnel in charge of various departments of an industrial enterprise acquire, in the performance of their duties, considerable managerial experience and represent a ready source of potential candidates for top management positions. In connection with this source it might be mentioned, however, that, under the regime of family control, management is generally selected from within the controlling family, and family bonds also determine, to a large extent, advancement in the hierarchy. Moreover, because of the greatly centralized nature of management in a family concern, there is less scope for younger men to acquire experience in leadership and decision making.

Foreign-owned enterprises are also important in this connection. Many young men, nationals of the host countries, with adequate educational background but little experience in business, enter employment in foreign establishments where they may be trained for executive positions. There is, however, great diversity in the policies of foreign companies concerning employment and training of local personnel. The extreme case occurs when such companies keep the management of local subsidiaries as much as possible in the hands of their own nationals; in some cases this is because the home office of the foreign company is unaware of the availability, or distrusts the capacity, of local personnel to fill executive positions. On the other hand, many foreign concerns frequently make a point of replacing foreign executive staff by nationals as soon as the latter become available. These firms start first with "imported" management but take pains to select local candidates who, after being given suitable training, are placed in managerial positions.

Commerce and banking are considered to be other sources of top industrial management personnel, in view of the opportunities provided by these occupations to develop executive ability. Difficulty sometimes arises in regard to personnel recruited from these branches of activity since, as mentioned, the general outlook and attitude in matters of business policy developed in trade or finance may prove to be somewhat of a handicap in industry. A serious effort at adaptation, together with technical training, may often be required.

Government Service. It is considered that experience gained by civil servants in the higher positions in public administration often provides them with a good background to qualify as candidates for top managerial positions in industry.

Professions. Another possible source is provided by professions, which are not necessarily limited to those involving technical or scientific training. Nontechnical professions—for example, law and accounting—have often provided excellent managerial personnel.

Foreign Management Personnel. The importing of foreign personnel may constitute an immediate solution to the problem of management. Under this heading come immigration of trained individuals, staffing of foreign enterprises by nationals of the home country, and hiring of managers from similar industries abroad. Provision of foreign staff for new industrial enterprises, as a transitional arrangement until local managerial cadres have been trained, is frequently of particular urgency. As one method of recruitment, it is well known that foreign manufacturers of industrial equipment are often ready to cooperate with their customers in providing experienced technical staff or assisting in locating suitable individuals; such an arrangement might also cover management personnel. However, this type of assistance is generally available only to the larger enterprises, and it is also difficult to obtain it in cases where the equipment of the new enterprise originates from a number of sources.

A possible source of recruitment of foreign personnel which does not appear to have been fully exploited might be retired staff members of large and medium-sized concerns in the developed countries. These persons, who are usually between the ages of sixty and sixty-five, have wide experience which may range from service as chairmen, presidents, or vice presidents of companies to higher-level foremanship, They might be induced to work for a few years in the underdeveloped countries at a remuneration which would not be excessive as compared to their experience. While they may not always be familiar with conditions in underdeveloped countries, their training and experience in their home countries would often give them the necessary flexibility in adapting themselves to local conditions.

As an alternative to recruitment of foreign personnel, mention may be made of the services of specialized consultant firms which provide management teams on a contractual basis for specified periods of time.

There should be no hesitation in employing foreign consultants in the survey and engineering work relating to large or complicated industrial schemes which are beyond the capacity of local engineers. The extra expenditure involved in the employment of foreign consultants is more than offset by the savings which will result from the selection of a proper site, the accurate preparation of estimates, and the purchase of the right type of plant and machinery. Great care, however, needs to be exercised in the selection of competent foreign consultants and in the drawing up of the terms of the consultancy agreement. In some instances underdeveloped countries have been badly disappointed by inexperienced and unscrupulous consultants, and consultancy agreements have been found to be expensive and somewhat one-sided. The essential safeguards are to ensure that the consultants have adequate staff and have had practical experience in the design and erection of industrial plants, not only in North America and Europe but also in the less developed countries of Asia, Africa, or South America. The consultancy agreement should extend to the surveying or checking of preliminary investigations already carried out by local engineers, the preparation of a comprehensive project report, the drawing up of specifications, designs, and plant layout, and so on. In preparing these specifications, care should be exercised to see that the selection of the plant and machinery is not restricted to any one make or country and that a wide choice is available in respect to both quality and price. The consultant should also be required to assist in the preparation of invitations to tender and in the adjudication of the tenders received. Other provisions of the consultancy agreement must necessarily depend upon the nature of each industry, the size of the investment involved, and the extent to which the country concerned is able to undertake the project on its own. Normally, it is a wise safeguard to have the assistance of qualified consultants in inspecting the plant and machinery received from the manufacturer, in supervising the erection of the plant and the performance tests, in training local staff, and if need be in the initial operation of the plant. In the case of a really large and complicated industrial venture, it may be worthwhile to enter into "turnkey" contracts with the manufacturers. These contracts provide not only for the supply of plant and machinery and the training of technical staff, but also for the operation of the plant for two or three years. To make such a contract effective, it is necessary to provide for performance guarantees both in respect to the time scheduled for the completion of a project and in assuring rated production within a specified period of time.

Lower-echelon Management Personnel. The principal source of middle management personnel—at least as far as the more technical functions are concerned—is to be found among graduates of universities and technical and business schools, and among supervisors who have risen from the ranks. As to the methods of recruitment of personnel in this category, in one case which has been cited, a local university recommended a group of students of potential management caliber, from which a number of trainees was selected on the basis of interviews. In another case, a preliminary screening of university graduates was made on the basis of written applications; the promising candidates were then interviewed for final selection by a committee composed of academic and business people. In still another instance, several skilled workers with adequate general education were selected on the basis of interviews and given on-the-job training for a period of several months; they were then placed in jobs with some managerial responsibility.

There appears to be a need for developing suitable devices to facilitate impartial screening and selection of candidates for managerial posts from the ranks of students and graduates of engineering schools, universities, and business schools. Recruitment of candidates would be facilitated if they were systematically informed of existing openings; the establishment of an appropriate register of vacancies might also be considered. As to the composition of the screening boards, these should include individuals appointed by academic institutions and industry, also independent persons of high caliber.

Managerial Cadres for Smaller Enterprises. The problems of recruitment and selection discussed above apply mainly to larger enterprises; in the case of smaller plants the problems are different. Smaller plants are largely run by owner-managers who may originally have been skilled workers, foremen, or graduates of technical schools, or who may have come from nonindustrial occupations, such as trade. Supply of managerial talent in this sector is in many cases governed by the principle of "the survival of the fittest," which may not necessarily be considered the best or the most desirable criterion. There appears to be a need for a major effort on the part of the public authorities to supply the managerial needs of small-scale industry by promoting suitable training schemes.

Training. The major function of the training program—whether combined with existing facilities or set up on an *ad hoc* basis—would be to provide trainees with a basic knowledge of modern managerial functions and techniques. The training might preferably take place after working hours and be of short duration. Special programs might also be provided for training of foreman cadres. As to methods of training, these may include round-table conferences, seminars, and—whenever practicable—visits to plants and in-plant work. In training foremen, formal instruction might be included in the curriculum, in view of the educational level of some of the trainees.

In several instances in which enterprises have successfully trained abroad their technical and administrative personnel, the training involved a combination of postgraduate study with in-plant activities in foreign companies, training in the plants of manufacturers of equipment, under equipment purchase contracts, or similar methods. Clearly, smaller plants are likely to be at a disadvantage in this respect, because they have greater difficulty in establishing the necessary contacts with foreign firms, and also because the authorities are not always aware of their needs. Cases have been cited by technical assistance experts of governments being reluctant to provide the necessary support for training of personnel from smaller enterprises. Foreign exchange to cover the cost of trainees abroad would be disallowed by the exchange authorities either because such training needs were not recognized or because other training projects, relating to large-scale industry, were given priority. The attention of governments should be drawn to the importance of proper recognition of the needs of smaller plants in this field.

In connection with the more advanced type of training for higher-caliber personnel, attention is drawn to the existence of well-organized management training programs in a number of industrialized countries.

As far as the long-run aspects of management training are concerned, the development of adequate managerial cadres would require—in addition to the development of specialized training facilities—some reorientation of the curricula of academic institutions engaged in technical education, whereby schools of engineering, universities, and similar institutions of higher technical education would teach students the elements of organization and administration of enterprises. At the present time the programs of study too often fail to do justice to these disciplines. It might also be recalled here that in few underdeveloped countries is management considered as a career in itself, and appropriate incentives, such as attractive employment opportunities and scales of pay and professional prestige, are indicated in order to stimulate the interest of potential talent in this field.

Labor-Management and Internal Relationships[2]

Managerial Policy and Internal Relationships. Industrialists in many parts of the world are observing more and more the success of a type of management which centers its interest primarily on the human beings through which it operates rather than on the things—materials, facilities, money—which, however essential, are controlled by those human beings. The motivations behind human conduct in any society are decisive factors in the development of the managerial element in that society, and the character of management thus varies from society to society and from country to country. Management itself can be explained and evaluated in terms of its effect on human motivation and productivity.

[2] From "Some Problems in the Organization and Administration of Public Enterprises in the Industrial Field," 1954, pp. 46–54, passim; C. R. Wynne Roberts, "Labour Aspects of Management," in *Industrialization and Productivity*, Bulletin 2, March, 1959, pp. 42–45.

The Will to Work. In any organization, and in any culture, the worker must satisfy certain basic emotional needs in order to be productive and attain what is often called "job satisfaction." In the early stages of economic development a spirit of adventure, pride in the achievements of newly won national independence, personal sacrifice for the good of the community, or even a sense of power derived from material achievement, may be the dominant factor in building up this sense of satisfaction. In a more complex society the worker looks for a sense of security derived from regular wages, regular employment, and a feeling that his work is thereby adequately valued; for a sense of success—the feeling that he is making progress, that he is producing something worthwhile and acceptable and is thus making adequate use of his skill and ability; and for a sense of being accepted as a member of the group and of receiving recognition not just for achievement but for his personal worth and significance.

Recent social science research in advanced industrial countries shows that the will to work is best stimulated in an environment of that character by a process of direction by consent, an approach to leadership in conformity with democratic political traditions. Scientific measures of productivity in industrial enterprises in various countries show that the highest productivity is usually secured when the worker sees his objectives clearly and is convinced that they are desirable, accepts the idea that he can achieve these objectives cooperatively, has some choice in the methods used, and is able to see and participate in the final results of the work.

Key Organization Problems. The first area in which we can profitably explore the effects of this humanistic concept of management, as opposed to the mechanistic approach, is in matters of organizational arrangement and subdivision of labor. Perhaps a few organizational problems will serve as illustrations.

The first problem is that of flexibility. One of the advantages of separate corporate entities for public enterprises is that internal organization and management policies can be left to the inventiveness and adaptation of the individual management of each organization. That this latitude breeds success is consistent with the idea that responsible human beings with a definite goal can achieve considerable success when provided with certain guidelines and when trusted to work out the method for themselves. Even where there are two enterprises of the same type under common governmental authority, there is an advantage in substantial autonomy for each, modified only by general policy guides and clear-cut accountability for results.

Next in importance is the problem of size. Public enterprises in the less developed countries are probably smaller in size on the average than those in more advanced industrial communities. Normally this should give them an advantage. A small enterprise can remain closer to its human problems. Greater versatility of staff is required, with resultant greater informality and flexibility in operation. It is much easier to stimulate employee pride, to reach the wellsprings of cooperation and teamwork. The smaller the unit the less excuse has management for poor communication—the mire in which the will to work is so often bogged.

A third problem is clarity of objectives. The need for clear understanding by the worker of the direction in which he is working, of how his work fits in with other operations, and of the reasons why it is essential is a cardinal principle of motivation. A sense of achievement and security can hardly be obtained without it. This applies both to the individual worker and to groups of workers.

A much-discussed organizational problem is the span of control. Attempts have been made to deduce a mathematical formula to determine the number of immediate subordinates or the number of subsidiary functions which can be controlled by a single executive or senior supervising officer. The problem is not capable of a general solution because so much depends on the variety of functions involved. For example, a managing director responsible for coordinating the work of a group which includes more than one technical specialist may find it impossible to deal with more than a small group of heads of departments. On the other hand, in a department store in the United States actual experiments proved that the manager would successfully deal with a large number of departmental supervisors, in one instance as many as thirty, by encouraging them to deal with much of their work under delegated authority, so that the matters which they brought to him, though important, were sufficiently few in number for him to give them personal attention.

If it is impracticable to give the senior a wide span of control, it becomes necessary to introduce one or more intervening layers of supervision, providing him with a number of assistants, each of whom in turn coordinates the work of a group of supervisors in the next layer below. When this type of organization becomes necessary, the choice of functions which go directly to the chief executive becomes important. In addition to the main productive activity or the main service given by the enterprise, he should, for example, give some personal attention to such important problems as budget or personnel, and the hierarchy must be so arranged that these matters come within his immediate direction. The opposite arrangement, whereby a large group of supervisors report directly to a manager in charge, gives great scope for their individual initiative, since the manager has little opportunity to give any one of them a great deal of his time. This situation makes careful selection of supervisors extremely important, and it also tends to produce men of initiative who subsequently make good candidates for higher management.

In any type of organization the critical element is of course the capacity and skill of the supervisors. Devolution of authority has a considerable value; often personal capacity is not discovered until it is given an opportunity.

The auxiliary staff services are of considerable importance in the smooth running of headquarters and are broadly of two types:

1. Operations which run horizontally throughout the organization and require central leadership and direction, such as personnel practices, public information, legal interpretation, budgeting and financial control, provision of supplies or materials, maintenance of buildings and equipment, etc.

2. Services in the immediate office of the principal executive designed to conserve his time—reducing by preliminary discussion the number and complexity of issues that must be put before him; clarifying misunderstandings where possible; explaining the executive's decisions, where these must be

repeated to various groups; collecting information and digesting reports and data to facilitate executive decision; drafting decisions or policies for executive review; and screening visitors and correspondence, thereby shifting as many matters as possible to other parts of the organization.

The need in large organizations for special auxiliary units concerned with the managerial services of personnel, public information, legal analysis, budget and finance, purchasing, and housekeeping has long been recognized. In organizations of less than 1,000 employees these can often be combined into one or two units. They not only serve and advise the executive; they can act for him where he delegates authority.

The second category of auxiliary services, which can best be provided through personal staff assistants and secretarial staff, is equally vital to allow the executive to devote his time to general policy.

Decision Making: A Process of Communication and Delegation. Much of what has been said already touches upon the elements of decision making. Before effective action is achieved, it must be decided what is to be done, how it is to be done, and who is going to see that it is done. If the organization is so small that control is vested in a single individual, he will have no difficulty in disposing of all three problems. Once these responsibilities have to be divided between two or more people, even if one individual is in ultimate charge, there at once arises a problem of communication, and the efficiency of the organization is then determined by the efficiency of its communications. It should always be remembered that a good organization is oriented in terms of persons so that the making of decisions is primarily a process engaged in by people, affecting people, and influenced by the attitudes of people. Decisions must be based on the information received at the point where they are made, so that they are critically dependent upon the channels of communication and staff participation. The quality of decisions is also dependent on the capacity of those who have to take them and on the reliance placed upon these individuals by superior authority. The problem arises more with executive management than with the formulation of policy. In the nationalized industries of the United Kingdom, for instance, formulation of policy is frequently in the hands of boards, whereas executive management is entrusted as far as possible to individuals such as the area general managers of the Coal Board or the district managers of the Gas and Electricity Boards.

Communications and employee participation are of vital importance in reaching decisions. If we consider the basic reasons for the motivation of employees, we quickly realize that executives cannot afford to make decisions in an ivory tower, insulated from the knowledge, the feelings, and the aspirations of their subordinates. Technical decisions must, of course, be made on the basis of technical information and the professional judgment of specialists; but decisions become less and less technical and more and more far-reaching as they rise higher and higher in the hiearchy. The more far-reaching they are, the more the human factor must be taken into account.

Many management experts refer to employee participation as if it were confined to those administrative problems which relate to personnel policies such as working conditions, pay, or supervisory practices. If we are to interpret decision making from the humanistic point of view, we must regard employee participation as a regular method of work in all the daily decisions of an organization. The following are some of the means of achieving it:

1. Staff meetings should be regular and frequent. Supervisors should not be afraid of having too many discussions with employees. Even the foreman of an unskilled labor force, although he might find group meetings impractical, should encourage employees to express opinions on working methods.

2. Wherever possible, each supervisor should try to lead his unit to a group decision on any matter which affects general work policy or standards, rather than reserve this prerogative for himself.

3. Employee suggestions for work improvement should be stimulated up and down the line. Management should praise supervisors who elicit employee ideas.

4. Employees should be asked individually to help estimate what their individual production goals should be.

5. The head of the organization should hold mass meetings of employees several times a year, out of doors if necessary, wherever the work arrangements permit.

6. If at all possible, an employee newspaper or bulletin should be published regularly, containing current information about the goals and success of the enterprise and matters of human interest concerning individual employees.

7. Serious group problems of discipline, laxity, malingering, or the like should be discussed frankly and openly with the groups of employees affected, in an attempt to obtain their solution of the difficulty.

If such practices as these become a natural and habitual part of the working environment, they can go a long way toward providing both top management and rank-and-file employees with an understanding of working aims and of each other's problems and feelings, and toward satisfying the workers' emotional needs for sympathetic identification with the aims of the organization.

Employee organizations and trade unions also serve a constructive purpose because:

1. They provide a convenient means of assessing employee group opinion on personnel policy and of negotiating with employees.

2. They provide a vehicle, set up by the employees, from which representation can be secured on labor-management committees such as the Whitley Councils in the United Kingdom, the Works Councils in Germany, and similar instruments in the public enterprises of other countries.

Delegation of authority also assists in the making of decisions. Authority may be delegated down the line, following the functional hierarchy and the layers of supervision within a given location, and it may be delegated to executives in charge of units at other locations. The latter process is often referred to as decentralization. Delegation and decentralization refer essentially to the same method—a fanning out of decision making so that employees at various levels in the organization can take action without awaiting prior approval by their superiors.

In a study of the nationalized coal industry of the United Kingdom this statement has been made: "Decentralization is not simply an aim which can be achieved by organizational changes, but is primarily a problem of the adjustment of human relationships." This suggests that the advantages of maximum delegation of authority to act are achieved (1) by improving the efficiency and speed of action of individuals within an enterprise, and (2) by motivating those who are given authority to take a genuine interest in and responsibility for their work.

The human element is the primary consideration, as well as the limiting factor in delegation. Delegation can go only so far as an employee is equipped to exercise the judgment that is required. This presupposes (1) the necessary personal knowledge and capacity, (2) training in the aims and policies of the enterprise, and (3) definite standards, defined in writing wherever possible, by which the employee makes the decisions. The success of training and the setting of standards in obtaining greater efficiency through delegation of authority illustrates how such activities pay for themselves.

In any event, delegation should go as far as human conditions and relationship will permit. In the enterprises of every country of the world there is all too often a failure to give adequate responsibility to individuals and to make full use of the human resources already in the organization.

Other Problems of Supervisionm The importance of good supervision is implicit in all that has been said, but there are some significant aspects of supervision and human relations yet to be emphasized.

One of the vital concerns of management is how it selects and develops those who are expected to lead others. Studies and experience in the highly industrialized countries suggest the following:

1. Productive supervision requires a person with emotional maturity and stability and a fundamental respect for the dignity and worth of human personality. He must have an interest in working through other people.
2. Supervisors should not be selected on the basis of their technical ability alone or their productivity as individuals. If supervision is an important requirement of the job to be filled, then the successful candidate should possess the qualities necessary to good supervision.
3. Various kinds of aptitude tests have been found useful in weeding out employees who are not intellectually or emotionally suited for supervisory work, but they are only one factor in selection.
4. Classroom training in supervision can improve a supervisor's organization of work in his unit and his intellectual appreciation of the foundations of good human relations, but it is not likely to change his behavior if he is failing through his own emotional shortcomings.

The motives which lead an employee to do his best work are highly individualized. They vary with the nature of the organization, the attitudes of other employees, the period in the organization's history, and the stage in an employee's career. Any form of recognition of an individual for unusual effort must be handled in such a way that cooperation among workers is not jeopardized.

For these and other reasons, the transplanting from one country to another of systems of awards and rewards which have been found successful, both cash and honorary, must be approached with caution.

Success in the use of special awards and recognition of individual merit is more dependent on the qualities of supervision and leadership than on any other condition. Here again, a consciousness of human needs and feelings is the most important consideration.

Senior management in any enterprise must not only motivate its workers but must assure itself that operations are being carried out in accordance with established policy. This is less of a problem where morale is high, but even under the best conditions there must be well-defined methods of inspection.

Where standards and policies have been clearly defined with employee participation, management has a sound basis for the inspection of results. Where it has delegated authority commensurate with individual responsibility and capacity, it can properly inspect production and performance through periodic reports, surveys by staff specialists, statistical controls, fiscal accounting records, and even periodic interviews with key employees and supervisors. Employees up and down the line will welcome inspection procedure and will be accountable when they have been trusted with responsibility which they can understand, when they have something to say about how the work is to be performed, when they are commended for good work, and when they feel that management is interested in their welfare.

Conclusion. This has not been an exhaustive treatment of all the problems and issues of managerial policy and relationships. It endeavors primarily to suggest that an enterprise is most successful when its leadership is thoroughly conscious that its principal means of operation is through human beings and that each of these persons has a will of his own and is entitled to respect for the worth of his individual personality. Testing every management decision and method against this criterion is, in the long run, the simplest approach to enlisting the enthusiasm and cooperation of a working force.

How to Increase the Workers' Role in the Development of Industrial Efficiency. In order to operate with full effectiveness, an undertaking must have, in addition to sufficient financial, material, and managerial resources, a labor force physically and mentally suited to the tasks it has to perform and adequately trained and properly motivated to carry out these tasks well.

The extent to which each of these essential conditions is attained depends on a number of factors, the most important of which, in any country, appears to be the attitude of the employers and top management concerned. However well-qualified and willing the workers themselves may be and however cooperative the governments and trade unions, the initiative lies squarely with the employer, public or private; if he fails to take it, no one else can do so with the same effectiveness. Conversely, the employer or manager with a sound understanding of the problems of getting the best from his personnel and with the will to try may rapidly achieve a high degree of efficiency, even in the case of initially untrained and inexperienced people.

The problems of effective utilization of the abilities of the worker and of achieving satisfactory human relations between employer and employed are far from being solved even in the most industrially advanced countries. In these countries there exist, however, formally organized media of communication between employers and employed, and a considerable body of knowledge has been accumulated on factors affecting informal relationships between management and labor and on the use and development of workers' abilities and skills.

This is not generally the case in underdeveloped areas, although in every country may be found a few enterprises outstandingly managed by men of ability and imagination. Nevertheless, it is in the area of personnel management—in its broadest sense, which includes human relations—that some of the greatest problems of industrial operation in underdeveloped countries occur. Some of these problems relate to the development of labor's capabilities and involve managerial responsibilities for the selection and training of workers; others concern the motivation of employers and employees and involve the responsibility of management for winning the cooperation of its manpower.

Selection and Training of Workers. In very few enterprises in underdeveloped countries is any attempt made at systematic selection or training of workers. In many instances employees are recruited on the basis of a personal relationship or friendship with a supervisor or someone else already employed in the enterprise. Few firms have adopted selection tests. In a limited number of countries schemes for vocational guidance for young people have been put into operation, but the employment situation is often such that they are forced to take the first available opening. In any case, such schemes as exist are generally restricted to a few centers of industry.

In most underdeveloped countries, little formal vocational training in industry is so far provided, and formal apprenticeship in industry as opposed to handicraft is rather the exception than the rule. Where it does exist, apprentices are often treated as laborers or shop boys rather than future workers and are left to their own devices to pick up the skills for their future occupations. Teaching is haphazard and depends on the goodwill and teaching ability of the skilled men with whom they are put to work. While this situation is improving, especially in the larger enterprises, progress is slow because of many deep-rooted obstacles.

One of the obstacles is the attitude of employers. In general, they are not interested in giving their workers formal training, even when this might be provided by technical assistance experts working in their plants, and they may even oppose the setting up of institutes for this purpose. This reluctance appears to arise from a fear that if they train a man he will at once demand higher wages or will leave them for a competitor prepared to offer higher pay. It also seems to arise from ignorance of the nature of industrial skills, of the way in which they are acquired, and of their importance in carrying out manufacturing processes; this ignorance in turn stems from the backgrounds and interests of many employers, which often prompt them to concentrate upon the commercial and financial aspects of industrial operation rather than upon those relating to production. The problem is sometimes complicated by widespread illiteracy and the aversion of literate people to manual labor.

In the countries where they have been established, centers for vocational training of young workers and adults are generally sponsored or assisted by the government. As a rule, the schemes are of limited scope, as regards both the number of trades taught—metal trades are often preferred—and the number of workers trained. The primary aim, at first, is to train instructors who will in turn train staff for other centers or pass on their knowledge when they return to industry. Only in large enterprises is it feasible, occasionally, to provide international experts and instructors to set up and operate special departments for the direct training of operating personnel.

The serious lack of skilled personnel in industry indicates the need for plant managers to train workers in their own plants, using foremen and other skilled workers for that purpose. Unfortunately, the latter are not always capable of transmitting their own knowledge effectively. First aid can be provided in this respect by a training-within-industry job instruction program—a device limited in scope but yielding quick returns. Large-scale training in these programs has been carried out by ILO experts in India, Yugoslavia, Israel, Burma, Pakistan, and other countries.

Experience shows that while employers are reluctant to take part in promoting schemes for vocational training, they are generally willing—at least, the more enlightened among them—to have their workers trained once such schemes have been set up. The problem remains of educating the majority of employers to appreciate the nature of their own requirements for skilled personnel and to overcome their inertia or their reluctance to take the necessary action.

The training of operatives can be appreciably facilitated and the requirements for skilled labor reduced when programs of work simplification are adopted by enterprises. By breaking up complex operations, it is possible to concentrate the efforts of skilled workers on those phases which demand particular skills, so that the tasks that do not call for high qualifications and can be quickly taught can be performed by unskilled or semiskilled workers (for example, handling and transporting). The training time can be reduced by the use of motion studies to simplify the more complex phases of the operations. The training of staff specialists to carry out this work is the special field of activity of productivity missions, productivity centers, and similar organizations, many of which have been set up and assisted by the International Labor Organization.

Motivation. Proper selection and training will enable a worker to develop his capabilities. This, however, is not enough: for an enterprise to be productive, its employees should want to use their capabilities to the full. In industrially advanced countries with adequate numbers of skilled workers in many trades, employers have found that, in addition to being available, labor should be cooperative. Perhaps a more important cause of loss of output than strikes—of which every country has a history—is a conscious policy often practiced by workers of limiting their output, usually because of a fear of rate cutting or of "working themselves out of their jobs." This loss cannot be measured. Sometimes, particularly in the case of piecework, output may be restricted to a level agreed upon among the workers or to a level considered by a worker as sufficient to provide him with a certain income he wants to earn. Considerable loss of output may also be caused by workers who would keep to themselves short cuts or improvements in methods which they have discovered and which, if applied, would raise substantially the productivity of the plant. Over and above the loss due to restrictions, there may often be loss due to excessive scrap or faulty work owing to sheer indifference on the part of the workers to quality requirements.

In industrial countries, conditions may develop in which even enlightened employers fail to enlist the cooperation of their workers; tense relations and industrial strife usually have a long history and are concentrated in particular industries or areas. Most underdeveloped countries have no such histories, and the bulk of their labor force has no industrial tradition, being drawn predominantly from agricultural occupations. Unions are often, though by no means always, weak. Action to develop sound labor-management relations resulting in proper motivation of workers lies squarely on the shoulders of employers and managements. The history of industrial relations in the more advanced countries suggests that unless this opportunity is seized and made use of at the start, industry may have to contend with continuing noncooperative attitudes of labor in an atmosphere of bitterness and suspicion.

The task of convincing managements in underdeveloped countries, including managements of public enterprises, of this important truth is not always easy. The predominantly commercial and financial outlook of many industrialists tends to make them consider labor as just another commodity whose services are to be bought as cheaply as possible. Where the industrialist has a landowning background, he may tend to think of his workers in almost feudal terms, and although he may give them greater recognition as indivduals than employers of other types, he may be prompted to impose his will as a right and to expect unquestioning obedience. Other traditional attitudes stemming from caste or class tend to make relations between managers and workers difficult and distant.

The first impressions which an employee receives of a plant where he is hired may condition his outlook toward his employers for the whole duration of his stay. In most industrially advanced countries, induction procedures have become an accepted technique of personnel management, but in underdeveloped countries little is done except in the few enlightened enterprises to help the new worker adjust himself to his surroundings or to explain to him the workings of the enterprise and his role in it. Yet most countries in the process of industrializing are faced with the problem of integrating into industry workers who hitherto have had no contact with it and have lived in remote rural areas. Although there is some awareness of this problem, it does not seem to have greatly impressed the people most concerned with the issue. Indeed, many employers in underdeveloped countries do not see it at all.

The transition from an agricultural way of life with its varied tasks and self-imposed disciplines to the regimentation of industrial life is usually very abrupt. It is made harder if the worker has to leave his home to live in a city, usually under conditions depriving him of the social satisfactions which would offset the frustration and unhappiness of his working hours. In particular, the move from a small society, in which, poor as he may be, he has a recognized status and is accepted as an individual, into one in which he becomes a mere cipher is likely to set up psychological tensions and to be the cause of deep discontent. The well-known phenomena of high labor turnover, prolonged absenteeism, and occasional apparently irrational acts of violence—which are to be found in industry in underdeveloped countries—may well be caused by failure on the part of both workers and management to provide for a proper adjustment to the new conditions.

Working conditions affect not only the motivation of the worker but his very capacity to do his work. The conditions in most industrial establishments in the countries under discussion, especially in the smaller plants, are such that the worker simply cannot perform with full effectiveness, even if he would. Anybody who has made visits to factories in tropical countries has been able to see workshops with little or no ventilation, weaving sheds wet with live steam, lack of drinking water, and often hopelessly inadequate working space. Workers sit in rows outside the buildings, absenting themselves from the workplace in order to keep cool. Good working conditions are a prerequisite to any attempt to improve methods of work or to install incentive schemes.

A report of the ILO meeting of experts on industrial and human relations lists a number of measures which can be taken to influence relations within the enterprise and to raise morale. Some of these—for instance, incentive schemes—require highly trained staff for their effective application, and steps should be taken in underdeveloped countries to ensure that adequate facilities for training such staff are available. Whatever steps are taken, this should be done in consultation with the workers or their representatives. Consultation at all levels is something which can be undertaken without specially trained staff. Workers in underdeveloped countries have the same basic attitudes as workers anywhere else, and they are more likely to cooperate with management if the reasons for management action are explained to them. An example of this is provided in the report of an expert sent by the International Labor Organization to undertake training in work study and industrial engineering in the transport workshops of a Asian country. It was his constant practice, as a first step, to call together management, supervisors, and workers' representatives and to explain what he proposed to do and why. Before any technical improvements had been introduced in the shops, a marked rise in output became noticeable. Questioned on this, the union secretary stated: "We were enabled to understand the reasons for many things for the first time; we explained these reasons to the workers, and they accepted them where they had formerly been hostile." It is quite possible that in this case the procedure used by the outside expert was successful because he was trusted by the workers. This points to the fact that it is of little use for management to attempt joint consultation unless it is prepared to do so sincerely and is ready to carry out any promises made. Broken promises to workers would permanently impair relations within the undertaking.

Effective motivation depends largely on a proper attitude of top management toward labor and upon the transmission of this attitude through middle management to supervisors. The frequent failure of the training-within-industry job instruction program in many undertakings can be directly traced to the fact that the attitudes and behavior toward subordinates taught to supervisors under this program were not duplicated in the behavior of their own superiors toward them. The fact that enlightened attitudes toward employees yield improved efficiency has been demonstrated by advanced firms in all countries. Unfortunately, in too many cases employers fail to realize this fact or lack the energy to act on it. The failure of Robert Owen over a century ago in Great Britain to convince his fellow employers of the necessity of good management-labor relations is still repeated everywhere today.

Measurement of Management[3]

"Measurement" as consciously applied to management is a new phenomenon. For a long time management was taken to be an "art" pure and simple, the successful application of which depended entirely on the inherent capacity of the person who was entrusted with the job. But with the increasing size and growing complexity of business enterprises, it became necessary to devise tools which would enable management to fulfill its role by methods other than purely personal knowledge and observation. The scientific method came to be applied to the problems of management and this naturally led to an attempt at using objective and precise criteria for helping and judging the performance of management. This was especially so because the management function in a modern business enterprise came to be exercised by different persons operating at different levels and in different capacities, instead of by a single person as in the past. The separation of ownership and operational management required the owners to perform the function of selecting managerial personnel and judging their efficiency of operation. The actual management itself was too complicated to be carried out by any one person on his own. The head of the management organization had to delegate many management functions to subordinates specialized in particular functions or individual parts of the whole enterprise; and such delegation led to the creation of multiple tiers in the management hierarchy. This made it necessary for the higher level of management to lay down definite objectives for the lower levels to pursue and to try to assess how far these objectives were being effectively attained. All this has necessitated the increasing use of "measurement of management."

The criteria for measuring management efficiency can be broadly divided into two categories:

1. General indices, which are based on a money measure and provide some overall index of efficiency.
2. Particular indices, which would indicate efficiency in regard to a particular part of the enterprise or the use of a particular input.

Profitability. The criterion that is most easily and obviously applied is that of the "profitability" of the enterprise. In private enterprise this criterion is almost the only one used by shareholders, because their basic motive in investing their money is to participate in the profits of the enterprise. Therefore they ultimately judge the efficiency of the management that they have set up by the profits that it has been able to make on their behalf. Of course it is true that shareholders may not judge efficiency of management entirely by measuring the profits made in a particular year so much as by assessing the profit possibilities as developed by the management over a period of time, yet the basic importance of the criterion remains.

It is obvious that the profit made by an enterprise will depend con-

[3] From "Public Industrial Management in Asia and the Far East," 1960, pp. 30–36, 136–138.

siderably on the price policy it pursues. Unless there is considerable competition in the market for its products, prices will be determined to a considerable extent not automatically in the market but by the deliberate policy of the producer. If maximization of profits is the only objective set by the enterprise, and if it is permitted to pursue it, then the rate of net profit may be high; if there is some governmental regulation of prices, the rate of profit is likely to be lower; and if the main objective is not to make profit but to ensure supply of the product at a price which sometimes may even be lower than cost, the net profit may be either negligible or nonexistent. It is obvious that in such instances profitability is not a useful measure of management efficiency. It may further be mentioned that the usefulness of this measure will depend very much upon appropriate provision for meeting all costs, including proper depreciation.

Cost Reduction. In public industrial enterprises where the maximization of profit is not the objective, a good alternative to the measure of profitability may be that of cost reduction. This would also be a general measure covering the whole enterprise. If standard norms regarding the cost of production are laid down for all the main products of the enterprise, the efficiency of management could be judged by the management's success in keeping actual costs within these limits. Obviously the extent to which this will be a useful measure will depend upon the care with which the norms are set up. If they are based purely on historical costs, they may provide only a very rough measure of management efficiency. Even so, cost norms based on historical costs may have to be used in the earlier stages of an enterprise before other norms based on detailed study are built up, as this latter process may take time. Some experience regarding the actual working of the enterprise will have to be available before they are possible. If prices of most inputs remain at the same level, such norms will provide a rough basis for measuring efficiency; even if prices are fluctuating, costs at fixed prices of inputs can be specially calculated to provide a basis for comparison. There are usually some reserves in any production process which can enable an efficient management to improve upon its performance. Therefore the success of management can to a certain extent be judged fairly by its capacity to reduce costs below the norms established on the basis of previous history. The difficulty is that as management succeeds in utilizing these reserves and thus eliminating waste, such efforts will yield progressively diminishing returns, especially as year after year the norms themselves will be brought down according to the cost levels actually attained. If cost reduction as compared to cost norms historically established is to be the sole measure of management efficiency and every achievement in cost reduction is to lead to a further lowering of norms, management may be induced not to achieve too much cost reduction in any given year.

Therefore while cost norms based on purely historical data may be useful at the beginning, an early attempt should be made to calculate standard costs for the various inputs, based on a proper study of the processes of production. The general cost norms will then be a total of these with allowance for overhead. Obviously this will mainly serve the purpose of providing a general measure of overall management for the benefit of the external controlling authority. The itemized standard costs will be more useful for measuring efficiency for the purpose of bringing about improvements.

An important disadvantage of any overall measure of efficiency, like profitability or cost reduction, is that in a complex undertaking where a number of different products are produced and there are a large number of constituent parts of the undertaking the overall measure may conceal the state of efficiency or inefficiency of particular sections of the enterprise. This indicates the necessity for maintaining separate accounts for the different parts of the undertaking.

Internal Norms. The measurement of management should also provide criteria by which the higher management of a production unit will be able to check on the operational efficiency of the operating units under its control and to indicate the correctives necessary to improve their efficiency.

For this purpose a large number of norms, standards, and so on will have to be evolved, suited to the needs of the particular production unit. By detailed study of operations, a series of norms regarding input-output relations can be laid down for every workshop, for various definable parts of a workshop, and to a certain extent for small groups of workers or even individual workers. The setting up of such norms is obviously a complicated problem. Technical studies will help in setting standards regarding the use of raw materials, power, spare parts, and so on. Setting those for labor utilization will be a more complicated task. It will require studies regarding the whole process of production, the flow of material, division of operations, and the manner and technique of carrying out various processes. It will also require a considerable degree of cooperation from the personnel operating at various levels. The man with the stopwatch has been a hated figure in many industrial units, and unless management takes care to see that the workers are able to take a positive attitude toward such a study of operations, the study may be difficult to organize. It has now been accepted that it is necessary for management to take the workers into its confidence and obtain their consent if labor norms are effectively to be set up and used for improving efficiency.

Organizational Problems. In using the various methods detailed above for measurement of management, a prerequisite is the setting up of proper organizational machinery for establishing norms, for revising them on the basis of experience gained, and for judging to what extent the norms have been satisfied in actual operation. One type of organization will be mainly technological. The suppliers to the plant may provide certain criteria about utilization of raw materials and so on. Technological research by a special organization in the industry will have to go further into these problems so as to find out better ways of improving technical efficiency and then to set up ways of judging whether these methods are being followed. A production unit will also need to organize a work study department for setting standards of labor utilization and for conducting studies regarding operations and flow of material. The necessity for a cost accounting department in production units no longer needs to be emphasized. Financial audit has, it is now accepted, not only the purpose of ensuring that there is no misappropriation of resources but also that there is proper provision for depreciation, that all the costs which should be met from revenue are included in the profit and loss accounts, that there is an appropriate allocation of common costs as between different activities, and so on. Obviously this would be principally the task of what is called "internal audit" and would require internal organizations to be set up by higher management for the purpose of providing it with these measurements for efficiency.

It should be pointed out that if the laying down of these various criteria and the general use of measurement of management are to be effective in improving efficiency, this cannot be done merely by exhorting management at various levels to attain the objectives laid down. It is true that when definite quantitative criteria exist for judging management efficiency, management will try to show good performance, as it will know that these criteria provide definite and precise indications of the extent to which it succeeds or fails. But unless the controlling authority is to rely entirely on the weapon of removal, which is obviously an instrument to be used rarely and with great care, various types of incentive will have to be devised and effectively applied to emphasize the importance of attaining the objectives laid down. If monetary awards of various types are related to the satisfactory attainment of such objectives, the objectives themselves will come to have a much greater and more obvious significance to the personnel operating in the enterprise. All those concerned should be given a clear picture of the criteria by which their efficiency will be judged, and fairly regular information should be supplied to them as to their actual attainments. If proper methods are used to publicize norms and actual attainments, this may provide a healthy basis for competition among various operation elements in the enterprise; it might create greater interest in the fulfillment of norms.

Use of Modern Accounting Systems. Management accounting, involving the analysis, tabulation, and presentation of data arising from economic activity in an enterprise, includes the processes formerly known as financial, historical, or conventional accounting, budgetary control, cost accounting, material and stores accounting, and internal audit. The modern concept of accounting has adopted a forward-looking approach instead of a backward-facing philosophy and is very much concerned in evaluation of the predetermined plan by using available statistical and accounting information to compare the result of actual performance with that expected, both in quantitative and financial terms. The variations from the standards or targets initially set are studied and possible corrective measures indicated. This comparison of "promise" with "performance" has been further developed to concentrate mainly on exceptional deviations, and this is often referred to as "control by exception."

Speed and frequency of preparation of financial reports is particularly important even at the sacrifice of absolute accuracy, as management is vitally concerned with knowing trends of results quickly, rather than having to wait for more accurate results. There is a need regularly to review the types, frequency, and effective use of reports, and top management, in particular, must not be overloaded with too much or too detailed information.

Appraisal of Performance. Appraisal of measurement of performance of an enterprise is a team effort, but the effectiveness of appraisal depends on suitable diagnosis of statistical and accounting data, particularly by using budgetary control and cost accounting techniques. In this connection, accounting must be regarded as a service to management and not as an executive function; the accountant must form part of the whole team of management if the best results are to be achieved.

There appears to be a need for a regular review of the methods of appraisal to check their effectiveness or utility. Further, the cost of accounting and reporting must not outweigh its usefulness in any enterprise. No level of management should be expected to account for results which are beyond its control; methods of responsibility, accounting, and direct costing may be needed.

Interim methods can be evolved to enable management to receive certain essential accounting information. For example, it is possible for cash receipts and payments to be compared with a cash budget; attention can be paid to control of credit and review of current assets and current liabilities, especially levels of cash, stocks, work in progress, and so on. If possible, estimated production statements should be compiled, as estimated figures are better than none at all. Much valuable statistical information is usually available and can be used for measuring performance.

The need to give priority to the maintenance of current records, in preference to arrears, is particularly important, so that recent accounting data are available to management in order to enable it to make decisions from day to day.

One way to improve accounting techniques is by employing consulting firms or advisers to review present accounting systems and to recommend and install new systems suitable to the particular enterprise. These need not be elaborate but should be designed to fulfill the requirement of each case. The possibility of effective use of mechanized accounting might be explored, particularly as this can often result in speedy and more accurate production of necessary figures.

Management Controls[4]

Management controls referred to in this section include financial or historical accounting, budgetary control, cost accounting, stores accounting and material control, and internal or management audit.

In larger enterprises, basic control information is generally available. Most of these concerns maintain a well-developed accounting organization and have fully qualified accounting staffs. However, in public enterprises, accounting methods and records are sometimes patterned upon procedures in use in the administrative agencies of the government, and these are not always suited to the purposes of industry. Medium-sized enterprises generally maintain a system of financial accounting and—to a lesser extent—some cost accounting and control procedures, supplementing their accounting staff when necessary with occasional outside professional help, for example, for the preparation of annual financial statements. In small-scale enterprises it is unusual for even a minimum system of accounting to be kept.

There is a tendency on the part of the average manager to rely mainly on

[4] From "Management of Industrial Enterprises in Underdeveloped Countries," 1958, pp. 29–31, passim.

financial accounting and to overlook the value of proper integration of costing and financial accounts, which would considerably increase the usefulness of the accounting system as a whole. In many cases it is not realized that greater use could be made even of financial accounting for purposes of management control, particularly in smaller enterprises, which, because of their limited resources, cannot always afford the expense of more elaborate cost records. To serve that purpose, financial accounts would have to be compiled at regular intervals and made available as soon as possible after the end of the accounting period. They would need to be set up in such a way as to make comparable the data for corresponding periods.

There is also considerable room for improvement in the use of budget techniques for control purposes. To that end management should be educated in the necessity of planning ahead and translating the plans into financial terms, of keeping under continuous review the comparison of the actual with the planned results and the reasons for any discrepancies. It would also appear that enterprises in underdeveloped countries would greatly benefit by developing materials control accounting.

The foregoing raises an important point, namely, that in addition to developing the accounting basis for controls it is necessary for management to make effective use of the control information thus provided. Many enterprises maintain accounting records largely to comply with the requirements of tax legislation or of credit institutions. Professional organizations of accountants—in countries where they exist—perform an extremely valuable task by bringing home to management of enterprises the potentialities offered by the proper use of accounting information. Cases can be cited of enterprises going to considerable trouble and expense in setting up elaborate accounting systems, with little regard to the practical usefulness of the information for purposes of management control.

The effectiveness of the control is clearly related to the general organization of the enterprise. In particular, proper delegation and definition of functions and circulation of relevant information to all levels of management are essential prerequisites. Top management should not be overburdened with detailed control data while the needs of lower-echelon management for information on costs, sales, and procurement relevant to the performance of their duties remain unsatisfied because little or no control information reaches their level. It should be noted in this connection that information provided by the accounting system is also a useful device for training lower-echelon personnel, as well as for measuring their performance. It gives them a better appreciation of their role in the activities of the firm as a whole and makes possible a more rational approach to operational problems.

An important factor in the effectiveness of the control system is the relationship of the accountant to other members of the management team. For technical and accounting personnel better to appreciate one another's problems, closer cooperation between them is necessary. This might be achieved by means of frequent staff meetings and discussions at various management levels. A better understanding of the value of accounting controls might be achieved if engineers and technical personnel were encouraged to familiarize themselves with the principles of cost accounting and budgeting.

As to the supply of professional skill in accounting, large-scale enterprises are generally able to set up accounting systems either by recruiting senior accounting personnel from abroad or by training nationals in foreign countries. For smaller enterprises, the situation is generally less satisfactory, and the provision of accounting services to this category of enterprise is an urgent need. It is suggested that the governments of underdeveloped countries make the fullest use of international assistance facilities in this field, and that accounting services should be considered one of the key functions of the management service institutes referred to earlier. It should be the role of these institutes to assist small and medium-sized enterprises in introducing and using modern accounting methods; they should also promote, and assist in, training of local personnel.

Selection of Plant and Machinery[5]

Some of the operational difficulties experienced by industrial enterprises are due to the selection of plant and machinery not properly suited to the conditions of underdeveloped countries; sufficient care is not taken at the outset to ensure that the size of the plant is commensurate with the potential market and yet is sufficiently large to ensure economic cost of production. National pride has occasionally led to some of these enterprises being made into expensive showpieces. In other instances, the plant is basically too small to produce manufactured goods at competitive prices. Another common failing is the tendency to buy the most modern and automatic machinery available in Western countries, overlooking the fact that such plant may not be appropriate in countries where labor is cheap but lacks technical skill and operating experience. While it is essential that modern and up-to-date machinery should be purchased, it is no less important to ensure that the plant is suitable for the climatic and other conditions of the countries of southern Asia and the Far East. Since most of these countries are short of foreign exchange but have an abundant labor supply, it may be advantageous to utilize labor-intensive rather than capital-intensive plant and machinery. The saving in wages resulting from the use of highly automatic machinery in the United States and Western Europe is frequently offset in underdeveloped countries by the high initial capital cost of the equipment and the practical difficulties experienced in operating the plant with comparatively uneducated and unskilled workers. In most of these countries, it may be preferable to utilize less automatic but well-tried machinery which can be easily operated and maintained by the workers and foremen normally available in newly industrialized countries.

A further precaution in the case of large factories is the provision of adequate workshops where necessary repairs can be carried out and where it may be possible to fabricate simple parts and other equipment needed in an emergency. Numerous cases have been reported where publicly owned factories have stopped production for want of relatively inexpensive equipment or spare parts. On the other hand, one must also avoid building up large inventories of stores, as this results in the unnecessary locking up of capital and is reflected in high overhead costs. It is here that technical knowledge and

[5] From "Public Industrial Management in Asia and the Far East," 1960, pp. 40–41.

operating experience prove most useful in ensuring adequate provision of essential requirements without excessive outlays of working capital.

Management of Production Facilities and Quality Control[6]

Management of Production Facilities. This covers some of the more important areas of industrial management, in which basic decisions are made on such problems as plant capacity and selection of equipment and plant design, as well as on the organization and supervision of current operations. Some of these problems involve long-term commitments incurred prior to the start of operations; others deal with current planning and control of production. The two sets of problems are closely related and affect the results of the enterprise.

Design and Utilization of Equipment. A well-known aspect of the problem of the transfer of technology to underdeveloped countries is the need for adapting processes and equipment developed in industrialized countries to the local environment. Experts in the field have cited instances of production equipment which is well suited to the needs of industrialized countries but whose performance fails to measure up to expectations in the industrial environment of underdeveloped countries. The problem seldom arises in the case of large-scale industrial operations, since technical processes, including plant design, are fairly standardized in this type of operation. However, even in such cases, a certain flexibility exists in the design of equipment for some ancillary operations, for example, materials handling. By making such operations more labor-intensive, substantial savings in capital might be achieved. In view of the scarcity of capital resources in newly industrializing countries in relation to their needs, detailed studies of appropriate factor proportions, dealing with the possible combinations of capital and labor in major industrial processes, would appear to be extremely useful.

The problem of equipment specially designed to meet the conditions of underdeveloped countries does, however, frequently arise in small-scale industries. There are generally few prototype plants in industrialized countries, and even when available, they may often be too complex to operate and maintain in less developed countries. In purchasing equipment the small entrepreneur is not always in a position to exercise his own judgment—as, for instance, in the case of a changeover to more mechanized operations involving a different level of competence. He can also seldom afford outside paid advice and has to rely on the advice of importers or manufacturers' agents, who may not necessarily be objective. There is, therefore, a real need for the provision of competent engineering advice on design and procurement of equipment for small-scale industry.

It also appears desirable to collect and disseminate, on a systematic basis, engineering and economic data on equipment in a certain number of industries.

In the design of plant for small-scale industry, it is sometimes found that major economies, or better and more uniform quality, can be realized if a particular step is carried out on a large scale. Where a complicated and

[6] From "Management of Industrial Enterprises in Underdeveloped Countries," 1958, pp. 17–24, passim; William R. Pabst, Jr., "Use of Statistical Quality Control in the Industry of Underdeveloped Countries," in *Industrialization and Productivity*, Bulletin 3, March, 1960, pp. 56–58.

expensive piece of equipment is required for a certain purpose, or other facilities are found to be necessary which are beyond the means of a single plant, a possible solution would be the establishment of common facility services, for instance, using the device of industrial estates—a well-known feature of the organization of small-scale industry in some countries.

As another problem in design of plant, it may be noted that plants are sometimes designed to meet existing demand and fail to take advantage of potential opportunities for economies, either in scale or by the application of improved techniques, where an expanding market for the industry's output could reasonably be anticipated. Conversely, the minimum size for economic operation may be such that the establishment of a plant is not warranted by the existing or foreseeable demand for the product. Thus, studies of the relationship between size of plant and investment and cost of production in given industries appear to be an important field of investigation for the purposes of both industry programming and investment decisions of individual enterprises.

Attention should also be focused on the problem of improving the rate of utilization of existing equipment, the importance of which as a "capital-saving" device in underdeveloped countries need hardly be stressed. One approach to this problem would be through the use of methods of work study. These methods make it possible to analyze machine utilization and to set standards of labor output and plant utilization on which production programs may be based.

Another way of improving the rate of utilization of equipment is to increase the hours worked by machines, either through the use of overtime or by the device of multiple shifts. In this regard, it is recognized that certain economic and social factors are involved, as well as purely technical considerations. Thus, in some newly industrializing countries, many workers would be reluctant to engage in night work; this applies especially to the more recent arrivals who have not yet adapted to industrial work discipline. The introduction of night shifts may be further hampered by inadequate public services and lack of other facilities, such as urban transportation and meals. Problems of a social nature also arise. For all these reasons, the introduction of multiple-shift operations represents a complex problem, the solution of which involves cooperation between management, labor, and public authorities.

Seen from the cost point of view of the individual enterprise, the introduction of additional shifts might be expected to lead to higher labor costs. Higher rates of pay, or bonuses based on regular attendance, would be necessary to attract labor to night-shift work, and the required plant facilities to accommodate additional shifts would be a further source of expenditure. Nevertheless, it is considered that the additional cost might be more than offset by savings resulting from better utilization of equipment.

Raw Materials. One source of difficulty in industrial production in underdeveloped countries is the poor and uneven quality—and sometimes the uncertain supply of raw materials. The poor quality is often due to the primitive methods of production and production control prevailing in the primary producing industries. Irregularity of supply is largely the result of poorly organized markets and defective distribution, including transport and storage facilities. Industrial efficiency suffers from both these factors as regards the establishment and maintenance of proper quality standards in production and regular production schedules. Enterprises often attempt to overcome the deficiencies in the supply situation by keeping high inventories of raw materials, requiring considerable outlays of working capital and expensive storage facilities. This leads, in the last analysis, to higher cost of production.

The attention of governments is also drawn to the fact that manufacturing activities are, in some cases, seriously hampered by indiscriminately applied restrictions on imports of raw materials and uncertainties as to future government policies in the matter of such imports. Abrupt shifts in foreign sources of supply, which may be dictated by exchange policies, also often have a disruptive effect upon production and create serious problems of management. It is considered that, even in stringent exchange situations, a more flexible policy might be justified for certain imported materials which, while being used in small amounts, thus involving an insignificant outlay in foreign exchange, are nevertheless key components of the manufacturing process whose elimination would greatly affect the quality of the final product. Dyes for textiles and certain alloys for castings are examples of such materials.

Quality Control: Use of Specifications and Standards. There are several factors responsible for the often inferior quality of manufactured goods in underdeveloped countries. One of these is the use of defective raw materials, noted above. Another is that the goods are produced with inadequate, obsolete, or worn-out equipment. The related problem of inadequate maintenance is reflected in poor performance of the machinery. The final factor is the extent to which management is prepared to enforce a rigorous system of quality control throughout the production process.

Industry standards in regard to quality control are generally low. Even where they exist, they are usually limited to the finished product stage, and little or no effort is made to control the intermediary stages. As regards larger enterprises, the adoption of higher quality standards in production is related to the improvement in the general quality of management. No specific suggestions appear to be indicated on the enterprise level, except perhaps to draw the attention of management to the importance of the problem. On the national level, the adoption of standard specifications would greatly facilitate the task of management in introducing quality control techniques into their plants.

The problem of specifications and standards is closely related to quality control. In some countries, while no formal national standards exist, some specifications are used in industry, based on makeshift arrangements or on norms developed by a few large, well-known firms. In some cases foreign standards, known through imports, come to be adapted in the course of time. The multiplicity of standards originating from different sources may introduce a degree of confusion and is often a source of annoyance to producers and users alike. Uniform quality specifications would greatly facilitate quality control and simplify many production problems. They would also facilitate marketing and distribution and increase the confidence of consumers in the products of industry. Standardization would be particularly helpful in promoting exports. Finally, it is considered that the enforcement of uniform standards would be an important step toward reducing excessive diversification of products—a well-known weakness in most underdeveloped countries and a source of inefficiency and waste that industry can ill afford.

There appears, however, to be some difference of opinion as to the advisability of establishing standards at an early stage of industrialization. Extensive and careful experimentation with materials and products and long experience in use are often required before standards can be established. Standardization would also have to be approached with considerable caution in situations where consumer tastes are in a state of flux. It is likely that the need for standards would be felt first of all in producer goods industries, in consumer goods industries serving organized markets, such as textiles, and in export industries.

It is considered that practical action should preferably be undertaken by the industries directly concerned. The prevailing practice is for standardization institutes to be established by the respective industries, with the assistance of engineering societies and with active support from governments. The institutes coordinate and direct the technical work, including research, and are also active as clearance centers for information on standardization work conducted internationally. They perform a particularly useful task in promoting "standards consciousness" among manufacturing enterprises and an awareness of the problem among the public.

Maintenance and Repair of Equipment. Industrial maintenance has two aspects: preventive maintenance and repair. The former involves periodic inspection of equipment and facilities for such upkeep as inspection indicates; the latter involves repair after breakdown. Because of inadequate maintenance, industry in many underdeveloped countries suffers from an unduly high rate of depletion of capital assets and a chronic waste of productive capacity which even economically stronger countries could hardly afford. As regards preventive maintenance, it is found by many technical assistance experts that, in some industries, this tends to be neglected to the point where equipment breaks down and has to be replaced. Many instances are also reported where, because of poor preventive maintenance, the consumption of spare parts is excessively high, necessitating considerable outlay of foreign exchange for replacement.

In many cases the lack of attention to preventive maintenance is caused by neglect or indifference to this problem on the part of management. There may be unwillingness to engage in an expense which does not appear to yield immediate returns, and there is often a tendency to consider the maintenance department as an unnecessary burden upon the enterprise.

In so far as poor maintenance is a matter of attitude, this could be overcome by a process of education which would also encourage management to make every possible use of outside advice on, and assistance in, introducing sound maintenance practices. There may be, however, a less subjective reason, such as shortages of skilled maintenance labor and technicians. This could be remedied, in the short run, by the use of trained personnel from abroad, who would train local personnel. A longer-run approach to the problem is the setting up of adequate training facilities for maintenance personnel.

Another important factor in maintenance is the problem of spare parts. Management is not always fully aware of the necessity for carrying adequate inventories of spare parts. In many cases, however, the fault also lies with a too rigid application of import controls by the exchange authorities. In importing new equipment, enterprises often experience difficulties in obtaining additional exchange for spare parts. Instances have been cited by technical assistance experts in the field of new factories being set up without a single spare part in stock.

In many countries, the spare parts situation is aggravated by the fact that existing physical plant is extremely heterogeneous as regards age, type, and country of origin. This makes procurement of parts a complex and, in the case of obsolescent equipment, an impossible task. In this connection, it is suggested that an effort should be made by industry to standardize basic equipment as much as possible, as far as its origin is concerned. It is recognized, however, that this is a slow process which also involves the active cooperation of the public authorities with respect to their import control policies.

The problem of repair has two aspects: capacity of plant repair shops and availability of trained personnel. Because outside facilities are often inadequate and spare parts and equipment difficult and slow to obtain, plant repair shops are often engaged in production of replacement parts and even in duplicating complete pieces of equipment, and, particularly in the large enterprises, elaborate mechanical facilities are set up at considerable investment expense. From a rational point of view, this often represents duplication and poor utilization of scarce investment resources; from the point of view of the individual enterprise, establishment of costly facilities is reflected in high production costs. On the whole, the situation illustrates the effects of inadequate external economies upon the economics of industry. Training in maintenance involves both inculcating sound maintenance principles in managers and teaching correct practices and procedures to technical and operative personnel.

A possible solution to the repair problems of small-scale enterprises might be the establishment of central or pooled maintenance shops serving the needs of several cooperating plants. Central maintenance units of this kind could be established in close proximity to the plants and could be equipped to manufacture parts, if necessary, in addition to providing facilities for repair work. It is suggested that the establishment of pooled repair facilities might be considered within the framework of the industrial estates to which reference was made earlier.

Introducing Quality Control in a Plant. Once management is convinced of the value of quality control, the question arises of how to introduce it. How should a quality control section be organized and staffed? Should some simple problems be tackled first so that the success achieved would stimulate more difficult endeavors? Should quality control charts be made for every machine and process? To all these questions, the answer is that any of these approaches might be appropriate under given circumstances, bearing in mind that there is no easy way to bring into any plant, whatever its size, what is essentially a revolutionary procedure. Psychological obstacles and technical limitations are to be reckoned with—for example, fear of innovations, and difficulties of communicating with those who may be affected by the changes and of having to train or retrain people. A rather extended period of time is normally required before a new system is established and accepted. Quality control cannot be simply added to an enterprise; if it is to be effective, changes must be introduced in basic organization concepts and methods.

The problem of how to introduce a quality control system was probed by the author in a review of about one hundred plants in some thirty different industries in India. In nearly all cases the objective was to present to management a practical course of action divided into convenient steps, each of which could be implemented in one or two months. In all the industries considered, with the exception of jute and cotton manufacturing, the following five steps which provide, in a sense, a check list of those areas in which the greatest gains can be achieved, were proposed as a normal order of procedure:

1. Measure outgoing quality.
2. Determine scrap and rework rates.
3. Assess utilization of machinery and equipment.
4. Evaluate incoming materials.
5. Establish a quality control framework.

In the case of cotton and jute, step 3—study of utilization of machinery—appears to be the most effective first step because immediate gains in spinning and weaving efficiency can thereby be quite easily won.

Step 1: Measure Outgoing Quality. In nearly all the companies surveyed, the first step in initiating quality control was the development of a means of measuring product quality in relation to the desired specification and to consumer needs and wishes. The reason for this is twofold. First, this provides management with information useful in comparing present quality both with that achieved in the past and that obtained in similar facilities; second, the final product reflects the influence of all the process factors in the plant. In making chairs, sewing machines, fans, soaps, jute and cotton textiles, shoes, and in nearly every other instance, the first question is whether the final product meets both the customer's and the firm's standards of quality and cost. Quality control investigation will show to what extent this is the case and will indicate which process factors must be dealt with to improve the product and reduce its costs.

Measuring outgoing quality is not a simple thing. First, standards of product must be developed or made explicit, and methods for determining product quality must be evolved. A usual procedure is to make a classification of defects, grading the types of departure from specifications or objectives according to their importance. This must be properly engineered in order to reflect a correct evaluation of the material. The point at which final product quality can be determined must also be considered. For instance, in many industries, as in the manufacture of chairs and office equipment, the final coat of paint may hide objectionable details, so that, to express a final quality judgment, examination should be made before and after painting. "Acceptance sampling" methods are particularly appropriate for evaluating the outgoing product, since accurate examination of a few items is more important than casual inspection of large numbers; routine inspection is normally inadequate for the accurate measurement of outgoing quality.

While it is important to measure outgoing quality, it is equally important to determine how good the measure is. What is needed is a measure of quality that is invariant as between inspectors and invariable over time, so as to minimize errors. Very often the error among the inspectors is greater than the variation of the material on which they are working. Like any gauging or measuring process, an inspection evaluation is not proper or useful until the error of measurement is small relative to the variability of the objects being measured. It is not unusual to find screening inspection less than 50 percent efficient, as shown above in the cases of the glass and jute industries. Many techniques are available to resolve these differences, the direct experiment being foremost.

Step 2: Determine Scrap and Rework Rates. Whether or not product quality is satisfactory, the existence of scrap and rework justifies the introduction of quality control. The rate of scrap should be measured and classified by cause, as in the case of defective products at the stage of final product quality evaluation. Scrap is usually encountered at intermediate stages of the process, as a result of improper casting, improper machine setting, and many other causes. It is usually possible to determine from technical sources the causes of all possible types of scrap. Grading can then be introduced to determine those phases in the process where stronger controls are needed. These phases may sometimes be revealed by use of control charts, frequency distributions, and other devices. When causes cannot be easily determined, it may be necessary to resort to direct experiments as a preliminary step.

Some scrap is unavoidable, and its minimum amount may be determined by engineering methods or by comparison with similar operations either within the plant or in similar industries. The way scrap is disposed of sometimes hides its nature and its magnitude. In the case of "stuck" plates in a pottery plant, nothing can be done except to dispose of the material by dumping or destroying it, while molds rejected before baking and glazing can be reused as raw material. In soap plants, rough cakes rejected at the cutting stage go back into the vats as raw material. The volume of "return" or "rework" is seldom considered as important as that of material actually discarded, although it does involve costly labor, machine, and plant time. A considerable volume of rework must be scrutinized with the same care as actual scrap in order to achieve the most efficient processing.

Step 3: Assess Utilization of Machinery and Equipment. Relatively simple quality control methods are available for measuring the rate of machine utilization. The method commonly used, known as the "ratio delay method" of sampling or "snap-check reading," consists of noting or recording the number of machines or other equipment which are not in operation at the time the observer passes by. A given number of observations may be made per day at random time-intervals, and a summary of these sample observations, as provided in a control chart, gives quite readily a measure of the percentage of machines in operation.

This method can be used, for instance, to measure the rate of utilization of machine tools in a light machinery manufacturing plant or of typewriters in an office. It is used extensively in cotton and jute mills to provide a rapid measure of the efficiency of the spinning or weaving department by counting the number of "ends down," the number of individual spindles on which the thread is broken, or the number of looms stopped.

Such measurements of machinery utilization should be supplemented by information as to the causes of stoppage. These can be catalogued, and the stopped machines can then be denoted by cause by a system of code numbers. In some textile mills snap-check studies have been used to compare the causes of stoppage in a certain number of the most productive looms with those in a corresponding number of the least productive ones. Differential studies of this kind provide the basis for remedial action to raise the level of output of the more inefficient machinery, whether by training machine operators, improving maintenance or repair procedures, providing better facilities for handling material, installing better lighting, or adopting any of the numerous other measures which influence productivity.

Step 4: Evaluate Incoming Materials. Quality control methods are useful for controlling the quality of incoming raw materials and purchased parts. Raw materials control may be relatively complex in some cases, such as that of jute manufacturing, where the level of spinning and weaving efficiency determines in large part the necessary raw materials mix. Consistent with color and grade conditions, cheaper raw materials may be used provided that these can be spun without undue loss in processing efficiency. Control charts relating raw material costs to spinning or weaving efficiency may contribute toward achieving a controlled situation in which raw material and processing costs would be best combined by introducing certain changes in the raw materials used. It is sometimes possible to have a pilot line in which raw material mixes can be tried in actual practice, but even if this is used, formal quality control methods would still provide a better basis for decision making. Control charts employing correlation theory are important in such instances.

Step 5: Establish a Quality Control Framework. The last and probably the most important objective of a quality control survey in a plant is the setting up of an organization for solving quality control problems. Such an organization may vary from a sizable group in a large plant to a few people working possibly part time in a small establishment; regardless of its size, it must enjoy direct management support and interest. In a small concern, the best way of introducing quality control is to train its management. In the author's experience, nearly all managers who attended training courses were able to initiate effective programs in their own enterprises. The manager's subordinates collected the necessary information, and the manager himself scrutinized and interpreted it. Success achieved in solving one problem led to the tackling of another, and little by little relatively effective quality control measures were introduced throughout the plant. A manager of a shoe factory who was satisfied with the quality of his production undertook, after the completion of his training, a final product evaluation which revealed, to his astonishment, that in spite of thorough inspection of partly finished and final products, more than 10 percent of the latter failed to meet specifications. This led him to take the necessary steps in the tanning process and in the cutting procedures to attain a controlled process within specifications. Where quality control functions are entrusted to a team not immediately connected with management, it should enjoy an independent status and should not be under direct supervision of those whose efforts it is trying to evaluate. When quality control is entrusted to an operating division of a company, it is usually unable to deal effectively with major quality problems and is reduced to a routine application of techniques. The same situation sometimes occurs when, for instance, quality control is introduced by the owners of a plant without first winning the confidence and support of the managerial personnel. To be successful, a program of quality control should win a minimum degree of cooperation from both supervisory staff and labor. It is their operations that are to be examined and improved. This may have major effects upon their jobs and earnings, and to avoid suspicion and opposition what is being done should be explained by management and accepted by those concerned.

TECHNICAL ASSISTANCE, AGRICULTURAL DEVELOPMENT, AND INNOVATION

Stanley Andrews

Introduction

At the end of 1962, more than forty thousand people were carrying out technical assistance assignments in some 109 countries of the world. Fully two-fifths to one-half of that number were directly concerned with agricultural development and with industrial phases of development, irrigation, fertilizer manufacturing, processing, and transportation directly related to agriculture. This vast army of technical personnel came from or operated under the sponsorship and support of the United States government, other governments such as that of France, with some twenty thousand personnel engaged abroad in technical services, international and private banks, the International Development Bank, United Nations specialized agencies, private business groups, foundations, and missionary societies. More than two thousand of these experts involved in agricultural development came from the United States. Their assignments ranged all the way from teaching an Indian on the Alto Plano in Bolivia how to make a better hitch of his oxen to a five-inch plow to the use of isotopes in agricultural research to detect fertilizer absorption by a plant. Estimates developed from a conference of international experts on personnel needs in technical assistance in all phases meeting in Rome in 1962 predicted that the number of agricultural experts needed would be doubled and possibly tripled in ten years. The successful introduction of a simple innovation in agricultural production, for example, usually sets off a chain reaction which requires more and more technical services and new categories of personnel qualified in the new services which such innovation develops.

Mr. Andrews is a consultant and agricultural expert.

Early in the Point Four program of the United States government, a certain South American nation wanted to explore the possibility of cereal grain production in the interior of the country. Two top-flight wheat-seed breeding and production experts requested by the country were sent. It was quickly determined that a high-producing variety of wheat could be successfully grown. Seed was developed, tractor stations to break the new lands were laid out and manned, training and maintenance depots were established, and local technicians were trained to operate the machinery and installations. Wheat was grown in abundance. However, the area is subject to heavy rain squalls, and wheat must be kept under cover in good warehouses or it spoils. Distributive and marketing systems in the country were based on handling grain from the ports to the inland, not from the inland to the ports. There were no local buyers, and no government machinery to buy, store, transport, and process this wheat. A project brilliant in its initial stages became a first-rate headache. Dozens of additional experts, vast added expenditures of money, and extensive transportation, distributive, and processing facilities were required before the initial innovation paid off. As countries learn the value of fertilizer, they will have to learn how to make it, distribute it, and provide either through private or government channels the credit and the facilities for the complete job. In many instances "super-specialists" will have to be employed, such as the man recently required to work with Thailand to develop a variety of rice which would respond to the use of fertilizer in the soils of Thailand, where the traditional rice varieties in that country would not respond.

Every day someone makes a list of the qualities which are required of the successful innovator—the man who has accepted the challenge and somehow come out along with the host country without a disaster of some kind. These check lists for evaluation are backed by no real empirical data with which to judge either the man or the factors involved in the success or failure of the innovation. Indeed, there is scarcely any unanimity on success in the eyes of both the technician or administrator and those most involved, the nationals of the host countries. Few technicians have been sent home as failures because they were not technically qualified. Along with the problem of fitting the right technical competence into the job, our ignorance of the personal qualities needed to provide social change, which is an essential part of technical innovation if it is to stick, is even greater.

While practically all newly developing countries have higher education in some form, however limited, it is nearly always in the classical or liberal arts mold and woefully weak on the technical or vocational side. This probably stems from the traditional view held in most predominantly rural cultures that agriculture is at the bottom of the list as a desirable way of life and that law, medicine, or just plain liberal arts philosophy or government service provide status. Even in those countries which have moved cautiously into agriculture, engineering, business administration, and the vocational arts, enrollment in agriculture courses is notoriously low. One South American country, with its national income almost wholly dependent on agriculture and with potential agricultural resources per capita greater than almost any country in the world, graduates less than fifty persons in agricultural courses per year.

It is conservatively estimated that this country will need an average of 1,000 a year over the next twenty years just to man the new institutions and educational needs now being developed in the country.

One African nation finds itself with less than 100 graduates possessing any kind of agricultural education, and yet that country must sell abroad products of the soil to survive. This situation in itself demands a vast reservoir of manpower and knowledge from the outside to maintain the *status quo*. If these areas are to grow and develop in step with the vastly expanded needs of the growing populations in all countries, literally thousands of qualified technical personnel must come from the outside.

Ownership Patterns. While limitation to the field of government-sponsored development leaves out the important element of development by private interests within a country and also eliminates concession-type agricultural development, these forms of private ownership widely used during the long colonial history of many of the new and less developed economies are either gone completely or on the way out in nearly every country in the world. The existing large private estates in most countries have been taken over or are in the process of being taken over by government and in some instances broken up into smaller units. The concession-type development, such as the Goodyear plantations in Indonesia or the Dutch sugar concession in Ethiopia, are rarities in modern-day agricultural development.

The basic problems of human behavior under the concession or estate type of agricultural development are about the same as for the government-sponsored general type of project or program now being undertaken in practically all developing countries. However, the manager or corporation which owns the estate and the outside firm or agency which manages a concession to develop a special crop, such as sugar in the Philippines or coffee in Brazil, have strict control over what actually happens. The problem of introducing a new crop, an innovation in markets or production, or some other change is handled by the command route rather than by persuasion and education, though there must be elements of both even in a command situation. The same situation prevails on a hacienda or large plantation. The owner or his manager decides on a course of action, a change of crops, or an expansion or refinement of the operation. He orders that this be done. With his ability to mobilize the materials, resources, and other services to back up the innovation—perhaps it is the introduction of a new machine or a new variety of seed—and through his control over the people who actually do the work through his corps of supervisors, the change or innovation takes place more or less rapidly and reasonably completely, even though it may be accompanied by grudging acceptance and sometimes outright protest from the workers.

With the breakup of the haciendas and estates, particularly in some of the countries of Latin America, South and Southeast Asia, and the Middle East where land reform has been introduced, the problem of introducing innovation and change becomes vastly more complicated. The administrator, technician, or specialist working with a host government or a subdivision of a government, state, or province, finds himself with little or no structure or framework with which to work. There is no channel of communication or chain of command. He must try to communicate his ideas and aspirations to produce change to the several thousand new landowners or managers or occupiers of the small plots of land which used to be a large estate or government concession.

The land reform program in one country recently seized and broke up some three thousand estates or concessions on government land and divided it among three hundred thousand peasants who for over four hundred years had never owned land. Their main experience with land possession had consisted in the tillage rights on a small parcel of land which the landlord, government, or concessionaire could cancel on a moment's notice. The sheer problem of communication with so large a number of smallholders becomes a major problem, to say the least.

With this limitation on the type of sponsorship of a technician, specialist, or administrator going abroad, we shall turn to the kind of person he should be and the kind of knowledge he should possess on taking up an international assignment in agricultural development.

Selection and Orientation

The technical competence required of the overseas technician or manager varies greatly among countries and even projects within a given country. However, it is generally conceded that high professional competence in the field or facet of agricultural development to which the person is assigned is a must. This is so even though in most instances the overseas technician will use only a small part of the knowledge he possesses on a given project. It is important that his knowledge extends beyond the immediate needs of the situation. This is largely because there are a few persons in every country who are knowledgeable about almost any area of agriculture. Although few in number, they are often more specialized and knowledgeable than the technician coming out to assist them in agricultural development.

The American or Western technician must pass the "intellectual test" with this small number of the elite, who are usually in positions of power in government or universities. This in effect constitutes winning the respect of the intellectual power structure of the country. After this hurdle has been surmounted, work at the actual project level rarely ever goes beyond a rather low or median technical level in the average less developed country.

The candidate for an overseas assignment should be challenged and motivated concerning the central task to be undertaken rather than the so-called glamor aspects of a foreign assignment—travel, higher pay, greater status, relatively high living standards, and the so-called respect which the ruling classes of most countries are assumed to carry.

As a technical assistance organ, he needs the ability to accept innovation himself if he is going to introduce innovation and change to other people. Paradoxically, the person seeking to introduce innovation is often so completely possessed of his own competence and correctness that he sees no way of accomplishing a task, anywhere or in any place, except through his own concept of what is needed. This is a fatal characteristic, because if there is anything which the average overseas technician or manager must learn, it is to change himself and be flexible, both in thought and action, in a new and often strange environment and culture.

The ability to listen sympathetically to fellow technicians and workers of the host country is another job requirement of the development officer. The author has interviewed many technicians of the countries in which Americans are working as to their feeling about their American counterparts. There is general appreciation of the strictly personal qualities of the American and often awe at what he seems to know. Underlying the general high regard, however, the host country technician often complains that Americans seem to think that nothing in the country is worth considering; that they will not stop to listen to the other side but are bent on "doing it my way." A high ministry official once told the author, "You treat us like second-class citizens in our own country." Unfortunately, with their brash and aggressive manner added to the fact that they often have the power to release or withhold funds to support a project of some kind, Americans have at times literally imposed their own approaches to development on an area or a particular problem. The approach is tolerated but not accepted by the local people. Sometimes, therefore, after the technician has gone home, his innovation will be abandoned.

These are all qualities which show up in varying degrees when the individual reaches his post assignment. Present personnel selection methods rarely weigh more than the professional competence factor. Occasionally candidates are turned down for lack of motivation and overt lack of consideration for people of other cultures. The other necessary qualities listed above are difficult to detect, though sometimes this may be indicated in the preassignment orientation, if such is given.

Orientation

Preassignment Training. The problem of how to prepare an individual for best performance in an overseas assignment is one which has baffled every government, corporation, or foundation from the missionary society and government agency to the colonial administrator and the international development corporation working in a foreign country. Theories vary all the way from having the prospective overseas worker immersed in the statistics and the economies of the country and fluent in its language to giving him a complete course in cultural anthropology and even psychology. Experience over the years seems to indicate that a whole multitude of elements have some bearing on the individual's ability to accomplish his assigned task in another culture or environment with success. There appears to be no single predominating cause which predestines success or failure. If there is a single important element which carries through both successes and failures, it might be described as "how the individual behaves within another social system," assuming that some technical competence, motivation, cultural empathy, and organizing and operating ability are present.

The following conclusions may be reached:

One may have studied and absorbed all the economic, geographic, political, and statistical information about a country and its people prior to his assignment and yet find it of little value in meeting the problems faced on the job. While it follows that some information is beneficial, mere *information about it* is not sufficient for even the person of high professional competence to carry out his assignment adequately.

Fluency in the local language is desirable, but too much fluency, while of considerable advantage to the possessor of it, often defeats the main purpose of good communication. Here again some smattering of language is absolutely necessary, and a willingness and persistence in improving language ability after one reaches the country is highly desirable. This does two things to break down barriers of communication, namely, (1) it shows that the technician has interest enough in his job to try to learn the local language, and (2) it not only gives the host counterpart an opportunity to "help the technician to learn the language" but it gives him an opportunity to learn English as well. Further, it shows that the local counterpart or technician has something worth contributing to the American or Western side of the program.

There is of course the school which holds that being completely absorbed and learned in the culture and anthropology of the country is the answer. This can be a false assumption, depending largely on how the overseas technician uses his knowledge. If he becomes an amateur anthropologist, he soon becomes so concerned with the many facets of the culture that he exaggerates the differences between his own culture and that of the host country. This widens the personal gap and opens the door for even more misunderstanding and missed signals. If he has enough of a flair and an understanding of cultural anthropology to notice the likenesses rather than the differences between his culture and the host country, this interest is desirable. He must become a participant in whatever he is trying to do involving the host country people rather than a detached observer, as is all too often the case of the amateur anthropologist.

Perhaps the greatest single need and the most desirable attribute in any American working in another country is to have the patience to seek out why things are being done as they are and to get an understanding of the forces which cause change to take place or stall in a given situation. There are key groups or individuals in every bureaucracy, whether it be a government bureaucracy or a counterpart of that in a business structure, who make things happen. Recognition of this is far more desirable than the typical American approach of just "busting in" and doing it yourself. Patience in seeking out the channels and the power structure through which things actually get done is probably one of the most difficult problems for an American. Certainly it is the most difficult art to teach. We feel that even if the art cannot be taught, orientation courses can at least be constructed so as to alert the technician to some of the signals which will help him recognize these forces and make use of them.

Different Orientation for Different Categories of Overseas Personnel. While there are certain basic social, cultural, and political areas which are more or less common to all persons going abroad, the orientation given a "foreign service officer" is not necessarily good for the agricultural technician or for the administrator going out, for example, to assist a country in its land reform problems. This follows from the roles each must play in their respective assignments. He "must at all times represent and present the American viewpoint," the interest and the policies of the American government. In this role he represents certain political, social, and economic views. On the other hand, the agricultural technician must, if he is effective, play down his political, economic, and often social views and the idea that he is representing America in the political sense. He has been sent out to work with other technicians in the country on projects conceived in, for, and by that country. His role as a representative of the American viewpoint, other than in know-how or technology, is purely secondary.

This does not mean that he must "go native," accepting and espousing completely the viewpoint and customs of the host country. On the contrary, American or visiting technicians should hold to the basic conduct which they would be expected to follow in their own country. The host technician should be allowed to explain and tell about his country, and the overseas technician should listen and try to find something in it to which he can give respect and praise.

Early Orientations. The orientation given most of the early participants in the Marshall Plan effort in Europe was based largely on complete economic and industrial information about the country to which the American was assigned. Aside from the usual lectures on habits and customs related to eating, housing accommodations, and social life, little else was given.

When the Point Four program was inaugurated in 1951 for underdeveloped countries, such orientation as was given stressed in addition the cultural and sociological aspects of the country. In the case of agriculture, many of the technicians recruited from the ranks of the extension service and the land grant agricultural colleges had no orientation at all. The assumption was that these individuals were competent professionally and were working largely with rural people in America, hence they would perform adequately in a foreign assignment. This on the whole proved to be only partially true, though it is conceded that possibly the agricultural technicians were perhaps better able to "take hold of a situation" and get things moving than some of their colleagues in other disciplines. Even they had their severe limitations. The general tendency was for the American technician or administrator to attempt to transfer the American structure and levels of technology with which he was familiar rather than to adapt and build on, or to apply the principles which made his particular specialty work in the United States.

With these generalizations on some of the pitfalls in orientation and selection before us, let us now turn to the situation as it actually exists in some eighty or ninety countries of the world in which American, Western European, and United Nations technical specialists and administrators in agriculture are working—primarily in government-sponsored programs and projects in agriculture.

Situation in Undeveloped Areas

Location. A majority of the underdeveloped countries which are today importing technical know-how in agricultural development are located in tropical and semitropical areas of the earth. This is a band around the earth ranging from the Equator to the 40th parallel north and to the 20th parallel south. Here live about 1,935 million of the human beings on the globe.

Temperatures and rainfall range from those of the hot wet rainforests to those of the hot dry deserts, with a multitude of variations in between depending on mountains, location of river valleys, and other physical factors. Soils range from the deep black silt in the valleys to lateral white clay and leached soils on the hills and the dry sands and rock of desert and semiarid areas.

People. Native and original indigenous populations predominate in all the areas, with the usual sprinkling of west and central Europeans whose ancestors conquered and colonized the area and introduced a considerable smattering of Western technology, customs, and structures at the upper levels of the government and the economy. In addition, there is a large percentage of mixed types who generally stand socially and economically between the elite and the original indigenous population and do not seem to belong to either. Even in this century there is not much movement from one group to another except in a few isolated countries. Illiteracy is high, ranging from around 60 percent in southern Asia and Latin America to more than 95 percent in most of Africa.

The urban areas are heavily westernized in a commercial and industrial sense, and the streets of Bangkok or Singapore or La Paz, stripped of some of the strictly local cultural features, look little different from Des Moines or Austin so far as utilities, streets, office buildings, consumer goods in the stores, and the general trappings of commerce and industry are concerned. Usually one of the great religions predominates in an area—Hindu, Buddhist, Moslem, or Christian, the latter in the case of Latin America, dominated largely by the Catholic faith. In nearly all countries are found Catholic groups started by missionaries hundreds of years ago, and likewise there are Protestant groups of varying size and frequency sprinkled in nearly every country. Most people—outside the urban areas—live in rural villages and on farm land which they do not own. They usually live in houses which belong to a landlord or, in the case of some parts of Asia and the Middle East, to the man who owns the entire village or series of villages. There is little consciousness on the part of the village people of anything resembling government service, and the impression generally is that government, whether by a dictator or a freely elected representative of the people, is somehow a sort of policeman.

Washington State University a few years ago conducted a series of studies in Pakistan villages to determine (1) the so-called political consciousness of the village people, and (2) their concept of what the government meant to them. Very few in the political study were conscious of any political loyalties or attachments to any political structure other than the local head man or the seniors in the village. This seemed to be more of a family affair than a political party concept. About the only image the villagers seemed to have of government was provided by the policeman who came occasionally to settle a row or arrest somebody and by the tax collector who came annually to the villages to collect taxes. There was no concept at all of a government service for schools, roads, agricultural extension, or health, all of which, with other government-supported aids, are generally common to the West.

One-crop Economies. The economic and agricultural development of these areas has a sort of duality. The people in the villages produce more or less what they eat, with just a little more at times to spare. There is very little commercial agriculture except when the little extra above what is required to live upon is sold, traded, or bartered for the scant necessities of village life. On the other hand, there are vast and very efficient one-crop estates which developed largely out of private enterprise operating on a concession basis. They were developed because somebody saw a chance to make money out of the commercial production of rubber, coffee, tea, cotton, abaca, sugar, cocoa, or some other industrial agricultural crop. This usually coincided with the aims, needs, and desires of the home country. Out of this grew the so-called one-crop economies which, for better or worse, plague nearly every less developed country in the world. This program has become even more acute with the rise, since World War II, of about fifty-two nations. These new nations are now sovereign and independent. They have all the problems of continuing production of this one crop for export to secure foreign exchange in payment of the bills for their new embassies, armies, airplanes, and trappings of sovereignty. At the same time they must rearrange their economies to produce food for their growing populations, some of which they used to buy through the exchange generated by the export crop. There is the further tendency of these new nations to want to industrialize at once, usually at the expense or neglect of their agricultural production.

While there is commercial farming at a high technical level on the estates, village agriculture is inadequately served with markets, and the kind of distribution system which makes possible the pull and attraction of profit to provide the needed input supplies (including credit) essential to modern and maximum agricultural production. Interest rates on farm production loans are usually excessively high by the standards of more developed economies. When translated into supplies and provided to the tenant or peasant in the village, these rates at times run to 180 to 200 percent per year.

Repair parts for even the simplest kind of agricultural implement must usually be forged and made in the village or in a larger town nearby, or shipped from some depot in the capital city. In the case of major tractor parts or more sophisticated machine parts, these usually have to come from the country of origin of the tractor or other equipment. The ownership of land is usually the highest aspiration of the villager. The tillage right to land under a cash rent arrangement is something to dream about.

These observations are of necessity rather broad and general, but we hope they give the prospective candidate for an overseas assignment in agriculture some idea of the base from which he will have to start his agricultural innovation.

Where to Start

How Do We Start? Let us assume that our candidate has been selected, has been briefed on his assignment, and has some general knowledge of the country. He has been informed whether his assignment will require the planning and development of an entirely new project or merely the carrying forward of a project already started. In some cases it may be a new facet of an old and going program.

He is now in the country, and has perhaps (if everything has worked out) found a place to live; his furniture will be arriving soon, and he has gone through his initial run-down with the mission or with the local representative of the agency with which he is associated under the host country assignment. Being an American he will want to "get going." No doubt his fingernails are already bitten down as a result of impatience with his own colleagues. In some instances the manager or technician works within the U. S. agency involved and "goes across the street" to advise and assist his host country counterpart on some agreed plan of action or project. In other instances he works directly in the host country agency involved in the project. In rare instances he will be in charge of the project for both countries. Getting hold of something to do is a very critical problem. Often the man responsible for the project from the host government side is timid, sometimes hostile and suspicious. He usually presents an outward show of confidence but is often insecure and afraid of his own ability and his place in his own government. The very fact that this American has come out to be his "adviser" places him in a psychological position of inferiority, not to mention the manner which the average American assumes, usually without thinking. The very size and brashness of most Americans place the usually smaller-stature host country counterpart at a disadvantage. If the host country technician has at some time visited the United States, that is all to the good. If he has obtained his impressions from American movies, or perhaps has never been exposed to anything American, then the problem becomes difficult.

In some countries literally hundreds of American and UN technicians have been requested through government channels to assist in agricultural projects or programs. They have arrived in the country, been briefed and cordially greeted by local personnel, and been given an office either in their own mission or in the host country ministry or agency concerned with their project. They have gone to the office and have sat back waiting for the agency or someone in it to ask their assistance. They have waited not for mere days, but at times for weeks and even months, with nothing being asked of them. These are extreme cases, but they happen every day. This means that the first real task of the manager or technician is to establish communication with someone concerned in the project program.

Communication Comes First. By "establishing communication" we mean a kind of mutual behavior which wipes away the suspicion that "this fellow is out to get my job or show me up as a fool before my superiors." It means finding some common ground of respect for each other as persons—not the back-slapping, kidding kind of fellowship, but a sort of intuitive feeling that "this fellow is real," that "we are both interested in getting our task accomplished and will support and help each other."

It is difficult for an American, but the more he can "lead by walking two steps behind," and the more he can build up his counterpart in the eyes of the host country power structure and bureaucracy, the more likely is he to promote a mutual exchange of ideas and feedback through his colleague, without which the average American technician is blundering around in the dark. Once a true working relationship has been established at the power center of the agency or project which makes possible the genuine planning and implementation of a project, the next and most important step is to get in communication with the people upon whom the whole success of the enterprise or project depends—the actual workers and producers on the soil.

As we have discussed above, communication, or "cultural traffic," as the sociologist would call it, between the elite of the government and the people in the villages is limited. The formal channel reaches down to about the regional level, and the village people move up to about the local district level, but there is nothing in between. Programs and projects usually originate, under the present system, at the top—sometimes in far-off Washington in the mind of some aggressive planner who thinks he knows what is good for the country. Papers are drawn up, arguments are batted around the table, papers are approved, implementation is scheduled, and a whole avalanche of paper is passed around among people mostly at the seat of government. Rarely, if ever, does the content of these plans reach the villager in a form which he can understand.

As an example, a few years ago officials in a country which was deficient in wheat and bread grains determined by experiments with ammonium sulfate in one of their research stations that the application of 200 pounds of ammonium sulfate to an acre of timeworn land would raise their cereal yield about 25 percent. The statisticians at the top figured out that by applying this much fertilizer per acre to their existing cereal acreage they could more than become self-sufficient in one year. So as a start the country imported (they had no fertilizer manufacturing facilities) some 300,000 tons of ammonium sulfate. A gigantic "food campaign" was launched in the press. There was a great stir at the many levels of bureaucracy about this ammonium sulfate and the "grow more food campaign." Production in that year actually declined, though in this instance mostly from dry weather. High officials were quite astounded to learn that little of the fertilizer was even taken out of the warehouses and that the farmers, or fellaheen, as they were called in this country, paid not the slightest attention to all the noise. This was most understandable on looking closer. First, illiteracy is high. Newspapers rarely move out of the large urban centers, and radio at that time was rare in the villages. Most of the farmers had had no experience in using ammonium sulfate on cereals. Up to this time all fertilizer was used on the industrial crops—tea, cotton, jute, and sugar. On top of that, the government-fixed price of grain was very low. This was a policy to protect the city population against the squeeze of high food costs. With the sulfate at $160 per ton and interest at 12 to 50 percent even to the landlord, it was not likely that much fertilizer would be used. So the campaign flopped miserably largely because the one person—the actual worker on the land—who could make the scheme succeed was never really in on it and certainly not an active part of it.

Most Americans working in agriculture in this country are hardly conscious of the vast communications complex which makes possible the kind of rapid spread of technical information which is characteristic of our present-day society. Notice the high rate of literacy, newspapers, magazines, technical journals, radio, TV, extension agents, vocational agricultural teachers, and, not to be overlooked, the excellent publicity and educational work done by the commercial firms, cooperatives, and others who manufacture and sell fertilizer, insecticides, seed, and other supplies to farm people. Think what the situation is where none of these things exist.

The mere knowledge of a product or practice introduced by even the most advanced communication methods is not enough. The product or practice must be easily available to the only person who can make it effective, that is, the direct tiller of the soil, or the man who actually makes the decision and does or directs the work. This means a distributive system which will place the item, product, or practice within reach of the potential user. One may readily demonstrate the superiority of a Japanese rice hoe for the cultivation of potatoes in Bolivia, as has been done, but the hoe, costing $2.75, is in Japan and of no value until it is in the hands of the Alto Plano Indian. Even with the vast complex and rapid interchange of information and people in the communication complex of the most Westernized societies and with the equally vast and aggressive commercial distribution systems, there are thousands of farms relatively untouched. It is a personal opinion that if the U. S. Technical Assistance program had spent its first five years assisting countries to establish channels of communication with their own people before any real technical assistance or development work in agriculture was undertaken, the programs in most countries would probably be much farther advanced than they are now.

The problem still exists. Not only must top-level interpersonal communication take place in planning and implementation, but the sort of constructive and motivating contact with the actual people of the country that develops a sense of participation is imperative. In agricultural development the elite must view the masses in the villages as something more than peasants to be pushed around and exploited. It must find ways of motivating them for participation in economic development.

Planning and Its Pitfalls

The Shopping List. While establishing the right sort of basis for work with our counterpart and acquainting ourselves with the real communication channels and "how things get done in our host country," we have no doubt begun to discover something about this project, program, or task for which we were recruited. It is an understatement to say that by now we have discovered that the things which apparently we are supposed to undertake with, in, and for the host country have little or no resemblance to the things which were included in our job description or reported to us by the recruitment officer at home.

There is usually some sort of a country plan in the developing countries. It is sometimes nothing more than a "shopping list" of the things the country would like to have or like to do. In some cases it is what an outside planning group thinks the country should have. Indeed, in some countries the planning or development boards blandly say that it is "our job to make a plan, but somebody else's responsibility to find the means of implementing it." There seems to be little real coordination between the planners and the persons or agencies responsible for marshaling the resources and carrying out the multitude of separate operations and projects which must be carried out if a national agricultural development plan amounts to anything more than a paper plan.

Flexibility Is a Must. It is exceedingly unlikely that the new technician will find on arrival in a country a ready-made structure or project in which to use his particular talents. As a matter of fact, he will often find not even a project plan. As often as not he is without a counterpart and is called upon to develop a project which will not only (hopefully) fill some actual need in a country's agricultural development but will more often have to fit the ideas of somebody at a desk in Washington or Rome or some other directing center of technical assistance.

The country's master plan may be designed to increase and strengthen cooperatives, or implement a land reform or land distribution program. Perhaps the program is to improve livestock or marketing or to increase cereal production. There are hundreds of places where some small beginning can be made toward an objective as broad as this. The tendency is for the technician to begin to look for facets of the program where his particular specialty will fit—poultry, livestock, plant breeding, or disease control, for example—and then go about planning and developing a project that fits his talents in an area where he feels competent. This is often sold to the "powers that be" as something of high priority. As often as not second-country resources are put behind the effort, and sometimes these projects stand out as really significant accomplishments on a relatively small scale. Too often projects are hardly under way before the technician leaves the country for another assignment. Failure to plan within the context of the basic elements within the country, or failure to give proper weight to the many alternatives and establish priorities in relation to other elements of the developing country, is probably the outstanding negative characteristic of all technical assistance efforts in agriculture over the past ten years. This to some extent was necessary when few countries had any plan. Few had ever had any resource studies or surveys, let alone a soil map and basic information on markets and production possibilities, which are essential to fully developed program plans. Technicians and their counterparts thus developed projects which were often brilliantly implemented. In some instances these projects represented the beginning of programs which have had a profound effect on the country's agricultural development.

Two Examples. Some years ago country X experienced a severe shortage of poultry products in its principal city markets. Poultry in that country is and was somewhat of a small-flock, scavenger operation. A poultry man was requested and sent to that country. (It happened to be in South America, where chickens are a prime item in the diet of the upper classes.) Our poultry specialist decided to do something quick and dramatic. A large consignment of baby chicks was flown in from the United States and quickly installed in improvised brooder houses. The beginning of a colony-type poultry operation for the production of broilers and eggs was instituted. Unfortunately it was soon discovered that these high-bred and expensive baby chicks would not do well on the local feed. High-priced feed had to be imported from the United States. In almost no time the limited but important luxury market for high-quality poultry and eggs in the principal city of that country was flooded. The egg market dropped sharply. This situation (1) made the local and small peasants who depended on selling a few eggs for a small income very unhappy, and (2) brought the price of eggs so low that the plant could not operate on expensive feed imported from the United States.

It took first nearly ten years to develop a local feed supply and next to get some spread of this better poultry among the local village people, who must sell something if they are to survive on their little farms. The big plant operation has long since gone, but the residual of the project is in the better poultry that eventually reached the smallholders.

In another country a sheep and wool management specialist was requested by the host country ministry, and a really able and highly skilled man came down. Years before, an American technician working in an experimental station had introduced new strains of animals in the local flocks. This phase of the effort was exceedingly successful. The second phase was to provide better markets for the meat and especially the wool. Sheep in this particular country were usually sheared on an average of about once every five years, by a rather crude system of using a razor blade or sharpening a piece of tin can and literally shaving the wool from the live sheep. Our specialist, used to the most modern techniques of the West, had brought into the country (at considerable expense) a mobile diesel-powered electric clipping machine whereby six or seven sheep could be sheared on the platform at once. It was demonstrated at a few places in the first year. In the second year the machine and its trained crew were advertised in the villages, and the local farmers brought in their sheep to be sheared by this new and glamorous machine. Some twenty-five thousand head were sheared. By that time the technician's two-year term was out. He went home. No one came to replace him and the whole program lapsed, largely as a result of overlooking three main items in the project plan.

1. There is no use shearing sheep and bundling up the wool if there is no marketing system to take it away. Previous to this project the only market for wool was for local village industries and handicrafts, along with hand-spun and hand-woven clothing. The wool from 25,000 sheep would last a long time.

2. Gasoline, oil, and repair parts for the mobile unit were almost unattainable in that country without dollar exchange and the most elaborate and expensive methods of getting these materials out of the United States.

3. The technician left the country before the local people were trained to operate and care for the machine, and especially before the village people really understood what this was all about.

Now, seven years after the first effort, another "sheep man" is in the country. This time he is starting in on an outlet in world markets for the wool if it is finally removed from the sheep. By now the villagers are a little more sophisticated about money; originally they would not exchange their wool for money but wanted barter goods. Now they will take a little money if they see something which they want to buy and can spend it immediately.

Barriers. Instances like the above can be cited by the dozen. They result from the failure of specialists or technicians to look or plan beyond their immediate special interest and competence. Furthermore, the projects were clearly isolated from other parts of agricultural development. They were small pieces of the national plan, perhaps, but not really related to it in the broad development aspects. However, there are barriers other than the technician's own tendency to be narrow that sometimes throw a well-planned project out of gear.

In country Y an American technician went out at the request of the host government, also on a sheep improvement program. This man was more of a generalist and not a super-specialist. There were some things he did not know about breeding and herd management. He soon found the one person in that country who had received a doctor's degree in animal husbandry. The two men started work with the scanty resources provided by the provincial government and the little farmers who had sheep in a series of villages. Their first step was improvement of quality of the animals. This was done by introducing into the district some high-bred rams. The offspring were annually spread to other villages, and in a short period of three or four years there was a noticeable improvement in the meat quality of the animals showing up on market day at the various urban centers. Wool had likewise improved in quality, but under the hit-and-miss marketing system in vogue in the country the villager got no more for his superior wool than he got from the rag-tag wool of his indigenous sheep. A part of the plan was improvement in the packaging and marketing of wool. In the four years of this operation a well-planned program was projected, including shearing at special centers, washing and cleaning the wool, grading it in uniform lots, and the collection of these lots in a central place to sell by auction. This called for some improved equipment for shearing sheep and washing the wool. More than a year before this phase of the project started, the United States technician requested through channels the proper equipment to make possible the rounding out of four or five years of effort in improving meat and wool quality in that district. As things sometimes happen—too often in fact—his requisition for equipment was mislaid somewhere in the bureaucracy of the United States mission or in Washington, and only two weeks before shearing time was he notified that the equipment request had been lost or ignored by the authorities. It involved a simple expenditure of less than $100 for some hand shears and twine to bind the bundles of graded wool. With shearing scheduled, a wool auction floor already set up, and buyers over the country notified, the whole project was near collapse. Here improvisation came into play. By scrounging for old shears and actually having the village blacksmiths make some crude shears, the shearing demonstration went off on schedule in the entire district covered by the project. The shearing made possible the rest of the project. The *New York Times* that fall carried a small international dispatch of how the first wool auction in the history of that country had been held and how the producers had received an average of 5 cents more per pound for wool than in previous years. The technician has long since come home. Not only have the sheep been improved, but also an improved marketing system, with the widest sort of producer participation, is now going ahead. Farmers are improving their flocks steadily because they are benefiting from these innovations in the marketplace.

While Americans generally are adept and ingenious in operational planning—and American industrial enterprise is based securely on the most detailed project planning—American technicians, both industrial and agricultural, are sometimes singularly devoid of the genius for the broad and detailed economic development planning required if a new country with little outside capital from private or government services is to progress. We are not adept at making the maximum use of the scant manpower, technology, and property resources which the average less developed country possesses. This probably grows from the fact that, except on a project basis, such as that of the Tennessee Valley Authority, the river development work of the Army Engineers, and some excellent project planning by the Soil Conservation Service, planning per se is something of a nasty word in the United States lexicon. Some American university economists together with agencies of foreign countries have created brilliant overall economic plans, often in great detail and in great volume, but the practical implementation of such plans is usually something else. An examination of several such country plans within recent years has convinced the author that too much emphasis is placed on the assistance that must come from the outside. There is not enough setting up of priorities on the basis of what can be done in the event that outside assistance is not forthcoming.

Host People Must See a Need. A cardinal rule for any technician developing a specific project or a larger development plan should be, first, to select what seems to be the greatest need as seen by the host country and to estimate how much may be accomplished with the resources at hand. It must then be determined what priority this project should have for a call on the scant resources of the country compared with other projects probably equally important in the minds of the local people. Projects may always be expanded and accelerated with the coming of new and added resources.

In this connection not only the host technician but the host government or private enterprise group is vitally important. They must *want* to do something pretty badly, and they must *believe* that something can be accomplished. The creating of this confidence and general attitude is probably the most important role of the average imported technician, manager, or specialist. One of the key ingredients of community development programs is the matter of people gaining confidence in what they can accomplish for themselves with very little outside help, or none at all.

Here again the power structure and "how things get done" in a country come into play. In most former colonial countries, even with a democratic system of government, there is a tendency for everything to be relayed from the top down. Orders are issued and mayors and district officials appointed by the central government. Taxes are collected from the local village and paid to the central government. Then funds are parceled back to the village by the central government, if they come back at all. There was not until recently, in many countries, any local machinery or authority whereby local units of government could vote taxes and collect anything more than voluntary funds for local improvements and development. This is changing in some areas, particularly in India, Pakistan, the Philippines, and in one or two Middle Eastern countries.

To schedule steps of broad economic development planning is clearly beyond the visiting technician or manager's power. Not only is there usually an American mission plan, in some form, in every country where United States technicians are assigned to work, but the local country plans must also be considered; these often differ in priorities and short-term objectives. The two must be reconciled. The technician or administrator usually confines his effort to the immediate project and the immediate special area of his concern, often with too little regard for what a successful implementation of such a project would do for the rest of the economy.

An Example. Corn is the principle item of diet among the villagers and some of the urban population of country Z. The corn is of very low quality, and the yields are critically low. When weather conditions are not right, corn supply becomes a critical problem for the country. Corn in this economy is strictly a locally used item and is not exported. The balance between a critical shortage or a surplus is very fine. After consultation with host government technicians, the United States technician decided to introduce hybrid corn to an area especially adapted for corn growing in that country. Tests had been made at the local experimental station to determine the best varieties for this area. A hybrid-corn campaign was launched by the United States agricultural mission and the local authority. Within two years the whole district was planting hybrid corn. As was expected, the yields were doubled, sometimes trebled or quadrupled, with the hybrid varieties. During the first year things went well, because there was a shortage of carry-over corn and the villagers were happy to fill their bins again. However, in the second year the whole country was literally flooded with corn. Everybody had corn, and nobody wanted any. Much of the crop stood in the field and was never picked. The village women did not like the hard kernels which they had to pound with a pestle to make meal for bread. To cut a long story short, for a number of years anyone suggesting the use of hybrid corn in that area was running a great risk! Now some seven or eight years later some of the strains of this hybrid experiment have carried over into the native corn, and while the yields are not as high, they are better. The general corn supply is better; it is kept in some sort of a balance by the low yields, the weather, and the rising population of the area. Yet here was a scientifically sound, carefully planned, highly successful effort to develop and introduce hybrid corn. The final result was not what the planners had hoped for. How to detect these signals and how to guard against moving technology too fast are additional factors in this business of planning. Even a plan highly successful in our eyes and on our standards may be a complete failure in the eyes of those who must live with the innovation.

Below is a series of points of personal behavior as well as action planning which, if observed, will assist the overseas technician to be more effective in his assignment.

Personal Behavior

"Know Thyself": A Good Basis upon Which to Start

1. By this is meant a sort of self-analysis, first, of why you are undertaking the assignment—money, getting away from home or from an unpleasant home

situation, professional improvement, travel, or a sense of responsibility to help out in the present world situation. Be honest; even if the answer is not very flattering to your ego, it will be worthwhile.

2. Try to understand your own situation and why you are as successful in your home job as you are. You will discover that it is not entirely you or your undoubted ability. A whole host of other things help you to succeed in your particular job. There is somebody to take care of the taxes or payroll money; somebody sees that you have an office, probably a secretary, a filing cabinet, heat, lights, a telephone. Able helpers compile the statistics or information you need; you have an assistant; somebody helps you get your transportation, and somebody either requests or arranges for your meetings or classes or particular tasks. Even a system or regulation tells you when to come to the office or go home. You are a part of a structure and a system which support your effort. Weigh all these helpers against your accomplishments and the part they play in your success. Then try to picture yourself in a foreign country with probably none of these things to back you up. Your ego will be reduced to about the right size after a little of this sort of self-examination.

Know Your Own Country

1. Be familiar with the current issues in your own country and particularly the current international talk. You will be amazed at the questions you will be asked. You will not rate well unless you know as much as the questioner about them.

2. Learn as much as you can about the country to which you are going. Don't depend on somebody lecturing to you or giving you the information. If you are really interested, you will read books, and there are many of them on every country. Don't become an authority—try simply to get the feel of the area to which you will eventually go. Be ready to learn. Do not establish a rigid image, good or bad, before you see the country and its people.

3. Learn as much of the language as you can; if nothing else, acquire the ability to say good-morning and order a meal or perhaps find the direction to a place or building. The chances are you will need and use an interpreter for your official contacts. No doubt you will have to use an interpreter for technical matters as long as you are in the country, but language ability for general conversation helps break down barriers, makes your hosts feel that you are interested in the country, and gives them an opportunity to help you learn more. (As a footnote here, if your are lucky enough to be assigned an interpreter, treat him as a real equal. His mastery of your language along with his own is an ability which you do not possess. He should be treated as a person on that basis. All too often really brilliant and highly educated people acting as interpreters for Americans are treated as office boys, taxi drivers, or household servants.)

4. Expect to get your real knowledge of the country after you are there and from the people themselves. This usually means outside the capital and big cities. This is not done during a briefing session or a trip out to a village with your camera over your shoulder to take pictures of the "natives." It takes time and patience to listen and to seek out from the people the really important things in the country from their standpoint—*not* yours.

5. Be yourself. Do not put on a false show of affability or go overboard for the foreign person. He will be embarrassed. Accord him the same respect that you expect him to accord you.

6. Try to seek out the points upon which you are alike, rather than exaggerating the differences between you and your host.

7. Don't say, "We do it this way in the United States," or even look at some fine object and say, "We also have this in the United States." Let your host tell you of some of his values and the things in his country in which he takes pride. Share that pride and do not talk about the United States unless asked. When asked, be prepared, so that you can really tell him something about your country that he does not know.

8. Last, remember you may be in a country foreign to you, but actually *you* are the foreigner. You are the guest of another country. Act as you would expect a guest to act in your home.

On Planning and Implementation

Have Patience, and Look Before You Leap

1. Before introducing innovation into the confusion and change which already exist, take the time to find out why things are being done the way they are. *Do Not* start on a major change unless you can explain the most practical reasons for it and thereby convince your host technicians. Particularly the farmer, who has to make the major change, must become convinced that your innovation means something better for him. Then move only at his speed, rather than the speed which is your idea of how he should move.

In country after country technicians, managers, and specialists have literally jammed through in short order projects involving a major change in a whole social and economic system, thinking they have really accomplished something, only to return ten years later and find the project either forgotten or just then becoming an accepted part of the social and economic system.

United States technicians especially seem to forget how many years it took us here in the United States, under the most favorable circumstances, to reach our present technical competence and production efficiency. This will not be accomplished overnight in any country, and ten years is a short time at best to expect a system actually to take hold.

2. Study the power structure of the country. Too often we align ourselves with a fellow technician who is part of a structure, but there is little knowledge of how the local resources in men, money, and authority move anything more than paper from one desk to another. Look for the keys which make things move.

As an example of this, when preparing for military government assignments during the war prospective candidates were given the most elaborate and detailed treatment of the pattern of government and the relationship between central, provincial, and national government structure, the police power, local and state, and a whole list of services which might be called upon to implement whatever was to be undertaken by military government. In Italy, for instance, it was soon discovered that the *podesta,* or mayor of a village or a large city, was the key man; without him and his power to operate and delegate, you would accomplish nothing. All the other trappings meant nothing if an action did not fit into the administrative or power structure of the *podesta*. The same thing is true in economic development, whether sponsored by the government or by a development corporation.

3. Plan and build your project or program into a going structure, one that is legally based (and budget-supported) in the government or even in the development corporation body. Do not hang your project onto a structure without making it an integral part of it, for in the absence of such integration the host agency will feel no responsibility for continuing the project or program when your money runs out. There will be no legal or budget basis for its continuance, and the chances are that it will collapse after the departure of you or your successors who feed it money.

This building into a social and political structure is slow and frustrating, but it is the only way to make your program work with the help of the indigenous technicians who have a real status in it. In several countries new agencies have been set up outside government structures and often staffed with local government or development corporation technicians. Invariably the technicians leave, even though they may receive bigger salaries than other government officials. They are cut off from the professional bureaucracy where they get their status, promotions, and fringe emoluments, the basis for being professional. They know that American involvement in the project will some day cease to exist and that they will be left in the cold by their own professional group. Therefore project integration should be considered a *First Priority* even if it may hold back the innovation for a few years.

4. Finally, analyze the facilities, services, and the assistance which you have introduced in demonstrating your innovation or change of method to see where these services will come from when they cease to be available from the outside in the form of money and technical services.

As an example, the Japanese system of rice production was introduced and successfully demonstrated in a Southeast Asian country ten years ago. Farmers exposed to this demonstration were enthusiastic about it. Yet the method or system has not been adopted widely. Why? Because the farmers are mostly illiterate and must be shown personally, step by step, the intricate and highly successful Japanese system. It involved not only great manual skills but the extensive use of insecticides, fertilizer, herbicides, and the use of simple hand equipment to apply the various sprays, plus simple but hard-to-get special hand tools for cultivation. When all these things were present and their use visually demonstrated, the system was taken up quickly by the farmers. Unfortunately there were not, and never will be, enough persons trained in the Japanese system to give every farmer a personal demonstration. Next the commercial and government distribution system for the inputs of insecticides, seed, and fertilizer was not functioning sufficiently to make indispensable items readily available to farmers. Even if they existed physically in the village, credit or funds with which to buy these required items were lacking. This example teaches us to *provide in planning* for the supply of the required sustaining services and supplies to introduce innovation as a permanent change in the social and economic system. This takes planning, yes—but imaginative implementation too. The author was partially instrumental, ten years ago, in introducing the short-handled Japanese rice hoe to replace the wooden spade used by the Bolivian Indians in cultivating their small patches of land. They liked the hoe, and with it they were able to cultivate not only better but much faster than with the wooden spade. The hoe cost only $2.75 in Japan, but aside from a government grant and an actual gift of the hoe to the smallholder there was no way for very many Indians to benefit from this simple innovation. It has taken ten years for even a small fraction of the farmers to acquire this particular important item of cultivation. In the meantime, up-to-date tractors and other machinery have been introduced in the large estates which are in the process of being broken up. This breaking up of estates in Bolivia and in many other countries of the world, for example, Mexico, Japan, Iran, Iraq, South Korea, and Egypt, as an element of political and social change, presents an added challenge to the technician and so-called "change agent" working in an underdeveloped country. Solutions are needed to maintain the production of these areas while the breakup is maturing and the new owners are not yet capable of operating their new possessions efficiently. What substitutes for management, furnishing of supplies, credit, and markets, which the owner or manager of the larger estate represents, will make it possible for the many new smallholders to operate the land effectively and efficiently? Some have tried supervised credit as one means of holding the general production plan formerly followed by the larger unit. In Japan the truly strong and aggressive local leadership through peasant-owned and -controlled cooperatives developed by the new owners on the basis of the old mutual aid societies, were essential contributing factors of the highly successful land reform there. Japan, along with southern Italy, is one of the few places where agricultural production has consistently increased every year since land reform rather than decreased as in most other countries. This is another illustration of the change in technical assistance requirements as social and political change sweeps over many of the newly developing areas.

Conclusion

The foregoing discussion has perhaps overemphasized the negative in attempts by Western-oriented personnel to introduce major agricultural innovations in some of the less developed countries where cultural and socioeconomic systems differ from those generally existing in the West.

We have emphasized the need for planning beyond the immediate short-term project. We have said that significant technical change may have impressive social, economic, and even political repercussions and that change imposed from the top rarely sticks in its original form without a long period of supervision and administration by the imposing power. Some innovation has been imposed, as in the case of the Communist countries, but not too successfully from a productive standpoint. In other countries, the sections supplying aid in the form of technical assistance and capital goods have imposed innovation through the ability to grant or withhold funds from a particular project. Ten years of experience in two essentially different approaches to economic development have brought recognition of factors other than the mere introduction of capital, which was the programming objective of the Marshall Plan, and the enhancement of human skills or the transfer of know-how, which was the base for the Point Four program. Neither alone is enough, nor are both together. Development of any kind involves more than capital or skills, though both are elements in the process. Development begins with an attitude of leaders and people. It proceeds from there to the introduction of skills and capital which may set in motion far-reaching cultural, economic, and social change, which in turn affects every aspect of individual and community behavior. Agricultural development then becomes a mixture of political, social, ideological, and economic variables. This requires time.

The speed of change and innovation, provided other factors such as resources and institutions are favorable, depends largely on the ability of the population to absorb and apply knowledge. Recognition and consideration of these in-between elements, which are not capital or skills, are perhaps the prime ingredients in successful long-term agricultural development. They are elements to be recognized not only by the agricultural innovator or technician but by the local government itself as it starts on the road to modernization of the agriculture in its country.

PRODUCTIVITY AND INCOME OF RURAL LABOR—FARM PROBLEMS IN UNDERDEVELOPED ECONOMIES

Elias H. Tuma, Ph.D.

Introduction

The ultimate objective of economic activity is to improve economic welfare of the people by increasing their real income and the consumption of goods and services they desire.

Per capita real income of the rural population may be raised by redistributing incomes from urban to rural sectors and/or by increasing their productivity. However, incomes of rural labor may be raised also by redistributing incomes within the rural community. Redistribution has usually been a primary objective of agrarian reform, but not so the raising of labor productivity, which is the topic of this paper.

Assuming that factor remuneration depends on its productivity, this study proposes that redistribution is inadequate to raise the real income and standard of living of rural labor in underdeveloped countries; to do so it is imperative to raise labor productivity and improve the quality of its performance.

Labor productivity may be measured by the rate of return per unit of input, or by the labor-time input per unit of output or of cultivated land. Increased productivity implies higher return per unit of labor time or lower labor input per unit of land without reducing total production, or even increasing it. In either case, higher productivity of labor means better performance and, given the positive relation assumed between productivity and remuneration, higher labor income and standard of living.

Dr. Tuma is Assistant Professor at the University of Saskatchewan, Saskatoon, Canada. He takes this opportunity to thank Professors Gustave E. von Grunebaum and Richard N. Farmer for their kind and helpful comments on an earlier draft of this paper.

Productivity may be increased by improving performance either quantitatively or qualitatively, or both. The quantitative approach involves no change of techniques or of capital investment. It tends to reduce surplus or unused labor time by its more intensive use and by increasing the actual time contributed by employed labor.[1] Such reduction of the number of workers employed on a given land area tends to increase their productivity and hence their income. The displaced workers must, of course, seek work elsewhere.

The qualitative approach involves adoption of techniques that are either laborsaving or nonlaborsaving.[2] Laborsaving techniques imply mechanization and substitution of capital for labor. Nonlaborsaving techniques include measures such as use of better seeds, more fertilizer, and easier-to-handle hand tools. However, these innovations may increase productivity only to a limited extent, since the quality and skills of labor will not necessarily be substantially affected.

Here we shall deal with five factors that contribute to higher labor productivity. All of them may be subsumed under the concept of agrarian reform, as follows: management of agrarian reform, mechanization, transportation, supervised rural credit, and agrarian planning.

Management of Agrarian Reform

Management here refers to the administration and implementation of reform in general or of any specific measure in the program. Theoretically, the role of management is secondary, since the major reform policies are usually predetermined by the political authorities in the form of law. It is usually established in advance whether the reform should have any direct impact on productivity and income of rural labor, implicitly if not explicitly. However, like most other laws, effectiveness of the reform law depends on the discretion and reinterpretation of its executors. They are capable of bringing it to a successful consummation, as well as of reducing its impact substantially. First we shall discuss some possible weaknesses of management and then suggest means of avoiding them.

Internal and External Factors. Failure of the management to promote labor productivity may be due to internal or to external factors, or to a combination of the two.

1. The internal factors are those inherent in the managing machinery itself. For example, the managers are usually political appointees and, therefore, tend to focus attention on the political and stabilizing functions of reform, to the neglect of the main problems plaguing the rural economy. In Mexico the reformers broke up efficiently run estates, thus reducing production and productivity, in order to spread employment and pacify the peasants. In post-emancipation Russia, obsessed with the political objectives

[1] Employment time should be distinguished from work time; some members of peasant families are ipso facto employed on the farm, yet their actual work time is less than full, and they are therefore underemployed.

[2] Nonlaborsaving techniques are to be distinguished from labor-using techniques; the former imply no change in labor-use intensiveness, while the latter imply an increase.

of the reform, the reformers compromised with the former landlords to the extent that the land recipients had to pay more in redemption than the market value of the land they received; the redistributive impact of the reform was nil or even negative.

Sometimes the management is understaffed, both in numbers and in qualifications. Understaffing is a serious handicap, especially when the reform requires expert advice or speedy implementation if it is to be effective. The usual results are procrastination, arbitrariness, and disappointment.

2. The external factors are beyond the control of management, yet they render its job impossible. For example, loopholes in the reform law and the need for its reinterpretation permit arbitrariness and infiltration of reactionary elements into the reform machinery, to the disadvantage of the prospective beneficiaries. In the name of democracy, itself an ambiguous concept, composition of the land commissions in Japan was left to local communities that were greatly influenced by former landlords or their agents. Obstruction of the reform by these people was overcome only when the Supreme Commander of the Allied Forces saw fit to interfere. Another classical example is the ambivalent attitude of the reformers in Mexico toward the *ejido*[3] between 1925 and 1935.

Sometimes the management is handicapped by lack of finances, by social conservatism, or by lack of rapport with the public, all of which make efficient management very difficult.

Some Suggestions. There is no formula for dealing with these problems, most of which are human as much as they are technical. Solutions and detailed instructions can be formulated only within the framework of the specific environment and reform measure, and only by or in cooperation with the field worker. However, the following general suggestions may be helpful.

1. The reform law should be precise in defining the reform objectives, the processes of its implementation, and the land and tenure groups to be affected. If precision should be difficult to embody in the framework of a general reform law, the executors of the reform may supplement the law with a separate code or set of rules and definitions providing the precision needed and also allowing for the local and regional differences in the objectives and methods of reform. Adopting such a code would guide execution and reduce the need for reinterpretation of the law, also the possibility of conflict or arbitrary decisions. Precision is particularly important when a reform measure is made to depend on the degree of efficiency of production, the need of the farmer for help, or the political and social status of the peasant vis-à-vis a landlord. By explaining what "efficiency" or "need for help" means, what land is to be redistributed, or what landlord rights are to be compensated, conflict, arbitrary decision, and prolonged adjudication may be avoided. These pitfalls

[3] The *ejido* system of tenure originally applied to common landholdings of the Indian villages of Mexico. Since the beginning of the reform, the term has been used to characterize two types of these villages, the collective and the individual. In the collective *ejido* crop land, pastures, meadows, and forests are held and operated in common; in individual *ejidos* crop land is parceled out to the members and is operated individually by them, while pastures and woodlands are held in common.

in the law were common in France after the Revolution, in pre-Soviet Russia, and in Mexico since the present reform has started.

2. Managers and decision makers should be chosen on the basis of their expertise rather than their political affiliation. It may be advisable to appoint outsiders or people who have no vested interests in preserving the prereform agrarian structure to fill decision-making positions. While these experts may consult with local people, the decision should be theirs alone. Thus it would be possible to avoid the problems met with in Mexico and Japan, where people with vested interests were on the committees that decided which and how much land was to be redistributed. However, it should be emphasized that former landlords and estate managers should be recruited whenever possible in order to make use of their technical experience in local agriculture. The experience of Egypt in appointing former estate managers to guide agricultural cooperatives has been encouraging.

3. The reform should be implemented in stages, each stage to be completed within a specified period of time. Such staging permits periodic evaluation of the efficiency of implementation, as well as helping to detect failures in time to correct them. The reform stages actually represent the pace of reform or the rate of introducing change, which depends on the available resources and on the readiness of the rest of the economy to bear the impact of change. For example, labor productivity may be raised by capital investment only if capital is available, but even then it may be unwise to invest if this would displace many more rural workers than can be absorbed elsewhere. Similarly, it may be difficult to introduce machinery if skilled workers are lacking, but it may be as futile to train people if they cannot be put to use in the near future. In other words, since agrarian reform replaces the market mechanism in guiding rural development, it is imperative that managers take into consideration the conditions of supply and demand expected during and after reform, so as to maintain a certain degree of balance between agriculture and other sectors. It is easy to see that had such planning been applied to the Mexican reform, the chaos and procrastination characterizing it would have been greatly reduced.

4. Since agrarian reform touches upon different aspects of rural life, its implementation should be guided and its effects evaluated by experts from different disciplines. It is most useful to look upon reform management as a team effort in which the economist, sociologist, educator, public health officer, and others are equally important and useful. This approach enriches the fund of knowledge at the disposal of management and provides a check on efficiency of implementation. Just to take one example: it is quite important that attention be given to children and young people deprived of farm work as a result of new labor legislation. Yet labor legislation and the building of facilities for displaced youth cannot be done by the same person, hence the need for teamwork.

5. Finances for executing the reform should be designated in the national budget concurrently with passage of the reform law, or at least before embarking upon its execution. Insufficiency of funds delays execution, reduces the confidence of those in the reforming agency, and probably affects popular cooperation with the reformers. India, for example, is reported to have found it hard to implement its reform program for lack of funds to pay

compensation and set up the necessary agencies. Japan could not execute the Owner-Farmer Establishment Law rapidly because of "insufficient budgetary appropriation." Insufficient funds for rural credit have been reported in many countries where the law provides for them. In such cases the reform cannot be expected to succeed. Therefore, to make the reform a reality, and to facilitate its management, funds should be allocated in accordance with the timing and requirements of the reform plan.

6. Finally, it is most important to isolate the political from the economic and social objectives of reform and to recognize that only by increasing productivity of labor can the basic rural problems be solved. The public should also be informed of the potentialities of the reform to avoid false expectations and subsequent disappointments, also to promote cooperation between the field worker and his clients.

Mechanization

Mechanization means the substitution of mechanical for manual power and, as such, the reduction of labor input per unit of output or of land. It also implies that the labor kept on the job must have higher skills to operate the machinery, hence higher labor productivity and income. Yet, in spite of these obvious advantages, mechanization of agriculture in underdeveloped countries has been slow. Several reasons may account for this:

1. There are contradictions between mechanization, which displaces labor, at least in the short run, and agrarian reform policies of spreading employment and pacifying the peasants. Inadequate planning, lack of resources, and obsession with matters such as equality and redistribution, political stability, and the fight against extremist tendencies preclude the introduction of labor-saving techniques, even if the workers remain underemployed and poorly paid.

2. It is considered economically more efficient to utilize less of the scarce resources, capital and land, and more of the abundant resource, labor, and to maximize output per land unit rather than per unit of labor. Therefore, intensification and not mechanization is often recommended. This, of course, assumes perfect substitutability of these factors, which is doubtful.

3. Mechanization requires skills, funds, and large-scale farm operation, all of which rarely exist in underdeveloped countries. Therefore, it is impractical and unfeasible to mechanize while these hindrances prevail.

Many people are persuaded by these arguments, and national policies have often excluded mechanization accordingly. However, the arguments are too general. Mechanization or lack of it must depend on specific factors such as climate, terrain, crops, land-labor ratio, attitude of the community, and, most important of all, on the individual farming enterprise. One cannot mechanize tropical agriculture, rice paddies, or tomato picking until the appropriate machinery has been invented. Furthermore, these general arguments are themselves not convincing and even deficient. Lack of skills and finances, along with an appropriate scale of operation, are structural problems that can be adjusted by agrarian reform; these will not be discussed here. We shall deal only with the theoretical and policy issues.

4. Spreading employment without increasing the productive capacity of the economy precludes higher labor productivity and income. It sustains

underemployment, reduces potential saving, and tolerates stagnant agriculture. Such has been the dilemma of most underdeveloped overpopulated countries, even where agrarian reform has been implemented. The classical contrasting examples are Britain, Scandinavia, and the United States on one side, and on the other Japan and Egypt, where productivity and income of farm labor have remained at or near subsistence levels in spite of their highly intensive agriculture.

5. Economic efficiency is relative and can be evaluated only from the standpoint of the proposed objective. Efficiency from the standpoint of national policy is not necessarily the same from the individual or entrepreneurial point of view, or from that of labor or the tiller of the land. Labor may be redundant in the economy as a whole, the short-run supply being fixed, but not so on the individual farm. Even members of the peasant family, if relieved of their duties, may seek outside employment and need not take future unemployment for granted.

On the other hand, intensification and mechanization are not mutually exclusive, nor are they substitutes. They may actually be complementary to each other and implemented in different degrees of intensity. Nor does mechanization necessarily reduce total employment; it may increase it by extending cultivation to marginal and submarginal land and by creating jobs for maintaining and servicing the machinery.

Finally, the economic efficiency argument against mechanization overlooks the interdependence between agriculture and other sectors of the economy and considers the rural problems as peculiar to that sector. Specifically, it ignores the possibility that marginal returns may be higher to labor outside agriculture and to capital inside it than otherwise. If so, it would be more efficient economically to transfer labor *from* agriculture and capital *to* it until the marginal returns of each factor are equalized in both sectors.

6. The final decision to mechanize and the solution of the relevant problems belong, however, to the individual enterprise. Therefore, whether to mechanize or not, and how to mechanize, may be decided upon as follows:

a. Mechanization must be evaluated in the context of the individual farm rather than of national agriculture. Economic efficiency of production is a problem of business management which is responsible for the producing unit, whether individual, cooperative, or collective.

b. If monetary returns to the farmer may be increased by mechanization, it should be adopted. Only then can the farmer afford to pay higher wages or to receive them as the tiller of his land. The farmer should therefore take account of money costs and returns and apply the techniques that render the highest profit, whatever the factor combination or the national policy on employment. Reports on the sugar industry in the Caribbean show that mechanization was recommended by a majority of the investigating commissions and committees in spite of the "abundance" of low-wage labor.[4]

[4] See, for example, Cedric O. J. Matthews, "Agricultural Labour and Mechanisation," *Caribbean Economic Review*, vol. 3, nos. 1 and 2, October, 1951.

c. The type of machinery, its horsepower, and methods of utilization should be decided with expert help after a thorough study of the local environment.

d. Mechanization should be introduced in stages to give the farmer and his helpers time to adapt to the new techniques. However, once a job is being mechanized, it should be mechanized fully.

e. The farmer should also take into consideration the nonmonetary effects of mechanization, such as better sanitation in the absence of animals, saving of space and of land formerly used for feed and now usable for other purposes, and the impact of regularity and certainty of production. If anticipated results are encouraging, the farmer may proceed with mechanization.

Transportation

Except for differences in degree, the impact of transportation on labor performance and income is the same whichever type is being utilized. The choice between types depends on local conditions. Generally, the impact falls in three categories: physical productivity, value productivity, and socioeconomic change.

1. Physical productivity of labor may be increased by the creation of roads, as an example, by saving time and energy which may be expended for higher production. Saving of time and energy may be up to 50% of current input, especially when the farm is distant from the village or market or when it is fragmented and requires the farmer to commute.

Building roads extends resource use to uncultivated and uninhabited areas or permits colonization of new land when such is obstructed by isolation and inaccessibility. Opening new frontiers is a classical example. However, building the road is only one step; its maintenance and use are equally important in providing employment for otherwise unemployed people.

2. The impact on value productivity derives from extension of the market. When means of transportation are available, rural products will find new markets in city and town rather than go to waste by spoilage or reach the market only after losing their freshness and thus much of their market value. The farmer will also be able to take advantage of changes in the market and the structure of demand for agricultural products, varying his production accordingly. The money returns may thus be increased.

3. Most important, however, is the impact on socioeconomic change. Connection between country and city may be the catalyst of change and economic development. The worker will now have a market for the product of his labor and for his labor itself. Geographic mobility, given the demand for his services, becomes possible.

Through contact with the city, the demonstration effect—the knowledge of and longing for new products—may stimulate a search for new sources of income, better skills, and probably a whole new way of life.

For entrepreneurs, including self-employed peasant farmers, contact with the city and assurance of a market may be strong enough stimuli to specialize and commercialize production and introduce new techniques.

The construction of means of transportation is usually accompanied by many difficulties. That is why it is usually undertaken by public authorities. The large amounts of capital and the complicated planning necessary are obvious difficulties. Less obvious but more important, however, are the following observations:

1. Roads are useless unless automotive vehicles are available and sufficiently used to justify the investment; the same applies to railways, airports, and other means of transportation. Therefore, the decision to build roads or railways implies a decision to invest in the vehicles that go with them. However, such investment is known to follow almost automatically.

2. To the local inhabitants roads are always useful and justified, but the same is not true to the national policy makers. They have to evaluate the efficiency of investment against the alternatives and in terms of the returns.

3. A decision needs to be made on the type of transportation to be constructed—whether it be a road for cars, a railway, or even an airport as the United States has thought fit for Afghanistan. This will depend on the uses projected, the type of cargo, the distances to be covered, and on the anticipated volume of haulage.

4. Probably the most difficult problem is to justify road building, or any other means, on a purely economic basis, especially if the road connects small isolated communities with each other or even with the city. In such cases the economic returns may be small relative to the investment. Yet most rural communities in underdeveloped countries are of this type. It is only when seen in a broader perspective and in a dynamic framework that such communications construction will be justified. Transportation means must be seen as stimuli of social and economic change, which in turn will reflect positively on rural performance and living standards. This was clearly experienced in England, where navigable waterways have usually been mentioned as primary factors in its early industrialization and development.

5. Finally, the individual farmer and the local community can play a significant role in the development of transportation. In fact, without their cooperation the benefits hoped for will remain a dream. The farmer can contribute accessible resources, including labor, and help maintain the road in the neighborhood of his farm. However, to derive direct benefits from it, he must connect his farm with the main road as well as facilitate communication on the farm itself. Otherwise, use of the road will be limited and cumbersome. In other words, the farmer should understand that the road is his and not the government's.

Supervised Rural Credit

Strictly speaking, rural credit benefits rural labor only in the latter's capacity as entrepreneurs—self-employed farmers—and only indirectly as wage labor. It affects the workers only to the extent that the credit is utilized by managers of the farms in new investment. Borrowing to cover current expenses, to compensate for crop failure, or to consume against future income will at best only prevent deterioration. As investment, rural credit has the same impact as any other investment, regardless of the source. The main feature to be treated here is the *supervision* of rural credit.

Supervision implies that credits will be used according to a plan approved by the lending agency. Supervised credit differs from regular credit in its function as an aid to the farmer in minimizing risk of failure, educating him in management, and setting examples to other farmers. Its success depends on the qualifications of the supervisor and of the farmer, on cooperation between them, and on the credit terms.

The Supervisor. The supervisor need not be an expert. It is enough if he is able to evaluate the feasibility of the project to be financed by relying on available data. For example, he should understand the functioning of the market and should assess the marketability of the product, the applicability of the proposed techniques, and the suitability of soil and climate for the particular crops.

The supervisor needs to know the applicant. Often such knowledge is acquired from prejudiced or misinformed local people. The author recalls cases when credits were extended on the basis of backing by the head of the village although the alleged farmer neither farmed the land himself nor intended to invest in it. Certainly such cases are exceptions, but they are enough to warn that in order to avoid misuse of resources the supervisor should acquaint himself with the community as well as with the applicant.

The Farmer. The farmer needs not only to have the skill or intention to undertake the project but also to be aware of the benefits and risks anticipated. Often a farmer embarks on a project only because someone else in the village did the same, or because his friend or neighbor suggested it. Regardless of the potentials of the project, unless the farmer himself is aware of them, he may not be able to put the resources to efficient use.

Cooperation between the Two. Cooperation between the supervisor and the farmer is the most important precondition of successful use of supervised credit. If the farmer is willing to inform the supervisor of developments at regular intervals and the latter is willing to evaluate them, it is unlikely that serious mistakes or waste of resources will go undetected for long.

To facilitate cooperation and to realize the objectives of supervised credit, the terms of credit should provide for:

1. Sufficient flexibility to permit periodic modification as decided jointly by the parties concerned, including the supervisor.
2. Adequate time for completion of the project before the farmer is required to pay the loan. Short-term credits, a year or less, are useless as means of guidance.
3. Adequate finances to be determined in proportion to the estimated cost of the project. However, the loan should not cover total costs, except when it is intended for colonization of new land or for movement of people according to a national plan.
4. Financing by stages according to the needs and progress of the project, each new stage to be preceded by successful completion of an earlier stage.

Terms of Credit. Finally, the terms of credit should be put in a simple enough form for the farmer to understand his rights and obligations. While the administration of supervised credit may be complicated and costly, its impact is tremendous, and investment in it is worthwhile.

Agrarian Planning

According to John D. Black, planning is the opposite of "*drifting*—to pass from doing one thing to the next that happens to come to hand with little or no thinking ahead as to where one wants to get and how to get there."[5] Thus, planning implies setting an objective and heading toward it. One may add that by planning one attempts to regulate the rate or speed with which he arrives at the objective.

Agrarian planning can be national, regional (sectoral), or local—on the level of the farm or producing unit. Its impact on performance and income of rural labor depends on which of these forms is applied and on the substance of the plan. National and regional planning, unless the latter is undertaken by a community of farmers with common interests, as in a cooperative, have nothing inherent in them to benefit the worker. National planning in Soviet Russia increased productivity and total production, but the income of labor remained the same or decreased. In contrast, planning in Sweden and Norway always made rural welfare a focal point and succeeded in raising the standard of living of the workers. Generally, national and regional planning influence the rural living standard according to whether or not they improve productivity of the worker and permit him a larger share of the product, and according to the extent to which they integrate the rural sector with the rest of the economy. We shall not deal with this type of planning.

Farm or local planning affects labor by increasing both productivity and the product value. It affects the standard of living of wage labor if it results in quantitative or qualitative improvement in the use of labor, as discussed above. The more interesting case, however, is that of the self-employed farmer, whether tenant or owner, as long as he tills the land and receives the product of his labor. If, then, planning leads to mechanization, intensification of labor use, crop rotation, better seed selection, better marketing, more efficient use of credits, or any such measure, its effects are bound to favor the worker and raise his income and living standard.

While detailed planning must be done separately for each farm, to be successful local planning must observe certain general principles, among which are the following:

The Planner. The planner must be the farmer himself, or his managing agent. He may, of course, seek outside help, but the final decision must be his own so that he will know what he plans for and how to get to it.

The Plan. The plan must be feasible. The planner should view the producing unit within the framework of the region and the economy—at least as these are defined by his market. He should have an estimate of his resources in physical and monetary terms—the soil and the best suited crop; marketability of the product; accessibility of machinery and applicability of the

[5] J. D. Black et al., *Farm and Other Operating Land-use Planning*, Harvard University Press, Cambridge, Mass., April, 1955, p. 8.

techniques; availability of funds; and anticipated changes in the composition of the resources, including labor available in the plan period. These questions are related to the technical feasibility of the plan, regardless of the economic efficiency of the techniques or investments.

Its Economic Efficiency. Economic efficiency or profitability of the plan may be evaluated by constructing a budget indicating the estimated monetary values of all inputs and outputs, since efficiency of production requires maximization of the difference between costs and revenues. This may be an impossible job for the illiterate farmer. The budget, however, need not be too refined; the problem has to be faced, and attempts should be made to solve it.

Importance of Flexibility. The planner should know of alternative objectives and methods of implementation. Knowledge of alternative objectives makes the decision harder but also more defensible. Being aware of alternative methods and techniques promotes efficiency and permits modification of the plan during implementation should obstacles arise.

Evaluation. To reduce the risk of failure and permit periodic evaluation, the plan must be set up for short and long periods and be organized in stages. Each stage should define the work to be done, the methods to be used, and the results to be expected. The actual results may then be evaluated in terms of expectations and by comparison with results obtained on other farms of similar structure.

A Problem in Education. The major difficulty is probably to convince the farmer that he needs a plan and that he should abide by it once it has been adopted, especially when the plan introduces new techniques. He may be growing olives, tobacco, or rice, having used the same techniques for centuries. Why should he change, and how can he be convinced that it is to his advantage to substitute machinery for the half-starved animals he uses, or for his sons, who have taken over his responsibilities and allowed him to lead a leisurely though poorly remunerated life?[6] This is a problem in education and social dynamics and can best be treated in that context. Two points may, nevertheless, be suggested:

1. The farmer may be reminded that he needs a plan, and that he is capable of setting up his own plan based on available advice. Suggesting alternatives and pointing out results from other experiences may be of great advantage to him.

2. By example and by gradual transfer of responsibility, it may be possible to convince the farmer of the benefits of alternative techniques. This is

[6] Skepticism of new techniques and innovations is well illustrated in a dialogue between two Chinese workers: "Comrade Wang, is it possible that you believe you know more than our Chairman Mao?" Comrade Wang retorts: "Comrade Li, there are many things that Chairman Mao knows which I do not know. But rice is our livelihood and perhaps it is not his. He is gentlefolk and I am not. His father was a landowner, but mine was a farmer. And my grandfather was a farmer and my ancestral fathers before that. These fields have been planted to rice for thousands of years. And not just to any rice but to the special rice which grows best in our earth here. . . ." Pearl S. Buck, "A Field of Rice," *Saturday Evening Post,* Dec. 29, 1962, p. 34.

suggested by an experiment in an Arab village in Israel.[7] Showing the farmer that the tractor permits deep plowing, that machinery can cultivate land inaccessible with oxen and horses, that the value of the product may be increased by the regularity and certainty of production assured by the new techniques, also that technical and financial assistance is more accessible to efficient farmers—all these may be convincing arguments. The exact approach, however, must be designed to fit the specific community under consideration.

BIBLIOGRAPHY

Bishop, C. E.: "The Rural Development Program and Underemployment in Agriculture," *Journal of Farm Economics, Proc.*, vol. 42, no. 5, pp. 1196–1206, December, 1960.

Brinser, A., and R. G. Wheeler: "Farm Planning as a Basis for Extending Agricultural Credit," *Journal of Farm Economics*, vol. 30, pp. 243–258, May, 1948.

Dumont, René: *Types of Rural Economy*, Methuen & Co., Ltd., London, 1957, especially chaps. I, VII, XII, and Conclusion.

Heyman, Hans, Jr.: "Air Transport and Economic Development: Some Comments on Foreign Aid Programs," *American Economic Review*, vol. 52, no. 2, pp. 386–395, May, 1962.

Kaufmann, J. H.: "Planning for Transport Investment, in the Development of Iran," *American Economic Review*, vol. 52, no. 2, pp. 396–404, May, 1962.

OEEC: *Farm Management*, manual on the preparation of national and regional handbook for use in farm-management advisory work, Project 395/1, Paris, 1958.

———: *Farm Management in the United States*, Project 395/B, Paris, 1958.

Owen, W.: "Transportation and Economic Development," *American Economic Review, Proc.*, vol. 49, no. 2, pp. 179–187, May, 1959.

———: "Transportation and Technology," *American Economic Review, Proc.*, vol. 52, no. 2, pp. 405–413, May, 1962.

Ruopp, P. (ed.): *Approaches to Community Development*, W. Van Hoeve Ltd., The Hague, 1953.

Saab, G.: *Motorisation de l'agriculture et dévelopment agricole au Proche-Orient*, Sedes, Paris, n.d., especially chaps. VI–IX.

Tuma, E. H.: *Twenty-six Centuries of Agrarian Reform: A Comparative Analysis*, University of California Press, Berkeley, Calif., 1965.

[7] This excellent experiment is reported on by the American Friends Service Committee; it was conducted in the Arab village of Tur'ān between 1950 and 1955. Frank Hunt of the American Friends Service Committee has kindly put a photostat copy of the report at the author's disposal.

IMPROVING SMALL FAMILY FARMS

Dr. Lorand D. Schweng

Introduction

Most of the farms in less developed countries are small family farms, although not necessarily subsistence farms. Their surpluses are individually small, but, owing to the large number of such farms, when taken together they often account for an important part of national production, if not of the volume of production that appears on the market. Agriculture in these countries is the most important economic activity.

The small farmers themselves are by far the largest occupational and social group. Their level of living—their economic progress, as reflected in increased production, increased purchasing power, increased demand for the goods and services produced by other sectors of the economy—is an important factor affecting the rate of progress of the whole nation and country.

Agricultural development plans tend to look upon agriculture in the abstract. Even when they treat the large-farm and small-farm sectors separately, seldom do they pay sufficient attention to the fundamental differences between the two. Certainly the large farms and the small family farms produce crops, livestock, and livestock products subject to the same laws of nature, and better resource use, better technology, better farm management are the ways to increase production on both; but the small family farm, which is characteristic of less developed countries, is not a minute replica of the large farm. The difference in size and in scale of operations does not show how fundamentally different the two types of farm are. Failure to recognize this fact has doomed many technically impeccable agricultural development plans and farm improvement programs.

At the time of writing, Dr. Schweng was associated with the Guayana Project of the Joint Center for Urban Studies of the Massachusetts Institute of Technology and Harvard University, Corporación Venezolana de Guayana, Caracas.

The purpose of this paper is to take a brief look at the small family farm and the conditions under which it operates, and to examine how the conventional measures used in farm improvement programs would have to be adapted to suit their peculiarities and special nature.

Small Family Farms and Their Setting

Small farmers live in hamlets or villages, and their fields lie around the hamlet or village. The "farm" is not a visible unit, except perhaps on an aerial photograph, because it consists of a lot in the village, where the house stands, and a small field or garden adjacent to or near the lot. The fields themselves are scattered over a larger area, are often small and of irregular shape, and are at a considerable distance from the house, often accessible only on foot or with animals. The farmer would have grazing rights on the communal pasture of the village, when there is one. When the village has woods, he has the right to collect firewood or get some timber from it.

Where the farmers live on homesteads, the farm is at least a visible unit, but it is not easily accessible, because the homesteads are often scattered and separated by large tracts of savannah or bush. Even when they are contiguous, they seldom have good access to the nearest all-weather road.

Illiteracy and physical isolation, along with the difficulties of movement and communication, make the world of the small farmers a narrow one. They live in closely knit communities which bind them together, with their traditions and mores, even in technical matters. They learn farming as part of their life, as part of their general culture. Technical operations are firmly embedded in their traditions, have symbolic significance, and are rituals.

The abundant resource of the farm is family labor. As other employment is virtually unavailable, family labor has low opportunity cost. The guiding principle in organizing their operations is to cope with the peak demands for labor with as little outside help as possible. The concern of the small farmers is survival and not profit maximization. Small family farms are thus economic units but not enterprises in the normally accepted sense of the word.

Because of the smallness of the farms their margin of safety is narrow, and the farmers are reluctant to take risks. Their planning horizon is restricted both in space and time. The one near, accessible market, or perhaps the intermediary who comes to buy their produce, limits their choice of crops. The present and near future loom large, while the more distant future is discounted at a rate which greatly reduces the attractiveness of long-term future benefits. The smallness of the scale of operations makes the farmers acutely aware of the constraints under which they operate. The number of constraints is enhanced by the general state of the economy and by their distrust and sometimes fear of the outside world and the agents who represent it.

There is great variation among less developed countries, just as there is often great variation in any one country. But even if one particular statement does not apply to every country and every small family farm and even if the general picture that emerges may need readjustment in one particular case, this summary of the special peculiarities of the small family farm will, it is hoped, be sufficiently accurate to support the arguments and recommendations presented.

Officials who are concerned with small family farms and whose task it is to work out plans to improve them, or the agents whose duty it is to implement programs of farm improvement, are from a different world, even when originally they come from a village or were born on a small family farm. Education in the towns, plus the habits and ways of thought acquired in the process, create a gulf between them and their kith and kin in the village, whose outlook they do not share and often can no longer understand.

Agricultural colleges in less developed countries teach principles which apply to all farms. But in teaching technology they teach advanced methods, i.e., those evolved in countries where the general conditions are different and where the farms are different from the small family farms of less developed countries. In farm management the discussion is usually restricted to the problems of larger commercial farms. A small family farm, producing largely for subsistence, seems to have no problems worth discussing; it is held to be the relic of an antiquated past doomed to disappearance.

Yet there is no hope that small family farms will fast disappear. Even Japan, whose rate of industrial development has not been rivaled by any other similar country, has not succeeded in reducing the number of farms or its farm population. Small family farms are here to stay for some time. In order to assure a better life for the farmers they will have to produce more—first, to provide more food for the farmers themselves, because many of them do not now have enough to eat, and also to provide larger surpluses for the markets. Economic development depends to a large extent on the extension of the exchange economy, but the changeover from producing food primarily for one's own consumption to producing cash crops is a difficult one. The success of such an effort does not depend only on changes in crops, technology, and farm organization but also on the efficient operation of marketing organizations and other services which the farmers can seldom provide for themselves without outside assistance.

Improving Technology

Primitive technology is generally held to be the principal cause of the low output of small family farms. Mechanization, the introduction of better crop varieties, the use of fertilizer, pesticides, and insecticides, and the introduction of better livestock are thought to be the answer.

These are methods which could increase production, but with some qualifications. Mechanization makes farm work lighter, increases the amount of work a man can perform in a given time, and enables him to expand his operations by cultivating larger areas of land, but it also requires cash and facilities for maintenance. There is no reason why farm work should remain backbreaking. But the saving of labor and time beyond the point where it enables planting to be on time or reduces losses in harvesting is costly when the time saved has no economic value, or when the use of machinery has neither increased production (by doing the work better) nor increased the cultivated area, because no more land was available for cultivation anyway and the machines did a rougher job than hand labor.

Far more attention has been given to improving farm machinery for big jobs than to improving hand implements and small machines. Also, large farm machinery has attracted the attention of authorities in less developed countries more than improved hand implements. In many cases splendid, expensive large machines stood idle most of the time or went out of service and soon had to be abandoned for lack of maintenance and repair facilities. More discrimination in investment would have spared farmers from serious losses, if not ruin, and governments could have spent the funds saved on more effective ways of improving agriculture.

Without the use of fertilizer or better methods of cultivation, better-yielding varieties can soon exhaust the soil and cease to yield more. Apart from this, the small farmer values a safe yield more than an eventual large one; hardiness and resistance to pests and diseases are for him so important that he is prepared to sacrifice large yields for lower but safer ones. Also, people who produce food for their own consumption, not food that goes through elaborate processing, are particular about its taste and have marked preferences which seldom enter into the thinking of the producers of better-yielding varieties.

Pesticides and insecticides occupy an important role in programs destined to help the small farms, provided the farmers can be protected against being sold fakes and are taught how to use them properly. The dangers of using poisonous chemicals on small farms where the household and farm work are inextricably mixed and where animals forage and graze freely are much greater than on larger farms.

In livestock management the popularization of highly bred stock has become the symbol of progress and the fact that the better stock will not produce more and better meat, milk, or eggs unless properly fed and cared for is often overlooked. For the small farmer, hardiness is often more important than a capacity for high yields requiring systems of feeding and management which he cannot cope with or afford. Even without improvement the native breeds often respond well to better feeding and management, and they could be developed by breeding to yield more and retain their hardiness and adaptation to the climate. Breeding animals for good production under conditions that could be provided on small farms deserves greater attention than the breeding of animals for record production under exceptional conditions or the popularization of imported breeds which often do not adapt themselves easily and well to the new climate and farm conditions.

Until recently the management problems of small family farms received little attention. With labor seemingly abundant it was thought that there was no problem. Yet there is a very real problem because of the great variation in labor requirements, the unfavorable ratio of effective working time to total time (due to the fragmentation and distance of fields and the topography and layout of the farms), and, finally, the relatively small flexibility of a small labor force. We must repeat: Operations on small farms are organized to enable the family to cope with the peak requirements for labor with as little outside help as possible. This is a rational aim considering that the labor requirements of the whole community vary in much the same manner over the season, and outside help would not be easily available when most needed. As time is not measured with any great exactness and records are not kept, an appraisal of the situation and help through advice in this field is very difficult. Data obtained on experimental farms are of no avail for the small family farms, because they usually refer to plantation crops and not to those grown on small farms. Even when they do refer to such crops, the layout of the fields, the manner of planting, the spacing of the plants, the implements used, and the manner of operation are different. Yet, without such information, no sound advice can be given. The observation of small farms is usually restricted to census-type surveys. Only continuous observation or the setting up of experiments with farms as a whole can provide the information needed and can, at the same time, enable those interested to test improved farm plans in the field. There are several ways in which such observations and experiments can be carried out. If they were carried out in different countries under different conditions, they could greatly add to our knowledge of the management problems of small family farms and would make it easier to improve them.

Methods for Improving Small Family Farms

Agricultural Extension. The conventional methods used for improving small family farms are the extension service, supervised credit, cooperatives, and agricultural education.

Organizing an agricultural extension service in a less developed country is more difficult and requires even greater care than in a highly developed country where agriculture is carried on larger, market-oriented farms.

First, the technical training of future extension agents acquaints them with a technology that is not applicable to small family farms. It makes them emphasize in their work technical efficiency and technological improvement. This gives them a point of view which is very different from that of the small farmer, who looks upon crops and techniques from the point of view of return and possible risk.

The agents' level of education also creates a cultural barrier between them and the small farmer. The prestige that goes with an office and a desk in less developed countries tends to make the agents impressed with their own authority and makes them prefer consultation in the office, impersonal distributing of leaflets, showing of films, and giving of lectures to dirtying their clothes and hands and teaching a farmer by actually doing things with him on his farm.

Even when the agents are well trained, their effectiveness is reduced by the difficulties of transport, the distances involved, the small scale of operations of the individual farm, and the time involved in giving individual attention to a small farmer. Yet it is on this that their prestige and success will depend. The distribution of leaflets can have only a limited role, not only because most farmers are illiterate but also because it requires more than reading ability to accept advice from somebody unknown. Nor can moving films and sound films be as effective with audiences who are not used to such films, even when the subjects and method of presentation take full account of the conditions in which small farmers work, and this is not always the case. Building up prestige and winning the farmers' confidence takes time and demands prowess in the skills the farmers know and can appreciate rather than a show of learning. Success depends at least as much on human qualities as on professional qualifications.

In building up an extension service and setting suitable standards, more attention ought to be paid to the actual level of the farmers to be served than to the pattern of service practiced in advanced countries where conditions are different. Greater value ought to be attached to men with good practical training and good human qualities, to the professional "noncommissioned officer" rather than to the "staff officer." Every effort should be made to make the extension agent a true field worker rather than a bureaucrat preoccupied with paper work.

Supervised Credit. Increase in production generally needs inputs like better seeds, fertilizers, insecticides, or pesticides that require a cash outlay. Maybe a better implement is needed, or a well or building has to be constructed or improved. Even when the best use is made of local materials, which, regrettably, have fallen into disrepute with "progressive" technicians, some parts or some materials still have to be purchased. At the same time, changing over from annual crops to permanent crops that take years to bring forth economic yields requires forgoing the income derived from the annual crops. Small farmers seldom have enough cash for such operational expenses, much less for larger and longer-term investments.

Given the small farmers' inability to handle money and the temptations of the shops in the nearest large town where they have to go to buy the necessary perquisites, coupled with their inferior position vis-à-vis the merchants, and it can be seen that loans in cash have considerable risks attached to them. Considering the limited planning horizon of the small farmer, it is difficult for him to draw up a plan to use a loan for long-term investments profitably.

The bad experience of agricultural banks with loans to small farmers made the idea of supervised credit popular. Here again, ensuring that this instrument works efficiently and that supervision does not defeat its purpose by costing more than the risks it is intended to reduce presents problems that are solved more easily in advanced countries, with clients who are larger and more business-minded farmers, than in less developed countries with small family farmers.

Small farmers are reluctant to contract loans against the security of their land. This attitude is understandable, because the loss of land is in most cases irreparable and means more than a financial loss—it entails loss of status in the community. Often they do not own land and cannot offer it as a security. For reasons discussed in connection with the extension service, the drawing up of a farm plan, the supervision of its execution, the release of the installments of the loan, and the control of the use of the funds are difficult to execute. The banks must of necessity be in the center of districts and are far removed from the farms; the postal service cannot be relied on, and each step involves a longer trip by the farmer or the supervisor of the bank, usually during a period when time is precious. The sums involved are small, which makes control expensive.

To make the system cheap and effective, formalities would have to be reduced to a minimum, and control would have to be decentralized and vested in men who are intimately acquainted with the manner of operation of the small family farms and the farmers themselves. This is one area in which cooperatives could help a great deal.

Cooperatives. With the emphasis on improvements in technology, cooperatives in less developed countries are thought of primarily as effective instruments for bringing about improvements in technology and the benefits of economies of scale by making small farmers pool their lands. Protagonists of land reforms often think that the beneficiaries of the reform could turn divided-up large estates into cooperative enterprises.

Experience has shown that small farmers are attached not to the land as such but to the individual plots they own; they are reluctant even to exchange plots to consolidate their holdings. To make them pool their lands for the purpose of mechanization and the benefit of large-scale operations is even more difficult. It is well-nigh impossible to persuade former farm servants and laborers who have come into possession of the lands of a divided-up large estate to continue to operate it or parts of it as a large unit; the discipline required by such an operation would remind them too much of the regime that had passed. But producers' cooperatives can help farmers a great deal in getting their supplies by assuring better quality, lower prices, and more favorable terms of payment. They could be helpful in purchasing implements and machinery which would be beyond the reach of the individual farmer, although in this field there are limits to the benefits because most of the implements and machines would be needed at the same time. Credit is an ideal field for cooperative activity, and so is the marketing of the farm produce. Cooperatives could do much to standardize production and reduce the small farmer's risks by providing a guaranteed market for his products and by helping in the changeover from subsistence to commercial farming.

In the rural communities of many underdeveloped countries, forms of cooperation and of mutual help once existed but are now the abandoned victims of "progress." Often they could not fit well into more advanced forms of organization that were being favored by the government and were being propagated or foisted on the communities with the help of more or less gentle pressure. However, streamlined, centrally controlled systems are likely to operate with a very much lower efficiency in the general climate of a less developed country, if for no other reason than the difficulties of communication and the loss of personal contact so essential to small farmers for the success of a truly cooperative venture.

Agricultural Education. With the best of effort, improving or changing the age-old technologies and patterns of management of established adult farmers is a difficult task and holds out limited hope of success. Greater possibilities lie in evoking new interests and in inculcating new habits in the new generation.

Generally the aim of educational authorities is to make the population literate, and most less developed countries find it difficult enough to provide elementary education for all children in rural areas and to keep them in the schools long enough to master the three Rs. Secondary and technical education are the privilege of a few. The usual requisite in vocational schools is six years of elementary education, and even this is the exception rather than the rule. In all less developed countries, agricultural schools are few and far between, and only an infinitesimally small fraction of the total number of farmers, or even of those who in any one year are about to take over the farms of their fathers, pass through an agricultural school. The purpose of the existing agricultural schools is, in fact, although not always admittedly, to train boys for jobs as foremen of larger farms, or for government jobs, rather than for operating small family farms. The agricultural colleges which require higher entrance qualifications avowedly aim at that.

Almost without exception the agricultural schools are in or near a town. The accommodation they provide is beyond anything dreamt of in the village and farms. The schools have rather large farms, much larger than the common type of family farm, and usually have more expensive large equipment than can be found on the best-equipped large, mechanized farms of the country. Of the crops grown on small family farms, only those are grown and studied which are also plantation crops. The livestock of the farm is composed of pure-bred foreign breeds or high-grade improved breeds. The sheds, stables, and sties are elaborate, expensive buildings, the like of which can only be found on the best large farms of the country, provided the owner is rich and likes to spend money on his farm without consideration of return. In instruction, the emphasis is on a solid theoretical foundation. There are exercises in farm work; there are schools where the farm is at some distance from the school and the pupils are taken for these exercises in buses.

Schools of this type make their pupils reluctant to return to their native villages and farms and equip them with knowledge which would be practically useless on a small farm should they choose to return. Such schools do not even prepare their students for the task of improving small family farms as extension agents or for planning the improvement of such farms as agricultural administrators, because their knowledge of technology is restricted to a type which is inapplicable to small family farms; of the management of such farms they know practically nothing.

If agricultural education is to serve its purpose, the schools will have to be in the midst of rural areas and not in towns. Besides giving the indispensable minimum in "theory," they will have to make their pupils adept in the use of implements and equipment that are within the reach of the ordinary run of small farmers, and instead of teaching technology in the abstract they will have to inculcate working habits.

I believe that in agricultural education civilians could learn a great deal from the military. Illiterate farmer boys in less developed countries are taught with great success to handle efficiently the most complicated equipment and weapons for purposes of destruction. Without a "theoretical base" they learn how to use them in a functional way even under difficult "battle" conditions. Their teachers are noncommissioned officers who have no theoretical base and in their turn were taught by officers. Only the officers have a broader and better theoretical background, but they are still adept in handling the instruments and weapons efficiently.

Administrators in charge of agricultural education would do well to pause and think about the reasons for the success of the military in teaching techniques of destruction to illiterate farmer boys and adapt some of these techniques for teaching these boys how to grow more food, raise better animals, and make life happier on small family farms.

It is an irony of fortune that in countries where the military does run vocational schools to prepare conscripts for their return to civilian life, when designing the schools and curricula the staff make exactly the same mistakes as civilian administrators.

Summary and Conclusions

In the brief space allotted to this topic, an attempt has been made to present a brief sketch of the principal characteristics of the small farms and examine critically the conventional methods used for improving them.

The gist of the argument is that small family farms are not minute replicas of large farms but units which are different not only in size and in scale of operations but also in their nature. The greatest resource of the small family farm is, within limits, its very smallness and the relative abundance of labor. The greater attention the small farmer can devote to his crops and his livestock the better is he enabled to achieve high returns per unit of land, which is the scarcest factor. Plans to improve small family farms should be based on recognition of this fact. Instead of making these farms adopt a technology for which they are not fitted or trying to merge small farms into real or phony cooperatives in an attempt to make them benefit from large-scale operations, small farmers should be taught how to increase their output per unit of land. Increasing output in relation to the scarcest factor will enable small farmers to increase their output per man year. In trying to introduce modern improvements in technology and better management, the peculiarities of small farms and small farmers should be scrupulously recognized and respected.

To work well, the methods used must be custom-tailored. No general system of organization and method applies to all countries, all regions, all groups of farmers. Because of this, it has been thought best to emphasize here the special characteristics of small family farms as they exist in less developed countries and point to the weak and critical points in the conventional methods of farm improvement programs which are likely to cause trouble. Thus, by examining carefully the family farms of their own countries, administrators will hopefully be able to recognize the situation frankly and devise, with realism, the methods best suited in the particular environment.

Small farmers of the traditional type are often blamed for their primitive methods and backward attitudes. But masters of the new technology and advocates of progress have seldom stooped to establish themselves on small family farms to show that they could do better under the same conditions as the ordinary farmers. The advanced level of farming in some countries is due not only to the technology developed by them but to the fact that educated and trained people were willing to live in rural areas, use the better methods, and live a different life under exactly the same conditions as their ill-instructed fellow farmers. They taught not by advising but by setting an example. To raise the bread the leaven must be mixed with the dough and go through the oven.

BIBLIOGRAPHY

Allen, Harold B.: 1954. *Rural Reconstruction in Action,* Cornell University Press, Ithaca, N.Y.

Bauer, P. T., and B. S. Yamey: 1957. *The Economics of Under-developed Countries,* James Nisbet and Co., London.

Belshaw, Horace. 1959. *Agricultural Credit in Economically Under-developed Countries,* FAO, Rome.

Binns, Sir Bernard O.: 1950. *Consolidation of Fragmented Agricultural Holdings,* FAO, Rome.

Brossard, Dario B.: 1954. *Manual de crédito agrícola suvervisado,* FAO, Rome.

Digby, Margaret, and R. H. Gretton: 1957. *Cooperative Marketing for Agricultural Producers,* FAO, Rome.

Dumont, René: 1957. *Types of Rural Economy,* Methuen & Co., Ltd., London.

Edwards, David: 1961: *An Economic Study of Small Farming in Jamaica,* University College of the West Indies, Institute of Social and Economic Research, Kingston, Jamaica.

Gourou, P.: 1953. *The Tropical World,* Longmans, Green & Co., Ltd., London.

Heilman, John: 1953. *El crédito agrícola planeado y supervisado,* Consejo de Bienestar Rural, Caracas.

Hill, George W., and others: 1959. *La vida rural en Venezuela,* Tipografía Vargas, Caracas.

Japan FAO Association: 1958. *Agriculture in Japan,* Tokyo.

Jolly, A. L.: 1952. "Unit Farms," *Tropical Agriculture,* vol. 29, nos. 7–12, pp. 172–179, July–December.

———: 1955. "Small Scale Farm Management Problems," *Tropical Agriculture,* vol. 32, pp. 80–87, April.

———: 1955. "Peasant Experimental Farms," *Tropical Agriculture,* vol. 32, no. 4, pp. 257–273, October.

Lewis, A. B.: 1954. "El fomento de recursos agrícolas," in *Desarrollo agrícolo y económico de la zona del Mantara en el Perú,* International Development Service Inc., New York (mimeographed).

———: 1955. *Agriculture in Santa Ana Mixtan, Guatemala* (mimeographed).

Lewis, Arthur W.: 1955. *The Theory of Economic Growth,* George Allen & Unwin, Ltd., London.

Makal, M.: 1955. *Village in Anatolia,* Vallentine, Mitchell and Co., Ltd., London.

Mead, Margaret (ed.): 1953. *Cultural Patterns and Technical Change,* UNESCO, Paris.

Nair, Kusum: 1962. *Blossoms in the Dust: The Human Factor in Indian Development,* Frederick A. Praeger, Inc., New York.

Najafi, Nazmeh, and Helen Hinckley: 1959. *New Life for a Persian Village,* Victor Gollancz, Ltd., London.

OEEC: 1950. *Agricultural Advisory Services in European Countries.*

———: 1951. *The Mechanization of Small Farms in European Countries.*

———: 1954. *Development of Agricultural Advisory Services in Europe since 1950.*

Redfield, Robert, and W. Lloyd Warner: 1940. "Cultural Anthropology and Modern Agriculture," in *Farmers in a Changing World,* U.S. Department of Agriculture Yearbook of Agriculture, pp. 983–993.

Rodríguez, Sandoval Leonides: 1949. *Vida económica social del Indio libre de la Sierra Ecuatoriana,* The Catholic University of America Press, Washington, D.C.

Skrubbeltrang, F.: 1953. *Agricultural Development and Rural Reform in Denmark,* FAO, Rome.

Tax, Sol: 1953. *Penny Capitalism: A Guatemalan Indian Economy,* The Smithsonian Institution, Washington, D.C.

Tschajanoff, A. W.: 1923. *Die bauerliche Landwirtschaft,* Springer-Verlag OHG, Berlin.

———: 1923. *Die Lehre von der bauerlichen Wirtschaft,* Springer-Verlag OHG, Berlin.

Warriner, Doreen: 1939. *Economics of Peasant Farming in Southeast Europe,* Oxford University Press, London.

———: 1948. *Land and Poverty in the Middle East,* Royal Institute of International Affairs, London.

Whetton, Nathan L.: 1948. *Rural Mexico,* University of Chicago Press, Chicago.

Wiser, William H., and Charlotte V. Wiser: 1951. *Behind Mud Walls,* Agricultural Missions Inc., New York.

Yang, Martin: 1945. *Chinese Village,* Columbia University Press, New York.

GRAIN STORAGE

Stephen S. Easter

The commonly accepted conception of a warehouse would not make a suitable grain store. It is interesting to think back on the role of grain storage in the dawn of civilization. Obviously the trend from precariously fed nomadic tribes to comfortably established farmers could not have been attained without means of growing definite grain crops and storing them safely from harvest to harvest. In many places this storage was accomplished with little difficulty, as the primary problem was one of keeping the grain dry. As communities grew closer and populations increased, the problems of storage increased. Larger amounts were involved. Travelers carried grain as staple food over all the known world. Unfortunately harmful insects and rodents were also carried and disseminated at the same time, until now the same insects and to a lesser extent the same rodents are found attacking grain all over the world, regardless of their original source.

The problems of storage have changed. In the early stages communities and countries were mere subsistence producers with minor movements of grain. Now vast quantities of grain move annually all over the world. Means of cheap transport and cheap handling are of major importance. There is a need for standards to ensure uniformity in grain shipped over a period of years. All these things and others must be considered in grain storage. Already, then, there is clearly seen to be a need for various specialists to cooperate in solving the problem. Entomologists, biochemists, zoologists, engineers, economists, and others must pool their knowledge.

In some countries the desire for adequate storage has been motivated by a need to control prices of basic foods. In one small country the prices fluctuated to triple the amount between harvests. This caused great hardship on the poor farmers and poor consumers. This country, Costa Rica, now has a storage system tied together with price control. When the purchase price of

---

Mr. Easter is a Consultant for the United Nations. This article is from his previously written "Grain Storage," in *Formulation and Economic Appraisal of Development Project*, 1951, vol. II, pt. IV, pp. 559–566.

grain in the open market falls below a set figure, the government buys grain—corn and beans—and stores it. If the selling price in the open market exceeds a set figure, stocks are released for sale. In this manner the prices of these two basic foods are maintained at a fairly constant level. It should be emphasized that this would be impossible without safe storage of the corn and beans; stocks would not be available at variable time intervals for release. Prior to the installation of a sound storage plant the system did not work in Costa Rica owing to heavy losses from insect damage.

Several other countries have recently started grain storage systems. They have found that it is not a simple proposition but requires much study before the actual construction can begin. First of all there must be statistics on production so that the magnitude can be judged. How much grain must be handled? How much will be needed in the producing area and how much will be surplus? What is the population? What is the trend in population? These and other questions must be answered by the economist. Sometimes these figures are available, sometimes not; in the latter case, the storage needs of a city or other center of population may be determined by a knowledge of the consumption rate of basic food. This information is to be gained from nutritionists. The location of storage sites must be determined by the pooled knowledge of various men—construction engineers, economists, and perhaps entomologists, as the climate in different areas could be a factor in the favorable or unfavorable conditions for insect growth. The actual siting of plants, selection of material, blueprinting, etc., must lie in the hands of competent experienced engineers after the functional design is planned by the people responsible for the grain handling. It must become obvious that no one specialist could possibly be competent to handle all these aspects of the storage problem.

After a storage plant is built, there is still a great need for the attention or supervision of some specialists. Men must be trained in modern efficient methods of grain handling to, during, and from storage; an incompetent manager can be an expensive luxury. The handling cost alone may be the key to a successful system. In the organization and operation of a grain storage system in areas where insect losses are high, the management can do more cheap, efficient insect control by sanitation, rotation of stocks, and sound storage procedure than by chemicals. It is frequently found that poor management offsets all the advantages of a well planned and constructed installation. Lack of trained personnel should be a factor in planning a grain storage system. One modern installation might be a logical start where personnel could be trained for future installations.

Handling should be considered further. It is customary where labor is cheap to disregard the aggregate cost of such labor. Attention may be paid to the low wage of the individual worker rather than the cost of a particular operation. Grain can be most cheaply handled in bulk where machinery can replace manpower. Under certain conditions it may not be economic to do so. Again there is a need for analysis by competent specialists.

What should storage provide? Primarily, good adequate storage should provide protection against insects, weather, and rodents. In tropical areas of high rainfall, protection against weather is an absolute necessity. In addition the storage system should provide facilities for cleaning, weighing, drying, and handling the grain properly and at low cost. There are, of course, other considerations, but these are major to a technician.

It will probably be beneficial to discuss in detail a specific problem in grain storage. The present study of grain storage in Pakistan should be an excellent example.

The problem can quickly be divided into three parts:

1. The domestic storage of wheat in the various centers of consumption
2. The farm storage of the entire country, estimated to be 60% of the total
3. The export of 400,000 tons of wheat annually from Karachi

The first two are important but would require more time than is available here to study the needs of farm storage and the extent to which present methods suffice. There is a still more important factor in the time and manpower which would be needed in extension to effect any material change in methods, providing that simple economic improvements were known. No more will be discussed concerning these two. The third topic is simpler and will be reviewed at some length with proposals for its solution.

A few basic facts should be considered first:

1. The export wheat (400,000 tons) is grown in the Punjab or Sind.
2. Some storage facilities exist in Punjab and Sind.
3. There is an adequate rail system which can deliver 5,000 tons per day in Karachi.
4. No storage facilities exist in Karachi.
5. The storage conditions in Karachi are infinitely worse than those in Punjab or Sind, because of the climate there.
6. There is a possibility that India may be a major market for the export of wheat.
7. The market in India is directly connected by railroad and lies close to the Punjab.

On the examination of these facts it becomes obvious that large storage facilities are not needed at Karachi. The only need here is for modern handling equipment with temporary storage sufficient to load about two ships. There is a great need for handling facilities, oversized, necessary to weigh, clean, bin, or deliver grain directly to ships. "Temporary" storage relates here to time and not to construction. The most modern bulk-handling installation is needed. The present sheds cannot be considered as grain stores at all, and as shown later are actually more costly than the most modern installations. Any extensive grain stores should be built in the Punjab, where most of the wheat is grown. The size and location is a study in itself, but certainly further construction should be of modern type and not costly makeshift warehouses suitable for nonperishable commodities. The economics of operation over a period of time should be the determining factor, rather than the initial cost. At present most of the grain in Pakistan is stored in jute bags containing about 224 pounds each. This bag lasts at most one year, must less if handled often. This bag is a storage unit differing only in size from a concrete or steel bin. It does not protect grain from insects, weather, or rodents. Its handling cost is high, as it does not fit into machine handling. Yet its cost is far greater than either steel or concrete. Over a period of ten years or less the cost of the bags in dead storage would alone pay for either steel or concrete bins. The bag at present costs U.S.$0.51 each, or $5.10 per ton of storage space. Small steel bins can be bought in the United States for a cost of from $10 to 15 per ton of storage. Modern plants equipped with all the necessary machines can be built complete in steel or concrete for about $35 to 70 per ton storage. The bag cost goes on each year for ever. The cost of the bin, including investment charges, is soon paid for. No consideration need be taken of the great savings from other losses in order to justify good modern storage where grain is now stored in bags.

Improved storage is needed in the Punjab and Sind. Concrete bins here have already proved their value. Expansion will require time and capital. In the meantime the needs are clear at Karachi as a standing point for the export handling. In Karachi at present grain intended for export is all handled in bags, making it necessary to handle it several times before ultimate delivery on board ship. The amount of handling varies, with only the usual minimum considered. Without any disruption of the present system of shipping from the producing area in bags, grain intended for export could be received at a storage terminal and handled thenceforward in bulk at minor cost. Such handling would include cleaning, automatic weighing, temporary storage, and delivery to the ship directly in bulk. The savings to be gained by a terminal will come directly from

1. The saving per ton handled in handling costs
2. The saving per ton stored in bulk by reducing the number of bags necessary

These can be determined quite accurately. There will also be other savings:

1. A reduction in the loss from insects, rodents, and fungus, which is considerable but difficult to assess accurately
2. Maintenance of high quality in the grain in order to command higher prices and ensure uniform delivery of clean dry grain
3. Reduction of time now lost in loading ships by inadequate handling
4. Reduction in mechanical losses from excessive handling

Some handling costs have been obtained from the port of Karachi, but it has been impossible to verify them. Some estimates have had to be made. These are indicated. The differences in cost of handling in the port are shown per ton for present methods and by bulk, in order to make it simple to calculate the savings based on volume.

Procedure by present methods	*Cost per 100 bags (10 tons)* Rs.	A.	P.
Unloading from wagons (box cars) and stacking in piles 10 bags high (higher piles cost more)	3	0	0
Unstacking, unsacking, weighing, bagging, and sewing for export movement of bags to ships	12	4	0
Loading in wagons	3	0	0
Railroad shunting charges to dockside	5	8	0
Unloading wagons and transfer to ship, emptying bags in hold, estimated	6	4	0
Total cost of port handling per 10 tons (cost per ton: Rs. 3, or $0.90)	30	0	0

Note: Grain may remain for months in open storage.

Procedure using modern bulk methods	*Cost per 100 bags (10 tons)* Rs.	A.	P.
Emptying bags only at wagon door to pit	1	0	0
Receiving, weighing, cleaning, and binning (½ cent per bushel)	6	2	0
Loading in wagons—eliminated	0	0	0
Shunting—eliminated	0	0	0
Loading in ships directly in bulk (¼ cent per bushel)	3	1	0
Total cost per 10 tons (cost per ton: Rs. 1–0–4, or $.31)	10	3	0

The estimated net saving per ton handled is therefore $0.59.

At present there is wheat stored in Karachi which is so badly damaged by insects that it would be unwise to export it except as a distress cargo at a greatly reduced price. This is in the interest of future sales. Wheat was examined which was fully 50% destroyed by insects; this was not an average but representative of the worst infested bags. Lacking sufficient samples to judge, it appeared that all the wheat in the port was infested and that the net loss might easily exceed 10%. Part of the loss was compensated for by a gain in weight due to absorption of water from the humid port atmosphere. This water is a poor substitute for the wheat consumed. It is reasonable to expect that any wheat stored in the open in Karachi for three months will sustain a loss of from 5% upwards due to insect attack.

The loss due to rodents cannot be assessed here. They are said to be present and to be causing some damage, but the greatest damage is usually caused by the cutting of bags and resultant spillage, rather than by direct consumption of grain. A modern grain storage plant in Karachi would reduce the loss from insect damage to a minor or negligible figure, eliminate the loss from heating, and exclude rodents completely.

With the use of adequate cleaning and classifying equipment, uniformly graded grain could be prepared which in time would be marketed more readily as its reputation was established. The wheat of Punjab and Sind contains a very low moisture content in the vicinity of 9 to 9.5%. This rises rapidly during storage in Karachi to 11.0% or higher, dependent on the time in outside storage. The covered sheds do not retard this gain in weight. With storage in tight bins until delivery to the ships, this low moisture content could be maintained and should bring a premium in price or demand.

The present system of loading ships is slow and costly. The costs of loading have been presented already, but the time of loading is important also. It was stated that as much as fifteen days might be required to load a large ship, which is very costly to the shipping company. With a modern grain plant the loading time should be reduced to not more than four days for boats up to 9,000 tons. This would reduce or possibly eliminate demurrage charges, which could conceivably amount to several thousand dollars per ship by extended delays. Such demurrage charges would be a direct cost to Pakistan. Port charges on tonnage handled are not included, as they would logically remain roughly the same whether grain was handled in bulk or bag. There might be a reduction for bulk handling, as the busy dockside wharf would not be used.

Finally, bulk handling in the port of Karachi would reduce a minor but constant loss due to spillage and leakage from the handling of bags.

It is quite obvious that large static or dead storage facilities are not needed in Karachi for the export grain, as said before. What is needed is temporary storage sufficient to load the maximum number of ships likely to be loaded at one time. The more this load can be distributed over the year, the smaller the plant needed. It would appear that a minimum of 20,000 tons might be logical, as this would permit the loading of two normal ships of 9,000 tons and leave some space for working capacity and off-grade grain from the cleaners. It must be kept in mind that a plant of 20,000 tons will handle a far greater tonnage of wheat if properly managed. If the load of shipping could be evenly spaced throughout the year, a plant of this size could quite readily handle the entire 400,000 tons for export. The plant should be equipped to receive wheat from wagons by emptying bags directly from the wagon door into pits or hoppers. From here the grain would be handled only in bulk and by suitable machinery. Equipment would consist mainly of automatic scales, cleaning machines, lofters or elevators, conveyors, and a small drier for insurance. Storage would be in vertical bins of 500 to 1,000 tons capacity each. Delivery of grain would be over the scales directly to ships. The railroad can deliver 5,000 tons per day. The plant should be able to handle 2,000 in full operations daily.

The cost of such a plant might be from $750,000 to 1,500,000, depending on many factors which only engineers experienced in this type of construction could determine. Assume it will cost $1,500,000, the maximum.

The benefits directly to be derived are as follows:

1. Assume that only 200,000 tons will be handled annually at a saving in handling cost per ton of $0.59.	
Assumed saving	$118,000
2. The saving in bags will be greater than the static storage capacity, as much handling is eliminated, but take only the static storage of 20,000 at $5.10.	
Assumed saving	102,000
3. By better management in the port, losses from insects, rodents, and fungi could be reduced without a modern plant. The saving, therefore, should be considered very conservatively at 2.5%, not the 12.5% or more which may take place. On November 2, 1950, wheat in Lahore was quoted at 8/12 to 9 per maund, or $71.04 per ton at 2.5%, or $1.77. This again should be saved on every ton handled from storage in Karachi. Much would come directly from Punjab, so this should again be conservatively based on static storage.	
20,000 tons at $1.77	35,400
4. By cleaning, classifying, and maintaining low moisture, grain would improve in quality (not assessable).	
5. By rapid loading of ships there should be a definite saving in port demurrages (not known, but can be determined).	
6. A definite saving in mechanical handling loss of ¼ of 1%, estimated on 200,000 tons at $71.04	35,520
Total annual savings based on 200,000 tons	$282,920

It is obvious that a plant of the kind portrayed could pay for itself in six to seven years, including interest charges on the investment. It should be noted that in all figures the most conservative estimates have been used. Operating costs are included in the bulk handling per ton. A more careful study would probably show a still more favorable report for a modern plant.

The storage system does not stop with the construction of modern plants. There must be much additional work and study to improve the whole system, including the grain itself. Luckily there is already one excellent variety of wheat grown extensively in the Punjab and Sind. In future the wheat breeders may replace this with an even better variety.

The transport may be improved. At present all grain is carried in railroad wagons in bags. Possibly water transport may be developed, and certainly grain will soon be carried in bulk with a considerable saving. Much of the infestation in grain begins in transport and is transmitted from cargo to cargo. The bag is the worst offender, as insects find excellent refuge here.

There will be a need for study by experts in marketing to ensure constant world markets at fair prices. There must be establishment of uniform grades and standards so that there will be an incentive to farmers to produce high-quality wheat.

Improvement is needed in the handling of wheat before it reaches storage. Agricultural engineers have a wide field for improving threshing methods—not necessarily by buying expensive combines but by introducing small hand-powered machines to take the place of bullocks. In this way the crop can be threshed without contact with the ground, resulting in cleaner grain of higher quality for market.

These are only a few of the related phases of agriculture which indirectly or directly affect a grain storage system. It should become obvious that all scientists concerned, regardless of their specialization, must cooperate to attain the desired end.

DEVELOPMENT OF RURAL PATTERNS IN ISRAEL

Dr. Raanan Weitz

The ancient Jews were a nation of peasants. When they were exiled from their land, history cut them off from the soil, and they were transformed into town dwellers in urban occupations. Their desire to return to the homeland was identified with their desire to return to agriculture. For that reason, when the Jews immigrated to Palestine, the new arrivals always hoped to turn to farming.

Arab agriculture, as it existed in Palestine, was based on a feudal system and on extensive farming. It provided the farmer with subsistence only. The Arab peasant was, in the main, a tenant of rent-collecting landowners.

The new farmers from among the Jewish immigrants hailed from central and eastern Europe and belonged to a generation that had revolted against ancestral traditions and the ways of life of the small townlets. Their purpose was to establish a society based on moral and spiritual principles: nationally owned land, the labor of the farmer's family, mutual assistance and full co-operation, pride of the working man in his work, and the ascendancy of the spirit over matter. It was on these general principles that three new rural patterns were evolved.

1. The *kibbutz* is a collective agricultural settlement. Both production and consumption are communal. All the members benefit from the public services provided by the kibbutz. Cooking, laundering, and education of the children are conducted on a joint basis. The kibbutz is administered by an annually elected secretariat.

2. The *moshav* is a settlement based on the family farm. Each family has a plot of land of its own, and both production and consumption are within the

Dr. Weitz is Director of the Settlement Department of the Jewish Agency for Israel.

range of the family. Nonetheless all the families in the settlement are affiliated in a cooperative union that looks after marketing, purchases, mutual assistance, and all the public services of the community.

3. The *moshav shitufi* is a settlement in which production is cooperative. Nonetheless, it is based on the family, for each family lives its life separately and receives its share of income in accordance with the schedule of work put into the farm as a whole.

All three forms were established by the free choice of the members, and in this they are basically different from the collective patterns or cooperatives to be found in Communist countries.

Mixed farming is the basis of all the Israeli forms of settlement. In other words, farming is based on a large number of branches, no outstanding priority being accorded to any definite branch. Such mixed farming enjoys a number of advantages:

1. Assurance of income in case any of the other branches should suffer from some natural calamity
2. A balancing of the work schedule
3. The possibility that the farm might be cultivated by the farmer's own family alone
4. The possibility of preserving the fertility of the land by a suitable rotation of crops

In early phases of land settlement, such mixed farming was extensive. As water resources were developed, however, it became intensive and made possible a considerable reduction in the area of land required for the subsistence of an agricultural family.

Each agricultural settlement constituted a closed and independent unit which was economically and socially self-sufficient and could exist independent of its surroundings. Such a unit included all the economic, social, and security services required for its existence during the Mandatory period in Palestine. The various forms of agricultural settlement were linked in an organizational network by means of national central cooperatives, which looked after marketing, purchases, credits, and so forth.

On the establishment of the State of Israel, far-reaching changes were brought about in the social and economic conditions of the rural regions.

The most important change was the appearance of a new human element. Whereas until the foundation of the State the majority of the settlers in Jewish villages had been of Western origin, with the surging waves of immigrants that arrived from Middle Eastern, African, and Asian countries there came people who brought with them the social-patriarchal background of their countries of origin. Many lacked all technical and vocational skill, whether in agriculture or in any other branch of endeavor, and were accustomed to a low standard of living. Very soon it became apparent that there is a considerable internal and basic difference between the technological and organizational systems that are an outcome of Western culture and the social structure and mode of life of the Afro-Asian immigrant. There exists in Oriental society a certain natural internal opposition to the employment of methods originating in Western traditions. Hence any plan imposed and directed by experts of a Western mode of thought will not ensure the desired results. Indeed, all the forms of settlement that existed in Israel were found to be unsuitable for the absorption of the immigrants from Asia and Africa, and so the need arose for new systems of development and an adaptation of the systems of transferring knowledge and guidance to their special mode of life.

An additional change occurred in economic conditions. The rise in the general standard of living and the necessity for balancing such a rise among the agricultural population, as well as the need to increase the volume of exports, made it imperative to launch new systems of agricultural production based on increased efficiency, specialization, and the utilization of the natural resources peculiar to every region in the country. The result was a departure in the structure of the agricultural farm from one of multicultural mixed farming to specialized farming exploiting the special conditions of the particular region.

These changes gave an impetus to the creation of new rural organizational patterns, of which the principal are:

1. The creation of suitable conditions for the development and cooperation of the internal leadership in the village. The traditional patriarchal structure is based on ethnic units led from within. It is necessary, therefore, to gain the confidence of this leadership and to induce it to follow what is necessary for economic progress. One must also take steps to induce the creation of a new leadership from among the young generation, at the same time preventing any decline in authority which might impair all the efforts at rural development.

2. The creation of conditions to attract and settle a suitable team of experts and public servants within rural regions. Such a team is composed primarily of teachers, nurses, instructors, mechanics, etc., who come from outside the area. They will gradually be replaced by local people who have acquired the necessary knowledge and know-how. The creation of such conditions may stop the exodus of the progressive and more educated elements from the rural regions, especially at a time when they are most needed there.

3. The establishment of economic, educational, cultural, and consolidative services that are both efficient and inexpensive. Assuring the continuity and stability of the rural stratum is possible only if the settler is guaranteed adequate services at a cost comparable to those accorded to urbanites. Likewise, if we want to build up an economy capable of competing with the market and to improve the quality of the produce, we must necessarily provide special services relevant to the nature of regional production. These must be intended for the region as a whole, not only for one single village, and will therefore be more efficient and at the same time inexpensive.

4. Economic changes and the transition to the production of industrial crops necessitate the introduction of industries in the agricultural region. Agricultural produce requiring processing (cotton, sugar beets, etc.) should preferably be processed in the region where it is produced in order to effect savings in transportation cost, etc. In addition, to ensure rural social stability and prevent migration from the villages to the towns, it is necessary to develop in rural regions various industries which will be able to absorb surplus manpower and supply additional employment and sources of livelihood to the farmer's family, or to those who were forced to abandon agriculture in favor of

nonagricultural vocations. In this way, the structure of the rural community will be preserved.

Relying on these principles, Israel has produced a new approach to the development of the rural regions, based on comprehensive rural planning.

"Comprehensive planning" means the linking of agriculture, industry, and services within a certain region and an examination of their relationship and mutual influences from the economic, social, organizational, civic, and security, as well as environmental, points of view.

The basic nucleus is the special regional structure in which the individual agricultural settlement no longer constitutes an independent socioeconomic unit but only one link in a composite regional structure. A suitable number of agricultural settlements are linked to a rural center. In such centers are located all the economic, consumer, and social services which the settler needs. The concentration of all these services for a number of settlements means greater efficiency and reduces their cost. The center also includes a special residential quarter for the public servants and professional people serving the farmers in the district. Their concentration in one special residential quarter creates a social atmosphere in keeping with their requirements and attaches them to the agricultural region. We have called this basic nucleus a "composite rural structure."

A number of such nuclei constitute a settlement region, at the center of which a regional town is situated. Here the large industrial concerns and the more central institutions intended to serve the whole region are located—for example, factories for the processing of agricultural produce, a regional secondary school, a hospital, a regional experimental station, and all the required government institutions.

At a later stage of development, suitable industries are also established in the rural centers. In this way, it is possible to obtain a new link between the farmer and those engaged in other vocations and to guard against creating a gap between the farmer and the remainder of the population.

With the introduction of this new planning, the systems of implementation were improved upon, and new ones were tried out.

In the first place, teamwork was introduced into the region. Such teams included experts in the economic, agricultural, and communal spheres. Joint work and a joint study of the regional problems bring about coordination and collaboration in all the local problems and lead to an organized and desirable related development of the rural community in all walks of life. The team is headed by an expert in composite rural planning.

Secondly, a suitable system of guidance was introduced, established in accordance with the nature of the settlers. Experience and research have shown that it is necessary to adapt the methods of agricultural guidance to every type of settler and to every standard of vocational know-how. It is often necessary to maintain several different kinds of guidance in one settlement in accordance with the ethnic origins of the settlers and their level of knowledge. Guidance methods were therefore adapted to the social structure and particular origins of the people.

Thirdly, in order to teach the settlers new agricultural methods and at the same time to avert crises, the system of the "directed transition farm" was introduced. The settlement is directed over a certain period in the form of an agricultural farm, and each settler receives wages for his work. In this way, the income of the settler is secured, even though he lacks vocational know-how, and is not in a position to cope with the work on his land. On the other hand, in this way he acquires the required vocational techniques and gradually passes over to the cultivation of his family farm.

The composite rural development method was introduced in certain new experimental regions and was later transferred to a whole region, "the Lachish Zone." Only after the success of this method was proved was it introduced into more veteran agricultural regions.

THE USE OF TOOLS IN SELF-HELP PROGRAMS

Frank L. Goffio

"Helping people to help themselves" is a timeworn phrase in danger of losing its meaning through constant repetition. It is a phrase bandied about too loosely by many people engaged in foreign aid or technical assistance. It is nevertheless a very basic expression of what we attempt to accomplish by an effective distribution of tools in a program of self-help.

CARE, the Cooperative for American Relief Everywhere, Inc., was formed in 1945 as a private, nonprofit organization which focused its attention upon the widespread hunger in Europe. In 1950, after the European relief program had helped to improve conditions on the stricken continent, CARE expanded its mission to include other underprivileged areas of the world, areas in which the standards of living barely matched the minimum requirements for human growth and development.

Although its campaign to relieve hunger effectively filled an immediate need, it was soon recognized that this type of relief was essentially temporary in character, providing no solution to the longer-range problems of productivity among the underdeveloped nations. A more permanent solution had to be found. By examining the economic realities of the countries in which they served, CARE mission personnel, working with outside specialists, made recommendations which led to the formulation of a program known simply as "self-help."

Two principles underlie this program. There is, first of all, the belief that many people in the underprivileged areas of the world are victims of circumstance rather than indolence and that, given the proper impetus, they are eager to improve their economic situation through their own efforts. Secondly, it is felt, the proper impetus to stimulate greater productivity is effective programming of necessary tools and equipment.

Mr. Goffio is Executive Director of CARE, Inc. (Cooperative for American Relief Everywhere), a nonprofit organization for relief, rehabilitation, and reconstruction.

CARE's self-help program today, financed by one-third of the donations received at the organization's world headquarters in New York, has been broadened to include thirty-six countries of the world. Funds expended for the purchase of fifty different kinds of standard self-help kits—woodworking kits, mason's kits, electrical workshops, educational kits—and a wide variety of nonstandard items ranging from toothpaste to piglets, X-ray machines, and fire-fighting equipment, total almost $34 million since the inception of the program.

Program Criteria

An exacting set of criteria are applied to self-help programs in countries which have requested assistance. Designed to bring about community-level changes in agricultural production, health and sanitation conditions, educational levels, and technical skills, self-help projects must meet the following guidelines:

1. *Need.* The program should aim at meeting basic, high-priority social and economic needs. Emphasis should be on stimulating permanent improvement as against temporary relief.
2. *Supplemental assistance.* In order to achieve a significant impact upon basic social and economic problems, the self-help program should stress the supplementing of existing programs of government and other agencies by providing essential equipment otherwise unavailable.
3. *Cost.* The costs of a program should be considered in relation to the number of improvements expected and the number of beneficiaries involved (per capita cost).
4. *Ability to utilize.* Adequate supervision should be available to ensure proper utilization of equipment supplied. Complexity of equipment should be commensurate with the technical and economic ability of the beneficiaries to use and maintain it. Equipment for training purposes should be provided only when there is assurance that new skills can and will be utilized.
5. *Beneficiary participation.* Programs should embody contributions by the beneficiaries themselves. A *quid pro quo* in terms of labor, material, or a revolving fund system must exist so that the area of impact will be extended.
6. *Community organization.* Programs should aim at assisting communities or groups of beneficiaries engaged in a common effort.
7. *Multiplier effect.* Programs should embody a multiplier effect, whereby the assistance extended further stimulates cooperation and development within or beyond the immediate project.
8. *Local responsibility.* Self-help programs should aim at developing an awareness of and a sense of responsibility for basic problems on the part of the beneficiaries, local groups and agencies, and government bodies. The assistance extended is of particular value when it can aid local groups to translate general concern into realistic, well-organized programs.

Program Areas

The broad people-to-people self-help program administered by CARE reaches out into eight sectors vital to local development:

1. Agricultural and industrial production
2. Community development
3. Education
4. Health and medical relief
5. Emergency or disaster relief
6. Refugee resettlement and assimilation
7. Vocational training
8. Social welfare

At the present time CARE is conducting self-help programs in Afghanistan, Algeria, British Honduras, Ceylon, Chile, Colombia, Costa Rica, Cyprus, Dominican Republic, Ecuador, Egypt, Greece, Guatemala, Haiti, Honduras, Hong Kong, India, Iran, Iraq, Israel, Italy, Jordan, Korea, Liberia, Libya, Malaysia, Mexico, Pakistan, Panama, Philippines, Poland, Sierra Leone, Tunisia, Turkey, Vietnam, and Yugoslavia.

While CARE insists that trained personnel be on hand to instruct the recipients in the most effective use of the tools, it does not directly participate in the training procedures. Wherever possible, CARE seeks out local technicians, or technical personnel from the Food and Agriculture Organization, the United Nations Children's Emergency Fund, the United Nations Relief and Works Agency, the World Health Organization, the Peace Corps, the U.S. Agency for International Development, or host government technicians to give proper supervision to a particular program. Each project is then worked out by the local CARE mission and submitted to New York headquarters for careful review.

Program Effectiveness

The introduction of CARE tools through a self-help program has helped bring about significant changes in productivity, health, and education on the local level. Typical examples include:

1. *Farm implements.* Donations of 24,408 plows and wheel hoes and 48,301 packages containing 259,228 hand tools have provided enough farm implements to help 320,000 farmers and their families increase crop yields and raise family incomes.

2. *Preserving jars.* Distribution of 7,638 packages totaling 353,740 quart and 41,816 pint jars to farm women who have preserved 374 tons of food every harvest season, helping to feed almost 33,000 farm families throughout the year.

3. *School kits.* Shipments of 277,685 packages of writing materials in four areas of Asia help educate 277,685 children.

4. *Sewing machines.* Gifts of 6,534 sewing machines to vocational schools, community centers, and village workshops help 131,000 women, men, and young people make their own clothing and qualify for jobs as seamstresses and tailors.

5. *Woodworking kits.* Introduction of 11,045 woodworking kits containing 237,120 tools helps train and equip 110,000 men and boys to build village improvements and earn their living as carpenters.

6. *Midwife equipment.* Donations of 8,120 kits and replacement packages

of instruments and sterile supplies help protect the lives of 161,766 newborn babies and assure proper instruments for thousands of additional births.

7. *Mobile health units.* Previous shipments of 66 mobile health units are helping in the examination and treatment of 1,500,000 people and in the demonstration of proper health techniques to 6 million people each year.

These programs, however, have not always met with uniform success, and it may be useful to review briefly here several examples, discussing the impact of each program upon the beneficiaries and the pitfalls which were encountered in the administration of the program.

Panama: Fishing Cooperatives

In Panama, an important self-help program was responsible for the formation of the country's first fishing cooperatives. These cooperatives were developed to assist fishermen who, although determined to improve their economic conditions, lacked the necessary capital to make effective progress in their fishing techniques.

Panama was singled out for this series of pilot projects because of the poverty within its fishing industry. Protein deficiency, with its resultant effects in malnutrition and tubercular diseases, had become a serious problem in the country. The primitive methods employed by the Panamanian fishing industry had not been able to produce sufficient quantities of fresh or dried fish to alleviate this shortage. As a result, the government of Panama was forced to allocate $800,000 out of a total annual budget of $67 million for the importation of fish for domestic consumption. Those unable to afford the imported fish had to purchase the locally dried product, often rotten and germ-infected due to improper treatment.

It was found that the Panamanian fishing industry is largely composed of fishermen who were originally farmers but were driven to the sea for lack of work on the farms. Most of them live in conditions described by observers as "subhuman" and risk considerable exploitation by middlemen through whom they must deal to market their fish in the interior of the country. Moreover, the methods they employ to obtain their catch are those of a people who have not had long experience with the sea. Their fishing boat, or *cayuco*, is a small, unstable dugout canoe without sails, which prevents the fisherman from venturing far out to sea or handling a large net, and the type of net used limits their fishing to beaches and therefore to seasonal catches.

Faced with these economic conditions and the disorganized structure of the fishing villages, CARE officials felt that outboard motors could not be granted outright to fishermen who had never handled them before and had no idea how to repair and maintain them or how to market the additional catch obtained by the use of the motors. To ensure proper use of the donation, it was decided that the most logical solution would be the formation of a cooperative along the same basic lines as those followed by the various agricultural, fishing, and housing cooperative organizations in other countries. These ordinarily include the establishment of a "revolving fund," in which equipment or supplies given by CARE constitute the basic capital of the cooperative, enabling members to increase their own profits. Under cooperative by-laws, the members are in turn required to invest a portion of their increased profits back into the revolving fund, so that other needy members may purchase whatever equipment they require.

Since these were to be the first fishing cooperatives in Panama, the program was cosponsored by the Panamanian Department of Fisheries and the Agricultural Extension Department. They assisted in the formation of the cooperative, while the Food and Agriculture Organization of the United Nations supplied an expert to provide guidance on the most appropriate type of fishing boat for Panama.

The villages of El Higo and El Farallon were chosen for the pilot project. A credit cooperative had already been established in El Higo under the guidance of the Agricultural Extension Department. Interest had also developed among the villagers of El Farallon, who had long been served by a CARE milk distribution program.

Under a cooperative structure, the incorporated cooperative organization retains title to any material received from CARE, renting it out to its members for a percentage of their additional income. However, since the organizers of the cooperatives in El Higo and El Farallon did not want to lose the support of the most enthusiastic participants, the boat owners, or to upset the traditionally individualistic economic structure of the villages, it was decided that most of the boats, outboard motors, and nets received from CARE would be sold by the cooperative to the four or five boat owners in each village on a long-term credit basis, with repayment made to the cooperative as a percentage of the daily catch. Furthermore, each fisherman was to contribute whatever he could each week toward the purchase of a full $5 share in the cooperative. The capital accumulated from this repayment would form the basis of a revolving fund which could eventually be used for cooperative development in other fishing villages. Each boat owner was to be responsible for all incurred expenses and would divide his catch with the six or seven members of his crew, giving 60% to the crew and taking 40% for himself.

The Panamanian project was furnished with sixteen outboard motors, varying from 18 to 25 horsepower, for use by these cooperatives, and it has obtained the services of a master boat carpenter, who taught the villagers to build a 22-foot New England–type dory boat under specifications set by an FAO marine engineer. This type of boat is easily erected by those inexperienced in boatbuilding and is sufficiently rugged for use in Panama's waters. Twelve of these boats were built by the villagers.

During the formation of the cooperatives, two nylon drift gill nets were distributed to the fishermen as substitutes for the cumbersome beach nets they had been using. Overcoming their initial hesitation and skepticism, the fishermen found that the new nets not only increased their catch of fish but, much to their surprise, also brought in more lobsters than they had been able to obtain by using lines, hooks, and lobster traps. On one day, for example, the fishermen caught 127 pounds of lobster with the new gill nets as compared with 112 pounds caught at best by the hook-and-line methods. The net also enabled them to increase their daily catch of fish to 1,091 pounds, compared with the 192 pounds obtained with the old beach nets. Made of nylon, the new gill nets are able to stand up for a considerably longer period of time without repairs. For this reason, the old nets are now being replaced with nylon ones while the fishermen become accustomed to the use of drift gill nets and lampara seins.

The organization and development of fishing cooperative projects in El Higo and El Farallon has not proceeded without difficulty. Although Mr Roberto Chiari, then president of Panama, had given his full support to the projects, there were several instances of unsuccessful government agency attempts to monopolize the sale and purchase of the fish. In addition, Communist elements denounced the projects for working outside the Communist framework as cooperative ventures in private enterprise, while, on the other hand, the capitalist element criticized them as an outgrowth of communism. The confidence of the American and Panamanian governments, CARE, and private enterprise in both countries, however, has been expressed by joint investment already totaling over $90,000 and by their close cooperation to assure the success of these pilot projects. The Fisheries Office of the U.S. Department of State has called these "the only true fishing cooperatives in Latin America," and President Kennedy took a personal interest in these cooperatives as one of the first successful examples of Alliance for Progress assistance.

Colombia: A Community Development Project

CARE's community development enterprise in Colombia has also attempted to bring about measurable accomplishments of real significance. In cooperation with the country's *Accion Communal* program, it is elevating conditions of rural life through improved agricultural techniques, better housing and community facilities, and the modernization and improvement of education.

The town of Candelaria was selected for one of these community development pilot projects. A *municipio* of some twenty thousand people, it is representative of many localities in the rural lowlands of the upper Cauca valley.

In order to create a healthier environment in the poverty-stricken town, an integrated program focusing on health, home, agriculture, and economic productivity was needed. The solution was a cooperative venture between the pilot health center at the nearby University of Valle School of Medicine and the extension services of the CVC, a Cauca Valley development service similar to the Tennessee Valley Authority in the United States.

Financial support for acquisition of the tools and equipment was limited. In turning to CARE for help, Colombian authorities expected, from earlier experience, that the agency would seek to provide it in the most effective manner.

For nutritional improvement CARE supplied substantial quantities of milk. But, in addition, it made available some $16,000 worth of other materials and supplies, including 10,000 chicks for enlarging agricultural earnings, an audio-visual trailer for health, home, and agricultural education, 200 sets of agricultural hand tools, vaccines for fighting endemic diseases (tetanus, diphtheria, whooping cough), midwife kits for helping newly trained midwives to improve childbirth standards, and laboratory equipment for the central clinic.

The project was also extended into six adjoining towns. In each of these a small medical center has been erected. The School of Medicine now has five recent graduates making the rounds of these substations, along with a physician-director at the Candelaria clinic, a dentist, a public health nurse, and several auxiliaries.

The CARE-supported community development program in Candelaria is making significant changes in every sector of the town's life. Housing conditions, water pollution, education, drainage and flood control, and economic and home improvement activities are daily demonstrating the effectiveness of carefully programmed self-help assistance.

Iran: Plows and Agricultural Hand Tools

The productivity of soil and labor in any underdeveloped area is very largely determined by the form of the implements employed in soil cultivation. Iran is no exception. The marginal farmer in Iran has virtually no agricultural equipment except for his wooden drag or clod-crusher, plus a few simple hand tools. His continued use of a primitive plow is primarily due to its cheap cost and ease of construction, use, and repair, but his plow is hardly suited to the optimum yields and increased per capita income which are so desperately needed in the rural areas of Iran. Generally of shallow draft, this wooden plow prevents the soil from being turned over deeply enough to kill weed growth and to provide good seedbed preparation.

Indeed, the lack of modern hand tools and of mechanized farming techniques is largely responsible for the fact that Iran has 78% of its population producing only two-thirds of the country's food requirements (compared to 8% in the U.S. producing a massive annual surplus) and that Iran's annual growth rate in agricultural production is only 3.3% (compared to the 3.6% average for other countries of the Middle East). A graphic example of these poor conditions is provided by the production of Iran's major food staple, wheat, which, with barley, occupies 4 out of the 6 million hectares of land currently under cultivation. Yet, in spite of the enormous concentration of manpower devoted to wheat farming, Iran must continue to import wheat.

For these reasons CARE undertook a two-part program of agricultural assistance to Iran in 1959, working primarily through the Agricultural Extension Service and Education Programs of the Iranian Government and with local agencies in the community development field.

The first segment of this program involved the distribution of $22,000 worth of agricultural hand tools to farm youth organizations throughout Iran in the early part of 1960. It was felt that such a program, placed under the effective administration of the Agricultural Extension Service, could have far-reaching effects in terms of training young Iranian farmers in the use of modern farm implements.

The tools distributed included a standard agricultural tool kit (consisting of a hoe, rake, spade, and cultivator) plus castrators, sheep shears, syringes, dusters, sprayers, and scythes, all of which could be used by the farm youth club members in their own projects. It was found that the arrival of these tools had a significant impact upon club membership, which increased by 67% from the 1960 figure of 4,284 to 7,139 in 1961, while the number of clubs themselves increased from 219 in 1960 to 379 in 1961 (73%). Moreover, the number of projects in which the original recipient clubs engaged, such as vegetable gardening, citrus farming, field crops, poultry, and sheep and cattle farming, increased by 73% from 1960 to 1961.

Apart from the educational benefits derived from these tools, they also helped the recipient clubs gather funds to expand into new activities. Tools were loaned out to members, who sprayed stables, castrated livestock, sheared sheep, or vaccinated poultry for local farmers, using the income to buy new tools and repair the ones they received from CARE.

The success of this particular program was reflected in a report made by the U.S. Agency for International Development mission in Iran, which stated that "general response to this program has been good, and, in some cases, the accomplishments of specific clubs utilizing this equipment have been outstanding, mainly in the field of poultry vaccination, castration of lambs, kid goats, and calves, and in the shearing of sheep."

In 1960 CARE also attempted to meet the Iranian farmer's need for a better plow with the purchase of 1,166 specially designed CARE plows for distribution to farmers in four areas of the country. It was hoped that, through demonstration, these plows would change the farmer's suspicious and conservative attitude toward metal plows and would encourage local production of these plows by village blacksmiths.

Unfortunately, this program proved to be only of limited success, and the reasons for its failures may well serve as a guide to other administrators involved in this kind of program. CARE depends, wherever possible, upon local technical experts and local agencies for the planning and administration of its self-help programs, but in this particular case these groups did not prove to be competent. While several farmers who received the plows reaped the obvious benefits of increased crop production and training in the use of metal plows, most of the plows were not used at all, because of their faulty design and the improper timing of their distribution. The design of these plows and the details of the plow programs had been worked out by local technicians and local agencies during three years of testing and demonstration. In one area, however, the plows eventually distributed were not strong enough for the hard soil, while in another the plows, designed to be pulled by horses, were distributed by a local agency to farmers who used oxen. In a third area, oxen-drawn plows were distributed to farmers who used oxen, but, because of the time lag between the initial planning of the project and its final implementation, tractors had become available to the farmers in that area through local machinery cooperatives. The undistributed plows from each area had to be collected and stored for use in other areas of Iran.

Korea: Livestock, Seed, Fertilizer

Tools are but one approach to the problem of insufficient agricultural production. In Korea the emphasis of CARE programming has been on livestock, seed, and fertilizer to refugee assimilation projects sponsored by the Korean government, projects designed to resettle refugees from Communist North Korea by providing them with arable land.

Typical of these projects is the assistance provided in 1961–1962 to Cheju Do island, situated 90 miles off the southeast coast of Korea. Refugee families had settled in Cheju Do five years before, having been driven out of North

Korea by Communist guerrillas. Trying to extract a living from 30 acres of upland under cultivation, they were able to produce only three months' worth of their annual food requirements. They therefore decided to raise their yields, as well as their incomes, by introducing potato and red bean crops (the most profitable crops in the area), by reclaiming 60 acres of wasteland near their settlement, and by initiating a community effort to breed piglets and chickens.

Acting at the request of the Governor of Cheju, CARE assisted these farmers by providing them first with three bullocks and three unweaned calves in August, 1961, enabling the farmers to cultivate more rapidly the land already cleared. In December they were provided with 100 bags of potato seed, 100 bags of red bean seed, and 150 bags of fertilizer. Four months later the CARE representative in Korea reported that the farmers, despite a severe winter, had been able to place an additional 42 acres under cultivation, which, combined with the 30 acres already cleared, gave each family an average of 2.75 acres (good by Korean standards). Their increase in land and in income was then estimated as follows:

Item	Land increase, acres	Estimated income increase, $
Sweet potato	10	2,210
Potato	6	575
Red bean	20	575
Upland rice	6	387
Total	42	3,747

By December, 1962, it was reported that the two cows had given birth to new calves in July, bringing the total bullock population up to eight, and that the three unweaned calves had now grown to the extent that they could participate in field work. An additional 6 acres had been cleared, making a total of 48 toward the goal of 60, and the additional income was used for the purchase of seed and the construction of pig-pens.

CARE then provided 23 piglets and 260 chickens for the project. Of these, the 17 female pigs produced twice a year as of March, 1963, and the chickens began laying at this time. The breeding and raising of the pigs and chickens is a cooperative effort on the part of the farmers, who share equally in the proceeds.

The aid investment in this project totaled $2,065 to date, but, as can be seen from the figures, the economic yield has been and will be far greater. Although control was exercised by the provincial government officials and local agricultural advisers, most of the administration of the project was effectively carried out by the farmers themselves.

Iran: Sewing Machines

A recent survey made of the credit position of villagers in the rural areas of Iran revealed that the average village family has a continued indebtedness of approximately $130. Multiply this figure by the 2,500,000 rural families, and the total indebtedness, which in itself represents only the accumulated results of borrowing over several years and is thus just a fraction of the farmers' needs, amounts to well over $300 million.

One approach taken by the Government of Iran to meet this problem was the establishment in 1958 of the Home Demonstration Agent Program, which now extends its services to rural families in eleven of Iran's fourteen provinces. Under this program, home demonstration agents, usually women, visit the rural areas and train village women in such activities as sewing, food preparation and preservation, home improvement, vegetable gardening, child care, and first aid, all of which could be used to enlarge their families' incomes.

CARE became involved with this program in 1959 by providing each of 196 village workers with a set of materials that included a sewing machine, a needles trades kit, agricultural hand tools, preserving jars, and a first aid kit. Of these items, the most successful was the sewing machine, primarily because of its demonstration value.

Because of the effectiveness of the Iranian program and the use to which the village workers put the sewing machines, it was found that in many cases women who learned to sew went on to purchase new sewing machines of their own and began turning out shirts, pajamas, blouses, children's clothes, etc., which not only filled the needs of their families but could be produced for sale, thereby creating new income for their families. In one year, over 62,400 pieces of clothing had been made by the women who were trained on CARE sewing machines. To these economic benefits were attached the social benefits of increased prestige within the village, a factor which helped to attract other women into the Home Demonstration Center and to gain the confidence of the villagers, who are normally suspicious of outsiders. This, then, was an example of a successful program effectively administered by local agencies.

To sum up, tools, like food, can be distributed endlessly. There will always be a need for them in every developing country. The primary problem faced by a voluntary agency engaged in material assistance, then, is to devise programs ensuring the most effective use of these tools, programs which require active participation on the part of the recipients, programs which work directly on the community organization, and encourage on the part of the villagers a sense of individual responsibility for their own welfare.

Furthermore, it should be remembered that CARE's emphasis on applying donor funds volunteered by the American public to the supply of low-cost implements and equipment has been based on two important premises. First of all, this approach provides an efficient way of relating directly to the hopes and strivings of the individuals and communities in terms which the recipients can understand and use. The supply of a village water pump, for example, is more manifest, to those who are grievously in need of water, than the long-term dam-building project for irrigation or power which may be far too sophisticated to stimulate a local sense of participation in facing up to the problem at hand.

This is not to deny the validity of high-level capital investment in what is called infrastructure. But it does seem apparent that since the rich have become richer and the poor poorer in many developing countries, the degree of emphasis on heavy capital projects may be due for reconsideration. At the local level of life, in village or slum, it must often appear that many heavy capital-investment projects are of more benefit to the elite than to those most deeply in need of opportunity. The thesis of a self-help program is that the development process can also be started in very practical and simple ways at the other end of the economic spectrum, while investment in national infrastructure might be continued on a meaningful scale.

The CARE self-help program is geared to the ability of peoples whose lives have been spun out in a different historical context from that of the industrialized countries. The important thing about the development process is that it stimulates not only a response but an actual working partnership between the "giver" and the "receiver." Low-level investment in tools that emerging peoples understand and put directly to work seems to provide a simple means to develop that kind of partnership. It is not something superimposed, but something which directly requires the response of people who are primed for the first step forward. The important thing is that the priming for the step forward—through local education, initiative, and sensitive preparation—produces a sense of individual and community responsibility.

MARKETING PESTICIDES OVERSEAS

Dr. Ernest R. Marshall

The Place of Business in the New Economies

In the United States both agriculture and business have undergone many changes. New machines, new chemicals, and new products have wrought many outstanding improvements. They have brought about a technological revolution. However, in many places overseas the differences have been even greater. In many newly emerged countries the rise of nationalism has also brought about a change in government. Some of these new governments are of a more socialistic or paternal nature than we have been accustomed to, which does not necessarily mean that this is an obstacle to marketing. In fact, in some of these countries it may be not only desirable and necessary, but even helpful to those interested in marketing products there. During their rise to freedom the normal business channels may have dried up, or they may never have existed. Thus, it is logical for both the nation's own citizens and outside businessmen to turn to the government—the citizen in order to gain a window to the outer world and the businessman in order to gain outlets within the country. Indeed, there are cases where the government has found it expedient to step in to save business and the economy, as we shall see later in the case of Ghana.

The People

The standard of living in some of the newer nations is, by Western yardsticks, tragically low. For instance, in South Korea the average farm consists of only about 2 acres and the annual income for farm dwellers is about $50. In parts of Africa the cash income may run even lower. This makes it difficult for

Dr. Marshall is Manager of Agricultural Chemicals of the Union Carbide International Company.

the people to offer much of a market for manufactured goods—or even fertilizers and insecticides with which to raise their production and consequently their supply of food and/or cash income.

In the low-income areas sickness and disease are often coupled with this basic situation—malaria, dysentery, typhus, encephalitis, yellow fever, parasite disease, and others take their toll and further sap the strength of the individuals so that the people are unable to work hard and so raise their incomes and standards of living.

Further, with a low income level comes a low level of education, so that the need for trained personnel becomes even more critical. In most new countries the number of educated people is limited, and the few that are available are needed to build the framework of the new government. Thus, a trained agronomist who is badly needed at the grass-roots level may become an ambassador, and an entomologist may become a cabinet minister.

This has happened many times, and as a consequence a great void has developed in the technical fields where struggling young nations seriously need help. One cannot rely upon the help of an educated and sympathetic county agricultural agent to bring one's story to the farmer, as is the case in the United States, simply because there are no county agents!

Perennial Shortage of Food

In many of the less developed countries there is also a perennial shortage of food, which further aggravates the situation we have just discussed. Hungry people do not have the energy and the will to work as hard as they otherwise could, nor do they take as much interest in their own advancement as they might.

This shortage of food is brought about by several factors, one of the basic ones being low productivity. For example, in the Sudan, which incidentally is relatively better off than many other areas, a reasonable figure for corn production is about 20 bushels to the acre. Under comparable conditions, American production can go up to 100 bushels per acre, with the U.S. record being in the neighborhood of 300 bushels.

Another basic problem is proper storage. In parts of Africa corn is stored on the cob by hanging it on racks in the open or on trees—open to attack by whatever comes along. In not all countries is the storage method so trusting. Yet most of them allow ample room for improvement. Severe losses are also incurred in many of these countries from spoilage caused by moisture on one hand and desiccation on the other. A terrific toll is also taken by insects, birds, and rodents because of the lack of proper protection. We shall discuss this more fully later.

In many parts of the world commercial fertilizers are virtually unknown. Natural manures may be used, but at best they can only return to the soil what was taken out. In practice, however, this is not the case, and many nutrients never get back to the soil. Likewise, there is no compensation for leaching or runoff and no provision made for primary deficiencies.

Pesticides—insecticides and fungicides—are, if anything, even less known. In some cases locust attacks are still being combatted with fans, flails, and sticks. Modern insecticides like Malathion, DDT, or our own Sevin, which helped save the Egyptian cotton crop in 1961, are as uncommon as the proverbial hen's teeth.

Add to this primitive methods of culture (burning off the accumulated humus in clearing land, using land until it is worn out and then moving on, preparing the soil by barely scratching it with a stick, harvesting grain with a sickle, and winnowing by throwing it into the air), and it is easy to see why food and other crop production is low.

Lack of Incentives

With the economic and political changes taking place throughout the world, there is often a lack of incentive to work. The Ghana cocoa crop is a good example. Cocoa is the major crop in Ghana and represents about 60 percent of the country's dollar income. Even though British experiments had shown that by the use of the simplest of fertilizer and pest control practices the yield could run as high as 2,000 pounds to the acre, the normal returns were only about 250.

Following independence from Great Britain, cocoa growers discovered they needed only the return from the sale of about 250 pounds to buy enough staples to satisfy their basic wants and desires from one year to the next. Therefore, they harvested only enough to supply these minimum cash needs. The remainder of the crop, if any, was left to rot on the ground. Yet the government desperately needed the funds the unharvested cocoa would have brought.

To solve this problem, the government finally abolished the private buying of cocoa beans, and all beans were then purchased by government agencies. But the government did not pay world market prices; instead, it paid the growers only a fraction of the price previously paid by the private buyers and pocketed the difference, a big boost to the government's income. At the same time, the growers found that to purchase their year's staples they had to harvest much more cocoa. In order to do this, they had to fertilize and control insects. To assist them, the government arranged for the purchase and availability of suitable products. This saved the government and marked the first step toward establishing widespread pest control and feeding practices in Ghana, which, in two years alone, markedly increased both cocoa yields and national income.

Business Overseas

We are, of course, interested in the question of what part American businessmen are playing in the international chemical market. It is a big market. With the possible exception of soybeans, there is no single major crop in the United States that is not exceeded abroad both in total acreage and as a potential market for agricultural chemicals. In the case of cotton, for instance, the United States' 12 million acres is less than one-fifth of the Free World's 65 million acres. Thus, while the annual consumption of pesticides used overseas is several times that of the United States, if overseas farmers ever approach the per capita production of American farm workers, their use of pesticides will be astronomical.

But let us not assume that these markets can be had just for the asking.

Competition is very keen. First, a lack of registration requirements, or weak laws regarding labeling and residue control, greatly reduce the development costs of many chemicals. Second, in some countries, politics alone may determine which pesticides will be used and which not. Third, credit terms offered by competitors are often unrealistic according to American standards. In some markets European suppliers offer as much as 360 days credit! In addition, through tradition or former political ties (not to mention preferential tariffs) foreign manufacturers have had a decided advantage over their American competitors.

Another serious handicap to American penetration of the foreign markets has come from our own ineffectual methods. For instance, until recently most American producers wishing to sell pesticides relied upon the antiquated system of sending a traveling salesman through the area once or twice a year to book orders. Usually he knew little about local conditions or how to give technical assistance—and his time was too limited, even if he did have the knowledge and inclination to help. So he based his selling effort upon price. At the same time, our foreign competitors were making complete studies of the market, their competition, and credit terms, and were determining what should be done in the way of sales development. They often organized chains of outlets for distribution, and some even provided planes or other equipment for wide-scale application of their pesticides.

More and more American chemical suppliers have adopted or are adopting a more realistic approach. Looking ahead, it appears that those U.S. firms that are ready to bear the cost of sound market development and research in the field of agricultural chemicals will be able to build large markets overseas. But they must build upon a sounder basis than in the past. Each major market must be supplied with continuous technical support, a sales development program, and the proper type of distribution system necessary to supply the proper chemicals to the farmers in that particular country.

Some mention should also be made of the export-import agents. They certainly have a place in the marketing program, but they can often be harmful not only to the manufacturers but also to local distributors in the countries they supply. They rarely make the outlay of capital necessary for proper market development, nor do they set up an effective distribution system. Hence, they usually sell at a low price—sometimes with little or no profit on the merchandise—and make their profit through manipulation of the currency, which is completely demoralizing in markets where stable prices are badly needed. Though they can often ferret out orders that would otherwise be lost, they seldom take a long-term view. They tend to take their profits and turn quickly to the next deal.

Additional Factors to Keep in Mind

Potential suppliers must keep in mind several points:

1. We must be aware of political trends. Each market has its own political and business characteristics. We cannot expect to impose our methods or systems upon other societies. Rather, we must adapt ourselves to the market conditions existing in each one. What is considered an entirely normal business practice in one country may be illegal in others.

2. Language can be a serious barrier. Even though some people in nearly every country speak English, we must not expect business discussions to be held in English around the world. It is a definite aid to business if those responsible for marketing in a particular country can speak the language, or at least a closely related and favored language.

3. Sales development often involves such problems as registration, labeling, tolerances, etc. Companies should not rely upon their distributors to bear all the trouble and expense. No distributor can possibly have as great an interest in promoting a product as its manufacturer, nor does he usually have the financial resources or technical staff.

4. Credit and import licenses are also important factors in international trade. To compete with those who offer up to 360 days credit, a flexible policy must be developed. In Central America, for instance, credit is often more important than price. In other places, such as India, Burma, Indonesia, and Colombia, the availability of import licenses is a serious problem.

5. Acquiring the proper personnel and training them adequately constitutes a primary requirement. Wherever possible, it is advisable to hire nationals. Their English may not be the best, but they do know their countries, they speak the languages, and their salaries and costs are usually less than those of Americans.

Chemicals to the Rescue

Why do pesticides offer such a good market overseas? When insects strike in vast numbers, they can do a tremendous amount of damage. For example, the U.S. Department of Agriculture's data on outbreaks in Africa and the Near East are almost unbelievable. Workers found as many as 6,000 egg-pods of the Moroccan locust per square yard, and during a campaign against migratory locusts in western Turkey collectors gathered 430 tons of eggs and 1,200 tons of locusts in three weeks.

The following is an example of what can be accomplished by using pesticides. In the summer of 1961 armyworms spread through the fertile valley of the Nile. Not only did they threaten to wipe out the entire cotton crop, one of the two main pillars of the Egyptian economy (the other is the Suez Canal), but they also broadened their attack to include most of the food crops. This would have spelled complete disaster for Egypt.

Fortunately, however, Union Carbide had tested its new insecticide, Sevin, in Egypt for two years and had demonstrated its effectiveness to the Egyptian government officials. Therefore, when the outbreak assumed alarming proportions (25 percent of the cotton crop was already destroyed), the Egyptian government sent an urgent call to Union Carbide to airlift more than 2 million pounds of the chemical at once.

Union Carbide received the first call in New York late Friday afternoon. Immediately the production plants were put on a twenty-four-hour schedule, and every available truck was put to hauling the chemical to New York's Idlewild Airport. Next every available cargo plane was pressed into service, including those of the U.S. Military Air Transport Service, and before the emergency was over, more than $2 million worth of the chemical was flown to Cairo, making it the biggest commercial airlift in history. Not only the chemical but every available technician was flown in to help instruct the Egyptian workers in how to apply the insecticide.

This particular chemical was insisted upon because it is extremely effective for cotton insects, and unlike most others it is relatively safe to handle, even by the most inexperienced workers. This was doubly important, because much of the insecticide was applied with hand-operated sprayers, and no masks or protective clothing were used.

Deterioration and loss of grain in storage is also a very great problem abroad. According to the United Nations Food and Agricultural Organization (FAO) world cereal grain production (1956), not including the U.S.S.R., was 756 million metric tons, of which at least 10 percent, or 75,600,000 tons, was destroyed by insects, rodents, and fungi. At an average ration of 800 grams daily per person, this would feed an additional 255 million people for one full year. Even in such a relatively advanced country as Australia, during World War I 3½ million tons of grain in emergency storage suffered a $2½ million damage from insects before control measures could be taken, and it cost another $1½ million to bring them under control—a total loss of $4 million. Even today in the United States it has been calculated that each rat alone costs the farmer $6 a year.

The most critical areas are the humid tropics. But all warm climates are particularly susceptible to such losses (Southeast Asia, the Near and Middle East, Africa, Latin America, etc.) and can ill afford them.

In parts of Egypt, for instance, some grain is still stored in ditches and covered by sand. Except for adding physical "dirtiness," this works fairly well if it is safe from infiltrating water and pests. However, when it is not, the loss from weevils, termites, and fungi can be extremely heavy. A second method is that of storing it in sacks under heaps of straw or chaff, but in such cases infestation is easy, inspection difficult, and the fire hazard great. Another and even more primitive method still used in places is the *shouna* system handed down from the ancient Egyptians—simply storing heaps or sacks in the open, enclosed by a fence or wall and exposed to rain, birds, rats, insects, higher water, dust, and excrement from the creatures attacking it.

In China, too, much of the grain is stored in heaps on the floor, enclosed in open-ended bamboo cylinders, and in miscellaneous boxes, baskets, etc. Nor are these two countries exceptions. Such practices are quite widespread.

Fortunately, however, the Food and Agricultural Organization is attacking the storage problem on several fronts. It is encouraging local design and demonstration of inexpensive and efficient storage facilities. It is promoting effective methods of pest control and is working intensively on the training of local personnel to put these measures into effect.

Governments, too, are taking steps to correct these losses. For example, Ghana inaugurated the selling of chemicals like Lindane dust in brightly colored 4-ounce packets suitable for treating 100-pound sacks of maize or corn, and Kenya has been experimenting with the mixing of chemicals like Malathion with grain in storage and has sought protection by covering exposed grain with polyethylene sheeting.

The government of Burma, through its State Agricultural Marketing Board, has embarked upon a vast improvement program aimed at securing its position as the leading rice exporter. It is working on the proper drying of the grain, improved storage facilities, and the use of chemicals, fumigants, etc., to eliminate the loss from insects, rodents, and funguslike organisms.

If There Were No Chemicals

Occasionally one hears the cry that chemical sprays and other pest controls are not needed—that the world would be better off without them. Nothing could be more misleading. If the insects' own enemies could control them, why did Egypt have so much trouble, or Turkey, or even the United States? Why did early Nebraskans suffer from a swarm of locusts variously estimated at half a mile high, 100 miles wide, and 300 miles long, or why was the eastern United States infested with canker worms as recently as the early 1960s? In fact, if modern pest control were ever stopped, it would no longer be possible to feed the 182 million people in the United States. Its population-carrying capacity would rapidly drop back toward the less than 1 million the country supported when first discovered.

With respect to sickness alone, Dr. E. F. Knipling of the U.S. Department of Agriculture estimates that no less than 100 million illnesses have been prevented through the use of chemicals for the control of malaria, typhus, dysentery, and several other diseases.

The Solution

So far, we have presented some of the problems inherent in the less developed countries: the poverty of the people, lack of education, low food production, inability to store food properly, and the difficulties involved in doing business in those countries. Now the problem resolves itself into how to raise the standard of living in those countries through increased production of food and other crops so that not only the populace but prospective businessmen, both domestic and foreign, may realize the maximum trade and benefits therefrom. Some suggested approaches are as follows:

1. There is a need for more trained personnel. This may be accomplished by strengthening those agricultural schools and colleges which already exist and by establishing more. For example, while Sudan turns out about 60 agricultural college graduates and Paraguay about 125 per year (1960–1961), both could profitably use several times as many with ease.

But this is a long-term project. What is needed now is a short-term cure as well. Countries like the United States can help by bringing more students to study in American institutions—this has the added advantage of also giving the students an understanding of American ways. Established missionary groups can be given additional support not only for the expansion of their schools but for more "grass roots" or extension-service–type teaching. Further, many countries could benefit by greater emphasis upon our American governmental agricultural missions to foreign countries and upon our Peace Corps.

In addition to these, however, chemical and other industrial concerns doing business in these countries should lend all the assistance they can. This can be done by sending technicians to work at all levels within these countries, as did Union Carbide in the Egyptian cotton emergency, and by helping the local citizens set up effective marketing and distribution systems.

2. Biological control of insects and diseases is often advocated. Early entomologists were essentially naturalists. They preached a gospel of biological pest control, having little or no other means at their disposal. In some cases biological methods have been conspicuously successful, in many others a complete failure. Among successful examples are the introduction of the Australian lady beetle into the California orange groves to control the cottony-cushion scale and the use of a minute internal wasp parasite to stop the woolly apple aphid in the Pacific Northwest.

Perhaps the most conspicuous example of success has been the control of the screwworm in cattle in the southern United States. Millions of male flies were raised, sterilized by irradiation, and released. Upon mating with the females, no progeny resulted, and the numbers were radically reduced. However, this required complete specialized laboratories and highly trained personnel.

Somewhat simpler to carry out, but far less effective, has been the attack upon the Japanese beetle by spreading a powder containing spores of the milky disease. In some places and in some seasons this has been rather effective, but in the eastern United States, where the infestation first started early in the century, the pest is still with us.

An example of still less effective biological control is found in the case of the European corn borer, which entered the United States about 1908. Scientists have worked ever since to find weak spots in its biology. Every new lead was pursued for years, and yet the only really promising method has been the spraying or dusting with spores of *Bacillus thuringiensis* in Europe. But the fact remains that if spraying must be resorted to, chemical controls are usually cheaper and less dependent upon weather for effectiveness.

3. A third method of raising production levels is through the creation of better and more productive crop plants. This is often quite effective in bringing about larger yields, but such a program usually takes many years and requires highly qualified personnel. The time can be shortened by importing improved varieties, but this is not always successful because the improved varieties may not be adapted to local growing conditions. To develop disease or insect resistance by breeding and selection is possible but still more difficult. Also, there have been cases where many years were spent breeding resistance to a certain insect or disease only to find a new pest appear and virtually wipe out the crop.

4. This leaves the chemical control of insects and diseases the prime method of raising production and, consequently, the standard of living in most less developed countries.

This is only a brief discussion of some of the problems associated with the international agricultural chemical market and the summary of a few successes we have enjoyed. However, we are convinced that agricultural chemicals will play a very large part in the world markets of the future. Many potential fields remain virtually untapped. There is a need for weedkillers for rice, sugar cane, coffee, and many other crops, as well as for soil sterilants, nematocides, etc. In order to meet the challenge successfully we must supply new products, technical assistance, effective distribution systems, and a flexible marketing policy tailor-made for each specific market. If we do these things, the future of export sales of agricultural chemicals looks extremely bright, and the prospects of bringing health, prosperity, and economic well-being to the people of many more nations seem most promising.

CROP SPRINKLING IN TROPICAL AFRICA

W. Brunner, Dipl. Ing.

H. Schmidt, Dr. Agr.

R. W. Hagemann

Water Management: A Vital Problem

On the entire African continent the growing of crops is first and foremost a water problem: 80% of all arable land in Africa suffers from extreme climatic conditions, especially from water shortage. In the subtropical regions of North Africa the problem is how to make the most profitable use of the limited quantities of water available in order to irrigate the maximum possible area of land, but the decisive question in Central Africa is to ensure that the available moisture will be distributed in an expedient way, corresponding to the physiological conditions of the crops concerned.

When we refer to irrigation, we generally mean surface irrigation and think in terms of furrow or flood irrigation as the main types. Check, border, or basin irrigation are also types of surface irrigation, but they are developed locally where special conditions of topography, type of soil, or crop may exist.

Surface irrigation, no matter the type, requires level ground; in other words, the field should be free from undulations. Moreover, the field should have a slight slope to let the water flow across it without permitting a runoff or too rapid a percolation. Unfortunately not many fields meet these requirements, and if we have to irrigate, we must level and smooth the land—a costly

---

Mr. Brunner is a Certified Agricultural Engineer.

Dr. Schmidt is an expert on irrigation.

Mr. Hagemann is an agricultural engineer.

operation. With any surface irrigation method it is essential that the water must be applied at a rate exceeding the percolation rate of the soil. Such a method must inevitably cause considerable water loss either by evaporation from the canals, open ditches, furrows, and ponds or by ditch seepage, percolation, and surface runoff from the fields. The greatest hazard from all types of surface irrigation is, however, the slow but steady removal of topsoil by soil erosion. Topsoil is always carried away whenever there is runoff from a field, because water has to be applied at a rate exceeding the percolation rate of the soil. Another point yet to be mentioned is that any surface irrigation system which consists of a number of canals, flumes, ditches, or other field obstructions cuts the field into small plots. This type of "land fragmentation" prevents the use of large-size farm machinery and makes general field cropping operations difficult.

Sprinkler Irrigation

For almost twenty years, an irrigation system which gives freedom from all the troubles brought about by surface irrigation has been in common use throughout the world and has proved very successful. This system is called "sprinkler" or "overhead" irrigation. This is an improved form by which water is applied to the land just like natural rainfall. Sprinkler irrigation has nothing to do with the method of bombarding clouds to induce rain that is publicized by the "rainmakers." Sprinkling is the method of producing "rain" from ground-stored or river water. It does not have to rely on clouds. Sprinkling will work in small units on any size of plot and is particularly worthwhile—in comparison with the rainmakers' method—if there are no clouds. Thus, sprinkling can replace the old surface irrigation method as well as the ultramodern method of bombarding clouds, because the area of operation, amount of water, and time of operation can be readily controlled.

A sprinkler irrigation system includes all the equipment necessary to pump, convey, and distribute the water onto the land to be irrigated. Thus, it generally consists of the pumping plant, the pipe system, and the sprinklers. The pumping plant consists of the pump with the suction device and the power unit. Usually, a horizontal-shaft centrifugal pump driven by an electromotor petrol engine or an air-cooled diesel engine is used. The piping is of thin-walled lightweight steel or aluminum. The pipes are connected by means of a folding stirrup fixed to the male part of the fitting, and the coupling is sealed with a replaceable rubber gasket placed in the female part, thus ensuring a positive seal at high and low pressures. Rotary sprinklers are rainers which distribute water radially at recommended spacings and pressures; they are the types most commonly used.

Today, all common crops have been or are being irrigated successfully by sprinkling. In comparison with surface irrigation methods, overhead does not only affect the yield in quantity, but also in quality irrigation. A better stand is obtained, the soil is better protected against sunshine, and the quality of the crop is increased while labor and pumping costs decrease.

As to the cost of a sprinkler irrigation system, much has been said about this subject by people who evidently have in mind only the purchasing, maintenance, and operating costs, without giving thought to the saving of labor and water or to the additional profit (better quality, higher yield) resulting from the use of the sprinkler system. To offset the overall cost of running a sprinkler system, we have to keep in mind the cost of the ditch and furrow construction in surface irrigation systems and the labor cost of keeping the canals and ditches open and weed-free. We have also to consider the amount of water saved in comparison with the surface method, the quantity of fertilizer saved through no more leaching by too deep penetration, the land area saved by not having the necessary canals and ditches, the topsoil saved by reducing soil erosion troubles, and, above all, the increased production and quality.

The Mannesmann Corporation has built extensive sprinkler installations in both North and Central Africa, gathering a considerable amount of experience over many years. In Morocco and other North African countries the use of overhead irrigation reduced water requirements to one-third or even one-fourth of the amount required with orthodox surface irrigation methods. In other words, the cultivated area of arable land, which, in principle, is abundantly available and of great fertility, could be increased three- to fourfold.

Central African Experience

No less successful is crop sprinkling in Central Africa, where it is applied to offset the effects of dry spells and droughts.

Bananas. The sprinkling of banana plantations presents considerable technical difficulties as regards the installation of the sprinklers, since banana trees have a large leafage, attain a height of up to 6 meters, and are frequently planted on hilly terrain. Sprinkling can be greatly facilitated here by using portable sprinkler systems featuring laterally interconnectable quick-coupler pipes with appropriately shaped connecting pieces and riser pipes on which the sprinkler heads are mounted.

Recently, positive results were achieved in South America with under-tree sprinkling in banana plantation using portable and semiportable sprinkler systems. Hereby the a/m difficulties can be avoided, and the expensive riser pipes will be economized. Operation is simplified. The disadvantage of less perfect water distribution when sprinkler jets hit the banana trunks is easily outbalanced by the advantages of the under-tree sprinkling. This system has not been applied in Africa so far, but experiments will soon be conducted to find out about the applicability of under-tree sprinkling there.

Under tropical conditions bananas need some 500 to 600 mm (20 to 24 in.) of supplemental moisture under a rotation schedule of from seven to nine days on light soils. On medium soils, the application may be reduced to 450 to 500 mm under a rotation schedule of from ten to fourteen days. The individual maximum rates of application should not exceed 50 mm (2 in.) on light soils or 60 mm on medium soils. Sprinkling of banana trees may be expected to yield a relative production increase of from 50 to 70%.

Coffee. Coffee crops are sprinkled mainly to increase production and improve quality. Production increases of from 50 to 120% are no rarity. Under tropical African conditions, coffee crops need some 250 to 300 mm of supplemental moisture annually on medium soils. A rotation schedule of two to three weeks has proved sufficient. The individual rates of application should not exceed 50 to 60 mm.

Incidentally, sprinkling also has a remarkable effect on the coffee blossom. Coffee blooms fairly promptly seven days after a rain shower, which in the ecological habitat of the coffee bush is produced with certainty by the monsoon. However, in the Central African regions these showers do not occur with such regularity as to guarantee good crops. Premature showers on the still undeveloped buds produce premature, sparse blossoming. Belated showers have little effect, since by then the buds have already begun to drop off in their unopened state. Showers of inadequate intensity likewise produce only unsatisfactory blossoming.

Similar conditions exist with respect to the showers still required after the blossoming, which must occur some ten to twenty days after the blossoming showers. Without them, fructification will remain unsatisfactory, and fruits already developing will be shed. Sprinkling enables the planter to eliminate the accidental results of natural rain showers and to give the coffee rain whenever it needs it, which of course leads to corresponding production increases.

Tea. As a leaf-producing plant, the tea bush is a great water consumer, and crop yields vary greatly with rainfall during growth. The annual precipitation figures for the typical tea-growing regions (not below 4,000 mm, or 160 in.) would in themselves be high enough for continuously good crops; however, conditions are adversely affected by the irregular distribution of precipitation, the frequently only moderate water storage capacity of the soils, and the occasionally considerable evaporation. Tea is mostly sprinkled on a ten-day rotation schedule in relation to the picking of the leaves, with good results being achieved by individual application rates of from 25 to 30 mm.

The effectiveness of tea crop sprinkling lies not so much in absolute yield increases as in the smoothing of the production graph. During the rainy season the tea plant yields large amounts of fresh leaves of relatively low quality which require high processing costs and yet fetch only moderate prices. In the dry season, on the other hand, the amount picked is only about one-third as much as in the rainy season, with quality being correspondingly better and prices higher, whilst the overall volume is low. Sprinkling enables the planter to increase dry-season yields without sacrificing too much of the dry-season quality. The tea yield graph is thus smoothed out as well.

Cocoa. An average annual precipitation of about 1,200 to 1,500 mm (48 to 60 in.), if evenly distributed, is sufficient for the cocoa tree. However, this even distribution is not found everywhere. Even as near the Equator as 1.5° south or north there exists a pronounced dry season of some two months—from June to August—and a less pronounced one from January to February. The cocoa tree reacts to such dry spells with a yellowing of its foliage and a decrease in yields. After some twenty rainless days the cocoa tree will begin to wilt. If the rainless period continues for sixty or more days, one must reckon with the loss of a considerable number of trees. Until recently there existed no remedy against the drop in yield caused by the annual dry spells, nor against the constantly recurring catastrophic years with prolonged droughts of more than sixty days.

It is customary to provide a good deal of natural shade for cocoa plantations. With this aim in mind, a number of trees of the primary forest are left standing when the forest is cleared, whereupon a secondary forest consisting of cocoa trees is planted. In the Congo, growers have succeeded in achieving (in years with normal precipitation) production increases of some 30% as compared with the nonsprinkled reference plots. This, however, is not actually a true production increase but rather a case of crop preservation over the dry spell, during which the cocoa blossom and often already budding fruits usually dry up and are shed.

The summer of 1958 brought a prolonged drought culminating in a totally rainless period of seventy-five days. This drought constituted the most severe test for cocoa sprinkling. The harvest report of a cocoa plantation in the Congo records a 74% decrease caused by the drought on a 65-hectare plot as compared with production figures for the three preceding years. On the other hand, the yields achieved on three different sprinkled plots of a combined 135-hectare area amounted to 127, 107, and 95% respectively, or to an average 110% of the figures for the preceding three-year period. Whereas on the sprinkled plots the average number of cocoa fruits harvested per hectare was 14,890, the corresponding figure for the nonsprinkled reference plot was only 3,595. Sprinkling thus produced a 414% production increase. In this connection it must be considered that in the three reference years average yields on the test plots deviated by only 0.05% from the overall average yield, a fact which throws the results obtained into even greater relief. This extremely satisfactory result was achieved by sprinkling the crop for some thirty days. The application rate did not exceed 150 mm (6 in.).

One may assume that an extension of the sprinkling period to approximately fifty to sixty days would yield even better results.

The net value of the extra yield produced by sprinkling amounted to roughly DM1,100 per hectare (gross extra yield DM1,185), a sum which approximately equals the equipment cost of the sprinkler installation.

Not included in the above calculation is the indirect profit derived from the preservation of the productive capacity of the cocoa trees and of the trees themselves. After the catastrophic summer of 1958, some 150,000 cocoa trees (i.e., about 7.5% of the total in the plantation) had to be newly planted on the nonsprinkled parts of the plantation. Apart from the value of the plant material and the labor costs, one must take into account a three-year loss of production until the young trees start bearing fruit. Furthermore, one must also consider the decrease in yield in the next years, caused by the loss of strength of those trees which did not die and did not have to be replaced. There is no doubt that the sprinkler system in this one year alone not only fully paid for itself and its installation but moreover yielded a considerable net profit. However, such years of particularly pronounced dryness do not occur more than once every twelve to fifteen years.

It has been calculated that application of from 100 to 150 mm of supplemental moisture during the dry season requires that the extra yield thereby obtained should amount to no less than 100 to 150 kg of cocoa per hectare if it is to cover the costs of sprinkling. These costs comprise the amortization of the sprinkling equipment, the interest on initial capital outlay, power costs, etc. A production increase of from 100 to 150 kg of cocoa per hectare corresponds to a 20% raise in yield on fields of average productivity. Since one may normally expect yield to rise 30% through sprinkling, one may also be confident that the capital invested will pay high dividends.

Future developments, however, transcend what has been achieved so far. The ever-increasing scarcity and higher costs of labor force the plantations to apply more intensive growing techniques. First experiments with intensive cocoa cultivation seem to indicate that yields may be doubled in this way, provided, however, that the fullest possible use is made of crop sprinkling.

Sugar Cane. It is most surprising to learn that Africa as a whole does not produce enough sugar to meet its own requirements. To a number of African states the necessity of importing sugar is a growing burden on the national budget, as sugar consumption goes up regularly and rapidly as soon as the standard of living starts to rise.

Production of cane sugar is possible and profitable in large areas of tropical and subtropical Africa, and the installation of sprinkler irrigation requires investigations of the results. In East Africa (Uganda and Tanganyika) sprinkler irrigation is conducted on a large scale already, and results are most encouraging. It can be expected that sugar cane cultivation with sprinkler irrigation will spread widely in years to come. Exact figures on the effectiveness of sprinkler irrigation are known from the most important integrated sprinkler system in Africa (perhaps in the world). It was started in 1959 and continuously extended; in August, 1963, it will reach a covered area of more than 2,650 hectares (6,500 acres). It was found that the yield in sugar, given in pounds per acre per month, increased from 471 to 819 by sprinkling.

To make this nearly incredible figure understood, some basic data must follow. Without irrigation, cane yields were reported to average 50 tons/acre, plant crop (twenty months), 40 tons/acre, first ratoon (eighteen months), and 30 tons/acre, second ratoon (eighteen months). This adds up to 120 tons/acre in fifty-six months, or 2.14 tons/acre/month; the corresponding yield in commercialized sugar is 471 lb/acre/month.

The introduction of sprinkler irrigation not only increased yields but also shortened the growing period of the cane. Comparative figures for the a/m yields in those parts of the plantation which were irrigated by sprinkling are 65 tons/acre, plant crop (seventeen months), 60 tons/acre, first ratoon (fifteen months), 50 tons/acre, second ratoon (fifteen months), totaling 175 tons/acre in forty-seven months, or 3.72 tons/acre/month. This means 819 lb/acre/month, which is 74% more than the nonirrigated cane yielded.

It should be added, for the sake of completeness, that parallel experiments were conducted with surface irrigation (furrow irrigation) on the same plantation. Results did not nearly reach those of sprinkling, although investments and running costs were actually higher.

Operation and Management

For the operation of sprinkler irrigation systems as described, one has to bear in mind that the handling of the equipment and the operation and maintenance of pumping sets (especially with diesel engines) have to be as simple as possible in regions with mostly unskilled labor. This important question must be taken into consideration at the outset when planning the various schemes.

Great care has to be taken in training the supervision staff as well—not only from the mechanical side but also from the agronomic point of view, as it is most important to determine the optimum amount of water needed by the crop throughout its growth cycle to give optimal production at harvest. The water requirements at various stages of growth depend on the size and age of the plant and on prevailing climatic conditions, i.e., sunshine, temperature, relative humidity of the atmosphere, and wind velocity, which all influence the rate of evaporation from the leaves and soil surface. The total amount of water thus evaporated is termed "consumptive use" or "evapotranspiration." Evapotranspiration is usually expressed in "inches of water" per hour, week, or month and gives an indication of the amount of water required by the plant for optimum growth.

In summing up, it may be said that water, as a growth factor, and sprinkling, as the most modern and rational technique of crop irrigation, are of decisive importance in Central Africa. The profitable growing of crops stands and falls with the supply and suitable distribution of water. Agriculture in these regions can be intensified only by mastering the water factor, so that great tasks await crop sprinkling in this important developing area.

BIBLIOGRAPHY

Lehmann, F.: "Just Like Natural Rain," *India Magazine.*

———: *Beregnungstachenbuch* (The Pocketbook of Sprinkling), Mannesmann-Landtechnik, GmbH, Düsseldorf.

van Beveren: *Beregnungstechnik von Heute und Morgen* (Sprinkling Technology of Today and Tomorrow), Mannesmann-Landtechnik GmbH, Düsseldorf, 1959.

———: *Erfolge der Beregnung in den tropischen und subtropischen Gebieten Afrikas* (Successes of Sprinkling in the African Tropical and Subtropical Regions), Mannesmann-Landtechnik, GmbH, Düsseldorf, 1959.

FISH CULTURE IN DEVELOPING COUNTRIES

C. F. Hickling, Sc.D.

Fish culture, which originated in ancient China and in medieval Europe, has been introduced into a number of developing countries since the war as a measure by which large crops of fish can be produced in small bodies of water and by which land unsuitable for agriculture can often be profitably used. As against fishing in natural waters, fish culture has the advantage that the ponds are the property of the owner, who alone has the use of the fish raised in them.

Among these countries may be mentioned the Congo, the Rhodesias, the Cameroons, Kenya, Tanganyika, and Uganda in Africa; Indonesia, Thailand, and the Philippines in Asia; and others in the Caribbean and South America.

The usual way of introducing fish culture has been to send an expert on an advisory mission concerning the practicability of fish culture in the territory, the most promising places in which to start, and the species of fish and management techniques most likely to succeed. This preliminary visit may be followed up by the appointment of a hired expert who sets up one or more experimental and demonstration units, if the technique is being tried there for the first time. When a successful technique has been evolved, instruction is given to locally recruited extension and field officers whose job is to foster fish culture in the districts within their jurisdiction.

When deliberately sponsored by a government, fish culture is usually taken over by the Agricultural Department or a fisheries subdivision of that department. In this case there is central direction, but the demonstration units and extension programs may be conducted on a regional basis under that central direction. Religious missions have sometimes made fish culture a part of their educational program and usually link up with the government program.

Suitable Situations for Fish Culture

Often there are ready-made impoundments of water which can be stocked with suitable fish and managed to some degree. Hydroelectric dams are of

Dr. Hickling is an authority on fish culture.

limited value in this regard, because they are generally deep or very deep; not only may the lower levels of water have little or no oxygen and so be incapable of supporting any fish life, but fishing on a commercial scale may be difficult. Such dams may grow their own fish fauna, which is based on the original river fauna, but its species composition is probably altered by the change in the environment from a flowing river with a seasonably changing level to static, lakelike conditions. This is visibly happening in the new Lake Kariba, where already after three or four years, and even before the lake has reached its final level, the fish fauna has changed from a dominance of predators in the original river to a good balance between predators and nonpredators in the lake. There may be scope for adding suitable fish to such dams where there is an unfilled ecological niche; for example, there may be no efficient plant-eating fish naturally present.

Irrigation dams offer better possibilities. They are often extensive and fairly shallow, so that the water is usually warm and well oxygenated. Such dams also usually contain a natural fish fauna which may include valuable species. But there have been outstandingly successful transplantations of fish to such dams, resulting in the creation of important fisheries. There are other bodies of water which by chance may have a poor natural fauna of fish, and where the transplantation of suitable species may create valuable fisheries;[1] in Lake Tempé in the Celebes, for example, deliberate stocking with several suitable fish species, where the lake formerly had a fish fauna of little value, raised fish production from 0.4 to 10.5 million kg in a decade. Such fisheries need some management, but have the advantage that little capital cost is involved.

Irrigation schemes are favorable situations for the development of fish culture because here also the capital works needed to impound and regulate the water supply and to bring it in channels over the land have already been made. Though irrigation schemes are devised for the raising of land crops or rice, they often include areas unsuitable for agriculture because of drainage difficulties or excessive soil salinity. Several valuable species of fish will tolerate salinities too high for any of the usual land crops. The common carp will flourish in water with a salinity of 2,500 parts per million, or 2.5 parts per mille, and so will the Chinese major carps. *Puntius javanicus,* a weed-eating member of the carp family, tolerates 9 parts of salt per mille, and *Tilapia melanopleura* and *T. macrocheir* tolerate 7 to 13. *Tilapia mossambica* flourishes in salinities as high as those of the sea, namely, about 30 to 35 parts per mille. So land commanded by irrigation water which is too saline for irrigated crops could be profitably laid down in fishponds cultivating any or all of the above fish. As to waterlogged land, the soil of fishponds must by definition be impervious to water.

Capital expenditure is needed in such a case to construct the ponds, and it may be necessary to raise the water by a few feet from the level of the irrigation channels. This will maintain a depth of 3 ft in the ponds while still allowing a complete emptying of the pond by gravity, when needed, into the

[1] See C. F. Hickling, *Tropical Inland Fisheries,* Longmans, Green & Co., Ltd., London, 1961.

existing drainage channels of the irrigation scheme. Such costs, however, should not be high, because a small diesel or electric pump will raise a very large volume of water to the height of 5 or 6 ft, which is all that would be needed.

As will be shown later, fish culture can be combined with hog and poultry raising, sewage disposal, and market gardening, where it results in a saving of expense because the fish are grown on the waste products of the main business and tended by labor already available; in this way it adds to income without a proportionate increase in costs.

It is not suggested that good agricultural land is unsuitable for fish culture, but obviously a new idea is better shown as a profitable use for poor land than as a competitor for the use of good land, which may in any case be inadequate for food growing.

The human factor must also be considered. The most favorable situation is where there is already a tradition of small-livestock animal husbandry. The small amount of care and management needed for success with fish culture would offer no difficulty to such people. Where they are inexperienced or indifferent to the care of livestock, extensive demonstration and propaganda may be needed. This would be the case in most African territories, for instance. Though progress might be slow, experience has shown that interest does grow, and the need for increased supplies of first-class animal protein may justify the expenditure and effort involved.

Where fish culture cannot be tied in with some existing agricultural scheme but has to be started on its own, a good location would be close to the headwaters of streams near forested, marshy, or cultivated land where there would be an assurance of water and flooding would be unlikely. Where it has to be started on low ground with some risk of floods, the outer embankments at least should be made high enough to keep floods out. Fish culture is also worth considering in delta country as a part of the schemes for reclamation of such country. Ponds suitably sited in relation to tidal levels can be filled with water at high tide and emptied for harvest at low tide. At a distance back from the sea, the water at high tide is likely to be fresh, or at least brackish, and it has been shown that several important cultivated fish tolerate brackish water. There is also the possibility in such situations of useful supplementary crops of prawns, as the young stages may be carried into the ponds with the inflowing water.

No incentives are usually offered to the population for starting fish culture, though prizes may usefully be offered at agricultural shows for the best exhibits in the fish culture field. The prospect of an assured supply of fish under his own control and for his own use, with perhaps a surplus to trade, may be sufficient incentive to an enterprising man. Governments recognize that fish culture offers a ready means of supplying animal protein in diets where people live remote from natural sources of fish. Because of the rapid rates of growth and reproduction in fish, results can be won more rapidly than with most other kinds of livestock. In some cases there has been a spontaneous development of fish culture, and in such cases the government may intervene to direct and improve the practice.

Fish culture may be used to help out with compulsory rationing where governments stipulate that labor employed in private or public enterprise must be fed a stated quantity of first-class protein, such as meat or fish. Such workers include those in diamond and copper mining and smelting, or those employed by sugar, and sisal estates. Apart from this, some employers have found that the prospect of a regular ration of fish is an inducement in recruiting and holding labor, giving them a competitive advantage where labor is scarce. In some cases, even, a specialist officer may be employed to take charge of fish procurement.

When the "squatters" were resettled in new villages in Malaysia during the bandit war, fishponds were included in the plans of many such new villages, in conjunction with pig and poultry raising.

Since fish culture in the developing countries is almost invariably on the peasant subsistence scale, no provision may be needed for marketing. This will not arise until the scale of fish culture increases to the point where the fish cannot be disposed of at the pond site.

Fish Culture as a Sideline of Other Farming Activities

Only in the more advanced countries, as, for example, in Europe and Israel, is fish culture practiced on a large scale, with pond areas totaling hundreds or even thousands of acres. Exceptions to this are found in Indonesia and the Philippines, where the brackish-water pond systems do cover thousands or hundreds of thousands of acres, also in Hong Kong, where a great city assures a good market near at hand, and there are some fish farms 60 acres in area. But in undeveloped countries generally the scale of individual fishponds is very small and may consist of one or several ponds of a total area of less than 1 acre. Large-scale fish farms, like other large agricultural ventures, need plenty of capital and working capital and an infrastructure of good communications, cheap transport, and a good market easily accessible. On the peasant scale, the capital for construction may be represented by the labor put in by the fish culturist and his friends and family. Such costs are easier to meet when the venture represents part of a smallholding, since labor costs are shared with other activities and the fish can be fed, at least in part, by the waste products at hand. These other activities may include hog, duck, and chicken raising and market gardening. In silk-growing areas fish culture may be further combined with the culture of mulberries, with the fish being fed in turn on the feces of the silkworms and on the silkworms themselves when the silk is spun off. Silkworms are extremely nutritious and in fact may be used directly as human food.

This combination of smallholding and fishponds results in an intensive use of the land, while at the same time fertility is conserved; here, then, is a field where the agriculturalist and the fishery worker can join efforts. Hog and poultry pens are usually built over the ponds on piles driven into the pond bottom, and the feces, urine, and washings of the hogs, along with the droppings of the poultry, fall into the water through slats in the floor. The feces are probably mainly consumed directly by the fish as food, and when the fish in turn pass them on, the residual nutrients as well as the liquid urine and washings act as fertilizer in the water, increasing the production of plant and animal life, much of which (especially crustacea and insects) is useful fish food. The vegetable trash from the market garden is put into the pond to feed the vegetarian fish which are usually stocked, and the pond itself may be used as a reservoir of water for the garden. Finally, the pond mud may be scraped out at intervals and spread as a fertilizer on the soil, since it is rich in plant nutrients and its removal serves to deepen the pond.

An intensively worked smallholding will produce more food than the operator needs for his own use, so its successful introduction needs a cash market close at hand.

Fish culture can also be a valuable sideline for large-scale commercial pig farms, dairies, and poultry farms. Ponds can be run on the waste products of the main business and with the existing labor force, thus salvaging waste materials which may greatly increase the profits of the business without adding to expenditure. In the case of dairies, the washings of the cowsheds can be led into fishponds, where they will act as fertilizer. Grains or oilcakes used as supplementary food for the cattle would be available as supplementary food for the fish as well, with the advantage of bulk purchase.

An account of a pig, fruit, and fish farm at Bayan Lepas on the island of Penang in Malaysia has been published.[2] Over 500 pigs at a time are raised there in piggeries of modern design on properly blended rations. The capital cost was Malayan $32,000 (say, US $10,600) and of this about one-third was for the fishponds, concrete channels, and sluices. The ponds had an effective producing area at the time of 2.65 acres, though they have since been increased to about 6 acres. A small stream has been dammed so as to divert water down concrete channels through the piggeries and on into the fishponds. This water carries with it the washings of the pigs and sties and the feces. Fruit trees are planted around the ponds. The ponds are stocked with fish, and some wild fish also find their way in. The annual production of fish fed with the waste products of the pigs works out at the very high figure of 3,260 lb per acre. Of these, the small trash fish and wild fish are fed to the pigs, and the better fish are sold. Moreover, the leafy plant *Ipomoea reptans*, a relative of the sweet potato, is grown in these well-fertilized ponds and produces heavy crops which are cut and fed to the pigs. The capital cost of the 2.65 acres of ponds, including purchase of the land and fencing, was Malayan $11,600 (say, US $3,900), and the gross income from the sale of the fish was Malayan $5,939, or 59 percent on capital. Net income was $1,419, or 12.2 percent on capital; since then the pond acreage has been doubled, and expenditure has been cut by dispensing with the two watchmen. But even at the lower pond acreage and including the wages of the men, the fishponds increased the gross income of the whole business from $71,240 to $77,379, in Malayan currency.

Fishponds are also a valuable way of salvaging waste nutrient materials in sewage, also industrial wastes such as the washings of milk factories, slaughterhouses, and distillery residues. These all contain so much organic matter that their disposal into streams may lead to serious pollution, with death of fish and foul anaerobic conditions. But if led suitably diluted through fishponds, the organic matter is oxidized and the nutrient materials released to produce good feeding conditions for fish. Because fishponds should be shallow

[2] Le Mare, *Malayan Agricultural Journal*, vol. 35, no. 3, July, 1952.

in relation to their area, the oxidation of the organic matter is rapid, and the content of dissolved oxygen should not fall to a point dangerous to most cultivated fish. At all events, in a number of countries sewage disposal is successfully linked with fish culture; there are large or very large crops of fish to sell and an effluent is produced which compares very favorably in purity with that produced by other methods of sewage treatment.

Fish culture can be combined with rice growing in two different ways. Where there is a wet fallow between crops, the flooded rice fields are in effect fishponds and can be stocked as such. The banks, or *bunds,* may be raised so as to hold a greater depth of water, and two or more small fields may be joined to make one large fish-raising pond. The trash on the fields left over from the rice crop acts as a fertilizer, but growing rice plants are pulled up. In a four- to six-month growing period a worthwhile crop of fish can be obtained. Alternatively or additionally, fish may be grown with the rice crop; during the drainage of the rice fields for weeding, the fish take refuge in trenches dug round the perimeter of the field or down the center. In such shallow water, however, the fish are very vulnerable to birds and other pests, and the short period of flooding and the interruptions due to the culture of the rice tell against the production of large fish, since in such cases the rice is the main crop and its requirements have priority. But during the growth of the rice valuable quantities of fish fingerlings can be raised for sale to fish culturalists or for transplantation to the following flood fallow.

There is a tendency toward a growing antagonism between rice and fish in this mixed culture; for the modern trend, which will eventually find its way into developing countries, is to use fertilizers for the rice, such as cyanamide and sulfate of ammonia, which are toxic to the fish, also pesticides such as aldrin, dieldrin, and endrin, which are extremely toxic. Moreover, large quantities of water are needed. Still, the possibilities of using flooded rice fields at least for the raising of fingerlings are worth considering in rice-growing countries.

Investment Required and Returns Possible

In most underdeveloped countries fish culture is on a peasant scale and may in any case be combined with other activities. No accounts are likely to be kept, so it is difficult to discover what capital is needed and what are the returns. The case of the Bayan Lepas pig and fish farm quoted above is an exception because this venture is a sideline of a group of experienced businessmen, but there are cases in the literature which point to the fact that fish culture is profitable. For example, in south China the rent charged for fishponds was higher than that for cultivated land; while in Java it has been said that a peasant cultivator might allow his landlord the whole profits of the rice crop in return for the right to run the rice field as a fishpond in the off season. The mere fact that fish culture is done on such an extensive scale shows that it must be profitable.

Schuster[3] gives some data, applicable to 1940 values, in which the selling

[3] Schuster, *Fish Culture in Brackish-water Ponds of Java,* Indo-Pacific Fisheries Council Special Publications, no. 1, FAO, 1952.

price of these ponds varied with known productivity from Fl. 343 for good ponds to Fl. 20 per acre for poor ponds. As to profitability, Schuster gives as an example an estimate of income and expenditure per acre of a brackish-water fishpond in east Java at the price levels of 1950. Gross earnings from the sale of fish and other products of the pond were 281 florins, and the owner's profit 84. No entry is made for interest and amortization of capital, though land rent is taken into account.

Lin[4] estimates that the experienced fish farmers in Hong Kong could, on 1940 values, make a profit of HK$30 to 55 per *mow* (1/5 acre) annually; rent accounts for nearly one-third of all expenses, which are reckoned at HK$70 per *mow*.

Depasse[5] gives data on the profitability of fishponds in the Congo quoting values as in 1956, before the Congo became independent. He estimates the cost of construction at Fr. 40,000 to 100,000 per hectare and assumes an average of Fr. 70,000. Amortization in ten years requires Fr. 7,000 per annum; the selling price of the fish is estimated at Fr. 15 per kg, and of fish food at Fr. 1 per kg, with a conversion rate of 7.

A good natural pond in which the water is not fertilized and the fish are not given supplementary food would produce about 500 kg per hectare per annum, valued at Fr. 7,500. Expenses would come to Fr. 8,250 including the 7,000 for amortization. So even under good natural conditions a pond would be run at a loss of Fr. 750. But, at the other extreme, heavy feeding of the fish and fertilization of the water could produce a fish crop of 5,000 kg per hectare per annum valued at Fr. 75,000 against expenses of Fr. 50,500 giving a profit of Fr. 24,500 per hectare per annum. Of these expenses, Fr. 31,500 are for the purchase of food and Fr. 9,000 for maintenance. Amortization is still Fr. 7,000 but is now a minor item in costs. According to Depasse's figures, a pond in which the fish are intensively fed could give a return of about 35 percent net on capital.

A final example can be quoted from Liu,[6] who gives results obtained in a pond of 6,065 sq m, or about 1½ acres, in which the fish, chiefly the mollusk-eating black carp, *Mylopharyngodon piceus,* were fed snails and bivalves gathered locally, and the grass carp, *Ctenophyngodon idella,* which was also stocked, was fed vegetation. A great weight of these foods was fed, and the fish crop was one of the heaviest for which detailed records are available, namely, 4,572 kg net—a rate of 7,538 kg per hectare, or 6,724 lb per acre. The net profit was given as 36 percent on expenses, which however did not take account of any rent or amortization. In a second pond, 3,657 sq m in area, where the grass carp was the principal fish stocked, the food consisted of aquatic plants gathered locally, chiefly *Vallisneria, Myriophyllum,* and *Potamogeton,* and no less than 1,913 baskets

[4] Lin, "Fish Culture in Ponds in the New Territories of Hong Kong," *Journal of Hong Kong Fisheries Research Station,* vol. 1, no. 2, 1940.

[5] Depasse, "Monographie piscicole de la Province Orientale," *Bulletin Agricole du Congo Belge* 47, no. 4, 1956.

[6] Liu Chien-Kang, "On the Productivity of Two Experimental Fishponds Managed with Traditional Methods of Chinese Pisciculture," *Acta Sinica,* 1955, no. 1. This article is in Chinese with an English summary.

of these weeds were fed. The fish crop again was very high, namely, 1,101 kg, or at a rate of 3,011 kg per hectare. In this case, the net profit was about 12 percent on expenses, again excluding rent and amortization.

It would however be true to say that in underdeveloped countries at the peasant level fish culture would tend to develop either on a subsistence basis or on a barter basis, and cash might not be the main consideration. Capital expenditure would probably consist largely of labor, chiefly that of the fish culturalist who would excavate and embank the pond or ponds; and whether he would be willing to undertake this would depend on his desire to have fish at his disposal. Certainly ponds would be best as part of a smallholding, because in such a case the smallholder is already in possession of the tools and can call on labor. If however a loan is needed to pay extra labor, cash transactions do arise, since the borrower must raise money, probably on the sale of a part of the fish, to repay loan and interest. In a capitalized and large-scale fishpond business it has been estimated that not more than one-third of the cash revenue from the ponds should be payable on interest and amortization if the business is to pay its way; on the peasant scale this should be less, say, 20 percent.

But a problem facing anyone seeking to introduce fish culture as a source of first-class protein in a territory new to it is to attempt to forecast what the rate of fish production will be and what prices the fish will fetch. If fish is a popular food and there is a reasonable amount of money in circulation, a fair assumption would be about one shilling, say 14 cents, per pound. In a warm tropical climate, especially where suitable cheap supplementary fodders are available on site, a fish crop of the order of 2,000 lb per acre per annum could reasonably be hoped for. Gross income would then be about £100, or, say, £280 per acre of pond and pro rata for smaller areas. If not more than 20 percent of this gross income should be devoted to interest and amortization of a loan, and the latter is assumed to be 7 percent, then the ponds cannot bear capital costs in excess of about £300, or, say, £280 per acre. But hand labor is usually cheap in rural areas, and it should be possible to do the work for this sum. Though small ponds may be more expensive per unit area than large ponds, it should still be feasible to construct them within these limits.

Where fish culture is unknown in a territory, it is often necessary to set up a demonstration unit where training can also be done. Where the territory already has agricultural demonstrators for extension work, such personnel are highly suitable for training in fish culture, since this is a form of stock raising. But it is difficult to do costed trials at such stations. They are made to higher standards than would be needed in commercial ponds and so have higher capital costs. Staff are also usually more numerous than would be the case in a business, and there is the salary of the expert in charge. The best that can usually be done is to produce notional figures; but at all events such stations can show the results possible with good management. A good situation for a demonstration unit would be at an agricultural station, such as are established in many developing countries. There, dung and cheap fodders are likely to be on hand, also plenty of vegetable trash, as well as watchmen and labor quarters.

Participants for training may come forward spontaneously; headmen or farmers become interested after seeing the demonstration units and express the wish to start. There may be funds to assist in the capital cost of pond construction, as in loans at a low rate of interest for part or all of the cost. On the more usual peasant scale, however, the labor of construction may be provided by the beneficiary himself.

It is not possible to suggest the acreage of ponds required. For the subsistence of the owner and his family, a very small pond will suffice if well managed. Gruber[7] showed that ponds only 2 acres in area (200 sq m, or, say, 1/20 acre) could each produce 45 to 51 kg of fish annually, using as fertilizer and fodder only the wood ashes of the family hearth and the household kitchen scraps. This weight of fish was produced by feeding 550 to 650 kg of such scraps. So even as small a pond as this could give the owner a fish meal per week.

Where fishponds are a part of a smallholding, their size is a matter of convenience of maintenance, since they add to earnings while at the same time the owner is not wholly dependent on them for his living. The same applies to fishponds attached to piggeries and dairies; they can be as large as can be profitably run on the wastes of the main business. As shown above for the Bayan Lepas pig and fish farm, 500 pigs provided enough waste to maintain 6 acres of ponds at a profit, and a larger acreage could certainly have been added, for the overspill of the ponds strongly fertilized a large area of rice fields adjacent to the farm and much increased its rentable value.

Where a man proposes to earn his living wholly by fish culture, a viable unit could hardly be less than 10 acres, and 20 would be better; therefore capital costs would be substantial, and would not be less than about £5,000, or $14,000, probably more. Such ventures are less likely in the developing countries than the smaller-scale ponds associated with some other farming activities.

General Principles

Any piece of water will support only a certain quantity of fish, which can be called the *maximum standing crop*. In natural water without treatment it will vary with the temperature; it will be higher in warmer than in cooler climates, because the growth of all organisms in the water is more rapid at higher temperatures. It will also vary with the acidity of the water, which should always be tested. Acid waters are unproductive, and very acid waters are toxic to fish. On better soils, and with less acid water, fish crops should be of the order of 100 to 500 lb, but these would not be economical, as the Congo example quoted showed. By adding fertilizer, these crops can be raised to 800 to 2,000 lb in a warm climate, which allows a long growing period. The essential fertilizer is phosphate; about 30 lb P_2O_5 per acre is probably the best dosage. In acid conditions, this is best given as basic slag, but where the water is neutral or alkaline or has been made so, it is best given as

[7] Gruber, "Considérations sur l'amélioration des rendements en pisciculture congolaise," *Bulletin Agricole du Congo Belge* 51, no. 1, February, 1960.

triple superphosphate, because the transport costs per unit of P_2O_5 are less than with ordinary super or basic slag.[8]

Though they greatly increase the standing crops of fish and so the fish crops, the use of fertilizers adds to costs and in fact involves a cash transaction which could cause difficulties in a primitive economy. Organic manures, especially dung and night-soil, are the fertilizers used at present because they are usually available and may cost nothing (hence the value of tying fishponds to smallholdings and piggeries). But it was shown at Malacca in the most convincing way that 30 lb of P_2O_5 gives better results as a fishpond fertilizer per acre than 7 tons of cow dung. If a group of men bought phosphate fertilizer on a cooperative basis, the cost would be much reduced, and this would be a most desirable development, as it would free the dung for use on the land where it has soil-conditioning properties of great value.

With the use of phosphate fertilizer in this way, fish culture would become marginally economic. If cheap fodders are available for the fish, with or without the use of fertilizer, the fish crop can be raised to 2,000 to 4,000 lb per acre per annum, and even more, as has already been shown—the fish crop being in proportion to the food fed and its nutrient value. The food conversion rate varies greatly and is rarely less than 5:1. In the Congo example quoted above, it was taken as 7:1. So foddering the fish will be economical only if the cost of the fodder delivered to the site is not more than about 1/10 of the estimated value of the fish produced.

There is a wide range of possible fish fodders.[9] They include rice bran, the sweepings of mills and grain offals, oil-seed residues of all kinds, soybean factory residues, beer residues and brewer's grains, spoilt or damaged grains and foodstuffs, and household scraps; for vegetable-eating fish, leafy trash and grasses of all kinds are used. Such foods should not be too fibrous, since much of the fiber may be indigestible, nor should they contain too much water, because large quantities will be needed and transport costs will be high. Guinea grass can very usefully be grown on any waste land near the ponds as a food for vegetarian fish, as it grows rapidly and crops heavily.

It was previously stated that no piece of water will support more than a certain weight of fish, the maximum standing crop. In practice, the pond is fished out before the maximum standing crop is reached, because the growth in weight of the fish slows down as their increase begins to press on the food supply available, and this means a loss of earning time. The profit in fish culture lies in stocking a pond with a small weight of young fish and making them grow as fast as possible to near the maximum standing crop, when they are harvested by draining or fishing out the pond.

The best fish to use are those that do not breed freely in the raising ponds, or at least not until they have reached an acceptable weight. They should be cropped before they breed. Breeding is best done in separate small breeding ponds, the fingerlings being transplanted to the raising ponds. One breeding

[8] A summary of the results obtained with these fertilizers is given in the annual reports of the Tropical Fish Culture Research Station at Batu Berendam, Malacca, Malaysia, and copies can be had from the station.

[9] These are listed, together with their composition and digestibility, in C. F. Hickling, *Fish Culture*, Faber & Faber, Ltd., London, 1962.

pond should be able to supply many raising ponds, and in the case of the small operator it would be better to buy the fingerlings rather than raise his own. The raising of fingerlings as a catch crop in rice fields has already been mentioned.

The tilapias are good table fish, which unfortunately mature in ponds at a small size, often at less than 1 oz, and breed very freely. A pond stocked with tilapias will quickly fill up with small fish, few of which will exceed 1 oz in weight. Where the local demand is for small fish, this does not matter and very heavy crops can be got. In these cases, the ease of breeding and feeding the tilapias makes them an attractive proposition. But where the market expects fish of a larger individual weight, tilapias may give disappointing results.

The common carp is still unrivaled as a culture fish. It grows fast and is a catholic feeder, and it has proved acceptable wherever it has been introduced. It will not usually breed in ponds until it has reached a weight of 1 lb or more; well grown fish can fairly easily be induced to spawn in breeding ponds and produce a great number of offspring. Another good fish is *Puntius javanicus*, a member of the carp family which can feed on soft vegetation; this fish will sometimes breed spontaneously in sandy ponds, especially after heavy rain, but even so it reaches a good weight before it breeds. Its breeding in special ponds is easy.

The fastest-growing and most valuable of all pond fish are the major Indian and Chinese carps; all grow fast to great weight, and none breed naturally in captivity. The supply of fingerlings for pond stocking comes from an ancillary fry-catching industry which catches and sorts the fish from their natural breeding places and transports them for sale to fish culturalists. But these fish are now being bred in captivity by inducing spawning with hormone injections, so that, in future, some of these excellent fish can be bred and raised anywhere in the world where conditions are suitable.

From the practical angle, given suitable water and a favorable site, it is best to set a reasonable target figure for fish production. For example, in a warm year-round climate with neutral or alkaline water, 2,000 lb net of fish per acre and per annum might be a reasonable aim. If the demand is for a ½ lb fish, then stocking should be at a rate of 4,000 fingerlings per acre, plus, say, 25 percent addition to allow for mortality. Having fertilized the water, feeding might be done at a rate of 5 percent of the estimated weight of the fish daily; this can be estimated by sampling at monthly intervals and weighing the fish sampled. When the desired weight is reached, the fish can be harvested, and mortality and growth rates and yields can be checked. On these first results, the next run can be planned, until a suitable technique is evolved which can be propagated by extension work in the territory.

MEETING THE NATION'S NEEDS IN MANAGEMENT EDUCATION

Frederic E. Pamp, Jr., Ph.D.

No country in the world today can be pointed out as the ideal in education for management. To speak only of the United States, two recent detailed studies have handled the U.S. educational system for management rather roughly. Top executives complain about the quality of general educational preparation both in those recruited for business firms and those who should be candidates for promotion to top manager or general manager positions.

Compared with European education, U.S. education as a whole is seen as far too specialized. Americans see Great Britain and the countries of Western Europe as turning out very good higher specialists with a sound background of general education, but too few of them, and giving to the rank and file too little access to the possibility of such training. Americans try to educate *everybody*, to give equal opportunity to everybody to get to the top. Yet this effort is criticized as having developed an alarming superficiality in the general education system and a shocking degree of finicking specialization in technical education and training—a specialization which begins too early and is allowed to proliferate too superficially and to neglect the standards necessary for future progress.

Many countries are faced with desperate shortages of technicians and engineers and a surplus of lawyers and broadly educated graduates. There is no doubt that the developing countries need technicians and specialists, and need them—as we say—yesterday. They must attack the problem in two dimensions. They must build technical schools and at the same time train technicians and specialists outside the educational system as such—in industry, on the job, and in short courses serving industry.

Dr. Pamp is Vice President of American Management Association, New York.

It is perhaps not generally recognized that the United States faced this same problem in the field of management education after World War II (to a lesser degree than is the case with the developing countries, it is true, but the difficulty was no less real). However, with the speed of development of technology and of the "universe" of markets in which it operates, U.S. management has accepted the fact that it must conduct training and education for technicians and managers as a continuing effort. Moreover, it is agreed that as the complexity of problems increases, the effort must increase.

The view of the future which gives the necessary present-day perspective and operating principles to most of the industries based on advanced technology has been put thus: "Nothing could be more wildly impractical and nothing more destructive to the future of an individual or of society than an education designed to prepare people for specific vocations and professions, or to facilitate their 'adjustment' to the world as it is. To be practical, an education now must prepare a man for work that doesn't yet exist and whose nature can't even be imagined."[1]

I should like to discuss here the implications of this area of continuing education and the basic needs which it serves.

It must be said further that any society, any nation's industry, must look beyond the provision of technical skills and specializations, without neglecting their development, to the overriding necessity of training and educating *managers*. We call this concern Manager Development. United States industry has gone through, and is still going through, fads and styles and changing philosophies embraced by this term. This is no place to go into details on objectives and programs. We can, however, say that the critical problem is not the training of technicians and specialists; it is the education and development of managers. In a sense we can say that if the latter is provided for, we can be sure the former will also be taken care of.

Training Specialists

In discussing the supply of specialists we are talking about training; in planning to meet the shortage of managers, we are talking about education. The specialist is *trained* in a technique. A manager may continue to practice his specialty. It is important that be begins by having a specialty of some sort, but the "Vital Shift," as Lawrence A. Appley has called it, forces him to enter a new dimension of thought and action when he begins to manage an enterprise, or even a part of an enterprise. It can, I think, be demonstrated (1) that the manager must be *educated* rather than trained for that dimension, and (2) that a seminar and course program of the type developed and continued by the American Management Association and its members in the United States is in all countries peculiarly well suited to the special characteristics of management in its aspect as a discipline and to the special educational needs of the manager himself.

Under the telescoping impact of scientific development, the present organization of technical education must be progressively broadened to continue

[1] Charles E. Silberman, "The Remaking of American Education," *Fortune*, April, 1961, p. 127.

to serve as a base for producing the number and kind of specialists who will be needed. But in approaching the problem of producing managers we must talk about education as distinguished from training.

Education for Managers

J. W. Platt, Chairman of the Advisory Council on Education for Management of Great Britain, makes the distinction in an article entitled, "Preparing Men for Business Careers" in the London Times of June, 1961. He speaks of the pursuit of efficiency as the area of the specialist in tools and techniques, which ". . . occupy very little of the day-to-day attention of higher management. . . . The second is education which concentrates on the development of the individual to enable him to make the best use of his powers and be always able to bring a suitably trained mind to bear on the unexpected problems which he must constantly face. . . . The latter . . . has always been the sphere of the universities."

However, the mature manager has neither the time nor the inclination to return to the university, nor even the patience to return to the status of the student sitting under the professor. Since, on the other hand, the preparation of the manager for larger responsibilities should be a continuing process, it is clear that some new form of educational stimulus to growth must be found and put to use by business. This sort of program has in fact been developed by the American Management Association during the past ten years in response to the specific needs of U.S. industry.

We can recognize that education is more than the accumulation of facts and techniques. It is also a modification of the sensibility, a rise in the level of organization of the organism. It results in a new and better control of the self and the outer world. It seeks understanding by development of a set of higher meanings.

We can link this idea very aptly with the concept of management. We can truly say that the manager is to the specialist (management is to technique) as education is to training. Management is a command of controlling concepts.

Management is a science in the sense that its elements can be reduced to certain principles and that it is susceptible to an orderly reasoned approach and to certain repeatable controls and procedures. There is no denying the fact, however, that it is not and can never become an exact science. In the words of Peter Drucker, it is a "practice." Over the years, certain principles of management (as distinguished from skills or techniques) continue to be deduced and evolved from successful practice, but from year to year there is really no agreement on what they are or how far they apply in different sets of circumstances. The same management principles can produce different results in different circumstances. In fact one can now defend the thesis that the controlling element in management is the situation itself and that the essence of management is the way the manager, the leader, establishes control over that situation, and makes a new combination of elements which he directs toward the objectives of the enterprise. It is tempting to call management "existential" rather than "scientific."

Developing Leadership

The core of the problem, to which all commentaries seem to return, is leadership. We in the United States have spent millions of dollars since 1945 on research to define the qualities and elements of leadership. We have produced acres of descriptive terms, but no real agreement on how leadership can be developed. We in management would do well to look at the experience of the military through many centuries. Military academies teach the art and science of strategy and leadership, and they have on the whole done well in turning out professionals who have mastered their skills and techniques and perform adequately. When war comes the professionals go out and practice their science, guided by the principles they have been taught. But then comes a Lee or a Jackson, a T. E. Lawrence, a Rommel, or a Mao tse Tung, and we have to rewrite the Book.

So it is with management. The good manager always realizes that he is rewriting the Book. Under the pressure of necessity and events he must seize on and exploit new developments which make new combinations of the old elements. He must train himself to see implications in events that others do not see; if he assumes that the Book is already written, that everything about his particular company and his job is in the Book, he will not be a manager, in the best sense, but a technician. What provides the resources for his action is education rather than training. It is true that the manager trains himself to be aware of significant patterns of events and people, but the backdrop of conceptual skill and imagination is far more complex than can be encompassed by the term "training."

The AMA Program

The American Management Association began and developed for some thirty years in the image of a professional association, which it still is—an association of managers who wished by sharing their experiences and experiments, to build management toward a science. They set out, that is, to write the Book.

In 1950, under the leadership of its president, Lawrence A. Appley, AMA—in attempting to increase the usefulness of the traditional exchange of experience—developed its seminar program of workshops and orientations. This development in effect translated instruction into mutual education. In attempting to devise a type of meeting which would enable executives to go deeper into special subjects in a more intensive, small-group, personal atmosphere than is possible at large scientific lecture conferences, AMA found that it had peculiar resources for developing a special kind of mutual adult education, as a base for instruction and training. It turned out that this was a type of education peculiarly adapted to the special characteristics of management as a discipline. What happened was that the seminar as it developed set up situations in which managers could develop themselves as they helped develop others.

We at AMA see it as normal and necessary that the company should have an internal manager training program where the manager learns the accepted techniques and policies of that company in that industry, preferably in the light of established principles of management.

In the smaller company, the ends of such a training plan can be met by more informal means, such as personal coaching, for example.

Combating Parochialism

If the manager never leaves his company to learn, he may be well adapted to it and to the limited universe of principles it embodies, but his company will eventually suffer from a limitation on its ability to realize and cope with the rapidly changing elements of its environment. The company owes it to its own survival to make that man grow as close as possible to his own potential. For the man's own sake, and that of the company, he must be freed from parochialism and enabled to measure and match himself against his peers. It is not enough to have friendly meetings and discussions to "exchange views." During this time he must in some way demonstrate his ability to translate the things he learns of other companies' thinking and techniques into principles usable by his own company, to solve a group problem, to justify the techniques used by his company, or to lead a group to a new ground of knowledge and action.

The AMA Workshop Seminar brings fifteen experienced executives (no more than one from a company) together for 2½ days to pool their experience, under the chairmanship of two discussion leaders (usually executives like themselves), on one specific subject. No record is kept; no conclusions are voted, but as these men follow a discussion outline, they compare their companies' approach to the problem; they find new dimensions open to them all; they attack or defend this problem as part of a team. While they learn facts and approaches from other companies, it is more important that they are challenged to compare their own company, their own abilities, with these others. More important, this form forces the man himself to generalize his concepts. In semantic terms, he is forced, in order to communicate, into a higher level of generalization. No longer can he use the vocabulary of X company in Y industry: he must find some common terms to convey what he is saying to a man similarly limited to W company in Z industry. So he must talk general principles; he uses the language of *management*. He is in a process of education rather than training. This process represents a forced increase of control over a part of management, and since this higher level of control has been reached through the evolving of general principles, the principle remains to be used when the particular conditions have changed.

Similarly, in the AMA Orientation Seminar, while the registrant listens to concise presentations on particular areas of the seminar's full subject by experienced executives, he is also encouraged to challenge these presentations, to question, to discuss. He is given the opportunity to present his own experience and views, and as much time is given to discussion, either in the whole or in small working groups, as to speakers. In the AMA Management Course small-group problem solving is a large part of the course, and an entire week is taken up in actually meeting management problems in simulation with the aid of a computer, the so-called Business Game. AMA's Executive Action Course consists almost entirely of a group's moving toward understanding of motivation for action in management situations through successive problem and self-examination sessions.

In detailed, unhurried talk with other managers, testing his ideas against theirs, hammering out principles together, the individual manager can come to a realization of his own strength and weaknesses. Self-realization is perhaps the single most important element in education.

He can come to know too the strength of the winds of competition for his company and his industry. Today they blow from many directions and with greatly increased strength.

Development by Learning: Group Leadership

All I have said has been about the manager who is a registrant, as AMA calls him. But more than 90% of the men who are asked by the various division managers of AMA to speak, to lead groups, and to act as seminar chairman, are also working executives. For them the process is also educational, even more so than for the registrant. This man must, in an orientation seminar or at the management course, justify himself as a manager, also his company, to his peers. We find that the best companies in the United States think that having their executives chosen to act as speaker or leader of an AMA seminar is not only a tribute to the standing of the company and a means for making the company favorably known, but a valuable stimulant to the man himself toward progress in his job.

Adult Education

One more point, and it is an important one: This is adult, pragmatic education. Men speak to each other as equals in a search for comprehension and control; it is not the all-knowing professor instructing the schoolboy, pouring information into a basically resistant ear. That psychological block is gone in cooperative seminars.

Yet these seminars are not allowed to be ignorance compounded. Some new subjects, like Operations Research or Finance and Accounting for the Nonfinancial Executive are put in settings where instruction takes precedence. Thus they are treated as orientation seminars or courses. The Financial Executive's Job may be a workshop seminar, with only qualified executives admitted, or an orientation with a minimum of prepared presentations.

Above all, this experience of attending a seminar gives a man a creative break in his routine, a chance to step back and look at himself, at his job, in perspective. And it is a sharp practical perspective, with pressures applied to make the most of the opportunity. Even if he misses many of these effects, as Mr. Appley has said, "It is impossible for a competent executive to spend any appreciable amount of time in deliberating with others on the performance of his work without his working better."

Applying the Program Abroad

The need for multifaceted organization for the promotion of management education has been recognized in the developing countries, notably those of Latin America and Asia. We at AMA have had literally hundreds of calls for help from these countries in the years since the war and have done what we could, with private means, to help. Some portion of U.S. aid funds has been used in various parts of the world to develop business schools and curricula and, notably in Latin America, to foster the development and growth of management societies.

In some cases, business managers have felt that university economics departments have reached out a heavy academic hand and turned such business schools away from direct concentration on management and the practical problems of industrial development. This represents a friction which, like that between basic and applied research, will always be with us and can yet be fruitful.

Association and University

It is open to question, however, whether national management societies and other nonacademic centers of management training have sufficiently realized and exploited the differences between their purposes and abilities and those of the academic institutions.

Even more basic is the question of whether, except in certain larger countries like India or Japan, these associations can ever become large enough to be truly effective. Their "market," for one thing, is too small; the number of executives who are potential "customers" cannot provide sufficient income to the association to assure top-quality staff and services. Moreover, the stock of industrial and managerial experience within the country is also limited, and the members of the association are soon repeating to each other what they already know. While the association can and should be bringing new knowledge and techniques into the country, it has difficulty in paying the costs involved.

These associations must each face sooner or later the problem of building and conserving vitality of program and financial support. They are already choosing in some cases between being or becoming the "club" of top managers only, or the training center for supervisors and not many others. Whichever they choose, their full effectiveness will be impaired, as well as their contribution to the country's development.

There is a solution, which the International Management Association has suggested as a program to the Alliance for Progress. Strong regional Management Centers would offer seminars and short courses all year round, on all areas of management, to the executives of all the countries in a given region. Speakers and leaders for these programs would come from all the countries regionally represented, as well as from the United States and Europe if necessary. Thus successful techniques and specialized management knowledge would be more rapidly spread. The executive from Peru who goes to a seminar in the center, say, in Mexico City, can be the speaker at the next meeting of the Peruvian Management Association and share what he learned.

At the same time this center would be developing and sending out to the associations and productivity centers of the whole region materials for national programs for middle and lower managers and supervision. These would include printed materials, case studies, course outlines and readings, movies, and TV tapes.

Thus a group of countries would be breaking down the parochialism which now inhibits their more rapid development; at the same time they would be pooling their best knowledge and experience.

Can this work? On a national basis it *has* worked in Brazil for over four years now. Management Center do Brasil, established by the International Management Association with the support of the American Management Association and the Richardson Foundation of the United States, has run over 200 seminars and courses in its quarters in São Paulo. Over 2,000 executives have attended from almost as many companies. The interesting fact is that it has not been found necessary to import a single "expert" or speaker from the United States to staff these seminars. There is already in Brazil sufficient management knowledge to staff a full program of management education. The working executives who have this knowledge are ready to share it, if it is made possible for them to do so. A management center can make it possible and do it for a whole group of countries.

THE POLICY OF INTERNAL MANAGEMENT DEVELOPMENT

Ernst Wolf Mommsen

We live in a world in which, despite the yearning for freedom and individualism, all sociological trends, even all thinking and consequently all individual decisions, are increasingly influenced by collectivism. This may sound harsh, and perhaps it should be taken with a grain of salt. But we must realize that the ability of the individual to make decisions is steadily weakened, a fact which is at least partly due to technological progress. On the other hand, the relation and the subordination of the individual to an anonymous society are becoming increasingly important.

In the field of technology the trend toward larger and more complicated equipment necessitates the raising of enormous funds, with the effect that the role of the individual is diminishing and that technical research is done by large teams. The same trend is apparent in the field of distribution. The highly efficient department store has made its way into Europe. The latest development in this field—the supermarket, a completely rationalized unit—offers to the competing individual but a meager chance to retain his independence. The more time and distances are eliminated, the narrower grows the scope within which the individual can make a decision and operate on his own. We need only to think of the managerial independence of the branch manager in East Asia some thirty years ago, or of the chief engineer in charge of a large bridge or dam project in Egypt or Turkey; compare his independent decision-making power with the methods of division of managerial authority and responsibility that are customary in the big projects of today.

It may be argued that, on the other hand, the burden of responsibility resting on the individual is steadily growing as a result of this technological prog-

Assessor Mommsen is Director of Phoenix-Rheinrohr A.G., Düsseldorf.

ress. The machine that an individual is entrusted to operate very often represents an immense value in terms of money, and any error in operation may cause an enormous loss. But this argument does not hold water. Damaging a machine by error is not tantamount to decision making; there is no true choice of either yes or no.

Yet it is the "either or" alone that characterizes what we call a decision, and technology tries to eliminate possible mistakes by making the operation of these devices foolproof.

When looking at economic activities from this angle, we discover that nowhere in this world have people such a great freedom to take genuine individual decisions as in the top management of private enterprises. Of course, many true decisions are made at all levels. But as a result of our collectivized life and thinking, their effects are almost invariably paralyzed. To quote an example, who could claim to be capable of deciding on his own to be a reformer in the intellectual, political, or religious sphere without having secured the support of either a mass party, radio, television, or the giant press? Any individual decision—and they have been and still are taken in the above-mentioned fields—will as a rule result in frustration or resignation, unless these vast instruments can be employed.

All this is in sharp contrast to business. Here, there is still scope for genuine decisions which may even go as far as jeopardizing the existence of a big company. Hence the passionate controversies in many countries regarding the control of such companies, because of the dependence of a great number of people, even whole communities, on the fate of certain industries. The noteworthy fact that personal decisions are still possible to an unusually high degree in business was underlined by the eminent Protestant theologian, Bishop Lilje, in a remarkable speech made before a group of industrialists. From this fact he deduces that such freedom should be felt as a divine grace rather than as power, and that it involves a strong sense of responsibility as well as ethical considerations.

Freedom of Decision and Its Significance for Internal Management Development

Let us proceed on the assumption that latitude in personal decision making is at least comparatively wider for leading business executives than for other people in our increasingly collectivized world. What are the conclusions to be drawn?

1. The greater the freedom to decide, the greater the risk to take wrong decisions. Parenthetically, it should be added that this freedom at the same time encourages great and gallant deeds which, in a collectivized society, are often stifled in favor of a compromise.

2. This risk places increased responsibility on those who have been entrusted with a position of this kind, likewise on those who feel they are qualified for such a position.

What, then, is this responsibility for the one who actually has freedom to decide, that is to say, for the top businessman? I propose to answer the question by putting forward some more theses.

To be in a leading position in business means not merely to take decisions. It also implies that executives should allow decisions to develop. It is wrong to believe that in our world, which tends to become more and more complex, the individual could take it upon himself in the long run to make solitary decisions. Nor is this what he is expected to do. Leading positions should be filled by men possessing superior knowledge, and the ability to activate the knowledge of others; men possessing intuition and initiative, and the ability to instill these in others; and by men having the courage to take decisions, and the ability to enable others to prepare those decisions by mustering all their knowledge, so that they will be as effective as possible.

From these factors everything else must be derived: advanced studies by executives (for instance, in the United States, university classes held by men in leading industrial and political positions), the necessity of fostering teamwork, and, finally, careful control and guidance of the staff and recruits.

On the other hand, there are those who hope to be called to a leading position, or at least feel they are capable of filling one. Right from the beginning they will have to realize the responsibility involved in the positions they desire to attain. Once they have become aware of this factor, they must take every opportunity to improve their knowledge, to verify their views, and above all to increase their imaginative powers, which enable them to anticipate the problems of tomorrow. It is nothing but clear thinking that, in a final analysis, will pave the way for them and eventually lead to success. Certainly, the "big chance" does play an important part in life. There are other factors, too, which facilitate the rise of one man while another has to do without them. All the same, everyone who in himself feels the call to a leading position should keep in mind that the majority of men who have actually been called to do executive work have gone the way of strenuous effort, profound knowledge, and the willingness to employ all their physical and mental powers.

The Basic Aspects of Management Development

Thus we may say that the problem of developing management personnel must be solved for both types of personnel, the ambitious ones and the others. Training is as necessary for the one who holds a leading position (he will have to improve his own management qualities as well as those of his staff) as for the one who feels able to fill such a position, unless he prefers to stick to a routine job.

These, then, are the basic conclusions governing management development:

1. Business gives the individual a greater freedom to take decisions than does any other branch of activity under the present social situation.

2. This fact involves additional responsibilities for the one actually taking such decisions, as well as for the one who feels he is able to do so.

3. Business leadership does not only require personal courage to take decisions. More than that, for the correctness of the decision it is important that it should have been prepared by teamwork so that it is supported by a common sense of responsibility.

4. Control over the actual state of affairs and the provident anticipation of tomorrow's situation, combined with the decisions based upon these, cannot be derived from a responsibility for the fate of the company alone; it is also

the result of that higher sense of responsibility that has its roots in the greater freedom to decide.

5. The obligation of leading men to improve their own knowledge and also the knowledge of those who participate or will in future participate in their decisions—and such persons must be looked for at all levels of a company's staff—is not merely a corollary to the higher sense of responsibility as outlined above, but is an integral part of the concept of management.

The Principal Obligations of Management

What exactly are the primary duties of management? Here again, I should like to outline the term "management" by stating a few brief theses.

Management implies:

1. Determination of the company's objectives
2. Determination of the company's policy
3. Control of the company's affairs
4. Observation of external influences
5. Continual decisions regarding modification or extension of the company's objectives and business policy, based upon company control and observation of external influences

Naturally, these factors require many additions or complements. Also, I am fully conscious of the fact that by giving such theses I have simplified the complex management problem. However, I feel justified in doing so for the purpose of arriving at a concise description of management development tasks.

Internal Management Development

In planning intense management development we must consider the following:

1. Internal management training is not necessarily confined to the company's premises—it may just as well take place outside the company. This includes courses on an intercompany level and visits to and experience in foreign countries, as well as university studies supported by the company. Internal training does not merely include "measures." It may also be derived from the day-by-day example of the organization as such.

2. Advanced internal training, whatever its form, may pursue various objectives:

a. It should enable the individual to broaden his intellectual scope and give him a chance to show that he has learned on the job, in order to facilitate his advancement.

b. In a world of increasingly more complicated technical processes it should enable the individual to adapt himself to new technological and economic processes, so that he may cope with future problems challenging him.

c. It should enable the individual to get insight into far-reaching problems in order to give him (particularly if he is a specialist) an understanding of the broad pattern in the midst of which his activities take place. Thereby he should become an intellectual buttress for his environment.

d. It should make the individual as well as the company feel that the training facilities provide every opportunity for the advancement of junior executives.

e. For the company, it should make sure that a continuous flow of up-to-date technical and economic information will train a team of junior managers to seek and define future objectives and to anticipate and reduce future risks, if necessary by overriding the old generation.

f. It should also make for increasing solidarity among such members of the staff as take part in the training, thereby fostering the formation of teams.

g. Finally, it should provide the basis for an all-round occupation of the individual executive, both in order to protect the company's interests and as a safeguard against setbacks in his own special branch of activity.

h. Any internal management training serves not merely the company but the whole community. Versatility and the active promotion of his personal development make it possible for the individual executive to be employed in other jobs in other lines, even in rival companies. In the same way as all business activities and all economic objects of a company must be an integral part of our social order, all internal training will have to serve the wider task of developing our social structure, a task that cannot be separated from our economic activities.

3. No doubt the above-mentioned functions of internal management training will make it quite plain that here, as in business policy, nothing must be left to chance; such training should be the object of far-reaching planning within the company. In fact, it should be an essential part of the organization problems to be solved by a company.

It can be said that a well-organized company which undertakes long-term planning with regard to its business policy and objectives must of necessity become aware of the personnel problems that are to be solved in order to reach these objectives. Such problems include the preparation of the staff for these objectives by means of basic training, advanced training, and confrontation with the present and future situation.

The Various Methods of Internal Management Training

In the first place, there is the ideal. Every generation had its ideal with which it associated certain social concepts. Yet the image of entrepreneurs was long distorted as a result of doctrines dating back to the period of social struggles, industrial disputes, and lockouts. Even today it is being distorted by Communist demagogy and by grave mistakes made on our own part.

While in the United States the names of great men of business are mentioned with pride, there is a certain reluctance to do so in Europe. This is a fact deserving serious thought, because it involves a certain danger for economic development.

Leading men who fail to be models to others by refusing to take on public responsibilities or to have any social conscience cannot hope to develop the type of executive necessary for responsible management, not even with an optimum of organizational means.

In the same way that economy in operations was often regarded as a business ideal by past generations, the ideals of contributing to the welfare of society and serving the public, consequently of influencing the way day-to-day work is performed, leave their hallmark on a company today.

Important aspects of internal organization favoring management training are the following:

1. Definition of the long-term business policy and organic integration of the long-term personnel policy into it.

2. Definition of the long-term personnel policy, at the same time indicating the possibilities for advancement, but also emphasizing future demands on the various divisions of the company. Example: Adaptation to the Common Market.

3. Laying open the facilities for management training and the requirements to be fulfilled for participating in the use of such facilities.

4. Selection of suitable personnel and guidance of those who have made use of such facilities.

5. Confrontation of superiors with training facilities and institutions.

6. Discussion groups composed of superiors and juniors, concerning methods of internal management training and application of what they have heard, seen, and learned.

7. Survey of one's own activities by comparing them with those of other companies.

It is an extremely difficult problem to define the long-term business policy and the long-term personnel policy which is derived from, and also adjusted to, management development.

In contrast to the United States, in Europe we practice a notorious secrecy in guarding company facts and figures. There actually are companies who believe they can do without any management development policy, who regard production and distribution as something almost natural. And if matters should once develop in a manner inconsistent with their own ideas and wishes, the first thing they do is call upon the government for action.

If, however, a company completely fails to lay open its future objectives, even to its own personnel, it cannot expect its staff to think or plan ahead. How should the personnel policy be framed, and what should a junior executive do to prepare himself for future duties? One example is the adjustment of a company to the new situation brought about by the Common Market. Certainly the considerations involved in this need not be presented publicly. Yet the main problems, such as location, raw material resources, sales and purchasing control, etc., must be the subject of far-reaching consultations within the company and must be solved in relation to training and staff.

This applies similarly to long-term personnel policy. Goals should be clear enough to enable efficient junior members of the staff to recognize their opportunities, to make the necessary preparations, and to take part in studies improving their knowledge. At the same time, the announcement of goals should make them believe firmly in the future of their company.

Senior members should also be shown what they are expected to do, what they are to make preparations for, and why they have to train their staff if they too are to fulfill their obligations in future.

Nothing that concerns facilities for internal management training should be left to mere chance. All plans for the future and the requirements of corporate development should be understood and should serve as a basis for managerial development.

Unfortunately, the care for those who have participated in management development programs has so far been woefully neglected. What is the use of the best training if the trainee, filled with ideas, returns to his job only to find that he cannot make use of what he has learned? Many juniors, returning from training courses and failing with everything they have studied just because the company is not willing to take advantage of it, are overcome by deep frustration. Hence, if there is to be some sense in internal training, and if it is to give satisfaction, the trainees should be given careful attention. This is a problem of human relations and organization.

It is suggested that, in the first place, the superior should be acquainted with the methods of internal training. Not only should he know that internal training is imperative, but he should also have an idea of the subjects of these studies so as to enable him to turn to good account the acquired knowledge of his subordinates.

Finally, I would like to emphasize particularly the necessity of comparing one's own methods and facilities of internal training with those of other companies here and abroad. Certainly, each company has its own ideas in this respect, which are determined by its objectives and by its top management. All the same, companies should try to avoid the risk of a "training routine" by a steady exchange of ideas with other companies, organizations, and institutions. This includes the assignment of members of the company's staff to institutions where men from various organizations and fields of activity meet for training purposes. It is a widespread mistake to believe that the best training is of necessity the one concentrated on company affairs. On the contrary, it is going *beyond* one's own special field that creates the far-sightedness requisite for leading men. Moreover, these men will breathe fresh air outside the company's confines. They will develop much more personality and will be encouraged to ask the well-known, and painful, "silly" (but so constructive) questions.

Conclusion

We must ask ourselves what the deeper significance of all management development programs is. At the beginning I mentioned the great possibility of taking free decisions which business offers. Now, in concluding, I am bound to emphasize the important part that business plays in the social evolution of the Free World. Private enterprise is in fact part of what we call the Free World. Any grossly erroneous decisions, any wrong attitude of leading businessmen toward their subordinates, and any failure to recognize the present social responsibilities resting upon us in the industrial field may endanger the present political status and, as a consequence, our freedom. Everyone in business, in particular present and future management, must therefore become aware of the importance of their own actions for our social structure.

Furthermore, we must realize that we are living in a world in which the social order is subject to increasingly rapid changes. Just as the gap between rich and poor becomes smaller and smaller, our social system evolves new aspects which we must not only recognize but also accept as desirable. It is not merely the prosperity of all social classes that matters. It is the higher degree of security that protects the individual in this new social order, yet also demands of him the obligation to defend this order as the result of a genuine political decision. We must come to realize that this is what we are expected to do in order to ensure security. And defense means the willingness to think and plan ahead. Imperturbability and comfortable satisfaction, lip service, even laziness, are the greatest dangers for our social order and our political freedom. Our economy, as well as private property, which is closely connected with our economic system, is an integral part of our political order. Within the framework of this order, managerial competence can make the greatest contribution to economic development and to public welfare. These contributions are necessary and will be made by a managerial group properly prepared by managerial development programs.

Whereas in the past only a few men had to look across national boundaries while the majority concentrated on national markets, there is bound to be an increasing number of men, for example, those concerned with the Common Market, who will have to look beyond that into still larger political and economic units. What is mere wishful thinking today will soon be reality, and wrong decisions based on misjudgment of future developments will be irreparable a few years from now.

Finally, the tendency toward shorter working hours must of necessity lead to an increasingly heavier burden for the man in a leading position. He has never been bound to working hours and never will be. Though in former times this may have been as asset, today it is a ponderous burden. That is why, particularly, leading men need collaborators qualified for leadership if they are to bear this personal burden and be gradually relieved of it.

CORRESPONDENCE TEACHING FOR UNDERDEVELOPED COUNTRIES

John C. Villaume

In Latin America, Africa, and Asia, the challenge is the same. Millions of workers must master job skills vital to the rapid economic development of their homeland; predominantly illiterate populations must be educated in the duties and the opportunities of citizenship in a non-Communist society.

But on each continent, their mastery of twentieth-century technology and their introduction to free institutions are frustrated by common problems. Resident schools are so few and far between, their faculties so small, and their facilities so limited, that they cannot hope to meet this challenge. Vast distances and inadequate transportation make it impossible for thousands of potential students to reach existing schools with any regularity. And few employed adults in these areas, no matter how desperate they are for training, can afford to give up a job to study full-time.

Nevertheless, measurable progress is being made as government and business leaders employ educational methods to dissolve the "iron curtain" of ignorance. One means that is proving most effective and economical in underdeveloped areas is correspondence study.

Earning Army of 50,000

Today, the largest American home study institute, the International Correspondence Schools of Scranton, Pennsylvania, and its affiliates count among their approximately 150,000 active students more than 50,000 young men and women in foreign countries. Many are hard at work in lands where education, particularly qualified technical instruction, is very difficult to come by. Their tuition costs, modest by American standards, are sometimes met

Mr. Villaume is President of International Correspondence Schools, Scranton, Pennsylvania.

entirely by the individual, but with increasing frequency governments and private companies are helping to defray them.

For example, in Central America employees of the Standard Fruit Company are enrolled in such correspondence training programs to upgrade a broad range of skills. Such subjects as diesel and gas motor technology, accounting, construction engineering, milling mechanics, and business administration are being taught to promising indigenous workers in the company with an employer-sponsored tuition refund plan for those who successfully complete their studies.

Since 1956, an ALCOA subsidiary in British Guiana has had a cooperative training plan resulting in some 150 correspondence enrollments—sixty-five of them just last year. The company pays the cost of training employees in more than a score of subjects, including industrial instrumentation, chemical production, and industrial electrical engineering, and this will equip the local staff to handle much skilled work in their area.

A U.S. management consultant firm charged with responsibility for helping a new African nation develop managerial classes for local government and industry turned to ICS for a program of correspondence instruction.

On the island of Aruba off the coast of South America, the Lago Oil and Transport Company's training supervisor heads a correspondence school. He supervises a group of employees studying a variety of correspondence courses who met weekly to take examinations graded in America.

A Flexible, Industry-tested Learning Method

In the United States today several thousand firms encourage employees to take job-related correspondence courses. More than 2 million Americans are enrolled in some 450 private correspondence schools. Moreover, home study offers special advantages which explain the fast-growing demand for sound correspondence instruction in underdeveloped as well as highly industrialized economies.

Students can obtain instruction that is not available locally—in skilled trades, business and engineering, and academic fields—and can study subjects of numerous educational levels. Since they need not travel to attend school but can learn at home in their own time, study does not interfere with regular employment; it meets the different needs of students with dissimilar backgrounds and abilities, permitting them to complete instruction in a short time or over a longer period depending on choice and learning speed.

In addition, it is a most economical way to train a group of workers in different fields simultaneously. Home study can be integrated into an in-plant training program, with examinations and progress checked regularly by company training personnel. Courses are specific and concentrated so that they can be tailored to short- and long-range training needs of a company or individual. Furthermore, top-quality up-to-date correspondence training, free from political, religious, or racial dogmatism, makes uniform technical and academic instruction available to people of every race, creed, and color.

It would be a mistake to think that correspondence education is primarily used on the most basic levels. Consider the actual case of a U.S. corporation engaged in manufacturing, selling, and servicing a variety of office machines and scientific equipment, including the most advanced and sophisticated of electronic computers. Recognizing that the final phases of such intricate instruction had to be handled on a face-to-face basis in the United States, this company set about recruiting personnel throughout the world wherever it does business.

Recruitment and training officials soon realized that by casting such a wide net, international in scope, they were bringing in prospective students with differing educational backgrounds. In addition to variations in aptitude, they uncovered widely divergent levels of training in such basic subjects as electricity and electronics. The application of time and expense to the training of students lacking a common background, after their arrival in the United States, was obviously uneconomical.

The company therefore enlisted the special services of the International Correspondence School's Diagnostic Testing. Thus were identified the areas where concentrated training was needed, as well as those where swift review would suffice. These students were then trained in their native lands via correspondence courses. Some of the courses taught were:

Magnetism and Electromagnetism
Transformers in Radio Receivers
Theory of Electron Tubes
Audio-frequency Amplifiers
Components and Circuits in Electronic Data Processing Machines

These topics, as well as a variety of more basic courses necessary to the understanding of more advanced subjects, were mastered by a great number of foreign students. No language barrier existed, since courses could be supplied in a number of foreign languages.

As a result, once they had completed their basic and intermediate training, the students could be brought to the United States for the most advanced phases of a course on electronic computers, and the company could be certain that all of them had attained virtually identical levels of knowledge. Advanced instruction in the United States was thus achieved with a minimum of both time and expense.

The details of these and many other ways in which correspondence study is being put to use by American firms operating abroad, and by underdeveloped nations seeking the education necessary for advancement, vary greatly from case to case. Requirements change; what one country or company needs today, it may have outgrown tomorrow, thanks to today's training. But certain basics underlie all these efforts.

Knowledge, the Key to Survival

"Human history," H. G. Wells once pointed out, "becomes more and more a race between education and catastrophe."

Nothing that has happened since this observation was made has done anything but underscore the power of Wells's insight. Certainly today the possibility of catastrophe is sharper than ever before, while, at the same time, the need for education has been heightened to a crucial necessity.

The underdeveloped and uncommitted nations hold the key to much of this planet's future. It is here that the race between education and catastrophe runs fastest. And it is here, as we have seen, that the new educational technique of correspondence training comes into play.

To understand the role this form of teaching is playing and will play to an increasing extent in the critical years that lie ahead for less developed nations, to understand the value of correspondence teaching, or "home study," let us examine the method in brief detail.

Like any educational process, correspondence study requires three basics —student, instructional material, and teacher.

Unlike other educational systems, however, in home study the teacher and student are separated by distance. No accredited correspondence school "teaches by mail." Teaching is done through the written word and the personalized instruction service which is part of any system of education. The mail is simply a carrier to bring student response to the teacher and the teacher's comments and advice to the student.

The essential characteristic of correspondence study, therefore, is not the fact that it is instruction by mail. Indeed, the correspondence method has always been used in resident instruction in certain subjects, and in many cases no other method is possible.

The chief features of the method are constant efforts by the student and correction by the teacher. As ordinarily applied in correspondence study, the method consists of the assignment by the instructor of definitely planned work, the writing out by the student of the results of his work, the correction and criticism by the instructor of the written lessons, and the suggestions and assistance upon points where the student needs such help.

The student is tested on the whole of every lesson. He not only recites the entire lesson but reduces it to writing, so that any error may be detected and corrected. The criticism by the instructor is also clearly and definitely written. No slipshod or evasive work, no bluffing, is possible for student or for instructor.

The hard grind which such methods require from students is such an ever-present fact, so much a part of correspondence study, and so seldom found in class work, that it more truly represents the essential feature of correspondence study than does postal transmission. An educator in South Africa, a country with a system of university correspondence education attracting several thousand students annually, recently wrote:[1]

> Whereas normally the young residential student attends a university because his parents decide on it, the external student makes his own decision from a sense of responsibility towards himself and his family. Obviously this must result in an entirely different approach towards university study and what it entails. The "chancers" who expect to obtain a degree without effort soon fall by the wayside. On the whole, the external student displays an exceptional degree of self-discipline, maturity and independent thinking. . . . (He) can be expected to do more self-study which in itself is more conducive to the right scientific approach than the "spoonfeeding" which the young residential student so often expects and obtains.

[1] F. E. Radel, "Correspondence Education in South Africa," *Home Study Review*, Fall, 1963, p. 13.

Correspondence study is also an *individual* method of instruction, almost the only one now practiced on any large scale. Except in correspondence study, individual instruction has given way to the class method, save for the favored few who are able to meet the higher cost of private tutoring.

In correspondence study each student receives continuous individual attention and assistance to meet his special needs throughout the course. Each examination submitted by an ICS student, for example, receives individualized personal attention. Supplementary instruction is given in marginal notes on the student's paper and in printed supplements, with additional comments and suggestions given in personally dictated letters.

The cost of correspondence study to the student can be kept low, because the preparation of the course material, the services of the instructor, and the supervision of the work, while administered individually, are also given to a number of other students. It thus preserves many of the economies of the class method without losing the personal character of individual instruction.

Further, in contrast to the classroom method, correspondence study does not hold some students back and drag others on too fast; no two minds are exactly alike or require exactly the same treatment.

Correspondence study is especially desirable for those who wish intensive instruction in special subjects. The home study course permits them to select what will serve their purpose without doing work that to them is useless or repetitious, although required by the courses planned for group instruction.

The specially prepared instruction text is the core of the correspondence course system. Texts are written by experts who are daily engaged in the type of work about which they are writing. An engineer employed by a public utility writes texts on power-plant operation for electrical engineering courses. This makes the text realistic, up to date, and authoritative.

The staff of correspondence educators then rewrites and edits this material to "build the teacher into the text." Student questions must be anticipated, and the language of the text must be simple, clear, and readable. Each text is profusely illustrated. ICS texts are written for the student, not for the teacher; they are teaching texts.

There has been some misunderstanding about correspondence school examinations, because the student has his text available during his examination. However, resident schools have long made use of open-book examinations. Persons taking the examination for professional engineering licensing are also permitted to bring as many reference books into the examination room as they desire. Many bring suitcases filled with reference texts!

Home Study: An Ancient Practice

The correspondence, or home study, approach to education is by no means new. It has been going on for a longer period than most of us realize. There is evidence that Buddhist priests in Japan were being trained by this method at the time of Christ, that correspondence education existed in ancient Rome. In the twelfth century, the idea flourished anew when an Italian university offered regular correspondence instruction.

Few people realize the tremendous scope of correspondence education or the extent of its influence on the world today. More than 3 million people throughout the world are studying by the correspondence method. In the United States, as many students enroll with private home study schools as enter all the college and university freshman classes. However, in many foreign countries correspondence education is making a far greater contribution to the entire educational picture than here in the United States. For example, in Sweden virtually all vocational education is available through correspondence programs. More than 300,000 people of a total population of 7 million are studying by the correspondence method.

A recent survey of correspondence education in Russia, according to the U.S. Office of Education, shows that more than 482,000 students were enrolled in high school and university-level correspondence courses in 1960. Annually, approximately four out of every ten Russians who graduate from institutes and universities win their degree as the result of successfully completing correspondence study programs.

In addition, Russia has stepped up its educational efforts and now needs more teachers. To meet the needs, elementary school teachers are being given additional training through correspondence. Secondary school students are also being taught by correspondence. Current figures are not available, but at last report 60,000 students were enrolled in eighty such schools.

There are more than 400 private home study schools in the United States, only 65 of which have been accredited. In addition, some 150 colleges and universities offer courses by the correspondence method. The accredited private correspondence schools have a student body of approximately 1,250,000, and the colleges and universities, about 200,000

The U.S. Armed Services operate some of the largest home study schools with a current student body of about 1,500,000. Virtually overnight, hundreds of thousands had to learn new skills essential to the military effort. Correspondence instruction for troops on the move and for those with limited or irregular study time proved so effective that several services later set up their own correspondence schools. During World War II, the U.S. Armed Forces Institute was formed to unify these educational activities. USAFI has been supplied with more than 15 million correspondence texts.

Job-related Training

Correspondence education is also widely used by business and industry. For example, students of the International Correspondence Schools are usually gainfully employed and are invariably interested in taking job-related courses that will help them on their present job and prepare them for the one immediately ahead. Consequently, 85% of these students are studying courses directly related to their present job or the one immediately ahead, attempting to improve their value to their employer.

In many significant respects, one can say that the educational *problems* of the future are being met by the educational *method* of the future.

Nowhere is this more true than in the less developed nations of the world. Having achieved political independence, governments and peoples now yearn to achieve economic independence as producing, progressing coequals.

The files of the International Correspondence Schools show an interesting pattern developing in many of these areas. We have seen that, in cooperation with home study institutions, both private industry and governments are working to help individuals learn and achieve. The pattern that is emerging is in the best traditions of the free enterprise system. It blends private and public initiative to enhance the individual's rightful place in society and affords a great opportunity to many correspondence students. They are able to better themselves and their nation through an educational method that reaches them with a foreign postmark.

They can benefit from education at home, and in so doing they bring the results of their private study to the job through which they are contributing to their country's economic development.

TRAINING FOR MANAGERS OF DEVELOPING COUNTRIES IN ISRAEL

Sylvia Kowitt

Israel, one of the newly emergent states, is still in the process of development, but in many ways new countries see in her an example to follow. More than seventy countries have requested Israel's cooperation in their development plans. In the years 1958–1962 over 6,000 people from developing countries have come to Israel for training, while 1,000-odd Israeli experts have been sent to foreign countries.

Israeli international cooperation is organized in fields where Israel has acquired particular expertise and experience. Limited in natural resources and faced with overwhelming demands for rapid development due to the influx of thousands upon thousands of immigrants, Israel had to utilize the latest scientific methods, combining them with ingenuity, flexibility, and a pioneering spirit. People from countries which had been bypassed by modern technology had to be taught the trades and skills demanded by the growing economy. A wasteland had to be made productive.

Among the first to turn to Israel were the Burmese, who sent whole families to Israel's cooperative villages to learn the special techniques of cooperative agricultural settlement. The Namsang (Shan States) Project called for the establishment of villages by demobilized soldiers on wide stretches of unclaimed wastelands. While Israeli experts were preparing surveys and plans in Burma, more than forty Burmese families lived and worked in Israeli moshavim (smallholders' cooperative settlements). After their year's training they returned to Burma to settle in cooperative villages in the Namsang region which were initially directed with the help of Israeli experts.

In 1958 there were 150 students from developing countries in Israel; in

---

Miss Kowitt is employed in the Information Office of the Department for International Cooperation, Jerusalem.

1959 the number rose to 300, and in 1960 to 650. In 1961, 1,250 people took part in the organized courses and individual training programs. During 1962 there were 1,600 in more than 30 courses, and in 1963, 2,270 students took part in some 40 courses.

For the years 1961–1962, students came from the following places:

Area	1961	1962
Africa	877	832
Asia	275	173
Latin America	16	115
Mediterranean region	82	349
Others		39

The question arises why other developing countries are attracted to Israel as a country for study and training. Leaders of newly independent countries see on their visits to Israel the tangible action and progress that permeates Israel's national life. There is no substitute, they say, for seeing and feeling development in the process. Beyond the techniques of development which any modern state can offer, they prize Israel's approach.

The chief ingredient in this approach is the pioneering spirit which has made possible national rehabilitation and the cultivation of a land neglected and laid waste for two thousand years. Jews returning to Israel after centuries of exile are motivated by a sense of mission. This is an important factor in considering Israel's program of cooperation. Israelis can be appealed to to make sacrifices and can be recruited on the grounds of patriotism. Cooperation experts and instructors impelled by the momentum of pioneering are ready to undertake often arduous tasks.

Because of its own history of persecution, Israel feels a particular kinship with the new states of Africa and Asia. In 1898, Theodore Herzl, father of modern Zionism, wrote in "Altneuland" a description of the Jewish State he envisaged, after which he said:

> There is still one other question arising out of the disaster of the nations which remains unsolved to this day, whose profound tragedy only a Jew can comprehend. That is the African question. Just call to mind all those terrible episodes of the slave trade, of human beings who merely because they were black were stolen like cattle, taken prisoner, captured and sold. Their children grew up in strange lands, the objects of contempt and hostility because their complexions were different. I am not ashamed to say, though I may expose myself to ridicule in saying so, that once I have witnessed the redemption of Israel, my people, I wish to assist in the redemption of the Africans. . . . In our country, we shall set up a great university to which students will come from Africa and Asia. . . .

Israel's program is flexible and suited to improvization. It operates with a minimum of red tape and is relatively fast-moving. The list of training courses is established on the request of the interested governments in the fall of each year, but courses may be added on request, and individual training schedules are worked out in accordance with specific needs.

When necessary, development services can work around the clock to organize a badly needed course in a hurry. Countries are not told to wait months or years—but their needs are met as soon as possible.

Instructors are recruited from various governmental and private institutions; kibbutzim (collective settlements) are often asked to release key experts in agriculture; schools and colleges lend their staff; classrooms and accommodations are arranged with the aid of local institutions.

The size and scope of projects in Israel are more akin to the limited actual possibilities in developing countries than the complex, large-scale, expensive models of more advanced nations. Many of the actual problems faced by this nation have to be tackled by other countries as well: the unification of diverse communities into a single nation, the establishment of a common language, the building of a common culture from diverse elements, imparting the idea of the dignity of agriculture, mobilizing the youth, providing medical and administrative personnel and services. Having taught new trades to immigrants ingathered from different backgrounds and levels of education, the country developed particular training methods based on intensive courses designed for immediate needs.

In the field of agriculture, for example, modern scientific methods have produced a fivefold increase in productivity since 1948, despite the fact that the country is semiarid. Farmers work closely with the scientists and base their work on precise calculations of needs for water, fertilizer, labor, and time; they keep up with latest developments through a widespread extension service. Through this approach, and by careful breeding, cattle, sheep, and poultry are among the most productive in the world. Experts and instructors are not bureaucrats but down-to-earth people who often work in overalls right in the fields.

In general the courses are short and intensive. Students, it is reasoned, should not be taken away from their jobs for too long, lest their readjustment on return be difficult. This also prevents any hardships for their families during their absence. Four months is the usual duration of shorter courses. The idea is to have trainees combine short, intensive periods of study with the opportunity to implement their new knowledge fairly quickly on the job.

The students are required to work very hard. Every hour is accounted for, and every activity has a definite purpose. The students are eager to learn, concentrate well, and respond favorably to long hours of study and practical work. On-the-spot observations which take them all over the country to varied regions and institutions are geared to the theoretical studies.

Students are cautioned not to adopt the demonstrated techniques blindly when they return. They are advised to adapt what they think may be of use to them, considering the specific conditions at home. Thus an evaluation of the differences and contrasts is essential.

Here is an example of methods used in training senior administrative officials for Africa. Work was divided into four main periods:

1. Principles of public administration, foundations of the state and of government, the economics of development.

2. Illustrations of theoretical studies by study of technical details and the introduction of practical subjects, such as political sociology, budgeting,

efficiency, planning and organization, public relations and administrative law.

3. Government and other offices—three weeks in three offices in accordance with an individual plan of study drawn up for each student on the basis of an analysis of his present occupation and future plans.

4. A period of summary of impressions and know-how acquired through discussions with principal lecturers and the planning of individual projects based on analyses of the offices inspected and on a comparison with work done in the students' offices and countries.

Groups were kept small for exercises and discussions. Two instructors were at their disposal at all times to aid them individually in the preparation of homework or to supplement class explanations.

There were six to eight hours of obligatory study daily, and lessons were held with the aid of visual means of instruction. In addition to a technical library at their disposal, 600 pages of material based on the lectures were also prepared for the students, and they were given this, as well as other educational aids, to take home.

Special emphasis in all training projects is placed on social organization, on developing a spirit of unity among the students and between them and the Israeli population. Little effort is made at actually refining a standard of behavior toward foreign guests. The local population itself is composed of people of many origins and different shades of color. It was ingathered from more than seventy countries, speaking different languages and bringing along different customs. Half of Israel's population comes from Africa and Asia. Differences, therefore, go largely unnoticed.

In Haifa, the municipality undertook a program of education in the city schools. When African trainees arrived in large numbers to attend the International Training Center in Community Services, they met a city which had been thoroughly acquainted with African customs, way of life, and history.

In Natanya, where the ORT Vocational School is located, a local teacher asked the African students to lecture in the schools about their homelands. The young men, some speaking Hebrew by now, told of their countries, providing a living lesson in geography and sociology. Residents of the town are invited to school parties and national celebrations.

Organization of the Program

The students are recipients of scholarships awarded by the state of Israel in programs requested by their respective governments.

In some cases, international organizations have channeled technical assistance through Israel's scholarship program. The Organization of American States, the International Labor Organization, the Food and Agricultural Organization, the United Nations Special Fund, the World Veterans Federation, the World Assembly of Youth, and UNESCO have also participated in the program. The World Health Organization directly aided in the establishment of the six-year course in medicine for English-speaking students from developing countries.

In general, the country of the student's origin or the international organization pays for travel expenses. Israel awards scholarships which cover complete costs of tuition, books, and room and board, with a monthly grant of pocket money.

There is a special Department for International Cooperation in the Israel Foreign Office, created to carry out its program within the framework of the Ministry for Foreign Affairs. With a staff of over forty and liaison officers at training centers throughout the country, the Department collaborates closely with other Ministries, official bodies, and institutes of higher learning.

The administrative machinery is fairly simple, with a decentralization of authority. There are two deputy directors; one, with his assistants, is directly responsible for the training program, while the other takes charge of the experts. Working with the deputy director are several specialists who deal with the students from certain areas—French-speaking Africa, English-speaking Africa, Latin America, the Mediterranean region, and Asia. A special officer is assigned to the students who come for individual training and to those who attend the courses for women in family and community development. In addition to the technical staff there is a follow-up office and a special publications department for promoting the program of cooperation for providing students and experts with background knowledge and professional and other material, and for publishing experts' reports and other data of the program.

Requests for training programs and/or expert advice are usually passed to the Department by the local diplomatic or consular representative of the particular government concerned. The Department then establishes a plan after consultations with the foreign government and Israeli institutions and Ministries.

Interministerial committees have been organized to consider requests for training, help work out the length, program, and budget of the course, engage instructors, and supervise the training program together with the Department for International Cooperation. Similar joint committees have been set up with ORT (the Organization for Rehabilitation through Training), the Hebrew University, and the Technion, Israel Institute of Technology.

Often experts will be sent to the country requesting assistance in order to determine more fully the specific needs and local conditions which should be taken into consideration when planning a course for that country. The Director of the Foreign Training Department of the Ministry of Agriculture, for example, visited East Africa after several courses in agricultural cooperation had terminated and graduates had returned home to their jobs. He went to evaluate the results—was the training useful on the job, was there anything to be learned for improving future courses? At the same time, he supervised the selection of new candidates for future courses.

When candidates have applied, their applications are reviewed by their own governments, which present a selected list to the Department. The institution giving the course, together with the Department for International Cooperation, then determines who will participate.

Formal academic education, while an asset, is usually not stressed as a requirement for admission to the shorter practical courses. Although an attempt is made to have an agreed scholastic level as a prerequisite, practical experience is considered a substitute for formal education. Attempts are made to have a balanced group in so far as experience, education, and languages are concerned, but usually this is not possible. Institutions of learning here have experience in teaching people with diverse educational backgrounds and cultural levels in the same classroom, and they have learned to make the best of such a situation.

In designing the program of courses, the Department makes every attempt to integrate these courses with concrete development projects planned or already under way abroad. For example, the training of Tanganyikan youth leaders paralleled the planning of a pioneer youth training center. The graduates of Israel's four-month course in youth leadership returned to Tanganyika with an instructor to work together. Ultimately, the Tanganyikan team would train local personnel and be able to take over completely from the Israeli instructors, who then returned.

Students are encouraged not to end their training with their return home but to continue on-the-job improvements and extension work. A follow-up program is organized which includes material and publications of professional interest sent largely through the institutions that conducted the course, or by relevant Ministries and the Department. Experts on their travels abroad to conduct survey missions or to assist in the selection of candidates often look up former students and try to be of help.

Aside from receiving professional material by mail, students remain in close touch with the institutions where they studied and will receive further advice should any problems arise. They often develop close personal ties with former teachers, tell of their lives, and exchange letters, greeting cards, or announcements of the birth of their children. Trainees have walked for many miles, with their families, to greet former teachers visiting in the area.

The students receive an alumni bulletin, *Shalom,* which brings them news of fellow students and keeps them in touch with their colleagues' developments. Numerous "Shalom Societies" have sprung up among returned trainees in Africa and Asia, where graduates of Israel's training programs organize professional and extension programs and often continue to study Hebrew and learn Israeli songs and dances.

The Program of Courses

The training program falls roughly into the categories outlined below:

Category	*Trainees by field* (1961)
Agriculture	415
Education and vocational training (carpentry, electricity, metalwork)	318
Cooperation and trade unionism	120
Administration	56
Community development	82
Academic studies	83
Special seminars devoted to problems of developing countries	27
Short study tours	30

In the majority of cases where courses are short and intensive, the language of instruction is English, French, or Spanish. In the six-year medical course and the four-year course on agricultural engineering, to save time from the lengthy and exacting curriculum, students are taught in English, rather than Hebrew—the language of matriculation in Israeli schools. However, at a later stage, the medical students will be able to join the regular Hebrew program after summer ulpan (intensive language training) courses and weekly lessons. In their clinical years they will work in the hospital wards with Israeli patients.

Students coming by boat from East African countries through the Red Sea port of Eilat begin classes aboard ship and spend the two weeks receiving orientation and theoretical lectures.

Agriculture. The course in agriculture during the past few years dealt with irrigation techniques, fisheries, poultry husbandry, agricultural instruction and extension work, cattle husbandry, agricultural planning and development, arid zone agriculture, and the use of fertilizers.

Participants are required to have a certificate of agricultural or secondary school training, or adequate experience in the field. Candidates who have worked as practical farmers are preferred. The language of instruction is English, French, or Spanish, although courses have also been taught in Persian and, on one occasion, lectures were translated into Japanese. The average number of participants in the course has been fixed at twenty-five.

Education and Vocational Training. Because of the urgent needs for middle-level manpower in order to mobilize a nation's human resources, these fields are of special importance to new and developing countries. Every effort is made in Israel's training program to provide instructors as well as skilled craftsmen.

At the ORT Vocational School in Natanya, a center has been opened for the training of foremen and instructors for vocational high schools in developing countries. Students are offered a basic, accelerated course in metalwork, electricity, carpentry, and agromechanics. Suitable students are permitted to continue for another two years in order to qualify as instructors. Students are taught in French or English, according to their country. Hebrew serves as the lingua franca between English- and French-speaking students. During one summer, an Ethiopian student at the Hebrew University who had mastered Hebrew came up to Natanya and, as a summer job, taught Hebrew to the African students at ORT.

There is also a year's intensive course for physical education teachers at the Wingate Institute for Physical Education. Four-month courses in telecommunications and, for secondary school teachers, on nuclear energy problems and their applications are also offered.

During their visits, leaders of developing countries have shown particular interest in youth organizations which channel the energy of the young toward national service, of special importance in countries where rapid social change upsets traditional patterns and exposes the young to many complex and contradictory demands.

In a few cases, African leaders have sent their own children to the four-month intensive courses for youth leaders which the Department has organized, in cooperation with the Ministry of Defense, in French, English, and Spanish. Incorporating some of the experience of Israel's pioneer youth organizations, NAHAL and GADNA, Ghana organized the Builders' Brigade and Togo an agricultural group to stem the tide of rural youth toward the cities; Tanganyika's TANU recently announced a program of national service. Graduates of Israel's courses have organized youth clubs in Sierra Leone, Kenya, Nigeria, and the Central African Republic.

Cooperation and Trade Unionism. Many sectors of the national economy have been developed as a result of cooperative enterprises and the strong trade union movement. Studies on cooperation and trade unionism are organized and conducted by the Histadrut (Israel General Federation of Labor) Afro-Asian Institute. There have been special seminars for various national groups from India, Dahomey, Guinea, French-speaking Africa, East Africa, Japan, Latin America, and Iran.

The regular program is divided into a two-course yearly cycle for French- and English-speaking students on trade unionism and cooperatives. More than thirty-seven countries have sent representatives, not including individuals and smaller study groups.

The course deals with the principles of cooperation, labor economics, the sociology of trade unions, economic development, agriculutral cooperation (in cooperation with the Foreign Training Department of the Ministry of Agriculture), and the role of cooperative organizations in a developing society.

Preference is given to candidates actively engaged in the trade unions or cooperative movement. The Institute is particularly interested in training people who can teach others once they return home. Women students are also encouraged. The languages of instruction vary according to the composition of the group. In addition to theoretical studies, workshops, discussion groups, and guided reading, there is extensive field work, along with tours and inspections of trade union branches, cooperative enterprises, state-owned or Histadrut-owned enterprises, and private businesses.

Special emphasis is placed on cooperative rural development. Students benefit from actually seeing whole regions in the process of development where Israel's aim is to achieve for the new villages a cultural, economic, and social level on a par with the larger urban centers.

Through observations, study tours, and active participation in the work and life of cooperative settlements, students learn the subject at first hand. Specialized training is organized in selected fields related both to the general study program and the specific tasks awaiting the student in his home country.

Administration. Short courses in administration for local government officials, city clerks, and executive officers of local councils, and an accelerated course in public administration, are offered in cooperation with the Union of Local Authorities, the Ministry of the Interior, and the Israel Institute of Productivity. Here, too, candidates must have secondary school certificates or adequate experience in the field.

Community Development. In courses dealing with the family and with community development, special attention is placed on how to involve women directly in national development. Israel has considerable experience in this field; a large part of Israel's development is recognized to be due to the active effort of the women who worked side by side with their men in complete equality. Courses also deal with the problems, stresses, and strains which the family and community face in societies undergoing rapid social change.

As a result of a highly useful seminar on the Role of Women in a Developing Society, held in Haifa in 1961, an International Center for Training in Community Services was opened in that city.

Supported jointly by the Department for International Cooperation and the Municipality of Haifa, the Center resulted from a resolution adopted at the end of the six-week seminar by the sixty-six women from more than twenty countries of Africa, Asia, and the Mediterranean, to establish "a center in Israel [for] promoting future national and international activities for the advancement of women."

The seminar for community leaders and the course for rural community workers are designed to show women how to take an active and increasingly definitive role in the development of their countries. Women are taught how to organize voluntary women's organizations. Courses are offered in home economics, handicrafts, kindergarten and nursery teaching, adult education, rural integration, and food and health supervision. Here, too, teaching is in French and English, and the courses run generally for four months.

Academic Studies. A series of undergraduate and postgraduate courses are offered in nursing and in medical and public health, in cooperation with the Ministry of Health and the Hadassah Medical Organization. Where students, such as in the midwifery course, are to stay in the host country for several years, they are taught Hebrew at an intensive ulpan course which enables them to attend regular classes and deal with patients.

As a result of many requests received from developing countries for admission to the Hebrew University–Hadassah Medical School, a special six-year course has been organized leading to an M.D. for English-speaking students from abroad. Representatives of WHO, which is participating in the course, and local committees, together with the Medical School, carefully screen applicants and approve those of high caliber. It is hoped that the students will ultimately form the nucleus of medical faculties in their home countries. For the first two years teaching is in English.

A four-year course leading to a B.Sc. in Agricultural Engineering is offered by the Technion, Israel Institute of Technology, for English-speaking students from developing countries. Students will specialize in soil and water construction or farm power and machinery.

Individual Training. In addition to courses enumerated above there are individual training programs specially designed to fit the individual student's needs—to give him the finishing touches for professional competence. A wide variety of fields have been open for individual training, such as radio, printing, education of the handicapped, food preservation and canning, marine and nautical trades, and postgraduate nuclear research.

In many cases, a follow-up period of specialized training in Israel is arranged for students who have finished a particular course.

Opportunities Offered by Joint Companies and Itinerant Courses. Another aspect of training opportunities is that offered by the joint companies. Some twenty joint companies have already been created in several countries of Africa and Asia. Many emerging nations prefer joint ventures to detached technical advice or financial help. The usual pattern has been that 60 percent of the share capital is owned by the host government and 40 percent by the outside interests. The joint ventures are usually engaged in construction, transportation, and the exploitation of water resources.

One of the objects of the joint undertaking is to train key personnel in the countries concerned to take over the management of the enterprise as quickly as possible. As soon as the company is developing satisfactorily, the Israeli share is liquidated, and the capital involved, together with the Israeli personnel, is freed for transfer to similar ventures elsewhere. Within the framework of the joint company, scholarship candidates are selected from among the employees. Thus, a Senegal-Israel electronics company brings promising employees to the counterpart firm in Israel and to the ORT Vocational School. Trainees may also go on to attend an institution of higher learning, such as the Israel Institute of Technology or the Hebrew University of Jerusalem. In these cases, the Israeli partner takes a direct interest in the students' training and welfare.

An experiment in itinerant courses was begun in 1962, as one way of meeting the growing need for accelerated training of skilled and middle-level manpower. These courses in the building and construction trades took place in five countries of West Africa and were made possible by the cooperation of the Israel Institute of Productivity and joint construction companies in which African countries and Israel are partners.

The success of this experiment has led to the planning and organization of similar itinerant courses in building and construction trades and possibly in such fields as agriculture, public health and sanitation, and youth leadership.

Special Seminars. Another method of training has been the judicious use of seminars. These are organized on various subjects of interest and provide an opportunity for people in the field to discuss their common problems, share ideas on the various approaches and methods, and meet with experts in the subject. A three-week course on the causation and prevention of crime in developing countries offered an opportunity for prominent criminologists and police officers, judges, and wardens of penal institutions to exchange ideas. Lectures were followed by study tours and observation periods. In the resolutions of the seminar, delegates advocated a permanent center to study the problems of developing countries.

After the seminar many of the participants remained in Israel, having requested an additional period of study. They were taken in hand by their counterparts and given daily practical guidance and experience among the Israeli police, in the courts, prisons, and rehabilitation centers.

Seminars have also been held on problems of rural youth in changing societies, the role of students in developing countries, and the role of women in a developing society.

Part of the theory behind the use of seminars is the encouragement of developing states to help each other. Government leaders and scientists from twenty-three African and Asian nations were invited to Israel to hold the first International Conference on Science in the Advancement of New States.

Also in attendance were leading scientists, including Nobel Prize winners, from more advanced states. In day and night meetings, which lasted for two weeks, these men explored the ways in which science might help newly developing regions. Between sessions, Prime Ministers and university presidents, health experts and soil scientists traded ideas.

In concluding the seminar, delegates unanimously decided to set up a permanent committee through which the new states would aid each other, and also established a clearing-house for exchange of information.

Every attempt is made to ensure the students' success in their studies. Special tutors (madrichim) are provided to attend to the students' various needs and to assist them in their acclimatization. They are at the students' disposal twenty-four hours a day to help them in their studies. At the same time, students are introduced into Israeli life. They are invited home by whole communities or individuals and take part in national festivals and national activities.

The whole country is behind the program of cooperation in a personal way. Israel is a small country with little formality and a great deal of familiarity. The program tends to overflow from the instructors who have the most immediate contact with the students to their families and communities.

As a developing country with limited means, Israel was until very recently a recipient of aid. Needing friends in the international community, Israel can now herself aid others with a sentiment based on friendship, cooperation, and the belief that the spread of knowledge and skills, together with the spirit of pioneering, is the foundation for higher living standards, better government, and understanding among peoples.

SELECTED BIBLIOGRAPHY

Growth Theory and General Works on Development Problems

Bauer, Peter T., and Basil S. Yamey: *The Economics of Underdeveloped Countries,* University of Chicago Press, Chicago, 1957.

Brannen, Ted: *Overseas Management,* McGraw-Hill Book Company, New York, 1965.

Fryer, D. W.: *World Economic Development,* McGraw-Hill Book Company, New York, 1965.

Harbison, Frederick, and Charles A. Myers: *Management in the Industrial World,* McGraw-Hill Book Company, New York, 1959.

Higgins, Benjamin: *Economic Development: Principles, Problems and Policies,* W. W. Norton & Company, Inc. New York, 1959.

Kindleberger, Charles P.: *Economic Development,* 2d ed., McGraw-Hill Book Company, New York, 1965.

Meier, Gerald M., and Robert E. Baldwin: *Economic Development: Theory, History, Policy,* John Wiley & Sons, Inc., New York, 1957.

Meier, Richard: *Developmental Planning,* McGraw-Hill Book Company, New York, 1965.

Singer, Hans W.: *International Development,* McCraw Hill Book Company, New York.

Walinsky, Louis J.: *The Planning and Execution of Economic Development,* McGraw-Hill Book Company, New York, 1963.

Country Studies

GENERAL

Harbison, Frederick, and Charles A. Myers: *La Dirección de Empresa en el Mundo Industrial,* McGraw-Hill Book Company, New York, 1962.

AFRICA

United Nations, Department of Economic and Social Affairs: *Economic Survey of Africa since 1950,* United Nations Publication 1959.II.K.1, New York, 1959.

BRAZIL

Kuznets, Simon S. (ed.): *Economic Growth: Brazil, India, Japan,* The Duke University Press, Durham, N.C., 1955.

BURMA

Hagen, Everett E.: *The Economic Development of Burma,* National Planning Association, Planning Pamphlet 96, Washington, D.C., 1956.

CHINA

Barnett, A. Doak: *Communist Economic Strategy: The Rise of Mainland China,* National Planning Association, Washington, D.C., 1959.

Hollister, William Wallace: *China's Gross National Product and Social Accounts, 1950–1957,* The Free Press of Glencoe, New York, 1958.

EGYPT

Harbison, Frederick, and Charles A. Myers: *La Dirección de Empresa en el Mundo Industrial,* McGraw-Hill Book Company, New York, 1962.

FRANCE

Clapham, John H.: *Economic Development of France and Germany, 1815–1914,* 4th ed., Cambridge University Press, New York, 1955.

HUNGARY

Balassa, Bela A.: *The Hungarian Experience in Economic Planning: A Theoretical and Empirical Study,* Yale University Press, New Haven, Conn., 1959.

INDIA

India Planning Commission: *Second Five Year Plan,* New Delhi, 1956.

India Planning Commission: *Third Five Year Plan: A Draft Outline,* New Delhi, 1960.

India Planning Commission: *Third Five Year Plan,* New Delhi, 1961.

Krishnaswamy, K. S., et al.: "Economic Development and Cultural Change in India," *Economic Development and Cultural Change,* Part I, vol. 7, no. 3, pp. 194–384, April, 1959.

INDONESIA

Higgins, Benjamin: *Indonesia's Economic Stabilization and Development,* Institute of Pacific Relations, New York, 1957.

Paauw, Douglas S.: *Financing Economic Development: The Indonesia Case,* The Free Press of Glencoe, New York, 1960.

ISRAEL

Patinkin, Don: *The Israel Economy: The First Decade,* Jerusalem Post Press, Jerusalem, 1960. Reprinted with minor corrections and the addition of an index and bibliography from the Fourth Report, 1957–1958, of the Falk Project for Economic Research in Israel.

ITALY

Saraceno, Pasquale: *The Vanoni Plan in Its Third Year: Results and New Perspectives,* Economic Development Institute, International Bank for Reconstruction and Development, Washington, D.C., 1957.

JAPAN

Lockwood, William W.: *The Economic Development of Japan: Growth and Structural Change, 1868–1938,* Princeton University Press, Princeton, N.J., 1954.

Ohkawa, Kazushi, et al.: *The Growth Rate of the Japanese Economy since 1878,* Hitotsubashi University, Institute of Economic Research, Economic Research Series, no. 1, Tokyo.

Rosovsky, Henry: *Capital Formation in Japan, 1868–1940,* The Free Press of Glencoe, New York, 1961.

Smith, Thomas C.: *The Agrarian Origins of Modern Japan,* Stanford University Press, Stanford, Calif., 1959.

LIBYA

International Bank for Reconstruction and Development: *The Economic Development of Libya,* report of a mission organized by the International Bank for Reconstruction and Development at the request of the government of Libya, The Johns Hopkins Press, Baltimore, 1960.

MEXICO

International Bank for Reconstruction and Development: *The Economic Development of Mexico,* report of the Combined Mexican Working Party, The Johns Hopkins Press, Baltimore, 1953.

NIGERIA

International Bank for Reconstruction and Development: *The Economic Development of Nigeria,* report of a mission organized by the International Bank for Reconstruction and Development at the request of the governments of Nigeria and the United Kingdom, The Johns Hopkins Press, Baltimore, 1955.

PAKISTAN

Andrus, James R., and Azizali E. Mohammed: *The Economy of Pakistan,* Stanford University Press, Stanford, Calif., 1958.

Pakistan Planning Commission: *The Second Five Year Plan* (1960–65), Karachi, 1960.

SWEDEN

Heckscher, Eli F.: *An Economic History of Sweden,* transl. by Göran Ohlin, Harvard University Press, Cambridge, Mass., 1954.

SWITZERLAND

Hunold, Albert C.: *The Industrial Development of Switzerland,* National Bank of Egypt, Cairo, 1954.

THAILAND

International Bank for Reconstruction and Development: *A Public Development Program for Thailand,* report of a mission organized by the International Bank for Reconstruction and Development at the request of the government of Thailand, The Johns Hopkins Press, Baltimore, 1959.

UNION OF SOVIET SOCIALIST REPUBLICS

Bergson, Abram (ed.): *Soviet Economic Growth: Conditions and Perspectives,* Harper & Row, Publishers, Incorporated, New York, 1953.

Bergson, Abram: "U.S.S.R. versus U.S.A.: Comparative Economic Trends," *Sankei Shimbun* (Tokyo), Jan. 1, 1960.

Nove, Alec: "The Pace of Soviet Economic Development," *Lloyds Bank Review* (London), n.s., no. 40, pp. 1–23, April, 1956.

U.S.S.R. AND EASTERN EUROPE

United Nations, Economic Commission for Europe: "The Planning and Finance of Investment in the Soviet Union and Eastern Europe" and "Investment

Programmes and Results in the Soviet Union and Eastern Europe," *Economic Survey in Europe in 1955*, chaps. 7 and 8, pp. 198–247, Geneva, 1956.

United Nations, Economic Commission for Europe: "The Long-term Plans of Eastern Europe and the Soviet Union, 1956 to 1960," *Economic Survey of Europe in 1956*, chap. 2, pp. 1–23, Geneva, 1957.

UNITED KINGDOM

Ashton, Thomas S.: *The Industrial Revolution, 1760–1830,* Oxford University Press, London, 1948.

Clapham, John H., and William H. P. Court: *Concise Economic History of Britain,* 2 vols, Cambridge University Press, London, 1957–1958.

UNITED STATES

Kroose, Herman E.: *American Economic Development*, Prentice-Hall, Inc., Englewood Cliffs, N.J., 1955.

Williamson, Harold F.: *The Growth of the American Economy,* 2d ed., Prentice-Hall, Inc., Englewood Cliffs, N.J., 1951.

VENEZUELA

International Bank for Reconstruction and Development: *The Economic Development of Venezuela,* report of a mission organized by the International Bank for Reconstruction and Development at the request of the government of Venezuela, Johns Hopkins Press, Baltimore, 1961.

YUGOSLAVIA

Bicanic, Rudolf: "Economic Growth under Centralized Planning: Jugoslavia—a Case Study," *Economic Development and Cultural Change* (Chicago), vol. 6, no. 1, pp. 63–74, October, 1957.

Industrial and Commercial Development

Alexander-Frutschi, Marian C.: *Small Industry: An International Annotated Bibliography,* The Free Press of Glencoe, New York, 1960.

Aubrey, Henry G.: "Small Industry in Economic Development," *Social Research* (New York), vol. 18, no. 3, pp. 269–312, September, 1951.

Baldwin, George B.: *Industrial Growth in South India: Case Studies in Economic Development,* The Free Press of Glencoe, New York, 1959.

Bryce, Murray D.: *Industrial Development,* McGraw-Hill Book Company, New York, 1960.

———: *Desarrollo Industrial,* McGraw-Hill Book Company, New York, 1961.

Eckaus, Richard S.: "Choice of Technology," *Economic Weekly* (Bombay), vol. 13, nos., 4/6, pp. 197–202, Feb. 4, 1961.

Ford Foundation, International Planning Team: *Report on Small Industries in India,* Ministry of Commerce and Industry, New Delhi, 1955.

Gorst, Sheila: *Cooperative Organization in Tropical Countries: A Study of Co-operative Development in Non-self-governing Territories under United Kingdom Administration, 1945–1955,* Basil Blackwell & Mott, Ltd., Oxford, 1959.

Hagen, Everett E.: *Handbook for Industry Studies,* The Free Press of Glencoe, New York, 1958.

Harbison, Frederick, and Charles A. Myers: *Management in the Industrial World,* McGraw-Hill Book Company, New York, 1959.

Holton, Richard H.: "Marketing Structure and Economic Development," *Quarterly Journal of Economics* (Cambridge), vol. 67, no. 3, pp. 344–361, August, 1953.

Hoover, Edgar M.: *The Location of Economic Activity,* McGraw-Hill Book Company, New York, 1948.

International Labor Office: *The Development of the Cooperative Movement in Asia,* report prepared for the Asian Regional Conference, Nuwara Eliya, Ceylon, January, 1950, Geneva, 1949.

Isard, Walter: *Location and Space-economy: A General Theory Relating to Industrial Location, Market Areas, Land Use, Trade, and Urban Structure,* The Technology Press of the Massachusetts Institute of Technology, Cambridge, Mass., and John Wiley & Sons, Inc., New York, 1956.

Kalmanoff, George: *Joint International Business Ventures in Colombia,* Columbia University, School of Law, Research Project on Joint International Business Ventures, Country Studies, no. 1, November, 1957, and supplement, March, 1959.

——— and Benjamin Retchkiman: *Joint International Business Ventures in Mexico,* Columbia University, School of Law, Research Project on Joint International Business Ventures, Country Studies, no. 5, New York, 1959.

Krishnaswamy, K. S.: *Small-scale Industry: The Indian Textile Industry,* paper, Economic Development Institute Seminar, Mar. 14, 1957, Washington, D.C., 1961.

Leubuscher, Charlotte: *The Processing of Colonial Raw Materials: A Study in Location,* H. M. Stationery Office, London, 1951.

Lewis, William A.: *Report on Industrialization and the Gold Coast,* Government Printing Department, Accra, 1953.

Nigeria, Federal Ministry of Commerce and Industry: *Report of the Advisory Committee on Aids to African Businessmen,* Federal Government Printer, Lagos, 1959.

Prakash, Om: "Industrial Development Corporations in India and Pakistan," *Economic Journal* (London), vol. 67, no. 265, pp. 40–48, March, 1957.

Rosen, George: *Industrial Changes in India: Industrial Growth, Capital Requirements, and Technological Change, 1937–1955,* The Free Press of Glencoe, New York, 1958.

Staley, Eugene, and Richard Morse: *Modern Small Industry for Developing Countries,* McGraw-Hill Book Company, New York, 1965.

Stead, William H.: *Fomento: The Economic Development of Puerto Rico,* National Planning Association, Planning Pamphlet 103, Washington, D.C., 1958.

Stepanek, Joseph E.: *Small Industry Advisory Services: An International Study,* The Free Press of Glencoe, New York, 1960.

Torres, J. Garrido, and Denio Nogueira: *Joint International Business Ventures in Brazil,* Columbia University, School of Law, Research Project on Joint International Business Ventures, Country Studies, no. 11, New York, 1959.

Wood, Richardson, and Virginia Keyser: *Sears, Roebuck de Mexico, S.A.: A Case Study,* National Planning Association, Washington, D.C., 1953.

Yamanaka, Tokutaro, and Yoshio Kobayashi: *The History of Small Industries, with Two Specific Surveys,* Science Council of Japan, Economic Series, no. 15, Tokyo, 1957.

Political, Psychological, Geographical, and Social and Cultural Factors

Alderfer, Harold F.: *Local Government in Developing Countries,* McGraw-Hill Book Company, New York, 1964.

Benjamin, Harold: *Higher Education in the American Republics,* McGraw-Hill Book Company, New York, 1965.

David, Henry P. (ed.): *International Resources in Clinical Psychology,* McGraw-Hill Book Company, New York, 1964.

———: *International Trends in Mental Health,* McGraw-Hill Book Company, New York, 1965.

Gourou, Pierre: *The Tropical World: Its Social and Economic Conditions and Its Future Status,* 2d ed., transl. by E. D. Laborde, Longmans, Green & Co., Ltd., London, 1958.

Hoselitz, Berthold F.: *Sociological Aspects of Economic Growth,* The Free Press of Glencoe, New York, 1960.

International Institute of Differing Civilizations: *Development of a Middle Class in Tropical and Sub-tropical Countries,* record of the 29th session, London, Sept. 13–16, 1955, Brussels, 1956.

Lamb, Helen B.: "Business Organization and Leadership in India Today," in Richard L. Park and Irene Tinker (eds.), *Leadership and Political Institutions in India,* pp. 251–267, Princeton University Press, Princeton, N.J., 1959.

Lee, Douglas H. K.: *Climate and Economic Development in the Tropics,* Harper & Row, Publishers, Incorporated, New York, 1957.

Lerner, Daniel, and Lucille W. Pevsner: *The Passing of Traditional Society: Modernizing the Middle East,* The Free Press of Glencoe, New York, 1958.

McClelland, David C.: *The Achieving Society,* D. Van Nostrand Company, Inc., Princeton, N. J., 1961.

Mead, Margaret (ed.): *Cultural Patterns and Technical Change: A Manual Prepared by the World Federation for Mental Health,* United Nations Educational, Scientific and Cultural Organizations, Paris, 1953.

Millikan, Max F., and Donald L. M. Blackmer (eds.): *The Emerging Nations: Their Growth and United States Policy,* Little, Brown and Company, Boston, 1961.

Schultz, Theodore W.: *The Economic Test in Latin America,* Cornell University, New York State School of Industrial and Labor Relations, Bulletin 35, Ithaca, N.Y., 1956.

Shils, Edward: "The Concentration and Dispersion of Charisma: Their Bearing on Economic Policy in Underdeveloped Countries," *World Politics* (Princeton), vol. 11, no. 1, pp. 1–19, October, 1958.

Slotkin, James S.: *From Field to Factory: New Industrial Employees,* The Free Press of Glencoe, New York, 1960.

United Nations, Economic Commission for Asia and the Far East: "Economic Development and Planning in Asia and the Far East: Social Aspects," *Economic Bulletin for Asia and the Far East* (Bangkok), vol. 10, no. 3, pp. 1–58, December, 1959.

United Nations Educational, Scientific and Cultural Organization: "Economic Motivations and Stimulations in Underdeveloped Countries," Part 1, *International Social Science Bulletin* (Paris), vol. 6, no. 3, pp. 369–476, 1954.

INDEX